Mercedes-Benz C-Class
Service and Repair Manual

A K Legg LAE MIMI and RM Jex

Models covered

(3511-384-10AF1)

Mercedes Benz C-Class Saloon and Estate models with 4-cylinder petrol engines,
and 4- and 5-cylinder diesel engines.

1.8 litre (1797 cc/1799 cc), 2.0 litre (1998 cc), 2.2 litre (2199 cc), and 2.3 litre (2295 cc) engines.
2.2 litre (2155 cc) and 2.5 litre (2497 cc) diesel engines (normally-aspirated and turbocharged).

Does not cover supercharged (Kompressor) or 6-cylinder petrol engines, C200 diesel or CDI 220 diesel engines, or AMG versions
Does not cover new C-Class models, introduced September 2000

ABCDE
F

© Haynes Publishing 2003

A book in the **Haynes Service and Repair Manual Series**

ISBN **978 0 85733 988 1**

British Library Cataloguing in Publication Data
A catalogue record for this book is available from the British Library.

Printed in Malaysia

Haynes Publishing
Sparkford, Yeovil, Somerset BA22 7JJ, England

Haynes North America, Inc
859 Lawrence Drive, Newbury Park, California 91320, USA

Printed using NORBRITE BOOK 48.8gsm (CODE: 40N6533) from NORPAC; procurement system certified under Sustainable Forestry Initiative standard. Paper produced is certified to the SFI Certified Fiber Sourcing Standard (CERT - 0094271)

Contents

LIVING WITH YOUR MERCEDES-BENZ C-CLASS

Roadside repairs

Weekly checks

Lubricants, fluids and tyre pressures

MAINTENANCE

Routine maintenance and servicing

Contents

Advanced driving

Many people see the words 'advanced driving' and believe that it won't interest them or that it is a style of driving beyond their own abilities. Nothing could be further from the truth. Advanced driving is straightforward safe, sensible driving - the sort of driving we should all do every time we get behind the wheel.

An average of 10 people are killed every day on UK roads and 870 more are injured, some seriously. Lives are ruined daily, usually because somebody did something stupid. Something like 95% of all accidents are due to human error, mostly driver failure. Sometimes we make genuine mistakes - everyone does. Sometimes we have lapses of concentration. Sometimes we deliberately take risks.

For many people, the process of 'learning to drive' doesn't go much further than learning how to pass the driving test because of a common belief that good drivers are made by 'experience'.

Learning to drive by 'experience' teaches three driving skills:

☐ Quick reactions. (Whoops, that was close!)
☐ Good handling skills. (Horn, swerve, brake, horn).
☐ Reliance on vehicle technology. (Great stuff this ABS, stop in no distance even in the wet...)

Drivers whose skills are 'experience based' generally have a lot of near misses and the odd accident. The results can be seen every day in our courts and our hospital casualty departments.

Advanced drivers have learnt to control the risks by controlling the position and speed of their vehicle. They avoid accidents and near misses, even if the drivers around them make mistakes.

The key skills of advanced driving are **concentration,** effective all-round **observation, anticipation** and **planning.** When **good vehicle handling** is added to

these skills, all driving situations can be approached and negotiated in a safe, methodical way, leaving nothing to chance.

Concentration means applying your mind to safe driving, completely excluding anything that's not relevant. Driving is usually the most dangerous activity that most of us undertake in our daily routines. It deserves our full attention.

Observation means not just looking, but seeing and seeking out the information found in the driving environment.

Anticipation means asking yourself what is happening, what you can reasonably expect to happen and what could happen unexpectedly. (One of the commonest words used in compiling accident reports is 'suddenly'.)

Planning is the link between seeing something and taking the appropriate action. For many drivers, planning is the missing link.

If you want to become a safer and more skilful driver and you want to enjoy your driving more, contact the Institute of Advanced Motorists at www.iam.org.uk, phone 0208 996 9600, or write to IAM House, 510 Chiswick High Road, London W4 5RG for an information pack.

Working on your car can be dangerous. This page shows just some of the potential risks and hazards, with the aim of creating a safety-conscious attitude.

General hazards

Scalding

• Don't remove the radiator or expansion tank cap while the engine is hot.
• Engine oil, automatic transmission fluid or power steering fluid may also be dangerously hot if the engine has recently been running.

Burning

• Beware of burns from the exhaust system and from any part of the engine. Brake discs and drums can also be extremely hot immediately after use.

Crushing

• When working under or near a raised vehicle, always supplement the jack with axle stands, or use drive-on ramps. *Never venture under a car which is only supported by a jack.*
• Take care if loosening or tightening high-torque nuts when the vehicle is on stands. Initial loosening and final tightening should be done with the wheels on the ground.

Fire

• Fuel is highly flammable; fuel vapour is explosive.
• Don't let fuel spill onto a hot engine.
• Do not smoke or allow naked lights (including pilot lights) anywhere near a vehicle being worked on. Also beware of creating sparks (electrically or by use of tools).
• Fuel vapour is heavier than air, so don't work on the fuel system with the vehicle over an inspection pit.
• Another cause of fire is an electrical overload or short-circuit. Take care when repairing or modifying the vehicle wiring.
• Keep a fire extinguisher handy, of a type suitable for use on fuel and electrical fires.

Electric shock

• Ignition HT voltage can be dangerous, especially to people with heart problems or a pacemaker. Don't work on or near the ignition system with the engine running or the ignition switched on.

• Mains voltage is also dangerous. Make sure that any mains-operated equipment is correctly earthed. Mains power points should be protected by a residual current device (RCD) circuit breaker.

Fume or gas intoxication

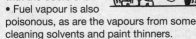

• Exhaust fumes are poisonous; they often contain carbon monoxide, which is rapidly fatal if inhaled. Never run the engine in a confined space such as a garage with the doors shut.
• Fuel vapour is also poisonous, as are the vapours from some cleaning solvents and paint thinners.

Poisonous or irritant substances

• Avoid skin contact with battery acid and with any fuel, fluid or lubricant, especially antifreeze, brake hydraulic fluid and Diesel fuel. Don't syphon them by mouth. If such a substance is swallowed or gets into the eyes, seek medical advice.
• Prolonged contact with used engine oil can cause skin cancer. Wear gloves or use a barrier cream if necessary. Change out of oil-soaked clothes and do not keep oily rags in your pocket.
• Air conditioning refrigerant forms a poisonous gas if exposed to a naked flame (including a cigarette). It can also cause skin burns on contact.

Asbestos

• Asbestos dust can cause cancer if inhaled or swallowed. Asbestos may be found in gaskets and in brake and clutch linings. When dealing with such components it is safest to assume that they contain asbestos.

Special hazards

Hydrofluoric acid

• This extremely corrosive acid is formed when certain types of synthetic rubber, found in some O-rings, oil seals, fuel hoses etc, are exposed to temperatures above 400°C. The rubber changes into a charred or sticky substance containing the acid. *Once formed, the acid remains dangerous for years. If it gets onto the skin, it may be necessary to amputate the limb concerned.*
• When dealing with a vehicle which has suffered a fire, or with components salvaged from such a vehicle, wear protective gloves and discard them after use.

The battery

• Batteries contain sulphuric acid, which attacks clothing, eyes and skin. Take care when topping-up or carrying the battery.
• The hydrogen gas given off by the battery is highly explosive. Never cause a spark or allow a naked light nearby. Be careful when connecting and disconnecting battery chargers or jump leads.

Air bags

• Air bags can cause injury if they go off accidentally. Take care when removing the steering wheel and/or facia. Special storage instructions may apply.

Diesel injection equipment

• Diesel injection pumps supply fuel at very high pressure. Take care when working on the fuel injectors and fuel pipes.

⚠️ *Warning: Never expose the hands, face or any other part of the body to injector spray; the fuel can penetrate the skin with potentially fatal results.*

Remember...

DO

• Do use eye protection when using power tools, and when working under the vehicle.

• Do wear gloves or use barrier cream to protect your hands when necessary.

• Do get someone to check periodically that all is well when working alone on the vehicle.

• Do keep loose clothing and long hair well out of the way of moving mechanical parts.

• Do remove rings, wristwatch etc, before working on the vehicle – especially the electrical system.

• Do ensure that any lifting or jacking equipment has a safe working load rating adequate for the job.

DON'T

• Don't attempt to lift a heavy component which may be beyond your capability – get assistance.

• Don't rush to finish a job, or take unverified short cuts.

• Don't use ill-fitting tools which may slip and cause injury.

• Don't leave tools or parts lying around where someone can trip over them. Mop up oil and fuel spills at once.

• Don't allow children or pets to play in or near a vehicle being worked on.

1993 model C180 Elegance Saloon

The Mercedes Benz C-Class was launched in the UK in October 1993. Developed from the very successful 190 series, the new C-Class attracted very favourable reviews, featuring as it does the traditional excellent Mercedes design and engineering combined with first-class build quality.

Only Saloon models were available initially, with a choice of 1.8 and 2.2 litre petrol engines, or 2.2 and 2.5 litre diesel engines, the latter available in normally-aspirated or turbocharged form. In a departure from previous Mercedes thinking, the C-Class was offered in four distinct trim levels - Classic, Esprit, Elegance and Sport - giving a wide range of 'ready-made' engine and trim permutations.

The 2.0 litre engine was added to the range in January 1994 and, in October 1995, airbags and a sophisticated security system were fitted to all models. August 1996 saw the introduction of the Estate models, with the normally-aspirated 2.3 litre petrol and 2.5 litre turbocharged diesel engines being added at the same time. The range received a minor facelift in July 1997, at which time side airbags were fitted to all models.

All engines are developments of well-proven engines which have appeared in many Mercedes-Benz vehicles. The engines covered in this manual are of double overhead camshaft 4-valves-per-cylinder design, mounted longitudinally ('north-south') with the transmission mounted behind the engine. Both manual and automatic transmissions are available, with a 5-speed electronically-controlled automatic available from August 1996 onwards.

Fully-independent suspension is fitted front and rear, with double front wishbones and the multi-link rear suspension first seen on the 190 series.

All models feature anti-lock brakes (ABS), power steering, central locking, electric mirrors, and a driver's airbag. As the range has developed, more equipment has been fitted as standard, with the most recent models featuring passenger and side airbags, electric front and rear windows, traction control and cruise control. An air conditioning system is available as an option.

Provided that regular servicing is carried out in accordance with the manufacturer's recommendations, the C-Class should prove very reliable and durable. The engine compartment is well-designed, and most of the items requiring frequent attention are easily accessible.

Your Mercedes C-Class manual

The aim of this manual is to help you get the best value from your vehicle. It can do so in several ways. It can help you decide what work must be done (even should you choose to get it done by a garage). It will also provide information on routine maintenance and servicing, and give a logical course of action and diagnosis when random faults occur. However, it is hoped that you will use the manual by tackling the work yourself. On simpler jobs it may even be quicker than booking the car into a garage and going there

twice, to leave and collect it. Perhaps most importantly, a lot of money can be saved by avoiding the costs a garage must charge to cover its labour and overheads.

The manual has drawings and descriptions to show the function of the various components so that their layout can be understood. Tasks are described and photographed in a clear step-by-step sequence. The illustrations are numbered by the Section number and paragraph number to which they relate - if there is more than one illustration per paragraph, the sequence is denoted alphabetically.

References to the 'left' or 'right' of the car are in the sense of a person in the driver's seat, facing forwards.

Acknowledgements

Thanks are due to Draper Tools Limited, who provided some of the workshop tools, and to all those people at Sparkford who helped in the production of this manual.

The following pages are intended to help in dealing with common roadside emergencies and breakdowns. You will find more detailed fault finding information at the back of the manual, and repair information in the main chapters.

If your car won't start and the starter motor doesn't turn

☐ If it's a model with automatic transmission, make sure the selector is in P or N.
☐ Open the bootlid or tailgate, lift up the right-hand cover, and make sure that the battery terminals are clean and tight.
☐ Switch on the headlights and try to start the engine. If the headlights go very dim when you're trying to start, the battery is probably flat. Get out of trouble by jump starting (see next page), using a friend's car.

If your car won't start even though the starter motor turns as normal

☐ Is there fuel in the tank?
☐ Is there moisture on electrical components under the bonnet? Switch off the ignition, then wipe off any obvious dampness with a dry cloth. Spray a water-repellent aerosol product (WD-40 or equivalent) on visible electrical connectors under the bonnet.
☐ Check for loose connections or blown fuses, by unclipping and removing the lids from the fuseboxes on either side of the engine compartment, at the rear. Check the fuses as described in Chapter 12, Section 3.
☐ Check the security and condition of the battery terminals. The battery is located on the right-hand side of the luggage compartment, next to the spare wheel; lift the floor covering for access.

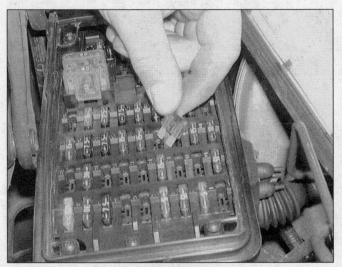

Checking the fuses

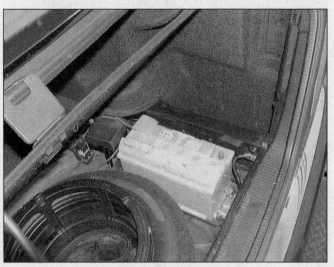

Battery location in luggage compartment

Jump starting

When jump-starting a car using a booster battery, observe the following precautions:

✔ Before connecting the booster battery, make sure that the ignition is switched off.

✔ Ensure that all electrical equipment (lights, heater, wipers, etc) is switched off.

✔ Take note of any special precautions printed on the battery case.

✔ Make sure that the booster battery is the same voltage as the discharged one in the vehicle.

✔ If the battery is being jump-started from the battery in another vehicle, the two vehicles MUST NOT TOUCH each other.

✔ Make sure that the transmission is in neutral (or PARK, in the case of automatic transmission).

 HAYNES HINT *Jump starting will get you out of trouble, but you must correct whatever made the battery go flat in the first place. There are three possibilities:*

1 *The battery has been drained by repeated attempts to start, or by leaving the lights on.*

2 *The charging system is not working properly (alternator drivebelt slack or broken, alternator wiring fault or alternator itself faulty).*

3 *The battery itself is at fault (electrolyte low, or battery worn out).*

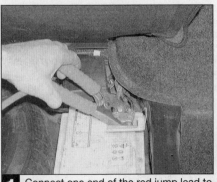

1 Connect one end of the red jump lead to the positive (+) terminal of the flat battery

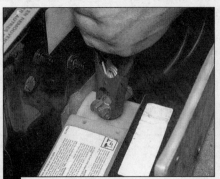

2 Connect the other end of the red lead to the positive (+) terminal of the booster battery.

3 Connect one end of the black jump lead to the negative (-) terminal of the booster battery

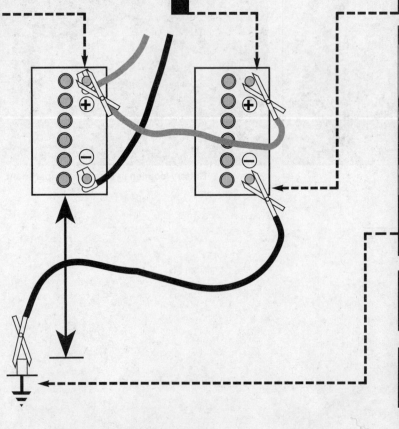

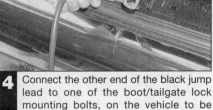

4 Connect the other end of the black jump lead to one of the boot/tailgate lock mounting bolts, on the vehicle to be started.

5 Make sure that the jump leads will not come into contact with the fan, drive-belts or other moving parts of the engine.

6 Start the engine using the booster battery and run it at idle speed. Switch on the lights, rear window demister and heater blower motor, then disconnect the jump leads in the reverse order of connection. Turn off the lights etc.

Wheel changing

 Warning: Do not change a wheel in a situation where you risk being hit by other traffic. On busy roads, try to stop in a lay-by or a gateway. Be wary of passing traffic while changing the wheel - it is easy to become distracted by the job in hand.

Preparation

- [ ] When a puncture occurs, stop as soon as it is safe to do so.
- [ ] Park on firm level ground, if possible, and well out of the way of other traffic.
- [ ] Use hazard warning lights if necessary.
- [ ] If you have one, use a warning triangle to alert other drivers of your presence.
- [ ] Firmly apply the parking brake and engage first or reverse gear (or Park on models with automatic transmission).
- [ ] Chock the wheels opposite the one being removed - a couple of large stones will do for this.
- [ ] If the ground is soft, use a flat piece of wood to spread the load under the foot of the jack.

Changing the wheel

1 The spare wheel and tools are stored in the luggage compartment. Lift up the boot floor panel, then unclip the jack from the mountings. Unscrew the liner inside the spare wheel anti-clockwise, then remove the spare wheel from its recess.

2 On models with steel wheels, either pull off the wheel trim, or lever it off using the end of the wheelbrace. Using the wheelbrace, slacken each wheel bolt by half a turn. Where anti-theft wheel bolts are fitted, a special adaptor will be required - this is provided in the toolkit.

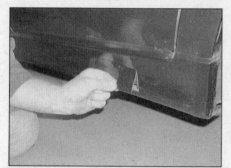

3 Unclip/remove the relevant access cover from the sill.

4 Fully insert the vehicle jack, making sure it is as upright as possible. Turn the jack handle clockwise until the wheel is raised clear of the ground.

5 Unscrew the wheel bolts and remove the wheel.

6 Fit the spare wheel and screw in the bolts. On models with alloy wheels, note that five shorter bolts are provided with the vehicle tools, for use with the steel spare wheel. On no account use the bolts for alloy wheels with the steel spare. Lightly tighten the bolts with the wheelbrace.

7 Lower the car to the ground. Securely tighten the wheel bolts in a diagonal sequence, then (where applicable) refit the wheel trim. The wheel bolts should be slackened and retightened to the specified torque (see Chapter 1A or 1B Specifications) at the earliest possible opportunity.

Finally...

- [ ] Remove the wheel chocks.
- [ ] Stow the damaged tyre or wheel, jack and tools in the correct locations in the car.
- [ ] Check the tyre pressure on the tyre just fitted. If it is low, or if you don't have a pressure gauge with you, drive slowly to the next garage and inflate the tyre to the correct pressure.
- [ ] Have the punctured wheel repaired as soon as possible, or another puncture will leave you stranded.

Identifying leaks

Puddles on the garage floor or drive, or obvious wetness under the bonnet or underneath the car, suggest a leak that needs investigating. It can sometimes be difficult to decide where the leak is coming from, especially if the engine bay is very dirty already. Leaking oil or fluid can also be blown rearwards by the passage of air under the car, giving a false impression of where the problem lies.

 Warning: Most automotive oils and fluids are poisonous. Wash them off skin, and change out of contaminated clothing, without delay.

 The smell of a fluid leaking from the car may provide a clue to what's leaking. Some fluids are distinctively coloured. It may help to clean the car carefully and to park it over some clean paper overnight as an aid to locating the source of the leak.
Remember that some leaks may only occur while the engine is running.

Sump oil

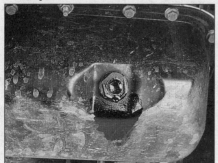

Engine oil may leak from the drain plug...

Oil from filter

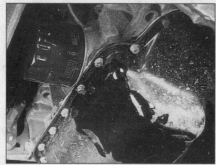

...or from the base of the oil filter.

Gearbox oil

Gearbox oil can leak from the seals at the inboard ends of the driveshafts.

Antifreeze

Leaking antifreeze often leaves a crystalline deposit like this.

Brake fluid

A leak occurring at a wheel is almost certainly brake fluid.

Power steering fluid

Power steering fluid may leak from the pipe connectors on the steering rack.

Towing

When all else fails, you may find yourself having to get a tow home - or of course you may be helping somebody else. Long-distance recovery should only be done by a garage or breakdown service. For shorter distances, DIY towing using another car is easy enough, but observe the following points:
☐ Use a proper tow-rope - they are not expensive. The vehicle being towed must display an ON TOW sign in its rear window.
☐ Always turn the ignition key to the 'on' position when the vehicle is being towed, so that the steering lock is released, and the direction indicator and brake lights will work.

☐ Towing eyes are provided at the front and rear of the vehicle, on the right-hand side. Do not attach the tow-rope to anything else.
☐ Before being towed, release the handbrake and select neutral on the transmission.
☐ Note that greater-than-usual pedal pressure will be required to operate the brakes, since the vacuum servo unit is only operational with the engine running.
☐ On models with power steering, greater-than-usual steering effort will also be required.
☐ The driver of the car being towed must keep the tow-rope taut at all times to avoid snatching.
☐ Make sure that both drivers know the route before setting off.

☐ Only drive at moderate speeds and keep the distance towed to a minimum. Drive smoothly and allow plenty of time for slowing down at junctions.
☐ On models with automatic transmission, the car must not be towed (with the rear wheels on the ground) further than 30 miles (50 km), or faster than 30 mph (50 km/h). The selector lever **must** be placed in neutral (N). If in doubt, do not tow with the driven wheels on the ground, or transmission damage may result.

Introduction

There are some very simple checks which need only take a few minutes to carry out, but which could save you a lot of inconvenience and expense.

These *Weekly checks* require no great skill or special tools, and the small amount of time they take to perform could prove to be very well spent, for example;

☐ Keeping an eye on tyre condition and pressures will not only help to stop them wearing out prematurely, but could also save your life.
☐ Many breakdowns are caused by electrical problems. Battery-related faults are particularly common, and a quick check on a regular basis will often prevent the majority of these.

☐ If your car develops a brake fluid leak, the first time you might know about it is when your brakes don't work properly. Checking the level regularly will give advance warning of this kind of problem.
☐ If the oil or coolant levels run low, the cost of repairing any engine damage will be far greater than fixing the leak, for example.

Underbonnet check points

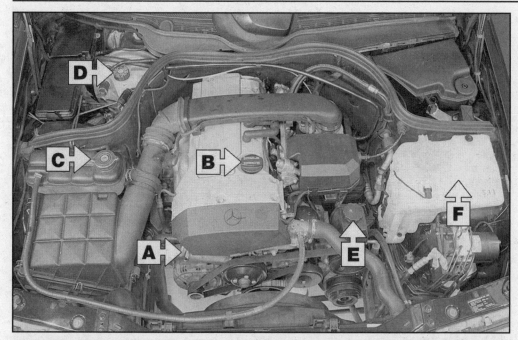

◀ Petrol engines

A *Engine oil level dipstick*
B *Engine oil filler cap*
C *Coolant expansion tank*
D *Brake and clutch fluid reservoir*
E *Power steering fluid reservoir*
F *Screen washer fluid reservoir*

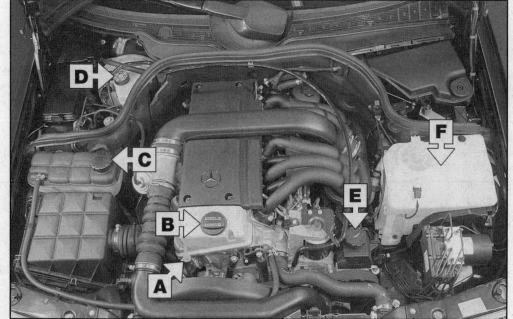

◀ Diesel engines

A *Engine oil level dipstick*
B *Engine oil filler cap*
C *Coolant expansion tank*
D *Brake and clutch fluid reservoir*
E *Power steering fluid reservoir*
F *Screen washer fluid reservoir*

Engine oil level

Before you start

✔ Make sure your car is on level ground.
✔ Check the oil level before the car is driven, or at least 5 minutes after the engine has been switched off.

 If the oil is checked immediately after driving the vehicle, some of the oil will remain in the upper engine components, resulting in an inaccurate reading on the dipstick!

The correct oil

Modern engines place great demands on their oil. It is very important that the correct oil for your car is used (See Lubricants and fluids on page 0•17).

Car Care

● If you have to add oil frequently, you should check whether you have any oil leaks. Place some clean paper under the car overnight, and check for stains in the morning. If there are no leaks, the engine may be burning oil, or the oil may only be leaking when the engine is running.
● Always maintain the level between the upper and lower dipstick marks. If the level is too low, severe engine damage may occur. Oil seal failure may result if the engine is significantly overfilled by adding too much oil.

1 The engine oil dipstick and filler cap are both located towards the front of the engine (see *Underbonnet check points* for exact location). Pull out the dipstick, and wipe it with a clean rag. Push it back into its tube, then remove it again and hold it vertically, with the handle uppermost.

3 Oil is added through the oil filler hole in the top of the camshaft cover. Unscrew or lift off the oil filler cap.

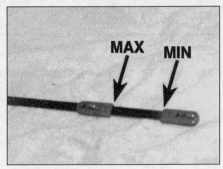

2 Check that the oil level is between the MIN and MAX markings on the dipstick.

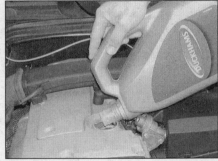

4 Top-up the level, using a funnel if preferred to reduce spillage. Add the oil slowly, checking the level on the dipstick often. Don't overfill (see *Car care* - left).

Coolant level

 Warning: DO NOT attempt to remove the expansion tank pressure cap when the engine is hot, as there is a very great risk of scalding. Do not leave open containers of coolant about, as it is poisonous.

Car Care

● With a sealed-type cooling system, adding coolant should not be necessary on a regular basis. If frequent topping-up is required, it is likely there is a leak. Check the radiator, all hoses and joint faces for signs of staining or wetness, and rectify as necessary.

● It is important that antifreeze is used in the cooling system all year round, not just during the winter months. Don't top-up with water alone, as the antifreeze will become too diluted.

1 Not all models have a separate coolant reservoir (expansion tank). Where one is fitted, it is located on the right-hand inner wing. Before removing the radiator/expansion tank cap, **wait until the engine is cold**. Slowly unscrew the cap, to release any pressure present in the cooling system, and remove it.

2 On models with no expansion tank, the coolant level must reach the mark inside the radiator filler neck. Add a mixture of water and antifreeze to the radiator until the coolant is at the correct level. Refit the cap and tighten it securely

3 On models with an expansion tank, the coolant level is visible through the reservoir body - it should be up to the black (upper) section. If topping-up is required, add the coolant mixture until the level is correct, then refit the cap and tighten it securely.

Brake and clutch fluid level

Note: *The brake and clutch hydraulic systems share the same reservoir.*

Warning:
● *Brake fluid can harm your eyes and damage painted surfaces, so use extreme caution when handling and pouring it.*
● *Do not use fluid that has been standing open for some time, as it absorbs moisture from the air, which can cause a dangerous loss of braking effectiveness.*

HAYNES HINT *The fluid level in the reservoir will drop slightly as the brake pads wear down, but the fluid level must never be allowed to drop below the MIN mark.*

Before you start:
✔ Make sure that your car is on level ground.

Safety First!
● If the reservoir requires repeated topping-up, this is an indication of a fluid leak somewhere in the brake or clutch system, which should be investigated immediately.
● If a leak is suspected, the car should not be driven until the braking system has been checked. Never take any risks where brakes are concerned.

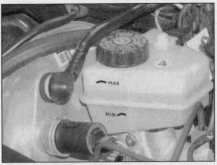

1 The MAX and MIN marks are indicated on the reservoir. The fluid level must be kept between the marks at all times.

2 If topping-up is necessary, first wipe clean the area around the filler cap to prevent dirt entering the hydraulic system. Unscrew the reservoir cap and carefully lift it out of position, holding the wiring connector plug and taking care not to damage the level sender float. Inspect the reservoir; if the fluid is dirty, the hydraulic system should be drained and refilled (see Chapter 1A or 1B).

3 Carefully add fluid, taking care not to spill it onto the surrounding components. Use only the specified fluid; mixing different types can cause damage to the system. After topping-up to the correct level, refit the cap securely and wipe off any spilt fluid. Reconnect the fluid level wiring connector.

Power steering fluid level

Before you start:
✔ Park the vehicle on level ground.
✔ Set the steering wheel straight-ahead.
✔ The engine should be turned off.

HAYNES HINT *For the check to be accurate, the steering must not be turned once the engine has been stopped.*

Safety First!
● The need for frequent topping-up indicates a leak, which should be investigated immediately.

1 The reservoir is mounted on top of the power steering pump, on the left-hand side of the engine. A dipstick is incorporated in the filler cap. Wipe clean the top of the fluid reservoir, then unscrew and remove the reservoir cap and dipstick.

2 Wipe the dipstick clean, then screw the reservoir cap fully back into position. Unscrew the cap once more, remove the dipstick and check the fluid level, which should be between the MAX and MIN marks. Note that there are two sets of marks - the 20° marks for checking the fluid when cold, and the 80° marks for fluid at operating temperature.

3 If topping-up is necessary, use the specified type of fluid - do not overfill the reservoir. When the level is correct, securely refit the cap. Start the engine and wait for the fluid level in the reservoir to stabilise before proceeding. With the engine running, turn the steering wheel fully left and right several times, returning to the straight-ahead position. Wait for the level to stabilise, then check the fluid level once more, and top-up if necessary. Switch off the engine on completion

Washer fluid level

☐The windscreen washer reservoir also supplies the headlight washers, where fitted.
☐On Estate models, a separate reservoir for the tailgate washer is fitted in the left-hand side compartment of the luggage area.

☐Screenwash additives not only keep the windscreen clean during foul weather, they also prevent the washer system freezing in cold weather - which is when you are likely to need it most. Don't top up using plain water

as the screenwash will become too diluted, and will freeze during cold weather. *On no account use coolant antifreeze in the washer system - this could discolour or damage paintwork.*

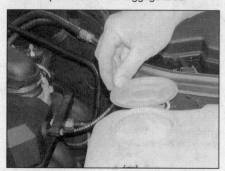

1 The windscreen and headlight washer fluid reservoir is located on the left-hand side of the engine compartment. Release the cap and observe the level in the reservoir by looking down the filler neck.

2 When topping-up the reservoir, a screenwash additive should be added in the quantities recommended on the bottle.

3 On Estate models, don't forget to check the tailgate washer reservoir as well. This is located behind the trim panel on the left-hand side of the luggage area.

Wiper blades

Caution: Take care during the fitting of a new blade that the wiper arm does not accidentally strike the windscreen or tailgate glass.

Note: *Fitting details may vary according to model, and according to whether genuine Mercedes wiper blades have been fitted. Use the procedures and illustrations shown as a guide for your car.*

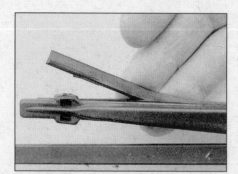

1 Check the condition of the windscreen wiper blade; if cracked or showing any signs of deterioration, or if the glass swept area is smeared, renew it. Wiper blades should be renewed annually.

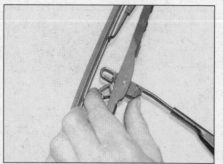

2 To remove a wiper blade, pull the arm fully away from the glass until it locks. Press the locking button at one end of the blade, and slide the blade out. Keep the locking button pressed while fitting the new blade, sliding it in between the lugs on the wiper arm - when fully inserted, release the locking button.

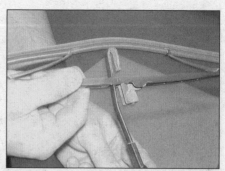

3 On Estate models, don't forget to check the rear wiper blade as well. Swivel the blade through 90°, press the locking tab with your fingers and slide the blade out of the arm's hooked end.

Tyre condition and pressure

It is very important that tyres are in good condition, and at the correct pressure - having a tyre failure at any speed is highly dangerous. Tyre wear is influenced by driving style - harsh braking and acceleration, or fast cornering, will all produce more rapid tyre wear. As a general rule, the front tyres wear out faster than the rears. Interchanging the tyres from front to rear ("rotating" the tyres) may result in more even wear. However, if this is completely effective, you may have the expense of replacing all four tyres at once! Remove any nails or stones embedded in the tread before they penetrate the tyre to cause deflation. If removal of a nail does reveal that

the tyre has been punctured, refit the nail so that its point of penetration is marked. Then immediately change the wheel, and have the tyre repaired by a tyre dealer.

Regularly check the tyres for damage in the form of cuts or bulges, especially in the sidewalls. Periodically remove the wheels, and clean any dirt or mud from the inside and outside surfaces. Examine the wheel rims for signs of rusting, corrosion or other damage. Light alloy wheels are easily damaged by "kerbing" whilst parking; steel wheels may also become dented or buckled. A new wheel is very often the only way to overcome severe damage.

New tyres should be balanced when they are fitted, but it may become necessary to re-balance them as they wear, or if the balance weights fitted to the wheel rim should fall off. Unbalanced tyres will wear more quickly, as will the steering and suspension components. Wheel imbalance is normally signified by vibration, particularly at a certain speed (typically around 50 mph). If this vibration is felt only through the steering, then it is likely that just the front wheels need balancing. If, however, the vibration is felt through the whole car, the rear wheels could be out of balance. Wheel balancing should be carried out by a tyre dealer or garage.

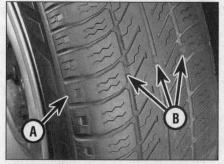

1 Tread Depth - visual check
The original tyres have tread wear safety bands (B), which will appear when the tread depth reaches approximately 1.6 mm. The band positions are indicated by a triangular mark on the tyre sidewall (A).

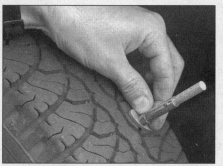

2 Tread Depth - manual check
Alternatively, tread wear can be monitored with a simple, inexpensive device known as a tread depth indicator gauge.

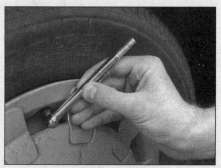

3 Tyre Pressure Check
Check the tyre pressures regularly with the tyres cold. Do not adjust the tyre pressures immediately after the vehicle has been used, or an inaccurate setting will result.

Tyre tread wear patterns

Shoulder Wear

Underinflation (wear on both sides)
Under-inflation will cause overheating of the tyre, because the tyre will flex too much, and the tread will not sit correctly on the road surface. This will cause a loss of grip and excessive wear, not to mention the danger of sudden tyre failure due to heat build-up.
Check and adjust pressures
Incorrect wheel camber (wear on one side)
Repair or renew suspension parts
Hard cornering
Reduce speed!

Centre Wear

Overinflation
Over-inflation will cause rapid wear of the centre part of the tyre tread, coupled with reduced grip, harsher ride, and the danger of shock damage occurring in the tyre casing.
Check and adjust pressures

If you sometimes have to inflate your car's tyres to the higher pressures specified for maximum load or sustained high speed, don't forget to reduce the pressures to normal afterwards.

Uneven Wear

Front tyres may wear unevenly as a result of wheel misalignment. Most tyre dealers and garages can check and adjust the wheel alignment (or "tracking") for a modest charge.
Incorrect camber or castor
Repair or renew suspension parts
Malfunctioning suspension
Repair or renew suspension parts
Unbalanced wheel
Balance tyres
Incorrect toe setting
Adjust front wheel alignment
Note: *The feathered edge of the tread which typifies toe wear is best checked by feel.*

Battery

Caution: Before carrying out any work on the vehicle battery, read the precautions given in Safety first! at the start of this manual.

✔ Make sure that the battery tray is in good condition, and that the clamp is tight. Corrosion on the tray, retaining clamp and the battery itself can be removed with a solution of water and baking soda. Thoroughly rinse all cleaned areas with water. Any metal parts damaged by corrosion should be covered with a zinc-based primer, then painted.

✔ Periodically (approximately every three months), check the charge condition of the battery as described in Chapter 5A.

✔ On batteries which are not of the maintenance-free type, periodically check the electrolyte level in the battery - see Chapter 1A or 1B.

✔ If the battery is flat, and you need to jump start your vehicle, see *Roadside repairs*.

HAYNES HiNT

Battery corrosion can be kept to a minimum by applying a layer of petroleum jelly to the clamps and terminals after they are reconnected.

1 The battery is located next to the spare wheel, in the luggage compartment. The exterior of the battery should be inspected periodically for damage such as a cracked case or cover.

3 If corrosion (white, fluffy deposits) is evident, remove the cables from the battery terminals (refer to *Disconnecting the battery*), clean them with a small wire brush, then refit them. Automotive stores sell a tool for cleaning the battery post . . .

2 Lift off the terminal covers, and check the tightness of battery clamps to ensure good electrical connections. Also check each cable for cracks and frayed conductors.

4 . . . as well as the battery cable clamps.

Bulbs and fuses

✔ Check all external lights and the horn. Refer to the appropriate Sections of Chapter 12 for details if any of the circuits are found to be inoperative.

✔ Visually check all accessible wiring connectors, harnesses and retaining clips for security, and for signs of chafing or damage.

HAYNES HiNT *If you need to check your brake lights and indicators unaided, back up to a wall or garage door and operate the lights. The reflected light should show if they are working properly.*

1 If a single indicator light, stop-light or headlight has failed, it is likely that a bulb has blown and will need to be replaced. Refer to Chapter 12 for details. If both stop-lights have failed, it is possible that the stop-light switch is faulty (see Chapter 9).

2 If more than one indicator light or headlight has failed, it is likely that either a fuse has blown or that there is a fault in the circuit (see Chapter 12). The main fuses are located in the fuseboxes on the left- and right-hand sides of the engine compartment, at the rear. Additional fuses are located in the luggage compartment, in front of the battery.

3 To replace a blown fuse, simply pull it out using the plastic tweezers provided. Fit a new fuse of the same rating (see Chapter 12). If the fuse blows again, it is important that you find out why - a complete checking procedure is given in Chapter 12.

Lubricants and fluids

Engine

Petrol	Multigrade engine oil, viscosity SAE 10W/40 to 15W/50, to CCMC G4 or API SG
Diesel	Multigrade engine oil, viscosity SAE 10W/40 to 15W/50, to CCMC PD2 or API CE
Cooling system	Ethylene glycol based antifreeze
Manual transmission	Automatic transmission fluid (ATF)
Automatic transmission	Automatic transmission fluid (ATF)
Final drive unit	Hypoid gear oil SAE 90 or 85W/90
Braking system	Hydraulic fluid to SAE J1703F or DOT 4
Power steering	Mercedes-Benz Lenkgetriebeol (000 989 88 03) **only**
General greasing (wheel bearings, etc)	Lithium-based molybdenum disulphide grease

Choosing your engine oil

Engines need oil, not only to lubricate moving parts and minimise wear, but also to maximise power output and to improve fuel economy.

HOW ENGINE OIL WORKS

• *Beating friction*

Without oil, the moving surfaces inside your engine will rub together, heat up and melt, quickly causing the engine to seize. Engine oil creates a film which separates these moving parts, preventing wear and heat build-up.

• *Cooling hot-spots*

Temperatures inside the engine can exceed 1000° C. The engine oil circulates and acts as a coolant, transferring heat from the hot-spots to the sump.

• *Cleaning the engine internally*

Good quality engine oils clean the inside of your engine, collecting and dispersing combustion deposits and controlling them until they are trapped by the oil filter or flushed out at oil change.

OIL CARE - FOLLOW THE CODE

To handle and dispose of used engine oil safely, always:

OIL CARE
0800 66 33 66
www.oilbankline.org.uk

• *Avoid skin contact with used engine oil. Repeated or prolonged contact can be harmful.*
• *Dispose of used oil and empty packs in a responsible manner in an authorised disposal site. Call 0800 663366 to find the one nearest to you. Never tip oil down drains or onto the ground.*

Tyre pressures

At the time of writing, Mercedes-Benz do not provide a definitive list of recommended tyre pressures for all C-Class models. Refer to your owner's handbook, or the information appearing inside the fuel filler flap. If there is still any doubt, refer to a Mercedes-Benz dealer for the most up-to-date information

Chapter 1 Part A:
Routine maintenance & servicing - petrol models

Contents

Degrees of difficulty

| Easy, suitable for novice with little experience | | Fairly easy, suitable for beginner with some experience | | Fairly difficult, suitable for competent DIY mechanic | | Difficult, suitable for experienced DIY mechanic | | Very difficult, suitable for expert DIY or professional | |

Lubricants and fluids

Refer to *Weekly checks*

Capacities

Engine oil

Including oil filter .... 5.8 litres

Cooling system

Without air conditioning .... 8.0 litres
With air conditioning .... 8.5 litres

Transmission

Manual transmission .... 1.5 litres
Automatic transmission:
    Fluid change .... 5.5 litres
    From dry .... 6.6 litres

Final drive unit

All models .... 1.1 litres

Power-assisted steering

All models (approximate) .... 1.0 litre

Fuel tank

All models:
    Total .... 62 litres
    Reserve .... 7 litres

Cooling system

Antifreeze mixture:
    50% antifreeze .... Protection down to –37°C (5°F)
    55% antifreeze .... Protection down to –45°C (–22°F)

Note: *Refer to antifreeze manufacturer for latest recommendations.*

Ignition system

Spark plugs:	Type	Electrode gap
All engines	Bosch F 8 KTCR	1.0 mm

Brakes

Brake pad friction material minimum thickness .... 2.0 mm

Torque wrench settings

	Nm	lbf ft
Engine oil drain plug	25	18
Manual transmission filler/level plug	60	44
Oil filter cap	25	18
Roadwheel bolts	110	81
Spark plugs	27	20

The maintenance intervals in this manual are provided with the assumption that you, not the dealer, will be carrying out the work. These are the minimum maintenance intervals recommended by us for vehicles driven daily. If you wish to keep your vehicle in peak condition at all times, you may wish to perform some of these procedures more often. We encourage frequent maintenance, because it enhances the efficiency, performance and resale value of your vehicle.

If the vehicle is driven in dusty areas, used to tow a trailer, or driven frequently at slow speeds (idling in traffic) or mainly for short journeys, shorter maintenance intervals are recommended.

When the vehicle is new, it should be serviced by a factory-authorised dealer service department, in order to preserve the factory warranty.

Later Mercedes C-Class models are equipped with a Service Indicator System (ASSYST). Approximately one month before a service is due, a spanner will appear on the indicator display together with the remaining distance or time. If the service is not performed on time, the display will flash with a minus sign. The *distance* between services can vary between 10 000 miles (15 000 km) and 20 000 miles (30 000 km), and the *time* between services can vary between 365 and 730 days, according to how the car is used (frequent starting, distance covered on journeys, etc). The system itself calculates the best service intervals and shows the information on the display. If the annual distance covered is in excess of 14 000 miles (22 000 km), the service display will be in distance, however if the annual distance covered is less than 14 000 miles (22 000 km), the service display will be in days.

After carrying out a service, the Mercedes-Benz dealership will reset the Service Indicator. To reset the system yourself, carry out the following.

1 *Insert the ignition key and turn it to position 2. Immediately press button 0 on the instrument panel twice within one second.*
2 *Turn the ignition key back to position 1.*
3 *Press and hold button 0, then turn the key to position 2 (keeping the button pressed). The display will show the current remaining distance or time, and after 10 seconds an acoustic signal will sound. The new starting distance or time will appear for about 10 seconds on the display.*
4 *Release button 0.*

Every 250 miles or weekly
☐ Refer to *Weekly checks*

Every 10 000 miles (15 000 km) - Service A on display
☐ Renew the engine oil and filter (Section 3)
☐ Check coolant antifreeze/inhibitor (Section 4)
☐ Check front brake pads for wear (Section 5)
☐ Check front brake discs for wear (Section 6)
☐ Check the seat belts (Section 7)
☐ Lubricate all hinges, locks, aerial and sunroof (Section 8)
☐ Check the operation of the windscreen/headlight washer system(s) (as applicable) (Section 9)
☐ Renew the pollen filter (Section 10)

Every 14 000 miles (22 000 km) - Service B on display
Note: *Carry out the following work in addition to that described for Service A*
☐ Check the battery electrolyte level (Section 11)
☐ Check all underbonnet components and hoses for fluid leaks (Section 12)
☐ Check the air conditioning system (System 13)
☐ Check the auxiliary drivebelt (Section 14)
☐ Lubricate the throttle linkage (Section 15)
☐ Check the rear brake pads for wear (Section 16)
☐ Check the rear brake discs for wear (Section 17)
☐ Check the operation of the parking brake (Section 18)
☐ Rotate the roadwheels position (Section 19)
☐ Check the steering and suspension components for condition and security (Section 20)
☐ Check for damage and corrosion (Section 21)
☐ Check the headlight beam adjustment (Section 22)
☐ Check the rear driveshaft gaiters (Section 23)
☐ Check the exhaust system and mountings (Section 24)
☐ Renew the windscreen wiper blades (Section 25)
☐ Carry out a road test (Section 26)

Every 20 000 miles (30 000 km) or 2 years
☐ Check the engine idle speed and mixture settings (Section 27)
☐ Lubricate the trailer coupling (tow bar) ball and socket (Section 28)

Every 30 000 miles (50 000 km) or 2 years
☐ Renew the evaporative emission control charcoal canister (Section 29)
☐ Check the clutch friction disc wear - manual transmission models (Section 30)
☐ Check the automatic transmission fluid level (Section 31)
☐ Check the manual transmission fluid level (Section 32)
☐ Check the condition of the propeller shaft rubber coupling (Section 33)

Every 40 000 miles (60 000 km) or 4 years
☐ Renew the spark plugs (Section 34)

Every 50 000 miles (80 000 km) or 4 years
☐ Renew the air filter element (Section 35)
☐ Renew the fuel filter (Section 36)
☐ Check final drive unit oil level (Section 37)

Every 2 years, regardless of mileage
☐ Renew the brake fluid (Section 38)

Every 3 years, regardless of mileage
☐ Renew the coolant (Section 39)

Underbonnet view of a 2.0 litre model

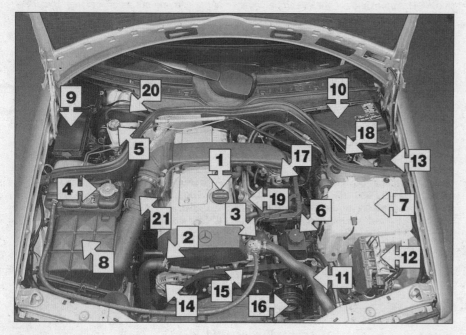

1   Engine oil filler cap
2   Engine oil dipstick
3   Oil filter
4   Coolant expansion tank
5   Brake fluid reservoir
6   Power steering fluid reservoir
7   Windscreen/headlamp washer fluid
    reservoir
8   Air filter
9   Fusebox
10 Engine management ECU and wiring
    connector box
11 Radiator top hose
12 Brake ABS unit
13 Diagnostic socket
14 Alternator
15 Auxiliary drivebelt
16 Air conditioning compressor
17 Throttle body
18 Accelerator cable
19 Fuel rail
20 Brake vacuum servo unit
21 Air mass meter

Underbonnet view of a 1.8 litre model

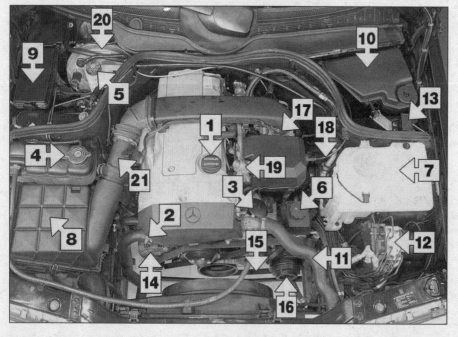

1   Engine oil filler cap
2   Engine oil dipstick
3   Oil filter
4   Coolant expansion tank
5   Brake fluid reservoir
6   Power steering fluid reservoir
7   Windscreen/headlamp washer fluid
    reservoir
8   Air filter
9   Fusebox
10 Engine management ECU and wiring
    connector box
11 Radiator top hose
12 Brake ABS unit
13 Diagnostic socket
14 Alternator
15 Auxiliary drivebelt
16 Air conditioning compressor
17 Throttle body
18 Accelerator cable
19 Fuel rail
20 Brake vacuum servo unit
21 Air mass meter

Front underbody view of a 2.0 litre model

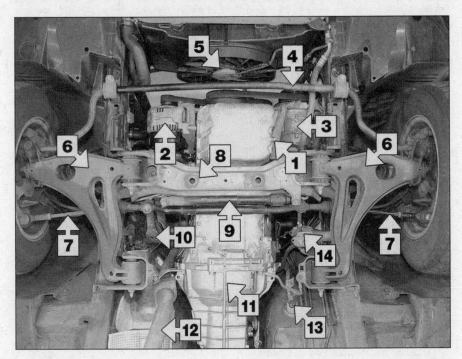

1 Engine oil drain plug
2 Alternator
3 Air conditioning compressor
4 Anti-roll bar
5 Electric cooling fan
6 Front suspension lower arm
7 Steering track rod
8 Subframe
9 Steering damper
10 Steering gear
11 Manual transmission
12 Exhaust system front pipe
13 Main wiring connector in passenger footwell from battery in luggage compartment
14 Steering idler

Rear underbody view of a 2.0 litre model

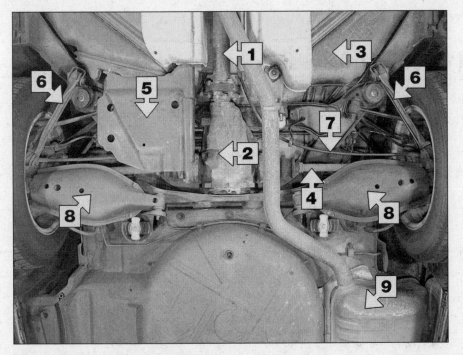

1 Propeller shaft
2 Final drive unit
3 Fuel tank
4 Driveshaft
5 Cover for fuel pump and fuel filter
6 Rear suspension radius arm
7 Handbrake cable
8 Rear suspension lower arm
9 Exhaust tailpipe

1 Introduction

This Chapter is designed to help the home mechanic maintain his/her vehicle for safety, economy, long life and peak performance.

The Chapter contains a maintenance schedule, followed by Sections dealing with each task in the schedule. Visual checks, adjustments, component renewal and other helpful items are included. Refer to the accompanying illustrations of the engine compartment and the underside of the vehicle for the locations of the various components.

Servicing your vehicle in accordance with the above recommendations and the following Sections will provide a planned maintenance programme, which should result in a long and reliable service life. This is a comprehensive plan, so maintaining some items but not others at the specified service intervals will not produce the same results.

As you service your vehicle, you will discover that many of the procedures can - and should - be grouped together, because of the particular procedure being performed, or because of the proximity of two otherwise-unrelated components to one another. For example, if the vehicle is raised for any reason, the exhaust can be inspected at the same time as the suspension and steering components.

The first step in this maintenance programme is to prepare yourself before the actual work begins. Read through all the Sections relevant to the work to be carried out, then make a list and gather all the parts and tools required. If a problem is encountered, seek advice from a parts specialist, or a dealer service department.

2 Regular maintenance

If, from the time the vehicle is new, the routine maintenance schedule is followed closely, and frequent checks are made of fluid levels and high-wear items, as suggested throughout this manual, the engine will be kept in relatively good running condition, and the need for additional work will be minimised.

It is possible that there will be times when the engine is running poorly due to the lack of regular maintenance. This is even more likely if a used vehicle, which has not received regular and frequent maintenance checks, is purchased. In such cases, additional work may need to be carried out, outside of the regular maintenance intervals.

If engine wear is suspected, a compression test (refer to the relevant Part of Chapter 2) will provide valuable information regarding the overall performance of the main internal components. Such a test can be used as a basis to decide on the extent of the work to be carried out. If, for example, a compression test indicates serious internal engine wear, conventional maintenance as described in this Chapter will not greatly improve the performance of the engine, and may prove a waste of time and money, unless extensive overhaul work is carried out first.

The following series of operations are those usually required to improve the performance of a generally poor-running engine:

Primary operations

a) Clean, inspect and test the battery (See Weekly checks and Section 11).
b) Check all the engine-related fluids (See Weekly checks).
c) Check the condition of the auxiliary drivebelt (Section 14).
d) Renew the spark plugs (Section 34).
e) Check the condition of the air filter, and renew if necessary (Section 35).
f) Check the fuel filter, and renew if necessaryr (Section 36).
g) Check the condition of all hoses, and check for fluid leaks (Section 12).

If the above operations are not fully effective, carry out the following secondary operations:

Secondary operations

All items listed under Primary operations, plus the following:

a) Check the charging system (see Part A of Chapter 5).
b) Check the ignition system (see Part B of Chapter 5).
c) Check the fuel system (see Part A of Chapter 4).

Every 10 000 miles (15 000 km) - Service A on display

3 Engine oil and filter renewal

1 Frequent oil and filter changes are the most important preventative maintenance procedures which can be undertaken by the DIY owner. As engine oil ages, it becomes diluted and contaminated, which leads to premature engine wear.

2 Before starting this procedure, gather together all the necessary tools and materials. Also make sure that you have plenty of clean rags and newspapers handy, to mop up any spills. Ideally, the engine oil should be warm, as it will drain better, and more built-up sludge will be removed with it. Take care, however, not to touch the exhaust or any other hot parts of the engine when working under the vehicle. To avoid any possibility of scalding, and to protect yourself from possible skin irritants and other harmful contaminants in used engine oils, it is advisable to wear gloves when carrying out this work. Access to the underside of the vehicle will be greatly improved if it can be raised on a lift, driven onto ramps, or jacked up and supported on axle stands (see Jacking and vehicle support). Whichever method is chosen, make sure that the vehicle remains level, or if it is at an angle, so that the drain plug is at the lowest point. Where necessary remove the splash guard from under the engine.

3 Working in the engine compartment, locate the oil filter/housing on the front left-hand side of the engine. Place a wad of rag around the housing to absorb any spilt oil, then unscrew the oil filter cap. It is recommended that a filter removal tool is obtained (see illustration) as this can be used to tighten the cap to its specified torque when fitting the new filter element. Note: By removing the cap, the oil will drain from the housing into the sump.

4 On early models, lift the old oil filter element out from the housing (using the handle provided), and discard it. On later models, the element is withdrawn with the oil filter cap, and can then be separated and discarded.

5 Working under the vehicle, unscrew the

3.3 Using a filter cap removal tool - the tool locates on the cap flats

sump drain plug about half a turn **(see illustration)**. Position the draining container under the drain plug, then remove the plug completely. If possible, try to keep the plug pressed into the sump while unscrewing it by hand the last couple of turns **(see Haynes Hint)**.

6 Recover the sealing ring from the drain plug.

7 Allow some time for the old oil to drain, noting that it may be necessary to reposition the container as the oil flow slows to a trickle. Remove the oil filler cap from the camshaft cover.

8 After all the oil has drained, wipe off the drain plug with a clean rag. Renew the sealing washer. Clean the area around the drain plug opening, then refit and tighten the plug **(see illustration)**.

9 Remove the old oil and all tools from under the car, then refit the splash guard and lower the car to the ground.

10 Wipe out the oil filter housing and cap using a clean rag, then locate a new O-ring on the cap **(see illustration)**.

11 On early models, locate the new element in the housing with the handle at the top. On later models, carefully press the new element into the cap, making sure that the indented end is entered first **(see illustration)**.

12 Screw on and tighten the cap to the specified torque **(see illustrations)**.

13 Remove the oil level dipstick then fill the engine, using the correct grade and type of oil (see *Recommended lubricants and fluids*). An

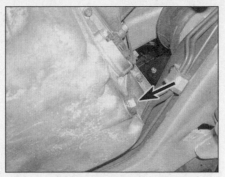

3.5 The sump drain plug is located on the left-hand side of the sump

oil can spout or funnel may help to reduce spillage. Pour in half the specified quantity of oil first, then wait a few minutes for the oil to fall to the sump. Continue adding oil a small quantity at a time until the level is up to the lower mark on the dipstick. Finally, bring the level up to the upper mark on the dipstick. Insert the dipstick, and refit the filler cap.

14 Start the engine and run it for a few minutes; check for leaks around the oil filter cap and the sump drain plug. Note that there may be a delay of a few seconds before the oil pressure warning light goes out when the engine is first started, as the oil circulates through the engine oil galleries and the new oil filter, before the pressure builds up.

15 Switch off the engine, and wait a few minutes for the oil to settle in the sump once

As the drain plug releases from the threads, move it away sharply so the stream of oil from the sump runs into the container, not up your sleeve.

more. With the new oil circulated and the filter completely full, recheck the level on the dipstick, and add more oil as necessary.

16 Dispose of the used engine oil safely, with reference to *General repair procedures* in the Reference section of this manual.

4   Coolant antifreeze/inhibitor check

Warning: Wait until the engine is cold before starting this procedure. Do not allow antifreeze to come in contact with your skin, or with the painted surfaces of the vehicle. Rinse off spills immediately with plenty of water.

1 A tester will be required to check the coolant strength; these can be obtained relatively cheaply from most motor accessory shops.

2 With the engine completely cold, unscrew and remove the filler cap from the coolant expansion tank. Follow the instructions supplied with the tester and check the coolant mixture is sufficient to give protection down to temperatures well below freezing. If the coolant has been renewed at the specified intervals this shouldn't be a problem. However, if the coolant mixture is not strong enough to provide sufficient protection it will

3.8 Refitting the oil drain plug together with a new sealing washer

3.10 Fitting a new O-ring to the groove in the filter cap

3.11 Fitting the new element in the cap on later models

3.12a Fitting the element and cap on later models

3.12b Tightening the oil filter cap to the specified torque

be necessary to drain the cooling system and renew the coolant (see Section 39).

3 Once the test is complete, check the coolant level is correct (see *Weekly checks*) then securely refit the pressure cap.

5 Front brake pad check

1 Firmly apply the parking brake, then jack up the front of the car and support it securely on axle stands (see *Jacking and vehicle support*). Remove the front roadwheels **(see Haynes Hint)**.

2 For a comprehensive check, the brake pads should be removed and cleaned. The operation of the caliper can then also be checked, and the condition of the brake disc itself can be fully examined on both sides. Refer to Chapter 9 for further information.

3 If any pad's friction material is worn to the specified thickness or less, *all four pads must be renewed as a set.*

6 Front brake disc check

Refer to Chapter 9, Section 6.

7 Seat belt check

1 Carefully examine the seat belt webbing for cuts or any signs of serious fraying or deterioration. If the seat belt is of the retractable type, pull the belt all the way out, and examine the full extent of the webbing.

2 Fasten and unfasten the belt, ensuring that the locking mechanism holds securely and releases properly when intended. If the belt is of the retractable type, check also that the retracting mechanism operates correctly when the belt is released.

3 Check the security of all seat belt mountings and attachments which are accessible, without removing any trim or other components, from inside the vehicle.

HAYNES HINT

For a quick check, the thickness of the friction material of the brake pad can be measured through the aperture in the caliper body

8 Lubricate hinges, locks, aerial and sunroof

1 Lubricate the hinges of the bonnet, doors and tailgate with a light general-purpose oil. Similarly, lubricate all latches, locks and lock strikers **(see illustration)**. At the same time, check the security and operation of all the locks, adjusting them if necessary (see Chapter 11).

2 Lightly lubricate the bonnet release mechanism and cable with a suitable grease.

3 If an electric aerial is fitted, extend the aerial and remove all traces of dirt from its mast. Lubricate the aerial mast with a light general-purpose oil and retract the aerial.

4 On models with a sunroof, slide the roof fully back and clean the sunroof guide rails. Apply a smear of fresh multi-purpose grease to the rails and close the sunroof.

9 Windscreen/headlight washer system check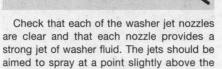

Check that each of the washer jet nozzles are clear and that each nozzle provides a strong jet of washer fluid. The jets should be aimed to spray at a point slightly above the centre of the screen/headlight. On the

8.1 Lubricating the door locks

windscreen washer nozzles where there are two jets, aim one of the jets slightly above the centre of the screen and aim the other just below to ensure complete coverage of the screen. If necessary, adjust the jets using a pin.

10 Pollen filter renewal

1 The air entering the vehicle's ventilation system is passed through a very fine pleated-paper air filter element, which removes particles of pollen, dust and other airborne foreign matter. To ensure its continued effectiveness, this filter's element must be renewed at regular intervals. Failure to renew the element will also result in greatly-reduced airflow into the passenger compartment, reducing demisting and ventilation capability.

2 Remove the passenger side lower facia panel, as described in Chapter 11, Section 41.

3 The cover which fits over the lower edge of the pollen filter is secured by two sliding catches. Slide the catches so that the cover is released, and remove the cover from under the facia **(see illustrations)**.

4 Withdraw the pollen filter element from its location under the facia, noting which way round it fits **(see illustration)**.

5 Fit the new filter into position, noting any direction-of-fitting markings which may be present, and secure the cover with the sliding catches.

6 Refit the passenger side lower facia panel using a reversal of the removal procedure in Chapter 11.

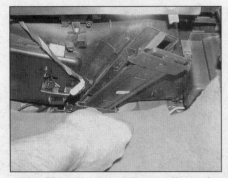

10.3a Slide the two catches to release the lower panel . . .

10.3b . . . then remove the lower panel from under the facia

10.4 Removing the pollen filter element

Every 14 000 miles (22 000 km) - Service B on display

11 Battery electrolyte level check

1 Where a standard battery is fitted, the level of the electrolyte may be checked and if necessary topped-up. On some batteries, MIN and MAX marks are printed on the side of the battery and the level may be checked without removing the cell covers. Where there are no exterior marks, remove the cover(s) from the top of the cells and check that the level of the electrolyte is approximately 2 or 3 mm above the internal plates. Some batteries have a plastic internal level indicator.
2 If necessary, top up the cells using distilled or de-ionised water.
3 Refit the cell cover(s).

12 Hose and fluid leak check

1 Visually inspect the engine joint faces, gaskets and seals for any signs of water or oil leaks. Pay particular attention to the areas around the camshaft cover, cylinder head, oil filter and sump joint faces. Bear in mind that, over a period of time, some very slight seepage from these areas is to be expected - what you are really looking for is any indication of a serious leak **(see Haynes Hint)**. Should a leak be found, renew the offending gasket or oil seal by referring to the appropriate Chapters in this manual.
2 Also check the security and condition of all the engine-related pipes and hoses. Ensure that all cable-ties or securing clips are in place and in good condition. Clips which are broken or missing can lead to chafing of the hoses, pipes or wiring, which could cause more serious problems in the future.

3 Carefully check the radiator hoses and heater hoses along their entire length **(see illustration)**. Renew any hose which is cracked, swollen or deteriorated. Cracks will show up better if the hose is squeezed. Pay close attention to the hose clips that secure the hoses to the cooling system components. Hose clips can pinch and puncture hoses, resulting in cooling system leaks.
4 Inspect all the cooling system components (hoses, joint faces, etc) for leaks. A leak in the cooling system will usually show up as white- or rust-coloured deposits on the area adjoining the leak. Where any problems of this nature are found on system components, renew the component or gasket with reference to Chapter 3.
5 Where applicable, inspect the automatic transmission fluid cooler hoses for leaks or deterioration.
6 With the vehicle raised, inspect the fuel tank and filler neck for punctures, cracks and other damage. The connection between the filler neck and tank is especially critical. Sometimes a rubber filler neck or connecting hose will leak due to loose retaining clamps or deteriorated rubber.
7 Carefully check all rubber hoses and metal fuel lines leading away from the petrol tank. Check for loose connections, deteriorated hoses, crimped lines, and other damage. Pay particular attention to the vent pipes and hoses, which often loop up around the filler neck and can become blocked or crimped. Follow the lines to the front of the vehicle, carefully inspecting them all the way. Renew damaged sections as necessary.
8 Closely inspect the metal brake pipes which run along the vehicle underbody. If they show signs of excessive corrosion or damage they must be renewed.
9 From within the engine compartment, check the security of all fuel hose attachments and pipe unions, and inspect the fuel hoses and vacuum hoses for kinks, chafing and deterioration.

10 Check the condition of the power steering fluid hoses and pipes.

13 Air conditioning system check

1 Locate the air conditioning sight glass, which is situated on top of the receiver/drier unit **(see illustration)** at the front, left-hand side of the engine compartment (see Chapter 3, Section 12).
2 Start the engine, allow it to idle and turn on the air conditioning at the control panel.
3 Carefully wipe clean the sight glass, and observe the fluid.
4 The fluid seen in the sight glass should be clear, and free of bubbles.
5 If fluid cannot be seen flowing, if there are bubbles, or if the fluid appears discoloured, the vehicle should be taken to a Mercedes-Benz dealer or air conditioning specialist for diagnosis and/or re-charging.
6 Note that it is advisable to use the air conditioning system all year round, to prevent problems which can arise through lack of use. In cold weather, the air conditioning can be used in conjunction with the heater, to provide rapid windscreen demisting.

14 Auxiliary drivebelt check and renewal

Drivebelt checking - general

1 Due to its function and construction, the auxiliary drivebelt is prone to failure after a period of time, and should be inspected periodically to prevent problems.
2 There are two lengths of drivebelt fitted, one for models with air conditioning and a

A leak in the cooling system will usually show up as white - or rust - coloured deposits on the area adjoining the leak

12.3 Heater hoses at the engine compartment bulkhead

13.1 Air conditioning sight glass

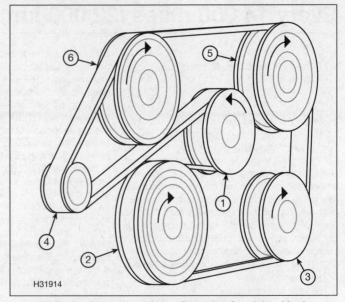

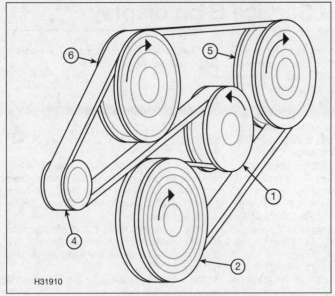

14.2a Auxiliary drivebelt configuration (models without air conditioning)

1	Tensioner pulley	5	Power steering pump pulley
2	Crankshaft pulley	6	Coolant pump pulley
4	Alternator		

14.2b Auxiliary drivebelt configuration (models with air conditioning)

1	Tensioner pulley	4	Alternator
2	Crankshaft pulley	5	Power steering pump pulley
3	Air conditioning compressor	6	Coolant pump pulley

shorter version for models without **(see illustrations)**. The drivebelt is of multi-rib type and drives the alternator, power steering pump, coolant pump and, where fitted, the air conditioning compressor. It is automatically tensioned by an idler pulley which incorporates a damper to cushion engine pulses.

3 If desired to improve access for belt inspection, where applicable, remove the viscous cooling fan and cowl as described in Chapter 3.

4 With the engine stopped, using an electric torch if necessary, check the drivebelt for cracks and separation of the belt plies. Also check for fraying and glazing, which gives the belt a shiny appearance. Both sides of the belts should be inspected, which means the belt will have to be twisted to check the underside. Turn the engine using a socket on the crankshaft pulley bolt so that the whole of the belt can be inspected.

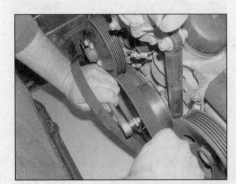

14.7 Removing the auxiliary drivebelt

5 Where removed, refit the viscous cooling fan and cowl as described in Chapter 3.

Drivebelt renewal

6 Where applicable, remove the viscous cooling fan and cowl as described in Chapter 3, to improve access.

7 Engage a spanner or socket with the nut in the centre of the tensioner pulley, then lever the tensioner anti-clockwise to relieve the tension in the belt **(see illustration)**.

8 Hold the tensioner in position with the spanner/socket, and slide the belt from the pulleys. If necessary, the tensioner can be retained in its released position by inserting a suitable bolt or metal dowel through the holes provided.

9 Fit the new belt around the pulleys, starting with the crankshaft pulley. Check that the belt is correctly seated on all the pulleys.

10 Release the spanner/socket, and allow the tensioner to move into position against the belt.

11 Where removed, refit the viscous cooling fan and cowl as described in Chapter 3.

15 Throttle linkage lubrication

1 Remove the plastic cover from the throttle linkage on the inlet manifold.

2 Lightly lubricate the linkage balljoints and sockets with clean engine oil. On automatic transmission models, also lubricate the control pressure cable linkage.

3 Refit the plastic cover.

16 Rear brake pad check

1 Chock the front wheels, then jack up the rear of the car and support it securely on axle stands (see *Jacking and vehicle support*). Remove the rear roadwheels.

2 As with the front brake pads, the thickness of pad linings can be checked quickly through the aperture at the rear of the caliper.

3 For a comprehensive check, the brake pads should be removed and cleaned. The operation of the caliper can then also be checked, and the condition of the brake disc itself can be fully examined on both sides. Refer to Chapter 9 for further information.

4 If any pad's friction material is worn to the specified thickness or less, *all four pads must be renewed as a set.*

17 Rear brake disc check

Refer to Chapter 9, Section 7.

18 Parking brake check

1 Chock the front wheels, then jack up the rear of the car, and support it on axle stands (see *Jacking and vehicle support*).

2 Release the parking brake fully, and select neutral.

3 Have an assistant gradually apply the parking brake, counting the number of clicks from the ratchet, while you check to see at what point the rear wheel begins to drag, and then locks. Repeat this check on the other rear wheel.

4 The rear wheels should both lock at the same point - if not, either the shoes need adjusting, or one of the rear cables is binding.

5 Both rear wheels should be fully locked within ten clicks from the ratchet mechanism.

6 When the parking brake is released, both rear wheels should be free to turn. Remember that there will be some drag from the rear axle and propeller shaft, however.

7 If necessary, adjust the parking brake as described in Chapter 9. Check that the parking brake cables are free to move easily and lubricate all exposed linkages/cable pivots.

19 Roadwheels rotation

Note: *This procedure is part of the Mercedes-Benz service schedule, and is important for ensuring even tyre wear. However, if this procedure is followed, it will logically result in the expense of replacing all four tyres at once. Providing a regular check is made on the tyre tread depth, some owners will find it more satisfactory to replace tyres in pairs as they wear out. Even on a rear-wheel-drive car, the front tyres generally wear faster than the rears.*

1 Jack up the front and rear of the vehicle and support it on axle stands (see *Jacking and vehicle support*).

2 To ensure even tyre wear, move the wheel positions front to rear on each side of the car.

3 Lower the car to the ground and tighten the wheel bolts to the specified torque.

20 Steering and suspension check

Front suspension and steering check

1 Raise the front of the vehicle, and securely support it on axle stands (see *Jacking and vehicle support*).

2 Visually inspect the balljoint dust covers and the steering linkage gaiters for splits, chafing or deterioration. Any wear of these components will cause loss of lubricant, together with dirt and water entry, resulting in rapid deterioration of the balljoints. Also check that the steering box mountings are tightened to the specified torque settings (see Chapter 10).

3 Check the power steering fluid hoses for chafing or deterioration, and the pipe and hose unions for fluid leaks. Also check for signs of fluid leakage under pressure from the steering box, which would indicate failed fluid seals within the steering box.

4 Grasp the roadwheel at the 12 o'clock and 6 o'clock positions, and try to rock it **(see illustration)**. Very slight free play may be felt, but if the movement is appreciable, further investigation is necessary to determine the source. Continue rocking the wheel while an assistant depresses the footbrake. If the movement is now eliminated or significantly reduced, it is likely that the hub bearings are at fault. If the free play is still evident with the footbrake depressed, then there is wear in the suspension joints or mountings. Note that the front hub bearings are adjustable (See Chapter 10).

5 Now grasp the wheel at the 9 o'clock and 3 o'clock positions, and try to rock it as before. Any movement felt now may again be caused by wear in the hub bearings or the steering track-rod balljoints. If the inner or outer balljoint is worn, the visual movement will be obvious.

6 Using a large screwdriver or flat bar, check for wear in the suspension mounting bushes by levering between the relevant suspension component and its attachment point. Some movement is to be expected as the mountings are made of rubber, but excessive wear should be obvious. Also check the condition of any visible rubber bushes, looking for splits, cracks or contamination of the rubber.

7 With the car standing on its wheels, have an assistant turn the steering wheel back-and-forth about an eighth of a turn each way. There should be very little lost movement between the steering wheel and roadwheels. If this is not the case, closely observe the linkage joints and mountings previously described, but in addition, check the steering column universal joint/coupling for wear, and the steering box itself.

Front and rear shock absorber check

8 Check for any signs of fluid leakage around the shock absorber body, or from the rubber

20.4 Check for wear in the hub bearings by grasping the wheel and trying to rock it

gaiter around the piston rod. Should any fluid be noticed, the shock absorber is defective internally, and should be renewed. **Note:** *Shock absorbers should always be renewed in pairs on the same axle.*

9 The efficiency of the shock absorber may be checked by bouncing the vehicle at each corner. Generally speaking, the body will return to its normal position and stop after being depressed. If it rises and returns on a rebound, the shock absorber is probably suspect. Examine also the shock absorber upper and lower mountings for any signs of wear.

21 Underbody check

Note: *This check should be carried out by a Mercedes-Benz dealer in order to validate the vehicle corrosion warranty.*

1 With the vehicle raised and securely supported, carry out a thorough check of the vehicle underbody sealant for signs of damage. If any area of the underbody sealant shows visible damage, the affected area should be repaired to prevent possible problems with corrosion occurring at a later date.

2 Thoroughly check the underbody for signs of corrosion.

3 Lower the car to the ground.

22 Headlight beam adjustment check

Accurate adjustment of the headlight beam is only possible using optical beam-setting equipment, and this work should therefore be carried out by a Mercedes-Benz dealer or service station with the necessary facilities.

Details of the headlight adjuster system are given in Chapter 12, Section 15.

23 Driveshaft gaiter check

1 With the vehicle raised and securely supported on stands, slowly rotate the rear roadwheel. Inspect the condition of the outer constant velocity (CV) joint rubber gaiters, squeezing the gaiters to open out the folds. Check for signs of cracking, splits or deterioration of the rubber, which may allow the grease to escape, and lead to water and grit entry into the joint. Also check the security and condition of the retaining clips. Repeat these checks on the inner CV joints **(see**

23.1 Check the driveshaft inner CV joints

illustration). If any damage or deterioration is found, the gaiters should be renewed (see Chapter 8).

2 At the same time, check the general condition of the CV joints themselves by first holding the driveshaft and attempting to rotate the wheel. Repeat this check by holding the inner joint and attempting to rotate the driveshaft. Any appreciable movement indicates wear in the joints, wear in the driveshaft splines, or a loose driveshaft retaining nut.

24 Exhaust system check

1 With the engine cold, check the complete exhaust system from the engine to the end of the tailpipe. The exhaust system is most easily checked with the vehicle raised on a hoist, or suitably supported on axle stands, so that the exhaust components are readily visible and accessible.

2 Check the exhaust pipes and connections for evidence of leaks, severe corrosion and damage. Make sure that all brackets and mountings are in good condition, and that all relevant nuts and bolts are tight. Leakage at any of the joints or in other parts of the system will usually show up as a black sooty stain in the vicinity of the leak.

3 Rattles and other noises can often be traced to the exhaust system, especially the brackets and mountings. Try to move the pipes and silencers. If the components are able to come into contact with the body or suspension parts, secure the system with new mountings. Otherwise separate the joints (if possible) and twist the pipes as necessary to provide additional clearance.

25 Windscreen wiper blade renewal

Mercedes-Benz recommend that the windscreen wiper blades should be renewed at this interval, regardless of their apparent condition. Refer to *Weekly checks* for details.

26 Road test

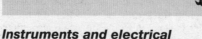

Instruments and electrical equipment

1 Check the operation of all instruments and electrical equipment.

2 Make sure that all instruments read correctly, and switch on all electrical equipment in turn, to check that it functions properly.

Steering and suspension

3 Check for any abnormalities in the steering, suspension, handling or road 'feel'.

4 Drive the vehicle, and check that there are no unusual vibrations or noises.

5 Check that the steering feels positive, with no excessive 'sloppiness', or roughness, and check for any suspension noises when cornering and driving over bumps.

Drivetrain

6 Check the performance of the engine, clutch (where applicable), gearbox/transmission, propeller shaft and driveshafts.

7 Listen for any unusual noises from the engine, clutch and gearbox/transmission.

8 Make sure that the engine runs smoothly when idling, and that there is no hesitation when accelerating.

9 Check that, where applicable, the clutch action is smooth and progressive, that the drive is taken up smoothly, and that the pedal travel is not excessive. Also listen for any noises when the clutch pedal is depressed.

10 On manual gearbox models, check that all gears can be engaged smoothly without noise, and that the gear lever action is not abnormally vague or 'notchy'.

11 On automatic transmission models, make sure that all gearchanges occur smoothly, without snatching, and without an increase in engine speed between changes. Check that all the gear positions can be selected with the vehicle at rest. If any problems are found, they should be referred to a Mercedes-Benz dealer.

Braking system

12 Make sure that the vehicle does not pull to one side when braking, and that the wheels do not lock when braking hard.

13 Check that there is no vibration through the steering when braking.

14 Check that the parking brake operates correctly without excessive movement of the foot pedal, and that it holds the vehicle stationary on a slope.

15 Test the operation of the brake servo unit as follows. With the engine off, depress the footbrake four or five times to exhaust the vacuum. Hold the brake pedal depressed, then start the engine. As the engine starts, there should be a noticeable 'give' in the brake pedal as vacuum builds up. Allow the engine to run for at least two minutes, and then switch it off. If the brake pedal is depressed now, it should be possible to detect a hiss from the servo as the pedal is depressed. After about four or five applications, no further hissing should be heard, and the pedal should feel considerably harder.

Every 20 000 miles (30 000 km) or 2 years

27 Idle speed and mixture check

Refer to Chapter 4A, Section 12.

28 Trailer coupling lubrication

1 Check the trailer coupling for security on the tow bar. Remove the cover and lubricate the tow ball with grease, then refit the cover.

Every 30 000 miles (50 000 km) or 2 years

29 Evaporative emission control charcoal canister renewal

1 Refer to Chapter 4C, Section 2.

30 Clutch friction disc check

1 Provision is made for assessing the wear of the clutch friction disc linings without removing the clutch or transmission assembly from the vehicle.
2 The check is carried out from below the clutch slave cylinder, and requires the use of a special checking gauge, which can easily be made from a strip of scrap metal or tin-plate, to the dimensions shown (see illustration).
3 After fabricating the checking tool, proceed as follows.
4 Apply the parking brake, then jack up the front of the vehicle, and support securely on axle stands (see Jacking and vehicle support).
5 Insert the forked end of the gauge into the machined slot between the slave cylinder flange and the bellhousing.
6 Push the gauge into the slot until the forked end contacts the slave cylinder pushrod.
7 If the two notches on the checking gauge are not visible, the friction disc linings are in a satisfactory condition. If the two notches are visible, the driven disc linings have reached their wear limit, and the clutch assembly must be renewed (see illustrations).
8 On completion of the check, remove the gauge and lower the vehicle to the ground.

31 Automatic transmission fluid level check

1 Note that on some later models, the top of the fluid level dipstick tube is fitted with a tamperproof cap incorporating a red plastic clip. The clip is broken when the cap is removed, and a new clip must be fitted when the cap is refitted. The dipstick is **not** fitted inside the tube, but must be obtained as a separate tool (number 140 589 15 21 00) from a Mercedes-Benz dealer. The alternative is to take the vehicle to a dealer for the fluid level check.
2 In order to check the automatic transmission fluid level, the transmission must be at operating temperature (fluid temperature 80°C). Operating temperature is reached after driving for approximately 10 miles. **Do not** attempt to check the fluid level on a cold transmission.
3 With the transmission at operating

temperature, ensure that the vehicle is parked on level ground.
4 With the engine running at idle speed, ensure that the transmission selector lever is in position P, and apply the parking brake.
5 Where applicable, pull out the locking pin securing the dipstick in its tube.
6 Remove the fluid level dipstick and wipe it with a lint-free cloth, then re-insert it (see illustrations).

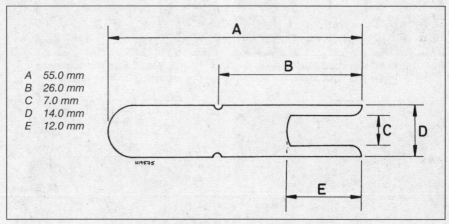

A   55.0 mm
B   26.0 mm
C   7.0 mm
D   14.0 mm
E   12.0 mm

30.2 Clutch friction disc wear checking gauge

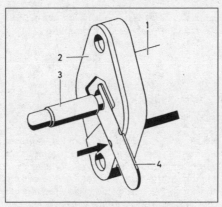

30.7a Checking clutch friction disc wear - linings in satisfactory condition

1   Slave cylinder
2   Slave cylinder shim
3   Pushrod
4   Checking gauge
Arrow indicates notches on gauge not visible

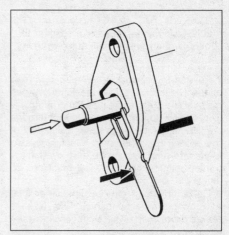

30.7b Checking clutch friction disc wear - linings worn

Light arrow   Pushrod movement as
                 wear takes place
Dark arrow   Notches on gauge visible

31.6a Pull out the automatic transmission fluid level dipstick . . .

31.6b . . . and wipe with a clean cloth

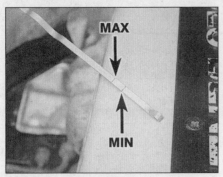

31.7 The fluid level should be between the MIN and MAX marks

31.8 Topping-up the automatic transmission hydraulic fluid

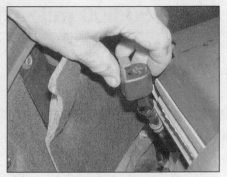

31.9 Fit the filler tube cap, then depress the tamperproof clip

32.2 Using a long nut and a spanner to unscrew the transmission fluid level/filler plug

33.2 Propeller shaft coupling at final drive

right-hand side of the transmission. A hexagonal key should be used to unscrew the plug, but a tool can be improvised using a long nut, or a length of hexagonal bar, and a spanner **(see illustration)**.

3 The fluid level should just be up to the bottom of the level/filler plug hole.

4 If necessary, top-up the level until fluid just begins to run out of the level/filler plug hole (see *Recommended lubricants and fluids*).

5 When the level is correct, refit the plug, and tighten securely.

7 Pull out the dipstick once more, and read off the fluid level. The level should be between the MIN and MAX marks **(see illustration)**.

8 If topping-up is necessary, top-up through the filler tube **(see illustration)**, using fluid of the specified type (see *Recommended lubricants and fluids*). **Do not** overfill the transmission - the fluid level must not be above the MAX mark.

9 On completion, refit the dipstick or filler tube cap (as applicable). Fit a new tamperproof clip where necessary **(see illustration)**.

32 Manual transmission fluid level check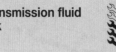

Note: *A hexagonal key, or a suitable alternative (see text) will be required to unscrew the transmission level/filler plug.*

1 Jack up the front and rear of the vehicle and support it on axle stands (see *Jacking and vehicle support*); ensure the vehicle is level.

2 Place a suitable container beneath the transmission level/filler plug, located on the

33 Propeller shaft rubber coupling condition check

1 Chock the front wheels, then jack up the rear of the vehicle and support it on axle stands.

2 Carefully check the propeller shaft front and rear rubber couplings for signs of damage and deterioration **(see illustration)**. Look for deterioration in the form of splitting, cracking or perishing. Damage may also be caused by oil or grease contamination.

3 If either of the couplings require renewal, refer to Chapter 8 for a description of the renewal procedure.

Every 40 000 miles (60 000 km) or 4 years

34 Spark plug renewal

1 The correct functioning of the spark plugs is vital for the correct running and efficiency of the engine. It is essential that the plugs fitted are appropriate for the engine (a suitable type is specified at the beginning of this Chapter). If this type is used and the engine is in good condition, the spark plugs should not need attention between scheduled replacement

intervals. Spark plug cleaning is rarely necessary, and should not be attempted unless specialised equipment is available, as damage can easily be caused to the firing ends.

2 Loosen the clips and remove the air inlet duct from between the air cleaner and inlet manifold.

Pre-12/94 models

3 Undo the screws and remove the cover from the top of the camshaft cover.

4 If the marks on the original-equipment spark plug (HT) leads cannot be seen, label

the leads to correspond to the cylinder the lead serves (No 1 cylinder is at the timing chain end of the engine). Pull the leads from the plugs by gripping the end fitting, not the lead, otherwise the lead connection may be fractured.

12/94-on models

5 Remove the ignition coils as described in Chapter 5B.

All models

6 Unscrew the plugs using a spark plug spanner, suitable box spanner or a deep

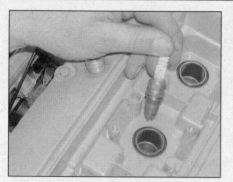

34.6 Removing the spark plugs

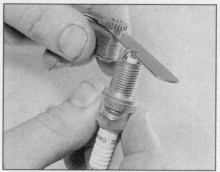

34.11 Measuring the spark plug electrode gap, using a feeler blade

34.12 Set the spark plug gap by carefully bending the electrode, using an adjusting tool

socket and extension bar **(see illustration)**. Keep the socket aligned with the spark plug - if it is forcibly moved to one side, the ceramic insulator may be broken off. As each plug is removed, examine it as follows.

7 Examination of the spark plugs will give a good indication of the condition of the engine. If the insulator nose of the spark plug is clean and white, with no deposits, this is indicative of a weak mixture or too hot a plug (a hot plug transfers heat away from the electrode slowly, a cold plug transfers heat away quickly).

8 If the tip and insulator nose are covered with hard black-looking deposits, then this is indicative that the mixture is too rich. Should the plug be black and oily, then it is likely that the engine is fairly worn, as well as the mixture being too rich.

9 If the insulator nose is covered with light tan to greyish-brown deposits, then the mixture is correct and it is likely that the engine is in good condition.

10 The spark plug electrode gap is of considerable importance as, if it is too large or too small, the size of the spark and its efficiency will be seriously impaired. The gap should be set to the value given in the

Specifications at the beginning of this Chapter. **Note:** *The electrode gap on multi-electrode spark plugs cannot be adjusted.*

11 To set the gap, measure it with a feeler blade and then bend open, or closed, the outer plug electrode until the correct gap is achieved. The centre electrode should never be bent, as this may crack the insulator and cause plug failure, if nothing worse. If using feeler blades, the gap is correct when the appropriate-size blade is a firm sliding fit **(see illustration)**.

12 Special spark plug electrode gap adjusting tools are available from most motor accessory shops, or from some spark plug manufacturers **(see illustration)**.

13 Before fitting the spark plugs **(see Haynes Hint)**, check that the threaded connector sleeves are tight, and that the plug exterior surfaces and threads are clean.

14 Tighten the plug to the specified torque using the spark plug socket and a torque wrench. Refit the remaining spark plugs in the same manner.

15 The remaining procedure is a reversal of removal.

It is very often difficult to insert spark plugs into their holes without cross-threading them. To avoid this possibility, fit a short length of 5/16 inch internal diameter rubber hose (arrowed) over the end of the spark plug. The flexible hose acts as a universal joint to help align the plug with the plug hole. Should the plug begin to cross-thread, the hose will slip on the spark plug, preventing thread damage to the cylinder head

Every 50 000 miles (80 000 km) or 4 years

35 Air filter element renewal

1 Release the coolant expansion tank purge hose from the clip on the top of the air cleaner cover, and move it to one side **(see illustration)**.

2 Release the spring clips securing the air cleaner cover to the main body and air mass meter **(see illustrations)**.

3 Lift the cover from the air cleaner, then withdraw the element, noting how it is fitted

35.1 Release the coolant expansion tank purge hose from the clip ...

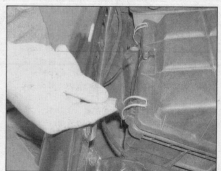

35.2a Release the spring clips ...

35.2b ... and plastic clip securing the cover to the main body ...

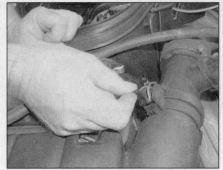

35.2c ... and release the clip securing the cover to the air mass meter

35.3 Removing the air cleaner element

37.2 Final drive unit oil level plug

(see illustration). It is not necessary to completely remove the cover from the air mass meter.

4 Wipe clean the interior surfaces of the cover and main body, using a dampened cloth.

5 Locate the new element in the main body, making sure it is seated correctly in the grooves, then refit the cover and secure with the clips.

6 Refit the purge hose in the clip on the top of the air cleaner cover.

36 Fuel filter renewal

Refer to the information in Chapter 4A, Section 4

37 Final drive unit oil level check

1 Either position the vehicle over an inspection pit, or jack up the front and rear of the vehicle and support it on axle stands (see *Jacking and vehicle support*). The vehicle must be level for the check to be accurate.

2 Clean the area around the filler/level plug on the left-hand side of the final drive unit (see illustration), then slacken and remove the plug from the housing (refer to Chapter 8, Section 2).

3 The oil level should be up to the lower edge of the filler/level plug aperture.

4 If necessary, top-up using the specified type of lubricant until the oil level is correct (see *Recommended lubricants and fluids*). Fill the final drive until oil starts to flow out and allow excess oil to drain out.

5 Once the final drive unit oil level is correct, refit the filler/level plug and tighten it securely. Lower the vehicle to the ground.

6 Note that frequent need for topping-up indicates a leakage, possibly through an oil seal. The cause should be investigated and rectified.

Every 2 years, regardless of mileage

38 Brake fluid renewal

 Warning: Brake hydraulic fluid can harm your eyes and damage painted surfaces, so use extreme caution when handling and pouring it. Do not use fluid that has been standing open for some time, as it absorbs moisture from the air. Excess moisture can cause a dangerous loss of braking effectiveness.

1 The procedure is similar to that for the bleeding of the hydraulic system as described in Chapter 9, except that the brake fluid reservoir should be emptied by siphoning, using a clean poultry baster or similar before starting, and allowance should be made for the old fluid to be expelled when bleeding a section of the circuit.

2 Working as described in Chapter 9, open the first bleed screw in the sequence, and pump the brake pedal gently until nearly all the old fluid has been emptied from the master cylinder reservoir.

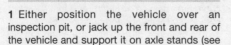

HAYNES HiNT *Old hydraulic fluid is usually much darker in colour than the new, making it easy to distinguish the two.*

3 Top-up to the MAX level with new fluid, and continue pumping until only the new fluid remains in the reservoir, and new fluid can be seen emerging from the bleed screw. Tighten the screw, and top the reservoir level up to the MAX level line.

4 Work through all the remaining bleed screws in the sequence until new fluid can be seen at all of them. Be careful to keep the master cylinder reservoir topped-up to above the MIN level at all times, or air may enter the system and greatly increase the length of the task.

5 When the operation is complete, check that all bleed screws are securely tightened, and that their dust caps are refitted. Wash off all traces of spilt fluid, and recheck the master cylinder reservoir fluid level.

6 Check the operation of the brakes before taking the car on the road.

Every 3 years, regardless of mileage

39 Coolant renewal

Cooling system draining

⚠️ *Warning: Wait until the engine is cold before starting this procedure. Do not allow antifreeze to come in contact with your skin, or with the painted surfaces of the vehicle. Rinse off spills immediately with plenty of water. Never leave antifreeze lying around in an open container, or in a puddle in the driveway or on the garage floor. Children and pets are attracted by its sweet smell, but antifreeze can be fatal if ingested.*

1 After allowing the engine to cool completely, cover the pressure cap with a wad of rag, and slowly turn the cap anti-clockwise to relieve the pressure in the cooling system (a hissing sound will normally be heard). Wait until any pressure remaining in the system is released, then continue to turn the cap until it can be removed **(see illustration)**.

2 Position a suitable container beneath the radiator, then fit a length of rubber hose to the drain nozzle. Open the drain plug (underneath the nozzle) by turning it with a large screwdriver and allow the coolant to drain through the hose, into the container **(see illustrations)**.

3 Reposition the container so that it lies beneath the engine block drain plug, which is located on the right-hand side of the cylinder block **(see illustration)**. (Certain engines are fitted with a drain plug with an integral nozzle, to which a length of rubber hose can be connected.) Open the drain plug by turning it with an open-ended spanner and allow the coolant to drain into the container.

4 Once all the coolant has drained, remove the drain hoses and close the cylinder block and radiator drain plugs.

Cooling system flushing

5 If coolant renewal has been neglected, or if the antifreeze mixture has become diluted, then in time, the cooling system may gradually lose efficiency, as the coolant passages become restricted due to rust, scale deposits, and other sediment. The cooling system efficiency can be restored by flushing the system clean.

6 The radiator should be flushed independently of the engine, to avoid unnecessary contamination.

Radiator flushing

7 To flush the radiator disconnect the top and bottom hoses and any other relevant hoses from the radiator, with reference to Chapter 3.

8 Insert a garden hose into the radiator top inlet. Direct a flow of clean water through the radiator, and continue flushing until clean water emerges from the radiator bottom outlet.

9 If after a reasonable period, the water still does not run clear, the radiator can be flushed with a good proprietary cooling system cleaning agent. It is important that the manufacturer's instructions are followed carefully. If the contamination is particularly bad, insert the hose in the radiator bottom outlet, and reverse-flush the radiator.

Engine flushing

10 To flush the engine, remove the thermostat as described in Chapter 3, then temporarily refit the thermostat cover. Adjust the heater control to the maximum setting.

11 With the top and bottom hoses disconnected from the radiator, insert a garden hose into the radiator top hose. Direct a clean flow of water through the engine, and continue flushing until clean water emerges from the radiator bottom hose.

12 On completion of flushing, refit the thermostat and reconnect the hoses with reference to Chapter 3.

Cooling system refilling

13 Before attempting to fill the cooling system, make sure that all hoses and clips are

39.1 Removing the pressure cap from the coolant expansion tank

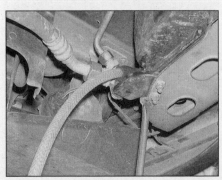

39.2b Attach a length of hose to the drain nozzle, and open the drain plug with a screwdriver

in good condition, and that the clips are tight. Note that an antifreeze mixture must be used all year round, to prevent corrosion of the engine components (see following sub-Section).

14 Remove the pressure cap, and fill the system by slowly pouring the coolant into the expansion tank (or radiator header tank) to prevent airlocks from forming.

15 If the coolant is being renewed, begin by pouring in a couple of litres of water, followed by the correct quantity of antifreeze, then top-up with more water.

16 Once the level in the expansion tank/header tank starts to rise, squeeze the radiator top and bottom hoses to help expel any trapped air in the system. Once all the air is expelled, top-up the coolant level to the MAX mark. Refit the pressure cap securely.

17 Start the engine and run it until the thermostat opens - the radiator top hose will begin to heat up as coolant flows through it to the top of the radiator.

18 Check for leaks, particularly around disturbed components. Check the coolant level in the expansion tank/header tank, and top-up if necessary. Note that the system must be cold before an accurate level is indicated. If the pressure cap is removed while the engine is still warm, cover the cap

39.2a View of the radiator drain plug from below

39.3 Engine block drain plug

with a thick cloth, and unscrew the cap slowly to gradually relieve the system pressure (a hissing sound will normally be heard). Wait until any pressure remaining in the system is released, then continue to turn the cap until it can be removed.

Antifreeze mixture

19 The antifreeze should always be renewed at the specified intervals. This is necessary not only to maintain the antifreeze properties, but also to prevent corrosion which would otherwise occur as the corrosion inhibitors become progressively less effective.

20 Always use an ethylene-glycol based antifreeze which is suitable for use in mixed-metal cooling systems. The quantity of antifreeze and levels of protection are indicated in the *Specifications*.

21 Before adding antifreeze, the cooling system should be completely drained, preferably flushed, and all hoses checked for condition and security.

22 After filling with antifreeze, a label should be attached to the expansion tank or header tank, stating the type and concentration of antifreeze used, and the date installed. Any subsequent topping-up should be made with the same type and concentration of antifreeze.

23 Do not use engine antifreeze in the windscreen/tailgate washer system, as it will cause damage to the vehicle paintwork. A screenwash additive should be added to the washer system in the quantities stated on the bottle.

Chapter 1 Part B:
Routine maintenance & servicing - diesel models

Contents

Degrees of difficulty

Easy, suitable for novice with little experience	**Fairly easy,** suitable for beginner with some experience	**Fairly difficult,** suitable for competent DIY mechanic	**Difficult,** suitable for experienced DIY mechanic	**Very difficult,** suitable for expert DIY or professional

Lubricants and fluids

Refer to *Weekly checks*

Capacities

Engine oil

2.2 litre engines	6.5 litres
2.5 litre engines	7.0 litres

Cooling system

Without air conditioning	8.0 litres
With air conditioning	8.5 litres

Transmission

Manual transmission	1.5 litres
Automatic transmission:	
Fluid change	5.5 litres
From dry:	
Type 722.42x	6.6 litres
Type 722.60x	9.3 litres

Final drive unit:

All models	1.1 litres

Power-assisted steering

All models (approximate)	1.0 litre

Fuel tank

All models:	
Total	62 litres
Reserve	7 litres

Cooling system

Antifreeze mixture:

50% antifreeze	Protection down to –37°C (5°F)
55% antifreeze	Protection down to –45°C (–22°F)

Note: *Refer to antifreeze manufacturer for latest recommendations.*

Pre-heating system

Glow plugs:

Engine code 604.910:	
Saloon models:	
Up to 01/95	Bosch 0 250 201 035
From 02/95	Bosch 0 250 201 038
Estate models with manual transmission:	
Up to engine number 006999	Bosch 0 250 201 035
From engine number 007000	Bosch 0 250 201 038
Estate models with automatic transmission:	
Up to engine number 034154	Bosch 0 250 201 035
From engine number 034155	Bosch 0 250 201 038
Engine code 605.910:	
Up to 01/95	Bosch 0 250 201 035
From 02/95	Bosch 0 250 201 038
Engine code 605.960	Bosch 0 250 201 038

Brakes

Brake pad friction material minimum thickness	2.0 mm

Torque wrench settings

	Nm	lbf ft
Auxiliary drivebelt tensioner lever bolt	10	7
Engine oil drain plug:		
M12 plug	30	22
M14 plug	25	18
Manual transmission filler/level plug	60	44
Oil filter cap	25	18
Roadwheel bolts	110	81

The maintenance intervals in this manual are provided with the assumption that you, not the dealer, will be carrying out the work. These are the minimum maintenance intervals recommended by us for vehicles driven daily. If you wish to keep your vehicle in peak condition at all times, you may wish to perform some of these procedures more often. We encourage frequent maintenance, because it enhances the efficiency, performance and resale value of your vehicle.

If the vehicle is driven in dusty areas, used to tow a trailer, or driven frequently at slow speeds (idling in traffic) or mainly for short journeys, shorter maintenance intervals are recommended.

When the vehicle is new, it should be serviced by a factory-authorised dealer service department, in order to preserve the factory warranty.

Later Mercedes C-Class models are equipped with a Service Indicator System (ASSYST). Approximately one month before a service is due, a spanner will appear on the indicator display together with the remaining distance or time. If the service is not performed on time, the display will flash with a minus sign. The distance between services can vary between 10 000 miles (15 000 km) and 20 000 miles (30 000 km), and the time between services can vary between 365 and 730 days, according to how the car is used (frequent starting, distance covered on journeys, etc). The system itself calculates the best service intervals and shows the information on the display. If the annual distance covered is in excess of 14 000 miles (22 000 km), the service display will be in distance, however if the annual distance covered is less than 14 000 miles (22 000 km), the service display will be in days.

After carrying out a service, the Mercedes-Benz dealership will reset the Service Indicator. To reset the system yourself, carry out the following.

1 Insert the ignition key and turn it to position 2. Immediately press button 0 on the instrument panel twice within one second.
2 Turn the ignition key back to position 1.
3 Press and hold button 0, then turn the key to position 2 (keeping the button pressed). The display will show the current remaining distance or time, and after 10 seconds an acoustic signal will sound. The new starting distance or time will appear for about 10 seconds on the display.
4 Release button 0.

Every 250 miles or weekly
- ☐ Refer to *Weekly checks*

Every 10 000 miles (15 000 km) - Service A on display
- ☐ Renew the engine oil and filter (Section 3)*
- ☐ Check coolant antifreeze/inhibitor (Section 4)
- ☐ Check front brake pads for wear (Section 5)
- ☐ Check front brake discs for wear (Section 6)
- ☐ Check the condition of the seat belts (Section 7)
- ☐ Lubricate all hinges, locks, aerial and sunroof (Section 8)
- ☐ Check the operation of the windscreen/headlight washer system(s) (as applicable) (Section 9)
- ☐ Renew the pollen filter (Section 10)

*Note: *Frequent oil and filter changes are good for the engine. We recommend changing the oil at half the mileage specified here, or at least twice a year if the mileage covered is a less.*

Every 14 000 miles (22 000 km) - Service B on display
Note: *Carry out the following work in addition to that described for Service A*
- ☐ Check the battery electrolyte level (Section 11)
- ☐ Check all underbonnet components and hoses for fluid leaks (Section 12)
- ☐ Check the air conditioning system (System 13)
- ☐ Check the condition of the auxiliary drivebelt (Section 14)
- ☐ Lubricate the throttle linkage (Section 15)
- ☐ Check the rear brake pads for wear (Section 16)
- ☐ Check the rear brake discs for wear (Section 17)
- ☐ Check the operation of the parking brake (Section 18)
- ☐ Rotate the roadwheels position (Section 19)
- ☐ Check the steering and suspension components for condition and security (Section 20)
- ☐ Check the underbody for damage and corrosion (Section 21)
- ☐ Check the headlight beam adjustment (Section 22)

Every 14 000 miles (22 000 km) - Service B on display (continued)
- ☐ Check the condition of the rear driveshaft gaiters (Section 23)
  Check the exhaust system and mountings (Section 24)
- ☐ Renew the windscreen wiper blades (Section 25)
- ☐ Carry out a road test (Section 26)

Every 20 000 miles (30 000 km) or 2 years
- ☐ Check the engine idle speed setting (Section 27)
- ☐ Lubricate the trailer coupling (tow bar) ball and socket (Section 28)

Every 30 000 miles (50 000 km) or 2 years
- ☐ Check the clutch friction disc wear - manual transmission models (Section 29)
- ☐ Check the automatic transmission fluid level (Section 30)
- ☐ Check the manual transmission fluid level (Section 31)
- ☐ Check the propeller shaft rubber coupling (Section 32)

Every 50 000 miles (80 000 km) or 4 years
- ☐ Renew the air filter element (Section 33)
- ☐ Renew the fuel filter and pre-filter (Section 34)
- ☐ Check final drive unit oil level (Section 35)

Every 2 years, regardless of mileage
- ☐ Renew the brake fluid (Section 36)

Every 3 years, regardless of mileage
- ☐ Renew the coolant (Section 37)

Underbonnet view of a 5-cylinder 2.5 litre turbo-diesel model

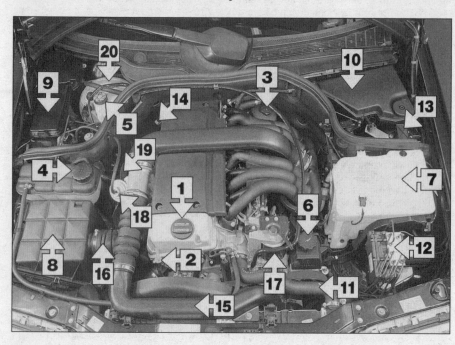

1 Engine oil filler cap
2 Engine oil dipstick
3 Oil filter
4 Coolant expansion tank
5 Brake fluid reservoir
6 Power steering fluid reservoir
7 Windscreen/headlamp washer fluid reservoir
8 Air filter
9 Fusebox
10 Engine management ECU and wiring connector box
11 Radiator top hose
12 Brake ABS unit
13 Diagnostic socket
14 Automatic transmission hydraulic fluid dipstick/filler tube
15 Air duct from intercooler to inlet manifold
16 Air duct from air cleaner to intercooler
17 Fuel filter
18 EGR unit
19 Turbocharger
20 Brake vacuum servo unit

Front underbody view of a 5-cylinder 2.5 litre turbo-diesel model

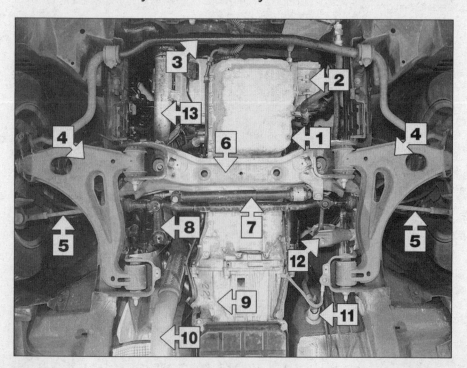

1 Engine oil drain plug
2 Air conditioning compressor
3 Anti-roll bar
4 Front suspension lower arm
5 Steering track rod
6 Subframe
7 Steering damper
8 Steering gear
9 Automatic transmission
10 Exhaust system front pipe
11 Main wiring connector in passenger footwell from battery in luggage compartment
12 Steering idler

Rear underbody view of a 5-cylinder 2.5 litre turbo-diesel model

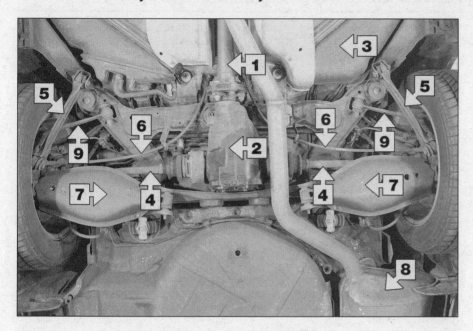

1 Propeller shaft
2 Final drive unit
3 Fuel tank
4 Driveshaft
5 Rear suspension radius arm
6 Handbrake cable
7 Rear suspension lower arm
8 Exhaust tailpipe
9 Rear suspension torque strut

1 Introduction

This Chapter is designed to help the home mechanic maintain his/her vehicle for safety, economy, long life and peak performance.

The Chapter contains a maintenance schedule, followed by Sections dealing specifically with each task in the schedule. Visual checks, adjustments, component renewal and other helpful items are included. Refer to the accompanying illustrations of the engine compartment and the underside of the vehicle for the locations of the various components.

Servicing your vehicle in accordance with the above recommendations and the following Sections will provide a planned maintenance programme, which should result in a long and reliable service life. This is a comprehensive plan, so maintaining some items but not others at the specified service intervals will not produce the same results.

As you service your vehicle, you will discover that many of the procedures can - and should - be grouped together, because of the particular procedure being performed, or because of the proximity of two otherwise-unrelated components to one another. For example, if the vehicle is raised for any reason, the exhaust can be inspected at the same time as the suspension and steering components.

The first step in this maintenance programme is to prepare yourself before the actual work begins. Read through all the Sections relevant to the work to be carried out, then make a list and gather all the parts and tools required. If a problem is encountered, seek advice from a parts specialist, or a dealer service department.

2 Regular maintenance

If, from the time the vehicle is new, the routine maintenance schedule is followed closely, and frequent checks are made of fluid levels and high-wear items, as suggested throughout this manual, the engine will be kept in relatively good running condition, and the need for additional work will be minimised.

It is possible that there will be times when the engine is running poorly due to the lack of regular maintenance. This is even more likely if a used vehicle, which has not received regular and frequent maintenance checks, is purchased. In such cases, additional work may need to be carried out, outside of the regular maintenance intervals.

If engine wear is suspected, a compression test (refer to the relevant Part of Chapter 2) will provide valuable information regarding the overall performance of the main internal components. Such a test can be used as a basis to decide on the extent of the work to be carried out. If, for example, a compression test indicates serious internal engine wear, conventional maintenance as described in this Chapter will not greatly improve the performance of the engine, and may prove a waste of time and money, unless extensive overhaul work is carried out first.

The following series of operations are those most often required to improve the performance of a generally poor-running engine:

Primary operations

a) Clean, inspect and test the battery (See Weekly checks and Section 11).
b) Check all the engine-related fluids (See Weekly checks).
c) Check the condition and tension of the auxiliary drivebelt (Section 14).
d) Check the condition of the air filter, and renew if necessary (Section 33).
e) Check the fuel filter and pre-filter, and renew if necessary (Section 34).
f) Check the condition of all hoses, and check for fluid leaks (Section 12).

If the above operations do not prove fully effective, carry out the following secondary operations:

Secondary operations

All items listed under *Primary operations*, plus the following:

a) Check the charging system (see Part A of Chapter 5).
c) Check the fuel system (see Part B of Chapter 4).
b) Check the preheating system (see Part C of Chapter 5).

Every 10 000 miles (15 000 km) - Service A on display

3 Engine oil and filter renewal

1 Frequent oil and filter changes are the most important preventative maintenance procedures which can be undertaken by the DIY owner. As engine oil ages, it becomes diluted and contaminated, which leads to premature engine wear.

2 Before starting this procedure, gather together all the necessary tools and materials. Also make sure that you have plenty of clean rags and newspapers handy, to mop up any spills. Ideally, the engine oil should be warm, as it will drain better, and more built-up sludge will be removed with it. Take care, however, not to touch the exhaust or any other hot parts of the engine when working under the vehicle. To avoid any possibility of scalding, and to protect yourself from possible skin irritants and other harmful contaminants in used engine oils, it is advisable to wear gloves when carrying out this work. Access to the underside of the vehicle will be greatly improved if it can be raised on a lift, driven onto ramps, or jacked up and supported on axle stands (see *Jacking and vehicle support*). Whichever method is chosen, make sure that the vehicle remains level, or if it is at an angle, so that the drain plug is at the lowest point. Where necessary remove the splash guard from under the engine.

3 Working in the engine compartment, locate the oil filter/housing on the rear left-hand side of the engine. Place a wad of rag around the housing to absorb any spilt oil, then unscrew the oil filter cap. **Note:** *By removing the cap, the oil will drain from the housing into the sump.* On early models the cap is secured to the housing with two nuts, however on later models the cap has its own thread and is screwed into the housing.

4 Lift the old oil filter element out from the housing (using the handle provided), and discard it **(see illustration)**.

5 Working under the vehicle, unscrew the sump drain plug about half a turn. Position the

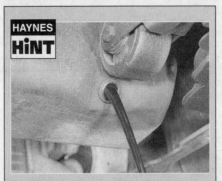

As the drain plug releases from the threads, move it away sharply so the stream of oil from the sump runs into the container, not up your sleeve.

draining container under the drain plug, then remove the plug completely. If possible, try to keep the plug pressed into the sump while unscrewing it by hand the last couple of turns **(see Haynes Hint)**.

6 Recover the sealing ring from the drain plug.

7 Allow some time for the old oil to drain, noting that it may be necessary to reposition the container as the oil flow slows to a trickle. Remove the oil filler cap from the camshaft cover.

8 After all the oil has drained, wipe off the drain plug with a clean rag. Renew the sealing washer. Clean the area around the drain plug opening, then refit and tighten the plug.

9 Remove the old oil and all tools from under the car, then refit the splash guard and lower the car to the ground.

10 Wipe out the oil filter housing and cap, using a clean rag, then fit a new oil filter element to the housing (with the handle at the top).

11 Fit a new O-ring to the cap then refit it and tighten the nuts or cap as applicable.

12 Remove the oil level dipstick then fill the engine, using the correct grade and type of oil (see *Recommended lubricants and fluids*). An oil can spout or funnel may help to reduce spillage. Pour in half the specified quantity of oil first, then wait a few minutes for the oil to fall to the sump. Continue adding oil a small quantity at a time until the level is up to the lower mark on the dipstick. Finally, bring the level up to the upper mark on the dipstick. Insert the dipstick, and refit the filler cap.

13 Start the engine and run it for a few minutes; check for leaks around the oil filter cap and the sump drain plug. Note that there may be a delay of a few seconds before the oil pressure warning light goes out when the engine is first started, as the oil circulates through the engine oil galleries and the new oil filter, before the pressure builds up.

14 Switch off the engine, and wait a few minutes for the oil to settle in the sump once more. With the new oil circulated and the filter

completely full, recheck the level on the dipstick, and add more oil as necessary.

15 Dispose of the used engine oil safely, with reference to *General repair procedures* in the Reference section of this manual.

4 Coolant antifreeze/inhibitor check

⚠️ *Warning: Wait until the engine is cold before starting this procedure. Do not allow antifreeze to come in contact with your skin, or with the painted surfaces of the vehicle. Rinse off spills immediately with plenty of water.*

1 A tester will be required to check the coolant strength; these can be obtained relatively cheaply from most motor accessory shops.

2 With the engine completely cold, unscrew and remove the filler cap from the coolant expansion tank. Follow the instructions supplied with the tester and check the coolant mixture is sufficient to give protection down to temperatures well below freezing. If the coolant has been renewed at the specified intervals this shouldn't be a problem. However, if the coolant mixture is not strong enough to provide sufficient protection it will be necessary to drain the cooling system and renew the coolant (see Section 37).

3 Once the test is complete, check the coolant level is correct (see *Weekly checks*) then securely refit the expansion tank cap.

5 Front brake pad check

1 Firmly apply the parking brake, then jack up the front of the car and support it securely on axle stands (see *Jacking and vehicle support*). Remove the front roadwheels **(see Haynes Hint)**.

For a quick check, the thickness of the friction material of the brake pad can be measured through the aperture in the caliper body.

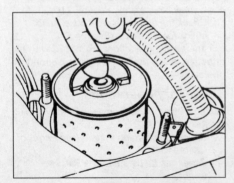

3.4 Lift out the oil filter element using the handle provided

2 For a comprehensive check, the brake pads should be removed and cleaned. The operation of the caliper can then also be checked, and the condition of the brake disc itself can be fully examined on both sides. Refer to Chapter 9 for further information.

3 If any pad's friction material is worn to the specified thickness or less, *all four pads must be renewed as a set.*

6 Front brake disc check

Refer to Chapter 9, Section 6.

7 Seat belt check

1 Carefully examine the seat belt webbing for cuts or any signs of serious fraying or deterioration. If the seat belt is of the retractable type, pull the belt all the way out, and examine the full extent of the webbing.

2 Fasten and unfasten the belt, ensuring that the locking mechanism holds securely and releases properly when intended. If the belt is of the retractable type, check also that the retracting mechanism operates correctly when the belt is released.

3 Check the security of all seat belt mountings and attachments which are accessible, without removing any trim or other components, from inside the vehicle.

8 Lubricate hinges, locks, aerial and sunroof

1 Lubricate the hinges of the bonnet, doors and tailgate with a light general-purpose oil.

Similarly, lubricate all latches, locks and lock strikers **(see illustration)**. At the same time, check the security and operation of all the locks, adjusting them if necessary (see Chapter 11).

2 Lightly lubricate the bonnet release mechanism and cable with a suitable grease.

3 If an electric aerial is fitted, extend the aerial and remove all traces of dirt from its mast. Lubricate the aerial mast with a light general-purpose oil and retract the aerial.

4 On models with a sunroof, slide the roof fully back and clean the sunroof guide rails. Apply a smear of fresh multi-purpose grease to the rails and close the sunroof.

9 Windscreen/headlight washer system check

Check that each of the washer jet nozzles are clear and that each nozzle provides a strong jet of washer fluid. The jets should be aimed to spray at a point slightly above the centre of the screen/headlight. On the windscreen washer nozzles where there are two jets, aim one of the jets slightly above the centre of the screen and aim the other just below to ensure complete coverage of the screen. If necessary, adjust the jets using a pin.

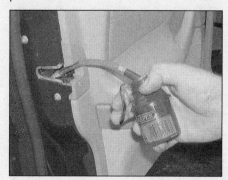

8.1 Lubricating the door locks

10 Pollen filter renewal

1 The air entering the vehicle's ventilation system is passed through a very fine pleated-paper air filter element, which removes particles of pollen, dust and other airborne foreign matter. To ensure its continued effectiveness, this filter's element must be renewed at regular intervals. Failure to renew the element will also result in greatly-reduced airflow into the passenger compartment, reducing demisting and ventilation capability.

2 Remove the passenger side lower facia panel, as described in Chapter 11, Section 41.

3 The cover which fits over the lower edge of the pollen filter is secured by two sliding catches. Slide the catches so that the cover is released, and remove the cover from under the facia **(see illustrations)**.

4 Withdraw the pollen filter element from its location under the facia, noting which way round it fits **(see illustration)**.

5 Fit the new filter into position, noting any direction-of-fitting markings which may be present, and secure the cover with the sliding catches.

6 Refit the passenger side lower facia panel using a reversal of the removal procedure in Chapter 11.

10.3a Slide the two catches to release the lower panel . . .

10.3b . . . then remove the lower panel from under the facia

10.4 Removing the pollen filter element

Every 14 000 miles (22 000 km) - Service B on display

11 Battery electrolyte level check

1 Where a standard battery is fitted, the level of the electrolyte may be checked and if necessary topped-up. On some batteries, MIN and MAX marks are printed on the side of the battery and the level may be checked without removing the cell covers. Where there are no exterior marks, remove the cover(s) from the top of the cells and check that the level of the electrolyte is approximately 2 or 3 mm above the internal plates. Some batteries have a plastic internal level indicator.
2 If necessary, top up the cells using distilled or de-ionised water.
3 Refit the cell cover(s).

12 Hose and fluid leak check

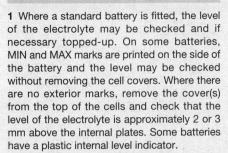

1 Visually inspect the engine joint faces, gaskets and seals for any signs of water or oil leaks. Pay particular attention to the areas around the camshaft cover, cylinder head, oil filter and sump joint faces. Bear in mind that, over a period of time, some very slight seepage from these areas is to be expected - what you are really looking for is any indication of a serious leak **(see Haynes Hint)**. Should a leak be found, renew the offending gasket or oil seal by referring to the appropriate Chapters in this manual.
2 Also check the security and condition of all the engine-related pipes and hoses. Ensure that all cable-ties or securing clips are in place and in good condition. Clips which are broken or missing can lead to chafing of the hoses, pipes or wiring, which could cause more serious problems in the future.

A leak in the cooling system will usually show up as white - or rust - coloured deposits on the area adjoining the leak

3 Carefully check the radiator hoses and heater hoses along their entire length **(see illustration)**. Renew any hose which is cracked, swollen or deteriorated. Cracks will show up better if the hose is squeezed. Pay close attention to the hose clips that secure the hoses to the cooling system components. Hose clips can pinch and puncture hoses, resulting in cooling system leaks.
4 Inspect all the cooling system components (hoses, joint faces, etc) for leaks. A leak in the cooling system will usually show up as white- or rust-coloured deposits on the area adjoining the leak. Where any problems of this nature are found on system components, renew the component or gasket with reference to Chapter 3.
5 Where applicable, inspect the automatic transmission fluid cooler hoses for leaks or deterioration.
6 With the vehicle raised, inspect the fuel tank and filler neck for punctures, cracks and other damage. The connection between the filler neck and tank is especially critical. Sometimes a rubber filler neck or connecting hose will leak due to loose retaining clamps or deteriorated rubber.

7 Carefully check all rubber hoses and metal fuel lines leading away from the petrol tank. Check for loose connections, deteriorated hoses, crimped lines, and other damage. Pay particular attention to the vent pipes and hoses, which often loop up around the filler neck and can become blocked or crimped. Follow the lines to the front of the vehicle, carefully inspecting them all the way. Renew damaged sections as necessary.
8 Closely inspect the metal brake pipes which run along the vehicle underbody. If they show signs of excessive corrosion or damage they must be renewed.
9 From within the engine compartment, check the security of all fuel hose attachments and pipe unions, and inspect the fuel hoses and vacuum hoses for kinks, chafing and deterioration.
10 Check the condition of the power steering fluid hoses and pipes.

13 Air conditioning system check

1 Locate the air conditioning sight glass, which is situated on top of the receiver/drier unit **(see illustration)** at the front of the engine compartment (see Chapter 3, Section 12).
2 Start the engine, allow it to idle and turn on the air conditioning at the control panel.
3 Carefully wipe clean the sight glass, and observe the fluid.
4 The fluid seen in the sight glass should be clear, and free of bubbles.
5 If fluid cannot be seen flowing, if there are bubbles, or if the fluid appears discoloured, the vehicle should be taken to a Mercedes-Benz dealer or air conditioning specialist for diagnosis and/or re-charging.
6 Note that it is advisable to use the air conditioning system all year round, to prevent problems which can arise through lack of use.

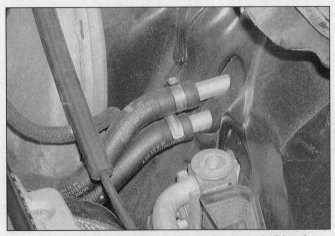

12.3 Heater hoses at the engine compartment bulkhead

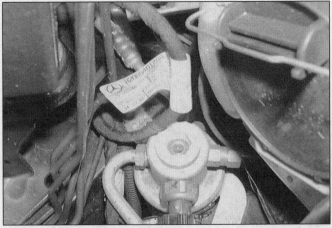

13.1 Air conditioning sight glass

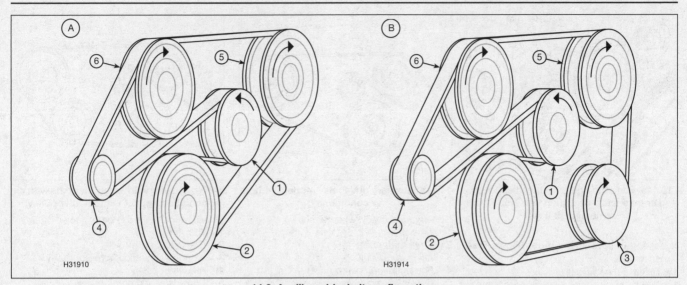

H31910 H31914

14.2 Auxiliary drivebelt configurations

A   Models without air conditioning
B   Models with air conditioning
1   Tensioner pulley
2   Crankshaft pulley
3   Air conditioning compressor
4   Alternator
5   Power steering pump
     pulley
6   Coolant pump pulley

In cold weather, the air conditioning can be used in conjunction with the heater, to provide rapid windscreen demisting.

14 Auxiliary drivebelt check and renewal

Drivebelt checking - general

1 Due to their function and construction, the belts are prone to failure after a period of time, and should be inspected periodically to prevent problems.

2 The number of belts used on a particular vehicle depends on the accessories fitted **(see illustration)**. Drivebelts are used to drive the coolant pump, alternator, power

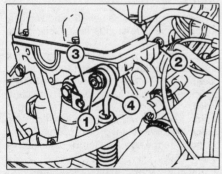

14.6 Auxiliary drivebelt tensioner components

1   Tensioner lever nut
2   Tensioner lever bolt
3   Tensioner lever
4   Tensioner spring

steering/suspension hydraulic pump, air conditioning compressor and air injection pump.

3 To improve access for belt inspection, if desired, remove the viscous cooling fan and cowl as described in Chapter 3.

4 With the engine stopped, using your fingers (and an electric torch if necessary), move along the belts, checking for cracks and separation of the belt plies. Also check for fraying and glazing, which gives the belt a shiny appearance. Both sides of the belts should be inspected, which means the belt will have to be twisted to check the underside. If necessary turn the engine using a spanner or socket on the crankshaft pulley bolt so that the whole of the belt can be inspected.

Drivebelt renewal

5 Remove the cooling fan blades and shroud, as described in Chapter 3.

6 Unscrew the nut from the end of the tensioner lever bolt **(see illustration)**.

7 Insert a suitable lever (approximately

12.0 mm diameter, and 300 mm long - eg, the wheel trim lever in the vehicle tool kit) into the hole in the tensioner lever, and press the lever anti-clockwise until the lever bolt can be slid back towards the inlet manifold.

8 Release the tensioner spring by pivoting the lever clockwise.

9 Push the idler pulley back, and withdraw the belt from the pulleys.

10 Fit the new belt as follows.

11 Raise the idler pulley slightly, and hold in position during the following procedure.

12 Form a loop in the belt, with the drive ribs on the outside, then slide the belt between the coolant pump and crankshaft pulleys **(see illustration)**.

13 Using the left hand, press the belt firmly into contact with the coolant pump pulley, then turn the coolant pump pulley anti-clockwise until the belt rides up onto the idler pulley **(see illustration)**.

14 Slide the belt over the idler pulley and the crankshaft pulley, then open out the remainder of the belt, and fit it around the

14.12 Form a loop in the belt and slide it between the coolant pump and crankshaft pulleys

14.13 Turn the coolant pump anti-clockwise until the belt rides up onto the idler pulley

14.14a Slide the belt over the idler pulley and crankshaft pulley, then fit it around the remaining pulleys

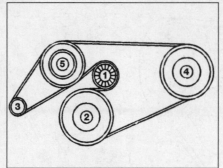

14.14b Auxiliary drivebelt - models without air conditioning

Fit belt round pulleys in order shown
1 Tensioner pulley
2 Crankshaft pulley
3 Alternator pulley
4 Power steering pump pulley
5 Coolant pump pulley

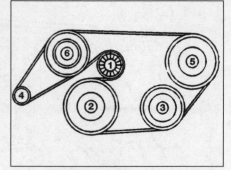

14.14c Auxiliary drivebelt - models with air conditioning, but without idler pulley

Fit belt round pulleys in order shown
1 Tensioner pulley
2 Crankshaft pulley
3 Air conditioning compressor pulley
4 Alternator pulley
5 Power steering pump pulley
6 Coolant pump pulley

remaining pulleys in the order shown **(see illustrations)**.
15 Release the idler pulley.
16 Press the tensioner lever as necessary to enable the lever bolt to be pushed into position.
17 Push the bolt back through the lever, checking that the tensioner spring locates correctly.
18 Refit the nut to the tensioner lever bolt, and tighten to the specified torque whilst counterholding the bolt.
19 Refit the cooling fan blades and shroud as described in Chapter 3.

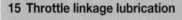

15 Throttle linkage lubrication

1 Lightly lubricate the linkage balljoints and sockets on the injection pump with clean engine oil. On automatic transmission models, also lubricate the control pressure cable linkage.

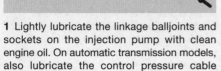

16 Rear brake pad check

1 Chock the front wheels, then jack up the rear of the car and support it securely on axle stands (see *Jacking and vehicle support*). Remove the rear roadwheels.
2 As with the front brake pads, the thickness of pad linings can be checked quickly through the aperture at the rear of the caliper.
3 For a comprehensive check, the brake pads should be removed and cleaned. The operation of the caliper can then also be checked, and the condition of the brake disc itself can be fully examined on both sides. Refer to Chapter 9 for further information.
4 If any pad's friction material is worn to the specified thickness or less, *all four pads must be renewed as a set.*

17 Rear brake disc check

Refer to Chapter 9, Section 7.

18 Parking brake check

1 Chock the front wheels, then jack up the rear of the car, and support it on axle stands (see *Jacking and vehicle support*).
2 Release the parking brake fully, and select neutral.
3 Have an assistant gradually apply the parking brake, counting the number of clicks from the ratchet, while you check to see at what point the rear wheel begins to drag, and then locks. Repeat this check on the other rear wheel.
4 The rear wheels should both lock at the same point - if not, either the shoes need adjusting, or one of the rear cables is binding.
5 Both rear wheels should be fully locked within ten clicks from the ratchet mechanism.
6 When the parking brake is released, both rear wheels should be free to turn. Remember that there will be some drag from the rear axle and propeller shaft, however.
7 If necessary, adjust the parking brake as described in Chapter 9. Check that the parking brake cables are free to move easily and lubricate all exposed linkages/cable pivots.

19 Roadwheels rotation

Note: *This procedure is part of the Mercedes-Benz service schedule, and is important for*

ensuring *even tyre wear. However, if this procedure is followed, it will logically result in the expense of replacing all four tyres at once. Providing a regular check is made on the tyre tread depth, some owners will find it more satisfactory to replace tyres in pairs as they wear out. Even on a rear-wheel-drive car, the front tyres generally wear faster than the rears.*
1 Jack up the front and rear of the vehicle and support it on axle stands (see *Jacking and vehicle support*).
2 To ensure even tyre wear, move the wheel positions front to rear on each side of the car.
3 Lower the car to the ground and tighten the wheel bolts to the specified torque.

20 Steering and suspension check

Front suspension and steering check

1 Raise the front of the vehicle, and securely support it on axle stands (see *Jacking and vehicle support*).
2 Visually inspect the balljoint dust covers and the steering linkage gaiters for splits, chafing or deterioration. Any wear of these components will cause loss of lubricant, together with dirt and water entry, resulting in rapid deterioration of the balljoints. Also check that the steering box mountings are tightened to the specified torque settings (see Chapter 10).
3 Check the power steering fluid hoses for chafing or deterioration, and the pipe and hose unions for fluid leaks. Also check for signs of fluid leakage under pressure from the steering box, which would indicate failed fluid seals within the steering box.
4 Grasp the roadwheel at the 12 o'clock and

6 o'clock positions, and try to rock it (see illustration). Very slight free play may be felt, but if the movement is appreciable, further investigation is necessary to determine the source. Continue rocking the wheel while an assistant depresses the footbrake. If the movement is now eliminated or significantly reduced, it is likely that the hub bearings are at fault. If the free play is still evident with the footbrake depressed, then there is wear in the suspension joints or mountings. Note that the front hub bearings are adjustable (See Chapter 10).

5 Now grasp the wheel at the 9 o'clock and 3 o'clock positions, and try to rock it as before. Any movement felt now may again be caused by wear in the hub bearings or the steering track-rod balljoints. If the inner or outer balljoint is worn, the visual movement will be obvious.

6 Using a large screwdriver or flat bar, check for wear in the suspension mounting bushes by levering between the relevant suspension component and its attachment point. Some movement is to be expected as the mountings are made of rubber, but excessive wear should be obvious. Also check the condition of any visible rubber bushes, looking for splits, cracks or contamination of the rubber.

7 With the car standing on its wheels, have an assistant turn the steering wheel back-and-forth about an eighth of a turn each way. There should be very little lost movement between the steering wheel and roadwheels. If this is not the case, closely observe the linkage joints and mountings previously described, but in addition, check the steering column universal joint/coupling for wear, and the steering box itself.

Front and rear shock absorber check

8 Check for any signs of fluid leakage around the shock absorber body, or from the rubber gaiter around the piston rod. Should any fluid be noticed, the shock absorber is defective internally, and should be renewed. **Note:** *Shock absorbers should always be renewed in pairs on the same axle.*

9 The efficiency of the shock absorber may be checked by bouncing the vehicle at each corner. Generally speaking, the body will return to its normal position and stop after being depressed. If it rises and returns on a rebound, the shock absorber is probably suspect. Examine also the shock absorber upper and lower mountings for any signs of wear.

21 Underbody check

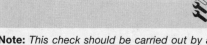

Note: *This check should be carried out by a Mercedes-Benz dealer in order to validate the vehicle corrosion warranty.*

1 With the vehicle raised and securely

20.4 Check for wear in the hub bearings by grasping the wheel and trying to rock it

supported, carry out a thorough check of the vehicle underbody sealant for signs of damage. If any area of the underbody sealant shows visible damage, the affected area should be repaired to prevent possible problems with corrosion occurring at a later date.

2 Thoroughly check the underbody for signs of corrosion.

3 Lower the car to the ground.

22 Headlight beam adjustment check

Accurate adjustment of the headlight beam is only possible using optical beam-setting equipment, and this work should therefore be carried out by a Mercedes-Benz dealer or service station with the necessary facilities.

Details of the headlight adjuster system are given in Chapter 12, Section 15.

23 Driveshaft gaiter check

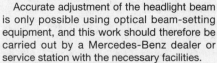

1 With the vehicle raised and securely supported on stands, slowly rotate the rear roadwheel. Inspect the condition of the outer constant velocity (CV) joint rubber gaiters, squeezing the gaiters to open out the folds. Check for signs of cracking, splits or deterioration of the rubber, which may allow the grease to escape, and lead to water and grit entry into the joint. Also check the security and condition of the retaining clips. Repeat these checks on the inner CV joints (see illustration). If any damage or deterioration is found, the gaiters should be renewed (see Chapter 8).

2 At the same time, check the general condition of the CV joints themselves by first holding the driveshaft and attempting to rotate the wheel. Repeat this check by holding the inner joint and attempting to rotate the driveshaft. Any appreciable movement indicates wear in the joints, wear in the driveshaft splines, or a loose driveshaft retaining nut.

23.1 Check the driveshaft inner CV joints

24 Exhaust system check

1 With the engine cold, check the complete exhaust system from the engine to the end of the tailpipe. The exhaust system is most easily checked with the vehicle raised on a hoist, or suitably supported on axle stands, so that the exhaust components are readily visible and accessible.

2 Check the exhaust pipes and connections for evidence of leaks, severe corrosion and damage. Make sure that all brackets and mountings are in good condition, and that all relevant nuts and bolts are tight. Leakage at any of the joints or in other parts of the system will usually show up as a black sooty stain in the vicinity of the leak.

3 Rattles and other noises can often be traced to the exhaust system, especially the brackets and mountings. Try to move the pipes and silencers. If the components are able to come into contact with the body or suspension parts, secure the system with new mountings. Otherwise separate the joints (if possible) and twist the pipes as necessary to provide additional clearance.

25 Windscreen wiper blade renewal

Mercedes-Benz recommend that the windscreen wiper blades should be renewed at this interval, regardless of their apparent condition. Refer to *Weekly checks* for details.

26 Road test

Instruments and electrical equipment

1 Check the operation of all instruments and electrical equipment.

2 Make sure that all instruments read correctly, and switch on all electrical

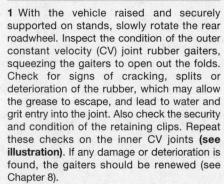

equipment in turn, to check that it functions properly.

Steering and suspension

3 Check for any abnormalities in the steering, suspension, handling or road 'feel'.
4 Drive the vehicle, and check that there are no unusual vibrations or noises.
5 Check that the steering feels positive, with no excessive 'sloppiness', or roughness, and check for any suspension noises when cornering and driving over bumps.

Drivetrain

6 Check the performance of the engine, clutch (where applicable), gearbox/transmission, propeller shaft and driveshafts.
7 Listen for any unusual noises from the engine, clutch and gearbox/transmission.
8 Make sure that the engine runs smoothly when idling, and that there is no hesitation when accelerating.

9 Check that, where applicable, the clutch action is smooth and progressive, that the drive is taken up smoothly, and that the pedal travel is not excessive. Also listen for any noises when the clutch pedal is depressed.
10 On manual gearbox models, check that all gears can be engaged smoothly without noise, and that the gear lever action is not abnormally vague or 'notchy'.
11 On automatic transmission models, make sure that all gear changes occur smoothly, without snatching, and without an increase in engine speed between changes. Check that all the gear positions can be selected with the vehicle at rest. If any problems are found, they should be referred to a Mercedes-Benz dealer.

Braking system

12 Make sure that the vehicle does not pull to one side when braking, and that the wheels do not lock when braking hard.

13 Check that there is no vibration through the steering when braking.
14 Check that the parking brake operates correctly without excessive movement of the foot pedal, and that it holds the vehicle stationary on a slope.
15 Test the operation of the brake servo unit as follows. With the engine off, depress the footbrake four or five times to exhaust the vacuum. Hold the brake pedal depressed, then start the engine. As the engine starts, there should be a noticeable 'give' in the brake pedal as vacuum builds up. Allow the engine to run for at least two minutes, and then switch it off. If the brake pedal is depressed now, it should be possible to detect a hiss from the servo as the pedal is depressed. After about four or five applications, no further hissing should be heard, and the pedal should feel considerably harder.

Every 20 000 miles (30 000 km) or 2 years

27 Idle speed check

Checking

1 Check that the adjustment of the accelerator cable is correct (see Chapter 4B).
2 Start the engine and run it until it reaches its normal operating temperature. With the parking brake applied and the transmission in neutral, allow the engine to idle. Check that all electrical consumers are switched off (including the air conditioning, where applicable).
3 Using a diesel engine tachometer, check that the engine idle speed is as quoted in the Specifications in Chapter 4B.

Adjustment

4 The idle speed is controlled electronically by the engine management ECU. If the idle speed is uneven or incorrect, the car should be taken to a Mercedes-Benz dealer or diesel specialist for the fault to be diagnosed using an instrument connected to the system diagnostic socket.

28 Trailer coupling lubrication

1 Check the trailer coupling for security on the tow bar. Remove the cover and lubricate the tow ball with grease, then refit the cover.

Every 30 000 miles (50 000 km) or 2 years

29 Clutch friction disc check

1 Provision is made for assessing the wear of the clutch friction disc linings without removing the clutch or transmission assembly from the vehicle.
2 The check is carried out from below the clutch slave cylinder, and requires the use of a special checking gauge, which can easily be made from a strip of scrap metal or tin-plate, to the dimensions shown **(see illustration)**.
3 After fabricating the checking tool, proceed as follows.
4 Apply the parking brake, then jack up the front of the vehicle, and support securely on axle stands (see *Jacking and vehicle support*).
5 Insert the forked end of the gauge into the machined slot between the slave cylinder flange and the bellhousing.
6 Push the gauge into the slot until the forked end contacts the slave cylinder pushrod.
7 If the two notches on the checking gauge are not visible, the friction disc linings are in a

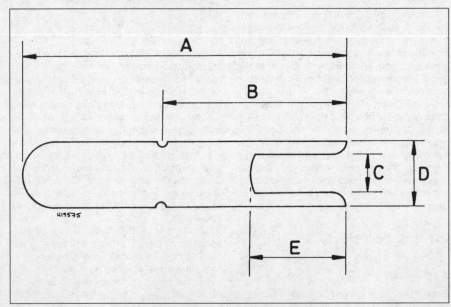

29.2 Clutch friction disc wear checking gauge

| A 55.0 mm | B 26.0 mm | C 7.0 mm | D 14.0 mm | E 12.0 mm |

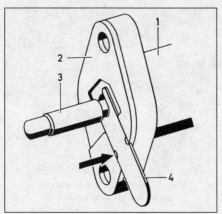

29.7a Checking clutch friction disc wear - linings in satisfactory condition

1   Slave cylinder
2   Slave cylinder shim
3   Pushrod
4   Checking gauge
Arrow indicates notches on gauge not visible

satisfactory condition. If the two notches are visible, the driven disc linings have reached their wear limit, and the clutch assembly

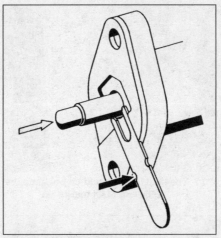

29.7b Checking clutch friction disc wear - linings worn

Light arrow   Pushrod movement as
                 wear takes place
Dark arrow   Notches on gauge visible

must be renewed **(see illustrations)**.
8 On completion of the check, remove the gauge and lower the vehicle to the ground.

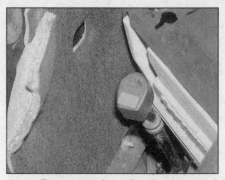

30.1a Tamperproof cap fitted to the top of the automatic transmission fluid level dipstick tube on later models

30 Automatic transmission fluid level check

1 Note that on some later models, the top of the fluid level dipstick tube is fitted with a tamperproof cap incorporating a red plastic clip **(see illustration)**. The clip is broken when the cap is removed, and a new clip must be fitted when the cap is refitted. The dipstick is **not** fitted inside the tube, but must be obtained as a separate tool (number 140 589 15 21 00) from a Mercedes-Benz dealer **(see illustration)**. The alternative is to take the vehicle to a dealer for the fluid level check.
2 In order to check the automatic transmission fluid level, the transmission must be at operating temperature (fluid temperature 80°C). Operating temperature is reached after driving for approximately 10 miles. **Do not** attempt to check the fluid level on a cold transmission.
3 With the transmission at operating temperature, ensure that the vehicle is parked on level ground.
4 With the engine running at idle speed, ensure that the transmission selector lever is in position P, and apply the parking brake.
5 Where applicable, pull out the locking pin securing the dipstick in its tube.
6 Remove the fluid level dipstick and wipe it with a lint-free cloth, then re-insert it **(see illustrations)**.

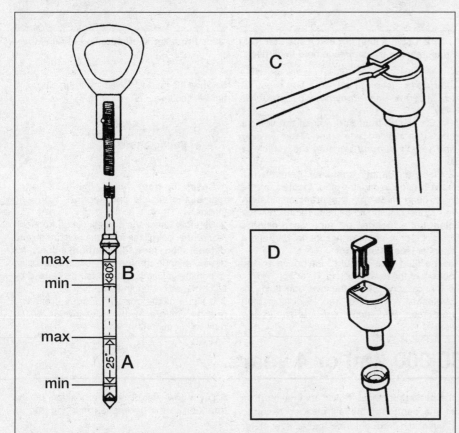

30.1b Automatic transmission dipstick

A   25°C (77°F)
B   80°C (180°F)
C   *Prise off the top of the tamperproof clip with a screwdriver, then press out the remaining part of the clip from the cap*
D   *Fit the cap to the dipstick tube, then press on the new tamperproof clip*

30.6a Pull out the automatic transmission fluid level dipstick . . .

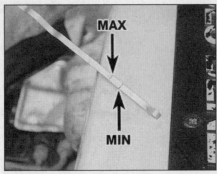

30.6b . . . and wipe with a clean cloth

30.7 The fluid level should be between the MIN and MAX marks

30.8 Topping-up the automatic transmission hydraulic fluid

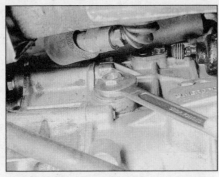

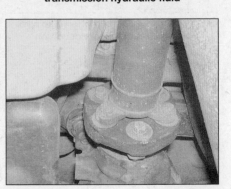

30.9 Fit the filler tube cap, then depress the tamperproof clip

31.2 Using a long nut and a spanner to unscrew the transmission fluid level/filler plug

32.2 Propeller shaft coupling at final drive

7 Pull out the dipstick once more, and read off the fluid level. The level should be between the MIN and MAX marks **(see illustration)**.

8 If topping-up is necessary, top-up through the filler tube **(see illustration)**, using fluid of the specified type (see *Recommended lubricants and fluids*). **Do not** overfill the transmission - the fluid level must not be above the MAX mark.

9 On completion, refit the dipstick or filler tube cap (as applicable). Fit a new tamperproof clip where necessary **(see illustration)**.

31 Manual transmission fluid level check

Note: *A hexagonal key, or a suitable*

alternative *(see text) will be required to unscrew the transmission level/filler plug.*

1 Jack up the front and rear of the vehicle and support it on axle stands (see *Jacking and vehicle support*); ensure the vehicle is level.

2 Place a suitable container beneath the transmission level/filler plug, located on the right-hand side of the transmission. A hexagonal key should be used to unscrew the plug, but a tool can be improvised using a long nut, or a length of hexagonal bar, and a spanner **(see illustration)**.

3 The fluid level should just be up to the bottom of the level/filler plug hole.

4 If necessary, top-up the level until fluid just begins to run out of the level/filler plug hole (see *Recommended lubricants and fluids*).

5 When the level is correct, refit the plug, and tighten securely.

32 Propeller shaft rubber coupling check

1 Chock the front wheels, then jack up the rear of the vehicle and support it on axle stands.

2 Carefully check the propeller shaft front and rear rubber couplings for signs of damage and deterioration **(see illustration)**. Look for deterioration in the form of splitting, cracking or perishing. Damage may also be caused by oil or grease contamination.

3 If either of the couplings require renewal, refer to Chapter 8 for a description of the renewal procedure.

Every 50 000 miles (80 000 km) or 4 years

33 Air filter element renewal

Turbo-diesel engines

1 Unscrew and remove the securing nuts from the air cleaner cover.

2 Lift off the air cleaner cover, together with

the packing material. Cover the intake orifice at the centre of the air cleaner base, to prevent dirt from entering the air flow meter and/or turbocharger.

3 Remove the filter element from the air cleaner.

4 Brush out all traces of dirt and debris from inside the air cleaner. Take care to prevent debris from falling down the intake orifice.

5 Lay a new filter element in position, paying attention to the orientation markings on its edge.

6 Refit the packing material and cover, then screw on the retaining nuts and tighten them securely.

Normally-aspirated engines

7 Slacken the hose clip and detach the ducting from the front of the air cleaner.

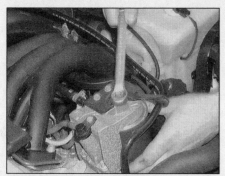

34.2a Unscrew the banjo bolt and remove the fuel filter canister

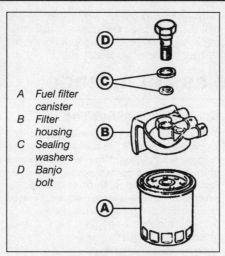

A Fuel filter canister
B Filter housing
C Sealing washers
D Banjo bolt

34.2b Fuel filter assembly

35.2 Final drive oil level plug

8 Prise open the spring catches and release the air cleaner cover.

9 Release the filter element from the air cleaner cover.

10 Brush out all traces of dirt and debris from inside the air cleaner.

11 Lay a new filter element in position in the air cleaner cover, with the folds of the filter element facing into the cover. Press the rubber seal firmly into the channel that runs around the inside edge of the air cleaner cover.

12 Fit the cover, together with the filter element, over the fixed section of the air cleaner cover. Secure the cover in position with the spring clips.

13 Reconnect the ducting to the front of the air cleaner cover, noting that the orientation arrow marked on the ducting must face the engine. Tighten the hose clip securely.

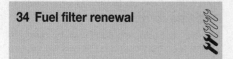

34 Fuel filter renewal

1 The fuel filter is located on the front left-hand side of the cylinder head. To minimise fuel spillage, position a small container or tray beneath the filter canister and pad the surrounding area with absorbent rags.

2 Support the fuel filter with one hand, then slacken and remove the banjo bolt from the

top of the fuel filter housing. Recover both O-ring seals and discard them - new items must be used on refitting **(see illustrations)**.

3 Remove the filter canister from the engine bay, keeping the mating face upwards to minimise fuel spillage.

4 With the filter removed, check that the restriction orifice in the fuel return line, on the mating surface of the filter housing, is clean and free from blockage.

5 Take the new filter canister and moisten the rubber seal with a little clean fuel.

6 Offer the filter up to the housing, then insert the banjo bolt (using new O-ring seals) and tighten it securely.

7 The pre-filter is positioned to the left-hand side of the fuel injection pump. Clamp off the fuel supply hose from the fuel tank downstream of the pre-filter, then slacken the clips and detach the fuel hoses from either side of the pre-filter. Fit the new unit in its place and tighten the hose clips securely.

8 Start and run the engine at idle and check around the fuel filter for fuel leaks. **Note: The fuel pump is self priming, but it may take a few seconds of cranking before the engine starts.**

9 Raise the engine speed to about 2000 rpm several times, then allow the engine to idle again. This should bleed the air bubbles from

the filter canister, but if the engine idle is at all rough or hesitant, repeat the action until the fuel system clears itself.

35 Final drive unit oil level check

1 Either position the vehicle over an inspection pit, or jack up the front and rear of the vehicle and support it on axle stands (see *Jacking and vehicle support*). The vehicle must be level for the check to be accurate.

2 Clean the area around the filler/level plug on the left-hand side of the final drive unit **(see illustration)**, then slacken and remove the plug from the housing (refer to Chapter 8, Section 2).

3 The oil level should be up to the lower edge of the filler/level plug aperture.

4 If necessary, top-up using the specified type of lubricant until the oil level is correct (see *Recommended lubricants and fluids*). Fill the final drive until oil starts to flow out and allow excess oil to drain out.

5 Once the final drive unit oil level is correct, refit the filler/level plug and tighten it securely. Lower the vehicle to the ground.

6 Note that frequent need for topping-up indicates a leakage, possibly through an oil seal. The cause should be investigated and rectified.

Every 2 years, regardless of mileage

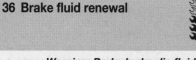

36 Brake fluid renewal

⚠ *Warning: Brake hydraulic fluid can harm your eyes and damage painted surfaces, so use extreme caution when handling and pouring it. Do not use fluid that has been standing open for some time, as it absorbs moisture from the air. Excess moisture can cause a dangerous loss of braking effectiveness.*

1 The procedure is similar to that for the bleeding of the hydraulic system as described in Chapter 9, except that the brake fluid reservoir should be emptied by siphoning, using a clean poultry baster or similar before starting, and allowance should be made for the old fluid to be expelled when bleeding a section of the circuit.

2 Working as described in Chapter 9, open the first bleed screw in the sequence, and pump the brake pedal gently until nearly all the old fluid has been emptied from the master cylinder reservoir.

3 Top-up to the MAX level with new fluid, and

 Old hydraulic fluid is usually much darker in colour than the new, making it easy to distinguish the two.

continue pumping until only the new fluid remains in the reservoir, and new fluid can be seen emerging from the bleed screw. Tighten the screw, and top the reservoir level up to the MAX level line.

4 Work through all the remaining bleed screws in the sequence until new fluid can be seen at all of them. Be careful to keep the master cylinder reservoir topped-up to above the MIN level at all times, or air may enter the system and greatly increase the length of the task.

5 When the operation is complete, check that all bleed screws are securely tightened, and that their dust caps are refitted. Wash off all traces of spilt fluid, and recheck the master cylinder reservoir fluid level.

6 Check the operation of the brakes before taking the car on the road.

Every 3 years, regardless of mileage

37 Coolant renewal

Cooling system draining

Warning: Wait until the engine is cold before starting this procedure. Do not allow antifreeze to come in contact with your skin, or with the painted surfaces of the vehicle. Rinse off spills immediately with plenty of water. Never leave antifreeze lying around in an open container, or in a puddle in the driveway or on the garage floor. Children and pets are attracted by its sweet smell, but antifreeze can be fatal if ingested.

1 After allowing the engine to cool completely, cover the pressure cap with a wad of rag, and slowly turn the cap anti-clockwise to relieve the pressure in the cooling system (see illustration) (a hissing sound will normally be heard). Wait until any pressure remaining in the system is released, then continue to turn the cap until it can be removed.

2 Position a suitable container beneath the radiator, then fit a length of rubber hose to the drain nozzle. Open the drain plug (underneath the nozzle) by turning it with a large screwdriver and allow the coolant to drain through the hose, into the container.

3 Position the container so that it lies beneath the engine block drain plug, which is located on the right-hand side of the cylinder block. (Certain engines are fitted with a drain plug with an integral nozzle, to which a length of rubber hose can be connected.) Open the drain plug by turning it with an open-ended spanner and allow the coolant to drain into the container.

4 Once all the coolant has drained, remove the drain hoses and close the cylinder block and radiator drain plugs.

37.1 Removing the pressure cap from the coolant expansion tank

Cooling system flushing

5 If coolant renewal has been neglected, or if the antifreeze mixture has become diluted, then in time, the cooling system may gradually lose efficiency, as the coolant passages become restricted due to rust, scale deposits, and other sediment. The cooling system efficiency can be restored by flushing the system clean.

6 The radiator should be flushed independently of the engine, to avoid unnecessary contamination.

Radiator flushing

7 To flush the radiator disconnect the top and bottom hoses and any other relevant hoses from the radiator, with reference to Chapter 3.

8 Insert a garden hose into the radiator top inlet. Direct a flow of clean water through the radiator, and continue flushing until clean water emerges from the radiator bottom outlet.

9 If after a reasonable period, the water still does not run clear, the radiator can be flushed with a good proprietary cooling system cleaning agent. It is important that the manufacturer's instructions are followed carefully. If the contamination is particularly bad, insert the hose in the radiator bottom outlet, and reverse-flush the radiator.

Engine flushing

10 To flush the engine, remove the thermostat as described in Chapter 3, then temporarily refit the thermostat cover. Adjust the heater control to the maximum setting.

11 With the top and bottom hoses disconnected from the radiator, insert a garden hose into the radiator top hose. Direct a clean flow of water through the engine, and continue flushing until clean water emerges from the radiator bottom hose.

12 On completion of flushing, refit the thermostat and reconnect the hoses with reference to Chapter 3.

Cooling system refilling

13 Before attempting to fill the cooling system, make sure that all hoses and clips are in good condition, and that the clips are tight. Note that an antifreeze mixture must be used all year round, to prevent corrosion of the engine components (see following sub-Section).

14 Remove the pressure cap, and fill the system by slowly pouring the coolant into the expansion tank to prevent airlocks from forming.

15 If the coolant is being renewed, begin by pouring in a couple of litres of water, followed by the correct quantity of antifreeze, then top-up with more water.

16 Once the level in the expansion tank/header tank starts to rise, squeeze the radiator top and bottom hoses to help expel any trapped air in the system. Once all the air is expelled, top-up the coolant level to the MAX mark. Refit the pressure cap securely.

17 Where applicable, unscrew the plug from the coolant sensor housing, on the upper surface of the cylinder head. As soon as coolant starts to flow out, refit the plug and tighten it. If none flows out, pour coolant into the hole vacated by the plug until it begins to flow back out. Refit the plug and tighten it securely. This removes any airlocks in the cooling system that might inhibit the operation of the coolant sensor(s).

18 Start the engine and run it until the thermostat opens - the radiator top hose will begin to heat up as coolant flows through it of the radiator when this happens.

19 Check for leaks, particularly around disturbed components. Check the coolant level in the expansion tank/header tank, and top-up if necessary. Note that the system must be cold before an accurate level is indicated. If the pressure cap is removed while the engine is still warm, cover the cap with a thick cloth, and unscrew the cap slowly to gradually relieve the system pressure (a hissing sound will normally be heard). Wait until any pressure remaining in the system is released, then continue to turn the cap until it can be removed.

Antifreeze mixture

20 The antifreeze should always be renewed at the specified intervals. This is necessary not only to maintain the antifreeze properties, but also to prevent corrosion which would otherwise occur as the corrosion inhibitors become progressively less effective.

21 Always use an ethylene-glycol based antifreeze which is suitable for use in mixed-metal cooling systems. The quantity of antifreeze and levels of protection are indicated in the Specifications.

22 Before adding antifreeze, the cooling system should be completely drained, preferably flushed, and all hoses checked for condition and security.

23 After filling with antifreeze, a label should be attached to the expansion tank or header tank, stating the type and concentration of antifreeze used, and the date installed. Any subsequent topping-up should be made with the same type and concentration of antifreeze.

24 Do not use engine antifreeze in the windscreen/tailgate washer system, as it will cause damage to the vehicle paintwork. A screenwash additive should be added to the washer system in the quantities stated on the bottle.

Chapter 2 Part A:
Petrol engine in-car repair procedures

Contents

Degrees of difficulty

Easy, suitable for novice with little experience	**Fairly easy,** suitable for beginner with some experience	**Fairly difficult,** suitable for competent DIY mechanic	**Difficult,** suitable for experienced DIY mechanic 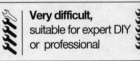	**Very difficult,** suitable for expert DIY or professional 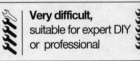

Specifications

General

Engine code:
1.8 litre fuel injection engine (10/93 to 6/96)	111.920
1.8 litre fuel injection engine (6/96 on)	111.921
2.0 litre fuel injection engine (1/94 to 5/97)	111.941
2.0 litre fuel injection engine (6/97 on)	111.945
2.2 litre fuel injection engine (10/93 to 10/96)	111.961
2.3 litre fuel injection engine (6/96 on)	111.974

Displacement:
1.8 litre engine (10/93 to 6/96)	1797 cc
1.8 litre engine (6/96 on)	1799 cc
2.0 litre engines	1998 cc
2.2 litre engine	2199 cc
2.3 litre engines	2295 cc

Bore:
1.8 litre engines	85.3 mm
2.0 litre engines	89.9 mm
2.2 litre engines	89.9 mm
2.3 litre engines	90.9 mm

Stroke:
1.8 and 2.0 litre engines	78.7 mm
2.2 litre engine	86.6 mm
2.3 litre engines	88.4 mm
Direction of engine rotation	Clockwise (viewed from front of vehicle)

General (continued)

No 1 cylinder location	Timing chain end
Firing order	1-3-4-2

Compression pressures:
  Standard:
Minimum	10.5 bars
Maximum	14.0 bars

  Economy:
Minimum	7.5 bars
Maximum	10.5 bars
Maximum difference between cylinders	1.5 bars

Compression ratio:
1.8 litre engine (10/93 to 6/96)	9.8 : 1
1.8 litre engine (6/96 on)	10.4 : 1
2.0 litre engine (1/94 to 5/97)	9.6 : 1
2.0 litre engine (6/97 on)	10.4 : 1
2.2 litre engine (10/93 to 10/96)	9.8 : 1
2.3 litre engine (6/96 on)	10.4 : 1

Camshaft

Camshaft bearing running clearance	0.05 to 0.15 mm

Camshaft bearing diameter:
Standard	28.00 to 28.02 mm
Oversize	28.50 to 28.52 mm

Camshaft bearing journal diameter:
Standard	27.95 to 27.96 mm
Oversize	28.45 to 28.46 mm

Endfloat:
New engine	0.070 to 0.150 mm
Wear limit	0.180 mm

Hydraulic tappets

Outside diameter (new)	34.965 to 34.975 mm

Cylinder head bolts

Thread diameter	M12
Length when new	102.0 mm
Maximum length	105.0 mm

Flywheel

Flywheel bolt:
Multi-spline bolt maximum shank length*	22.5 mm
Internal Torx bolt shank length	28.5 mm

Renew every time removed

Lubrication system

Minimum oil pressure:
At idle speed	0.3 bar
At 3000 rpm	3.0 bars

Torque wrench settings

	Nm	lbf ft
Air conditioning compressor mounting bolt	21	15
Armature retaining bolt (variable timing):		
Stage 1	5	4
Stage 2	Angle-tighten through a further 90°	
Automatic transmission hydraulic fluid hose union nut to radiator	20	15
Auxiliary drivebelt tensioner damper strut bolts	10	7
Auxiliary drivebelt tensioner pulley bolt	25	18
Auxiliary drivebelt tensioner	25	18
Big-end bearing cap bolts:		
Used bolts:		
Stage 1	30	22
Stage 2	Angle-tighten through a further 90 to 100°	
New bolts:		
Stage 1	40	30
Stage 2	Angle-tighten through a further 90 to 100°	

Torque wrench settings (continued)

	Nm	lbf ft
Camshaft bearing cap	21	15
Camshaft cover bolts	9	7
Coolant pump:		
M6 bolts	10	7
M8 bolts	25	18
Coolant pump pulley	10	7
Crankshaft pulley bolt	300	221
Crankshaft rear oil seal housing bolts	10	7
Cylinder block coolant drain plug	30	22
Cylinder head bolts:		
Stage 1	55	41
Stage 2	Angle-tighten through a further 90°	
Stage 3	Angle-tighten through a further 90°	
Engine-to-transmission bolts:		
Manual transmission:		
M10 x 40 mm bolts	55	41
M10 x 90 mm bolts	45	33
Automatic transmission:		
M10 bolts	55	41
M12 bolts	65	48
Flywheel/driveplate:		
Stage 1	45	33
Stage 2	Angle-tighten through a further 90°	
Front engine mounting bracket to cylinder block	20	15
Front engine mountings to crossmember (lower)	25	18
Front engine mountings to mounting brackets (upper)	55	41
Front timing cover to cylinder head:		
M6	10	7
M8	25	18
Main bearing cap bolts:		
Stage 1	55	41
Stage 2	Angle-tighten through a further 90 to 100°	
Oil drain plug	25	18
Oil filter cap	25	18
Oil pressure sensor to crankcase	15	11
Oil pump mounting bolts	25	18
Oil pump relief valve plug	50	37
Oil pump sprocket bolt	32	24
Power steering pump carrier	21	15
Power steering pump pulley	30	22
Rear engine mounting bracket to underbody	40	30
Rear engine mounting rubber to bracket	25	18
Rear engine mounting rubber to transmission casing	70	52
Sprocket nut to inlet camshaft (variable timing)	65	48
Sprocket or hub/plate bolt to camshaft:		
Stage 1	20	15
Stage 2	Angle-tighten through a further 90°	
Sump to crankcase:		
M6	10	7
M8	25	18
Sump to transmission	40	30
Thermostat housing:		
M6 bolts	10	7
M8 bolts	25	18
Timing chain cover front bolts	25	18
Timing chain cover upper bolts (to cylinder head)	25	18
Timing chain upper guide to cylinder head	10	7
Timing chain tensioner	80	59
Timing chain tensioner end piece	40	30
Transmission-to-sump bolt	40	30
Viscous fan:		
Fan to coupling	10	7
Coupling to bearing	40	30

1 General information

How to use this Chapter

This Part of Chapter 2 describes the repair procedures that can reasonably be carried out on the engine while it remains in the vehicle. If the engine has been removed from the vehicle and is being dismantled as described in Part C, any preliminary dismantling procedures can be ignored.

Note that, while it may be possible to overhaul items such as the piston/connecting rod assemblies while the engine is in the car, such tasks are not usually carried out as separate operations. Usually, several additional procedures are required (not to mention the cleaning of components and oilways); for this reason, all such tasks are classed as major overhaul procedures, and are described in Part C of this Chapter.

Part C describes the removal of the engine/transmission from the car, and the full overhaul procedures that can then be carried out.

Engine description

The engine is of four-cylinder in-line double overhead camshaft design, mounted in-line ('north-south') with the transmission on the rear of the engine.

The crankshaft is supported in five main bearings within the cast iron cylinder block. Crankshaft endfloat is controlled by thrustwashers fitted on either side of the centre main bearing.

The connecting rods are attached to the crankshaft by horizontally-split big-end bearings, and to the pistons by fully-floating gudgeon pins retained in the pistons by circlips. The alloy pistons are fitted with three piston rings; two compression and one oil control.

The camshafts are driven from the crankshaft sprocket by a double-row chain. A variable valve timing device is fitted to certain engines. The device consists of a piston located inside the inlet camshaft sprocket. The piston is splined to the sprocket and to the hub/plate with an intermediate gear, and the splines are helical to provide the necessary amount of advance or retard. An armature on the front of the device is operated by a solenoid located on the cylinder head front cover. The engine management ECU activates the solenoid, and the armature pulls out an internal plunger which uncovers oil supply holes to supply oil pressure to one side of the piston. The piston moves along the helical splines and the inlet camshaft valve timing is advanced or retarded. When the solenoid is de-activated, an internal spring forces the plunger back to uncover different oil supply holes in order to direct oil pressure to the other side of the piston.

The camshafts are supported in five bearings in the aluminium alloy cylinder head. The camshafts actuate the valves via hydraulically-operated tappets.

The oil pump is chain-driven from a sprocket on the front of the crankshaft.

Repair operations possible with the engine in the vehicle

The following operations can be carried out without having to remove the engine from the vehicle:

a) Removal and refitting of the cylinder head.
b) Removal and refitting of the timing chain and sprockets.
c) Removal and refitting of the camshafts.
d) Removal and refitting of the sump.
e) Removal and refitting of the big-end bearings, connecting rods, and pistons*.
f) Removal and refitting of the oil pump.
g) Renewal of the engine/transmission mountings.
h) Removal and refitting of the flywheel/driveplate.

* Although it is possible to remove these components with the engine in place, for reasons of access and cleanliness it is recommended that the engine is removed.

2 Compression test - description and interpretation

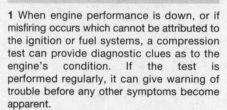

1 When engine performance is down, or if misfiring occurs which cannot be attributed to the ignition or fuel systems, a compression test can provide diagnostic clues as to the engine's condition. If the test is performed regularly, it can give warning of trouble before any other symptoms become apparent.

2 The engine must be fully warmed-up to normal operating temperature, the battery must be fully charged, and all the spark plugs must be removed (Chapter 1A). The aid of an assistant will also be required.

3 Disable the ignition system by removing the fuel pump relay, to ensure that no fuel is injected as the engine is cranked.

4 Fit a compression tester to the No 1 cylinder spark plug hole - the type of tester which screws into the plug thread is to be preferred.

5 Have the assistant hold the throttle wide open, and crank the engine on the starter motor. After one or two revolutions, the compression pressure should build up to a maximum figure, and then stabilise. Record the highest reading obtained.

6 Repeat the test on the remaining cylinders, recording the pressure in each.

7 All cylinders should produce very similar pressures; a difference of more than 1.5 bars between any two cylinders indicates a fault. Note that the compression should build up

quickly in a healthy engine. Low compression on the first stroke, followed by gradually-increasing pressure on successive strokes, indicates worn piston rings. A low compression reading on the first stroke, which does not build up during successive strokes, indicates leaking valves or a blown head gasket (a cracked head could also be the cause). Deposits on the undersides of the valve heads can also cause low compression.

8 Mercedes-Benz recommended values for compression pressures are given in the Specifications.

9 If the pressure in any cylinder is low, carry out the following test to isolate the cause. Introduce a teaspoonful of clean oil into that cylinder through its spark plug hole, and repeat the test.

10 If the addition of oil temporarily improves the compression pressure, this indicates that bore or piston wear is responsible for the pressure loss. No improvement suggests that leaking or burnt valves, or a blown head gasket, may be to blame.

11 A low reading from two adjacent cylinders is almost certainly due to the head gasket having blown between them; the presence of coolant in the engine oil will confirm this.

12 If one cylinder is about 20 percent lower than the others and the engine has a slightly rough idle, a worn camshaft lobe could be the cause.

13 On completion of the test, refit the spark plugs (see Chapter 1A) and fuel pump relay.

3 Engine assembly and valve timing marks - general information and usage

1 Valve timing on the Mercedes-Benz 111 series engine is set up at 20° ATDC, and not at TDC. At this position, tension from the valve springs is reduced enabling, for example, the camshafts to be removed without the danger of the timing chain jumping across the camshaft sprocket teeth.

2 Using a spanner on the crankshaft pulley bolt, turn the engine until the 20° ATDC mark on the pulley is aligned with the timing pointer on the timing cover. To check that the engine is positioned correctly, remove the oil filler cap and check that the No 1 cylinder inlet camshaft lobes are facing upwards at an angle. If they are not, turn the engine one compete turn and align the marks again.

3 If necessary, the camshafts can be locked in position by first removing the air cleaner (Chapter 4A) and camshaft cover (Section 4 of this Chapter). Check that the timing holes in the camshaft front bearing caps are aligned with the holes in the camshaft front drive flanges. Mercedes-Benz technicians use a special U-shaped tool to do this, however, the use of two suitable drill bits inserted

3.3 Inserting a bolt through the hole in the camshaft front bearing cap and into the flange

4.2 Removing the cover from over the thermostat housing

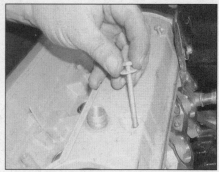

4.5a Unscrew the bolts . . .

through the holes will be sufficient **(see illustration)**.

4 If the timing chain is worn and stretched, it is possible that the timing holes may not align correctly with the crankshaft set at 20° ATDC. In this instance, it is permissible for the inlet camshaft to align between 20° and 30° ATDC, and for the exhaust camshaft to align between 25° and 35° ATDC. Note that incorrect fitting of the timing chain by one tooth on a camshaft sprocket will result in a change in crankshaft angle of approximately 20°.

4 Camshaft cover - removal and refitting

Removal

1 Remove the air cleaner-to-throttle body housing air duct.
2 Remove the cover from over the thermostat housing **(see illustration)**.
3 On pre-1994 models, unbolt the cover from the top of the camshaft cover, then identify the HT leads for position and disconnect them from the spark plugs. Move the leads to one side.
4 On 1994-on models, unbolt the cover from the top of the camshaft cover, then disconnect the low tension wiring from the

ignition coils. Disconnect the HT leads from the spark plugs of cylinders 2 and 4, then unbolt the ignition coils, and disconnect them from spark plugs 1 and 3.
5 Unscrew the bolts and lift the camshaft cover from the top of the cylinder head **(see illustrations)**. Recover the gasket from the groove in the cover.
6 If necessary the spark plug tube seals can be renewed. Use a screwdriver to prise them out from the camshaft cover, then use a suitable metal tube to drive the new ones into position. The outer metal perimeters of the seals are quite thin, and it will be necessary to use an exact fitting metal tube **(see illustrations)**.

Refitting

7 Clean the surfaces of the camshaft cover and cylinder head.
8 Locate the new gasket in the camshaft cover groove, then position the cover on the cylinder head. Insert the retaining bolts and hand-tighten them at this stage. Make sure that the gasket is still correctly located in the cover groove. To do this, feel around the rear of the cylinder head, particularly at the two recesses **(see illustrations)**.
9 Fully tighten the bolts and refit the cover over the thermostat housing.
10 On pre-1994 models, reconnect the HT leads to the spark plugs, and refit the cover to the camshaft cover. Tighten the bolts.

4.5b . . . and lift the camshaft cover from the top of the cylinder head

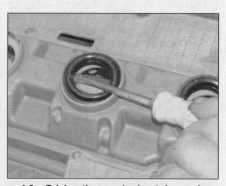

4.6a Prising the spark plug tube seals from the camshaft cover

4.6b Using a socket to drive in the new spark plug tube seals

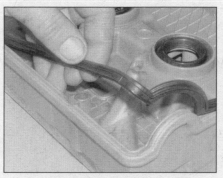

4.8a Locate the new gasket in the camshaft cover groove . . .

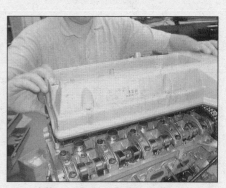

4.8b . . . then refit the cover . . .

4.8c . . . and insert the retaining bolts

4.8d Check that the gasket is correctly located at the rear of the camshaft cover

5.6a Removing the crankshaft pulley bolt and dished washers

11 On 1994-on models, refit the ignition coils to spark plugs 1 and 3, and reconnect the HT leads to spark plugs 2 and 4. Tighten the ignition coil mounting bolts and reconnect the low tension wiring. Refit the cover and tighten the bolts.

12 Refit the air cleaner-to-throttle body housing air duct and tighten the clips.

5 Crankshaft pulley/vibration damper - removal, inspection and refitting

Removal

1 Where fitted, remove the viscous fan as described in Chapter 3.

2 On models with a fan shroud, remove it from the rear of the radiator with reference to Chapter 3.

3 Remove the auxiliary drivebelt (and air conditioning compressor drivebelt where fitted) with reference to Chapter 1A.

4 Refer to Section 3 and set the engine to 20° ATDC, then turn the crankshaft back 20° so that the engine is at TDC and the Woodruff key for the crankshaft pulley/vibration damper is facing vertically upwards.

5 The crankshaft must now be held stationary while the pulley bolt is loosened. The bolt is tightened to a high torque. On manual

transmission models, one method of holding the crankshaft stationary is having an assistant depress the footbrake pedal with 4th gear engaged, or lever off the cover from the rear of the sump and insert a wide-bladed screwdriver between the starter ring gear teeth. Mercedes-Benz technicians use a special tool which is bolted to the sump, and a suitable home-made tool may be fabricated for this purpose. On automatic transmission models, remove the starter motor and insert a wide-bladed screwdriver between the starter ring gear teeth.

6 Unscrew the crankshaft pulley bolt then slide the pulley from the front of the crankshaft. Note the location of the dished washers under the head of the bolt. If the pulley is tight on the crankshaft, use a suitable puller to remove it. A two-legged puller which locates in the pulley holes is ideal. Alternatively, careful use of a screwdriver or levers may suffice (see illustrations).

7 If necessary, remove the Woodruff key from the groove in the nose of the crankshaft.

Inspection

8 Examine the oil seal contact surface of the pulley/vibration damper for an excessive wear groove. If evident, it is permissible to position the oil seal slightly further into the timing chain cover so that it runs on the unworn area of the pulley. Alternatively, the pulley should be renewed. The oil seal in the timing cover must

be renewed as a matter of course with reference to Section 14.

9 Note that the pulley/vibration damper on early models incorporates a smaller mass ring than on later models.

Refitting

10 Locate the Woodruff key in the groove in the nose of the crankshaft. Make sure that it is firmly pressed into position, and that its outer edge is parallel with the crankshaft so that the pulley/vibration damper will engage with it easily.

11 Wipe clean and lightly oil the seal contact surface of the pulley, then slide it fully onto the crankshaft, engaging it with the Woodruff key.

12 Lightly oil the threads of the crankshaft pulley bolt and the curved washers, then locate the washers on the bolt with their curved sides facing the bolt head. Insert the bolt and tighten it to the specified torque while holding the crankshaft stationary as for removal (see illustration). If necessary, press the access cover into the rear of the sump, or refit the starter motor.

13 Refit the auxiliary drivebelt (and air conditioning compressor drivebelt where fitted) with reference to Chapter 1A.

14 On models with a fan shroud, refit it to the rear of the radiator with reference to Chapter 3.

15 Where applicable, refit the viscous fan as described in Chapter 3.

5.6b Using a screwdriver to prise the crankshaft pulley

5.6c Removing the crankshaft pulley

5.12 Tightening the crankshaft pulley bolt to the specified torque

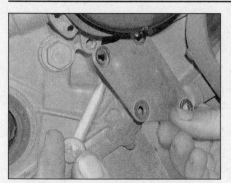

6.9a Removing the alternator support bracket . . .

6.9b . . . and air conditioning compressor support bracket

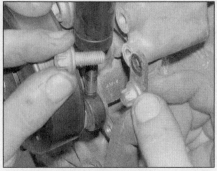

6.10a Unscrew the upper bolt . . .

6 Timing chain cover - removal and refitting

Removal

1 Disconnect the battery negative (earth) lead and position it away from the terminal. The battery is located in the rear luggage compartment.
2 Remove the camshaft cover as described in Section 4.
3 Remove the sump as described in Section 11.
4 Where fitted, remove the viscous fan as described in Chapter 3.
5 On models with a fan shroud, remove it from the rear of the radiator with reference to Chapter 3.
6 Remove the auxiliary drivebelt (and air conditioning compressor drivebelt where fitted) with reference to Chapter 1A.
7 Drain the cooling system as described in Chapter 1A.
8 On models with air conditioning, unbolt the compressor from the engine with reference to Chapter 3 and support it to one side. **Do not** disconnect the refrigerant lines from the compressor.
9 Unbolt the support bracket for the alternator and, where applicable, the air conditioning compressor **(see illustrations)**.
10 Unbolt the auxiliary drivebelt tensioner **(see illustrations)**.
11 Unbolt the thermostat housing and

recover the O-ring seal **(see illustrations)**.
12 Unbolt the front cover from the cylinder head.

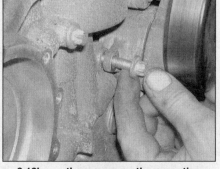

6.10b . . . then unscrew the mounting bolts . . .

6.11a Unbolt the thermostat housing . . .

13 Remove the coolant pump as described in Chapter 3 and recover the gasket **(see illustrations)**.

6.10c . . . and remove the auxiliary drivebelt tensioner from the left-hand side of the engine

6.11b . . . and recover the O-ring seal

6.13a Remove the coolant pump pulley . . .

6.13b . . . then unscrew the mounting bolts . . .

6.13c . . . and withdraw the coolant pump from the timing chain cover

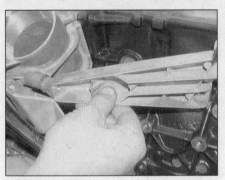

6.15 Removing the timing chain cover support bracket

6.26 Removing the air conditioning compressor mounting plate

6.27 Removing the timing chain cover from the front of the engine

14 Unbolt the pulley from the power steering pump. Hold the pulley stationary with an oil filter strap or with the auxiliary drivebelt.

15 Unbolt the timing chain cover support bracket from the left-hand side of the cylinder block **(see illustration)**.

16 Unbolt the support bar from the left-hand side of the engine, then on models with air conditioning, unbolt the compressor mounting bracket.

17 Unbolt the power steering pump and position it to the left-hand side of the engine compartment. **Do not** disconnect the hydraulic lines from the pump.

18 Using a spanner on the crankshaft pulley bolt, turn the engine until the 20° ATDC timing mark on the pulley is aligned with the timing mark on the timing cover. Insert suitable drills or metal dowels through the holes in the camshaft front bearing caps to lock the camshafts.

19 Use a dab of paint or a marker pen to mark the timing chain and the inlet and exhaust camshaft sprockets in relation to each other. This is necessary to ensure the chain is refitted correctly and the valve timing maintained.

20 Remove the timing chain tensioner as described in Section 8.

21 Hold the exhaust camshaft stationary using a spanner on the flats provided, then unscrew the three bolts and remove the

sprocket from the location peg on the camshaft flange. Release the sprocket from the timing chain. **Note:** *The sprocket retaining bolts must be renewed every time they are removed.*

22 Remove the inlet camshaft sprocket as described in Section 8.

23 Pull the guide rail pin from the front of the cylinder head. Mercedes-Benz technicians use a slide hammer tool which is screwed into the pin, however a universal slide hammer and bolt can be used **(see illustration 10.22)**, or alternatively it may be possible make up a removal tool using a long bolt, nut, large washers and metal tube. Locate the metal tube over the guide rail pin, and fit the nut to the bolt followed by the washers. Screw the bolt into the pin through the tube, then tighten the nut against the washers to extract the pin. **Note:** *If the pin has not been removed for some time, it can be very tight.*

24 Unscrew and remove the 4 upper bolts securing the timing cover to the cylinder head.

25 Unscrew the crankshaft pulley bolt, complete with dished washers, and slide the pulley from the front of the crankshaft. Note that the bolt is tightened to a high torque. The crankshaft must now be held stationary while the pulley bolt is loosened. On manual transmission models, one method of holding the crankshaft stationary is having an assistant depress the footbrake pedal with 4th gear engaged, or lever off the cover from the

rear of the sump and insert a wide-bladed screwdriver between the starter ring gear teeth. Mercedes-Benz technicians use a special tool which is bolted to the sump, and a suitable home-made tool may be fabricated for this purpose. On automatic transmission models, remove the starter motor and insert a wide-bladed screwdriver between the starter ring gear teeth.

26 Unbolt the air conditioning compressor mounting plate from the lower left-hand end of the timing chain cover **(see illustration)**.

27 Unscrew the remaining bolts and remove the timing chain cover from the front of the engine **(see illustration)**, taking care not to damage the front part of the cylinder head gasket. To ensure the bolts are refitted in the correct locations, make a drawing of their positions, or use a dab of paint on them to identify them. Remove the O-ring seals from their location on the inside of the cover. If the location dowels are loose, remove them also.

28 With the timing cover removed, use a pair of pliers to extract the chain tensioner oil reservoir non-return valve from the front of the cylinder block. Clean it and inspect for wear and damage, and if necessary, renew it.

29 It is recommended that the crankshaft front oil seal is renewed with reference to Section 14.

Refitting

30 Locate the chain tensioner oil reservoir non-return valve in its location in the front of the cylinder block.

31 Clean away all traces of old sealant, then apply new sealant to the mating surfaces of the timing cover, and fit two new O-ring seals **(see illustrations)**; make sure that no sealant is allowed to enter the oil supply chamber for the chain tensioner. If removed, refit the location dowels in the cylinder block. Clean the front part of the cylinder head gasket which contacts the timing cover.

32 Pull up the timing chain tightly so that it is located on the guides, then locate the timing cover on the front of the engine **(see**

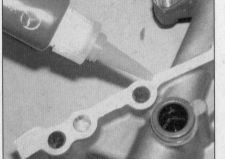

6.31a Apply sealant to the timing chain cover mating surfaces . . .

6.31b . . . and fit new O-ring seals

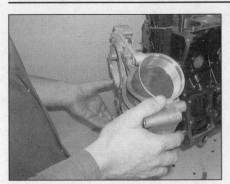

6.32 Fitting the timing chain cover

6.33 Tightening the timing chain cover bolts

6.35a Slide the crankshaft pulley onto the crankshaft . . .

illustration). **Note:** *If the chain is not pulled up, there is the possibility of a loop forming near the crankshaft sprocket.*

33 Insert the cover bolts in their previously noted positions and tighten to the specified torque **(see illustration)**.

34 Refit the air conditioning compressor mounting plate and tighten the bolts to the specified torque.

35 Slide the crankshaft pulley onto the front of the crankshaft and screw in the retaining bolt complete with dished washers. If it is tight, use a block of wood to drive it onto the crankshaft. Make sure that the curved sides of the washers face the bolt head. Hold the crankshaft stationary using the method used on removal, and tighten the bolt to the specified torque **(see illustrations)**. If necessary, press the access cover into the sump aperture, or refit the starter motor.

36 Insert the four upper bolts securing the timing cover to the cylinder head, and tighten to the specified torque.

37 Check that the crankshaft pulley timing marks are aligned correctly at 20° ATDC as previously described.

38 Apply sealant to the guide rail pin, then insert it in the front of the cylinder head making sure that it enters the top of the guide rail. Tap it fully into the head.

39 Refit the inlet camshaft sprocket with reference to Section 8. Note that the timing chain must be located on the sprocket as it is being refitted, since it is impossible to

fit it with the sprocket in place on the camshaft.

40 Locate the timing chain on the inlet camshaft sprocket so that the previously made marks are aligned.

41 Engage the exhaust camshaft sprocket with the timing chain so that the previously made marks are aligned, then offer the sprocket onto the exhaust camshaft and insert the new bolts. Hold the camshaft stationary with a spanner on the flats provided and tighten the bolts to the specified torque and angle.

42 Remove the locking drills/dowels then refit the front cover and spacers together with a new O-ring and tighten the bolts to the specified torque. Refit the chain tensioner as described in Section 8. Refit the camshaft cover as described in Section 4.

43 Refit the power steering pump and tighten the bolts.

44 Refit the support bar on the left-hand side of the engine, then on models with air conditioning, refit the compressor mounting bracket.

45 Refit the timing chain cover support bracket to the left-hand side of the cylinder block.

46 Refit the pulley to the power steering pump and tighten the bolts.

47 Refit the coolant pump as described in Chapter 3 **(see illustration)**.

48 Refit the front cover to the cylinder head and tighten the bolts. Also refit the thermostat housing together with a new O-ring seal and tighten the bolts.

49 Refit the auxiliary drivebelt tensioner and tighten the mounting bolts **(see illustration)**.

6.35b . . . using a block of wood to ensure it is fully entered

6.35c Insert the bolt and dished washers . . .

6.35d . . . and tighten to the specified torque

6.47 Refitting the coolant pump

6.49 Refitting the auxiliary drivebelt tensioner

50 Refit the support bracket for the alternator or air conditioning compressor and tighten the bolts.

51 On models with air conditioning, refit the compressor with reference to Chapter 3.

52 Refit the auxiliary drivebelt (and air conditioning compressor drivebelt where fitted) with reference to Chapter 1A.

53 Where fitted, refit the fan shroud to the rear of the radiator with reference to Chapter 3.

54 Where applicable, refit the viscous fan with reference to Chapter 3.

55 Refit the sump as described in Section 11.

56 Reconnect the battery negative lead.

57 Refill the cooling system as described in Chapter 1A.

7 Timing chain - inspection and renewal

Inspection

1 Remove the air cleaner assembly as described in Chapter 4A.

2 Remove the camshaft cover as described in Section 4.

3 Using a socket on the crankshaft pulley/vibration damper hub bolt, turn the engine so that the whole length of the chain can be progressively viewed at the camshaft sprocket.

4 The chain should be renewed if the sprocket or chain is worn, indicated by excessive lateral play between the links, and excessive noise in operation. It is wise to renew the chain in any case if the engine is to be dismantled for overhaul. Note that the rollers on a very badly worn chain may be slightly grooved. To avoid future problems, if there is any doubt at all about the condition of the chain, renew it.

Renewal

Note: *Removal of the timing chain using the following procedure entails the use of a portable electric grinder to cut through one of the chain links. Ensure that such a tool is available, as well as a new chain and new connecting link before proceeding.*

5 Disconnect the battery negative (earth) lead and position it away from the terminal. The battery is located in the rear luggage compartment.

6 If not already done, proceed as described in paragraphs 1 and 2.

7 Remove the spark plugs as described in Chapter 1A.

8 Remove the timing chain tensioner as described in Section 8. The engine will be positioned at 20° ATDC at this stage.

9 Before grinding away one of the links on the old timing chain, use two wooden wedges to temporarily lock the inlet and exhaust

camshaft sprockets and chains against the timing cover. During the following paragraphs the new timing chain will be attached to the old chain and drawn into position around the crankshaft and camshaft sprockets.

10 Cover the camshaft and the chain opening in the timing cover with clean rags.

11 Using a grinder, grind off the protruding lugs of one of the chain links at the top of the inlet sprocket - take care not to damage the sprocket.

12 Pull off the chain link plate, then push the link out towards the rear of the chain and recover the middle plate.

13 Remove the rags, taking care not to allow any swarf to drop down into the timing chain housing. Also remove the wooden wedges.

14 Using the new link, connect one end of the new timing chain to the end of the old chain on the inlet sprocket, in such a way that as the engine is turned (clockwise), the new chain will be drawn down, around the crankshaft sprocket, then up the other side. Fit the link from the rear of the sprocket and insert the middle plate (1.6 mm thick) at the same time. Ensure that the link is pushed firmly into position. If the old outer plate is a tight fit on the lugs, fit this as well, otherwise leave it off.

15 Using a socket on the crankshaft pulley/vibration damper hub bolt, slowly turn the crankshaft clockwise. Make sure that the old chain is kept engaged with the inlet sprocket so that the exhaust sprocket and camshaft also turns. The new chain must be fed onto the inlet sprocket and the old chain must be released from the inlet sprocket at the same time. The help of an assistant will make the procedure easier. Note that if the old chain is not kept engaged with the inlet sprocket, there is a chance that the valve springs will cause the sprocket to jump ahead of the rotation with the possibility of the chain becoming disengaged.

16 When both ends of the new chain are been engaged with the inlet sprocket, lock the inlet and exhaust camshafts with the wooden wedges and remove the old chain, taking care not to drop the link and middle plate. Make sure that the new chain remains firmly engaged with the inlet sprocket.

17 Fit the link and middle plate to join the ends of the new chain together, then fit the outer plate. Secure the outer plate to the link by riveting over the ends of the link pins. A special tool is available for this purpose, but it should be possible to achieve a satisfactory result using a ball-pein hammer, with a block of metal (or a second hammer) to support the rear of the chain - *take care not to damage the chain or the sprocket.*

18 Refit the timing chain tensioner as described in Section 8.

19 Using a spanner on the crankshaft pulley bolt, turn the engine until the 20° ATDC mark on the pulley is aligned with the timing pointer on the timing cover. The No 1 cylinder

inlet camshaft lobes should be both facing upwards at an angle. Check that the timing holes in the inlet and exhaust camshaft sprockets are correctly aligned with the holes in the camshaft front bearing caps. Use two suitable drill bits inserted through the holes to make the check (see Section 3).

20 If the holes are not correctly aligned, it is possible that the timing chain may have jumped one tooth during the fitting procedure, in which case it will be necessary to remove the exhaust camshaft sprocket with reference to Section 8 and reposition the chain before refitting the sprocket.

21 Refit the spark plugs as described in Chapter 1A.

22 Refit the camshaft cover as described in Section 4, then refit the air cleaner assembly.

23 Reconnect the battery negative lead.

8 Timing chain and oil pump chain tensioners, sprockets and guides - removal, inspection and refitting

Tensioner

Removal

1 Remove the top cover from the air cleaner and the air cleaner-to-throttle housing air duct.

2 Using a spanner on the crankshaft pulley bolt, turn the engine until the 20° ATDC mark on the pulley is aligned with the timing pointer on the timing cover. This will release any tension from the timing chain and ensure that it will not jump across any of the camshaft sprocket teeth when the tensioner is removed. To check that the engine is positioned correctly, remove the oil filler cap and check that the No 1 cylinder inlet camshaft lobes are both facing upwards at an angle.

3 Cover the alternator with a cloth rag as a precaution against anything falling into it.

4 Using an Allen key unscrew the timing chain tensioner end piece approximately one turn **(see illustration)**.

5 Unscrew the tensioner from the cylinder head and recover the washer **(see**

8.4 Unscrew the timing chain tensioner end piece approximately one turn . . .

8.5a . . . then unscrew the tensioner . . .

8.5b . . . and remove it from the cylinder head

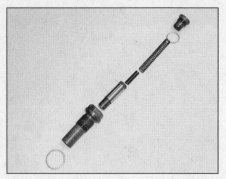

8.8 Timing chain tensioner components

illustrations). **Note:** *Once the tensioner has been unscrewed, it must be completely dismantled and reset.* **Do not** *attempt to re-tighten the tensioner in its housing at this stage, otherwise the timing chain will be over-tensioned.*

6 Completely unscrew the end piece from the tensioner. Recover the seal.
7 Remove the filler pin and main compression spring.
8 Push out the thrust pin and detent spring **(see illustration).**

Inspection

9 Thoroughly clean the tensioner components, and examine them for signs of damage or wear.
10 Check the condition of the springs, and renew if necessary.

11 Note that the oil reservoir of the timing chain tensioner is located in the front of the cylinder block, and is accessed by removing the timing cover. See Section 6 for more details.
12 Apply clean engine oil to the components as they are being reassembled.

Refitting

13 Insert the thrust pin and detent spring into the outer end of the tensioner housing until the pin's inner end is flush with the inner end of the housing.
14 Refit the tensioner together with a new washer, and tighten it to the specified torque **(see illustrations).**
15 Locate a new washer on the end piece and make sure it remains in position by using a little grease **(see illustration).**
16 Insert the main compression spring, filler

pin, and end piece, press in and screw on a few threads **(see illustration).**
17 Tighten the end piece to the specified torque **(see illustration).**
18 Refit the top cover to the air cleaner.

Camshaft sprockets
Removal

19 Remove the camshaft cover as described in Section 4.
20 Disconnect the water pump hose, then unbolt the thermostat housing from the front cover and recover the O-ring seal - note on the 111.945 engine it is necessary to unscrew the bolt securing the auxiliary drivebelt tensioner damper to the housing before removing the housing from the cylinder head **(see illustration).**

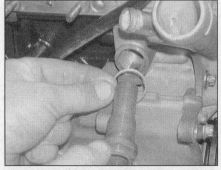

8.14a Refit the tensioner together with a new washer . . .

8.14b . . . and tighten to the specified torque

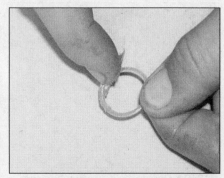

8.15 Use a little grease to hold the new washer on the end piece

8.16 Insert the main compression spring and filler pin . . .

8.17 . . . and tighten to the specified torque

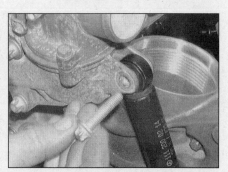

8.20 Unscrew the bolt securing the auxiliary drivebelt tensioner damper to the thermostat housing

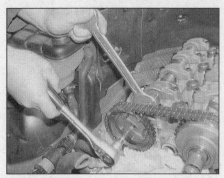

8.25a Hold the exhaust camshaft stationary while loosening the sprocket bolts

8.25b Releasing the exhaust camshaft sprocket from the timing chain

21 Unbolt the front cover from the cylinder head, and recover the O-ring. Check that the location dowels remain in the cover.

22 Using a spanner on the crankshaft pulley bolt, turn the engine until the 20° ATDC timing mark on the pulley is aligned with the timing mark on the timing cover. On engines with a variable valve timing device fitted to the front of the inlet camshaft, the device must be in its retarded position (ie when viewed from the rear, the dog in the upper cut-out must be on the left-hand side of the cut-out). Insert suitable drills or metal dowels through the holes in the camshaft front bearing caps to lock the camshafts. In this position the camshafts are not under any tension when the timing chain is removed. Note that it may be necessary to turn the crankshaft between 20° and 30° ATDC in order to get both camshaft

sprockets aligned with the bearing cap holes (refer to Section 3).

23 Use a dab of paint or a marker pen to mark the timing chain and the inlet and exhaust camshaft sprockets in relation to each other. This is necessary to ensure the chain is refitted correctly and the valve timing maintained.

24 Remove the chain tensioner as described earlier in this Section, then unbolt the upper chain guide from the front of the cylinder head.

25 Hold the exhaust camshaft stationary using a spanner on the flats provided, then unscrew the three Torx bolts and remove the sprocket from the location peg on the camshaft flange. Release the sprocket from the timing chain **(see illustrations)**. **Note:** *The sprocket retaining bolts must be renewed*

every time they are removed. Tie the timing chain to one side.

26 To remove the inlet camshaft sprocket on engines without variable valve timing, use the procedure described in paragraph 25.

27 On engines with a variable valve timing device on the front of the inlet camshaft, use the following procedure to remove the sprocket.

a) *Counterhold the armature (using a spanner on the flats provided) at the front of the inlet camshaft, and unscrew the securing bolt. Withdraw the armature **(see illustration)**. Discard the bolt, a new one must be used on refitting.*

b) *Unscrew the nut from the front of the camshaft while holding the camshaft stationary with a spanner on the flats provided, then withdraw the stepped collar. When unscrewing the nut, the camshaft can be counterheld on the flats provided **(see illustrations)**.*

c) *At this stage the piston of the variable valve timing device must be held on the camshaft while the outer sprocket is removed from its splines. To do this, either screw on a flanged nut or use a washer together with the collar securing nut. With the nut in position, slide the sprocket from the splined centre hub, at the same time releasing the timing chain from the sprocket teeth **(see illustrations)**. Tie the chain to one side using string or wire.*

d) *Unscrew the temporary nut, then*

8.27a Counterhold the armature and unscrew the bolt

8.27b Unscrew the nut . . .

8.27c . . . and withdraw the stepped collar

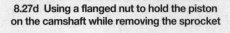

8.27d Using a flanged nut to hold the piston on the camshaft while removing the sprocket

8.27e Releasing the timing chain from the inlet camshaft sprocket

8.27f Unscrew the temporary nut . . .

8.27g . . . and withdraw the piston and spring

8.27h Unscrew the bolts . . .

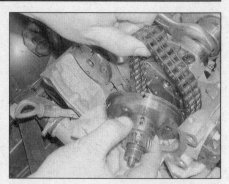

8.27i . . . and remove the hub/plate from the inlet camshaft flange

withdraw the piston, followed by the spring. Note that the smaller end of the spring locates on the inner hub of the device *(see illustrations)*.

e) Hold the inlet camshaft stationary using a spanner on the flats provided, then unscrew the three Torx bolts and remove the hub/plate from the location pin on the camshaft flange *(see illustrations)*. **Note:** *The sprocket retaining bolts must be renewed every time they are removed.*

f) If desired, working at the rear of the hub/plate remove the circlip, and withdraw the control plunger and spring *(see illustrations)*.

28 Note that the timing chain cannot become disengaged from the crankshaft sprocket, since the timing cover incorporates a retaining stub, however, it is recommended that the chain is kept tensioned by tying it to one side.

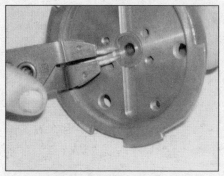

8.27j Extract the circlip . . .

8.27k . . . and remove the control plunger and spring

Note that the timing cover also incorporates an upper retaining stub, so that it is impossible for the chain to drop completely into the timing cover cavity with the timing cover in position.

29 If necessary, remove the locating pins from the ends of the camshafts.

Inspection

30 Examine the teeth on the inlet and exhaust sprockets for wear. Each tooth forms an inverted V. If worn, the side of each tooth under tension will be slightly concave in shape when compared with the other side of the tooth (ie, the teeth will have a 'hooked' appearance). If the teeth appear worn, the sprockets must be renewed.

Refitting

31 Refit the locating pins to the camshafts.
32 Engage the timing chain with the exhaust

camshaft sprocket, then refit the sprocket to the camshaft, insert the new bolts, and tighten to the specified torque and angle while holding the camshaft stationary with a spanner on the flats provided **(see illustrations)**.

33 On engines without variable valve timing, refit the sprocket to the inlet camshaft as described in the previous paragraph.

34 On engines with variable valve timing, refit the inlet camshaft sprocket using the following procedure.

a) Refit the control plunger and spring to the hub/plate and secure with the circlip.

b) Refit the hub/plate on the camshaft flange, insert the new bolts, and tighten to the specified torque and angle while holding the camshaft stationary with a spanner on the flats provided *(see illustrations)*.

8.32a Engage the timing chain with the exhaust camshaft sprocket . . .

8.32b . . . then refit the sprocket to the camshaft

8.34a Refit the hub/plate on the camshaft flange . . .

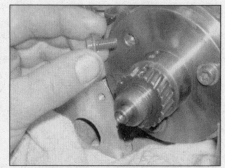

8.34b . . . insert the new bolts . . .

8.34c ... and tighten the bolts to the specified torque and angle

8.34d Refit the spring and piston ...

8.34e ... and temporarily hold with a nut

c) Locate the spring on the hub (small end first) and refit the piston on the hub/plate. It is necessary to press the piston against the tension of the spring when locating it

on the splines - note that there is a master spline to ensure correct alignment. Fit a temporary nut to hold the piston on the hub/plate (see illustrations).

d) Slide the inlet sprocket onto the piston hub splines - note there is a master spline to ensure correct alignment (see illustration). At the same time engage the timing chain with the sprocket making sure that the previously made marks are aligned with each other.

e) Unscrew the temporary nut, then refit the stepped collar followed by the retaining nut. Tighten the nut to the specified torque while holding the camshaft stationary with a spanner on the flats provided (see illustrations).

f) Refit the armature, insert the new bolt, and tighten to the specified torque while counterholding the armature with a spanner on the flats provided (see illustrations).

8.34f Slide on the inlet sprocket and engage it with the timing chain ...

8.34g ... refit the stepped collar ...

35 Refit the upper timing chain guide to the front of the cylinder head, and tighten the bolts to the specified torque, then refit the tensioner as described earlier in this Section.

36 Remove the locking drills/dowels then refit the front cover together with a new O-ring and tighten the bolts to the specified torque. At the same time refit the thermostat housing together with a new O-ring seal. On engine 111.945 refit the auxiliary drivebelt tensioner damper to the housing and tighten the bolt.

37 Refit the camshaft cover as described in Section 4.

Crankshaft sprocket

Removal

38 Disconnect the battery negative (earth)

8.34h ... and nut ...

8.34i ... refit the armature ...

8.34j ... and bolt ...

8.34k ... torque-tighten ...

8.34l ... and angle-tighten the bolt

lead and position it away from the terminal. The battery is located in the rear luggage compartment.

39 Remove the camshaft cover as described in Section 4.

40 Remove the sump as described in Section 11.

41 Where fitted, remove the viscous fan as described in Chapter 3.

42 On models with a fan shroud, remove it from the rear of the radiator with reference to Chapter 3.

43 Remove the auxiliary drivebelt (and air conditioning compressor drivebelt where fitted) with reference to Chapter 1A.

44 Drain the cooling system as described in Chapter 1A.

45 On models with air conditioning, unbolt the compressor from the engine with reference to Chapter 3 and support it to one side. **Do not** disconnect the refrigerant lines from the compressor.

46 Unbolt the support bracket for the alternator or air conditioning compressor.

47 Unbolt the auxiliary drivebelt tensioner.

48 Unbolt the thermostat housing from the front cover and recover the O-ring seal, then unbolt the front cover from the cylinder head.

49 Remove the coolant pump as described in Chapter 3.

50 Unbolt the pulley from the power steering pump. Hold the pulley stationary with an oil filter strap or with the auxiliary drivebelt.

51 Unbolt the bracket from the left-hand side of the cylinder head.

52 Unbolt the support bar from the left-hand side of the engine, then on models with air conditioning, unbolt the compressor mounting bracket.

53 Unbolt the power steering pump and position it to one side of the engine compartment. **Do not** disconnect the hydraulic lines from the pump.

54 Using a spanner on the crankshaft pulley bolt, turn the engine until the 20° ATDC timing mark on the pulley is aligned with the timing mark on the timing cover. Insert suitable drills or metal dowels through the holes in the camshaft front bearing caps to lock the camshafts.

55 Use a dab of paint or a marker pen to mark the timing chain and the inlet and exhaust camshaft sprockets in relation to each other. This is necessary to ensure the chain is refitted correctly and the valve timing maintained.

56 Remove the chain tensioner as described earlier in this Section.

57 Hold the exhaust camshaft stationary using a spanner on the flats provided, then unscrew the three bolts and remove the sprocket from the location peg on the camshaft flange. Release the sprocket from the timing chain. **Note:** *The sprocket retaining bolts must be renewed every time they are removed.*

58 Remove the inlet camshaft sprocket in the same manner as for the exhaust camshaft sprocket described in the previous paragraph.

59 Pull the guide rail pin from the front of the cylinder head. Mercedes-Benz technicians use a slide hammer tool which is screwed into the pin, however a universal slide hammer and bolt can be used **(see illustration 10.22)**, or alternatively it may be possible make up a removal tool using a long bolt, nut, large washers and metal tube. Locate the metal tube over the guide rail pin, and fit the nut to the bolt followed by the washers. Screw the bolt into the pin through the tube, then tighten the nut against the washers to extract the pin. **Note:** *If the pin has not been removed for some time, it can be very tight.*

60 Unscrew and remove the four upper bolts securing the timing cover to the cylinder head.

61 Unscrew the crankshaft pulley bolt, complete with dished washers, and slide the pulley from the front of the crankshaft. Note that the bolt is tightened to a high torque. The crankshaft must now be held stationary while the pulley bolt is loosened. On manual transmission models, one method of holding the crankshaft stationary is having an assistant depress the footbrake pedal with 4th gear engaged, or lever off the cover from the rear of the sump and insert a wide-bladed screwdriver between the starter ring gear teeth. Mercedes-Benz technicians use a special tool which is bolted to the sump, and a suitable home-made tool may be fabricated for this purpose. On automatic transmission models, remove the starter motor and insert a wide-bladed screwdriver between the starter ring gear teeth.

62 Unscrew the bolts and remove the timing cover from the front of the engine, taking care not to damage the front part of the cylinder head gasket. To ensure the bolts are refitted in the correct locations, make a drawing of their positions, or use a dab of paint on them to identify them. Remove the O-ring seals from their location on the inside of the cover. If the location dowels are loose, remove them also.

63 Hold the oil pump drivegear stationary with a suitable tool inserted in the drivegear holes, then unscrew the centre bolt. Remove the drivegear and chain from the oil pump and crankshaft.

64 Remove the chain tensioner arm, bush and spring from the pin on the lower front left-hand side of the cylinder block.

65 Swivel the guide rail as necessary and remove the timing chain from the crankshaft sprocket.

66 Using a suitable puller, remove the crankshaft sprocket from the front of the crankshaft. **Note:** *As from 01/1995 a rubber impregnated sprocket is fitted.*

67 Recover the two Woodruff keys from the slot in the nose of the crankshaft.

Inspection

68 Thoroughly clean the mating surfaces of the timing cover and cylinder block. Also clean the surfaces of the sump and crankcase. It is recommended that the crankshaft front oil seal is renewed as a matter of course. Refer to Section 14.

69 Refer to paragraph 30 for details of crankshaft sprocket inspection. Similarly, inspect the oil pump drive sprocket.

70 Inspect the oil pump drive chain and renew it if necessary. Examine the chain guides and if necessary renew them as described later in this Section.

Refitting

71 Insert the Woodruff keys in the slot in the nose of the crankshaft.

72 Align the groove in the crankshaft sprocket with the keys, then slide the sprocket fully onto the crankshaft. If it is tight, it may help if the sprocket is heated slightly with hot water.

73 Swivel the guide rail as necessary, then locate the timing chain on the crankshaft sprocket.

74 Refit the chain tensioner arm, bush and spring to the pin on the lower front left-hand side of the cylinder block.

75 Locate the oil pump drive chain on the crankshaft sprocket, then locate the oil pump sprocket in the chain and offer the sprocket onto the oil pump. Make sure that the groove in the sprocket locates correctly onto the driveshaft, then insert the retaining bolt and tighten to the specified torque while holding the sprocket stationary with a suitable tool.

76 Apply suitable sealant to the mating surfaces of the timing cover, and locate two new O-ring seals, holding them in position with the sealant, however, make sure that no sealant is allowed to enter the oil supply chamber for the chain tensioner. If removed, refit the location dowels in the cylinder block. Clean the front part of the cylinder head gasket which contacts the timing cover.

77 Pull up the timing chain tightly so that it is located on the guides, then locate the timing cover on the front of the engine. **Note:** *If the chain is not pulled up, there is the possibility of a loop forming near the crankshaft sprocket.*

78 Insert the timing cover front bolts and progressively tighten them to the specified torque, then insert the upper bolts and tighten them.

79 Slide the crankshaft pulley onto the front of the crankshaft and screw in the retaining bolt complete with dished washers. Make sure that the curved sides of the washers face the head of the bolt. Hold the crankshaft stationary using the method used on removal, and tighten the bolt to the specified torque. If necessary, press the access cover into the sump aperture, or refit the starter motor.

80 Apply sealant to the guide rail pin, then insert it in the front of the cylinder head making sure that it enters the top of the guide rail.

81 Refit the inlet camshaft sprocket with new bolts and tighten them to the specified torque.

82 Check that the crankshaft pulley timing

marks are aligned correctly at 20° ATDC as previously described.

83 Locate the timing chain on the inlet camshaft sprocket so that the previously made marks are aligned.

84 Engage the exhaust camshaft sprocket with the timing chain so that the previously made marks are aligned, then offer the sprocket onto the exhaust camshaft and insert the new bolts. Hold the camshaft stationary with a spanner on the flats provided and tighten the bolts to the specified torque.

85 Refit the chain tensioner as described earlier in this Section.

86 Remove the locking drills/dowels then refit the front cover and spacers together with a new O-ring and tighten the bolts to the specified torque.

87 Refit the camshaft cover as described in Section 4.

88 Refit the power steering pump and tighten the bolts.

89 Refit the support bar on the left-hand side of the engine, then on models with air conditioning, refit the compressor mounting bracket.

90 Refit the bracket to the left-hand side of the cylinder head.

91 Refit the pulley to the power steering pump and tighten the bolts.

92 Refit the coolant pump as described in Chapter 3.

93 Refit the front cover to the cylinder head and tighten the bolts. Also refit the thermostat housing together with a new O-ring seal and tighten the bolts.

94 Refit the auxiliary drivebelt tensioner and tighten the mounting bolts.

95 Refit the support bracket for the alternator or air conditioning compressor and tighten the bolts.

96 On models with air conditioning, refit the compressor with reference to Chapter 3.

97 Refit the auxiliary drivebelt (and air conditioning compressor drivebelt where fitted) with reference to Chapter 1A.

98 Where fitted, refit the fan shroud to the rear of the radiator with reference to Chapter 3.

8.105 Removing a timing chain guide rail from the pin on the front of the cylinder block

99 Where applicable, refit the viscous fan with reference to Chapter 3.

100 Refit the sump as described in Section 11.

101 Reconnect the battery negative lead.

102 Refill the cooling system as described in Chapter 1A.

Guide rails

Left- or right-hand guide rail

103 Remove the cylinder head as described in Section 10; the inlet and exhaust manifolds may remain attached.

104 Remove the timing cover as described in Section 6. The sump need not be removed if care is taken not to damage the area of the sump gasket which contacts the cover. If it is damaged, it will be necessary to remove the sump and renew the gasket. Note that the guide rail upper pin is removed during the timing cover removal procedure.

105 Pull the guide rail off of the pin on the front of the cylinder block (see illustration).

106 Examine the rail for signs of excessive wear, damage or cracks, and renew if necessary. Note that on the right-hand guide rail, the plastic panel is clipped in place and can be renewed separately.

107 Refitting is a reversal of removal, referring to Sections 6 and 10 as necessary.

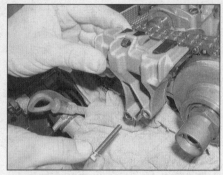

8.113 Unscrew the bolts and remove the guide pad from the front of the cylinder head

Guide pad on upper/front of cylinder head

108 Remove the air cleaner assembly as described in Chapter 4A.

109 Remove the camshaft cover as described in Section 4.

110 Where fitted, remove the viscous fan as described in Chapter 3.

111 Remove the timing chain tensioner as described earlier in this Section.

112 Unscrew the bolts and release the thermostat housing, then unbolt and remove the front cover from the cylinder head. Recover the O-ring.

113 Unbolt the guide pad from the cylinder head (see illustration).

114 Examine the pad for signs of excessive wear, damage or cracks. If necessary, the guide pad may be removed from the bracket (see illustration).

115 Refitting is a reversal of removal, referring to Chapters 3 and 4A, and to the timing chain tensioner refitting procedure given at the beginning of this Section. When refitting the front cover, use a new O-ring seal and apply suitable sealant to the mating surfaces of the cover and cylinder head (see illustrations).

Oil pump chain tensioner

116 Remove the timing cover as described in Section 6, and the sump as described in Section 11.

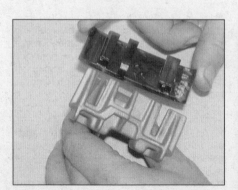

8.114 Removing the guide pad from the bracket

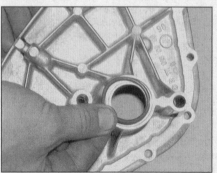

8.115a Fit a new O-ring seal to the front cover . . .

8.115b . . . then apply suitable sealant to the mating surfaces . . .

8.115c ... refit the cover ...

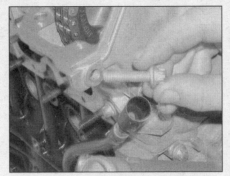

8.115d ... insert the bolts and tighten to the specified torque

8.119 Removing the oil pump tensioner from the pin on the front of the cylinder block

117 Remove the oil pump as described in Section 12.

118 Unhook the chain from the sprocket on the front of the crankshaft.

119 Note the location of the tensioner spring, then carefully release the spring with a screwdriver. Withdraw the tensioner and spring from the pin on the front of the cylinder block **(see illustration)**.

120 Refitting is a reversal of removal, referring to Sections 12, 11 and 6 as necessary.

9 Camshafts and hydraulic tappets - removal, inspection and refitting

Removal

1 Remove the camshaft cover as described in Section 4.

2 At this stage it is possible to carry out a basic check of the hydraulic tappets. Turn the engine as necessary so that the heel of the first camshaft lobe is positioned over the hydraulic tappet. Using a wooden or plastic tool, press down on the tappet and check that it feels firm. If it moves down, the internal components are not sealing correctly and the tappet must be renewed. Check the tappet of the second valve on that cylinder, then turn the engine as necessary to check the remaining tappets. **Note:** *Do not use*

excessive force to depress the tappets, otherwise the valves may open, giving a false indication.

3 Drain the cooling system as described in Chapter 1A.

4 Disconnect the coolant by-pass hose, then unbolt the coolant thermostat housing from the cylinder head front cover and move it as far forwards as possible. Recover the O-ring.

5 Disconnect the wiring from the variable valve timing coil, then unbolt the front cover from the front of the cylinder head. Recover the O-ring.

6 Use a dab of paint or a marker pen to mark the timing chain and the inlet and exhaust camshaft sprockets in relation to each other. This is necessary to ensure the chain is refitted correctly and the valve timing maintained. Also identify each camshaft with an I for inlet and E for exhaust.

7 Remove the chain tensioner as described in Section 8.

8 Unbolt the timing chain upper guide from the front of the cylinder head.

9 Remove the sprockets from the inlet and exhaust camshafts with reference to Section 8. **Note:** *The sprocket retaining bolts must be renewed every time they are removed.*

10 Using a spanner on the crankshaft pulley bolt, turn the engine clockwise until the 30° ATDC timing mark on the pulley is aligned with the timing mark on the timing cover. This will ensure that the camshafts can be rotated

without the valves touching the tops of the pistons.

11 Note that the camshaft bearing caps are numbered from 1 to 10, starting at the front of the exhaust camshaft.

12 Progressively unscrew the bearing cap bolts then remove the caps from the inlet and exhaust camshafts **(see illustrations)**.

13 Note the angled position of the camshaft lobes of No 1 cylinder as an aid to refitting, then carefully lift the inlet and exhaust camshafts from the cylinder head **(see illustrations)**.

14 Obtain sixteen small, clean containers, and number them 1 to 16. Using a rubber sucker, withdraw each hydraulic tappet in turn from the cylinder head, invert it to prevent oil loss, and place it in its respective container,

9.12a Progressively unscrew the bolts ...

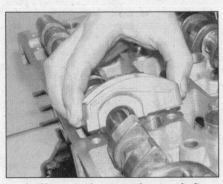

9.12b ... and remove the camshaft bearing caps

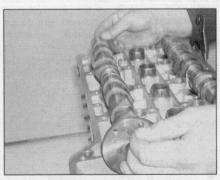

9.13a Removing the exhaust camshaft ...

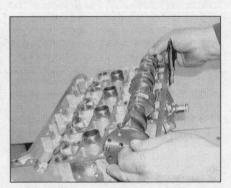

9.13b ... and inlet camshaft

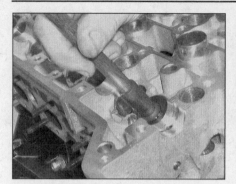

9.14a Use a rubber sucker . . .

9.14b . . . to remove the hydraulic tappets from the cylinder head

which should then be filled with clean engine oil **(see illustrations)**. Note: *Do not use a magnet to withdraw the tappets, as this will magnetise the upper surface causing swarf to be attracted to it.* Do not interchange the hydraulic tappets, or their rate of wear will be much increased. Do not allow them to lose oil or they will take a long time to refill on restarting the engine.

Inspection

15 With the camshafts and hydraulic tappets removed, check all components for signs of obvious wear (scoring, pitting, etc) and for ovality, and renew if necessary. Clean all the components thoroughly before making the check.

16 Measure the outside diameter of each tappet - take measurements at the top and bottom of each tappet, then a second set at right-angles to the first; if any measurement is significantly different from the others, the tappet is tapered or oval (as applicable) and must be renewed. Compare the outside diameter of the tappets with the information given in the Specifications. If the tappets or the cylinder head bores are excessively worn, new tappets and/or a new cylinder head will be required.

17 If the engine's valve components have sounded noisy, particularly if the noise persists after initial start-up from cold, there is reason to suspect a faulty hydraulic tappet. Only a good mechanic experienced in these engines can tell whether the noise level is typical, or if renewal of one or more of the tappets is warranted. If faulty tappets are diagnosed, and the engine's service history is unknown, it is always worth trying the effect of renewing the engine oil and filter (see Chapter 1A), using *only* good-quality engine oil of the recommended viscosity and specification, before going to the expense of renewing the any of the tappets.

18 Visually examine the camshaft lobes for score marks, pitting, and evidence of overheating (blue, discoloured areas). Look for flaking away of the hardened surface layer of each lobe. If any such signs are evident, renew the component concerned.

19 Examine the camshaft bearing journals and the cylinder head bearing surfaces for

signs of obvious wear or pitting. If any such signs are evident, renew the component concerned.

20 Using a micrometer, measure the diameter of each journal at several points. If the diameter of any one journal is less than the specified value, renew the camshaft.

21 To check the bearing journal running clearance, remove the hydraulic tappets, use a suitable solvent and a clean lint-free rag to clean carefully all bearing surfaces, then refit the camshafts and bearing caps with a strand of Plastigauge across each journal. Tighten the bearing cap bolts to the specified torque wrench setting (do not rotate the camshafts), then remove the bearing caps and use the scale provided to measure the width of the compressed strands. Scrape off the Plastigauge with your fingernail or the edge of a credit card - don't scratch or nick the journals or bearing caps.

22 If the running clearance of any bearing is found to be worn to beyond the specified service limits, fit a new camshaft and repeat the check; if the clearance is still excessive, the cylinder head must be renewed.

23 To check the camshaft endfloat, remove the hydraulic tappets, clean the bearing surfaces carefully, and refit the camshafts and bearing caps. Tighten the bearing cap bolts to the specified torque wrench setting, then measure the endfloat using a DTI (Dial Test Indicator or dial gauge) mounted on the cylinder head so that its tip bears on the camshaft right-hand end.

24 Tap the camshaft fully towards the gauge, zero the gauge, then tap the camshaft fully away from the gauge, and note the gauge reading. If the endfloat measured is found to be at or beyond the specified service limit, fit a new camshaft and repeat the check; if the clearance is still excessive, the cylinder head must be renewed.

Refitting

25 Note that from 10/1994 the hydraulic tappets were modified. The modified version is identified by red colour coding. Do not mix the old and new type tappets.

26 Locate the hydraulic tappets in their respective bores in the cylinder head.

27 Lubricate the camshaft journals with fresh

engine oil, then locate the inlet and exhaust camshafts in the cylinder head in their positions noted on removal. The lobes of the No 1 cylinder should be angled upwards and slightly inwards as noted on removal, and the timing holes in the front bearing caps and camshaft flanges must be aligned with each other.

28 Locate the bearing caps in their original positions, then insert the bolts and progressively tighten them to the specified torque. The tightening procedure must be carried out carefully so that the camshafts are not unduly stressed.

29 Turn the engine slightly anti-clockwise until the 20° ATDC timing mark on the pulley is aligned with the timing mark on the timing cover.

30 Refit the sprockets and timing chain to the inlet and exhaust camshafts with reference to Section 8.

31 Refit the timing chain guide to the front of the cylinder head and tighten the bolts securely.

32 Refit the chain tensioner as described in Section 8.

33 Apply suitable sealant to the mating surfaces, then refit the front cover to the front of the cylinder head together with a new O-ring. Tighten the bolts to the specified torque. Reconnect the wiring to the variable valve timing coil.

34 Refit the thermostat housing together with a new O-ring and tighten the bolts securely. Reconnect the by-pass hose and tighten the clip.

35 Refit the camshaft cover as described in Section 4.

36 Refill and bleed the cooling system with reference to Chapter 1A.

---

10 Cylinder head - removal, inspection and refitting

Removal

Note: *A new cylinder head gasket will be required on refitting, and new cylinder head bolts may be required - see text.*

1 Ensure that the engine is cold before attempting to remove the cylinder head.

2 Disconnect the battery negative (earth) lead and position it away from the terminal. The battery is located in the rear luggage compartment.

3 Raise the bonnet to the fully open position, as described in Chapter 11.

4 Drain the cooling system as described in Chapter 1A. Also unscrew the crankcase drain plug located on the side of the cylinder block, and drain the coolant.

5 Refer to Chapter 4C and disconnect the exhaust downpipe from the exhaust manifold. Note on some models, the manifold extends down to the right-hand side of the transmission, and where this is the case, it is

10.6a Disconnecting the crankcase ventilation hose and removing the air cleaner crosspipe

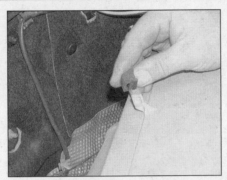

10.6b Removing the support rubbers from the camshaft cover

10.6c Removing the air cleaner from the right-hand side of the engine compartment

10.8 Disconnecting the crankcase ventilation hose from the left-hand side of the cylinder head

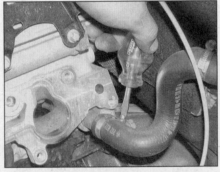

10.10 Disconnecting the coolant hose from the left-hand rear of the cylinder head

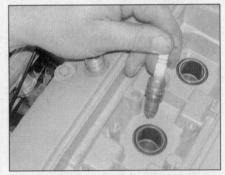

10.11 Removing the spark plugs

recommended that the complete manifold is removed from the cylinder head with reference to Chapter 4C.

6 Loosen the clips and remove the air cleaner crosspipe from the airflow meter and throttle housing. Disconnect the crankcase ventilation hose from the camshaft cover, and recover the support rubbers from the camshaft cover. Remove the air cleaner from the right-hand side of the engine compartment (see illustrations).

7 Unbolt the inlet manifold from the left-hand side of the cylinder head and support to one

side with reference to Chapter 4A. On engine codes 111.920, 111.941 and 111.961 it will be necessary to completely remove the inlet manifold.

8 Where applicable, disconnect the crankcase ventilation hose from the left-hand side of the cylinder head (see illustration).

9 Where applicable, unbolt the cable support from the left-hand side of the cylinder head.

10 Loosen the clip and disconnect the coolant hose from the left-hand rear of the cylinder head (see illustration).

11 Remove the camshaft cover as described

in Section 4 and the spark plugs as described in Chapter 1A (see illustration).

12 Disconnect the coolant hoses from the thermostat cover and bottom of the thermostat housing, and disconnect the coolant temperature sensor wiring, then unbolt the thermostat housing from the front cover noting the location of engine lifting eye. Remove the O-ring. Note that, on engines with an auxiliary drivebelt damper attached to the thermostat housing, it is necessary to remove the drivebelt and unbolt the damper before removing the housing (see illustrations).

10.12a Disconnecting the wiring from the coolant temperature sensor

10.12b Disconnecting the radiator top hose . . .

10.12c . . . air purge hose from the thermostat cover . . .

10.12d . . . and bottom of the thermostat housing

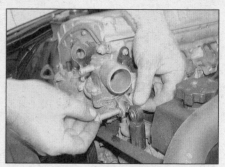

10.12e Unscrew the bolt securing the auxiliary drivebelt damper to the thermostat housing . . .

10.12f . . . then remove the mounting bolts (noting the engine lifting eye) . . .

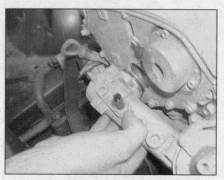

10.12g . . . and remove the thermostat housing from the front cover . . .

10.12h . . . and intermediate hose

1 Evaporative emission thermostatic valve
2 HFM and PMS coolant temperature sensor
3 Coolant temperature gauge sensor
4 Coolant temperature sensor with air conditioning/automatic climate control

10.12i Sensor locations on the thermostat housing (as applicable to engine)

10.13a Disconnect the wiring from the variable valve timing coil . . .

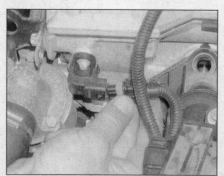

10.13b . . . and camshaft position sensor . . .

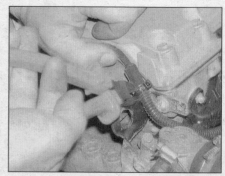

10.13c . . . then release the wiring from the cable tie

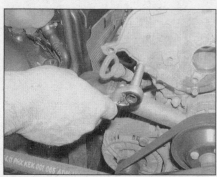

10.14a Unscrew the bolts . . .

10.14b . . . and remove the front cover from the cylinder head . . .

10.14c . . . then recover the O-ring seal

10.15 Unbolting the engine oil level dipstick tube from the cylinder head

10.17 Inserting bolts through the holes in the camshaft bearing caps to lock the sprockets in the timing position

10.18a Mark the inlet camshaft sprocket and timing chain in relation to each other . . .

13 Disconnect the wiring from the camshaft position sensor and variable valve timing coil, then release the wiring from the cable tie **(see illustrations)**.

14 Unbolt the front cover from the front of the cylinder head. Recover the O-ring **(see illustrations)**.

15 Unbolt the engine oil level dipstick tube from the cylinder head **(see illustration)**.

16 On automatic transmission models, unbolt the transmission fluid level dipstick tube from the cylinder head.

17 Using a spanner on the crankshaft pulley bolt, turn the engine until the 20° ATDC timing mark on the pulley is aligned with the timing mark on the timing cover. Insert

suitable drills or metal dowels through the holes in the camshaft front bearing caps to lock the camshafts **(see illustration)**. In this position the camshafts are not under any tension when the timing chain is removed.

18 Use a dab of paint or a marker pen to mark the timing chain and the inlet and exhaust camshaft sprockets in relation to each other **(see illustrations)**. This is necessary to ensure the chain is refitted correctly and the valve timing maintained.

19 Remove the chain tensioner as described in Section 8.

20 Unbolt the upper timing chain guide rail from the front of the cylinder head with reference to Section 8.

21 Remove the exhaust and inlet camshaft sprockets with reference to Section 8. Tie the timing chain to one side with string or wire. Note that the chain cannot come off of the crankshaft sprocket, because of a retaining tag on the timing cover, however, it is recommended that it is kept in tension to ensure that it remains in **full** engagement with the crankshaft sprocket while disconnected from the camshaft sprockets.

22 Pull the guide rail pin from the front of the cylinder head. Mercedes-Benz technicians use a slide hammer tool which is screwed into the pin, however a universal slide hammer and bolt can be used **(see illustration)**, or alternatively it may be possible make up a

10.18b . . . also similarly mark the exhaust camshaft sprocket

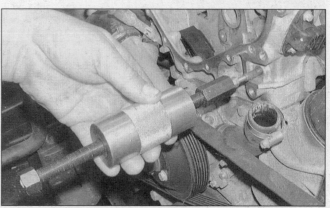

10.22 Using a universal slide hammer and bolt to remove the guide rail pin from the front of the cylinder head

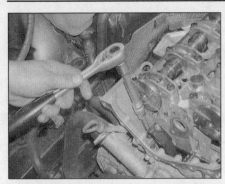

10.23 Removing the four upper bolts securing the timing cover to the cylinder head

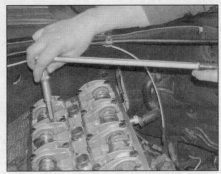

10.24a Loosen the cylinder head bolts (see text) . . .

10.24b . . . and remove them

removal tool using a long bolt, nut, large washers and metal tube. Locate the metal tube over the guide rail pin, and fit the nut to the bolt followed by the washers. Screw the bolt into the pin through the tube, then tighten the nut against the washers to extract the pin. **Note:** *If the pin has not been removed for some time, it can be very tight.*

23 Unscrew and remove the four upper bolts securing the timing cover to the cylinder head. The bolts are located in the recess at the front of the cylinder head **(see illustration)**.

24 Make sure that the engine is cold, then progressively unscrew the cylinder head bolts in two stages, using the reverse sequence to the tightening sequence **(see illustrations and illustration 10.41a)**.

25 With the help of an assistant, lift the cylinder head (complete with exhaust manifold, where applicable) from the block and remove from the engine compartment **(see illustration)**. If it is stuck, do not attempt to prise the head from the block with a screwdriver or similar tool as the mating surfaces will be damaged. Rock the head from side to side to release it. As the head is being removed, take care not to damage the timing chain guide rails.

26 Recover the cylinder head gasket **(see illustration)**. If necessary, remove the location dowels from the block.

Inspection

27 Refer to Chapter 2C for details of cylinder

head dismantling and reassembly. Where applicable, the exhaust manifold can be removed with reference to Chapter 4C.

28 The mating faces of the cylinder head and block must be perfectly clean before refitting the head. Use a scraper to remove all traces of gasket and carbon, and also clean the tops of the pistons. Take particular care with the aluminium cylinder head, as the soft metal is easily damaged. Also make sure that debris is not allowed to enter the oil and water passages. Using adhesive tape and paper, seal the water, oil and bolt holes in the cylinder block. To prevent carbon entering the gap between the pistons and bores, smear a little grease in the gap. After cleaning each piston, rotate the crankshaft so that the piston moves **down** the bore, then wipe out the grease and carbon with a cloth rag.

29 Check the block and head for nicks, deep scratches and other damage. If very slight, they may be removed carefully with a file. More serious damage may be repaired by machining, but this is a specialist job.

30 If warpage of the cylinder head is suspected, use a straight-edge to check it for distortion, with reference to Chapter 2C.

31 Clean out the bolt holes in the block using a pipe cleaner or rag and a screwdriver. Make sure that all oil and water is removed, otherwise there is a possibility of the block being cracked by hydraulic pressure when the bolts are tightened.

32 Examine the bolt threads and the threads

in the cylinder block for damage. If necessary, use the correct size tap to chase out the threads in the block.

33 The manufacturers recommend that the cylinder head bolts are measured, to determine whether renewal is necessary; however, some owners may wish to renew all the bolts as a matter of course.

34 Measure the length of each bolt from the base of the head to the end of the shank. If the bolt length is greater than the maximum specified, the bolts should be renewed.

35 Reassemble the cylinder head with reference to Chapter 2C. Where applicable, refit the exhaust manifold together with a new gasket with reference to Chapter 4C.

Refitting

Note: *A new cylinder head gasket will be required on refitting. The new gasket will be supplied in a sealed wrapper - do not remove the wrapper until the gasket is about to be fitted.*

36 Check that the camshafts are still locked with the drills or metal dowels, and the crankshaft 20° ATDC timing mark on the pulley is aligned with the timing mark on the timing cover.

37 If removed, refit the location dowels in the block.

38 Fit the new gasket over the dowels on the cylinder block, ensuring that it is fitted the correct way round **(see illustration)**.

39 Carefully lower the cylinder head onto the

10.25 Lifting the cylinder head from the cylinder block

10.26 Removing the cylinder head gasket from the block

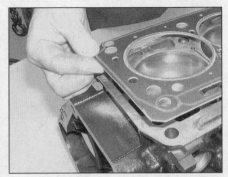

10.38 Locate the new cylinder head gasket on the cylinder block

block, while guiding the aperture in the front of the head over the timing chain guide rails **(see illustration)**. If necessary, engage the help of an assistant to hold the rails.

40 Oil the threads and the contact faces of the cylinder head bolts, then insert them and screw them into the cylinder block by hand **(see illustration)**.

41 Tighten the cylinder head bolts in the order shown **(see illustration)**. Tighten the bolts in the stages given in the Specifications - ie, tighten all bolts to the Stage 1 torque, then tighten all bolts to the Stage 2 angle, and finally tighten all the bolts to the Stage 3 angle **(see illustrations)**.

42 Insert the timing cover-to-cylinder head upper bolts and tighten them to the specified torque **(see illustration)**.

43 Apply sealant to the guide rail pin, then insert it in the front of the cylinder head making sure that it enters the top of the guide rail. Tap it fully into position using a soft metal drift and hammer **(see illustrations)**.

44 Refit the upper timing chain guide rail to the front of the cylinder head with reference to Section 8.

45 Refit the exhaust and inlet camshaft sprockets (using new bolts) with reference to Section 8, making sure that the marks on the timing chain and sprockets are aligned with each other.

46 Refit the chain tensioner as described in Section 8.

47 Remove the locking drills/dowels then refit the front cover together with a new O-ring and tighten the bolts to the specified torque.

48 On automatic transmission models, refit and tighten the bolt securing the transmission fluid level dipstick tube to the cylinder head.

49 Refit and tighten the bolt securing the engine oil level dipstick tube to the cylinder head.

50 Apply suitable sealant to the mating surfaces then refit the front cover to the front of the cylinder head and tighten the bolts to the specified torque.

51 Reconnect the wiring to the camshaft position sensor and variable valve timing coil, and secure it with a cable tie.

52 Refit the thermostat housing together with a new O-ring and tighten the bolts, then

10.39 Lowering the cylinder head onto the cylinder block

10.40 Inserting the cylinder head bolts

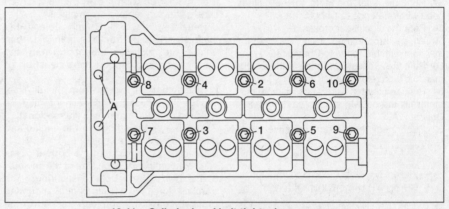

10.41a Cylinder head bolt tightening sequence

A Bolts securing cylinder head to timing cover

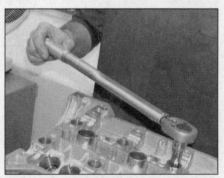

10.41b Torque-tightening the cylinder head bolts

10.41c Angle-tightening the cylinder head bolts

10.42 Torque-tightening the timing cover-to-cylinder head upper bolts

10.43a Apply sealant to the guide rail pin . . .

10.43b . . . then drive it into the front of the cylinder head

reconnect the hoses and tighten the clips. Where applicable, refit the auxiliary drivebelt damper to the thermostat housing and tighten the bolt.

53 Refit the camshaft cover with reference to Section 4 and the spark plugs as described in Chapter 1A.

54 Refit the coolant hose to the rear of the cylinder head and tighten the clip.

55 Where applicable, refit the cable support and tighten the bolt.

56 Where applicable, reconnect the crankcase ventilation hose to the left-hand side of the cylinder head. Make sure that the location arrows on the hose and flange are in line with each other.

57 Refit the inlet manifold to the cylinder head with reference to Chapter 4A.

58 Refit the air cleaner crosspipe.

59 Where applicable, refit the exhaust manifold with reference to Chapter 4C.

60 Refit the exhaust downpipe to the exhaust manifold with reference to Chapter 4C.

61 Refit and tighten the crankcase drain plug, then refill the cooling system as described in Chapter 1A.

62 Reconnect the battery negative (earth) lead.

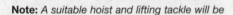

11 Sump - removal and refitting

Note: *A suitable hoist and lifting tackle will be*

required for this operation. A new sump gasket will be required on refitting.

Removal

1 Apply the parking brake, then jack up the front of the vehicle and support it on axle stands (see *Jacking and vehicle support*). Remove both front roadwheels.

2 Remove the front suspension anti-roll bar with reference to Chapter 10.

3 Drain the engine oil as described in Chapter 1A. On completion, check the copper washer and renew it if necessary, then refit the drain plug and tighten to the specified torque **(see illustration)**.

4 Where a cooling fan shroud is fitted, unbolt it and either position it over the viscous fan (where fitted) or remove it completely.

5 Refer to Chapter 4C and detach the exhaust downpipe from the manifold, then unbolt the exhaust mounting from the transmission and support the exhaust on an axle stand.

6 Disconnect the wiring from the oil level sensor. If necessary, the sensor may be removed from the sump **(see illustrations)**.

7 Attach a suitable hoist to the engine and take the weight of the engine.

8 Unscrew the bolts from the bottom of the engine mountings at each side of the engine.

9 Unscrew the bolts securing the transmission to the rear engine mounting bracket. Leave the bracket attached to the underbody.

10 Raise the engine and transmission as far as possible. Make sure it is adequately

11.3 Refitting the sump drain plug and copper washer

supported, as the next procedure involves working beneath the engine.

11 Unscrew the bolts securing the transmission to the rear of the sump, then unscrew the remaining sump-to-engine bolts and lower the sump from the cylinder block **(see illustration)**. Note the location of the bolts as they are of different lengths. Recover the gasket. If the sump is stuck, use a hide or wooden mallet to tap its sides in order to release it. Do not drive a screwdriver between the sump and cylinder block as this may damage the mating surfaces.

12 It is recommended that the oil and oil filter are renewed whenever the sump is removed. Before refitting the sump, it is a good idea to remove the oil filter in order to allow the oil to drain from the cylinder block oil gallery and internal oilways.

Refitting

13 Thoroughly clean the mating surfaces of the sump and cylinder block, then smear a little grease on the block and fit the gasket making sure that all of the holes align correctly. Refit the sump then insert all of the bolts finger-tight **(see illustrations)**. Now tighten the bolts securing the transmission to the sump to the specified torque. This will ensure the rear of the sump is correctly aligned with the transmission, as if it is not aligned correctly, vibration and noise may occur.

14 Tighten the remaining sump bolts to the specified torque.

15 Lower the engine and transmission onto

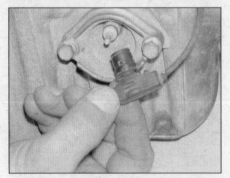

11.6a Disconnecting the wiring from the oil level sensor

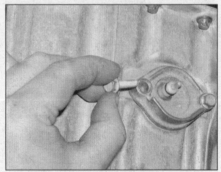

11.6b Unscrew the bolts and remove the oil level sensor . . .

11.6c . . . then recover the O-ring seal

11.11 Lowering the sump from the cylinder block

11.13a Locate the new gasket on the crankcase . . .

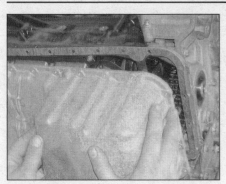

11.13b . . . then refit the sump . . .

11.13c . . . and insert the bolts

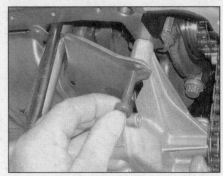

12.4a Unscrew the mounting bolts . . .

the mountings, insert the bolts, and tighten to the specified torque. Remove the hoist.

16 Reconnect the wiring to the oil level sensor.

17 Refer to Chapter 4C and refit the exhaust downpipe to the manifold.

18 Where applicable, refit the cooling fan shroud and tighten the bolts.

19 Refit the front suspension anti-roll bar with reference to Chapter 10.

20 Refit the front roadwheels and lower the car to the ground.

21 Renew the oil filter and refill the engine with oil with reference to Chapter 1A.

12 Oil pump and drive chain - removal, inspection and refitting

Oil pump

Removal

1 Remove the sump as described in Section 11. Note that this involves suspending the engine with a hoist.

2 On early models where the oil pump sprocket is bolted to the driveshaft, hold the sprocket stationary using a suitable tool inserted in the sprocket holes, then unscrew the securing bolt and recover the washer.

Withdraw the sprocket from the oil pump shaft and disengage it from the drive chain. On later models the sprocket is pressed onto the driveshaft, and the sprocket must be disengaged from the chain as the oil pump is being removed.

3 On early models, unscrew the bolt securing the oil pump to the rear support bracket.

4 Unscrew the mounting bolts, withdraw the oil pump from the bottom of the crankcase, and recover the O-ring seal **(see illustrations)**. On early models, recover the location dowels if necessary. Note, on later models, the oil pump mounting bolts also secure the baffle plate, and it may be helpful to loosen some of the baffle bolts to release the oil pump. On later models, disengage the sprocket from the chain as the pump is being removed.

Inspection

5 With the exception of the oil pressure relief valve components, the oil pump is a sealed unit. To remove the oil pressure relief valve components, proceed as follows. **Note:** *It is not necessary to remove the oil pump from the crankcase to remove the oil pressure relief valve components.*

6 Unscrew the relief valve plug. Take care, as the plug will be pushed out by the spring pressure when it reaches the end of the threads. Note that the plug has a tapered

shoulder and does not require a sealing ring.

7 Withdraw the spring, guide pin and piston, noting the orientation of the piston.

8 Thoroughly clean all components, and examine them for wear and damage. If there is any sign of excessive wear or damage, renew the appropriate component(s) - pay particular attention to the spring.

9 Also clean the oil pump intake strainer thoroughly, however, **do not** immerse the oil pump in cleaning solvent. Check that the piston moves freely in the pump bore.

10 Examine the drive chain for wear and damage. If necessary, renew the chain.

11 Reassemble the oil pump using a reversal of the dismantling procedure, lubricating each component with fresh engine oil before fitting. Tighten the relief valve plug to the specified torque.

12 With the oil pump upright, add fresh engine oil into the upper aperture while turning the pump shaft slowly **(see illustration)**. This will prime the oil pump so that normal oil pressure will be resumed as soon as possible after starting the engine.

Refitting

13 On early models, insert the location dowels in the crankcase.

14 Locate the oil pump on the crankcase together with a new O-ring seal, and insert the mounting bolts. Tighten the bolts to the

12.4b . . . and withdraw the oil pump from the bottom of the crankcase while disengaging the drive chain

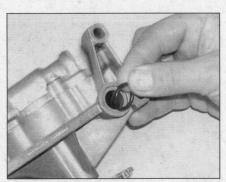

12.4c Recover the O-ring seal from the oil pump

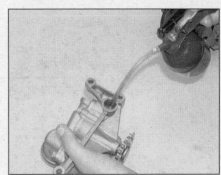

12.12 Priming the oil pump before refitting it

12.14 Torque-tightening the oil pump mounting bolts

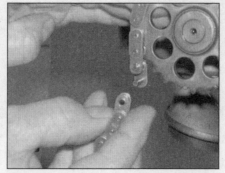

12.21 Connecting the new oil pump drive chain to the old chain

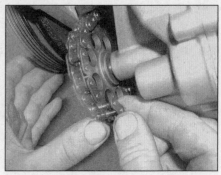

12.23a Fit the link . . .

specified torque **(see illustration)**. On later models, engage the sprocket with the chain while locating the pump on the crankcase.

15 On early models, insert and tighten the bolt securing the oil pump to the rear support bracket, then engage the sprocket with the chain, insert the bolt, and tighten to the specified torque. Note that the convex side of the sprocket must face the oil pump.

16 Refit the sump as described in Section 11. On later models, check that the baffle bolts are tight first.

Oil pump drive chain

Inspection

Note: *The following paragraphs describe renewal of the oil pump drive chain by removing one of the links and feeding the new chain up around the crankshaft sprocket. It is recommended that a chain link removal/refitting tool is obtained to do this, however it is possible to grind away a link and use a ball-pein hammer to fit the new link.*

17 Remove the sump as described in Section 11. Note that this involves suspending the engine with a hoist.

18 Before removing the oil pump drive chain, turn the crankshaft slowly and examine the chain and sprocket teeth for wear. If the chain links are loose and if the sprocket teeth are grooved where the chain rollers contact them, both the chain and sprocket must be renewed.

Renewal

19 Using the special tool, remove one of the links at the bottom of the chain, taking care not to damage the oil pump sprocket. Alternatively, grind away the lugs of one of the links and remove the link.

20 Unscrew the bolt and recover the washer, then remove the sprocket from the oil pump shaft.

21 Using the removable link supplied with the new chain, connect one end of the new chain to the end of the old chain so that the new chain will be drawn up over the crankshaft sprocket when the engine is turned clockwise **(see illustration)**. Fit the outer plate firmly onto the link to ensure the link stays in place.

22 Using a socket on the crankshaft pulley bolt, slowly turn the crankshaft clockwise until the new chain is located on the crankshaft sprocket and the link is at the bottom of the chain.

23 Remove the link and the old chain, then connect the two ends of the new chain together with the link. Fit the outer plate and secure by riveting over the ends of the link pins **(see illustrations)**. If not using the special tool, it should be possible to achieve a satisfactory result using a ball-pein hammer, with a block of metal (or a second hammer) to support the rear of the chain.

24 Check that the chain tensioner guide is located on the chain correctly.

25 Refit the sump as described in Section 11.

13 Flywheel/driveplate - removal, inspection and refitting

Removal

Note: *The flywheel/driveplate mounting bolts must be renewed on refitting.*

1 Remove the manual transmission (Chapter 7A) or automatic transmission (Chapter 7B).

2 On manual transmission models, remove the clutch as described in Chapter 6.

3 The flywheel/driveplate must be held stationary while the mounting bolts are loosened. To do this, have an assistant insert a wide-bladed screwdriver in the starter ring gear teeth through the access hole in the rear of the sump. On manual transmission models, Mercedes-Benz technicians use a special tool bolted to the sump incorporating serrations which engage with the ring gear teeth. Alternatively, make up a tool as shown **(see illustration)** and bolt it to a starter motor mounting hole.

4 Unscrew the mounting bolts, then lift the flywheel/driveplate from the rear of the crankshaft **(see illustrations)**. Note that the location dowel ensures the flywheel/driveplate can only be fitted in one position.

5 On automatic transmission models recover the locking plates from each side of the driveplate.

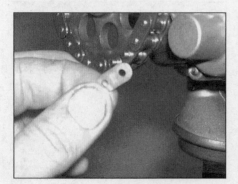

12.23b . . . and outer plate . . .

12.23c . . . then use the special tool to rivet over the ends of the link pins

13.3 Flywheel/driveplate holding tool made from a piece of metal

13.4a Unscrew the bolts . . .

13.4b . . . and remove the flywheel from the rear of the crankshaft

13.7 Spigot bearing in the centre of the flywheel

Inspection

6 If the teeth on the flywheel/driveplate starter ring gear are badly worn, it may be possible to fit a new ring gear, however this work should be entrusted to a Mercedes-Benz dealer who will have the necessary equipment to heat the new gear to the critical temperature in order to fit it. Over-heating the gear will affect its hardness, resulting in rapid wear. The old gear may be removed by drilling it and using a cold chisel to split it. Take care not to drill into the flywheel/driveplate.

7 On manual transmission models, if the clutch friction face of the flywheel is deeply scored, cracked or otherwise damaged, the flywheel must be renewed. However, it may be possible to have it surface-ground, but seek the advice of an engine reconditioning specialist. Check the condition of the spigot bearing in the centre of the flywheel or in the end of the crankshaft, and renew if necessary **(see illustration)**.

8 It is recommended that the flywheel/driveplate securing bolts are renewed whenever removed.

Refitting

9 Commence refitting by cleaning the mating faces of the crankshaft and flywheel/driveplate.

10 Make sure that the location dowel is in position in the end of the crankshaft. On automatic transmission models, fit the locking plate onto the crankshaft.

11 Locate the flywheel/driveplate onto the crankshaft, then insert the new mounting bolts (and further locking plate on automatic transmission models) and hand-tighten them.

12 Lock the flywheel/driveplate using the method employed during removal, then tighten the securing bolts progressively in a diagonal sequence to the specified torque first, then tighten all the bolts by the specified angle **(see illustrations)**.

13 On manual transmission models, refit the clutch as described in Chapter 6.

14 Refit the manual transmission (Chapter 7A) or automatic transmission (Chapter 7B).

14 Crankshaft oil seals - renewal

Crankshaft front oil seal

1 Remove the crankshaft pulley/vibration damper and inspect it as described in Section 5.

2 Measure and note the fitted depth of the oil seal in the timing chain cover.

3 Prise the oil seal from the cover using a hooked instrument **(see illustration)**. Alternatively, drill a small hole in the oil seal, and use a self-tapping screw and a pair of pliers to remove it.

4 Clean the seal location in the timing cover, and also clean the oil seal contact surface on the crankshaft pulley/vibration damper.

13.12a Torque-tightening the flywheel bolts

Examine the seal contact surface of the pulley/vibration damper for an excessive wear groove. If evident, refer to Section 5.

5 Dip the new oil seal in clean engine oil, and press it into the timing chain cover (open end first) to the previously-noted depth, using a suitable tube or socket **(see illustrations)**.

6 Refit the crankshaft pulley/vibration damper as described in Section 5.

Crankshaft rear oil seal

7 Remove the flywheel/driveplate as described in Section 13.

8 Note that from 02/95 the rear oil seal is vulcanised into the oil seal housing. On earlier models, the seal is available separate, however, each type of oil seal can be fitted to all engines. On later engines this can be an

13.12b Angle-tightening the flywheel bolts

14.3 Prising out the crankshaft front oil seal

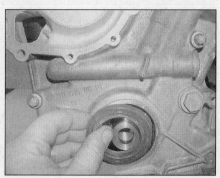

14.5a Locate the new oil seal in the timing cover . . .

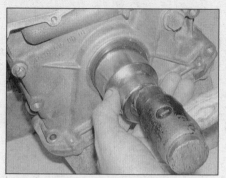

14.5b . . . and drive it into position using a socket or metal tube

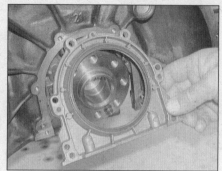

14.10 Removing the crankshaft rear oil seal housing

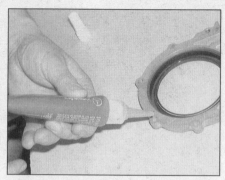

14.11 Applying sealant to the crankshaft rear oil seal housing

advantage, as the earlier type can fitted in order to position the seal away from an excessively worn groove in the rear of the crankshaft.

Housing with separate oil seal

9 Measure and note the fitted depth of the oil seal. Note carefully if there is any sign of oil leakage from the rear oil seal housing gasket on the crankcase.
10 Pull the oil seal from the housing using a hooked instrument. Alternatively, drill a small hole in the oil seal, and use a self-tapping screw and a pair of pliers to remove it (see illustration).
11 If leakage of oil from the oil seal housing was evident, unbolt the housing from the crankcase and recover the gasket (if fitted). Clean the components, then refit the housing together with a new gasket or using suitable sealant and progressively tighten the bolts to the specified torque (see illustration).
12 Examine the oil seal contact surface on the crankshaft for excessive wear indicated by a deep groove. If evident, the new oil seal should be located a further 3.0 mm into the housing so that it no longer runs over the groove.
13 Dip the new oil seal in clean engine oil, and press it into the housing (open end first) to the previously-noted or new depth, using a suitable tube or socket (see illustration). A piece of thin plastic or tape wound around the rear of the crankshaft flange is useful to prevent damage to the oil seal as it is being

fitted. Note that the seal must be fitted exactly at right-angles to the crankshaft flange to provide satisfactory sealing.
14 Remove the plastic or tape from the crankshaft.
15 Refit the flywheel/driveplate as described in Section 13.

Housing complete with vulcanised oil seal

16 Unbolt the rear oil seal housing from the crankcase and withdraw it over the rear of the crankshaft (see illustration).
17 Examine the oil seal contact surface on the crankshaft for excessive wear indicated by a deep groove. If evident, it is suggested that the earlier housing be obtained and fitted together with a new gasket, and the oil seal located a further 3.0 mm into the housing. Refer to paragraphs 9 to 15.
18 Wrap some tape or plastic sheeting around the rear of the crankshaft to protect the sealing lips of the oil seal as it is being fitted.
19 Clean the rear of the crankcase, then smear a little oil on the sealing lips of the oil seal.
20 Locate the housing over the rear of the crankshaft, using a twisting motion to ensure the sealing lip is not disturbed. Note that the housing is supplied complete with rubber sealing faces, and no sealant is required.
21 Insert the bolts and tighten them progressively to the specified torque.
22 Remove the plastic sheeting or tape from the crankshaft.

23 Refit the flywheel/driveplate as described in Section 13.

15 Crankshaft spigot bearing - renewal

1 On early manual transmission models, a ball-bearing is fitted to the end of the crankshaft to support the end of the transmission input shaft. On later models with a two-mass flywheel, the bearing is located in the centre of the flywheel. On high-mileage engines, the bearing may become dry and noisy, noticeable when the clutch is disengaged with a gear selected. To renew the bearing, proceed as follows.
2 Remove the clutch as described in Chapter 6.
3 Determine whether the bearing is located in the end of the crankshaft or in the centre of the flywheel. The crankshaft located bearing has an inner race, whereas on the flywheel located bearing it is possible to view the needle rollers of the bearing.

Crankshaft located bearing

4 The ball-bearing is protected by an end cover, also pressed into the end of the crankshaft. The cover can be removed together with the ball-bearing, or alternatively it can be prised out first.
5 Ideally, a slide hammer fitted with a suitable adapter should be used to withdraw the bearing and its cover from the end of the crankshaft. An alternative method which may work if the bearing is not too tight, is to fill the cavity behind the bearing with grease, then insert a close-fitting dowel rod through the bearing centre race. Use a hammer to drive the rod into the cavity, and the pressure produced will force the bearing from the crankshaft.
6 With the old bearing removed, thoroughly clean its location in the end of the crankshaft. There is no need to remove the spacer ring.
7 Tap the new bearing into position, up to the stop, using a tube or socket on the bearing outer race.
8 Tap the protective cover into position using

14.13 New oil seal fitted to the housing

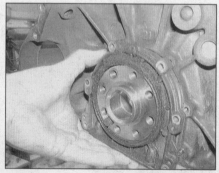

14.16 Removing the crankshaft rear oil seal (models manufactured from 02/95)

the tube or socket, until it contacts the bearing.

9 Refit the clutch as described in Chapter 6.

Flywheel located bearing

10 Remove the flywheel as described in Section 13.

11 Note the fitted depth of the needle bearing to ensure correct fitting.

12 Press or drive out the bearing.

13 Press or drive in the new bearing, using a metal tube on the outer part which locates in the flywheel. The open side of the bearing must face towards the clutch facing side of the flywheel.

14 Refit the flywheel as described in Section 13.

15 Refit the clutch as described in Chapter 6.

16 Engine/transmission mountings - inspection and renewal

Inspection

1 Three engine/transmission mountings are used, one on either side of the engine, and one under the rear of the transmission.

2 For improved access, raise the front of the vehicle and support it securely on axle stands (see *Jacking and vehicle support*).

3 Check the condition of the mounting rubber to see if it is cracked, hardened or separated from the metal at any point. Renew the mounting if any such damage or deterioration is evident. The mountings contain hydraulic oil, and must be renewed if oil leakage is evident.

4 Check that all the mounting bolts are securely tightened.

5 Using a large screwdriver or metal bar, check for wear in the mounting by carefully levering against it to check for free play. Where this is not possible, enlist the aid of an assistant to move the engine/transmission back and forth, or from side-to-side, while you observe the mounting. If excessive freeplay is found, check first that the fasteners are correctly secured, then renew any worn components as required.

Renewal

Front engine mountings

6 Support the engine, either using a hoist and lifting tackle connected to the engine lifting brackets, or by positioning a jack and interposed block of wood under the sump. Ensure that the engine is adequately supported before proceeding.

7 Unclip the cooling fan shroud from the radiator and either locate it on the viscous fan (where fitted) or remove it completely.

8 Remove the cover from over the thermostat housing at the front of the cylinder head.

9 If removing the left-hand mounting, unbolt the inlet manifold support bracket on models not fitted with a plastic manifold.

10 Unscrew and remove the engine mounting upper bolt.

11 Unscrew and remove the engine mounting lower bolt.

12 Raise the engine as necessary, taking care not to stretch the coolant hoses, and remove the mounting. If necessary, unbolt the mounting bracket from the side of the cylinder block **(see illustrations)**. On automatic transmission models, note the location of the wiring support on the right-hand bracket.

13 Refitting is a reversal of removal, but make sure that the location ear on the top of the mounting engages the cut-out in the mounting bracket, and tighten the mounting bolts to the specified torque.

Rear engine/transmission mounting

14 Raise the front of the vehicle and support it securely on axle stands (see *Jacking and vehicle support*).

15 Support the transmission using a jack and interposed block of wood.

16 Unbolt the mounting bracket from the underbody, then unscrew the bolts securing the mounting rubber to the rear of the transmission. Note the location of the splash guard support. Lower the bracket together with the mounting from the underbody. Note, on the manual transmission, the bolts screw into captive nuts, whereas on the automatic transmission the bolts screw directly into the transmission casing.

17 Unbolt the mounting rubber from the bracket.

18 Refitting is a reversal of removal.

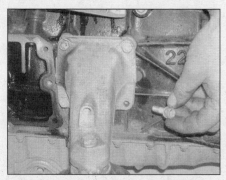

16.12a Unscrew the mounting bolts . . .

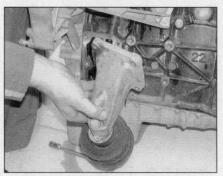

16.12b . . . and remove the left-hand front mounting from the cylinder block

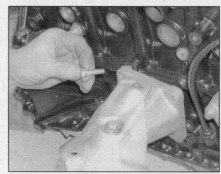

16.12c Removing the right-hand front engine mounting from the cylinder block

Notes

Chapter 2 Part B:
Diesel engine in-car repair procedures

Contents

Degrees of difficulty

Easy, suitable for novice with little experience	Fairly easy, suitable for beginner with some experience	Fairly difficult, suitable for competent DIY mechanic 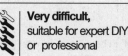	Difficult, suitable for experienced DIY mechanic	Very difficult, suitable for expert DIY or professional

Specifications

General

Engine code:	
2.2 litre (4-cylinder) engine	604.910
2.5 litre (5-cylinder) engine:	
Non-turbo	605.910
Turbo	605.960
Displacement:	
2.2 litre engine	2155 cc
2.5 litre engine	2497 cc
Bore:	
2.2 litre engine	89.0 mm
2.5 litre engine	87.0 mm
Stroke:	
2.2 litre engine	86.6 mm
2.5 litre engine	84.0 mm
Direction of engine rotation	Clockwise (viewed from front of vehicle)
No 1 cylinder location	Timing chain end
Firing order:	
2.2 litre (4-cylinder) engine	1-3-4-2
2.5 litre (5-cylinder) engine	1-2-4-5-3
Compression pressures:	
New compression pressure	29.0 to 35.0 bars
Minimum compression pressure	18.0 bars (approx)
Maximum difference between cylinders	3.0 bars
Compression ratio (all engines)	22.0:1

Camshafts

Endfloat:
  New engine . . . . 0.030 to 0.100 mm
  Wear limit . . . . 0.150 mm
Camshaft bearing running clearance:
  New engine . . . . 0.050 to 0.091 mm
  Wear limit . . . . 0.150 mm

Hydraulic tappets

Clearance between cam lobe and hydraulic tappet (Section 9) . . . . 0.40 mm maximum

Cylinder head bolts

Thread diameter M10
Length when new . . . . 102.0 mm or 115.0 mm
Maximum length . . . . 104.0 mm or 117.0 mm

Lubrication system

Minimum oil pressure:
  At idle speed . . . . 0.3 bar
  At 3000 rpm . . . . 3.0 bars

Flywheel/driveplate bolts

Minimum diameter . . . . 8.0 mm
Maximum length . . . . 22.5 mm

Torque wrench settings

	Nm	lbf ft
Auxiliary drivebelt idler pulley bolt	30	22
Auxiliary drivebelt tensioner damper strut bolts:		
Lower bolt	20	15
Upper bolt	25	18
Auxiliary drivebelt tensioner pivot pin	100	74
Big-end bearing cap nuts:		
Stage 1	40	30
Stage 2	Angle-tighten through a further 90 to 100°	
Camshaft bearing cap	15	11
Camshaft cover bolts	10	7
Camshaft housing to cylinder head	15	11
Camshaft sprocket	18	13
Coolant pump and housing	10	7
Crankshaft pulley to hub (early models)	25	18
Crankshaft pulley/vibration damper and hub:		
Stage 1	200	148
Stage 2	Angle-tighten by 90°	
Crankshaft rear oil seal housing bolts	10	7
Cylinder block coolant drain plug	30	22
Cylinder head bolts:		
Stage 1	15	11
Stage 2	35	26
Stage 3	Angle-tighten through a further 90°	
Stage 4	Wait for 10 minutes	
Stage 5	Angle-tighten through a further 90°	
Engine-to-transmission bolts:		
Manual transmission:		
M10 x 40 mm bolts	55	41
M10 x 90 mm bolts	45	33
Automatic transmission:		
M10 bolts	55	41
M12 bolts	65	48
Flywheel/driveplate bolts:		
Manual transmission models:		
Stage 1	45	33
Stage 2	Angle-tighten 90°	
Automatic transmission models:		
Stage 1:		
Hexagon bolts	35	26
Torx bolts	45	33
Stage 2	Angle-tighten 90°	

Torque wrench settings (continued)

	Nm	lbf ft
Front engine mounting bolts:		
M8	25	18
M10	40	30
Injection pipe union nuts	15	11
Main bearing cap bolts:		
M11 bolts:		
Stage 1	55	41
Stage 2	Angle-tighten through a further 90 to 100°	
M12 bolts	90	66
Oil baffle plate bolts	25	18
Oil drain plug:		
M12 plug	30	22
M14 plug	25	18
Oil filter cap	25	18
Oil level sensor to crankcase	20	15
Oil pressure sensor to oil filter	15	11
Oil pump mounting bolts	25	18
Oil pump relief valve plug	50	37
Oil pump sprocket	32	24
Oil spray nozzle to crankcase	10	7
Rear engine mounting crossmember to underbody	40	30
Rear engine mounting to transmission crossmember	25	18
Return tube to oil filter cap (early models)	25	18
Sump bolts to crankcase:		
M6	10	7
M8	25	18
Timing chain cover bolts:		
Upper (to cylinder head)	25	18
Timing chain cover to crankcase	10	7
Timing chain tensioner	80	59
Timing chain tensioner end piece	40	30
Transmission bellhousing bolts to sump	40	30
Viscous fan coupling to bearing body	45	33
Viscous fan to coupling	10	7

1 General information

How to use this Chapter

This Part of Chapter 2 describes the repair procedures that can reasonably be carried out on the engine while it remains in the vehicle. If the engine has been removed from the vehicle and is being dismantled as described in Part C, any preliminary dismantling procedures can be ignored.

Note that, while it may be possible physically to overhaul items such as the piston/connecting rod assemblies while the engine is in the car, such tasks are not usually carried out as separate operations. Usually, several additional procedures are required (not to mention the cleaning of components and oilways); for this reason, all such tasks are classed as major overhaul procedures, and are described in Part C of this Chapter.

Part C describes the removal of the engine/transmission from the car, and the full overhaul procedures that can then be carried out.

Engine description

The 4- and 5-cylinder diesel engines fitted are fundamentally the same, the only significant difference being the number of cylinders.

The engines are of in-line double overhead camshaft design, mounted in-line ('north-south') at the front of the vehicle with the transmission mounted on the rear of the engine.

On 4-cylinder engines, then crankshaft is supported in five main bearing within the cast iron cylinder block. Crankshaft endfloat is controlled by thrustwashers fitted on either side of No 3 main bearing. Similarly, on 5-cylinder engines the crankshaft is supported in six main bearings, and the endfloat thrustwashers are fitted either side of No 4 bearing location.

The connecting rods are attached to the crankshaft by horizontally-split big-end bearings, and to the pistons by fully-floating gudgeon pins retained by circlips. The alloy pistons are fitted with three piston rings; two compression and one oil control.

The exhaust camshaft is driven from the crankshaft sprocket by a double-row chain, and the inlet camshaft is gear-driven from the exhaust camshaft. The timing chain also drives the fuel injection pump.

The camshaft is supported in bearings in the cylinder head, and actuates the valves directly, via hydraulic valve lifters.

The oil pump is chain-driven from the front of the crankshaft. An oil cooler is located in the sump on early models, and on the oil filter housing at the left-hand rear of the cylinder block on later models.

Repair operations possible with the engine in the vehicle

The following operations can be carried out without having to remove the engine from the vehicle:

a) Removal and refitting of the cylinder head.
b) Removal and refitting of the timing chain and sprockets.
c) Removal and refitting of the camshaft.
d) Removal and refitting of the sump.
e) Removal and refitting of the big-end bearings, connecting rods, and pistons*.
f) Removal and refitting of the oil pump.
g) Renewal of the engine/transmission mountings.
h) Removal and refitting of the flywheel/driveplate.

* Although it is possible to remove these components with the engine in place, for reasons of access and cleanliness it is recommended that the engine is removed.

2 Compression and leakdown tests - description and interpretation

Compression test

Note: *A compression tester designed for diesel engines must be used for this test.*

1 When engine performance is down, a compression test can provide diagnostic clues as to the engine's condition. If the test is performed regularly, it can give warning of trouble before any other symptoms become apparent.

2 A compression tester specifically intended for diesel engines must be used, because of the higher pressures involved. The tester is connected to an adapter which screws into the glow plug or injector hole. On these engines, an adapter suitable for use in the injector holes is preferable. It is unlikely to be worthwhile buying such a tester for occasional use, but it may be possible to borrow or hire one - if not, have the test performed by a garage.

3 Unless specific instructions to the contrary are supplied with the tester, observe the following points.

a) *The battery must be in a good state of charge, the air filter must be clean, and the engine should be at normal operating temperature.*

b) *All the injectors or glow plugs should be removed before starting the test.*

c) *The stop solenoid must be disconnected, to prevent the engine from running or fuel from being discharged.*

4 There is no need to hold the accelerator pedal down during the test, because the diesel engine air inlet is not throttled.

5 Crank the engine on the starter motor. After one or two revolutions, the compression pressure should build up to a maximum figure, and then stabilise. Record the highest reading obtained.

6 Repeat the test on the remaining cylinders, recording the pressure in each.

7 The cause of poor compression is less easy to establish on a diesel engine than on a petrol one. The effect of introducing oil into the cylinders ('wet' testing) is not conclusive, because there is a risk that the oil will sit in the swirl chamber or in the recess in the piston crown instead of passing to the rings. However, the following can be used as a rough guide to diagnosis.

8 All cylinders should produce very similar pressures; a difference of more than 3.0 bars between any two cylinders indicates a fault. Note that the compression should build up quickly in a healthy engine; low compression on the first stroke, followed by gradually-increasing pressure on successive strokes, indicates worn piston rings. A low compression reading on the first stroke, which does not build up during successive strokes, indicates leaking valves or a blown head gasket (a cracked head could also be the cause). Deposits on the undersides of the valve heads can also cause low compression.

9 A low reading from two adjacent cylinders is almost certainly due to the head gasket having blown between them; the presence of coolant in the engine oil will confirm this.

10 If the compression reading is unusually high, the combustion chambers are probably coated with carbon deposits. If this is the case, the cylinder head should be removed and decarbonised.

11 Mercedes-Benz recommended values for compression pressures are given in the Specifications.

12 On completion of the test, refit the injectors or the glow plugs, and reconnect the stop solenoid.

Leakdown test

13 A leakdown test measures the rate at which compressed air fed into the cylinder is lost. It is an alternative to a compression test, and in many ways is better, since the escaping air provides easy identification of where a pressure loss is occurring (piston rings, valves or head gasket).

14 The equipment needed for leakdown testing is unlikely to be available to the home mechanic. If poor compression is suspected, have the test performed by a suitably-equipped garage.

3 Engine assembly and valve timing marks - general information and usage

> **Warning: When turning the engine, do not turn the engine using the camshaft sprocket bolts, and do not turn the engine backwards (ie, anti-clockwise).**

1 Top Dead Centre (TDC) is the highest point in the cylinder that each piston reaches as it travels up and down when the crankshaft turns. Each piston reaches TDC at the end of the compression stroke and again at the end of the exhaust stroke, but for valve timing TDC refers to the No 1 piston position on the compression stroke. No 1 piston is at the timing chain end of the engine.

2 Positioning No 1 piston at TDC is an essential part of many procedures, such as timing chain removal and camshaft removal.

3 Remove the camshaft cover as described in Section 4.

4 Using a socket on the crankshaft pulley/vibration damper hub bolt, turn the crankshaft clockwise until the O/T (TDC) mark on the crankshaft pulley/vibration damper is aligned with the pointer on the timing chain cover **(see illustration)**. For access to the bolt, it may be necessary to remove the viscous fan unit and radiator shroud as described in Chapter 3.

5 To check that the engine is positioned correctly, remove the oil filler cap and check that the No 1 cylinder inlet and exhaust camshaft lobes are pointing upwards. If they are not, turn the engine one compete turn and align the marks again.

6 If necessary, the camshafts can be locked in position. The inlet camshaft gear has a timing hole which aligns with a hole in the camshaft front bearing cap, and a suitable close-fitting drill should be inserted to lock the camshaft. With the inlet camshaft locked, the timing indentations (two 1.5 mm holes) on the fronts of the inlet and exhaust gears must be next to each other and aligned with the centre points of the camshafts. At TDC the timing marks on the camshaft gears will be aligned with each other when viewed from the front of the engine.

7 With the camshafts aligned as described, No 1 piston is at TDC on its firing stroke.

4 Camshaft cover - removal and refitting

Removal

1 Loosen the clips and remove the air inlet duct leading from the inlet manifold to the air cleaner/intercooler. It is only necessary to remove the section located over the camshaft cover **(see illustrations)**.

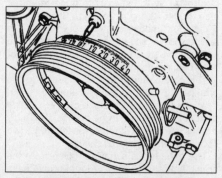

3.4 TDC (O/T) mark on crankshaft pulley/vibration damper aligned with pointer on timing chain cover

4.1a Loosen the clip at the intercooler end . . .

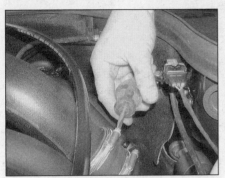

4.1b . . . and at the inlet manifold end . . .

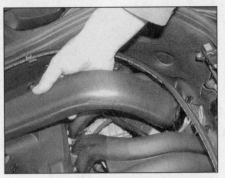

4.1c . . . and remove the air inlet duct from over the camshaft cover

4.2a Undo the screws . . .

2 Undo the self-tapping screws and withdraw the plastic cover from the top of the engine **(see illustrations)**.

3 Disconnect the crankcase ventilation hose at the front right-hand side of the camshaft cover, then unbolt the ventilation valve from the rear of the cover **(see illustrations)**.

4 Loosen the union nuts, and disconnect the fuel lines from the injectors. Also unbolt the fuel line support brackets from the left-hand side of the camshaft cover and loosen the fuel line union nuts on the injector pump. Carefully move the fuel lines to one side of the camshaft cover - if necessary remove them completely.

5 Unscrew the bolts then lift the camshaft cover away from the cylinder head **(see illustration)**.

6 Remove the cover gasket. Also remove the injector tube sealing O-rings. Do not remove the tubes unless the lower O-ring seals are leaking, otherwise oil may accumulate around the injectors.

7 Examine the condition of the gasket and O-rings, and renew if necessary.

Refitting

8 Clean the joint surfaces of the cover and cylinder head, then locate the gasket in the grooves in the camshaft cover, starting at the front and rear.

7 Check that the injector tubes are correctly

seated in the camshaft housing. If they have been removed, locate the lower O-ring seals on them, and position them in the camshaft housing making sure that the location lugs engage the cut-outs.

8 Locate the upper O-rings on the injector tubes.

9 Position the camshaft cover and gasket on the cylinder head, then insert the bolts and tighten them progressively to the specified torque.

10 Refit the fuel lines to the injectors and injector pump and tighten the union nuts to the specified torque. Refit the support brackets and tighten the bolts.

11 Refit the crankcase ventilation valve and hose to the camshaft cover and tighten the bolts securely.

12 Refit the plastic cover and tighten the self-tapping screws.

13 Refit the air inlet duct and tighten the clips.

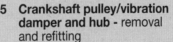

5 Crankshaft pulley/vibration damper and hub - removal and refitting

General

1 On early engines the vibration damper is located on the hub by a dowel, and the pulley

4.2b . . . and withdraw the plastic cover from the top of the engine

is bolted through the front of the vibration damper into the hub with 6 bolts. On later engines, the vibration damper, pulley and hub are combined as one unit.

Removal

2 Disconnect the battery negative (earth) lead and position it away from the terminal. The battery is located in the rear luggage compartment.

3 Apply the parking brake, then jack up the front of the vehicle and support it on axle stands (see *Jacking and vehicle support*). Remove the engine compartment undershield.

4.3a The crankcase ventilation hose locates on the top of the camshaft cover

4.3b The crankcase ventilation valve is located on the rear of the camshaft cover

4.5 A camshaft cover retaining bolt

5.4 The viscous fan unit

4 Remove the viscous fan unit as described in Chapter 3 **(see illustration)**.
5 With the auxiliary drivebelt still fitted, loosen the bolts securing the pulley to the coolant pump flange by half a turn each.
6 Remove the auxiliary drivebelt (and air conditioning compressor drivebelt where fitted) as described in Chapter 1B. On early models, release the auxiliary drivebelt tensioner by levering it up **(see illustrations)**.
7 Unscrew the bolts and remove the pulley from the coolant pump.
8 Refer to Section 3 and set the engine to TDC. This will ensure that the Woodruff key for the crankshaft pulley/vibration damper is positioned at the top of the crankshaft.
9 The crankshaft must now be held stationary while the pulley bolt is loosened. The bolt is tightened to a high torque. On manual transmission models, one method of holding the crankshaft stationary is having an assistant depress the footbrake pedal with 4th gear engaged, or lever off the cover from the rear of the sump and insert a wide-bladed screwdriver between the starter ring gear teeth. Mercedes-Benz technicians use a special tool which is bolted to the sump, and a suitable home-made tool may be fabricated for this purpose. On automatic transmission models, remove the starter motor and insert a wide-bladed screwdriver between the starter ring gear teeth.
10 Unscrew and remove the crankshaft pulley bolt and cone-shaped washer.
11 If necessary on early models, unscrew and remove the bolts securing the pulley to the vibration damper/hub, then withdraw the pulley and vibration damper from the hub. If loose, remove the location dowel from the hub.
12 Slide the crankshaft pulley/hub from the front of the crankshaft, using a suitable puller if it is tight.
13 If necessary, remove the Woodruff key from the groove in the nose of the crankshaft.

Inspection

14 Examine the oil seal contact surface of the pulley/vibration damper/hub for an excessive wear groove. If evident, it is permissible to position the oil seal slightly further into the timing chain cover so that it runs on the

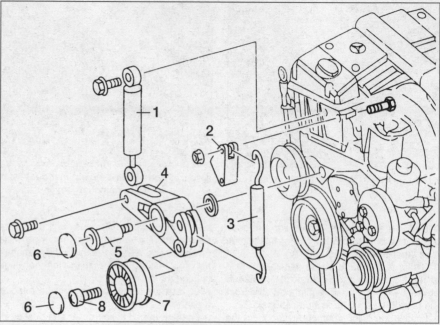

5.6a Auxiliary drivebelt tensioner components

1 *Damper*	4 *Tensioner lever*	6 *End cover*
2 *Bracket*	*bracket*	7 *Pulley*
3 *Tensioning spring*	5 *Pivot pin*	8 *Pulley bolt*

unworn area of the pulley. Alternatively, the pulley should be renewed. The oil seal in the timing chain cover must be renewed as a matter of course with reference to Section 14.

Refitting

15 Locate the Woodruff key in the groove in the nose of the crankshaft. Make sure that it is firmly pressed into position, and that its outer edge is parallel with the crankshaft so that the pulley/hub will engage with it easily.
16 Wipe clean and lightly oil the seal contact surface of the pulley, then slide it fully onto the crankshaft, engaging it with the Woodruff key.
17 If removed on early models, make sure that the location dowel is fitted in the hub, then locate the vibration damper on it, followed by the pulley. Insert the bolts and tighten to the specified torque.
18 Lightly oil the threads of the crankshaft

pulley bolt, then locate the cone-shaped washers on it and screw into the crankshaft. The convex sides of the washers must face the bolt head **(see illustration)**. Tighten the bolt to the specified torque while holding the crankshaft stationary using the method employed for removal.
19 On early models, refit the auxiliary drivebelt tensioner.
20 Refit the coolant pump pulley, and tighten the mounting bolts while holding the pulley stationary using an oil filter removal strap.
21 Refit the auxiliary drivebelt (and air conditioning compressor drivebelt where fitted) as described in Chapter 1B.
22 Refit the viscous fan unit as described in Chapter 3.
23 Refit the engine compartment undershield, then lower the car to the ground.
24 Reconnect the battery negative lead.

5.6b Auxiliary drivebelt tensioner and damper on the front of the engine

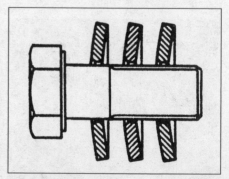

5.18 The convex side of the crankshaft pulley/vibration damper hub washers must face the bolt head

6 Timing chain cover - removal and refitting

Removal

1 Disconnect the battery negative (earth) lead and position it away from the terminal. The battery is located in the rear luggage compartment.

2 Apply the parking brake, then jack up the front of the vehicle and support it on axle stands (see *Jacking and vehicle support*). Remove the engine compartment undershield.

3 Drain the engine oil from the sump as described in Chapter 1B.

4 On turbocharged models, remove the air ducts from between the intercooler and air cleaner, and from between the intercooler and inlet manifold.

5 Remove the viscous fan unit (if fitted) as described in Chapter 3.

6 Before removing the auxiliary drivebelt, loosen the bolts securing the pulleys to the coolant pump and power steering pump by half a turn.

7 Remove the auxiliary drivebelt as described in Chapter 1B, and the tensioner as described in Section 8 of this Chapter.

8 Fully unscrew the bolts and remove the pulleys from the coolant pump and power steering pump.

9 Remove the brake vacuum pump from the front of the timing chain cover as described in Chapter 9. Recover the gasket.

10 Remove the camshaft cover as described in Section 4.

11 Refer to Section 3 and set the engine at TDC compression on No 1 cylinder. This is necessary in order to adjust the TDC sensor bracket on refitting. Ideally the crankshaft should be locked in this position during the removal of the timing chain cover. Mercedes-Benz technicians prise out the cover from the rear of the sump to bolt a special tool in position which engages the teeth of the starter ring gear.

12 Remove the crankshaft pulley/vibration damper/hub as described in Section 5.

13 On models fitted with an engine oil cooler, unbolt it from the right-hand side of the sump and recover the gasket. Tie the cooler to one side taking care not to strain the coolant hoses.

14 Unscrew the bolt securing the engine oil level dipstick tube to the front of the cylinder head.

15 Remove the alternator as described in Chapter 5A, then unbolt the alternator support bracket from the right-hand side of the cylinder block.

16 Unscrew and remove the bolts securing the sump to the bottom of the timing chain cover.

17 Loosen the remaining sump bolts by 2 or 3 turns.

18 Loosen the clips and disconnect the coolant hoses from the front of the cylinder head.

19 Unbolt the power steering pump and position it to the left-hand side of the engine compartment. **Do not** disconnect the hydraulic lines from the pump.

20 Unbolt the fuel filter from the left-hand side of the cylinder head, but leave the hoses connected to it. Support the filter to one side.

21 Pull the guide rail pin from the front of the cylinder head. Mercedes-Benz technicians use a special tool to do this, however a suitable bolt screwed into the pin should enable it to be removed.

22 Unbolt the auxiliary drivebelt tensioner and damper from the front of the cylinder block.

23 Mark the position of the injection pump on the rear of the timing chain cover (this is necessary to maintain the injection pump timing), then unscrew the retaining bolts.

24 Mark the position of the TDC sensor bracket on the timing chain cover, and note its position. Unscrew the bolts and remove the sensor and bracket. Position it to one side.

25 Working through the aperture in the top of the cylinder head, unscrew the two bolts securing the timing chain cover to the cylinder head. Recover the washers.

26 Unscrew the bolts and remove the timing chain cover from the front of the engine (**see illustration**), taking care not to damage the front parts of the cylinder head gasket and

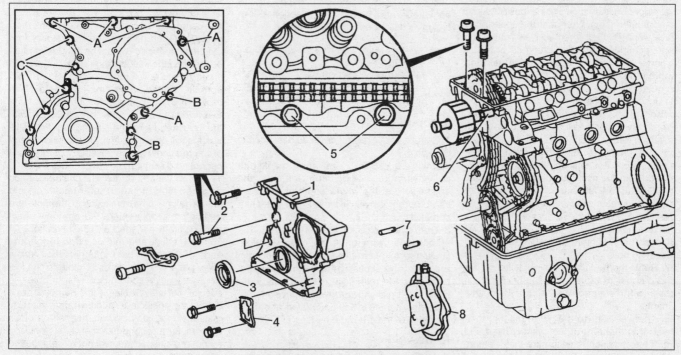

6.26 Timing chain cover components

1	Cover	4	Air conditioning compressor mounting plate
2	Bolts	5	Timing cover to cylinder head bolts
3	Crankshaft front oil seal	6	Upper guide pin (showing slide hammer)
		7	Location dowels
		8	Brake vacuum pump

A	M6x60 bolt and washer
B	M6x70 bolt and washer
C	M6x40 bolt and washer

sump gasket. To ensure the bolts are refitted in their correct locations, make a drawing of their positions, or use a dab of paint on them to identify them. If the two location dowels are loose, remove them also.

27 With the timing chain cover removed, it is recommended that the crankshaft front oil seal is renewed with reference to Section 14.

Refitting

28 Commence refitting by thoroughly cleaning away all traces of old sealant from the mating faces of the timing chain cover and cylinder block. Also clean the areas of the cylinder head gasket and sump gasket which contact the timing chain cover.

29 Carefully check the condition of the cylinder head gasket. If the gasket has been damaged during the removal procedure, the cylinder head should be removed in order to renew the gasket, as described in Section 10.

30 Similarly, carefully check the condition of the sump gasket. If the gasket has been damaged during the removal procedure, the sump should be removed in order to renew the gasket, as described in Section 11.

31 Apply sealant to the cylinder block mating face of the timing chain cover. Make sure that the two location dowels are correctly fitted.

32 Coat the lips of the crankshaft oil seal with clean engine oil, then slide the cover into position over the crankshaft. Take care not to damage the oil seal lips and the cylinder head and sump gaskets as the cover is fitted.

33 Insert all the retaining bolts, including the two upper ones, in their original positions and hand-tighten them. Note that the upper ones have washers. First, progressively tighten the bolts securing the timing chain cover to the cylinder block to the specified torque, then tighten the two upper bolts to the specified torque.

34 Insert the bolts securing the sump to the bottom of the timing chain cover. Progressively tighten all the sump bolts to the specified torque.

35 Refit the crankshaft position sensor mounting bracket, ensuring that the bracket is aligned with the marks made before removal. Ideally the adjustment of the crankshaft position sensor should be checked as described in Chapter 4B, Section 11, using a dial test indicator.

36 Insert and tighten the fuel injection pump mounting bolts.

37 Refit the auxiliary drivebelt tensioner and damper to the front of the timing chain cover with reference to Section 10 of this Chapter.

38 Apply sealant to the guide rail pin, then insert it in the front of the cylinder head and tap it into position making sure that it enters the top of the timing chain guide rail.

39 Refit the fuel filter to the left-hand side of the cylinder head, and tighten the bolts.

40 Refit the power steering pump and tighten the bolts.

41 Reconnect the two hoses (one large and one small) to the front of the cylinder head and tighten the clips.

42 Refit the alternator support bracket to the right-hand side of the cylinder block and tighten the bolts. Refit the alternator with reference to Chapter 5A.

43 Insert and tighten the bolt securing the dipstick tube to the cylinder head.

44 Refit the engine oil cooler (where fitted) to the sump together with a new gasket, and tighten the bolts.

45 Refit the crankshaft pulley/vibration damper/hub as described in Section 5.

46 Refit the camshaft cover with reference to Section 4.

47 Refit the brake vacuum pump to the front of the timing chain cover together with a new gasket as described in Chapter 9.

48 Refit the pulleys to the coolant pump and power steering pump. Use an oil filter removal strap to hold the pulleys stationary while the bolts are tightened.

49 Refit the auxiliary drivebelt as described in Chapter 1B.

50 Refit the viscous fan unit as described in Chapter 3.

51 On turbocharged models, refit the air ducts between the intercooler and air cleaner, and between the intercooler and inlet manifold.

52 Refit the engine compartment undershield and lower the car to the ground.

53 Reconnect the battery negative lead.

54 Refill the engine with the correct grade and quantity of oil, as described in Chapter 1B.

55 Check and adjust the injection pump timing as described in Chapter 4B.

7 Timing chain - inspection and renewal

Inspection

1 Remove the camshaft cover as described in Section 4.

2 Using a socket on the crankshaft pulley/vibration damper hub bolt, turn the engine so that the whole length of the chain can be progressively viewed at the camshaft sprocket.

3 The chain should be renewed if the sprocket is worn or if the chain is worn (indicated by excessive lateral play between the links, and excessive noise in operation). Note that the rollers on a very badly worn chain may be slightly grooved. To avoid future problems, if there is any doubt at all about the condition of the chain, renew it.

Renewal

Note: *Removal of the timing chain using the following procedure entails the use of a portable electric grinder to cut through one of the chain links. Ensure that such a tool is available, as well as a new chain and new connecting link before proceeding.*

4 Disconnect the battery negative (earth) lead and position it away from the terminal. The battery is located in the rear luggage compartment.

5 Remove the fuel injectors as described in Chapter 4B.

6 Remove the viscous fan and radiator shroud, as described in Chapter 3.

7 Remove the timing chain tensioner as described in Section 8.

8 Cover the camshafts and the aperture in the cylinder head with clean rags.

9 Using a grinder, grind off the protruding lugs of one of the chain links near the top of the camshaft sprocket - take care not to damage the sprocket.

10 Keeping both ends of the chain engaged with the sprocket, pull off the chain link outer plate and push the link out towards the rear of the chain. Recover the middle plate as the link is removed.

11 Remove the rags, taking care not to allow any swarf to drop down into the timing chain housing.

12 Using the new link, connect one end of the new timing chain to the tail end of the old chain, in such a way that as the engine is turned (clockwise), the new chain will be drawn over the sprocket, then down around the injection pump and crankshaft sprockets, and up the other side. Fit the link from the rear of the sprocket, and insert the middle plate (1.6 mm thick) at the same time. Ensure that the link is pushed firmly into position. If the old outer plate is a tight fit on the lugs, fit this as well, otherwise leave it off.

13 Using a socket on the crankshaft pulley/vibration damper hub bolt, slowly turn the crankshaft clockwise. The new chain must be fed onto the camshaft sprocket and the old chain must be released from the camshaft sprocket at the same time. The help of an assistant will make the procedure easier. Note that if the old chain is not kept engaged with the sprocket, there is a chance that the valve springs will cause the sprocket to jump ahead of the rotation with the possibility of the chain becoming disengaged.

14 When the end of the new chain has been engaged with the sprocket, remove the old chain, taking care not to drop the link and middle plate. Make sure that the new chain remains firmly engaged with the sprocket.

15 Fit the link and middle plate to join the ends of the new chain together, then fit the outer plate. Secure the outer plate to the link by riveting over the ends of the link pins. A special tool is available for this purpose, but it should be possible to achieve a satisfactory result using a ball-pein hammer, with a block of metal (or a second hammer) to support the rear of the chain - *take care not to damage the chain or the sprocket.*

16 Return the engine to TDC with reference to Section 3, and check that the timing holes in both camshafts are correctly aligned. If the holes are not correctly aligned, it is possible that the timing chain may have jumped one

tooth during the fitting procedure, in which case it will be necessary to remove the exhaust camshaft sprocket with reference to Section 8 and reposition the chain before refitting the sprocket. It will also be necessary to check the injection pump timing with reference to Chapter 4B.

17 Refit the timing chain tensioner as described in Section 8.

18 Refit the viscous fan and radiator shroud, as described in Chapter 3.

19 Refit the fuel injectors as described in Chapter 4B.

20 Reconnect the battery negative lead.

8 Timing chain tensioner, sprockets and guides - removal, inspection and refitting

Timing chain tensioner

Removal

1 Refer to Section 3 and set the engine to TDC on No 1 cylinder.

2 Working at the right-hand side of the engine, unscrew the tensioner body (**do not** unscrew the tensioner cover plug) from the cylinder head. Recover the sealing ring.

Inspection

3 Do not attempt to dismantle the tensioner assembly. If it is suspected that the tensioner is worn or faulty, the complete unit should be renewed.

Refitting

4 Before refitting the tensioner, the unit must be primed with oil as follows.

a) *Place the tensioner, with the plunger facing downwards in a container of engine oil. The oil level should be above the level of the collar so that the oil inlet is beneath the oil.*

b) *Press slowly down on the assembly (a hydraulic press may be required to achieve sufficient pressure) between seven and ten times until the plunger reaches the stop.*

c) *Once the tensioner has been primed, it should only be possible to compress the tensioner slowly, with it still immersed in the oil.*

5 Locate a new sealing ring on the tensioner, then screw it into position in the cylinder head and tighten to the specified torque.

Camshaft (exhaust) sprocket

Removal

6 Refer to Section 3 and set the engine to TDC on No 1 cylinder. Lock the inlet camshaft as described by inserting a drill through the camshaft front bearing cap into the gear (**see illustration**).

7 Use a dab of paint or a marker pen to mark the timing chain and the exhaust camshaft sprocket in relation to each other. This will help ensure that the chain is refitted correctly and the valve timing maintained.

8 Remove the timing chain tensioner as described earlier in this Section.

9 Hold the exhaust camshaft sprocket stationary using a suitable tool located in the sprocket cut-outs, then loosen the bolts securing the sprocket to the camshaft. **Do not** rely only on the drill located in the inlet camshaft sprocket to hold the sprocket.

10 At this stage the crankshaft and injection pump sprockets will still be at TDC, and the crankshaft must not be turned until the camshaft sprocket has been refitted. Use a length of wire to tie the upper part of the timing chain to the cylinder head to ensure the chain remains on the injection pump sprocket.

11 Unscrew the bolts and remove the sprocket from the location dowel on the camshaft flange. Remove the sprocket from the timing chain, and remove the dowel from the flange. **Note:** *The sprocket bolts must be renewed every time they are removed.*

Inspection

12 Examine the teeth on the sprocket for wear. Each tooth forms an inverted V. If worn, the side of each tooth under tension will be slightly concave in shape when compared with the other side of the tooth (ie, the teeth will have a hooked appearance). If the teeth appear worn, the sprocket must be renewed.

Refitting

13 Ensure that the camshaft and crankshaft timing marks are still aligned, as described in Section 3. If a new sprocket is being fitted, transfer the chain alignment mark from the old sprocket to the new.

14 Fit the location dowel to the hole in the exhaust camshaft flange.

15 Engage the sprocket with the chain, aligning the marks made on the chain and sprocket before removal, then locate the sprocket on the camshaft flange and engage it with the dowel.

16 Insert the bolts and tighten them to the specified torque while holding the sprocket stationary using the used tool for removal.

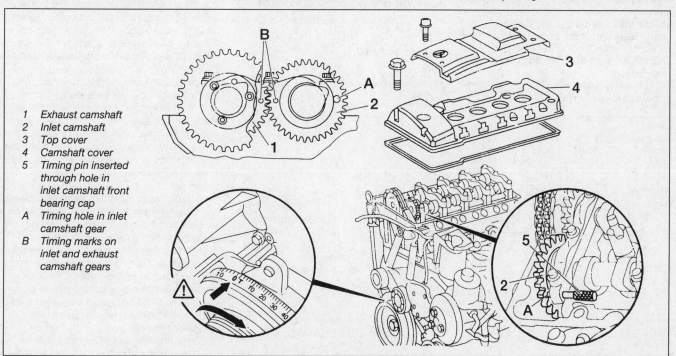

1 Exhaust camshaft
2 Inlet camshaft
3 Top cover
4 Camshaft cover
5 Timing pin inserted through hole in inlet camshaft front bearing cap
A Timing hole in inlet camshaft gear
B Timing marks on inlet and exhaust camshaft gears

8.6 Camshaft timing marks

Remove the wire used to tie the chain to the cylinder head.

17 Refit the timing chain tensioner as described earlier in this Section.

18 Using a socket on the crankshaft pulley/vibration damper hub bolt, turn the crankshaft through two complete revolutions, and check that the crankshaft and camshaft timing marks are still aligned with No 1 piston at TDC, as described in Section 3.

19 Remove the inlet camshaft locking drill, then refit the camshaft cover with reference to Section 4.

Crankshaft sprocket

Note: *A puller may be required to remove the sprocket.*

Removal

20 Remove the timing chain cover as described in Section 6. This procedure includes removal of the crankshaft pulley/vibration damper and Woodruff key, and the setting of the engine to its TDC position.

21 Remove the sump as described in Section 11.

22 Hold the oil pump sprocket on the oil pump stationary using a suitable tool engaged with the sprocket holes, then unscrew and remove the mounting bolts. Remove the sprocket from the oil pump drive flange and unhook the drive chain from the crankshaft sprocket on the front of the crankshaft. **Note:** *The oil pump chain drive sprocket is incorporated into the crankshaft sprocket.*

23 Remove the camshaft sprocket as described previously in this Section, however, in addition to marking the timing chain in relation to the camshaft sprocket, also mark it in relation to the injection pump sprocket and crankshaft sprocket. This is necessary to ensure the valve timing and injection pump timing is maintained, since it will also be difficult to ascertain the TDC position of the crankshaft with the timing chain cover removed.

24 Unhook the timing chain from the crankshaft sprocket and injection pump sprocket.

25 Slide the crankshaft sprocket from the front of the crankshaft. If it is tight, use a suitable puller, taking care not to damage the sprocket teeth. Alternatively, use two levers against the front of the cylinder block, positioning the levers diagonally opposite each other.

26 Recover the Woodruff key from the groove in the crankshaft.

Inspection

27 Refer to paragraph 12.

Refitting

28 Locate the Woodruff key in the crankshaft groove, making sure that the upper edge is parallel with the surface of the crankshaft.

29 Slide the crankshaft sprocket onto the front of the crankshaft and engage it with the Woodruff key. If necessary, use a suitable metal tube to tap it into position.

30 Engage the timing chain with the crankshaft sprocket and injection pump sprocket, making sure that the previously made marks are aligned with each other, then pull the chain up through the aperture at the front of the cylinder head.

31 Refit the camshaft sprocket as described earlier in this Section, making sure that the previously made marks on the chain and sprocket are aligned with each other. Check that the alignment marks are still correctly aligned.

32 Refit the oil pump drive chain and sprocket with reference to Section 12.

33 Refit the sump with reference to Section 11.

34 Refit the timing chain cover and crankshaft pulley/vibration damper as described in Section 6.

Fuel injection pump sprocket

35 The procedure is described in Chapter 4B.

Tensioner rail

Removal

36 Remove the cylinder head as described in Section 10.

37 Remove the timing chain cover as described in Section 6.

38 Remove the timing chain tensioner as described previously in this Section.

39 Remove the tensioner rail from its pin.

Inspection

40 Examine the tensioner rail for signs of excessive wear, damage or cracks, and renew if necessary.

Refitting

41 Locate the tensioner rail on the pin.

42 Refit the timing chain tensioner as described previously in this Section.

43 Refit the timing chain cover as described in Section 6.

44 Refit the cylinder head as described in Section 10.

9 Camshafts, camshaft housing and hydraulic tappets - removal, inspection and refitting

Camshafts

Removal

Note: If desired, before removing the camshafts, the condition of the hydraulic tappets can be checked as described in paragraphs 25 to 32. New camshaft endfloat control thrustwashers may be required on refitting.

1 Remove the exhaust camshaft sprocket as described in Section 8. Make sure that the timing chain remains engaged with the injection pump sprocket and crankshaft sprocket, using wire to tie it to one side.

2 Before removing the camshafts, it is important that the housing is bolted directly to the cylinder head with two bolts located in recesses beneath bearing caps 2 and 4 (4-cylinder engines) or beneath bearing caps 2 and 5 (5-cylinder engines). On models manufactured before 09/1994 the bolts are fitted by the factory as standard; on later models the bolts were discontinued and it will be necessary to obtain and fit them before removing the camshafts. **Note:** If the housing is not bolted to the cylinder head in this way, oil leaks may occur into the injector tubes. If there are existing oil leaks, the housing should be removed and the seals renewed as described later in this Section.

3 The camshaft bearing caps are numbered from the timing chain end of the engine. Check the bearing caps to ensure that marks are present, and if necessary make suitable marks using quick-drying paint or a centre-punch.

4 On models manufactured on or after 09/1994, the camshaft housing **must** be bolted to the cylinder head as follows. **Note:** The bolts can remain in position permanently. The bearing caps removed to fit the bolts **must** be refitted before following the camshaft removal procedure.

4-cylinder engine

a) *Progressively slacken and then remove the bolts from bearing caps 2 and 4 (see illustration).*

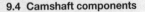

9.4 Camshaft components

1 Sprocket securing bolt
2 Exhaust camshaft sprocket
3 Exhaust camshaft and gear
4 Inlet camshaft and gear
5 Bearing cap
6 Camshaft housing

b) Lift off bearing caps 2 and 4, keeping them in order. Note that the bearing caps locate on dowels - if they are stuck, tap gently using a soft-faced mallet.

c) Insert two bolts (M7 x 41) in the special holes, and progressively tighten them to the specified torque.

d) Clean, then refit bearing caps 2 and 4, and progressively tighten the bolts to the specified torque.

5-cylinder engine

a) Progressively slacken and then remove the bolts from bearing caps 2 and 5.

b) Lift off bearing caps 2 and 5, keeping them in order. Note that the bearing caps locate on dowels - if they are stuck, tap gently using a soft-faced mallet.

c) Insert two bolts (M7 x 41) in the special holes, and progressively tighten them to the specified torque.

d) Clean, then refit bearing caps 2 and 5, and progressively tighten the bolts to the specified torque.

5 The camshaft bearing cap bolts must now be slackened according to the following information, and the camshafts removed.

 Warning: It is absolutely essential to observe the correct sequence when slackening the camshaft bearing cap bolts, because the camshafts are very sensitive to fracturing.

4-cylinder engine

a) Progressively slacken and then remove the bolts from bearing caps 1, 3 and 5.

b) Lift off bearing caps 1, 3 and 5, keeping them in order. Note that the bearing caps locate on dowels - if they are stuck, tap gently using a soft-faced mallet.

c) Progressively slacken the bearing cap bolts for bearing caps 2 and 4, in one-turn stages until all pressure on the camshaft is relieved. Take care not to allow uneven pressure on the camshaft as the bolts are unscrewed.

d) Lift off bearing caps 2 and 4, again keeping them in order.

e) Lift the inlet and exhaust camshafts from the camshaft housing and recover the thrustwashers from No 3 bearing location.

5-cylinder engine

a) Progressively slacken and then remove the bolts from bearing caps 1, 3, 4 and 6.

b) Lift off bearing caps 1, 3, 4 and 6, keeping them in order. Note that the bearing caps locate on dowels - if they are stuck, tap gently using a soft-faced mallet.

c) Progressively slacken the bearing cap bolts for bearing caps 2 and 5, in one-turn stages until all pressure on the camshafts is relieved. Take great care not to allow uneven pressure on the camshafts as the bolts are unscrewed.

d) Lift off the bearing caps 2 and 5, again keeping them in order.

e) Lift the inlet and exhaust camshafts from the camshaft housing and recover the thrustwashers from No 3 bearing location.

6 Remove the injector tubes from the camshaft housing, noting the position of the location lugs.

Inspection

7 Thoroughly clean the camshafts and the housing/caps.

8 Examine the camshaft journals and cam lobes for any sign of scoring, wear grooves or pitting, and if apparent, renew the relevant camshaft. Any damage of this nature may be attributable to a blocked oil passage in the cylinder head, and careful examination should be carried out to determine the cause.

9 To check the camshaft endfloat, ideally the camshaft housing should be removed, as described later in this Section, then locate each camshaft in the housing together with the thrustwashers. Using a DTI (Dial Test Indicator, or dial gauge), measure the endfloat and compare with the amount given in the Specifications. If the clearance is excessive, renew the thrustwashers.

10 Examine the bearing surfaces in the camshaft housing and bearing caps for excessive wear and scoring. If evident, renew the components together with the camshafts.

Refitting

11 On models manufactured on or after 09/1994, the bolts fitted in paragraph 4 can remain in position.

12 Refit the injector tubes to the camshaft housing, engaging the location lugs in the cut-outs.

13 Lubricate the camshaft journals and bearing locations in the camshaft housing/caps with clean engine oil. Also lubricate the hydraulic tappets.

14 Locate the inlet camshaft in the left-hand side of the camshaft housing together with the thrustwashers, then locate the exhaust camshaft in the right-hand side with its thrustwashers, at the same time engaging the gears at the fronts of the camshafts so that the timing marks are aligned (see Section 3).

15 Locate the bearing caps in position over the camshafts and tighten the securing bolts according to the following information, ensuring that the bearing caps are fitted to their original locations.

 Warning: It is absolutely essential to observe the correct sequence when tightening the camshaft bearing cap bolts, in order to avoid damage to the camshaft.

4-cylinder engine

a) Fit bearing caps 2 and 4, then insert the bolts, and tighten them progressively in one-turn stages to the specified torque. Take care not to allow uneven pressure on the camshaft as the bolts are tightened.

b) Fit bearing caps 1, 3 and 5, then insert the bolts, and tighten them progressively in one-turn stages to the specified torque.

5-cylinder engines

a) Fit bearing caps 2 and 5, then insert the bolts, and tighten them progressively in one-turn stages to the specified torque.

Take care not to allow uneven pressure on the camshaft as the bolts are tightened.

b) Fit bearing caps 1, 3, 4 and 6, then insert the bolts, and tighten them progressively in one-turn stages to the specified torque.

16 Refit the exhaust camshaft sprocket as described in Section 8.

Camshaft housing and hydraulic tappets

Removal

17 Remove the camshafts as described earlier in this Section. This procedure includes removal of the camshaft cover and injector tubes.

18 Extract the timing chain upper guide rail pin from the front of the cylinder head. Mercedes-Benz technicians use a slide hammer tool which is screwed into the pin, however an alternative tool can be made using a long bolt, nut, washers and metal tube. Locate the metal tube on the cylinder head over the pin, and fit the nut to the bolt followed by the washers. Screw the bolt into the pin, then tighten the nut to extract the pin.

19 Unscrew the two bolts and lift the camshaft housing from the cylinder head. Recover the O-ring seals - 4 on 4-cylinder engines, and 5 on 5-cylinder engines. The hydraulic tappets will not fall out of the housing if it is kept upright.

20 If necessary, remove the location dowels from the cylinder head.

21 Obtain a container with 16 compartments and fill it with clean engine oil. Number the compartments to indicate the location of the hydraulic tappets. Remove each hydraulic tappet in turn from the camshaft housing and immerse them in the oil in the container.

Inspection

22 Clean the camshaft housing and cylinder head and check for damage and wear. Also refer to paragraphs 7 to 9.

Hydraulic tappets - checking after removal

23 The operation of the removed hydraulic tappets can be checked as follows.

a) Press down firmly on the top of each tappet, using a blunt instrument such as a wooden hammer handle, for approximately 10 seconds.

b) Note how far the piston moves when depressed.

c) Repeat the operation for all the valve lifters in turn.

d) If any one tappet can be depressed more easily than the others, renew the relevant lifter.

24 Check the hydraulic tappets and the bores in the camshaft housing for wear and scoring. If any serious damage or wear is evident, the camshaft housing and tappets must be renewed.

Hydraulic tappets - checking in situ

25 Run the engine until it reaches normal operating temperature. Make sure the engine oil level is correct.

26 Remove the camshaft cover as described in Section 4 - take care as the engine will be hot.

27 Turn the engine to position No 1 piston at TDC, ensuring that crankshaft and camshaft timing marks are correctly aligned as described in Section 3.

28 Ensure that the valves are fully closed - ie, the cam lobes of No 1 cylinder are pointing upwards, then, using a soft metal or strong wooden rod, push down lightly on the tops of the No 1 cylinder hydraulic tappets.

29 Keep the valve lifter pressed down, and measure the clearance between the top of the valve lifter and the camshaft lobe, using a feeler blade.

30 If the clearance is greater than specified, the hydraulic tappet should be renewed.

31 Turn the crankshaft using a socket on the crankshaft pulley/vibration damper hub bolt, and repeat the checking procedure for the remaining cylinder hydraulic tappets. Each clearance must be checked with the relevant valve fully closed - ie, the cam lobe pointing upwards.

 Warning: When turning the engine, do not turn the engine using the camshaft sprocket bolt, and do not turn the engine backwards (ie, anti-clockwise).

32 When all the hydraulic tappets have been checked, refit the camshaft cover with reference to Section 4.

Refitting

33 Lubricate the hydraulic tappet bores in the camshaft housing with clean engine oil, then locate each hydraulic tappet in its original position in the housing.

34 Fit the camshaft housing location dowels in the cylinder head.

35 Locate new O-ring seals on the cylinder head, then lower the housing onto them and insert the two retaining bolts. Tighten the bolts progressively to the specified torque.

36 Apply sealant to the timing chain upper guide rail pin, then insert it into the front of the cylinder head and tap it in while guiding it through the top of the guide rail.

37 Refit the camshafts as described earlier in this Section.

---

10 Cylinder head - removal, inspection and refitting

Removal

Note: *A suitable hoist and lifting tackle will be required for this operation. New cylinder head bolts may be required - see text.*

1 Ensure that the engine is cold before attempting to remove the cylinder head, and note that the cylinder head is removed complete with the exhaust manifold.

2 Apply the parking brake, then jack up the front of the vehicle and support it on axle stands (see *Jacking and vehicle support*).

3 Disconnect the battery negative (earth) lead and position it away from the terminal. The battery is located in the rear luggage compartment.

4 Raise the bonnet to the fully open position.

5 Drain the engine oil and the coolant as described in Chapter 1B.

6 Remove the auxiliary drivebelt as described in Chapter 1B, then remove the drivebelt tensioner as follows:

a) *Pull off the plastic cover, unscrew the securing bolt, and remove the auxiliary drivebelt idler pulley.*

b) *Unscrew the securing bolts, and withdraw the tensioner damper strut. Recover any spacers and/or brackets from the bolts noting their locations.*

c) *Using a pair of pliers, unhook the tension spring, noting its orientation to aid refitting.*

d) *Where applicable, pull off the plastic cover, then unscrew the tensioner securing bolt and, slide off the spacer sleeve (if applicable).*

e) *Withdraw the tensioner, and recover the spacer (where applicable).*

7 Remove the camshaft cover as described in Section 4.

8 Remove the inlet manifold as described in Chapter 4B.

9 Loosen the clips and disconnect the coolant hose from the front of the cylinder head.

10 Identify the location of the vacuum pipes on the front of the cylinder head, then disconnect them.

11 Unbolt the exhaust downpipe from the exhaust manifold with reference to Chapter 4C. Recover the gasket.

12 Remove the timing chain tensioner as described in Section 8. This procedure includes setting the engine to TDC.

13 Remove the camshafts, and camshaft housing as described in Section 9.

14 Temporarily remove the filler cap from the fuel tank in order to release any vacuum, then refit it. Identify the fuel hoses on the preheater, then loosen the clips and disconnect them. Plug the ends of the hoses to prevent entry of dust and dirt.

15 At the left-hand rear of the cylinder head, disconnect the engine wiring harness.

16 On models with an oil cooler on the oil filter housing, unbolt and remove the oil filter housing from the left-hand side of the cylinder block and remove the oil cooler from the cylinder block. Recover the O-ring seals.

17 Unbolt the fuel filter from the left-hand side of the cylinder head, leaving the fuel hoses attached. Tie the filter to one side of the engine compartment.

18 Pull the upper guide rail pin from the front of the cylinder head. Mercedes-Benz technicians use a special tool to do this, however a suitable bolt screwed into the pin should enable it to be removed.

19 Remove the lower guide rail pin using the same method, then withdraw the guide rail

through the cylinder head aperture and from the timing cover. Note which way round the rail is fitted to ensure correct refitting - as the rail is removed, the guide pin holes are facing upwards.

20 Using a socket through the cylinder head aperture, unscrew and remove the two bolts securing the timing chain cover to the cylinder head. Recover the washers.

21 On turbocharged models, unscrew the union nut and disconnect the oil supply pipe from the turbocharger. Also, unscrew the flange bolts and detach the oil return pipe. Recover the gasket and O-rings. Loosen the clips and disconnect the air ducts from the turbocharger.

22 Make a final check to ensure that all relevant hoses and wires have been disconnected from the cylinder head.

23 Progressively loosen the cylinder head bolts, working in the reverse order to the tightening sequence **(see illustration 10.43)**.

24 Remove the cylinder head bolts, noting their locations, as different lengths of bolts are used **(see illustration)**.

25 Attach a hoist and lifting tackle to the cylinder head, and raise the hoist to just take the weight of the cylinder head. Note that Mercedes-Benz technicians use the bolt holes of the front and rear exhaust camshaft bearing caps to attach lifting eyes to the cylinder head.

26 Release the cylinder head from the cylinder block and locating dowels by rocking it. Do not prise between the mating faces of the cylinder head and block, as this may damage the gasket faces.

27 Carefully lift the cylinder head, complete with exhaust manifold, from the block, and manoeuvre it out from the engine compartment.

28 Recover the cylinder head gasket.

29 If necessary, remove the exhaust manifold with reference to Chapter 4C.

Inspection

30 Refer to Chapter 2C for details of cylinder head dismantling and reassembly.

31 The mating faces of the cylinder head and block must be perfectly clean before refitting the head. Use a scraper to remove all traces of gasket and carbon, and also clean the tops of the pistons. Take particular care with the cylinder head, as the metal is easily damaged. Also make sure that debris is not allowed to enter the oil and water passages. Using adhesive tape and paper, seal the water, oil and bolt holes in the cylinder block. To prevent carbon entering the gap between the pistons and bores, smear a little grease in the gap. After cleaning each piston, rotate the crankshaft so that the piston moves **down** the bore, then wipe out the grease and carbon with a cloth rag.

32 Check the block and head for nicks, deep scratches and other damage. If very slight, they may be removed from the cylinder block carefully with a file. More serious damage may be repaired by machining, but this is a specialist job.

33 If warpage of the cylinder head is suspected, use a straight-edge to check it for distortion, with reference to Chapter 2C.

34 Clean out the bolt holes in the block using a pipe cleaner or thin rag and a screwdriver. Make sure that all oil and water is removed, otherwise there is a possibility of the block being cracked by hydraulic pressure when the bolts are tightened.

35 Examine the bolt threads and the threads in the cylinder block for damage. If necessary, use the correct size tap to chase out the threads in the block.

36 The manufacturers recommend that the cylinder head bolts are measured, to determine whether renewal is necessary; however, some owners may wish to renew all the bolts as a matter of course.

37 Measure the length of each bolt from the base of the head to the end of the shank **(see illustration)**. If the bolt length is greater than the maximum specified, the bolts should be renewed.

Refitting

38 Where applicable, refit the exhaust manifold together with a new gasket with reference to Chapter 4C.

39 Check that the crankshaft is still set at TDC.

40 Locate the new cylinder head gasket on the block, making sure that it is the correct way up and positioned over the location dowels.

41 Raise the cylinder head using the hoist and lifting tackle, then lower it carefully onto the block.

42 Oil the threads and the cylinder head contact faces of the cylinder head bolts, then insert them and screw them into the cylinder block by hand. Ensure that the bolts are fitted to their correct locations as noted on removal. The 4 longer bolts (115.0 mm) are located on the left-hand side (ie, inlet manifold side).

43 Tighten the cylinder head bolts in the order shown **(see illustration)**, and in the stages given in the Specifications - ie, tighten all bolts to the

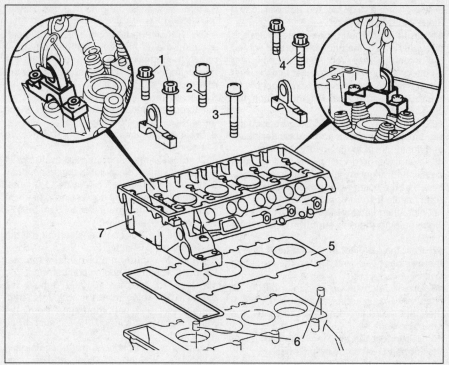

10.24 Cylinder head removal

1	Bolts for attaching lifting bracket	3	M10x115 cylinder head bolts	5	Cylinder head gasket
2	M10x102 cylinder head bolts	4	Bolts for attaching lifting bracket	6	Cylinder head location dowels
				7	Cylinder head

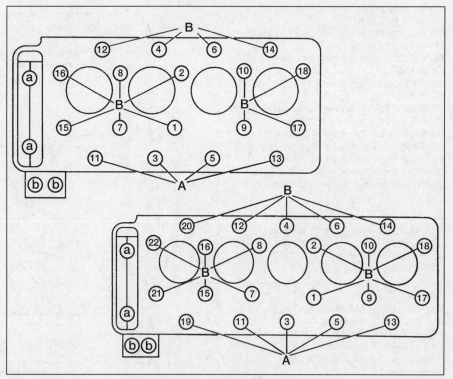

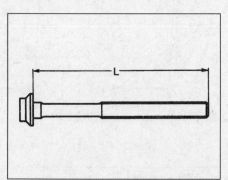

10.37 Measure the length (L) of the cylinder head bolts

See Specifications for maximum length

10.43 Cylinder head bolt tightening sequence

| A | M10x115 bolts | a | M8x50 bolts and washers (to timing chain cover) | b | M8x80 bolts and washers (fuel filter) |
| B | M10x102 bolts | | | | |

Stage 1 torque, then tighten all bolts to the Stage 2 torque, and so on.

44 On turbocharged models, reconnect the oil supply pipe to the turbocharger and tighten the union nut. Also, reconnect the oil return pipe together with a new gasket and O-rings, and tighten the flange bolts. Reconnect the air ducts to the turbocharger and tighten the clips.

45 Insert the two bolts and washers securing the timing chain cover to the cylinder head, and tighten them to the specified torque.

46 Insert the guide rail in the timing chain cover, and align the guide pin holes. Make sure that the guide rail is the correct way up. Apply sealant to the upper and lower guide rail pins, then carefully tap them into position while guiding them through the holes in the guide rail.

47 Refit the fuel filter to the left-hand side of the cylinder head, and tighten the mounting bolts.

48 On models with an oil cooler on the oil filter, refit the oil cooler to the cylinder block then refit the oil filter housing and tighten the mounting bolts.

49 Reconnect the engine wiring harness at the left-hand rear of the cylinder head.

50 Reconnect the fuel hoses to the preheater and tighten the clips.

51 Refit the camshaft housing and camshafts with reference to Section 9.

52 Refit the timing chain tensioner together with a new seal as described in Section 8.

53 Refit the exhaust downpipe to the exhaust manifold together with a new gasket with reference to Chapter 4C.

54 Reconnect the vacuum pipes to the front of the cylinder head.

55 Refit the inlet manifold as described in Chapter 4B.

56 Refit the camshaft cover as described in Section 4.

57 Refit the auxiliary drivebelt tensioner using a reversal of the removal procedure, then refit the drivebelt as described in Chapter 1B.

58 Reconnect the battery negative (earth) lead, and lower the car to the ground.

59 Refill the cooling system and refill the engine with oil with reference to Chapter 1B.

11 Sump - removal and refitting

Removal

Note: *A suitable hoist and lifting tackle will be required for this operation.*

1 Disconnect the battery negative (earth) lead and position it away from the terminal. The battery is located in the rear luggage compartment.

2 Apply the parking brake, then jack up the front of the vehicle and support it on axle stands (see *Jacking and vehicle support*).

3 Remove the engine compartment undershield.

4 On turbocharged models, unscrew the bolt securing the air inlet tube to the body front panel, then loosen the clip and remove the tube from the turbocharger pressure regulator.

5 Release the clips and remove the cooling fan shroud from the rear of the radiator. Place the shroud over the cooling fan.

6 Drain the engine oil with reference to Chapter 1B.

7 On models manufactured up to 30/06/94 and fitted with an oil cooler in the sump, drain the cooling system with reference to Chapter 1B, then unbolt the oil cooler and pipes and position it to one side (refer to Section 17). Recover the O-ring seals.

8 Remove the front suspension anti-roll bar as described in Chapter 10.

9 Unbolt the starter motor cable at the rear left-hand side of the engine compartment.

10 Refer to Chapter 4C and detach the exhaust downpipe from the manifold, then unbolt the exhaust mounting from the transmission and support the exhaust on an axle stand.

11 Attach a suitable hoist to the engine and take the weight of the engine and transmission. The lifting eyes are located on the left-hand side of the cylinder head, however, take care not to damage the front fuel injection pipe.

12 Unscrew the lower bolts from the front engine mountings, then unscrew the bolts securing the rear engine mounting crossmember to the underside of the transmission. Leave the crossmember attached to the underbody.

13 Raise the engine and transmission as far as possible, but do not stretch the coolant hoses excessively (if necessary, remove the

radiator from its mountings with reference to Chapter 3). Make sure the engine and transmission assembly is adequately supported, as the next procedure involves working beneath the engine.

14 Unbolt the earth cable from the rear of the sump, then unbolt the oil level switch wiring support and disconnect the wiring from the switch.

15 On automatic transmission models, unscrew the bolts securing the transmission fluid pipes and wiring to the sump.

16 Unscrew the bolts securing the transmission to the rear of the sump, then unscrew the remaining sump-to-engine bolts and lower the sump from the crankcase. Recover the gasket. Note that there are several bolt sizes fitted **(see illustrations)**. If the sump is stuck, use a hide or wooden mallet to tap its sides in order to release it. Do not drive a screwdriver between the sump and crankcase as this may damage the mating surfaces. Note that where a long deflector/baffle plate is fitted to the sump, it is necessary to unbolt the oil pump before lowering the sump **(see illustration)**; refer to Section 12. It may also be necessary to rotate the crankshaft to provide additional clearance.

17 Check that the location dowel is still fitted to the right-hand rear of the sump or in the crankcase. If it is loose, remove it and store in a safe place.

18 It is recommended that the oil filter and oil is renewed whenever the sump is removed. Before refitting the sump, it is a good idea to remove the oil filter in order to allow the oil to drain from the cylinder block oil gallery and internal oilways.

Refitting

19 Thoroughly clean the mating surfaces of

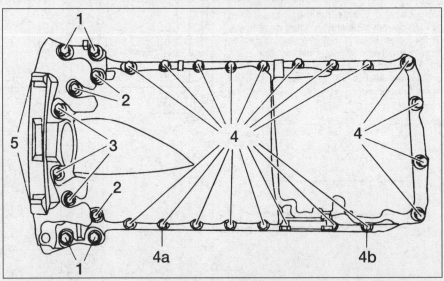

11.16a Sump bolt locations (604 engine)

1 *M8x40 bolt and washer*	4 *M6x20 bolt and washer*	4b *M6x75 socket-headed bolt*
2 *M6x35 bolt and washer*	4a *M6x20 socket-headed bolt*	*(automatic transmission)*
3 *M6x85 bolt and washer*	*(automatic transmission)*	5 *M10x40 bolt and washer*

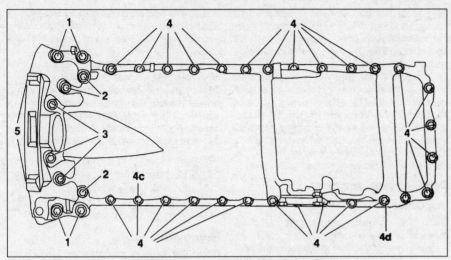

11.16b Sump bolt locations (605 engine)

1 M8x40 bolt and washer	*4a M6x20 socket-headed bolt*	*4c M6x20 socket-headed*
2 M6x35 bolt and washer	*(automatic transmission)*	*bolt (automatic*
3 M6x85 bolt and washer	*4b M6x75 socket-headed bolt*	*transmission)*
4 M6x20 bolt and washer	*(automatic transmission)*	*5 M10x40 bolt and washer*

the sump and crankcase, then smear a little grease on the crankcase and fit the new gasket, making sure that the bolt and dowel holes align with the holes in the gasket. Make sure the location dowel is fitted, then refit the sump to the crankcase and insert all of the bolts finger-tight. Now tighten the bolts securing the transmission to the sump to the specified torque. This will ensure the rear of the sump is correctly aligned with the transmission, as if it is not aligned correctly, vibration and noise may occur. Where a long deflector/baffle plate is fitted to the sump, refit the oil pump at the same time, with reference to Section 12.

20 Tighten the remaining sump bolts to the specified torque. On automatic transmission models, refit the transmission fluid pipes and wiring and tighten the bolts.

21 Reconnect the wiring to the oil level switch, then refit the wiring support bolt and tighten.

22 Refit the earth cable and tighten the bolt.

23 Lower the engine and transmission onto the mountings, insert the bolts, and tighten to the specified torque. Remove the hoist.

24 Refit the exhaust downpipe to the manifold, together with a new gasket, and tighten the bolts securely. Also refit the exhaust to the transmission and tighten the bolts.

25 Refit the starter motor cable to the left footwell terminal block and tighten the bolts.

26 Refit the front suspension anti-roll bar as described in Chapter 10.

27 On models manufactured up to 30/06/94, refer to Section 17 and refit the oil cooler and pipes to the sump together with new O-ring seals. Tighten the bolts securely.

28 Refit the cooling fan shroud and secure with the clips.

29 On turbocharged models, refit the air inlet tube to the pressure regulator and secure the tube to the body front panel.

30 Refit the engine compartment undershield, and lower the car to the ground.

31 Reconnect the battery negative lead.

32 Renew the oil filter and refill the engine with oil with reference to Chapter 1B.

33 On models manufactured up to 30/06/94, refill the cooling system with coolant with reference to Chapter 1B.

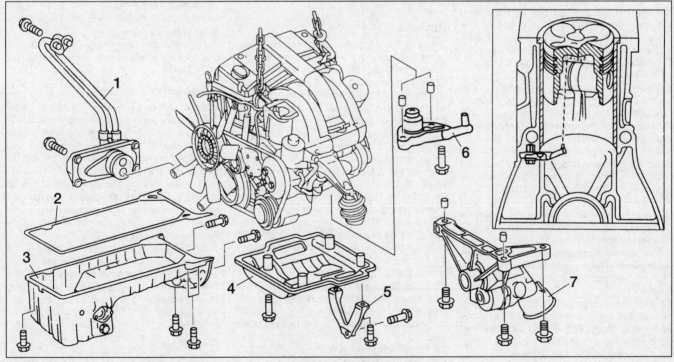

11.16c Sump removal

1 Oil cooler and pipes	*3 Sump*	*5 Oil pump support*	*6 Piston cooling oil spray jet*
2 Sump gasket	*4 Oil deflector plate/baffle*	*bracket*	*7 Oil pump*

12 Oil pump and drive chain - removal, inspection and refitting

Oil pump

Note: *It is not necessary to remove the oil pump from the crankcase to remove the oil pressure relief valve components.*

Removal

1 Remove the sump as described in Section 11. Note that this involves suspending the engine with a hoist. Note also that where a long deflector plate is fitted to the sump, the oil pump must be removed at the same time as the sump, as there is insufficient room to remove the sump first.

2 Hold the oil pump sprocket stationary using a suitable tool inserted in the sprocket holes, then unscrew the securing bolt and recover the washer. Withdraw the oil pump sprocket from the oil pump shaft.

3 Unscrew the bolt securing the oil pump to the support bracket.

4 Unscrew the mounting bolts and withdraw the oil pump from the bottom of the crankcase. Recover the location dowels if necessary.

Inspection

5 With the exception of the oil pressure relief valve components, the oil pump is a sealed unit. To remove the oil pressure relief valve components, proceed as follows.

6 Unscrew the relief valve plug. Take care, as the plug will be pushed out by the spring pressure when it reaches the end of the threads. Note that the plug has a tapered shoulder and does not require a sealing ring.

7 Withdraw the spring, guide pin and piston, noting the orientation of the piston.

8 Thoroughly clean all components, and examine them for wear and damage. If there is any sign of excessive wear or damage, renew the appropriate component(s) - pay particular attention to the spring.

9 Also clean the oil pump intake strainer thoroughly, however, **do not** immerse the oil pump in cleaning solvent. Check that the piston moves freely in the pump bore.

10 Examine the drive chain for wear and damage. If necessary, renew the chain as described later in this Section.

11 Reassemble the oil pump using a reversal of the dismantling procedure, lubricating each component with fresh engine oil before fitting. Tighten the relief valve plug to the specified torque.

12 With the oil pump upright, pour fresh engine oil into the upper aperture while turning the pump shaft slowly. This will prime the oil pump so that normal oil pressure will be resumed as soon as possible after starting the engine.

Refitting

13 Insert the location dowels in the crankcase.

14 Locate the oil pump on the crankcase dowels and insert the mounting bolts. Tighten the bolts to the specified torque.

15 Insert and tighten the bolt securing the oil pump to the support bracket.

16 Check that the sprocket is engaged with the drive chain correctly. The convex side of the sprocket must face the oil pump.

17 Locate the sprocket on the oil pump driveshaft and insert the securing bolt and washer. Tighten the bolt while holding the sprocket stationary as for removal.

18 Refit the sump as described in Section 11.

Drive chain - renewal

Inspection

Note: *The following paragraphs describe renewal of the oil pump drive chain by removing one of the links and feeding the new chain up around the crankshaft sprocket. It is recommended that a chain link removal/refitting tool is obtained to do this, however it is possible to grind away a link and use a ball-pein hammer to fit the new link. When renewing the chain it is recommended that the oil pump sprocket is renewed at the same time.*

19 Remove the sump as described in Section 11. Note that this involves suspending the engine with a hoist.

20 Before removing the oil pump drive chain, turn the crankshaft slowly and examine the chain and sprocket teeth for wear. If the chain links are loose and if the sprocket teeth are grooved where the chain rollers contact them, both the chain and sprocket must be renewed.

Renewal

21 Hold the oil pump sprocket stationary using a suitable tool inserted in the sprocket holes, then loosen the securing bolt.

22 Before removing the oil pump sprocket, use the special tool to remove one of the links at the bottom of the chain, taking care not to dislodge the chain from the crankshaft sprocket. Alternatively, grind away the lugs of one of the links and remove the link.

23 Unscrew the bolt and recover the washer, then remove the sprocket from the oil pump shaft.

24 Using the removable link supplied with the new chain, connect one end of the new chain to the end of the old chain so that the new chain will be drawn up over the crankshaft sprocket when the engine is turned clockwise. Fit the outer plate firmly onto the link to ensure the link stays in place.

25 Using a socket on the crankshaft pulley bolt, slowly turn the crankshaft clockwise until the new chain is located on the crankshaft sprocket and the link is at the bottom of the loop.

26 Remove the link and the old chain, then connect the two ends of the new chain together with the link. Fit the outer plate and secure by riveting over the ends of the link pins. If not using the special tool, it should be

possible to achieve a satisfactory result using a ball-pein hammer, with a block of metal (or a second hammer) to support the rear of the chain.

27 Locate the sprocket in the chain so that its curved side will face the oil pump.

28 Locate the sprocket on the oil pump driveshaft and insert the securing bolt and washer. Tighten the bolt while holding the sprocket stationary as for removal.

29 Refit the sump as described in Section 11.

13 Flywheel/driveplate - removal, inspection and refitting

Removal

Note: *The flywheel/driveplate mounting bolts must be renewed on refitting.*

1 Remove the manual transmission (Chapter 7A) or automatic transmission (Chapter 7B).

2 On manual transmission models, remove the clutch as described in Chapter 6.

3 The flywheel/driveplate must be held stationary while the mounting bolts are loosened. To do this, have an assistant insert a wide-bladed screwdriver in the starter ring gear teeth through the access hole in the rear of the sump. Mercedes-Benz technicians use a special tool bolted to the sump incorporating serrations which engage with the ring gear teeth.

4 Unscrew the mounting bolts, then lift the flywheel/driveplate from the rear of the crankshaft. Note that the location dowel ensures the flywheel/driveplate can only be fitted in one position.

5 On automatic transmission models recover the locking plates from each side of the driveplate.

Inspection

6 If the teeth on the flywheel/driveplate starter ring gear are badly worn, it may be possible to fit a new ring gear, however this work should be entrusted to a Mercedes-Benz dealer who will have the necessary equipment to heat the new gear to the critical temperature in order to fit it. Over-heating the gear will affect its hardness, resulting in rapid wear. The old gear may be removed by drilling it and using a cold chisel to split it. Take care not to drill into the flywheel/driveplate.

7 On manual transmission models, if the clutch friction face of the flywheel is deeply scored, cracked or otherwise damaged, the flywheel must be renewed. However, it may be possible to have it surface-ground, but seek the advice of an engine reconditioning specialist.

Refitting

8 Commence refitting by cleaning the mating faces of the crankshaft and flywheel/driveplate.

9 Make sure that the location dowel is in

position in the end of the crankshaft. On automatic transmission models, fit the locking plate onto the crankshaft.

10 Locate the flywheel/driveplate onto the crankshaft, then insert the new mounting bolts (and further locking plate on automatic transmission models) and hand-tighten them.

11 Lock the flywheel/driveplate using the method employed during removal, then tighten the securing bolts progressively in a diagonal sequence to the specified torque and angle. Tighten all the bolts to the specified torque first, then tighten all the bolts by the specified angle.

12 On manual transmission models, refit the clutch as described in Chapter 6.

13 Refit the manual transmission (Chapter 7A) or automatic transmission (Chapter 7B).

14 Crankshaft oil seals - renewal

Crankshaft front oil seal

1 Remove the crankshaft pulley/vibration damper/hub and inspect it as described in Section 5.

2 Measure and note the fitted depth of the oil seal in the timing chain cover.

3 Pull the oil seal from the cover using a hooked instrument. Alternatively, drill a small hole in the oil seal, and use a self-tapping screw and a pair of pliers to remove it.

4 Clean the seal location in the timing cover, and also clean the oil seal contact surface on the crankshaft pulley/vibration damper. Examine the seal contact surface of the pulley/vibration damper for an excessive wear groove. If evident, refer to Section 5.

5 Dip the new oil seal in clean engine oil, and press it into the timing cover (open end first) to the previously-noted depth, using a suitable tube or socket.

6 Refit the crankshaft pulley/vibration damper as described in Section 5.

Crankshaft rear oil seal

7 Remove the flywheel/driveplate as described in Section 13.

8 Note that from 02/95 the rear oil seal is vulcanised into the oil seal housing and cannot therefore be renewed separately. On earlier models, the seal is separate.

Models to 01/95

9 Measure and note the fitted depth of the oil seal. Note carefully if there is any sign of oil leakage from the rear oil seal housing gasket on the crankcase.

10 Pull the oil seal from the housing using a hooked instrument. Alternatively, drill a small hole in the oil seal, and use a self-tapping screw and a pair of pliers to remove it.

11 If leakage of oil from the oil seal housing was evident, unbolt the housing from the crankcase and recover the gasket. Clean the

components, then refit the housing together with a new gasket and progressively tighten the bolts to the specified torque.

12 Examine the oil seal contact surface on the crankshaft for excessive wear indicated by a deep groove. If evident, the new oil seal should be located a further 3.0 mm into the housing so that it no longer runs over the groove.

13 Dip the new oil seal in clean engine oil, and press it into the housing (open end first) to the previously-noted or new depth, using a suitable tube or socket. A piece of thin plastic or tape wound around the rear of the crankshaft flange is useful to prevent damage to the oil seal as it is being fitted. Note that the seal must be fitted exactly at right-angles to the crankshaft flange to provide satisfactory sealing.

14 Remove the plastic or tape from the crankshaft.

15 Refit the flywheel/driveplate as described in Section 13.

Models from 02/95

16 Unbolt the rear oil seal housing from the crankcase and withdraw it over the rear of the crankshaft.

17 Examine the oil seal contact surface on the crankshaft for excessive wear indicated by a deep groove. If evident, it is suggested that the earlier housing be obtained and fitted, together with a new gasket, and the oil seal located a further 3.0 mm into the housing. Refer to paragraphs 9 to 15.

18 Wrap some tape or plastic sheeting around the rear of the crankshaft to protect the sealing lips of the oil seal as it is being fitted.

19 Clean the rear of the crankcase, then smear a little oil on the sealing lips of the oil seal.

20 Locate the housing over the rear of the crankshaft, using a twisting motion to ensure the sealing lip is not disturbed.

21 Insert the bolts and tighten them progressively to the specified torque.

22 Remove the plastic sheeting or tape from the crankshaft.

23 Refit the flywheel/driveplate as described in Section 13.

15 Crankshaft spigot bearing - renewal

1 On early manual transmission models, a ball-bearing is fitted to the end of the crankshaft to support the end of the transmission input shaft. On later models with a two-mass flywheel, the bearing is located in the centre of the flywheel. On high-mileage engines, the bearing may become dry and noisy, noticeable when the clutch is disengaged with a gear selected. To renew the bearing, proceed as follows.

2 Remove the clutch as described in Chapter 6.

3 Determine whether the bearing is located in the end of the crankshaft or in the centre of the flywheel. The crankshaft located bearing has an inner race, whereas on the flywheel located bearing it is possible to view the needle rollers of the bearing.

Crankshaft located bearing

4 The ball-bearing is protected by an end cover, also pressed into the end of the crankshaft. The cover can be removed together with the ball-bearing, or alternatively it can be prised out first.

5 Ideally, a slide hammer fitted with a suitable adapter should be used to withdraw the bearing and its cover from the end of the crankshaft. An alternative method which may work if the bearing is not too tight, is to fill the cavity behind the bearing with grease, then insert a close-fitting dowel rod through the bearing centre race. Use a hammer to drive the rod into the cavity, and the pressure produced will force the bearing from the crankshaft.

6 With the old bearing removed, thoroughly clean its location in the end of the crankshaft. There is no need to remove the spacer ring.

7 Tap the new bearing into position, up to the stop, using a tube or socket on the bearing outer race.

8 Tap the protective cover into position using the tube or socket, until it contacts the bearing.

9 Refit the clutch as described in Chapter 6.

Flywheel located bearing

10 Remove the flywheel as described in Section 13.

11 Note the fitted depth of the needle bearing to ensure correct fitting.

12 Press or drive out the bearing.

13 Press or drive in the new bearing, using a metal tube on the outer part which locates in the flywheel. The open side of the bearing must face towards the clutch facing side of the flywheel.

14 Refit the flywheel as described in Section 13.

15 Refit the clutch as described in Chapter 6.

16 Engine/transmission mountings - inspection and renewal

Inspection

1 Three engine/transmission mountings are used, one on either side of the engine, and one under the rear of the transmission.

2 For improved access, raise the front of the vehicle and support it securely on axle stands (see Jacking and vehicle support).

3 Check the condition of the mounting rubber to see if it is cracked, hardened or separated from the metal at any point. Renew the mounting if any such damage or deterioration is evident. The mountings contain hydraulic

oil, and must be renewed if oil leakage is evident.

4 Check that all the mounting bolts are securely tightened.

5 Using a large screwdriver or metal bar, check for wear in the mounting by carefully levering against it to check for free play. Where this is not possible, enlist the aid of an assistant to move the engine/transmission back and forth, or from side-to-side, while you observe the mounting. If excessive freeplay is found, check first that the fasteners are correctly secured, then renew any worn components as required.

Renewal

Front engine mountings

6 Support the engine, either using a hoist and lifting tackle connected to the engine lifting brackets, or by positioning a jack and interposed block of wood under the sump. Ensure that the engine is adequately supported before proceeding.

7 Unclip the cooling fan shroud from the radiator and locate it on the viscous fan.

8 Remove the cover from over the thermostat housing at the front of the cylinder head.

9 If removing the left-hand mounting, unbolt the inlet manifold support bracket on models not fitted with a plastic manifold.

10 Unscrew and remove the engine mounting upper bolt.

11 Unscrew and remove the engine mounting lower bolt.

12 Raise the engine as necessary, taking care not to stretch the coolant hoses, and remove the mounting. If necessary, unbolt the mounting bracket from the side of the cylinder block. On automatic transmission models, note the location of the wiring support on the right-hand bracket.

13 Refitting is a reversal of removal, but make sure that the location ear on the top of the mounting engages the cut-out in the mounting bracket, and tighten the mounting bolts to the specified torque.

Rear engine/transmission mounting

14 Raise the front of the vehicle and support it securely on axle stands (see *Jacking and vehicle support*).

15 Support the transmission using a jack and interposed block of wood.

16 Unbolt the mounting bracket from the underbody, then unscrew the bolts securing the mounting rubber to the rear of the transmission. Note the location of the splash guard support. Lower the bracket together with the mounting from the underbody. Note on the manual transmission, the bolts screw into captive nuts, whereas on the automatic transmission the bolts screw directly into the transmission casing.

17 Unbolt the mounting rubber from the bracket.

18 Refitting is a reversal of removal.

17 Engine oil cooler - removal and refitting

Engines 604 and 605 manufactured up to 30/06/94

Removal

1 Apply the parking brake, then jack up the front of the vehicle and support it on axle stands (see *Jacking and vehicle support*). Remove the engine compartment undershield.

2 Drain the cooling system and engine oil as described in Chapter 1B.

3 Note the position of the clamps then unscrew the clamp bolt and disconnect the oil cooler external coolant pipes from the right-hand side of the coolant pump. Also disconnect the pipes from the oil cooler on the side of the sump. Recover the O-ring seals (**see illustration**).

4 Unscrew the mounting bolts and remove the oil cooler from the sump. Note the location of the pipe support on one of the bolts.

5 Remove the internal pipes leading to the oil pump, and recover the O-ring seals.

Refitting

6 Wipe clean the side of the oil pump and the side of the sump.

7 Dip the new O-ring seals in coolant (**do not** dip them in engine oil), then fit the seals to the internal and external pipes.

8 Refit the internal pipes with seals to the oil pump.

9 Locate a new O-ring seal on the oil cooler, then refit it to the side of the sump, making sure that the internal pipes are correctly located. Insert the bolts and tighten securely. Make sure the pipe support is located where noted on removal.

10 Refit the oil cooler external pipes together with new O-ring seals. Position the clamps as previously noted, then insert and tighten the clamp bolt.

11 Refit the engine compartment undershield and lower the vehicle to the ground.

12 Refill the engine with oil and coolant with reference to Chapter 1B.

Engine 605 manufactured from 01/07/94

Removal

13 Drain the cooling system as described in Chapter 1B.

14 Remove the inlet manifold as described in Chapter 4B. Also unbolt the manifold support from the oil filter.

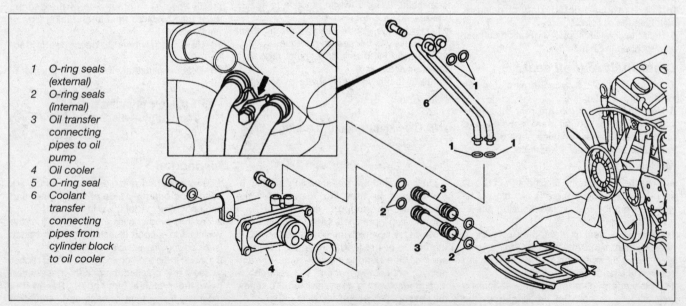

1 O-ring seals (external)
2 O-ring seals (internal)
3 Oil transfer connecting pipes to oil pump
4 Oil cooler
5 O-ring seal
6 Coolant transfer connecting pipes from cylinder block to oil cooler

17.3 Oil cooler on models manufactured up to 30/06/94

15 Position a suitable container next to the oil filter housing to place the filter element and cap into.

16 Unscrew the cap from the top of the oil filter housing. Remove the filter element. Note that with the cap removed, the oil filter oil will drain into the sump.

17 Unscrew the mounting bolts and remove the oil filter housing from the left-hand side of the cylinder block. Recover the gasket. Note the two location dowels, and the support bracket on one of the bolts. As the oil filter housing is being removed, disconnect the oil cooler from the cylinder block coolant tubes.

18 Unbolt the oil cooler from the side of the oil filter housing, and recover the O-ring seals **(see illustration)**.

19 Remove the coolant tubes from the cylinder block, and recover the O-ring seals.

20 Clean the oil filter and cylinder block mating faces, also the coolant tubes and apertures in the block.

21 Dip the new O-ring seals in coolant (**do not** dip them in engine oil), then fit the seals to the coolant tubes.

22 Fit the coolant tubes together with new O-ring seals to the cylinder block.

23 Refit the oil cooler to the side of the oil filter housing together with new O-ring seals. Tighten the bolt(s) securely.

24 Make sure that the two location dowels are in place, then locate a new gasket on the cylinder block.

25 Locate the oil filter housing on the cylinder block, at the same time locating the oil cooler and new O-ring seals on the coolant tubes. Insert the housing mounting bolts and tighten them securely.

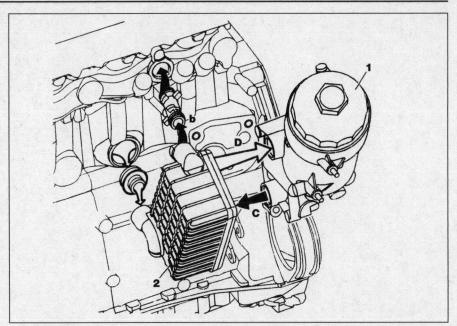

17.18 Oil filter housing and oil cooler on models manufactured from 01/07/94-on

1	*Oil filter housing*	*b*	*Coolant to crankcase*
2	*Oil cooler*	*C*	*Engine oil from oil filter*
a	*Coolant from crankcase*	*D*	*Cooled engine oil to oil filter*

26 Insert a new oil filter element in the filter housing.

27 Before refitting the oil filter cap, check that the bore through the return tube is clear. To do this, use a foot pump or air supply to blow through the hole at the top of the tube. It must be possible to feel air coming out of the bottom of the tube. If necessary, attempt to clear the tube with suitable wire, or if this does not clear it, renew the tube and cap.

28 Refit the oil filter cap and return tube, and tighten the nuts to the specified torque.

29 Refit the inlet manifold and support with reference to Chapter 4B.

30 Refill the cooling system with reference to Chapter 1B.

Chapter 2 Part C: Engine removal and general engine overhaul procedures

Contents

Degrees of difficulty

Easy, suitable for novice with little experience	**Fairly easy,** suitable for beginner with some experience	**Fairly difficult,** suitable for competent DIY mechanic

Difficult, suitable for experienced DIY mechanic	**Very difficult,** suitable for expert DIY or professional

Specifications

Cylinder head

Maximum gasket face distortion:
  Petrol engines:
    Longitudinal . . . . 0.15 mm
    Transverse . . . . 0.05 mm
  Diesel engines:
    Longitudinal . . . . 0.08 mm
    Transverse . . . . 0 mm
Minimum height after machining*:
  Petrol engines . . . . 97.8 mm
  Diesel engines . . . . 142.4 mm
*Note: *The total thickness of metal removed from the cylinder head and cylinder block mating faces combined must not exceed 0.5 mm for petrol engines or 0.4 mm for diesel engines.*
Swirl chamber protrusion (diesel engines) . . . . 7.6 to 8.1 mm
Valve seat width . . . . 0.9 to 1.1 mm
Valve seat angle . . . . 45°

Cylinder block

Cylinder bore diameter:
  Petrol engines:
    1.8 litre engines:

Standard A	85.300 to 85.306 mm
Standard X	85.307 to 85.312 mm
Standard B	85.313 to 85.318 mm
1st oversize A	85.550 to 85.556 mm
1st oversize X	85.557 to 85.562 mm
1st oversize B	85.563 to 85.568 mm
2nd oversize A	85.800 to 85.806 mm
2nd oversize X	85.807 to 85.812 mm
2nd oversize B	85.813 to 85.818 mm

    2.0 and 2.2 litre engines:

Standard A	89.900 to 89.906 mm
Standard X	89.907 to 89.912 mm
Standard B	89.913 to 89.918 mm
1st oversize A	90.150 to 90.156 mm
1st oversize X	90.157 to 90.162 mm
1st oversize B	90.163 to 90.168 mm
2nd oversize A	90.400 to 90.406 mm
2nd oversize X	90.407 to 90.412 mm
2nd oversize B	90.413 to 90.418 mm

    2.3 litre engines*:

Standard A	90.900 to 90.906 mm
Standard X	90.907 to 90.912 mm
Standard B	90.913 to 90.918 mm
2nd oversize A	91.413 to 91.406 mm
2nd oversize X	91.407 to 91.412 mm
2nd oversize B	91.413 to 91.418 mm

  Diesel engines:

2.2 litre engine	Not available at time of writing

    2.5 litre engine:

Standard grade A	87.000 to 87.006 mm
Standard grade X	87.006 to 87.012 mm
Standard grade B	87.012 to 87.018 mm
Oversize + 0.7 mm	Grades as above + 0.700 mm

Maximum cylinder bore ovality:

Petrol engines	0.05 mm
Diesel engines	0.07 mm

Maximum cylinder bore taper:

Petrol engines	0.05 mm
Diesel engines	0.07 mm

Cylinder block height:
  Petrol engines:

2.2 litre	289.35 to 289.45 mm
1.8 and 2.0 litre	292.35 mm
Diesel engines	299.62 mm

Maximum gasket face distortion:

Petrol engines	0.03 mm
Diesel engines	0.03 mm

No 1st repair size

Valves

Valve head diameter:
  Petrol engines:
    Inlet:

2.0 litre engines	42.90 to 43.10 mm
2.3 litre engine	45.90 to 46.19 mm
Exhaust	38.90 to 39.10 mm

  Diesel engines:

Inlet	37.90 to 38.10 mm
Exhaust	34.90 to 35.10 mm

Valve stem diameter;
  Petrol engines:

Inlet	7.955 to 7.970 mm
Exhaust	8.938 to 8.960 mm

  Diesel engines:

Inlet	7.955 to 7.970 mm
Exhaust	8.945 to 8.960 mm
Valve guide length	37.5 mm

Valve springs
Free length:
  Petrol engines . . . .   49.0 mm
  Diesel engines:
    Springs with yellow/green or violet/green colour marking . . . .   50.8 mm
    Springs with yellow/blue or violet/blue colour marking . . . .   50.0 mm

Pistons
Piston diameter:
  Petrol engines:
    2.0 litre engines:
      Standard 0 . . . .   88.968 to 88.982 mm
      Standard 1 . . . .   88.978 to 88.992 mm
      Standard 2 . . . .   88.988 to 89.002 mm
      Standard A . . . .   88.973 to 88.979 mm
      Standard X . . . .   88.978 to 88.986 mm
      Standard B . . . .   88.985 to 88.991 mm
      Oversize + 0.5 . . . .   Grades as above + 0.500 mm
      Oversize + 1.0 . . . .   Grades as above + 0.500 mm
    2.3 litre engine:
      Standard 0 . . . .   95.469 to 95.481 mm
      Standard 1 . . . .   95.479 to 95.491 mm
      Standard 2 . . . .   95.489 to 95.501 mm
      Standard A . . . .   95.473 to 95.479 mm
      Standard X . . . .   95.478 to 95.486 mm
      Standard B . . . .   95.485 to 95.491 mm
      Oversize + 0.5 . . . .   Grades as above + 0.500 mm
      Oversize + 1.0 . . . .   Grades as above + 0.500 mm
  Diesel engines:
    2.2 litre engine . . . .   Not available at time of writing
    2.5 litre engine:
      Standard grade A . . . .   86.970 to 86.976 mm
      Standard grade X . . . .   86.975 to 86.983 mm
      Standard grade B . . . .   86.982 to 86.988 mm
      Oversize + 0.7 mm . . . .   Grades as above + 0.700 mm
Piston protrusion (diesel engines):
  Minimum . . . .   0.735 mm
  Maximum . . . .   0.965 mm
Gudgeon pin clearance in small end bush . . . .   0.007 to 0.018 mm

Piston rings
End gaps:
  Petrol engines:
    Top compression ring . . . .   0.30 to 1.00 mm
    Second compression ring . . . .   0.25 to 0.80 mm
    Oil control ring . . . .   0.25 to 0.80 mm
  Diesel engines:
    Top compression ring . . . .   0.090 to 0.20 mm
    Second compression ring . . . .   0.050 to 0.15 mm
    Oil control ring . . . .   0.030 to 0.10 mm
Clearance in grooves:
  Petrol engines:
    Top compression ring . . . .   0.03 to 0.07 mm
    Second compression ring . . . .   0.015 to 0.040 mm
    Oil control ring . . . .   0.010 to 0.045 mm
  Diesel engines . . . .   Not available at time of writing

Main bearing cap bolts
Maximum length:
  Petrol engines . . . .   63.8 mm
  Diesel engines . . . .   Not available at time of writing

Big-end bearing cap bolts
Maximum length:
  Petrol engines . . . .   52.9 mm
  Diesel engines . . . .   Not available at time of writing

Crankshaft

Endfloat:	
Petrol engines	0.300 mm
Diesel engines	0.300 mm
Endfloat thrustwasher thicknesses	2.15, 2.20, 2.25, 2.35 and 2.40 mm
Main bearing journal diameters:	
Petrol engines:	
Standard	57.950 to 57.965 mm
Undersize 1	57.700 to 57.715 mm
Undersize 2	57.450 to 57.465 mm
Undersize 3	57.200 to 57.215 mm
Undersize 4	56.950 to 56.965 mm
Diesel engines:	
Standard	57.959 to 57.965 mm
Undersize 1	57.700 to 57.715 mm
Undersize 2	57.450 to 57.465 mm
Undersize 3	57.200 to 57.215 mm
Undersize 4	56.959 to 56.965 mm
Big-end bearing journal diameters:	
Petrol engines:	
Standard	47.955 to 47.965 mm
Undersize 1	47.705 to 47.715 mm
Undersize 2	47.455 to 47.465 mm
Undersize 3	47.205 to 47.215 mm
Undersize 4	46.955 to 46.965 mm
Diesel engines:	
Standard	47.950 to 47.965 mm
Undersize 1	47.700 to 47.715 mm
Undersize 2	47.450 to 47.650 mm
Undersize 3	47.200 to 47.215 mm
Undersize 4	46.950 to 46.965 mm
Radial play of crankshaft in main bearings:	
Petrol engines	0.015 to 0.03 mm
Diesel engines	0.080 mm
Radial play of big-end bearings on crankshaft:	
Petrol engines	0.03 to 0.05 mm
Diesel engines	0.080 mm

Torque wrench settings

See Chapters 2A (petrol) and 2B (diesel)

1 General information

Included in this Part of Chapter 2 are details of removing the engine from the car and general overhaul procedures for the cylinder head, cylinder block/crankcase and all other engine internal components.

The information given ranges from advice concerning preparation for an overhaul and the purchase of replacement parts, to detailed step-by-step procedures covering removal, inspection, renovation and refitting of engine internal components.

After Section 9, all instructions are based on the assumption that the engine has been removed from the car. For information concerning in-car engine repair, as well as the removal and refitting of those external components necessary for full overhaul, refer to Part A or B of this Chapter, as applicable, and to Section 6. Ignore any preliminary dismantling operations described in Parts A or B that are no longer relevant once the engine has been removed from the car.

Apart from torque wrench settings, which are given at the beginning of Parts A and B, all specifications relating to engine overhaul are at the beginning of this Part of Chapter 2.

2 Engine overhaul - general information

1 It is not always easy to determine when, or if, an engine should be completely overhauled, as a number of factors must be considered.

2 High mileage is not necessarily an indication that an overhaul is needed, while low mileage does not preclude the need for an overhaul. Frequency of servicing is probably the most important consideration. An engine which has had regular and frequent oil and filter changes, as well as other required maintenance, should give many thousands of miles of reliable service. Conversely, a neglected engine may require an overhaul very early in its life.

3 Excessive oil consumption is an indication that piston rings, valve seals and/or valve guides are in need of attention. Make sure that oil leaks are not responsible before deciding that the rings and/or guides are worn. Perform a compression test, as described in Part A or B of this Chapter (as applicable), to determine the likely cause of the problem.

4 Check the oil pressure with a gauge fitted in place of the oil pressure switch, and compare it with that specified in Part A or B. If it is extremely low, the main and big-end bearings, and/or the oil pump, are probably worn out.

5 Loss of power, rough running, knocking or metallic engine noises, excessive valve gear noise, and high fuel consumption may also point to the need for an overhaul, especially if

they are all present at the same time. If a complete service does not remedy the situation, major mechanical work is the only solution.

6 A full engine overhaul involves restoring all internal parts to the specification of a new engine. During a complete overhaul, the pistons and the piston rings are renewed, and the cylinder bores are reconditioned. New main and big-end bearings are generally fitted; if necessary, the crankshaft may be reground, to compensate for wear in the journals. The valves are also serviced as well, since they are usually in less-than-perfect condition at this point. Always pay careful attention to the condition of the oil pump when overhauling the engine, and renew it if there is any doubt as to its serviceability. The end result should be an as-new engine that will give many trouble-free miles.

Note: *Critical cooling system components such as the hoses, thermostat and coolant pump should be renewed when an engine is overhauled. The radiator should be checked carefully, to ensure that it is not clogged or leaking. Also, it is a good idea to renew the oil pump whenever the engine is overhauled.*

7 Before beginning the engine overhaul, read through the entire procedure, to familiarise yourself with the scope and requirements of the job. Overhauling an engine is not difficult if you follow carefully all of the instructions, have the necessary tools and equipment, and pay close attention to all specifications. It can, however, be time-consuming. Plan on the car being off the road for a minimum of two weeks, especially if parts must be taken to an engineering works for repair or reconditioning. Check on the availability of parts and make sure that any necessary special tools and equipment are obtained in advance. Most work can be done with typical hand tools, although a number of precision measuring tools are required for inspecting parts to determine if they must be renewed. Often the engineering works will handle the inspection of parts and offer advice concerning reconditioning and renewal.

Note: *Always wait until the engine has been completely dismantled, and until all components (especially the cylinder block/crankcase and the crankshaft) have been inspected, before deciding what service and repair operations must be performed by an engineering works. The condition of these components will be the major factor to consider when determining whether to overhaul the original engine, or to buy a reconditioned unit. Do not, therefore, purchase parts or have overhaul work done on other components until they have been thoroughly inspected. As a general rule, time is the primary cost of an overhaul, so it does not pay to fit worn or sub-standard parts.*

8 As a final note, to ensure maximum life and minimum trouble from a reconditioned engine, everything must be assembled with care, in a spotlessly-clean environment.

3 Engine removal - methods and precautions

1 If you have decided that the engine must be removed for overhaul or major repair work, several preliminary steps should be taken.

2 Locating a suitable place to work is extremely important. Adequate work space, along with storage space for the car, will be needed. If a workshop or garage is not available, at the very least, a flat, level, clean work surface is required.

3 Cleaning the engine compartment and engine/transmission before beginning the removal procedure will help keep tools clean and organised.

4 An engine hoist will also be necessary. Make sure the equipment is rated in excess of the weight of the engine (and transmission if both are being removed). Safety is of primary importance, considering the potential hazards involved in lifting the engine out of the car.

5 If this is the first time you have removed an engine, an assistant should ideally be available. Advice and aid from someone more experienced would also be helpful. There are many instances when one person cannot simultaneously perform all of the operations required when lifting the engine out of the vehicle.

6 Plan the operation ahead of time. Before starting work, arrange for the hire of or obtain all of the tools and equipment you will need. Some of the equipment necessary to perform engine removal and installation safely and with relative ease (in addition to an engine hoist) is as follows: a heavy duty trolley jack, complete sets of spanners and sockets (see *Tools and working facilities*), wooden blocks, and plenty of rags and cleaning solvent for mopping up spilled oil, coolant and fuel. If the hoist must be hired, make sure that you arrange for it in advance, and perform all of the operations possible without it beforehand. This will save you money and time.

7 Plan for the car to be out of use for quite a while. An engineering works will be required to perform some of the work which the do-it-yourselfer cannot accomplish without special equipment. These places often have a busy schedule, so it would be a good idea to consult them before removing the engine, in order to accurately estimate the amount of time required to rebuild or repair components that may need work.

8 Always be extremely careful when removing and refitting the engine. Serious injury can result from careless actions. Plan ahead and take your time, and a job of this nature, although major, can be accomplished successfully.

9 On all models, the engine is removed by lifting the assembly out from above the vehicle.

4 Petrol engine - removal and refitting

Removal

Note: *A suitable hoist and lifting tackle will be required for this operation.*

1 Disconnect the battery negative (earth) lead and position it away from the terminal. The battery is located in the rear luggage compartment.

2 Apply the parking brake, then jack up the front of the vehicle and support it on axle stands (see *Jacking and vehicle support*). Allow sufficient height for the hoist to lift the engine out of the engine compartment. Alternatively, the car can be lowered to the ground jjust before attaching the hoist. With the car raised, remove the engine compartment undershield.

3 Drain the cooling system and remove the radiator as described in Chapters 1A and 3. Unscrew the drain plug from the cylinder block and drain the coolant into a suitable container. On completion refit the plug and tighten.

4 Where fitted, remove the viscous fan coupling with reference to Chapter 3.

5 If necessary, drain the oil from the engine as described in Chapter 1A.

6 Remove the air mass meter as described in Chapter 4A, Section 10.

7 Remove the air mass meter-to-throttle body air duct, and also the air cleaner cover (see Chapter 4A).

8 On models with air conditioning, remove the guard plate from the condenser, then position a piece of strong card or similar over the condenser to protect it as the engine is being removed.

9 On the left-hand side of the engine compartment, disconnect the engine main wiring, and position the connector on the engine.

10 On engine code 111.920 disconnect the vacuum line from the PMS control unit. Also disconnect the two hoses from the fuel evaporative purge valve.

11 On engine code 111.961 disconnect the hose from the HFM system fuel evaporative purge valve on the carbon canister.

12 Disconnect the accelerator cable from the throttle housing as described in Chapter 4A.

13 Temporarily remove the fuel tank filler cap and refit it in order to release any pressure, then depressurise the fuel system with reference to Chapter 4A.

14 Unscrew the union nuts and disconnect the fuel feed and return lines from the fuel rail. Tape over or plug the lines and apertures to prevent entry of dust and dirt.

15 Disconnect the vacuum line from the inlet manifold/throttle body.

16 Disconnect the brake vacuum line at the inlet manifold/throttle body.

17 On automatic transmission models, disconnect the vacuum lines from the switch-over valve.

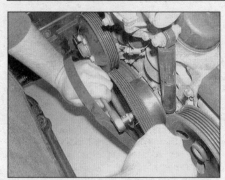

4.18 Removing the auxiliary drivebelt

4.19 Placing the windscreen washer reservoir to the left-hand side of the engine compartment

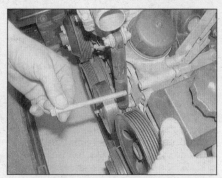

4.20 Unbolt the power steering pump from the left-hand side of the engine

18 Remove the auxiliary drivebelt with reference to Chapter 1A **(see illustration)**.
19 Unbolt the windscreen washer reservoir from the left-hand side of the engine compartment, and position it to one side **(see illustration)**.
20 Refer to Chapter 10 and unbolt the power steering pump from the left-hand side of the engine **(see illustration)**. Tie the pump to one side, in an upright position to prevent the fluid escaping.
21 On models with air conditioning, unbolt the air conditioning compressor and tie it to one side away from the engine **(see illustrations)**. If preferred, the compressor

can be unbolted as the engine is being lifted from the engine compartment. **Do not** disconnect the refrigerant lines from the compressor.
22 Loosen the clips and disconnect the coolant hose from the rear of the cylinder head, also disconnect the hoses located on the coolant pump **(see illustrations)**.
23 Remove the complete exhaust system as described in Chapter 4C.

Removal without transmission

24 Remove the inlet and exhaust manifolds as described in Chapters 4A and 4C. On automatic transmission models, tie the

transmission control pressure cable to one side.
25 Support the weight of the transmission with a trolley jack and interposed piece of wood.
26 Attach a suitable hoist to the two lifting eyes, and take the weight of the engine.
27 Unscrew and remove the bolts securing the engine front mountings to the suspension crossmember **(see illustration)**. Alternatively, the mountings can be removed completely.
28 Unscrew the bolts securing the transmission to the rear of the engine, noting the location of the earth cable and clutch

4.21a Disconnecting the wiring from the air conditioning compressor

4.21b Removing the air conditioning compressor from the left-hand side of the engine

4.21c Tie the air conditioning compressor to the side of the engine compartment

4.22a Disconnecting the bottom hose from the coolant pump

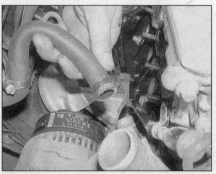

4.22b Disconnecting the heater hose from the coolant pump

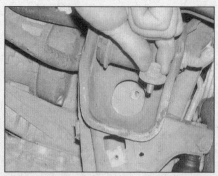

4.27 Removing the engine front mounting bolts from the suspension crossmember

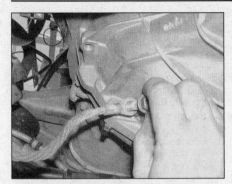

4.28 Note the location of the earth cable on the transmission-to-engine mounting bolt

4.29 Lifting the engine from the engine compartment

4.38 Lifting the engine and transmission from the engine compartment

slave cylinder hydraulic line **(see illustration)**. Access to the upper mounting bolts is best achieved from the rear of the transmission with an extension socket.

29 With the help of an assistant, draw the engine forwards from the transmission until the transmission input shaft is clear of the clutch, then lift the engine from the engine compartment, taking care not to damage the surrounding components and wiring **(see illustration)**. Move the hoist forwards and lower the engine to the ground.

Removal with transmission

30 Remove the exhaust heat shield from the underbody, then unbolt the front of the propeller shaft from the flexible joint on the rear of the transmission (refer to Chapter 8). On pre-1995 models loosen the nut on the propeller shaft centre bearing, then push the propeller shaft to the rear as far as possible.
31 Unbolt the earth cable from the transmission. Also disconnect all wiring plugs from the transmission.
32 On manual transmission models, fit a hose clamp to the hydraulic line leading to the clutch slave cylinder on the transmission (see Chapter 6). Unscrew the union nut and detach the hydraulic line from the slave cylinder. Tape over or plug the line and slave cylinder to prevent entry of dust and dirt. Alternatively, unscrew the slave cylinder mounting bolt and also unscrew the hydraulic pipe support from the left-hand side of the transmission bellhousing, then tie the pipe and slave cylinder to the transmission tunnel.
33 On manual transmission models, disconnect the gearchange levers from the transmission as described in Chapter 7A.
34 On automatic transmission models, disconnect the selector rod from the transmission as described in Chapter 7B. On models with the 722.60x transmission also disconnect the park lock interlock cable.
35 Attach a suitable hoist to the two lifting eyes, and take the weight of the engine and transmission. The hoist chains should be positioned so that the front of the engine will be tilted upwards slightly.
36 Temporarily support the transmission, then unscrew the bolts securing the engine rear mounting bracket to the underbody. If

necessary, the complete bracket may be removed from the transmission.
37 Unscrew the lower bolts from the engine front mountings.
38 With the help of an assistant, lift and tilt the engine and transmission to withdraw it from the engine compartment, taking care not to damage the surrounding components and wiring **(see illustration)**. It will be necessary to move the hoist forwards and guide the engine and transmission up through the engine compartment, taking care not to damage the surrounding components. Move the hoist forwards and lower the engine/transmission assembly to the ground.
39 To remove the transmission from the engine, refer to Chapters 7A or 7B as necessary.

Refitting

40 Before refitting the engine, check the condition of the engine/transmission mountings. In particular, check if they are compressed, are damaged or split, or have signs of oil leakage. If necessary, renew them with reference to Chapter 2A.
41 The refitting procedure is a reversal of removal, noting the following additional information.
a) *Tighten all nuts and bolts to the specified torque wrench settings, where given.*
b) *On automatic transmission models, adjust the selector rod as described in Chapter 7B.*
c) *On manual transmission models, bleed the clutch hydraulic system as described in Chapter 6.*
d) *Reconnect the propeller shaft to the flange on the rear of the transmission with reference to Chapter 8.*
d) *Refill the power steering fluid reservoir with fresh fluid and bleed the system as described in Chapter 10.*
e) *Ensure that all wiring, hoses and brackets are positioned and routed as noted before removal.*
f) *Reconnect and if necessary adjust the accelerator cable with reference to Chapter 4A.*
g) *On completion, refill the engine with oil, and refill the cooling system as described in Chapter 1A.*

5 Diesel engine - removal and refitting

Removal

Note: *A suitable hoist and lifting tackle will be required for this operation.*

1 Disconnect the battery negative (earth) lead and position it away from the terminal. The battery is located in the rear luggage compartment.
2 Apply the parking brake, then jack up the front of the vehicle and support it on axle stands (see *Jacking and vehicle support*). Allow sufficient height for the hoist to lift the engine out of the engine compartment. Alternatively, the car can be lowered to the ground just before attaching the hoist. With the car raised, remove the engine compartment undershield.
3 On turbocharged models, disconnect and remove the left- and right-hand air ducts to the intercooler. If necessary, remove the intercooler as described in Chapter 4B.
4 Drain the cooling system, then remove the radiator and viscous cooling fan as described in Chapters 1B and 3.
5 If necessary, drain the oil from the engine as described in Chapter 1B.
6 Remove the auxiliary drivebelt as described in Chapter 1B.
7 On air conditioning models, position a piece of strong card or similar over the condenser to protect it as the engine is being removed.
8 Identify then disconnect the vacuum hoses from the brake vacuum pump (exhauster), inlet manifold, brake servo unit, and vacuum control valve.
9 Loosen the clips and disconnect the coolant hoses from the rear of the cylinder head and from the thermostat housing on the front, right-hand side of the cylinder block.
10 Refer to Chapter 10 and unbolt the power steering pump from the left-hand side of the engine. Tie the pump to one side, in an upright position to prevent the fluid escaping.
11 Disconnect the engine wiring harness located on the left-hand side of the camshaft cover.

12 Briefly remove the filler cap from the fuel tank to relieve any pressure or vacuum, then unscrew the union nuts and disconnect the fuel supply and return lines from the injection pump.

13 On models with air conditioning, unbolt the compressor from the mounting bracket on the left-hand side of the engine, and support it to one side. **Do not** disconnect the refrigerant line from the compressor.

14 Remove the front section of the exhaust system as described in Chapter 4C.

Removal without transmission

15 On automatic transmission models, disconnect the control pressure cable and position it to one side.

16 Support the weight of the transmission with a trolley jack and interposed piece of wood.

17 Attach a suitable hoist to the two lifting eyes, and take the weight of the engine.

18 Unscrew and remove the bolts securing the engine mountings to the suspension crossmember. Alternatively, the mountings can be removed completely.

19 Unscrew the bolts securing the transmission to the rear of the engine, noting the location of the earth cable and clutch slave cylinder hydraulic line.

20 With the help of an assistant, draw the engine forwards from the transmission until the transmission input shaft is clear of the clutch, then lift the engine from the engine compartment, taking care not to damage the surrounding components and wiring. Move the hoist forwards and lower the engine to the ground.

Removal with transmission

21 Remove the exhaust heat shield from the underbody, then unbolt the front of the propeller shaft from the flexible joint on the rear of the transmission (refer to Chapter 8). On pre-1995 models loosen the nut on the propeller shaft centre bearing, then push the propeller shaft to the rear as far as possible.

22 Unbolt the earth cable from the transmission. Also disconnect all wiring plugs from the transmission.

23 On manual transmission models, fit a

hose clamp to the hydraulic line leading to the clutch slave cylinder on the transmission (see Chapter 6). Unscrew the union nut and detach the hydraulic line from the slave cylinder. Tape over or plug the line and slave cylinder to prevent entry of dust and dirt. Alternatively, unscrew the slave cylinder mounting bolt and also unscrew the hydraulic pipe support from the left-hand side of the transmission bellhousing, then tie the pipe and slave cylinder to the transmission tunnel.

24 On manual transmission models, disconnect the gearchange levers from the transmission as described in Chapter 7A.

25 On automatic transmission models, disconnect the selector rod from the transmission as described in Chapter 7B. On models with the 722.60x transmission also disconnect the park lock interlock cable.

26 Attach a suitable hoist to the two lifting eyes, and take the weight of the engine and transmission. The hoist chains should be positioned so that the front of the engine will be tilted upwards slightly.

27 Temporarily support the transmission, then unscrew the bolts securing the engine rear mounting bracket to the underbody. If necessary, the complete bracket may be removed from the transmission.

28 Unscrew the lower bolts from the engine front mountings.

29 With the help of an assistant, lift and tilt the engine and transmission to withdraw it from the engine compartment, taking care not to damage the surrounding components and wiring. It will be necessary to move the hoist forwards and guide the engine and transmission up through the engine compartment, taking care not to damage the surrounding components. Move the hoist forwards and lower the engine/transmission assembly to the ground.

30 To remove the transmission from the engine, refer to Chapters 7A or 7B as necessary.

Refitting

31 Before refitting the engine and transmission, check the condition of the engine/transmission mountings. In particular, check if they are compressed, are damaged or split, or have signs of oil leakage. If

necessary, renew them with reference to Chapter 2B.

32 The reconnection and refitting procedures are a reversal of removal, noting the following additional information.

a) Tighten all nuts and bolts to the specified torque wrench settings, where given.

b) On automatic transmission models, adjust the selector rod as described in Chapter 7B.

c) On manual transmission models, bleed the clutch hydraulic system as described in Chapter 6.

d) Reconnect the propeller shaft to the flange on the rear of the transmission with reference to Chapter 8.

d) Refill the power steering fluid reservoir with fresh fluid and bleed the system as described in Chapter 10.

e) Ensure that all wiring, hoses and brackets are positioned and routed as noted before removal.

f) Reconnect and if necessary adjust the accelerator cable with reference to Chapter 4B.

g) On completion, refill the engine with oil, and refill the cooling system as described in Chapter 1B.

6 Engine overhaul - dismantling sequence

1 It is much easier to dismantle and work on the engine if it is mounted on a portable engine stand. These stands can often be hired from a tool hire shop. Before the engine is mounted on a stand, the flywheel/driveplate should be removed, so that the stand bolts can be tightened into the end of the cylinder block/crankcase.

2 If a stand is not available, it is possible to dismantle the engine with it blocked up on a sturdy workbench, or on the floor. Be extra-careful not to tip or drop the engine when working without a stand.

3 If you are going to obtain a reconditioned engine, all the external components must be removed first, to be transferred to the replacement engine (just as they will if you are doing a complete engine overhaul yourself). These components include the following **(see illustrations)**.

a) Ancillary unit mounting brackets (oil filter, alternator, power steering pump, engine mountings, crankcase breather housing, etc.)

b) Thermostat and housing (Chapter 3).

c) Dipstick tube.

d) All electrical switches and sensors.

e) Inlet and exhaust manifolds (Chapters 4A, 4B and 4C).

f) Ignition coils and spark plugs (Chapters 1A and 5B).

Note: When removing the external components from the engine, pay close attention to details that may be helpful or important during refitting. Note the fitted

6.3a Unbolting the crankcase breather housing and removing the gasket from the left-hand side of the block

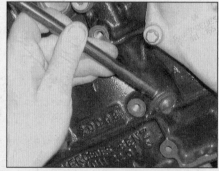

6.3b Removing the oil level dipstick tube from the cylinder block

position of gaskets, seals, spacers, pins, washers, bolts, and other small items.

4 If you are obtaining a 'short' engine (which consists of the engine cylinder block/crankcase, crankshaft, pistons and connecting rods all assembled), then the cylinder head, sump, oil pump, and timing chain will have to be removed also.

5 If you are planning a complete overhaul, the engine can be dismantled, and the internal components removed, in the order given below, referring to Part A or B of this Chapter unless otherwise stated.
  a) Inlet and exhaust manifolds (Chapter 4A, 4B or 4C).
  b) Timing chain, sprockets and tensioner.
  c) Cylinder head.
  d) Flywheel/driveplate.
  e) Sump.
  f) Oil pump.
  g) Piston/connecting rod assemblies (Section 13).
  h) Crankshaft (Section 11).

6 Before beginning the dismantling and overhaul procedures, make sure that you have all of the correct tools necessary. Refer to *Tools and working facilities* for further information.

7 Cylinder head - dismantling

Note: *New and reconditioned cylinder heads are available from the manufacturer, and from engine overhaul specialists. Be aware that some specialist tools are required for the dismantling and inspection procedures, and new components may not be readily available. It may therefore be more practical and economical for the home mechanic to purchase a reconditioned head, rather than dismantle, inspect and recondition the original head. A valve spring compressor tool will be required for this operation.*

Petrol engines

1 Remove the cylinder head as described in Part A of this Chapter.
2 Remove the inlet and exhaust manifolds as described in Chapters 4A and 4C.
3 Remove the camshafts and hydraulic tappets as described in Part A of this Chapter.
4 Unscrew the spark plugs from the cylinder head.
5 Using a valve spring compressor, compress the spring on each valve in turn until the split collets can be removed. Release the compressor, and lift off the spring cap and spring (**see illustrations**). If, when the valve spring compressor is screwed down, the spring cap refuses to free and expose the split collets, gently tap the top of the tool, directly over the spring cap, with a light hammer. This will free the retainer.
6 Using a pair of pliers or special removal

7.5a Removing the valve spring cap . . .

7.5b . . . and spring

7.6a Using a special tool to remove the valve stem oil seal

7.6b Removing the valve spring seat

tool, carefully extract the valve stem oil seal from the top of the guide, then lift off the spring seat (**see illustrations**).
7 Withdraw the valve through the combustion chamber (**see illustration**).
8 It is essential that each valve is stored with its collets, cap, spring, and spring seat. The valves should also be kept in their correct sequence, unless they are so badly worn that they are to be renewed. If they are going to be kept and used again, place each valve assembly in a labelled polythene bag or similar small container (**see illustration**). Label each bag No 1 inlet, No 1 exhaust, No 2 inlet, No 2 exhaust, etc, noting that No 1 valve is nearest to the timing chain end of the engine.

Diesel engines

9 Remove the cylinder head as described in Part B of this Chapter.
10 Remove the exhaust manifold as described in Chapter 4C.
11 If desired, remove the glow plugs as described in Chapter 5C.
12 Proceed as described in paragraphs 5 to 8.

8 Cylinder head and valves - cleaning and inspection

1 Thorough cleaning of the cylinder head and valve components, followed by a detailed

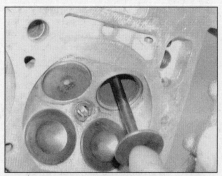
7.7 Removing a valve from the combustion chamber

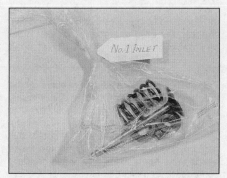
7.8 Store the valve components in a labelled bag

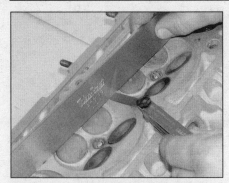

8.6 Use a straight-edge and feeler blade to check the cylinder head gasket face for distortion

8.15 Measuring a valve stem diameter

8.18 Using a suction valve-grindijng tool to grind in a valve

inspection, will enable you to decide how much valve service work must be carried out during the engine overhaul. **Note:** *If the engine has been severely overheated, it is best to assume that the cylinder head is warped - check carefully for signs of this.*

Cleaning

2 Scrape away all traces of old gasket material from the cylinder head.

3 Scrape away the carbon from the combustion chambers and ports, then wash the cylinder head thoroughly with paraffin or a suitable solvent.

4 Scrape off any heavy carbon deposits that may have formed on the valves, then use a power-operated wire brush to remove deposits from the valve heads and stems.

Inspection

Note: *Be sure to perform all the following inspection procedures before concluding that the services of a machine shop or engine overhaul specialist are required. Make a list of all items that require attention.*

Cylinder head

5 Inspect the head very carefully for cracks, evidence of coolant leakage, and other damage. If cracks are found, a new cylinder head should be obtained.

6 Use a straight-edge and feeler blade to check that the cylinder head gasket surface is not distorted **(see illustration)**. If it is, it may be possible to have it machined, provided that the cylinder head is not reduced to less than the specified height. Note also that, on diesel engines, the swirl chamber protrusion must be checked whenever the cylinder head surface is machined - see paragraphs 11 to 13.

7 Examine the valve seats in each of the combustion chambers. If they are severely pitted, cracked, or burned, they will need to be renewed or re-cut by an engine overhaul specialist. If they are only slightly pitted, this can be removed by grinding-in the valve heads and seats with fine valve-grinding compound, as described later in this Section. If the valve seats are re-cut, check that the valve recess dimensions, measured between

the plane of the cylinder head sealing face and the centre of the valve head, are maintained within the specified limits.

8 Check the valve guides for wear by inserting the relevant valve, and checking for side-to-side motion of the valve. A very small amount of movement is acceptable. If the movement seems excessive, remove the valve. Measure the valve stem diameter (see later in this Section), and renew the valve if it is worn. If the valve stem is not worn, the wear must be in the valve guide, and the guide must be renewed. The renewal of new valve guides should be entrusted to a Mercedes-Benz dealer or engine overhaul specialist, who will have the necessary tools available.

9 If renewing the valve guides, the valve seats should be re-cut or re-ground only *after* the guides have been fitted.

10 Examine the camshaft bearing surfaces in the cylinder head and the bearing caps for signs of wear or damage. If the bearings are excessively worn, consult a Mercedes-Benz dealer, or an engine overhaul specialist for further advice.

Swirl chambers - diesel engines

11 When inspecting the cylinder head, the swirl chamber protrusion should be checked - this is particularly important if the cylinder head face has been machined. If the swirl chamber protrusion is too great, the pistons may hit the swirl chambers when the engine is running, causing expensive damage.

12 Measure the protrusion of the swirl chamber from the sealing face of the cylinder head. If the protrusion is greater than the specified maximum, the protrusion can be altered by removing the swirl chamber, and fitting sealing spacers of varying thickness to achieve the specified protrusion.

13 Removal and refitting of the swirl chambers, and fitting of the appropriate spacers should be entrusted to a Mercedes-Benz dealer, or an engine overhaul specialist, due to the special tools required.

Valves

 Warning: The exhaust valves on most petrol and diesel engines are filled with sodium to improve

their heat transfer. Sodium is a highly reactive substance, and will ignite or explode spontaneously on contact with water (including water vapour in the air). These valves must NOT be disposed of as ordinary scrap. Seek advice from a Mercedes-Benz dealer when disposing of the valves.

14 Examine the head of each valve for pitting, burning, cracks, and general wear. Check the valve stem for scoring and wear ridges. Rotate the valve, and check for any obvious indication that it is bent. Look for pits or excessive wear on the tip of each valve stem. Renew any valve that shows any such signs of wear or damage.

15 If the valve appears satisfactory at this stage, measure the valve stem diameter at several points using a micrometer **(see illustration)**. Any significant difference in the readings obtained indicates wear of the valve stem. Should any of these conditions be apparent, the valve(s) must be renewed.

16 If the valves are in satisfactory condition, they should be ground (lapped) into their respective seats, to ensure a smooth, gas-tight seal. If the seat is only lightly pitted, or if it has been re-cut, fine grinding compound should be used to produce the required finish. Coarse valve-grinding compound should not be used, unless a seat is badly burned or deeply pitted. If this is the case, the cylinder head and valves should be inspected, to decide whether seat re-cutting, or even the renewal of the valve or seat insert (where possible) is required.

17 Valve grinding is carried out as follows. Place the cylinder head upside-down on a bench.

18 Smear a trace of (the appropriate grade of) valve-grinding compound on the seat face, and press a suction grinding tool onto the valve head **(see illustration)**. With a semi-rotary action, grind the valve head to its seat, lifting the valve occasionally to redistribute the grinding compound. A light spring placed under the valve head will greatly ease this operation.

19 If coarse grinding compound is being used, work only until a dull, matt even surface

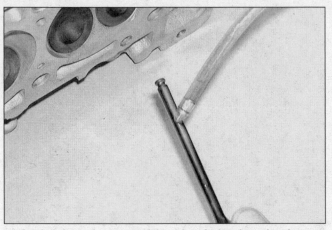

9.1 Lubricate the stems of the valves before inserting them

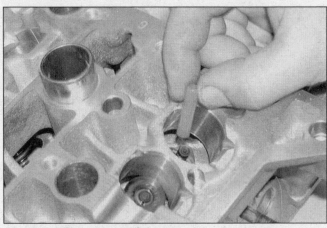

9.3a Locate the protective sleeve on the valve stem . . .

is produced on both the valve seat and the valve, then wipe off the used compound, and repeat the process with fine compound. When a smooth unbroken ring of light grey matt finish is produced on both the valve and seat, the grinding operation is complete. *Do not grind-in the valves any further than absolutely necessary*, or the seat will be prematurely sunk into the cylinder head.

20 When all the valves have been ground-in, carefully wash off *all* traces of grinding compound using paraffin or a suitable solvent, before reassembling the cylinder head.

Valve components

21 Examine the valve springs for signs of damage and discoloration. Check the free-length of the springs against the Specifications, and if necessary renew the springs. Where no figure is specified, if possible compare the length of the relevant valve spring with that of a new component.

22 Stand each spring on a flat surface, and check it for squareness. If any of the springs are damaged, distorted or have lost their tension, obtain a complete new set of springs. It is normal to renew the valve springs as a matter of course if a major overhaul is being carried out.

23 Renew the valve stem oil seals regardless of their apparent condition.

Hydraulic tappets

24 Refer to Part A or B of this Chapter for further details.

9 Cylinder head - reassembly

Note: *New valve stem oil seals should be fitted.*

Petrol engines

1 Lubricate the stems of the valves, and insert the valves into their original locations **(see illustration)**. If new valves are being fitted, insert them into the locations to which they have been ground.

2 Refit the spring seat.

3 Working on the first valve, dip the new valve stem seal in fresh engine oil. New seals are normally supplied with protective sleeves which should be fitted to the tops of the valve stems to prevent the collet grooves from damaging the oil seals. If no sleeves are supplied, wind a little thin tape round the top of the valve stems to protect the seals.

Carefully locate the seal over the valve and onto the guide. Take care not to damage the seal as it is passed over the valve stem. Use a suitable socket or tube to press the seal firmly onto the guide **(see illustrations)**. Remove the sleeve from the valve stem.

4 Locate the valve spring on top of the seat, then refit the spring cap. On engines where the spring is tapered, make sure that the large diameter end of the spring locates on the seat.

5 Fit the compressor tool, then compress the valve spring, and locate the split collets in the recess in the valve stem **(see illustration)**. Release the compressor, then repeat the procedure on the remaining valves.

> **HAYNES HiNT**
> *Use a little dab of grease to hold the collets in position on the valve stem while the spring compressor is released.*

6 With all the valves installed, support the cylinder head on blocks of wood and, using a hammer and interposed block of wood, tap the end of each valve stem to settle the components.

7 Refit and tighten the spark plugs (refer to Chapter 1A).

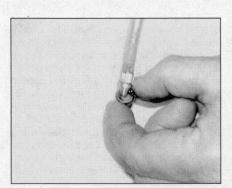

9.3b . . . then oil the new valve stem seal . . .

9.3c . . . and press it onto the valve guide

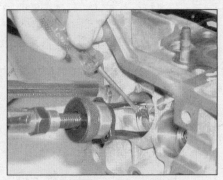

9.5 Fitting the split collets

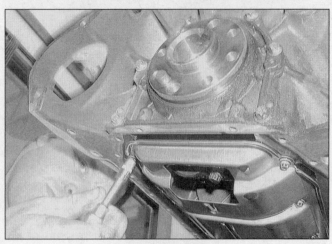
10.1a Unscrew the bolts . . .

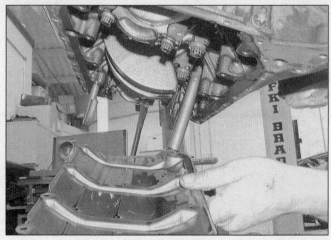
10.1b . . . and remove the oil baffle plate from the crankcase

8 Refit the hydraulic tappets and camshafts as described in Part A of this Chapter.
9 Refit the inlet and exhaust manifolds as described in Chapters 4A and 4C.
10 Refit the cylinder head as described in Part A of this Chapter.

Diesel engines

11 Proceed as described in paragraphs 1 to 6.
12 Where applicable, refit the glow plugs as described in Chapter 5C.
13 Refit the exhaust manifold as described in Chapter 4C.
14 Refit the cylinder head as described in Part B of this Chapter.

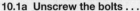

10 Piston/connecting rod assembly - removal

1 Remove the cylinder head, sump and oil pump as described in Part A or B of this Chapter (as applicable). Where fitted, unbolt and remove the oil baffle plate from the crankcase **(see illustrations)**.
2 If there is a pronounced wear ridge at the top of any bore, it may be necessary to remove it with a scraper or ridge reamer, to avoid piston damage during removal. Such a ridge indicates excessive wear of the cylinder bore.
3 Check the connecting rods and big-end caps for identification marks. Both rods and caps should be marked with the cylinder number on the inlet manifold side of each assembly. Note that No 1 cylinder is at the timing chain end of the engine. If no marks are present, using a hammer and centre-punch, paint or similar, mark each connecting rod and big-end bearing cap with its respective cylinder number on the flat machined surface provided - note on which side of the connecting rods the marks are made.
4 Similarly, check the piston crowns for a

direction marking. An arrow on each piston crown should point towards the timing chain end of the engine. On some engines, this mark may be obscured by carbon build-up, in which case the piston crown should be cleaned to check for a mark. In some cases, the direction arrow may have worn off, in which case a suitable mark should be made on the piston crown using a scriber - do not deeply score the piston crown, but ensure that the mark is easily visible.
5 Turn the crankshaft to bring piston Nos 1 and 4 (4-cylinder engines) or No 1 (5-cylinder engine), as applicable, to BDC (bottom dead centre).
6 Unscrew the bolts from No 1 piston big-end bearing cap. Take off the cap, and recover the bottom half bearing shell. If the bearing shells are to be re-used, tape the cap and the shell together.
7 Using a hammer handle, push the piston up through the bore, and remove it from the top of the cylinder block. On diesel engines, take care not to damage the piston cooling oil spay jets in the cylinder block as the piston/connecting rod assembly is removed. Recover the bearing shell, and tape it to the connecting rod for safe-keeping.
8 Loosely refit the big-end cap to the connecting rod, and secure with the bolts -

11.6 Removing No 3 main bearing cap and bearing shells

this will help to keep the components in their correct order.
9 On 4-cylinder engines, remove No 4 piston assembly in the same way before turning the crankshaft.
10 Turn the crankshaft as necessary to bring the remaining pistons to BDC, and remove them in the same manner.

11 Crankshaft - removal

1 Remove the sump, the timing chain cover, timing chain, crankshaft sprocket, and the flywheel/driveplate, as described in Part A or B of this Chapter.
2 Unbolt the crankshaft rear oil seal housing from the cylinder block. Recover the gasket.
3 Remove the pistons and connecting rods, as described in Section 10. If no work is to be done on the pistons and connecting rods, there is no need to remove the cylinder head, or to push the pistons out of the cylinder bores. The pistons should just be pushed far enough up the bores so that they are positioned clear of the crankshaft journals.
4 Check the crankshaft endfloat as described in Section 14, then proceed as follows.
5 On 4-cylinder engines, the crankshaft main bearing caps should be numbered 1 to 5 on the inlet side of the engine, starting from the timing chain end of the engine. Similarly, on the 5-cylinder engine, the main bearing caps should be numbered 1 to 6. If the bearing caps are not marked, mark them accordingly using a centre-punch. Note the orientation of the markings to ensure correct refitting.
6 Unscrew and remove the main bearing cap retaining bolts, and lift off each bearing cap **(see illustration)**. Recover the lower bearing shells, and tape them to their respective caps for safe-keeping.
7 Recover the lower endfloat control thrustwasher halves from either side of the

appropriate bearing cap, noting their positions, as follows.

a) **4-cylinder engine** - centre (No 3) main bearing.

b) **5-cylinder engine** - No 4 main bearing.

8 Lift the crankshaft from the crankcase.

9 Recover the upper bearing shells from the cylinder block, and tape them to their respective caps for safe-keeping. Similarly, recover the upper thrustwasher halves, noting their orientation.

12 Cylinder block/crankcase - cleaning and inspection

Cleaning

1 Remove all external components, brackets and electrical switches/sensors from the block **(see illustrations)**. Note the position of the power steering pump mounting bracket, as there must be a gap of 5.0 mm between it and the timing chain cover in order for the power steering pump to be fitted. For complete cleaning, the core plugs should ideally be removed. Drill a small hole in the plugs, then insert a self-tapping screw into the hole. Pull out the plugs by pulling on the screw with a pair of grips, or by using a slide hammer.

2 Scrape all traces of gasket from the cylinder block/crankcase, taking care not to damage the gasket/sealing surfaces.

3 Where applicable, remove the oil gallery plugs, and use new plugs when the engine is reassembled.

4 If the castings are extremely dirty, they should be steam-cleaned.

5 After the castings have been steam-cleaned, clean all oil holes and oil galleries one more time. Flush all internal passages with warm water until the water runs clear. Dry thoroughly, and apply a light film of oil to all mating surfaces, to prevent rusting. Also oil the cylinder bores. If you have access to compressed air, use it to speed up the drying process, and to blow out all the oil holes and galleries.

 Warning: Wear eye protection when using compressed air.

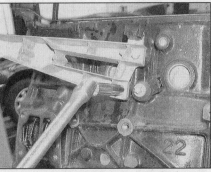

12.1a Unbolting the power steering pump mounting bracket from the left-hand side of the cylinder block

6 If the castings are not very dirty, you can do an adequate cleaning job with hot (as hot as you can stand!), soapy water and a stiff brush. Take plenty of time, and do a thorough job. Regardless of the cleaning method used, be sure to clean all oil holes and galleries very thoroughly, and to dry all components well. Protect the cylinder bores as described above, to prevent rusting.

7 Where applicable, the piston oil spray jets can be removed from the cylinder block for cleaning, however on later engines a special tool is required and it is recommended that an engine overhaul specialist carries out the work **(see illustration)**. To remove a jet on early engines, unscrew the securing bolt, recover the sealing ring (where applicable), and withdraw the jet from the cylinder block **(see illustration)**. The tool for removing the jets on later engines consists of an adapter which engages the base of the jet, and a slide hammer screwed into the adapter. Renew any jets which show signs of damage. Check the oil spray hole and oil passages for blockage.

8 All threaded holes must be clean, to ensure accurate torque readings during reassembly. To clean the threads, run the correct-size tap into each of the holes to remove rust, corrosion, thread sealant or sludge, and to restore damaged threads **(see illustration)**. If possible, use compressed air to clear the holes of debris produced by this operation.

9 Ensure that all threaded holes in the cylinder block are dry.

12.1b Removing the oil separator bracket from the left-hand side of the cylinder block

10 After coating the mating surfaces of the new core plugs with suitable sealant, fit them to the cylinder block. Make sure that they are driven in straight and seated correctly, or leakage could result.

> **HAYNES HiNT** *A large socket with an outside diameter which will just fit into the core plug can be used to drive core plugs into position.*

11 Where applicable, fit the new oil gallery plugs.

12 If the engine is not going to be reassembled right away, cover it with a large plastic bag to keep it clean; protect all mating surfaces and the cylinder bores as described above, to prevent rusting.

Inspection

13 Visually check the cylinder block/crankcase for cracks and corrosion. Look for stripped threads in the threaded holes. If there has been any history of internal water leakage, it may be worthwhile having an engine overhaul specialist check the cylinder block/crankcase with special equipment. If defects are found, have them repaired if possible, or renew the assembly.

14 Check each cylinder bore for scuffing and scoring. Check for signs of a wear ridge at the top of the cylinder, indicating that the bore is excessively worn.

12.7a Piston oil spray jet on a late engine

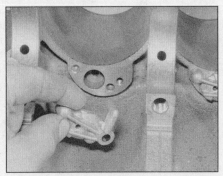

12.7b Removing a piston oil spray jet from an early engine

12.8 Clean damaged threads using a tap

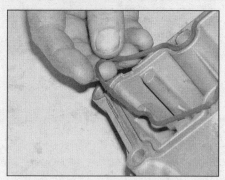

12.19 Use a new gasket when refitting the oil separator bracket

15 If the necessary measuring equipment is available, measure the bore diameter of each cylinder at the top (just under the wear ridge), centre, and bottom of the cylinder bore, parallel to the crankshaft axis.

16 Next, measure the bore diameter at the same three locations, at right-angles to the crankshaft axis. Compare the results with the figures given in the Specifications. If there is any doubt about the condition of the cylinder bores, seek the advice of a Mercedes-Benz dealer or engine reconditioning specialist.

17 If the cylinder bore wear exceeds the permitted tolerances, or if the cylinder walls are badly scored or scuffed, then the cylinders will have to be rebored by a suitably-qualified specialist, and new oversize pistons will have to be fitted. A Mercedes-Benz dealer or engineering workshop will normally be able to supply suitable oversize pistons when carrying out the reboring work. Note that the piston and bore size grades are stamped on the piston crowns, and on the adjacent cylinder head mating face of the cylinder block.

18 Inspect the upper surface of the cylinder block for damage. Use a straight-edge and feeler blade to check that the cylinder head gasket surface is not distorted. If it is, it may be possible to have it machined, provided that the cylinder block is not reduced to less than the specified height. Note also that on diesel engines, the piston protrusion must be checked whenever the cylinder head surface is machined - see paragraph 20.

19 After checking the cylinder block/crankcase, refit the items removed in paragraph 1. Use a new gasket when refitting the oil separator bracket **(see illustration)**.

Piston protrusion - diesel engines

20 When inspecting the cylinder block, the piston protrusion should be checked - this is particularly important if the cylinder head face has been machined. If the piston protrusion is too great, the pistons may hit the swirl chambers when the engine is running, causing expensive damage.

21 Measure the protrusion of the piston from

the sealing face of the cylinder head (a dial gauge should be used if possible). If the protrusion is greater than the specified maximum, consult a Mercedes-Benz dealer or an engine reconditioning specialist for advice - it is likely that the cylinder block will have to be renewed.

13 Piston/connecting rod assembly - cleaning and inspection

Cleaning

1 Before the inspection process can begin, the piston/connecting rod assemblies must be cleaned, and the original piston rings removed from the pistons.

2 Carefully expand the old rings over the top of the pistons. The use of two or three old feeler blades will be helpful in preventing the rings dropping into empty grooves **(see illustration)**. Be careful not to scratch the piston with the ends of the ring. The rings are brittle, and will snap if they are spread too far. They are also very sharp - protect your hands and fingers. Note that the third ring incorporates an expander. Always remove the rings from the top of the piston. Keep each set of rings with its piston if the old rings are to be re-used. Note which way up each ring is fitted to ensure correct refitting.

3 Scrape away all traces of carbon from the top of the piston. A hand-held wire brush (or a piece of fine emery cloth) can be used, once the majority of the deposits have been scraped away.

4 Remove the carbon from the ring grooves in the piston, using an old ring. Break the ring in half to do this (be careful not to cut your fingers - piston rings are sharp). Be careful to remove only the carbon deposits - do not remove any metal, and do not nick or scratch the sides of the ring grooves.

5 Once the deposits have been removed, clean the piston/connecting rod assembly with paraffin or a suitable solvent, and dry thoroughly. Make sure that the oil return holes in the ring grooves are clear.

13.2 Using a feeler blade to help remove a piston ring

Inspection

6 If the pistons and cylinder bores are not damaged or worn excessively, and if the cylinder block does not need to be rebored, the original pistons can be refitted. Measure the piston diameters, and check that they are within limits for the corresponding bore diameters. If the piston-to-bore clearance is excessive, the block will have to be rebored, and new pistons and rings fitted. Normal piston wear shows up as even vertical wear on the piston thrust surfaces, and slight looseness of the top ring in its groove. New piston rings should always be used when the engine is reassembled. Note that the piston and bore size grades are stamped on the piston crowns, and on the adjacent cylinder head mating face of the cylinder block.

7 Carefully inspect each piston for cracks around the skirt, around the gudgeon pin holes, and at the piston ring 'lands' (between the ring grooves).

8 Look for scoring and scuffing on the piston skirt, holes in the piston crown, and burned areas at the edge of the crown. If the skirt is scored or scuffed, the engine may have been suffering from overheating, and/or abnormal combustion which caused excessively high operating temperatures. The cooling and lubrication systems should be checked thoroughly. Scorch marks on the sides of the pistons show that blow-by has occurred. A hole in the piston crown, or burned areas at the edge of the piston crown, indicates that abnormal combustion (pre-ignition, knocking, or detonation) has been occurring. If any of the above problems exist, the causes must be investigated and corrected, or the damage will occur again. The causes may include incorrect ignition/injection pump timing, inlet air leaks or incorrect air/fuel mixture (petrol engines), or a faulty fuel injector (diesel engines).

9 Corrosion of the piston, in the form of pitting, indicates that coolant has been leaking into the combustion chamber and/or the crankcase. Again, the cause must be corrected, or the problem may persist in the rebuilt engine.

10 New pistons can be purchased from a Mercedes-Benz dealer or motor factor.

11 Examine each connecting rod carefully for signs of damage, such as cracks around the big-end and small-end bearings. Check that the rod is not bent or distorted. Damage is highly unlikely, unless the engine has been seized or badly overheated. Detailed checking of the connecting rod assembly can only be carried out by a Mercedes-Benz dealer or engine repair specialist with the necessary equipment.

12 The gudgeon pins are of the floating type, secured in position by two circlips. The pistons and connecting rods can be separated as follows.

13 Using a small screwdriver, prise out the circlips, and push out the gudgeon pin **(see**

13.13a Prise out the circlips . . .

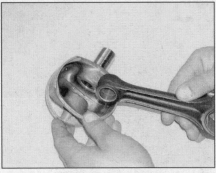

13.13b . . . then press out the gudgeon pin and separate the connecting rod

illustrations). Hand pressure should be sufficient to remove the pin. Identify the piston and rod to ensure correct reassembly. Discard the circlips - new ones must be used on refitting.

14 Examine the gudgeon pin and connecting rod small-end bearing for signs of wear or damage. It should be possible to push the gudgeon pin through the connecting rod bush by hand, without noticeable play. Wear can be cured by renewing both the pin and bush. Bush renewal, however, is a specialist job - press facilities are required, and the new bush must be reamed accurately.

15 The connecting rods themselves should not be in need of renewal, unless seizure or some other major mechanical failure has occurred. Check the alignment of the connecting rods visually, and if the rods are not straight, take them to an engine overhaul specialist for a more detailed check.

16 Examine all components, and obtain any new parts from your Mercedes-Benz dealer. If new pistons are purchased, they will be supplied complete with gudgeon pins and circlips. Circlips can also be purchased individually.

17 Position the piston in relation to the connecting rod as follows according to engine type.

a) On petrol engines, the connecting rod markings and the bearing shell retaining grooves must be on the inlet side of the engine, and the arrow on the piston crown must point towards the timing chain end of the engine.

b) On diesel engines, the cut-outs for the bearing shell locating tabs in the connecting rod and the bearing cap must be on the fuel injection pump side of the engine, and the arrow on the piston crown must point towards the timing chain end of the engine.

18 Apply a smear of clean engine oil to the gudgeon pin. Slide it into the piston and through the connecting rod small-end. Check that the piston pivots freely on the rod, then secure the gudgeon pin in position with two new circlips. Ensure that each circlip is correctly located in its groove in the piston.

14 Crankshaft - inspection

Checking crankshaft endfloat

1 If the crankshaft endfloat is to be checked, this must be done when the crankshaft is still installed in the cylinder block/crankcase, but is free to move.

2 Check the endfloat using a dial gauge in contact with the end of the crankshaft. Push the crankshaft fully one way, and then zero the gauge. Push the crankshaft fully the other way, and check the endfloat. The result can be compared with the specified amount, and will give an indication as to whether new thrustwasher halves are required **(see illustration)**. Note that all thrustwashers must be of the same thickness - refer to the

Specifications for the thicknesses of thrustwashers available.

3 If a dial gauge is not available, feeler blades can be used. First push the crankshaft fully towards the flywheel/driveplate end of the engine, then use feeler blades to measure the gap between the web of No 3 crankpin and the thrustwasher halves on 4-cylinder engines, or between the web of No 4 crankpin and the thrustwasher halves on the 5-cylinder engine.

Inspection

4 Clean the crankshaft using paraffin or a suitable solvent, and dry it, preferably with compressed air if available. Be sure to clean the oil holes with a pipe cleaner or similar probe, to ensure that they are not obstructed.

⚠️ *Warning: Wear eye protection when using compressed air.*

5 Check the main and big-end bearing journals for uneven wear, scoring, pitting and cracking.

6 Big-end bearing wear is accompanied by distinct metallic knocking when the engine is running (particularly noticeable when the engine is pulling from low speed) and some loss of oil pressure.

7 Main bearing wear is accompanied by severe engine vibration and rumble - getting progressively worse as engine speed increases - and again by loss of oil pressure.

8 Check the bearing journal for roughness by running a finger lightly over the bearing surface. Any roughness (which will be accompanied by obvious bearing wear) indicates that the crankshaft requires regrinding (where possible) or renewal.

9 If the crankshaft has been reground, check for burrs around the crankshaft oil holes (the holes are usually chamfered, so burrs should not be a problem unless regrinding has been carried out carelessly). Remove any burrs with a fine file or scraper, and thoroughly clean the oil holes.

10 Using a micrometer, measure the diameter of the main and big-end bearing journals, and compare the results with the Specifications **(see illustration)**. By measuring the diameter at a number of points around each journal's circumference, you will be able to determine whether or not the journal is out-of-round. Take the measurement at each end of the journal, near the webs, to determine if the journal is tapered.

11 Check the oil seal contact surfaces of the crankshaft for wear and damage. If the seal has worn a deep groove in the surface of the crankshaft, refer to Part A or B of this Chapter (as applicable).

12 If the crankshaft journals have not previously been reground, it may be possible to have the crankshaft reconditioned, and to fit undersize shells (see Section 18). If no undersize shells are available and the crankshaft has worn beyond the specified

14.2 Checking the crankshaft endfloat using a dial gauge

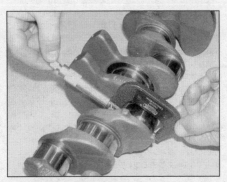

14.10 Measuring a big-end bearing journal diameter with a micrometer

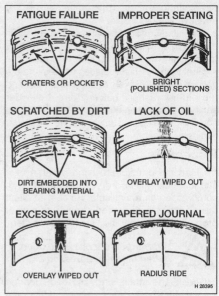

FATIGUE FAILURE — CRATERS OR POCKETS

IMPROPER SEATING — BRIGHT (POLISHED) SECTIONS

SCRATCHED BY DIRT — DIRT EMBEDDED INTO BEARING MATERIAL

LACK OF OIL — OVERLAY WIPED OUT

EXCESSIVE WEAR — OVERLAY WIPED OUT

TAPERED JOURNAL — RADIUS RIDE

H 28395

15.2 Typical bearing failures

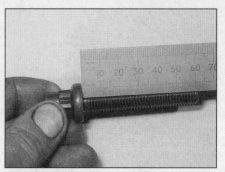

15.12 Measuring a main bearing cap bolt

limits, it will have to be renewed. Consult your Mercedes-Benz dealer or engine specialist for further information on parts availability.
13 Where the transmission input shaft spigot bearing is located in the end of the crankshaft, examine it for smooth running. If necessary renew it.

15 Main and big-end bearings, and bearing cap bolts - inspection

Bearings

1 Even though the main and big-end bearings should be renewed during the engine overhaul, the old bearings should be retained for close examination, as they may reveal valuable information about the condition of the engine. The bearing shells are graded by thickness.
2 Bearing failure can occur due to lack of lubrication, the presence of dirt or other foreign particles, overloading the engine, or corrosion **(see illustration)**. Regardless of the cause of bearing failure, the cause must be corrected before the engine is reassembled, to prevent it from happening again.
3 When examining the bearing shells, remove them from the cylinder block/crankcase, the connecting rods and the connecting rod big-end bearing caps. Lay them out on a clean surface in the same general position as their location in the engine. This will enable you to match any bearing problems with the corresponding crankshaft journal. *Do not* touch any shell's bearing surface with your fingers while checking it, or the delicate surface may be scratched.
4 Dirt and other foreign matter gets into the engine in a variety of ways. It may be left in the engine during assembly, or it may pass through filters or the crankcase ventilation

system. It may get into the oil, and from there into the bearings. Metal chips from machining operations and normal engine wear are often present. Abrasives are sometimes left in engine components after reconditioning, especially when parts are not thoroughly cleaned using the proper cleaning methods. Whatever the source, these foreign objects often end up embedded in the soft bearing material, and are easily recognised. Large particles will not embed in the bearing, and will score or gouge the bearing and journal. The best prevention for this cause of bearing failure is to clean all parts thoroughly, and keep everything spotlessly-clean during engine assembly. Frequent and regular engine oil and filter changes are also recommended.
5 Lack of lubrication (or lubrication breakdown) has a number of interrelated causes. Excessive heat (which thins the oil), overloading (which squeezes the oil from the bearing face) and oil leakage (from excessive bearing clearances, worn oil pump or high engine speeds) all contribute to lubrication breakdown. Blocked oil passages, which may be the result of misaligned oil holes in a bearing shell, will also oil-starve a bearing, and destroy it. When lack of lubrication is the cause of bearing failure, the bearing material is wiped or extruded from the steel backing of the bearing. Temperatures may increase to the point where the steel backing turns blue from overheating.
6 Driving habits can have a definite effect on bearing life. Full-throttle, low-speed operation (labouring the engine) puts very high loads on bearings, tending to squeeze out the oil film. These loads cause the bearings to flex, which produces fine cracks in the bearing face (fatigue failure). Eventually, the bearing material will loosen in pieces, and tear away from the steel backing.
7 Short-distance driving leads to corrosion of bearings, because insufficient engine heat is produced to drive off the condensed water and corrosive gases. These products collect in the engine oil, forming acid and sludge. As the oil is carried to the engine bearings, the acid attacks and corrodes the bearing material.
8 Incorrect bearing installation during engine assembly will lead to bearing failure as well. Tight-fitting bearings leave insufficient bearing running clearance, and will result in oil

starvation. Dirt or foreign particles trapped behind a bearing shell result in high spots on the bearing, which lead to failure.
9 *Do not* touch any shell's bearing surface with your fingers during reassembly; there is a risk of scratching the delicate surface, or of depositing particles of dirt on it.
10 As mentioned at the beginning of this Section, the bearing shells should be renewed as a matter of course during engine overhaul; to do otherwise is false economy. Refer to Sections 18 and 19 for details of bearing shell selection.

Main bearing cap bolts

11 The manufacturers recommend that the main bearing cap bolts are measured to determine whether renewal is necessary; however, some owners may wish to renew all the bolts as a matter of course.
12 Measure the length of each bolt from the base of the head to the end of the shank **(see illustration)**. If the bolt length is greater than the maximum specified, the bolts should be renewed.

Big-end bearing cap bolts

13 The manufacturers recommend that the big-end bearing cap bolts are measured to determine whether renewal is necessary, however, some owners may wish to renew all the bolts as a matter of course. It is strongly recommended that the bolts are renewed when reassembling the engine.
14 Press or tap the bolts out from the connecting rods.
15 Measure the length of each bolt from the base of the head to the end of the shank. If the bolt length is greater than the maximum specified, the bolts should be renewed.

16 Engine overhaul - reassembly sequence

1 Before reassembly begins, ensure that all new parts have been obtained, and that all necessary tools are available. Read through the entire procedure to familiarise yourself with the work involved, and to ensure that all items necessary for reassembly of the engine are at hand. In addition to all normal tools and materials, thread-locking compound will be needed. A suitable tube of liquid sealant will also be required for the joint faces that are fitted without gaskets.
2 In order to save time and avoid problems, engine reassembly can be carried out in the following order, referring to Part A or B of this Chapter unless otherwise stated. Where applicable, use new gaskets and seals when refitting the various components.
   a) *Crankshaft (Section 18).*
   b) *Piston/connecting rod assemblies (Section 19).*
   c) *Oil pump.*
   d) *Sump.*
   e) *Flywheel/driveplate.*
   f) *Cylinder head.*
   g) *Timing chain, tensioner and sprockets.*
   h) *Engine external components.*

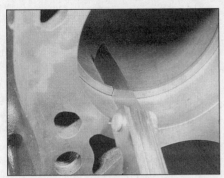

17.5 Measuring a piston ring end-gap

17.10 Fitting the oil control ring expander

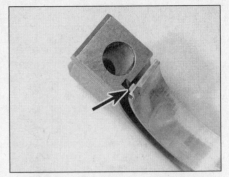

18.5 Ensure that the tab on each bearing shell (arrowed) engages with the notch in the cap

3 At this stage, all engine components should be absolutely clean and dry, with all faults repaired. The components should be laid out (or in individual containers) on a completely clean work surface.

17 Piston rings - refitting

1 Before fitting new piston rings, the ring end gaps must be checked as follows.
2 Lay out the piston/connecting rod assemblies and the new piston ring sets, so that the ring sets will be matched with the same piston and cylinder during the end gap measurement and subsequent engine reassembly.
3 Insert the top ring into the first cylinder, and push it down the bore using the top of the piston. This will ensure that the ring remains square with the cylinder walls. Position the ring near the bottom of the cylinder bore, at the lower limit of ring travel. Note that the top and second compression rings are different. The second ring is easily identified by the step on its lower surface.
4 Measure the end gap using feeler blades.
5 Repeat the procedure with the ring at the top of the cylinder bore, at the upper limit of its travel **(see illustration)**, and compare the measurements with the figures given in the Specifications.
6 If the gap is too small (unlikely if genuine Mercedes-Benz parts are used), it must be enlarged, or the ring ends may contact each other during engine operation, causing serious damage. Ideally, new piston rings providing the correct end gap should be fitted. As a last resort, the end gap can be increased by filing the ring ends very carefully with a fine file. Mount the file in a vice equipped with soft jaws, slip the ring over the file with the ends contacting the file face, and slowly move the ring to remove material from the ends. Take care, as piston rings are sharp, and are easily broken.
7 With new piston rings, it is unlikely that the end gap will be too large. If the gaps are too

large, check that you have the correct rings for your engine and for the particular cylinder bore size.
8 Repeat the checking procedure for each ring in the first cylinder, and then for the rings in the remaining cylinders. Remember to keep rings, pistons and cylinders matched up.
9 Once the ring end gaps have been checked and if necessary corrected, the rings can be fitted to the pistons.
10 Fit the piston rings using the same technique as for removal. Fit the bottom (oil control) ring first, and work up. When fitting the oil control ring, first insert the wire expander, then fit the ring with its gap positioned 180° from the protruding wire ends of the expander. Ensure that the rings are fitted the correct way up - the top surface of the rings is normally marked TOP **(see illustration)**. Arrange the gaps of the top and second compression rings 120° either side of the oil control ring gap, but make sure that none of the rings gaps are positioned over the gudgeon pin hole. **Note:** *Always follow any instructions supplied with the new piston ring sets - different manufacturers may specify different procedures. Do not mix up the top and second compression rings, as they have different cross-sections.*

18 Crankshaft - refitting and main bearing running clearance check

Selection of new bearing shells
1 If the original crankshaft is in good condition and is being refitted, new main bearing shells which are the same size as the removed shells should be fitted.
2 If the crankshaft has been reground, undersize bearing shells must be fitted. The appropriate shells are normally supplied by the engine reconditioning specialist.

Main bearing running clearance check
3 The running clearance check can be carried out using the original bearing shells. However,

it is preferable to use a new set, since the results obtained will be more conclusive in determining wear of the crankshaft journals.
4 Clean the backs of the bearing shells, and the bearing locations in both the cylinder block/crankcase and the main bearing caps.
5 Press the bearing shells into their locations, ensuring that the tab on each shell engages in the notch in the cylinder block/crankcase or bearing cap **(see illustration)**. Take care not to touch any shell's bearing surface with your fingers. If the original bearing shells are being used for the check, ensure that they are refitted in their original locations. Note that the bearings shells with oil grooves fit in the cylinder block, and the plain bearing shells fit in the bearing caps.
6 The clearance can be checked in either of two ways.
7 One method (which will be difficult to achieve without a range of internal micrometers or internal/external expanding calipers) is to refit the main bearing caps to the cylinder block/crankcase, with bearing shells in place. With the original cap retaining bolts tightened to the specified torque, measure the internal diameter of each assembled pair of bearing shells. If the diameter of each corresponding crankshaft journal is measured and then subtracted from the bearing internal diameter, the result will be the main bearing running clearance.
8 The second (and more accurate) method is to use a product known as Plastigauge. This consists of a fine thread of perfectly-round plastic, which is compressed between the bearing shell and the journal. When the shell is removed, the plastic is deformed, and can be measured with a special card gauge supplied with the kit. The running clearance is determined from this gauge. The procedure for using Plastigauge is as follows.
9 With the main bearing upper shells in place, carefully lay the crankshaft in position. Do not use any lubricant; the crankshaft journals and bearing shells must be perfectly clean and dry.
10 Cut several lengths of the appropriate-size Plastigauge (they should be slightly shorter than the width of the main bearings),

18.10 Plastigauge in place on crankshaft main bearing journal

18.13 Measure the width of the deformed Plastigauge using the scale on the card

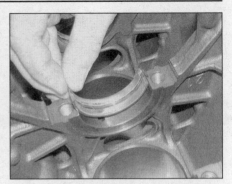

18.20a Place the bearing shells in the crankcase . . .

and place one length on each crankshaft journal axis **(see illustration)**.

11 With the main bearing lower shells in position, refit the main bearing caps. Starting with the centre main bearing and working outwards, tighten the original main bearing cap bolts progressively to their specified torque. Take care not to disturb the Plastigauge, and *do not* rotate the crankshaft at any time during this operation.

12 Remove the main bearing cap bolts and carefully lift off the caps, keeping them in order. Again, take great care not to disturb the Plastigauge or rotate the crankshaft. If any of the bearing caps are difficult to remove, free them by carefully tapping them with a soft-faced mallet.

13 Compare the width of the crushed

Plastigauge on each journal to the scale printed on the Plastigauge envelope, to obtain the main bearing running clearance **(see illustration)**. Compare the clearance measured with that given in the Specifications.

14 If the clearance is significantly different from that expected, the bearing shells may be the wrong size (or excessively worn, if the original shells are being re-used). Before deciding that different-size shells are required, make sure that no dirt or oil was trapped between the bearing shells and the caps or block when the clearance was measured. If the Plastigauge was wider at one end than at the other, the crankshaft journal may be tapered.

15 If the clearance is not as specified, consult your engine reconditioner for advice on obtaining different bearing shells.

16 After obtaining the new shells, repeat the running clearance checking procedure as described above.

17 On completion, carefully scrape away all traces of the Plastigauge material from the crankshaft and bearing shells. Use your fingernail, or a wooden or plastic scraper which is unlikely to score the bearing surfaces.

Final crankshaft refitting

Note: *It is recommended that new main bearing cap bolts are used when finally refitting the crankshaft.*

18 Carefully lift the crankshaft out of the cylinder block once more.

19 Where applicable, ensure that the oil spray jets are fitted to the cylinder block.

20 Place the bearing shells in their locations as described earlier. If new shells are being fitted, ensure that all traces of protective grease are cleaned off using paraffin. Wipe dry the shells and connecting rods with a lint-free cloth. Liberally lubricate each bearing shell in the cylinder block/crankcase and cap with clean engine oil **(see illustrations)**.

21 Fit the upper thrustwasher halves to the appropriate bearing location in the cylinder block as follows **(see illustration)**.

 a) *4-cylinder engines* - *centre (No 3) main bearing.*

 b) *5-cylinder engine* - *No 4 main bearing.*

Ensure that the oil grooves in the thrustwasher halves face out towards the crankshaft journals.

22 Lower the crankshaft into position **(see illustration)**.

> **HAYNES HiNT** *Use a little grease to hold the thrustwasher halves in position.*

23 Lubricate the lower bearing shells in the main bearing caps with clean engine oil. Make sure that the locating lugs on the shells engage with the corresponding recesses in the caps **(see illustrations)**.

24 Fit the main bearing caps to their correct locations, ensuring that they are fitted the

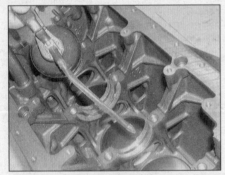

18.20b . . . and lubricate them with clean engine oil

18.21 Fitting the upper thrustwasher halves

18.22 Lowering the crankshaft into the crankcase

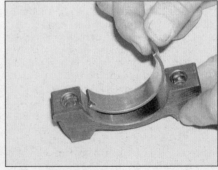

18.23a Locate the main bearing shells in the caps . . .

18.23b . . . and lubricate them with clean engine oil

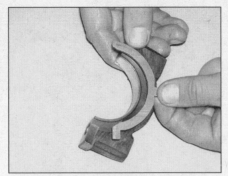

18.24a Fitting a thrustwasher half to a main bearing cap (use a little grease to hold the washer in position)

18.24b Fitting No 3 main bearing cap

correct way round. Ensure that the thrustwasher halves are in place on the appropriate bearing cap **(see illustrations)**.

25 Lightly lubricate the bolt threads, then fit the main bearing cap bolts **(see illustrations)**. Where applicable, ensure that the oil pick-up pipe support bracket is in place on the relevant bolts, as noted before removal. Tighten the bolts by hand only at this stage.

26 Progressively tighten the main bearing cap bolts to the specified torque, starting with the centre bearing cap, and working outwards. Observe the two tightening stages given in the Specifications **(see illustrations)**. If the bolts are angle-tightened, it is recommended that an angle-measuring gauge is used during this stage of the tightening, to ensure accuracy. If a gauge is not available, use a dab of white paint to make alignment marks between the bolt and bearing cap prior to tightening; the marks can then be used to check that the bolt has been rotated sufficiently during tightening.

27 Check that the crankshaft rotates freely.

28 Fit a new crankshaft rear oil seal to the housing, then refit the housing, using a new gasket, or suitable sealant, as applicable.

29 Refit the piston/connecting rod assemblies as described in Section 19.

30 Refit the flywheel/driveplate, crankshaft

18.25a Lightly lubricate the main bearing cap bolts . . .

18.25b . . . then insert them

sprocket, timing chain, timing chain cover and sump, as described in Part A or B of this Chapter.

19 Piston/connecting rod assembly - refitting and big-end bearing running clearance check

Selection of new bearing shells

1 If the big-end journals on the crankshaft are in good condition, new big-end bearing shells

which are the same size as the removed shells should be fitted.

2 If the crankshaft has been reground, undersize bearing shells must be fitted. The appropriate shells are normally supplied by the engine reconditioning specialist.

Big-end bearing running clearance check

3 Clean the backs of the bearing shells, and the bearing locations in both the connecting rod and bearing cap.

4 Press the bearing shells into their locations, ensuring that the tab on each shell engages in

18.26a Torque-tightening the main bearing cap bolts

18.26b Angle-tightening the main bearing cap bolts

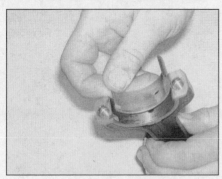

19.4a Inserting the bearing shells in the conrod . . .

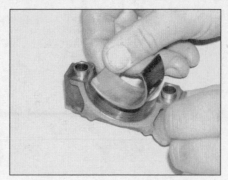

19.4b . . . and big-end bearing cap

19.14a Lubricating the pistons and rings . . .

the notch in the connecting rod and cap **(see illustrations)**. Take care not to touch the bearing surface of the shell with your fingers. If the original bearing shells are being used for the check, ensure that they are refitted in their original locations. The clearance can be checked in either of two ways.

5 One method is to refit the big-end bearing cap to the connecting rod, using the marks made or noted on removal to ensure that they are fitted the correct way around, with the bearing shells in place. With the original cap retaining bolts correctly tightened, use an internal micrometer or vernier caliper to measure the internal diameter of each assembled pair of bearing shells. If the diameter of each corresponding crankshaft journal is measured and then subtracted from the bearing internal diameter, the result will be the big-end bearing running clearance.

6 The second, and more accurate method is to use Plastigauge (see Section 18).

7 Ensure that the bearing shells are correctly fitted. Place a strand of Plastigauge on each (cleaned) crankpin journal.

8 Refit the piston/connecting rod assemblies to the crankshaft, and refit the big-end bearing caps, using the marks made or noted on removal to ensure that they are fitted the correct way around.

9 Refit the bearing cap nuts, and tighten the nuts to the specified torque in the two stages given in the Specifications. Take care not to disturb the Plastigauge, nor rotate the connecting rod during the tightening sequence.

10 Dismantle the assemblies without rotating the connecting rods. Use the scale printed on the Plastigauge envelope to obtain the big-end bearing running clearance.

11 If the clearance is significantly different from that expected, the bearing shells may be the wrong size (or excessively worn, if the original shells are being re-used). Make sure that no dirt or oil was trapped between the bearing shells and the caps or connecting rod when the clearance was measured. If the Plastigauge was wider at one end than at the other, the crankshaft journal may be tapered.

12 On completion, carefully scrape away all traces of the Plastigauge material from the crankshaft and bearing shells. Use your fingernail, or some other object which is unlikely to score the bearing surfaces.

Final piston/connecting rod refitting

Note: *A piston ring compressor tool will be required for this operation. Note that the following procedure assumes that the main bearing caps are in place.*

13 Ensure that the bearing shells are correctly fitted as described earlier. If new shells are being fitted, ensure that all traces of

the protective grease are cleaned off using paraffin. Wipe dry the shells and connecting rods with a lint-free cloth.

14 Lubricate the cylinder bores, the pistons, and piston rings, then lay out each piston/connecting rod assembly in its respective position **(see illustrations)**.

15 Start with assembly No 1. Make sure that the piston rings are still spaced as described in Section 17, then clamp them in position with a piston ring compressor **(see illustration)**.

16 Insert the piston/connecting rod assembly into the top of cylinder No 1. Ensure that the arrow on the piston crown points towards the timing chain end of the engine, and that the identifying marks on the connecting rods and big-end caps are positioned as noted before removal. Using a block of wood or hammer handle against the piston crown, tap the assembly into the cylinder until the piston crown is flush with the top of the cylinder **(see illustration)**. Where applicable, take care not to damage the piston cooling oil spray jets as the piston/connecting rod assemblies are refitted.

17 Ensure that the bearing shell is still correctly installed. Liberally lubricate the crankpin and both bearing shells. Taking care not to mark the cylinder bores or damage the piston oil jets (where fitted), pull the piston /connecting rod assembly down the bore and onto the crankpin. Refit the big-end

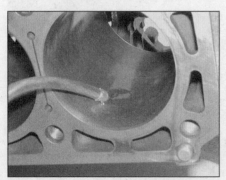

19.14b . . . and cylinder bores

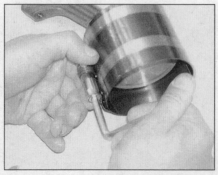

19.15 Fitting a piston ring compressor to the piston

19.16 Inserting a piston in its cylinder bore

bearing cap **(see illustration)**. Note that the bearing shell locating tabs must abut each other.

18 Lightly lubricate the bolt threads, then screw the big-end bearing cap bolts by hand into position in the connecting rods **(see illustration)**.

19 Progressively tighten the bolts to the specified torque and angle, observing the two tightening stages given in the Specifications **(see illustrations)**. It is recommended that an angle-measuring gauge is used to angle-tighten the bolts. If a gauge is not available, use a dab of white paint to make alignment marks between the bolt and bearing cap prior to tightening; the marks can then be used to check that the bolt has been rotated sufficiently during tightening.

20 Once the bearing cap bolts have been correctly tightened, rotate the crankshaft and check that it turns freely. Some stiffness is to be expected if new components have been fitted, but there should be no signs of binding or tight spots.

21 Refit the remaining piston/connecting rod assemblies in the same way.

22 Refit the oil pump, sump and cylinder head as described in Part A or B of this Chapter (as applicable).

20 Engine - initial start-up after overhaul

1 With the engine refitted in the vehicle, double-check the engine oil and coolant levels. Make a final check that everything has been reconnected, and that there are no tools or rags left in the engine compartment.

Petrol engines

2 Remove the spark plugs, then disable the fuel system and ignition system by removing the fuel pump relay, and disconnecting the ignition coil low tension wiring plug (see Chapter 5B).

3 Turn the engine on the starter until the oil pressure warning light goes out, then refit the spark plugs, refit the fuel pump relay and reconnect the wiring plug.

19.17 Refitting the big-end bearing cap

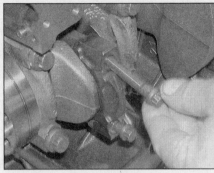
19.18 Fitting the big-end bearing cap bolts

19.19a Torque-tightening the big-end bearing bolts

19.19b Angle-tightening the big-end bearing bolts

Diesel engines

4 Disconnect the wiring from the stop solenoid on the fuel injection pump (see Chapter 4B), then turn the engine on the starter until the oil pressure warning light goes out. Reconnect the wire to the stop solenoid.

5 Prime the fuel system (see Chapter 1B).

6 Fully depress the accelerator pedal, turn the ignition key to position 2, and wait for the preheating warning light to go out.

All engines

7 Start the engine, noting that this may take a little longer than usual, due to the fuel system components having been disturbed.

8 While the engine is idling, check for fuel, water and oil leaks. Don't be alarmed if there are some odd smells and smoke from parts getting hot and burning off oil deposits.

9 Assuming all is well, keep the engine idling until hot water is felt circulating through the top hose, then switch off the engine.

10 After a few minutes, recheck the oil and coolant levels as described in the relevant part of Chapter 1, and top-up as necessary.

11 If new pistons, rings or crankshaft bearings have been fitted, the engine must be treated as new, and run-in for the first 500 miles (800 km). *Do not* operate the engine at full-throttle, or allow it to labour at low engine speeds in any gear. It is recommended that the oil and filter are changed at the end of this period.

Notes

Chapter 3
Cooling, heating and ventilation systems

Contents

Degrees of difficulty

Easy, suitable for novice with little experience	Fairly easy, suitable for beginner with some experience	Fairly difficult, suitable for competent DIY mechanic 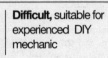	Difficult, suitable for experienced DIY mechanic	Very difficult, suitable for expert DIY or professional

Specifications

System type .... Pressurised, with crossflow radiator, auxiliary belt-driven thermo-viscous coupled cooling fan (electric fan on air conditioning models). Centrifugal water pump driven by auxiliary belt, bypass thermostat, radiator header tank or remote expansion tank.

General

Pressure cap opening pressure	1.4 bar
Thermostat:	
Petrol engines:	
Opening commences	87 ± 2°C
Fully open	102°C
Non-turbo diesel engines:	
Opening commences	85 ± 2°C
Fully open	94°C
Turbo-diesel engines:	
Opening commences	80 ± 2°C
Fully open	100°C
Coolant:	
Type	See end of *Weekly checks*
Cooling system capacity	See Chapter 1A or 1B Specifications

Torque wrench settings

	Nm	lbf ft
Alternator mounting bracket bolts	45	33
Automatic transmission fluid cooler unions	20	15
Belt tensioner damper bolts	25	18
Coolant pump housing bolts (diesel engine)	10	7
Coolant pump mounting bolts		
Petrol engines:		
M6 bolts	10	7
M8 bolts	25	18
Diesel engines	10	7
Coolant pump pulley bolts	10	7
Cooling fan to viscous coupling	10	8
Cylinder block drain plug	30	22
Thermostat housing mounting bolts:		
M6 bolts	10	7
M8 bolts	25	18
Viscous fan coupling nut/bolt	40	30

1 General information and precautions

General information

The cooling system is of pressurised type, comprising a pump, an aluminium crossflow radiator, a viscous cooling fan, and a thermostat. The system functions as follows. Cold coolant from the radiator passes through the hose to the coolant pump, where it is pumped around the cylinder block and head passages. After cooling the cylinder bores, combustion surfaces and valve seats, the coolant reaches the underside of the thermostat, which is initially closed. The coolant passes through the heater and is returned through the cylinder block to the coolant pump.

When the engine is cold, the coolant circulates only through the cylinder block, cylinder head, expansion tank and heater. When the coolant reaches a predetermined temperature, the thermostat opens and the coolant passes through to the radiator. As the coolant circulates through the radiator, it is cooled by the inrush of air when the car is in forward motion. Airflow is supplemented by the action of the viscous or electric fan as necessary. Upon reaching the bottom of the radiator, the coolant is now cooled and the cycle is repeated.

The coolant pump is mounted externally on the front of the engine, and is driven by the auxiliary drivebelt.

Coolant temperature information for the gauge mounted in the instrument panel, and for the fuel system, is provided by temperature sensors mounted in the thermostat housing (petrol models) or in the cylinder head (diesel models). A coolant level switch is fitted to the radiator header tank or expansion tank, as applicable.

On models without air conditioning, the viscous coupling to which the radiator cooling fan is bolted ensures that the system receives adequate cooling. When the underbonnet temperature is low, the coupling turns freely, and the fan rotates only slowly; as the temperature rises, the coupling stiffens up, causing the fan to turn faster.

On air conditioning models, an electric cooling fan is fitted in place of, or in addition to, the viscous unit. The fan serves a dual purpose, regulating both the engine coolant temperature and that of the air conditioning refrigerant in the condenser (which is mounted in front of the radiator). Partly because of these two roles, the fan is controlled via an electronic unit mounted at the left-hand front of the car (see Section 5 for details).

In general, older models fitted with a viscous cooling fan have a header tank and overflow pipe fitted on top of the radiator. Due to the theoretically greater variations in engine temperature (and therefore, in coolant expansion), models with an electric cooling fan also have a remote-mounted coolant expansion tank. The plastic expansion tank is located on the right-hand side of the engine compartment, and collects the coolant which is displaced from the system as it expands due to the rise in temperature. The displaced coolant is returned to the radiator as the system cools.

On models with automatic transmission, the transmission fluid passes through a heat exchanger in the base of the radiator, which cools the fluid before returning it to the transmission.

Similarly, diesel models are equipped with an engine oil cooler. On models up to July 1994, this is mounted on the sump and uses external pipework, while later models have a heat exchanger attached to the oil filter housing. In both cases, a supply of coolant is fed to the heat exchanger to cool the oil.

Although not strictly part of the cooling system, note that the power steering fluid rigid pipes pass in front of the radiator, and are cooled by the inrush of air when the car is moving, thus cooling the fluid.

The vehicle interior heater operates by means of coolant from the engine cooling system. Coolant flow through the heater matrix is regulated by solenoid valves, which are controlled by a temperature sensor at the front of the heater unit. Unusually, the heater matrix is divided into two separate sections, for the driver and front seat passenger. Accordingly, two solenoid valves are fitted into the coolant pipes which lead to the heater, providing independent control of coolant flow through the matrix halves (a further main supply valve is fitted on air conditioning models). Temperature control is further achieved by blending cool air from outside the vehicle (or from the air conditioning system) with the warm air from the heater matrix, in the desired ratio.

Refer to Sections 11 and 12 for information on the air conditioning system.

Precautions

 Warning: Do not attempt to remove the pressure cap, or disturb any part of the cooling system, while the engine is hot, as there is a high risk of scalding. If the pressure cap must be removed before the engine and radiator have fully cooled (even though this is not recommended), the pressure in the cooling system must first be relieved. Cover the cap with a thick layer of cloth, to avoid scalding, and slowly unscrew the pressure cap until a hissing sound is heard (be prepared to refit the cap quickly if bubbling noises are heard and hot coolant starts to come out). When the hissing stops, indicating that the pressure has reduced, slowly unscrew the pressure cap until it can be removed; if more hissing sounds are heard, wait until they have stopped before unscrewing the cap completely. At all times, keep your face well away from the pressure cap opening, and protect your hands.

 Warning: Do not allow antifreeze to come into contact with your skin, or with the painted surfaces of the vehicle. Rinse off spills immediately, with plenty of water. Never leave antifreeze lying around in an open container, or in a puddle in the driveway or on the garage floor. Children and pets are attracted by its sweet smell, but antifreeze can be fatal if ingested.

 Warning: The viscous cooling fan will be rotating all the time when the engine is running, while an electric fan could cut in even if the engine is not running (if the ignition is on). Be careful to keep your hands, hair, and any loose clothing well clear when working in the engine compartment - the fan blades are particularly sharp on these models.

2 Cooling system hoses - disconnection and renewal

1 The number, routing and pattern of hoses will vary according to model, but the same basic procedure applies. Before commencing work, make sure that the new hoses are to hand, along with new hose clips if needed. It is good practice to renew the hose clips at the same time as the hoses.

2 Drain the cooling system as described in Chapter 1A or 1B, saving the coolant if it is fit for re-use. Squirt a little penetrating oil onto the hose clips if they are corroded.

3 Release the hose clips from the hose concerned. The clip most commonly used on the Mercedes-Benz is the worm-drive clip, which is released by turning its screw anti-clockwise (see illustrations). The spring clip is released by squeezing its tags together with pliers, at the same time working the clip away from the hose stub. The 'sardine-can' clips are not re-usable, and are best cut off with snips or side cutters.

4 Unclip any wires, cables or other hoses

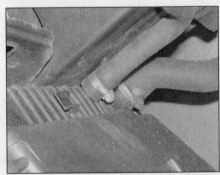

2.3a Radiator expansion tank and bottom hoses

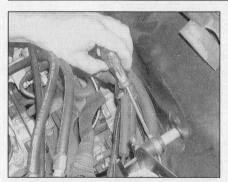

2.3b Unscrewing a heater hose worm-drive clip

3.3a Disconnect the air temperature sensor wiring plug . . .

3.3b . . . and unscrew the intercooler pipe mounting nut

which may be attached to the hose being removed. Make notes for reference when reassembling, if necessary.

5 Release the hose from its stubs with a twisting motion. Be careful not to damage the stubs on delicate components such as the radiator, or thermostat housings. If the hose is stuck fast, the best course is often to cut it off using a sharp knife, but again be careful not to damage the stubs.

6 Before fitting the new hose, smear the stubs with washing-up liquid or a suitable rubber lubricant to aid fitting. Do not use oil or grease, which may attack the rubber.

7 Fit the hose clips over the ends of the hose, then fit the hose over its stubs. Work the hose into position. When satisfied, locate and tighten the hose clips.

8 Refill the cooling system as described in Chapter 1A or 1B. Run the engine, and check that there are no leaks.

9 Recheck the tightness of the hose clips on any new hoses after a few hundred miles.

10 Top-up the coolant level if necessary (see *Weekly checks*).

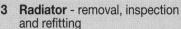

3 Radiator - removal, inspection and refitting

Removal

1 Refer to Chapter 1A or 1B and drain the cooling system.

2 On automatic transmission models, clamp the transmission fluid cooler hoses, ideally using proprietary hose clamps. Unscrew the hose unions from the base of the radiator (do not confuse the cooler hoses with the air conditioning pipes, where applicable). Carefully withdraw and cover the hoses.

3 On turbo-diesel models, loosen the hose clips at either end of the intercooler pipe which runs across the top of the radiator. Disconnect the wiring plug from the air temperature sensor, and unscrew the upper mounting nut **(see illustrations)**. Remove the pipe from the top of the radiator.

Models without air conditioning

4 Carefully prise out the retaining spring clips

securing the top of the fan shroud to the radiator. Disengage the shroud from the radiator, and either place it over the fan blades or remove it completely **(see illustrations)**.

5 Disconnect the wiring plug from the coolant level sensor in the radiator header tank **(see illustration)**, and move the wiring clear of the radiator.

6 If not already done, slacken the clips and disconnect the top and bottom hoses from the radiator.

7 Squeeze and release the plastic retaining catch at each end of the radiator, and slide them upwards to remove **(see illustration)**.

8 Where applicable, remove the spring clips securing the front air scoop to the top of the radiator, then lift the scoop upwards to

release the two locating lugs at the base of the radiator, and remove the scoop completely.

9 Pull out the two studs (where fitted) which locate the radiator in the lower mounting rubbers.

10 Check to make sure there is nothing still attached to the radiator, nor anything which will hinder its removal.

11 Carefully lift the radiator upwards out of its lower mountings, and withdraw it from the car. If the cooling fan has not been removed, take care not to damage the radiator fins (or the fan blades) as the radiator is removed.

Models with air conditioning

12 Refer to Chapter 11, Section 11, and remove the bonnet lock and crossmember.

3.4a Remove the fan shroud securing clips . . .

3.4b . . . and lift out the fan shroud

3.5 Disconnecting the coolant level sensor wiring plug

3.7 Release the radiator retaining clip from each end of the radiator

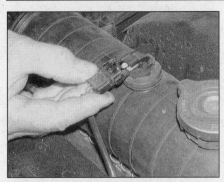

3.13 Unclip the expansion tank hose from the top of the radiator

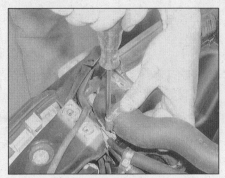

3.14a Slacken the hose clip . . .

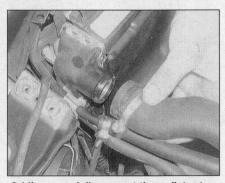

3.14b . . . and disconnect the radiator top hose

13 Release the coolant expansion tank hose from the clip on the upper panel, and lay it over the engine **(see illustration)**.
14 If not already done, slacken the clips and disconnect the top, bottom and, where applicable, the expansion tank hoses from the radiator **(see illustrations)**.
15 Remove the cooling fan as described in Section 5.
16 Where applicable, unclip and remove the grille cover from the front of the radiator.
17 Remove the two bolts securing the condenser to the top of the radiator **(see illustration)**; **do not** disconnect the condenser pipework.
18 Check to make sure there is nothing still attached to the radiator, nor anything which will hinder its removal.
19 Carefully lift the radiator upwards out of its lower mountings, and withdraw it from the car **(see illustration)**. Take care not to damage the radiator fins as the radiator is removed.

Inspection

20 Clear the radiator core of flies, small leaves or other debris by brushing or hosing. Check the condition of all hoses, clips, mountings and retaining spring clips, and renew as necessary.
21 Carefully examine the radiator for signs of leaks, corrosion of the alloy core, or damage to the plastic side, top or bottom compartments, as applicable. Should the radiator require attention, this work should be

left to a specialist due to the nature of its construction.

Refitting

22 Refitting the radiator is the reverse sequence to removal, noting the following points:
 a) *Ensure that the lower mounting lugs properly engage with the rubber mountings, and that (where applicable) the locating studs are pressed fully home.*
 b) *Make sure that the radiator and fan shroud retaining clips are a secure fit.*
 c) *On automatic transmission models, tighten the radiator fluid cooler unions to the specified torque.*
 d) *After fitting, fill the cooling system as described in Chapter 1A or 1B.*
 e) *On automatic transmission models, check the transmission fluid level as described in Chapter 1A or 1B.*

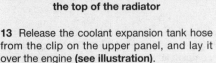

4 Thermostat - removal, testing and refitting

1 As the thermostat ages, it will become slower to react to changes in water temperature. Ultimately, the unit may stick in the open or closed position, and this causes problems. A thermostat which is stuck open will result in a very slow warm-up; a thermostat which is stuck shut will lead to rapid overheating.

2 Before assuming that the thermostat is to blame for a cooling system problem, check the coolant level. If the system is draining due to a leak, or has not been properly filled, there may be an air-lock in the system (refer to the coolant renewal procedure in the relevant part of Chapter 1).
3 If the engine seems to be taking a long time to warm up (based on heater output or temperature gauge operation), the thermostat is probably stuck open.
4 Equally, a lengthy warm-up period might suggest that the thermostat is missing - it may have been removed or inadvertently omitted by a previous owner or mechanic. Don't drive the vehicle without a thermostat - the engine management system's ECU will then stay in warm-up mode for longer than necessary, causing emissions and fuel economy to suffer.
5 If the engine runs hot, use your hand to check the temperature of the radiator top hose. If the hose isn't hot, but the engine is, the thermostat is probably stuck closed, preventing the coolant inside the engine from escaping to the radiator - renew the thermostat. Again, this problem may also be due to an air-lock (refer to the coolant renewal procedure in the relevant part of Chapter 1).
6 If the radiator top hose is hot, it means that the coolant is flowing and the thermostat is open. Consult the *Fault finding* section at the end of this manual to assist in tracing possible cooling system faults.
7 To gain a rough idea of whether the thermostat is working properly when the engine is warming up, without dismantling the system, proceed as follows.
8 With the engine completely cold, start the engine and let it idle, while checking the temperature of the radiator top hose. Periodically check the temperature indicated on the coolant temperature gauge - if overheating is indicated, switch the engine off immediately.
9 The top hose should feel cold for some time as the engine warms up, and should then get warm quite quickly as the thermostat opens.
10 The above is not a precise or definitive test of thermostat operation, but if the system does not perform as described, remove and test the thermostat as described below.

3.17 Remove the condenser securing bolts

3.19 Removing the radiator

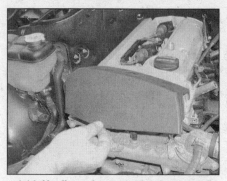

4.14 Unclip and remove the thermostat housing cover

4.15a Disconnect the radiator top hose . . .

4.15b . . . and the smaller bypass hose (where applicable) from the housing

Removal

11 The thermostat is located in a housing which is bolted to the side of the coolant pump. On petrol models, the thermostat and cover are one unit - do not attempt to separate the thermostat from the cover, or it will be damaged.

12 Disconnect the battery negative cable and position it away from the terminal. Drain the cooling system as described in Chapter 1A or 1B.

13 Where applicable, remove the screws and detach the plastic panel from above the radiator. Release the coolant hose from the clip on the upper panel.

14 On petrol models, unclip and remove the plastic cover fitted over the housing (see illustration).

15 Slacken the clip and detach the coolant hose(s) from the thermostat cover (see illustrations).

16 Unscrew the securing bolts, and remove the thermostat cover from the housing. If the cover is stuck to the housing, tap it gently, or carefully rock it back and forth to free it - do not lever between the mating faces. Recover the O-ring seal (see illustrations).

17 On diesel models, lift the thermostat from its housing, noting its orientation.

Testing

18 Check the temperature marking stamped

4.16a Unscrew the bolts and remove the thermostat housing (O-ring arrowed)

on the thermostat, or refer to the opening temperature quoted in this Chapter's Specifications.

19 Using a thermometer and container of water, heat the water until the temperature corresponds with the temperature marking stamped on the thermostat.

20 Suspend the (closed) thermostat on a length of string in the water, and check that maximum opening occurs within two minutes.

21 Remove the thermostat and allow it to cool down; check that it closes fully.

22 If the thermostat does not open and close as described, or if it sticks in either position, it must be renewed. Frankly, if there is any question about the operation of the thermostat, renew it.

4.16b Separating the thermostat from the housing

Refitting

23 Commence refitting by thoroughly cleaning the mating faces of the cover and the housing.

24 Refit the thermostat to the housing, noting that the spring-loaded side faces into the housing. On diesel models, the recess on the thermostat rim must be aligned with the rib on the housing cover (see illustration).

25 Lay a new seal in position on the housing, ensuring that it is correctly seated (see illustration).

26 Fit the cover to the thermostat housing, then refit the securing bolts, and tighten to the specified torque.

27 Further refitting is a reversal of removal. Refill the cooling system as described in Chapter 1A or 1B.

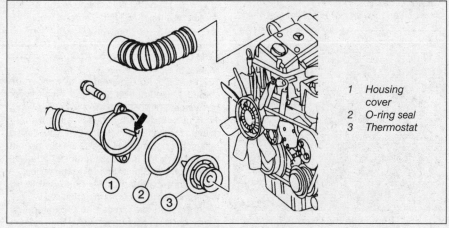

1 Housing cover
2 O-ring seal
3 Thermostat

4.24 Thermostat details on diesel engines - housing cover rib arrowed

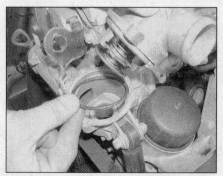

4.25 When refitting the thermostat, use a new O-ring seal

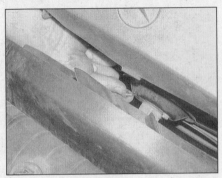

5.5a Where necessary, unscrew . . .

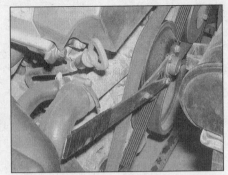

5.5b . . . and remove two of the cooling fan pulley bolts

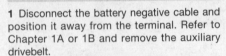

5.5c Bolt the holding tool (see Tool Tip) to the cooling fan pulley

5 Cooling fan - removal and refitting

1 Disconnect the battery negative cable and position it away from the terminal. Refer to Chapter 1A or 1B and remove the auxiliary drivebelt.

2 Where applicable, remove the screws and detach the plastic panels from above and below the radiator. Release the coolant hose from the clip on the upper panel.

Viscous fan - petrol models

3 If the shroud is to be removed as well as the fan, prise off the metal spring clips at the top, then lift the shroud to disengage the two lower locating lugs. Depending on model, it may now be possible to remove the shroud completely. If not, leave the shroud where it is for now, as moving it will interfere with removing the fan. Once the fan nut has been undone, the fan and shroud can be removed together.

4 If there is no requirement to remove the shroud, it need not be disturbed - the fan can be manoeuvred out with the shroud in place.

5 The coolant pump pulley must be held against rotation as the fan viscous pulley nut is loosened. On some models, flats are provided on the front face of the pulley, which can be gripped using a large open-end spanner or adjustable pliers. If not, make up a holding tool from a metal strip with two holes

drilled in it, then remove two of the pulley bolts, and bolt the tool to the pulley (see illustrations).

To make a fan pulley holding tool, obtain two lengths of steel strip about 6 mm thick by 20 to 30 mm wide or similar, one 400 mm long, the other 100 mm long (all dimensions approximate). Bolt the two strips together to form a forked end, leaving the bolt slack so that the shorter strip can pivot freely. At the end of each 'prong' of the fork, drill a hole to accept a slightly longer bolt of the same thread size as the pulley bolts just removed. We found it necessary to grind the ends of the fork legs to a taper, to avoid the legs overlapping. Bolt the fork legs through the holes in the pulley - the longer strip can then be held to prevent rotation as the fan nut is unscrewed

5.6 Using a large open-ended spanner to unscrew the fan pulley nut

5.7 Removing the viscous fan

6 Using a large open-end spanner, loosen the fan pulley nut, which has a **left-hand thread** - ie it unscrews **clockwise (see illustration)**. Special spanners are available from good tool stockists, specifically for this purpose. On our project car, the nut size was 36 mm - check before buying a spanner, however.

7 Unscrew the fan pulley nut completely, and remove the fan from the engine **(see illustration)**.

8 If required, the fan can be separated from the viscous unit by unscrewing the retaining bolts. Note that the fan has a rib cast on it, to ensure it will only fit to the viscous unit in one position; the front of the unit is also marked VORNE FRONT.

9 Refitting is a reversal of removal.

Viscous fan - diesel models

10 On four-cylinder models, the fan is removed using the same procedure as that described previously for petrol models. For five-cylinder models, proceed as described below.

11 On models with the turbo-diesel engine, release the clips securing the turbocharger air feed pipe at the base of the radiator and at the front of the engine, and remove the pipe.

12 If the shroud is to be removed as well as the fan, prise off the metal spring clips at the top, then lift the shroud to disengage the two lower locating lugs. Depending on model, it may now be possible to remove the shroud completely. If not, leave the shroud where it is for now, as moving it will interfere with removing the fan. Once the fan nut has been undone, the fan and shroud can be removed together.

13 If there is no requirement to remove the shroud, it need not be disturbed - the fan can be manoeuvred out with the shroud in place.

14 The coolant pump pulley must be held against rotation as the pulley bolt is loosened. Make up a holding tool from a metal strip with two holes drilled in it, then remove two of the pulley bolts, and bolt the tool to the pulley.

15 Unscrew the fan pulley bolt completely, and remove the fan from the engine.

16 If required, the fan can be separated from the viscous unit by unscrewing the retaining bolts. Note that the fan has a rib cast on it, to

5.18 Disconnecting the radiator cooling fan wiring plug

5.19 Removing one of the fan assembly securing clips

5.20 Lifting out the electric fan assembly

5.21 The fan motor is secured by three screws (arrowed)

5.25a Electric cooling fan control unit location under left-hand front wheel arch

5.25b Disconnecting the fan control unit wiring plug

ensure it will only fit to the viscous unit in one position; the front of the unit is also marked VORNE FRONT.

17 Refitting is a reversal of removal.

Electric fan - all models

18 Pull or prise the cooling fan wiring plug upwards to disconnect it **(see illustration)**.

19 Support the cooling fan assembly, then prise up and remove the two metal clips at the top of the radiator **(see illustration)**.

20 Carefully lift out the cooling fan assembly, and remove it from the engine compartment **(see illustration)**.

21 The fan motor is secured by three screws **(see illustration)**, while the fan itself is secured to the motor by a circlip.

22 Refitting is a reversal of removal.

Electric fan control unit

23 To gain access to the control unit, the front section of the left-hand front wheel arch liner must first be removed.

24 The front section of the wheel arch liner is secured by two bolts visible in the wheel arch, one bolt from underneath, and one from the side. Two further screws secure the liner to the lower edge of the bumper. Remove the liner from under the car.

25 Depress the top and bottom catches and disconnect the wiring plug from the front of the unit **(see illustrations)**.

26 Unscrew the two mounting nuts, and remove the unit from the car.

27 Refitting is a reversal of removal.

6.3a Coolant level sensor on radiator header tank . . .

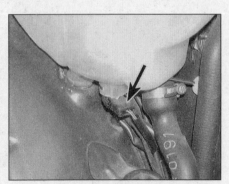

6.3b . . . and on base of expansion tank (arrowed)

6 Cooling system electrical switches - removal and refitting

Coolant level sensor

1 The sensor is mounted in the base of the coolant expansion tank, or on top of the header tank, as applicable. Before starting, ensure that the engine is cold.

2 On models with an expansion tank, refer to the relevant part of Chapter 1 and partially drain the cooling system, so that only the expansion tank is emptied.

3 Ensure that the ignition is switched off, then unplug the wiring from the coolant level switch at the connector **(see illustrations)**.

4 Remove the circlip and withdraw the sensor. Recover the O-ring seal if it is loose.

5 Connect a continuity tester, or a workshop multimeter, set to measure resistance across the sensor terminals. With the float held at the top of its travel, the contacts should be open-circuit. If the float is allowed to hang at the bottom of its travel, the contacts should close, indicated by a short-circuit.

6 Refit the level sensor by following the removal procedure in reverse, noting the following points:
a) Fit a new O-ring seal to the sensor body.
b) On completion, where necessary top-up the cooling system as described in Chapter 1A, 1B or Weekly checks.

6.8 Unclip and remove the plastic cover from the thermostat housing

6.9 Later models with air conditioning have just one sensor

6.16a Loosen the hose clips . . .

Temperature gauge coolant sensor

Petrol models

7 The temperature gauge sensor is screwed into the thermostat housing on the front of the engine.

8 Unclip and remove the plastic cover fitted over the housing **(see illustration)**.

9 On models without air conditioning, the gauge sensor is the sensor nearest the thermostat cover, and can be identified by its single wire connector. On early models with air conditioning, the sensor nearest the thermostat cover serves the air conditioning system, and the one next to it serves the temperature gauge. Later air conditioning models have just one sensor for both functions, the sensor being the one nearest the thermostat cover **(see illustration)**.

10 Ensure that the engine is cold, then refer to Chapter 1A and partially drain the cooling system. Alternatively, if the system is not drained, be prepared for some coolant loss when the sensor is removed.

11 Disconnect the wiring connector from the sensor, then unscrew the sensor and remove it from the housing. Recover the sealing ring.

12 Clean the threads of the sensor, and the location in the housing. Check the condition of the sealing ring, and fit a new one if necessary.

13 Refitting is a reversal of removal, noting the following points:
a) Use a smear of sealant on the threads, and tighten it securely.
b) On completion, top-up the cooling system as described in Chapter 1A or Weekly checks.

Diesel models

14 The sensor that drives the temperature gauge is threaded into the upper surface of the cylinder head, on the left-hand side of the engine, at the rear. Do not confuse it with the fuel system coolant temperature sensor, which is mounted nearby.

15 Ensure that the engine is cold, then refer to Chapter 1B and partially drain the cooling system.

16 On 5-cylinder models, loosen the hose clips at either end, and remove the air pipe

which runs across the top of the engine - this then allows access to the sensor, through the centre branches of the inlet manifold **(see illustrations)**.

17 Ensure that the ignition is switched off, then unplug the wiring from the sensor at the connector.

18 Unscrew the sensor from the cylinder head, and recover the sealing ring **(see illustration)**.

19 Refitting is a reversal of removal, noting the following points:
a) Use a new sealing ring.
b) On completion, top-up the cooling system as described in Chapter 1B or Weekly checks.

Fuel system coolant temperature sensor

Petrol models

20 The coolant temperature sensor used by the fuel system is located next to the temperature gauge sensor, in the third sensor location from the thermostat cover (on models without air conditioning, the first sensor location in the thermostat housing is blanked off).

21 Removal and refitting details are identical to the temperature gauge sensor, described previously in this Section.

22 Note that later models use the information provided by the temperature gauge sensor, and a separate sensor for use by the fuel system is not fitted.

Diesel models

23 The coolant temperature sensor used by the fuel system is located next to the temperature gauge sensor in the cylinder head.

24 Removal and refitting details are identical to the temperature gauge sensor, described previously in this Section.

25 Note that later models use the information provided by the temperature gauge sensor, and a separate sensor for use by the fuel system is not fitted.

7 Coolant pump - removal and refitting

Petrol models

Removal

1 Disconnect the battery negative cable and position it away from the terminal. Refer to Chapter 1A and drain the cooling system.

2 On models with a viscous fan, remove the cooling fan as described in Section 5.

3 Noting their locations, loosen the hose clips and disconnect the coolant hoses from the ports on the coolant pump.

4 Slacken, but do not remove, the bolts securing the coolant pump pulley.

5 Remove the auxiliary drivebelt as described in Chapter 1A.

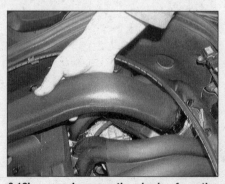

6.16b . . . and remove the air pipe from the top of the engine

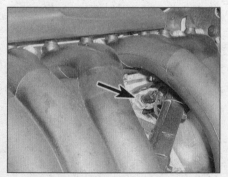

6.18 Coolant temperature sensor (arrowed) - 5-cylinder model shown

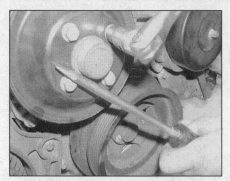

7.6 If necessary, use a screwdriver as shown when loosening the pulley bolts

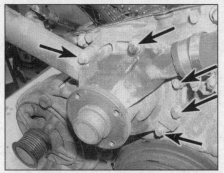

7.7 Five of the eight coolant pump bolts (arrowed)

7.8 Removing the coolant pump

6 Remove the bolts and washers, and take off the coolant pump pulley **(see illustration)**.

7 Loosen and remove the eight bolts securing the coolant pump, noting their locations, as they are of different lengths **(see illustration)**.

8 Lift off the pump, and where applicable, recover the gasket **(see illustration)**. The pump was originally fitted using sealant, but a paper gasket is available.

Refitting

9 Carefully clean the coolant pump and cylinder block mating surfaces, removing all traces of the old gasket or sealant. Take care to avoid scoring the surfaces, as this will cause leakage.

10 Refit the coolant pump by following the removal procedure in reverse, noting these points:

a) *If the pump is to be refitted using a bead of sealant instead of a gasket, apply the sealant in an even bead to the pump body only. Do not apply an excessive amount, as any excess may enter the pump and then the cooling system itself, which could block the radiator passages.*

b) *If a paper gasket was used, fit a new gasket when refitting* **(see illustration)**.

c) *Tighten the pump bolts in a diagonal sequence to the correct torque, noting the different figures for the different size bolts used.*

d) *Refit the viscous cooling fan with reference to Section 5.*

e) *Refit and tension the auxiliary drivebelt with reference to Chapter 1A.*

f) *On completion, refill the cooling system with reference to Chapter 1A.*

Diesel models

Removal

11 Disconnect the battery negative cable and position it away from the terminal. Refer to Chapter 1B and drain the cooling system.

12 On models with a viscous fan, remove the cooling fan as described in Section 5.

13 Slacken, but do not remove, the bolts securing the coolant pump pulley.

14 Remove the auxiliary drivebelt as described in Chapter 1B.

15 Remove the bolts and washers, and take off the coolant pump pulley.

16 Referring to Section 3 of Chapter 2B, set the engine to TDC on No 1 piston. Ensure that

the engine is not turned once this position has been set.

17 Paint or scribe alignment marks between the TDC sensor mounting bracket and the front of the engine, for use when refitting. Note that the pointer should be aligned with the TDC marking (0/T) on the vibration damper **(see illustration)**.

18 Unbolt the TDC sensor mounting bracket, and place it to one side. If preferred, trace the wiring from the sensor back to its wiring connector, and disconnect it.

19 Loosen and remove the eight coolant pump mounting bolts, then pull the pump from the housing, noting that it is located on two dowels. Recover the gasket, and discard it.

Refitting

20 Carefully clean the coolant pump and housing mating surfaces, removing all traces of the old gasket. Take care to avoid scoring the surfaces, as this will cause leakage.

7.10 Where applicable, fit a new gasket when refitting the pump

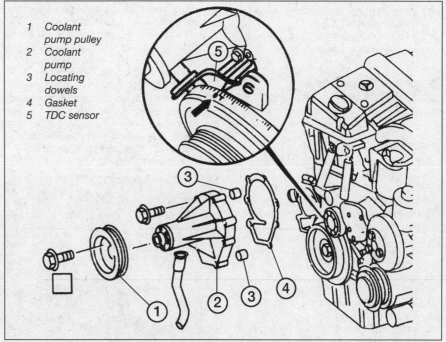

1 Coolant pump pulley
2 Coolant pump
3 Locating dowels
4 Gasket
5 TDC sensor

7.17 Coolant pump removal details

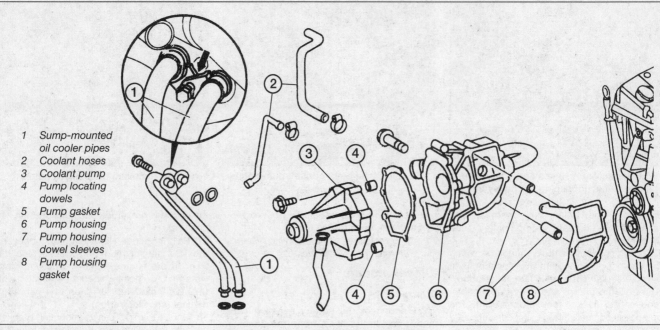

1 Sump-mounted oil cooler pipes
2 Coolant hoses
3 Coolant pump
4 Pump locating dowels
5 Pump gasket
6 Pump housing
7 Pump housing dowel sleeves
8 Pump housing gasket

8.5 Coolant pump housing removal details

21 Refit the coolant pump by following the removal procedure in reverse, noting these points:
  a) *Use a new gasket, and tighten the pump bolts in a diagonal sequence to the correct torque.*
  b) *Carefully align the marks made on the TDC sensor bracket when refitting it.*
  c) *Refit the viscous cooling fan with reference to Section 5.*
  d) *Refit and tension the auxiliary drivebelt with reference to Chapter 1B.*
  e) *On completion, refill the cooling system with reference to Chapter 1B.*

8 Coolant pump housing (diesel models) - removal and refitting

Removal

1 Proceed as described in Section 7, paragraphs 11 to 15 inclusive.
2 Refer to Chapter 5A and remove the alternator, together with its mounting bracket.
3 On models up to July 1994 with the sump-mounted oil cooler, remove the bolt securing the coolant pipes to the pump housing, noting how the mounting bracket is fitted. Prise the pipes out of the housing, and recover the O-ring seals.
4 Noting their fitted positions, loosen the hose clips and disconnect the coolant hoses from the pump housing.
5 Loosen and remove the seven bolts retaining the pump housing to the cylinder block, noting the locations of the bolts and of the two dowel sleeves **(see illustration)**.

6 Take off the housing, and recover the gasket (a new one must be used when refitting).
7 If required, the coolant pump can be unbolted from the housing - refer to Section 7 for more information.

Refitting

8 Carefully clean the pump housing mating surfaces, removing all traces of the old gasket. Take care to avoid scoring the surfaces, as this will cause leakage.
9 Refit the housing using a reversal of the removal procedure, noting the following points:
  a) *Use a new gasket, and tighten the housing bolts in a diagonal sequence to the correct torque. Ensure that the dowel sleeves are refitted to their original locations.*
  b) *When reconnecting the oil cooler pipes, use new O-rings, and coat them with fresh coolant (not oil).*

9.6 Unbolt the drivebelt tensioner damper from the housing

  c) *Refit the alternator and its mounting bracket using the information in Chapter 5A.*
  d) *Refit the cooling fan with reference to Section 5.*
  e) *Refit and tension the auxiliary drivebelt with reference to Chapter 1B.*
  f) *On completion, refill the cooling system with reference to Chapter 1B.*

9 Thermostat housing (petrol models) - removal and refitting

Removal

1 Disconnect the battery negative cable and position it away from the terminal. Drain the cooling system as described in Chapter 1A or 1B.
2 Remove the cooling fan as described in Section 5 - this is not essential on all models, but it does improve working room.
3 Unclip and remove the plastic cover fitted over the housing.
4 Disconnect the coolant hose(s) from the housing.
5 Noting the location of each, disconnect the wiring and vacuum connections from the switches and sensors on the housing - refer to Section 6 if necessary.
6 Unbolt the drivebelt tensioner damper from the end of the housing, and move it to one side **(see illustration)**.
7 Unscrew and remove the five housing mounting bolts, noting their locations as they are of different lengths. Two of the bolts are

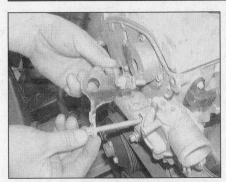

9.7 Two of the thermostat housing bolts also secure the engine lifting eye

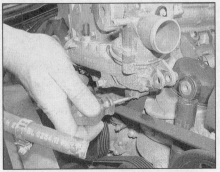

9.8 Loosen the hose clip under the thermostat location

9.9a Remove the housing from the front of the engine, noting the O-ring seal (arrowed) . . .

used to secure the engine front lifting eye **(see illustration)**.

8 Loosen the hose clip from the pipe at the base of the housing **(see illustration)**.

9 Remove the housing from the engine, lifting the pipe stub out of the hose and recovering the O-ring seal **(see illustrations)**.

Refitting

10 Refitting is a reversal of removal. Tighten the housing bolts to the specified torque.

10 Heater/ventilation components - removal and refitting

Facia vents

Side vents

1 Using a small screwdriver inserted through the vent grilles, release the tabs securing the speakers at either end of the facia **(see illustration)**. Lift up the speaker and disconnect the wiring plug.

2 Unscrew and remove the two screws in each speaker aperture which secure the facia vents **(see illustration)**.

3 Lift up the two retaining tabs at the base of each vent, and remove them from the ends of the facia **(see illustrations)**.

4 Refitting is a reversal of removal.

Centre vents

5 Remove the radio/cassette player as described in Chapter 12.

6 Remove the two screws above and below the radio aperture in the facia **(see illustration)**.

9.9b . . . and lifting it out of the hose

7 Pull the lower edge of the facia centre panel outwards, then unhook the side and top edges from the facia **(see illustration)**.

10.1 Release the speaker using a small screwdriver

10.2 Unscrew and remove the vent securing screws

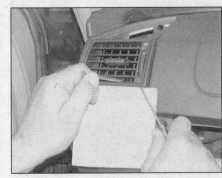

10.3a Lift up the tabs at the base of the vent . . .

10.3b . . . and prise the vent from its location

10.6 Facia centre panel securing screws (arrowed)

10.7 Removing the facia centre panel

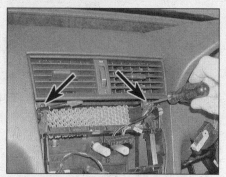

10.8a Remove the lower screws (arrowed) . . .

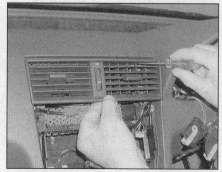

10.8b . . . then prise down the upper clips and remove the centre vent assembly

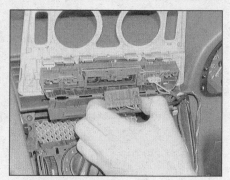

10.12 Disconnecting one of the facia centre panel wiring plugs

Removing the panel this far is sufficient to remove the centre vents; it is preferable, however, to remove the panel completely, as follows. Unclip the cover which fits over the switch panel wiring plugs. Noting their locations, disconnect the wiring from the switches, and remove the panel complete with switches.

8 The centre vents are secured by two screws at the bottom, and two clips at the top. Remove the screws and prise the clips downwards, then pull the centre vents from the facia **(see illustrations)**.

9 Refitting is a reversal of removal.

Heater control panel

10 Remove the radio/cassette player as described in Chapter 12.

11 Remove the two screws above and below the radio aperture in the facia.

12 Pull the lower edge of the facia centre panel outwards, then unhook the side and top edges from the facia. Unclip the cover which fits over the switch panel wiring plugs. Noting their locations, disconnect the wiring from the switches **(see illustration)**, and remove the panel complete with switches.

13 The heater control panel is secured by two screws and two clips at its top edge. Remove the screws, then prise the clips to the side and release the panel **(see illustration)**.

14 Pull the panel rearwards, disengaging the two operating rods at the rear from the heater unit.

15 Slide the locking lever to the side, and separate the large wiring plug at the rear of

the panel before removing it from the car **(see illustrations)**.

16 Refitting is a reversal of removal, taking care to engage the operating rods with the heater unit as the panel is refitted - this can be an awkward operation.

Heater blower motor

17 Remove the passenger lower facia panel as described in Chapter 11, Section 41.

18 Slide the two white plastic locking clips towards each other to release the blower motor access panel **(see illustration)**.

19 Disconnect the wiring plug, then lower the access panel down and remove it **(see illustrations)**.

20 Unscrew the two screws securing the blower motor resistor pack, then lower the

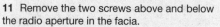

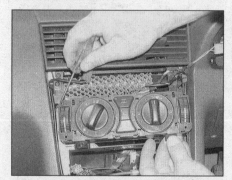

10.13 Remove the two screws, then prise the clips apart and remove the heater control panel

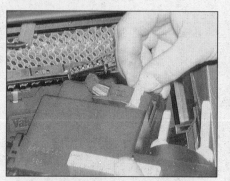

10.15a Slide the locking lever to one side . . .

10.15b . . . then disconnect the wiring plug from the heater control panel

10.18 Slide the two white clips towards each other

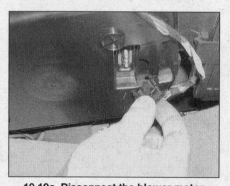

10.19a Disconnect the blower motor wiring plug . . .

10.19b . . . then lower the access panel

resistor pack and disconnect the two wires from it, noting which way round they are connected **(see illustrations)**.

21 Unscrew and remove the four Torx screws securing the blower motor, then lower it out from under the facia **(see illustrations)**.

22 Refitting is a reversal of removal, making sure that all wiring connections are securely remade.

Heater solenoid valves

Driver/passenger control valves

23 Wait until the engine is completely cold, then drain the cooling system as described in the relevant part of Chapter 1. Note, however, that draining the system may well not remove the coolant from the heater pipework, so some spillage is likely. Alternatively, if the coolant is not due for renewal, don't drain the system, and pack some rags around the hose connections at the valves before disconnecting them.

24 Disconnect the wiring plug from the valve unit **(see illustration)**.

25 Noting their locations for refitting, unscrew the hose clips and disconnect the three coolant hoses from the valves. Be prepared for coolant spillage, even if the system was drained.

26 Release the valve unit from its mounting bracket by compressing the two rubber mountings so that they will pass through the mounting bracket holes.

27 Refitting is a reversal of removal, noting the following points:
a) If necessary, use a little liquid soap (washing-up liquid) to ease the rubber mountings into place.
b) Make sure that the coolant hose connections are correctly and securely remade.
c) Refill or top-up the cooling system as necessary, as described in the relevant part of Chapter 1 or Weekly checks.

Main supply valve

28 The main supply valve is only fitted to models with air conditioning.

29 Wait until the engine is completely cold, then drain the cooling system as described in the relevant part of Chapter 1. Note, however,

10.20a Remove the two securing screws (arrowed) . . .

10.21a Remove the four Torx screws (arrowed) . . .

that draining the system may well not remove the coolant from the heater pipework, so some spillage is likely. Not draining the system is not an option in this case, as the low position of the valve will result in far more coolant being spilled.

30 Disconnect the wiring plug from the valve unit **(see illustration)**.

31 Noting their locations for refitting, unscrew the hose clips and disconnect the two coolant hoses from the valve. Be prepared for coolant spillage.

32 Release the valve unit from its mounting bracket by sliding off the rubber mounting.

33 Refitting is a reversal of removal, noting the following points:
a) If necessary, use a little liquid soap (washing-up liquid) to ease the rubber mounting into place.

10.20b . . . then lower the resistor pack and disconnect the wiring

10.21b . . . and remove the blower motor from under the facia

b) Make sure that the coolant hose connections are correctly and securely remade.
c) Refill the cooling system as described in the relevant part of Chapter 1.

Inlet air temperature sensor

34 A temperature sensor is fitted on the right-hand side of the heater unit, to monitor the temperature of the incoming air. On models with air conditioning, this sensor is mounted behind the evaporator, so that it effectively monitors the temperature of the refrigerated air.

35 Remove the facia as described in Chapter 11.

36 Disconnect the wiring plug at the right-hand side of the heater unit **(see illustration)**.

10.24 General view of the solenoid valves - wiring plug arrowed

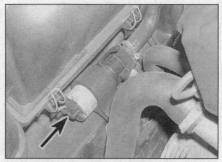

10.30 Main supply valve, seen from above with air cleaner removed - wiring plug arrowed

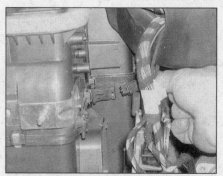

10.36 Disconnect the temperature sensor wiring plug at the right-hand side

10.37 Removing the inlet air temperature sensor

10.41 Disconnect the wiring plug from the front of the heater unit

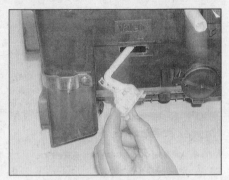

10.42 Removing the main outlet temperature sensor

37 Withdraw the sensor by tilting it backwards and downwards out of its location (see illustration).
38 Refitting is a reversal of removal.

Outlet air temperature sensors

Main (front) sensor

39 The outlet air temperature sensor fitted to the front of the heater unit actually contains two sensing probes - one for each side of the front passenger compartment. The heater matrix is divided internally into two sections, providing independent heating outputs to the driver and front seat passenger. The temperature sensor monitors heat output from both sections of the matrix, and regulates coolant flow through each section via the solenoid control valves.

10.47a Using a small screwdriver, release the retaining lugs . . .

40 Remove the heater control panel as described previously in this Section. Access is very awkward, but the only alternative is to remove the facia completely, as described in Chapter 11.
41 Disconnect the wiring plug from the sensor (see illustration).
42 Prise the sensor out from its location (see illustration). This is an awkward enough task even with the facia removed, as the sensor pipe bends around inside the heater unit, and there is only just sufficient room to manoeuvre it out.
43 Refitting is a reversal of removal.

Footwell (side) sensors

44 Temperature sensors are also fitted into the front footwell vents, at the sides of the heater unit.
45 Remove the centre console as described in Chapter 11.
46 Remove the driver's or passenger's lower facia panel, as described in Chapter 11, Section 41.
47 Using a small screwdriver, release the sensor retaining lugs, and pull out the sensor sideways (see illustrations).
48 Disconnect the wiring plug from the sensor, and remove it from the car (see illustration).
49 Refitting is a reversal of removal.

Heater unit

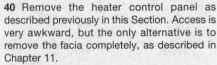 Warning: On models fitted with air conditioning, the air conditioning refrigerant MUST

be discharged prior to removal - see Section 11 for further details.
50 Drain the cooling system as described in the relevant part of Chapter 1.
51 Remove the facia as described in Chapter 11, and the steering column as described in Chapter 10.
52 Where fitted, remove the passenger airbag as described in Chapter 12.
53 In order to remove the heater unit, the facia support bar must be removed. This is a fairly major part of the car's structure, and its removal is a very involved operation. It is essential that the location and routing of all wiring is noted carefully as removal proceeds.
54 Noting their locations very carefully for refitting, disconnect the earth wires and various sections of wiring harness from the facia support bar. There are several cable-ties which must be cut through; feed the harness around the support bar in such a way that will allow the bar to eventually be removed. Note that the wiring plugs for the instrument panel can be dismantled by sliding off the end plate from the main wiring plug, and separating the smaller wiring plugs by sliding them apart (see illustrations).
55 On later models, there are various coloured vacuum hoses at the left-hand end of the heater unit which must be disconnected. To gain access to the connectors, the left-hand kick panel must be removed from the left-hand side of the passenger footwell. Pull off the rubber seal

10.47b . . . and remove the sensor from the side

10.48 Disconnect the wiring plug from the sensor

10.54a To separate the instrument panel wiring plug sections, slide off the end plate . . .

10.54b ... and pull the plug sections apart

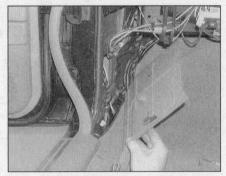
10.55a Remove the footwell kick panel ...

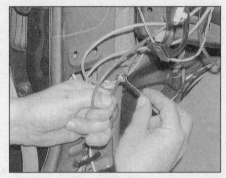
10.55b ... and separate the vacuum hose connections

from the door aperture, then remove the central screw from the panel, and release the panel from the two clips on the door aperture. Separate the vacuum connectors using a small open-ended spanner **(see illustrations)**.
56 Once the wiring harnesses have been sufficiently withdrawn, ease out the ducts which supply the facia end vents **(see illustration)**.
57 Once you are satisfied that the facia support bar is ready to be unbolted, move to the engine compartment and disconnect the supply hoses to the heater unit, as follows.
58 Remove the windscreen wiper motor and linkage as described in Chapter 12.
59 Remove the retaining screws and unclip the covers from the fuse and module boxes on the left- and right-hand sides of the engine compartment bulkhead **(see illustration)**.
60 Peel off the rubber weather seal fitted to the top edge of the bulkhead.
61 Withdraw the lower section of the windscreen cowl panel, which is secured by a number of screws and clips, and by two rubber 'nuts' in the centre **(see illustrations)**.
62 Prise out the wiring harnesses running to the fuse and module boxes to release them from the bulkhead centre section. Remove the centre section from the bulkhead by releasing the plastic clips at either end and pulling the panel upwards **(see illustrations)**.
63 Noting their locations very carefully, unscrew the hose clips and disconnect the coolant hoses for the heater unit at the bulkhead. There are two (supply) connections

10.56 Removing the passenger side vent duct

10.59a Remove the screws ...

10.59b ... and lift off the fuse/module box cover

10.61a The lower section of the cowl panel is held in by a number of clips ...

at the driver's side, one return connection at the passenger side **(see illustrations)**. Position some rags below all connections, as

there will still be some coolant spillage, either now or when the heater unit is finally removed.

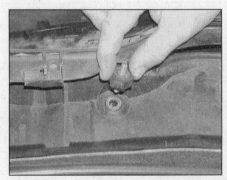
10.61b ... and by two rubber 'nuts'

10.62a Prise out the harness 'grommets' ...

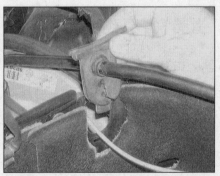
10.62b ... and lift the harnesses out of the bulkhead

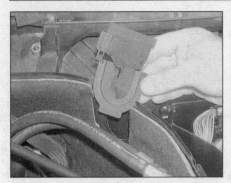

10.62c Unclip and remove the retaining clips . . .

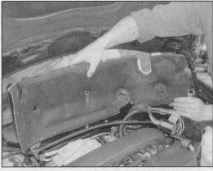

10.62d . . . and lift out the bulkhead centre section

10.63a Unscrew the hose clips from the heater supply pipes . . .

64 On models with air conditioning, the refrigerant pipes must now be disconnected at the point where they pass through the

10.63b . . . and from the return pipe (arrowed)

bulkhead. It is ESSENTIAL that the refrigerant has been discharged by a professional before this is done. Even so, it is recommended that

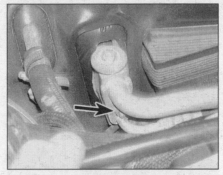

10.65a Unscrew the nut (arrowed) which secures the pipe retaining plate . . .

gloves are worn when separating the pipe connection, as some gas may still be present.
65 Unscrew the nut which secures the air conditioning pipe retaining plate, then pull the pipes out of the bulkhead, and recover the O-ring seals. New seals must be used when refitting. Cover the pipe ends to prevent dirt ingress **(see illustrations)**.
66 Returning to the inside of the car, remove the nuts and bolts which secure the facia support bar. There are two nuts/bolts at each end, two (shorter) bolts above the steering column location, and one at the centre. There are three nuts to remove - two in the centre, and one on the passenger side. Note that some of the fasteners are also used to secure earth leads **(see illustrations)**.
67 As the facia support bar is removed, the parking brake cable must be unhooked from

10.65b . . . then withdraw the plate and separate the air conditioning pipes

10.65c Cover the pipe ends (here using a finger cut from a rubber glove)

10.66a Facia support bar bolt at the centre . . .

10.66b . . . one at the side, with earth leads beneath . . .

10.66c . . . one above the steering column, again with earth leads . . .

10.66d . . . and a nut in the centre (not all fasteners shown)

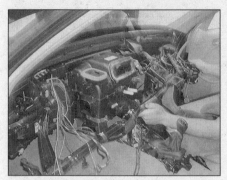

10.67 Removing the facia support bar

10.68 Disconnect the temperature sensor wiring plug at the right-hand side

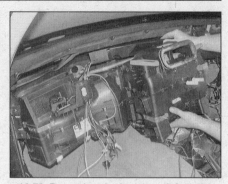

10.70 Removing the heater unit into the car

it. Feed the wiring harnesses over and around the bar as necessary, as the bar is removed **(see illustration)**. The help of an assistant is particularly useful here.

68 Disconnect the small wiring plug from the inlet air temperature sensor on the right-hand side of the heater unit **(refer to illustration 10.36)**.

69 Disconnect the outlet air temperature sensor wiring plug from the front of the unit, and the two wiring plugs (one on each side) from the temperature sensors in the footwell vents **(refer to illustrations 10.41 and 10.48)**.

70 With the aid of an assistant, carefully pull the heater unit into the car **(see illustration)**. As this is done, note that it will be necessary to release the main wiring harness which is cable-tied to the passenger side rear of the unit, and the harness plastic trunking, which is stuck to the top of the heater unit with heavy cloth tape. The assistant should also check that the heater (and where applicable) air conditioning pipes pass through the bulkhead safely.

71 Refitting is a reversal of removal, noting the following points:

a) *Work very methodically when refitting the heater unit, to ensure that nothing is overlooked. For instance, take care to re-attach the wiring harness plastic trunking when the unit is first offered into place.*

b) *Have an assistant manoeuvre the heater unit into the car, then have the assistant check very carefully that the heater (and where applicable) air conditioning pipes are correctly aligned with their respective holes in the bulkhead, before pushing the unit into place.*

c) *Use new seals when reconnecting the air conditioning pipes, where applicable.*

d) *Take care not to confuse the two heater supply hoses when reconnecting them. In all cases, tighten the hose clips securely. Inspect the hose ends carefully - if there are signs of splitting, consider fitting new heater hoses, to avoid future leaks.*

e) *It is advisable not to refit the windscreen cowl panels or wiper linkage until after the heater operation has been checked. Especially if a new heater matrix has been fitted, it may be necessary to relieve an airlock in the system by loosening the*

heater coolant connections (NOT the air conditioning pipes) to bleed off air.

f) *Route all wiring harnesses as noted during removal, and secure where necessary with new cable-ties.*

g) *On completion, refill the cooling system as described in the relevant part of Chapter 1, then run the engine and check the heater operation. It is not unknown for a heater not to work initially, due to the formation of an airlock (especially when a new heater matrix has been fitted). Follow the advice on dealing with airlocks given in the coolant renewal Section of Chapter 1A or 1B.*

Heater matrix

72 To judge by our project car, the heater unit must be removed as described previously in this Section in order to remove the heater

matrix. The access cover in the top of the heater unit would not come off when the heater unit was in place, due partly to the wiring harness plastic trunking which is securely wedged between the heater unit, windscreen and bulkhead, preventing access to the cover screws. When the matrix was finally removed on the bench, it became apparent that there would not be enough room for the matrix to be lifted out with the heater unit in place, and to try would risk damaging the matrix fins.

73 With the heater unit removed, unscrew and remove the four screws which secure the matrix access cover. There is one screw beside each top vent (lift off the foam surround for access) and two screws at the rear, over the pipes. Lift away the cover, and take off the pipe support section **(see illustrations)**.

10.73a Lift off the foam insulation . . .

10.73b . . . for access to the screw beside each vent outlet

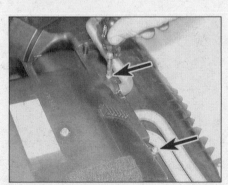

10.73c Remove the two screws (arrowed) at the rear . . .

10.73d . . . then lift off the access cover and pipe support plate

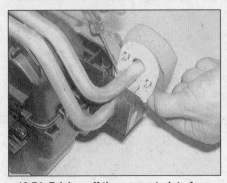

10.74 Prising off the support plate from the two inlet pipes

10.75a Remove the foam insulator . . .

10.75b . . . then undo two screws and remove the return pipe support

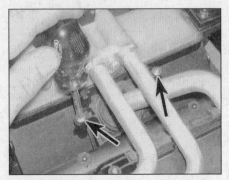

10.76 Remove two screws (arrowed) securing the heater pipework

10.77 Removing the heater matrix

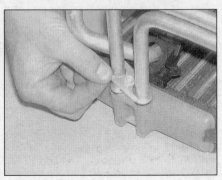

10.78a Unscrew the bolt, and remove the pipe retaining plate . . .

74 Prise off the plastic plate which locates the two heater supply pipes to the rear of the heater unit. Take off the plate, and recover the foam insulation **(see illustration)**.
75 Take off the foam insulator surrounding the single return pipe, then remove the two screws and slide the pipe retaining plate off the return pipe **(see illustrations)**.
76 Remove the two screws which secure the pipework to the top of the heater unit **(see illustration)**.
77 Taking care to support the heater pipework, lift the heater matrix out of the heater unit **(see illustration)**. Keep the matrix vertical, to avoid damaging the fins.
78 To remove the two heater supply pipes,

unscrew the bolt which secures the pipe retaining plate, and remove the plate. Carefully prise the two pipes out of the matrix, and recover the O-ring seals **(see illustrations)**. It is advisable to fit new seals as a matter of course, since all the dismantling work would have to be repeated, should the old seals leak when refitted.
79 The heater return pipe is retained in place by a large circlip, which can be extracted using pliers **(see illustration)**. Once again, it is advisable to fit a new O-ring seal.
80 Refitting is a reversal of removal. Note the points made in paragraph 71 when refitting the heater unit.

11 Air conditioning system - general information and precautions

An air conditioning system is fitted as standard equipment on later high-specification models, and was available as an optional extra on some lower-specification models. In conjunction with the heater, the system enables any reasonable air temperature to be achieved inside the car, it also reduces the humidity of the incoming air, aiding demisting even when cooling is not required.

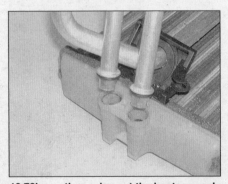

10.78b . . . then prise out the heater supply pipes . . .

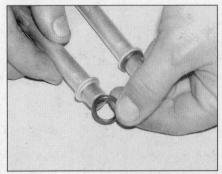

10.78c . . . and recover the O-ring seals

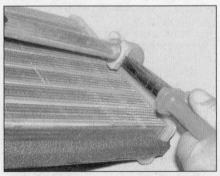

10.79 Removing the circlip which retains the heater return pipe

The refrigeration circuit of the air conditioning system functions in a similar way to a domestic refrigerator. A compressor, belt-driven from the crankshaft pulley, draws refrigerant in its gaseous state from an evaporator. The refrigerant heats up as a result of being compressed, but is then passed through a condenser (mounted in front of the engine radiator) where it loses heat and enters its liquid state. After dehydration, the refrigerant is passed through an evaporator (mounted alongside the heater/ventilation unit) where it is allowed to expand and reverts to being gas. This change of state has the effect of absorbing heat from the air passing over the evaporator fins, reducing its temperature. This cool air is mixed with warm air from the heater unit to achieve the desired cabin temperature. The refrigerant is directed back to the compressor and the cycle is then repeated.

Various subsidiary controls and sensors protect the system against excessive temperature and pressures. Additionally, engine idle speed is increased when the system is in use to compensate for the additional load imposed by the compressor. Electronic sensors detect the rotational speed differential between the engine and the compressor - if this becomes too great (due to a malfunctioning compressor), the compressor clutch is disengaged, to preserve the drivebelt.

Note: *The air conditioning electronic control system can only be tested using dedicated equipment. For this reason, it is recommended that problems with the operation of the air conditioning system are referred to a Mercedes-Benz dealer for diagnosis.*

 Warning: The refrigeration circuit contains pressurised liquid refrigerant. The refrigerant is potentially dangerous, and should only be handled by qualified persons. Refrigerant that is allowed to come into contact with the skin will cause severe frostbite. It is not itself poisonous, but in the presence of a naked flame (including inhalation through a lighted cigarette), it forms a poisonous gas. Uncontrolled discharging of the

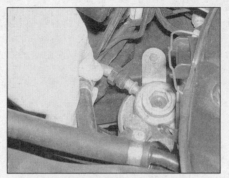
12.3a Disconnect the refrigerant lines (note the use of gloves) . . .

refrigerant is dangerous and is also extremely damaging to the environment. For these reasons, disconnection of any part of the system without specialised knowledge and equipment is not recommended.

Do not allow refrigerant lines to be exposed to temperatures in excess of 110°C (230°F), for example during welding or paint-drying operations.

Do not operate the air conditioning system if it is known to be short of refrigerant, or component damage may result.

12 Air conditioning system components - removal and refitting

 Warning: Refer to the previous Section before proceeding. Before carrying out any of the procedures detailed below, the air conditioning system MUST be professionally discharged by a garage or air conditioning specialist.

Note: *The car may be driven once the system has been discharged, but the air conditioning system should NOT be switched on, as this will cause damage to the compressor. The safest option is to have the system discharged where the car is to be worked on, and not move the car until the system has been recharged. With air conditioning becoming an increasingly common fitment, mobile air*

12.3b . . . and cover the pipe ends (here with a finger cut from a glove)

conditioning specialists are becoming more widespread.

Receiver/drier

1 The receiver/dryer is mounted at the front of the engine compartment, on the left-hand side (left as seen from the driver's seat).
2 Disconnect the wiring plug from the unit.
3 Gloves must be worn when disconnecting the refrigerant lines, even though the system will have been discharged at this point (refer to the warning at the start of this Section). Unscrew the unions on the two pipes, and disconnect them from the receiver/dryer. Recover the O-ring seals - new ones must be used when refitting. Cover the pipe ends, to prevent the entry of foreign matter **(see illustrations)**.
4 Unscrew the two mounting bolts, and lift the receiver/dryer out from its location **(see illustration)**.
5 It is most important that the openings on the receiver/dryer are covered over, so that they are air-tight. The unit contains silica gel, which will absorb moisture from the atmosphere all the time the openings are left uncovered. Eventually, this will mean that a new unit is required.
6 Refitting is a reversal of removal, noting the following points:
 a) *Use new O-ring seals when reconnecting the refrigerant lines, and tighten the unions securely.*
 b) *Have the system professionally recharged before attempting to use it.*

Condenser

7 Remove the radiator as described in Section 3.
8 Gloves must be worn when disconnecting the refrigerant lines, even though the system will have been discharged at this point (refer to the warning at the start of this Section). Unscrew the unions on the two pipes at the base of the condenser, and disconnect them **(see illustration)**. Recover the O-ring seals - new ones must be used when refitting. Cover the pipe ends, to prevent the entry of foreign matter.
9 Carefully lift the condenser out of its lower mountings, and remove it from the car, taking care not to damage the fins or pipework.

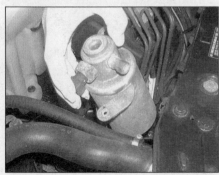
12.4 Unscrew the mounting bolts, and lift out the receiver/dryer

12.8 Showing the two refrigerant pipe unions at the base of the condenser

12.12a Slide the two clips at the front upwards and downwards respectively . . .

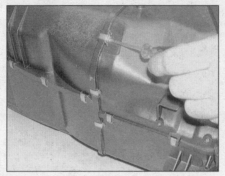

12.12b . . . release the clips on the vertical joint . . .

12.12c . . . and separate the blower housing from the heater unit

10 Refitting is a reversal of removal, noting the following points:
  a) Use new O-ring seals when reconnecting the refrigerant lines, and tighten the unions securely.
  b) Have the system professionally recharged before attempting to use it.

Evaporator

11 Remove the heater unit and heater matrix as described in Section 10.
12 The blower motor housing must be separated from the heater unit for access to the evaporator. Slide off the two clips at the front of the heater unit, then use a small screwdriver to prise off the small clips which run along the vertical joint between the heater unit and blower housing **(see illustrations)**.
13 Reach inside the heater unit, and release the temperature flap link rod from the end fitting on the operating rod **(see illustration)**.
14 Using a small screwdriver, prise off the small clips which secure the upper and lower halves of the heater unit casing. There are sixteen clips in total - take care that they do not fly off when they are released **(see illustration)**.
15 Remove the three screws which secure the top half of the heater unit casing. There are two screws on top of the unit, one behind each vent outlet, and one screw above the pipe connection at the rear of the unit **(see illustrations)**.
16 Lift the top half of the heater unit casing, and separate it from the lower half and the evaporator **(see illustration)**.
17 Lift the evaporator out of the casing, taking care not to damage the fins or side pipework **(see illustration)**.
18 Refitting is a reversal of removal. Refit the heater matrix and heater unit as described in Section 10.

Compressor

19 Remove the auxiliary drivebelt as

12.13 Disconnect the link rod from the end fitting (arrowed)

12.14 Releasing the clips securing the upper and lower halves of the heater casing

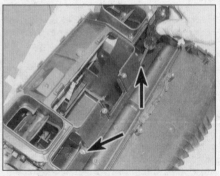

12.15a Remove the screw behind each top vent outlet (arrowed) . . .

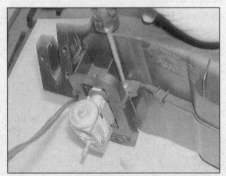

12.15b . . . and the one above the pipe connection at the rear

12.16 Lifting off the upper half of the heater casing

12.17 Lift out the evaporator, taking care not to damage it

described in the relevant part of Chapter 1.

20 Disconnect the wiring plug from the top of the compressor **(see illustration)**.

21 If the compressor is being removed as part of another procedure (such as engine removal), it is sufficient to remove the mounting bolts (see paragraph 22) and tie the compressor up to one side, without disconnecting the refrigerant lines. If the compressor is being removed completely, proceed as follows.

22 Gloves must be worn when disconnecting the refrigerant lines, even though the system will have been discharged at this point (refer to the warning at the start of this Section). Unscrew the unions on the two pipes on the compressor, and disconnect them. Recover the O-ring seals - new ones must be used when refitting. Cover the pipe ends, to prevent the entry of foreign matter.

23 Support the compressor (it is a heavy unit) and remove the mounting bolts. Depending on the exact type of compressor, and on the

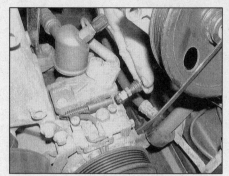

12.20 Disconnecting the wiring plug from the compressor

12.23 Removing the air conditioning compressor

engine to which it is fitted, there will be either three or four mounting bolts. Lift the compressor out of the engine compartment, and remove it **(see illustration)**.

24 It is advisable to cover the openings on the compressor while it is removed, to reduce oil loss and to prevent foreign matter from entering.

25 Refitting is a reversal of removal, noting the following points:

a) *Use new O-ring seals when reconnecting the refrigerant lines, and tighten the unions securely.*

b) *Tighten the mounting bolts securely.*

c) *Have the system professionally recharged before attempting to use it.*

Chapter 4 Part A:
Fuel system - multipoint petrol injection

Contents

Degrees of difficulty

Easy, suitable for novice with little experience		**Fairly easy,** suitable for beginner with some experience		**Fairly difficult,** suitable for competent DIY mechanic	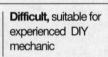	**Difficult,** suitable for experienced DIY mechanic		**Very difficult,** suitable for expert DIY or professional	

Specifications

General

System type:
  1.8 litre engines:

Up to 6/96 (111.920)	Bosch PMS sequential, closed-loop fuel injection/ignition system
From 6/96 (111.921)	Bosch HFM sequential, closed-loop fuel injection/ignition system.

  2.0 litre engines:

Up to 5/97 (111.941)	Bosch PMS sequential, closed-loop fuel injection/ignition system
From 6/97 (111.945)	Bosch HFM sequential, closed-loop fuel injection/ignition system.
2.2 litre (111.961) and 2.3 litre (111.974) engines	Bosch HFM sequential, closed-loop fuel injection/ignition system.

Torque wrench settings

	Nm	lbf ft
Anti-roll bar right-hand bracket	20	15
Camshaft position sensor	10	7
Crankshaft position sensor	10	7
Fuel filter union bolt/nut	26	19
Fuel gauge sender unit retaining ring	55	41
Fuel pump union bolt/nut	26	19
Fuel rail to cylinder head	25	18
Fuel tank strainer and return adapter	40	30
Fuel tank support straps:		
Right- and left-hand straps	40	30
Centre strap/bracket	20	15
Idle speed control actuator/throttle body	10	7
Inlet manifold-to-cylinder head bolts/nuts	20	15
Knock sensor	20	15
Lambda sensor	55	41

1 General information and precautions

Bosch HFM (**H**ot **F**ilm engine **M**anagement) and PMS (**P**ressure engine **M**anagement **S**ystem) are electronic engine management systems that primarily control the fuel injection and ignition. This chapter deals mainly with the fuel system components; the ignition system components are dealt with in Chapter 5B.

The major components of the fuel system are a fuel tank, an electric fuel pump, a fuel filter, fuel supply and return lines, a throttle body, a fuel rail, a fuel pressure regulator, four electronic fuel injectors, and an Electronic Control Unit (ECU), together with its associated sensors, actuators and wiring. The overall function of each of these components is outlined below.

The fuel tank is mounted horizontally beneath the loadspace floorpan. A fuel level sender unit is mounted in the bottom of the tank.

The fuel pump is of the electric, roller-cell type and is mounted under the floorpan at the rear of the vehicle. The pump motor is cooled by the fuel, in which both the pump and the pump motor are permanently immersed. The pump contains a non-return valve, which prevents the fuel supply line from emptying when the engine is switched off, and also isolates the fuel tank from the rest of the fuel system. The pump also contains a pressure relief valve, to prevent excessive fuel pressure build-up in the event of a restriction occurring.

The fuel pump delivers a constant supply of fuel through a cartridge filter to the fuel rail, at a slightly higher pressure than required - the fuel pressure regulator maintains a constant fuel pressure to the fuel injectors and returns excess fuel to the tank via the return line. This constant flow system also helps to reduce fuel temperature and prevents vaporisation.

The fuel injectors are electromagnetic valves, opened and closed by the Electronic Control Unit (ECU), which calculates the injection timing and duration according to engine speed, crankshaft position, throttle position, inlet air mass flow rate, inlet air temperature, coolant temperature and exhaust gas oxygen content information, received from sensors mounted on and around the engine.

Inlet air is drawn into the engine through the air cleaner, which contains a renewable paper and mesh filter element. From there, the air is drawn through the air mass meter. This device, unlike vane-type air flow meters, is sensitive to changes in air density. This means that when the vehicle is driven at high altitudes, the fuelling is adapted automatically to suit the 'thinner' air, without the need for separate barometric pressure measurement.

Idle speed control is achieved partly by an idle speed control module, mounted on the side of the throttle body and partly by the ignition system, which gives fine control of the idle speed by altering the ignition timing.

The exhaust gas oxygen content is constantly monitored by the ECU via the lambda sensor, which is mounted in the exhaust pipe, in front of the catalytic converter. The ECU then uses this information to modify the injection timing and duration to maintain the optimum air/fuel ratio - a result of this is that manual adjustment of the idle exhaust CO content is not necessary or possible. In addition, all models are fitted with a catalytic converter in the exhaust system - see Chapter 4C for details.

The ECU also controls the operation of the activated charcoal filter evaporative loss system - refer to Chapter 4C, Section 2, for further details.

It should be noted that fault diagnosis of the engine management system described in this Chapter is only possible with dedicated electronic test equipment. Problems with the systems operation should therefore be referred to a Mercedes-Benz dealer for assessment. Once the fault has been identified, the removal/refitting sequences detailed in the following Sections will then allow the appropriate component(s) to be renewed as required.

Precautions

 Warning: Many of the procedures in this Chapter require the removal of fuel lines *and connections, which may result in some fuel spillage. Before carrying out any operation on the fuel system, refer to the precautions given in Safety First! at the beginning of this manual, and follow them implicitly. Always switch off the ignition before working on the fuel system. Petrol is a highly-dangerous and volatile liquid, and the precautions necessary when handling it cannot be overstressed.*

Note: *Residual pressure will remain in the fuel lines long after the vehicle was last used. Before disconnecting any fuel line, first depressurise the fuel system as described in Section 11.*

2 Accelerator cable - removal, refitting and adjustment

Models with a direct control cable

Removal

1 Working in the engine compartment, remove the cover from the inlet manifold for access to the throttle linkage **(see illustration)**.

2 Disconnect the accelerator inner cable from the throttle relay lever by prising out the square retaining block and passing the inner cable through the slot in the lever **(see illustration)**.

3 Release the outer cable from its support bracket by compressing the lugs on the plastic retainer **(see illustration)**.

4 Working in the driver's footwell, remove the lower trim cover, then disconnect the inner cable from the pedal by pulling out the holder with the expanding pin.

5 Press the accelerator cable through the rubber grommet in the bulkhead and into the engine compartment.

6 Withdraw the cable from the engine compartment.

7 Check the condition of the rubber grommet and if necessary renew it by prising it from the bulkhead.

Refitting

8 Refit the cable by following the removal

2.1 Removing the cover from the throttle linkage on the inlet manifold

2.2 Releasing the inner cable from the throttle lever

2.3 Compress the plastic tabs to release the outer cable from the support bracket

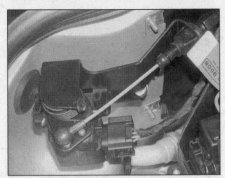

2.12 Accelerator cable (remote) attachment to the electronic module in the left-hand rear corner of the engine compartment

procedure in reverse, using a little grease to lubricate the moving parts. On completion adjust the operation of the cable as described in the following sub-section.

Adjustment

9 Check that the accelerator cable and linkage operate smoothly, without any stiffness or binding. Check that the cable is not kinked at any point along its length and lubricate the linkage if required.

10 With the linkage in the idle position, there should be 0.5 to 1.0 mm freeplay between the compression spring at the end of the accelerator cable inner and the plastic retaining block in the throttle guide lever. Turn the adjustment knob at the support bracket to achieve this, if necessary.

11 Adjustment of the throttle linkages should not be necessary, following renewal of the accelerator cable. If, however, the linkages have been disturbed, or are badly worn, adjust them as follows. Note that the adjustment affects the operation of the idle speed microswitch, so accurate adjustment is essential. Disconnect the connecting rod at one end, then check that the throttle lever is in its fully closed position. Offer the rod onto its pivot ball while checking that it is not under any tension. If necessary, adjust the length of the rod, then shorten the rod by turning the ball socket two complete turns. Refit the rod and lock the ball socket by tightening the locknut. On manual transmission models, fully depress the accelerator pedal and check that the lever on the throttle body is resting against the full throttle stop - if not, adjust the accelerator pedal stop inside the car. On automatic transmission models, fully depress the pedal, but do not operate the kickdown switch, then check that the lever on the throttle body is resting against the full throttle stop - if not, adjust the outer cable at the support bracket. After making an adjustment, check the clearance described in paragraph 10 again, however on automatic transmission models, make the adjustment at the pedal end of the cable, inside the car.
Note: *On models with cruise control, refer to Section 13.*

Models with remotely-located cable

Removal

12 Working in the left-hand rear corner of the engine compartment, release the inner cable socket from the ball on the electronic accelerator pedal module **(see illustration)**.
13 Release the outer cable from its support bracket by compressing the lugs on the plastic retainer.
14 Working in the driver's footwell, remove the lower trim cover, then disconnect the inner cable from the pedal by pulling out the holder with the expanding pin.
15 Press the accelerator cable through the rubber grommet in the bulkhead and into the engine compartment.
16 Withdraw the cable from the engine compartment.
17 Check the condition of the rubber grommet and if necessary renew it by prising it from the bulkhead.

Refitting

18 Refit the cable by following the removal procedure in reverse, using a little grease to lubricate the moving parts. On completion adjust the operation of the cable as described in the following sub-section, however, note that adjustment of the electronic module requires the use of a specialist Mercedes-Benz hand-tester. If the module has been renewed, or if its operation is suspect, the vehicle should be taken to a dealer for the adjustment.

Cable adjustment

19 Check that the accelerator cable and linkage operate smoothly, without any stiffness or binding. Check that the cable is not kinked at any point along its length and lubricate the linkage if required.
20 With the linkage in the idle position, there should be 0.5 to 1.0 mm freeplay at the end of the inner cable. If necessary, turn the adjustment nut at the end of the outer cable to achieve the correct freeplay.

3 Air cleaner and filter element - removal and refitting

Air filter element

Removal

1 Release the coolant expansion tank purge hose from the clip on the air cleaner cover, then prise open each of the cover retaining clips **(see illustrations)**.
2 Lift off the air cleaner cover and remove the air filter element **(see illustration)**.

Refitting

3 Clean out all debris from the inside of the air cleaner assembly.
4 Fit the new filter by following the removal procedure in reverse, ensuring that the filter element is fitted the correct way up, according to the markings on its upper surface.

3.1a Release the coolant expansion tank purge hose from the clip . . .

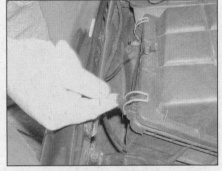

3.1b . . . then prise up the spring clips . . .

3.1c . . . and plastic clip to release the cover from the air cleaner body

3.2 Lift the cover and remove the air filter element

3.8 Disconnecting the inlet air duct from the front of the air cleaner

3.9 Pulling the air cleaner body from the rubber mountings

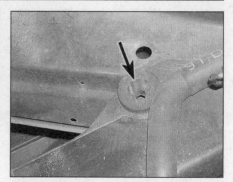

3.10 Air cleaner body mounting rubber

Air cleaner assembly

Removal

5 Remove the air filter element as described in the previous sub-Section.

6 On models with the HFM injection system, release the clip and disconnect the air cleaner cover from the airflow meter. Recover the O-ring seal.

7 On models with the PMS injection system, loosen the clip and disconnect the air cleaner cover from the airflow meter.

8 Disconnect the inlet air duct from the front of the air cleaner (see illustration).

9 Carefully pull the air cleaner body from the front mounting rubber grommet (see illustration).

10 Check the mounting rubber for damage and if necessary renew it (see illustration). On models with the HFM injection system, also check the O-ring seal between the air cleaner and airflow meter and renew it if necessary.

Refitting

11 Refitting is a reversal of removal.

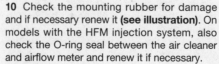

4   Fuel filter -
     removal and refitting

> *Warning: Observe the precautions in Section 1 before working on any component in the fuel system.*

Removal

1 The fuel filter is mounted in the fuel supply line, adjacent to the fuel tank (see illustration). Access is from the underside of the vehicle.

2 Temporarily remove the fuel tank filler cap in order to release pressure from the fuel system (refer to Section 11 and depressurise the fuel system if necessary). Disconnect the battery negative (earth) lead and position it away from the terminal. The battery is located in the rear luggage compartment.

3 With the vehicle parked on a level surface, apply the parking brake and chock the front roadwheels. Raise the rear of the vehicle and support it securely on axle stands (see *Jacking and vehicle support*).

4 Remove the screws and lower the protective cover away from the fuel pump(s) and filter. Note that one of the screws is accessed through a hole in the bottom of the cover (see illustrations).

5 Clamp the flexible fuel supply hose to the fuel pump, and the fuel filter outlet hose using proprietary hose clamps (see illustration). Position a suitable container beneath the filter to catch any spilled fuel.

6 Undo (or loosen) the central screw and release the mounting clamp plate from the bottom of the fuel pump and filter (see illustration).

7 Note the positional arrow on the filter body indicating the correct location, then release the clips and disconnect the inlet and outlet

4.1 The fuel filter (large diameter) is located next to the fuel pump (small diameter)

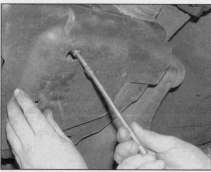
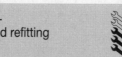

4.4a Undo the screws . . .

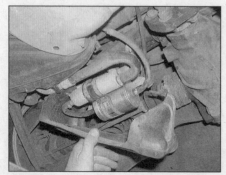

4.4b . . . and lower the protective cover away from the fuel pump and filter

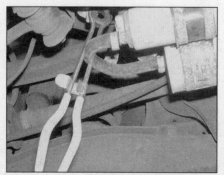

4.5 Using a hose clamp on the fuel pump-to-filter outlet hose

4.6 Removing the mounting clamp plate

4.7a Disconnect the inlet . . .

4.7b . . . and outlet hoses from the fuel filter

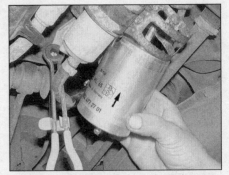

4.9 Make sure that the positional arrow is pointing towards the fuel flow to the front of the car

hoses from each end of the filter **(see illustrations)**. Withdraw the filter from under the car. Where necessary, recover the insulation sleeve. **Note:** *Some early models may be fitted with a union nut and bolt, together with copper washers, instead of normal hose fittings.*

Refitting

8 Refitting is a reversal of removal, but where necessary renew the insulation sleeve if it is damaged. Where a union nut and bolt is fitted, renew the copper washers and tighten the nut and bolt to the specified torque.

9 Where standard hoses are fitted, make sure that the positional arrow is pointing the correct way (ie, towards the fuel line leading to the front of the vehicle) **(see illustration)**.

5 Fuel gauge sender unit - removal and refitting

> ⚠ *Warning: Observe the precautions in Section 1 before working on any component in the fuel system.*

Removal

1 This work must be carried out with the fuel tank empty. This is best achieved by waiting until the tank is almost empty through the

course of normal driving. Any remaining fuel can be drained by unscrewing the drain plugs from the sender units before removing them.

2 Disconnect the battery negative (earth) lead and position it away from the terminal. The battery is located in the rear luggage compartment.

3 There are two fuel gauge sender units, each one located at the lower front of each half of the fuel tank. Chock the front roadwheels, then jack up the rear of the vehicle and support on axle stands (see *Jacking and vehicle support*).

4 Unbolt and remove the covers from the bottom front of each tank half, for access to the sender units.

5 Fit a hose clamp to the fuel supply hose, then loosen the clip and disconnect the hose from the left-hand fuel gauge sender unit **(see illustration)**.

6 Disconnect the fuel gauge wiring from each sender unit **(see illustration)**.

7 Unscrew the drain plugs from the sender units, and drain any remaining fuel from each half of the tank.

8 The retaining rings must now be loosened and removed. To do this, Mercedes-Benz technicians use a special tool which engages the holes in the ring. Ideally, this tool should be obtained, however it should be possible to fabricate a home-made version using metal bar and suitable-sized bolts.

9 With the rings removed, carefully withdraw the sender units from the fuel tank. Recover the special shaped gaskets. Note the location stud and groove to ensure correct refitting. When removing the left-hand sender unit, disconnect the internal pipes leading to each half of the tank.

Refitting

10 Refitting is a reversal of removal, but always renew the sender unit gaskets, and tighten the retaining rings to the specified torque.

6 Fuel pump(s) - removal and refitting

> ⚠ *Warning: Observe the precautions in Section 1 before working on any component in the fuel system.*

Removal

Models with a single fuel pump

1 The fuel pump is mounted on the underside of the floorpan, at the rear of the vehicle, adjacent to the fuel filter **(see illustration)**.

2 Refer to Section 11 and depressurise the fuel system.

3 Disconnect the battery negative (earth) lead and position it away from the terminal. The

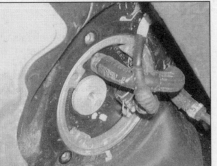

5.5 Fuel supply hose and sender wiring connected to the left-hand sender unit on the front of the fuel tank

5.6 Wiring connected to the right-hand sender unit on the front of the fuel tank

6.1 The fuel pump (small diameter) is located next to the fuel filter (large diameter)

battery is located in the rear luggage compartment.

4 Chock the front roadwheels, then jack up the rear of the vehicle and support on axle stands (see *Jacking and vehicle support*).

5 Working under the car, remove the screws and lower the protective cover away from the fuel pump and filter.

6 Use hose clamps to clamp the fuel supply hose to the fuel pump, and the fuel filter outlet hose. Do not use G-clamps as these may damage the hoses internally **(see Tool Tip)**.

TOOL TIP *If you don't have access to hose clamps, fit two 13 mm sockets over the jaws of a pair of Mole grips and use these to clamp the hose. The rounded sides of the sockets will prevent the wall of the hose being damaged.*

7 Remove the rear luggage compartment floor covering from inside the car, and lift the insulation from the floor for access to the fuel pump wiring. Disconnect the wiring at the connector, then prise the rubber grommet from the floor and feed the wiring through.

8 Position a container beneath the fuel pump to catch spilt fuel, then loosen the clip and disconnect the fuel supply hose from the fuel pump. Where fitted, also disconnect the ventilation hose from the fuel pump.

9 Loosen the clip and disconnect the fuel outlet hose from the fuel pump. **Note:** *Some models may be fitted with a union bolt and copper washers.*

10 Note the positional arrow on the fuel pump body indicating the fuel flow to the filter **(see illustration)**.

11 Unscrew the clamp bolt, release the clamp, and withdraw the fuel pump and plastic insulation sleeve. If necessary, the non-return valve may be unscrewed from the fuel pump outlet. Recover the sealing washer.

Models with twin fuel pumps

12 Some models are fitted with twin fuel pumps, mounted in series on the fuel tank side of the fuel filter. Removal of both pumps

6.10 The arrow on the fuel pump body must point towards the hose leading to the fuel filter

is similar to that already described in the previous paragraphs.

Refitting

13 Refitting is a reversal of removal, but renew the insulation sleeve if it is damaged. **Note:** *The fuel pump must **not** touch the mounting clamp, otherwise corrosion will occur.* Check the union copper washers and renew them if necessary. Tighten the union bolt to the specified torque. Note that the fuel pump incorporates a location lug which must engage the recess in the mounting bracket.

---

7 Fuel tank and expansion tank - removal and refitting

⚠ *Warning: Observe the precautions in Section 1 before working on any component in the fuel system.*

Fuel tank

Removal

1 The fuel tank must be emptied before the operation can be started. This is best achieved by waiting until the tank is almost empty through the course of normal driving. If necessary, any remaining fuel can be drained after supporting the vehicle on axle stands, by removing the drain plugs from the sender units in the bottom of each half section of the fuel tank. To do this remove the covers with reference to Section 5.

2 Park the vehicle on a level surface and chock the front roadwheels. Raise the rear of the vehicle, support it securely on axle stands (see *Jacking and vehicle support*) and remove the rear roadwheels.

⚠ *Warning: The use of an inspection pit is not advised; petrol vapours are heavier than air and can quickly build up on the floor of the pit, causing a potential hazard.*

3 Disconnect the battery negative (earth) lead and position it away from the terminal. The battery is located in the rear luggage compartment.

4 Remove the final drive unit as described in Chapter 8.

5 Remove the right-hand rear wheelarch liner, then loosen the clip attaching the filler neck to the fuel tank filler extension. Unscrew and remove the bolt securing the extension to the body.

6 Where necessary, remove the right-hand bracket of the anti-roll bar with reference to Chapter 10.

7 Remove the covers for access to the fuel gauge sender units at the bottom of each section of the fuel tank, if not already removed.

8 Fit a hose clamp to the fuel feed hose leading to the fuel pump, then loosen the union nut and disconnect the hose from the

tank. Also, where applicable, disconnect the ventilation hose from the fuel tank by loosening the clip.

9 Unscrew the nut and remove the vent line support bracket.

10 Support the fuel tank with a trolley jack and piece of wood to prevent damage.

11 Unscrew the nuts and remove the tank support straps.

12 Where necessary, remove the sound deadening mat from the tank.

13 Unscrew the nuts and remove the central shield from the front of the tank.

14 Loosen the clips and disconnect the vent lines from the upper left-hand side of the tank.

15 Carefully lower the fuel tank from the underbody, and remove from under the car.

16 Unscrew the fuel strainer from the tank and recover the O-ring seal.

17 Remove the gauge sender unit as described in Section 5.

18 Swill the tank out with clean fuel. If the tank shows signs of leakage, it should either be repaired by a specialist or renewed.

⚠ *Warning: Do not attempt to repair the tank yourself by welding, soldering or brazing. The tank will contain an explosive mixture of air and fuel vapour, even when emptied of liquid fuel.*

Refitting

19 Refit the fuel tank by reversing the removal procedure, but tighten all fixings to the correct torque, where specified.

Expansion tank

Removal

20 The fuel tank must be emptied before the operation can be started. This is best achieved by waiting until the tank is almost empty through the course of normal driving, and then draining out the remainder via the filler neck either by siphoning or by using a hand pump.

21 Disconnect the battery negative (earth) lead and position it away from the terminal. The battery is located in the rear luggage compartment.

22 Chock the front roadwheels, then jack up the rear of the vehicle and support on axle stands (see *Jacking and vehicle support*). Remove the right-hand rear roadwheel.

23 Remove the fuel tank filler cap.

24 Remove the right-hand rear wheelarch liner with reference to Chapter 11, Section 18.

25 Loosen the clip and disconnect the vent hose from the filler neck. Loosen the clip securing the main filler hose to the filler neck.

26 Unscrew the filler neck mounting bolt and nut.

27 Release the filler neck upper seal from the body, then pull the filler neck down and disconnect it from the filler hose.

28 Loosen the clip and disconnect the vent hose from the fuel expansion tank.

29 Unbolt the expansion tank mounting strap then tilt the tank down and withdraw it

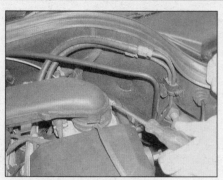

8.1a Loosen the clip . . .

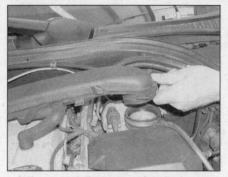

8.1b . . . and disconnect the air cleaner cross pipe from the throttle body

8.3 Disconnecting the fuel evaporative charcoal canister purge valve vacuum line from the throttle body

sufficiently far to access the air admission and vent hoses. Loosen the clips and disconnect the hoses.

Refitting

30 Refitting is a reversal of removal.

 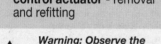

8 Throttle body/idle speed control actuator - removal and refitting

 Warning: Observe the precautions in Section 1 before working on any component in the fuel system.

Removal

1 Loosen the clips and remove the air cleaner cross pipe duct from between the air mass meter and throttle body/ idle speed control actuator **(see illustrations).**

2 Where applicable, disconnect and remove the crankcase ventilation hose from between the camshaft cover and the inlet manifold. Note the location arrows on the hose and inlet manifold.

3 Disconnect the vacuum line from the fuel evaporative charcoal canister purge valve **(see illustration).**

4 Unhook the throttle return spring.

5 Disconnect the throttle linkage intermediate

rod ball head from the throttle lever **(see illustration).**

6 Disconnect the wiring for the idle speed control actuator at the inlet manifold support bracket.

7 Unscrew the mounting bolts and withdraw the throttle body/actuator from the inlet manifold **(see illustrations).** Note the location of the support bracket.

8 Check the O-ring seal and if necessary renew it **(see illustration).**

Refitting

9 Refitting is a reversal of removal, but tighten the mounting bolts securely **(see illustration).**

---

9 Inlet manifold - removal and refitting

 Warning: Observe the precautions in Section 1 before working on any component in the fuel system.

Removal

1 Disconnect the battery negative (earth) lead and position it away from the terminal. The battery is located in the rear luggage compartment.

2 Loosen the clips and remove the air cleaner

8.5 Disconnecting the throttle linkage intermediate rod ball head from the throttle lever

8.7a Unscrew the mounting bolts . . .

8.7b . . . and lift the throttle body from the inlet manifold

8.8 Removing the throttle body O-ring seal

8.9 Refitting the throttle body to the inlet manifold

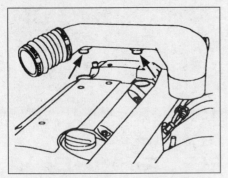

9.2 Release the inlet air ducting from the rubber mountings (arrowed) on the cylinder head cover

9.3a Disconnecting the fuel feed and return lines at the rear of the engine compartment

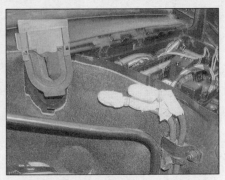

9.3b Seal the ends of the fuel lines with tape or polythene sheeting

cross pipe, at the same time releasing it from the rubber mountings **(see illustration)**.

3 Remove the fuel rail and injectors as described in Section 10. Alternatively, the fuel rail can be left in position and removed from the inlet manifold later. If this latter course of action is taken, disconnect the fuel feed and return lines at the rear of the engine compartment and tape over the ends of the lines **(see illustrations)**.

4 Unclip the wiring cable duct from the inlet manifold **(see illustration)**.

5 Unbolt the windscreen washer reservoir and position it to one side.

6 On models with a direct-type accelerator cable, remove the throttle body/idle speed control (LLR) actuator as described in Sec-

tion 8. Also where applicable disconnect the wiring from the partial inlet manifold preheater.

7 On models with a direct-type accelerator cable, unbolt the support bracket from the throttle linkage bracket **(see illustration)**.

8 On early models (pre 12/94) disconnect the wiring from the ignition coils, then unbolt and remove the coils. Refer to Chapter 5B if necessary.

9 Disconnect the evaporative purge valve vacuum hose from the inlet manifold **(see illustration)**.

10 Unscrew the union nut and disconnect the brake servo unit vacuum hose from the inlet manifold. Check that all vacuum hoses have been disconnected.

11 Unscrew the bolt securing the power steering pump bracket to the inlet manifold.

12 Disconnect the accelerator cable from the link on the inlet manifold, then remove it from the support.

13 On models with automatic transmission, disconnect the control pressure cable at the accelerator control.

14 On models with cruise control, disconnect the connecting rod.

15 Unbolt the throttle link bracket from the inlet manifold **(see illustrations)**.

16 Progressively unscrew the mounting nuts and bolts securing the inlet manifold to the cylinder head **(see illustration)**.

17 Withdraw the inlet manifold from the cylinder head and prise out the two gaskets

9.4 Unclip the wiring from the inlet manifold

9.7 Unscrew the bolt securing the support bracket to the throttle linkage bracket

9.9 Disconnecting the evaporative purge valve hose from the inlet manifold

9.15a Unscrew the bolts . . .

9.15b . . . and remove the throttle link bracket from the inlet manifold

9.16 Unscrewing the inlet manifold mounting bolts

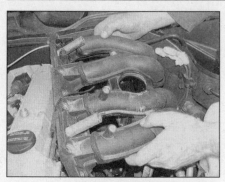

9.17a Removing the inlet manifold from the cylinder head

9.17b Removing the gaskets from the inlet manifold

10.2 Disconnecting the wiring from the air mass meter

from the grooves **(see illustrations)**. Clean the mating faces of the manifold and cylinder head.

18 If applicable, remove the partial preheater by unscrewing the bolt and removing the bracket. Carefully withdraw the preheater and recover the O-ring seal. Take care not to damage the contact pin or the plastic housing.

Refitting

19 Refitting is a reversal of removal, but use a new gasket and tighten all nuts and bolts to the specified torque, where given. Renew the O-ring seal on the partial preheater where applicable.

---

10 Bosch fuel injection system components - removal and refitting

Warning: Observe the precautions in Section 1 before working on any component in the fuel system.

Note: *If the ignition is switched on with a sensor disconnected, a fault may be registered in the memory of the system electronic control unit (ECU). If this occurs, the system may enter an 'emergency running' mode which could affect driveability and economy. Therefore, on completion of any procedures described in this Section, it is*

advisable to have the system checked by a Mercedes-Benz dealer and any faults in memory erased.
Note: *Refer to Section 12 for details of component fault diagnosis. If any of the following components are being removed because of a fault, it will be necessary to erase the fault from the ECU memory on completion.*

Air mass meter
Removal

1 The air mass meter is located on the rear of the air cleaner cover on the right-hand side of the engine compartment.
2 Unplug the electrical wiring from the sensor by turning the union nut anti-clockwise until it is felt to disengage and then separating the two halves of the connector **(see illustration)**.
3 Slacken the hose clip at the engine side of the sensor, then pull off the inlet ducting. Release the spring clips at the air cleaner side of the sensor and remove the sensor. Recover the O-ring seal **(see illustrations)**.

Refitting

4 Refitting is a reversal of removal, but fit a new O-ring seal.

Coolant temperature sensor
Removal

5 Refer to Chapter 1A and partially drain the cooling system. Ensure that the ignition is switched off.
6 The coolant sensor is located on the

thermostat housing at the front of the cylinder head. First, unclip and remove the plastic cover.
7 Disconnect the wiring from the sensor **(see illustration)**.
8 Unscrew the sensor from the housing and recover the O-ring seal.

Refitting

9 Refitting is a reversal of removal, but fit a new O-ring seal. On completion, top-up the cooling system.

Intake air temperature sensor
Removal

10 The intake air temperature sensor is located on the air duct between the air mass meter and the inlet manifold, at the manifold end.
11 Disconnect the wiring at the connector.
12 Compress the locking clips while slightly pressing in the sensor, then withdraw the sensor from the air duct. Recover the O-ring seal.

Refitting

13 Refitting is a reversal of removal, but fit a new O-ring seal.

Electronic control unit (ECU)
Removal

Caution: Electronic Control Units (ECUs) contain components that are sensitive to

10.3a Release the spring clips . . .

10.3b . . . and disconnect the air mass meter from the air cleaner

10.7 Disconnecting the wiring from the coolant temperature sensor on the thermostat housing

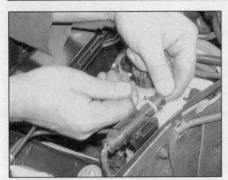

10.24 Disconnect the lambda sensor wiring . . .

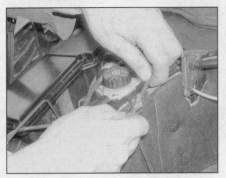

10.25 . . . and release the wiring from the bulkhead panel clip

10.26 Lambda sensor location on the exhaust manifold (2.0 litre engine)

the levels of static electricity generated by a person during normal activity. Once the multiway harness connector has been unplugged, the exposed ECU connector pins can freely conduct stray static electricity to these components, damaging or even destroying them - the damage will be invisible and may not manifest itself immediately. Expensive repairs can be avoided by observing the following basic handling rules:
a) Handle a disconnected ECU by its case only; do not allow fingers or tools to come into contact with the pins.
b) When carrying an ECU, earth yourself from time to time, by touching a metal object such as an unpainted water pipe, this will discharge any potentially damaging static that may have built up.
c) Do not leave the ECU unplugged from its connector for any longer than is absolutely necessary.

14 The ECU is located on the left-hand side of the bulkhead (right-hand side on LHD models). First, make sure that the ignition is switched off.
15 Remove the cover.
16 Where necessary, remove the windscreen washer fluid reservoir and position it to one side.
17 Disconnect the two wiring plugs from the ECU.
18 On the PMS system, disconnect the crankshaft position sensor wiring.

19 Unscrew the mounting bolts/nuts and withdraw the ECU from the bulkhead.

Refitting
21 Refitting is a reversal of removal, but on the HFM system insert the ECU into its mounting from below. Tighten the bolts/nuts securely.

Lambda sensor

Removal
21 The lambda (oxygen) sensor is located on the exhaust system manifold. First make sure that the ignition is switched off.
22 Apply the parking brake, then jack up the front of the vehicle and support it on axle stands (see *Jacking and Vehicle Support*).
23 Remove the right-hand bulkhead cover (left-hand on LHD models), then remove the cable duct for the sensor.
24 Disconnect the lambda sensor wiring **(see illustration)**.
25 Release the wiring from the bulkhead panel and unclip it from the cylinder head cover **(see illustration)**.
26 Using an open-ended spanner or a socket, unscrew the lambda sensor from the manifold **(see illustration)**. **Note:** *As a flying lead remains connected to the sensor after is has been disconnected, if the correct size spanner is not available, a slotted socket will be required to remove the sensor. Take care not to damage the wiring or the sensor tip, as it withdrawn.*

Refitting
27 Apply a little high temperature, anti-seize grease to the sensor threads - avoid contaminating the probe tip. Refit the sensor and tighten it to the specified correct torque. The remaining refitting procedure is a reversal of removal.

Fuel injectors and fuel rail

Removal
28 Refer to Section 11 and depressurise the fuel system. Disconnect the battery negative (earth) lead and position it away from the terminal. The battery is located in the rear luggage compartment.
29 Loosen the clips and remove the air cleaner cross pipe duct from between the air mass meter and inlet manifold.
30 Where applicable, disconnect and remove the crankcase ventilation hose from between the camshaft cover and the throttle body. Note the location arrows on the hose and inlet manifold.
31 Disconnect the vacuum hose from the fuel pressure regulator **(see illustration)**.
32 On early models (pre 12/94) disconnect the ignition HT leads at the coils.
33 Unscrew and remove the fuel line support bolt(s). Unscrew the union nut and disconnect the fuel feed line from the fuel rail, then unscrew the banjo union bolt and disconnect the return line. Recover the copper washers from the return line union **(see illustrations)**.

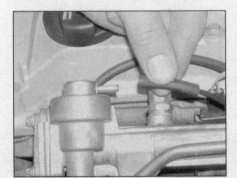

10.31 Disconnecting the vacuum hose from the fuel pressure regulator

10.33a Removing the fuel feed line support bolt from the fuel rail

10.33b Disconnecting the fuel feed line . . .

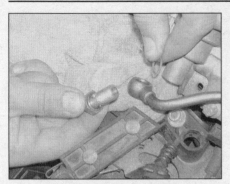

10.33c . . . and return line

10.34 Disconnecting the wiring from the fuel injectors

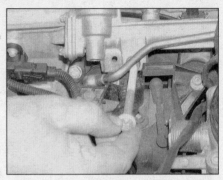

10.35 Unscrew and remove the mounting bolts . . .

34 Disconnect the wiring plugs from the injectors **(see illustration)**. To do this, depress the wire clips. Note that the wires are coloured for position.

35 Unscrew the fuel rail mounting bolts and recover the spacers **(see illustration)**.

36 Carefully pull out the fuel rail together with the injectors from the cylinder head. Recover the lower O-ring seals from the injectors **(see illustration)**.

37 To remove an injector from the fuel rail assembly, extract the relevant locking clip and withdraw the injector from its housing. Recover the upper O-ring seal **(see illustrations)**.

Refitting

38 Refitting is a reversal of removal, but renew the injector O-ring seals and oil them lightly before fitting. Tighten the fuel rail mounting bolts to the specified torque. When refitting an injector to the fuel rail, ensure the locking clip engages with the corresponding retaining lugs on the injector body.

Fuel pressure regulator

Removal

39 Refer to Section 11 and depressurise the fuel system. Disconnect the battery negative

(earth) lead and position it away from the terminal. The battery is located in the rear luggage compartment.

40 Disconnect the vacuum hose from the port on the fuel pressure regulator.

41 Using a pair of circlip pliers, remove the large diameter circlip and withdraw the pressure regulator from its housing. If necessary, use a screwdriver inserted through the aperture in the side of the regulator to release it. Be prepared for some fuel leakage - position a container under the unions and pad the surrounding area with absorbent rags.

42 Recover the large and small O-ring seals.

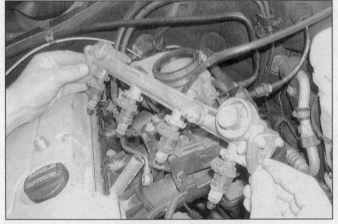

10.36a . . . then withdraw the fuel rail and injectors from the inlet manifold . . .

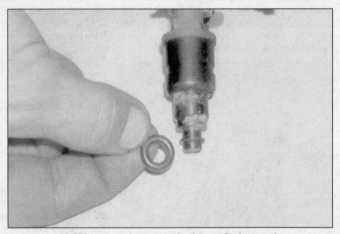

10.36b . . . and recover the lower O-ring seals

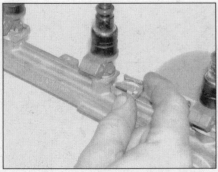

10.37a Extract the locking clip . . .

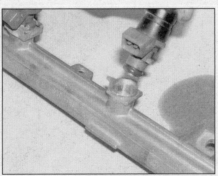

10.37b . . . withdraw the injector from its housing . . .

10.37c . . . and recover the upper O-ring seal

10.46 Disconnecting the wiring from the knock sensor

10.47 Removing the knock sensor from the left-hand side of the cylinder block

10.55 Disconnect the wiring . . .

Refitting

43 Refitting is a reversal of removal, but renew the O-ring seals and lightly oil them with clean engine oil before fitting.

Knock sensor

Removal

44 The knock sensor is located on the left-hand side of the cylinder block. First unbolt the windscreen washer reservoir and position it to one side.
45 Unbolt and remove the inlet manifold support bracket.
46 On early models, disconnect the wiring from the sensor by releasing the clip, then unbolt the wiring socket from the cylinder block. On later models, depress the clip and disconnect the wiring (see illustration).

10.58a . . . then unscrew the retaining bolt . . .

10.58b . . . and remove the crankshaft position sensor from the cylinder block

47 Note the position of the wiring socket on the sensor (to avoid straining the wire), then unscrew the mounting bolt and remove the knock sensor (see illustration).

Refitting

48 Clean the surfaces of the sensor and cylinder block. It is important that the sensor makes good contact with the cylinder block and is tightened to the correct torque, so also clean the threads of the mounting hole and bolt.
49 Locate the knock sensor on the cylinder block with the wiring socket in the previously noted position, then insert the bolt and tighten to the specified torque.
50 Refit the wiring socket to the block and tighten the bolts securely.
51 Reconnect the wiring and secure with the clip.
52 Refit the inlet manifold support bracket and tighten the bolt.
53 Refit the windscreen washer reservoir.

Crankshaft position sensor

Removal

54 The crankshaft position sensor is located on the left-hand rear of the cylinder block, above to the starter motor. Disconnect the battery negative (earth) lead and position it away from the terminal. The battery is located in the rear luggage compartment.
55 Disconnect the wiring from the sensor (see illustration). Where the wiring cannot be disconnected from the sensor, it may be necessary to disconnect it from the ECU. To

10.62a Unscrew the mounting bolt . . .

do this, first remove the cover from the left-hand side of the bulkhead for access to the ECU. On models with the HFM system, disconnect the sensor wiring leading to the ECU. On models with the PMS system, unbolt the windscreen washer fluid reservoir and position it to one side, then disconnect the sensor wiring from the ECU.
56 Where necessary on models with cruise control, remove the cruise control actuator.
57 If necessary for better access, remove the starter motor as described in Chapter 5A.
58 Unscrew the mounting bolt and remove the crankshaft position sensor (see illustrations).

Refitting

59 Refitting is a reversal of removal, but tighten the mounting bolt to the specified torque.

Camshaft position sensor

Removal

60 The camshaft position sensor is located on the left-hand front of the cylinder head, and it senses the rotation of the inlet camshaft. Disconnect the battery negative (earth) lead and position it away from the terminal. The battery is located in the rear luggage compartment.
61 Disconnect the wiring from the camshaft sensor.
62 Unscrew the bolt securing the sensor to the cylinder head, then withdraw the sensor, together with the spacer and O-ring (see illustrations).

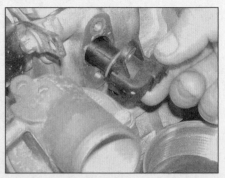

10.62b . . . withdraw the camshaft position sensor . . .

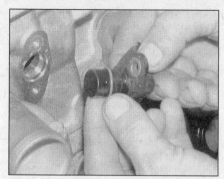

10.62c ... and recover the O-ring seal

Checking clearance and refitting

63 If a new sensor is being fitted, the clearance between the sensor and sprocket segment must be checked and adjusted using an appropriate spacer obtainable from a Mercedes-Benz dealer. For access to the sensor segment on the inlet camshaft sprocket, remove the camshaft cover and front cover, with reference to Chapter 2A, if a feeler blade is being used to check and adjust the clearance, however, note that this work is not essential if vernier calipers are being used, as described in the following paragraphs.

64 Set the engine to 20° ATDC with reference to Chapter 2A, Section 3. At this setting the sprocket segment will be positioned opposite the sensor mounting hole.

65 If necessary, temporarily remove the cap from the power steering fluid reservoir.

66 Using vernier calipers, measure and record the distance (A) from the sensor mounting face on the cylinder head to the segment on the inlet camshaft sprocket. Now measure the distance (B) from the mounting face on the sensor (without the spacer) to the inner end of the sensor. The difference between these two dimensions (A – B) will result in the clearance (C). The final clearance must be between 0.4 and 0.6 mm, but for the calculation 0.5 mm can be used.

Example 1: A greater than or equal to B

Dimension A	= 24.1 mm
Dimension B	= 23.8 mm
C (A – B)	= 0.3 mm
Desired clearance	= 0.5 mm
Less C	= 0.3 mm
Spacer thickness	= 0.2 mm

Example 2: A less than B

Dimension A	= 23.8 mm
Dimension B	= 24.1 mm
C (A – B)	= – 0.3 mm
Desired clearance	= 0.5 mm
Plus C	= 0.3 mm
Spacer thickness	= 0.8 mm

67 Locate the spacer on the sensor, then refit the sensor together with a new O-ring. Insert the mounting bolt and tighten to the specified torque.

68 Reconnect the wiring.

69 Reconnect the battery negative (earth) lead.

11 Fuel injection system - depressurisation

> **Warning: Observe the precautions in Section 1 before working on any component in the fuel system. Note that the following procedure will merely relieve the pressure in the fuel system - remember that fuel will still be present in the system components and take precautions accordingly before disconnecting any of them.**

1 The fuel injection system referred to in this Section is defined as the fuel pump(s), the fuel filter, the fuel rail, the fuel injectors, the fuel pressure regulator and the metal pipes and flexible hoses of the fuel lines between these components. All these contain fuel which will be under pressure while the engine is running and/or while the ignition is switched on. The pressure will remain for some time after the ignition has been switched off and must be relieved before any of these components are disturbed for servicing work. Ideally, for safety reasons, the engine should be allowed to cool completely before work commences.

2 Briefly remove and refit the fuel tank filler cap to release any pressure/vacuum in the tank.

3 A pressure release valve is located at the front of the fuel rail, beneath a dust cap. The valve is of Schrader type, as found on roadwheels, and ideally an adapter with a drain tube should be fitted to release the pressure. Alternatively, wrap some cloth rag around the valve and depress the valve core with a screwdriver to release the pressure. Make sure that fuel is not allowed to drip onto hot engine components **(see illustrations)**.

4 An alternative method of releasing the pressure is as follows. Refer to Chapter 12, Section 3, and locate the fuel pump relay. Remove the relay, then crank the engine for a few seconds. The engine may fire and run for a while, but continue cranking until it stops. The fuel injectors should have opened enough times during cranking to reduce the line fuel pressure. Place a suitable container beneath

the relevant connection/union to be disconnected, and have a large rag ready to soak up any escaping fuel not being caught by the container. It is advisable to clamp off the fuel supply hose to the fuel rail using a proprietary hose clamp. Slowly loosen the connection or union nut (as applicable) to avoid a sudden release of pressure and position the rag around the connection to catch any fuel spray which may be expelled. Once the pressure has been released, disconnect the fuel line and insert plugs to minimise fuel loss and prevent the entry of dirt into the fuel system.

12 Idle speed, exhaust CO content, and fault diagnosis

Experienced home mechanics equipped with an accurate tachometer and a carefully-calibrated exhaust gas analyser may be able to check the exhaust gas CO content and the engine idle speed, although the vehicle must be taken to a suitably-equipped Mercedes-Benz dealer or Bosch fuel injection specialist for assessment. Neither the air/fuel mixture (exhaust gas CO content) nor the engine idle speed are manually adjustable.

A diagnostics socket, located in the engine compartment under a cover next to the ECU, is incorporated in the engine management system wiring harness, to which dedicated electronic test equipment can be connected.

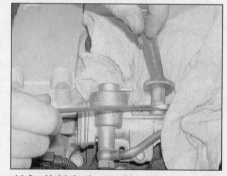

11.3a Hold the base with a spanner, while loosening the cap . . .

11.3b . . . then remove the cap from the pressure release valve on the fuel rail

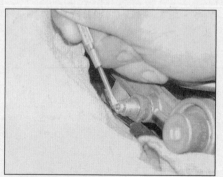

11.3c Use a small screwdriver to depress the valve and release the fuel pressure

The test equipment is capable of 'interrogating' the engine management system ECU electronically and accessing its internal fault log. In this manner, faults can be pinpointed quickly and simply, even if their occurrence is intermittent. Testing all the system components individually in an attempt to locate the fault by elimination is a time consuming operation that is unlikely to be fruitful (particularly if the fault occurs dynamically), and also carries high risk of damage to the ECU's internal components.

13 Cruise control system - general information and component renewal

General

1 The cruise control system is electronically-controlled by a control module. The main components of the system are the electronic control unit (ECU), electronic actuator, and switch. The system is controlled by the switch on the steering column, and there is also a switch on the brake pedal to disable the system. The actuator consists of an electric motor and gear drive, a one-way clutch, a potentiometer and an electromagnetic clutch.

2 If a fault occurs, have the system checked by a Mercedes-Benz dealer who will have the diagnostic equipment necessary to plug into the circuit. Do not attempt to check the system with analogue multi-meters as the electronic control unit will be damaged beyond repair.

Component renewal

Electronic actuator

3 Disconnect the battery negative (earth) lead and position it away from the terminal. The battery is located in the rear luggage compartment.

4 Remove the starter motor as described in Chapter 5A.

5 Unbolt and remove the inlet manifold support bracket.

6 Disconnect the wiring from the actuator. Also release the wiring from the conduit on the left-hand side of the engine compartment.

7 Unscrew the mounting bolts, then withdraw the actuator while disconnecting the link rod from the control mechanism lever.

8 Release the wiring strap at the bracket.

9 Unscrew the bolts and remove the actuator from the bracket. Recover the spacers and rubber grommets.

10 Release the tab washer and unscrew the nut, then remove the washer and control lever. If necessary, unscrew the nuts from the output shaft.

11 Refitting is a reversal of removal, but first check that the threaded bolt of the output shaft protrudes by 8.5 mm. If necessary, adjust the shaft. Finally, adjust the link rod as described later in this Section.

Pushbutton switch

12 Disconnect the battery negative (earth) lead and position it away from the terminal. The battery is located in the rear luggage compartment.

13 Remove the lower trim panel located beneath the steering wheel.

14 Remove the driver's airbag module as described in Chapter 12.

15 Remove the steering wheel as described in Chapter 10.

16 Remove the steering column shrouds, then disconnect the two wiring connectors for the pushbutton switch.

17 Undo the screws and remove the bracket from the steering column, then remove the pushbutton switch. Note the location of the wiring through the steering column tube.

18 Refitting is a reversal of removal.

Link rod adjustment

19 Before adjusting the link rod, thoroughly check the component parts for wear. Clean the moving parts and oil lightly.

20 Note that the throttle control was modified in 06/94.

21 Release the intermediate rod from the cruise control link rod, then make sure that the lever on the throttle body is at idle with the lever touching the stop. Hold the lever firmly against the stop.

22 Adjust the ball socket on the intermediate rod so that it is exactly aligned with the ball on the link rod, then adjust it back to shorten the link rod by 1.0 mm.

23 Refit the intermediate rod to the link rod.

Chapter 4 Part B:
Fuel system - diesel

Contents

Degrees of difficulty

Easy, suitable for novice with little experience	**Fairly easy,** suitable for beginner with some experience	**Fairly difficult,** suitable for competent DIY mechanic
Difficult, suitable for experienced DIY mechanic	**Very difficult,** suitable for expert DIY or professional	

Specifications

General
Injection .... Indirect
Idle speed (electronic idle speed control):
  4-cylinder engine .... 690 to 790 rpm
  5-cylinder engine .... 610 to 710 rpm
Maximum no-load engine speed (non-adjustable) .... 5200 to 5600 rpm
Smoke test opacity 1.9

Fuel injection pump
Type:
  2.2 litre normally aspirated engine .... Lucas R86 40A 030A distributor-type
  2.5 litre normally aspirated engine .... Bosch 0400 195 001 in-line
  2.5 litre turbo engine .... Bosch 0400 195 001 in-line
Start of delivery (with digital tester) .... 14° + 0.5° ATDC

Fuel injectors
Type:
  2.2 litre normally aspirated engine .... CAV LDC 001 R03
  2.5 litre normally aspirated engine .... Bosch 0430 211 997
  2.5 litre turbo engine .... Bosch
Opening pressures:
  2.2 litre normally aspirated engine:
    New .... 115 to 125 bars
    Minimum .... 100 bars
  2.5 litre normally aspirated engine:
    New .... 115 to 125 bars
    Minimum .... 100 bars
  2.5 litre turbo engine:
    New .... 115 to 125 bars
    Minimum .... 110 bars

Torque wrench settings

	Nm	lbf ft
Camshaft bearing cap	15	11
Camshaft cover	10	7
Camshaft gear	18	13
Camshaft sprocket	18	13
Fuel gauge sender unit retaining ring	55	41
Fuel heat exchanger	10	7
Fuel tank strainer and return adapter	40	30
Fuel tank support straps:		
Right- and left-hand straps	40	30
Centre strap/bracket	20	15
Injection pipe union nuts	15	11
Injection pump inspection hole plug:		
4-cylinder engine	25	18
5-cylinder engine	35	26
Injection pump sprocket bolt	45	33
Injection pump to front mounting bolts	25	18
Injection pump to rear mounting bracket	25	18
Injectors	40	30
Inlet manifold bolts:		
M5	10	7
M7	20	15
Pre-combustion chamber retaining ring	130	96

1 General information and precautions

General information

The major components of the fuel system are a fuel tank, a fuel injection pump and lift pump, engine-bay mounted filter, fuel supply and return lines and one fuel injector per cylinder. 4-cylinder engines are fitted with a distributor-type injection pump, where the fuel is pressurised in the distributor head at one end of the pump. 5-cylinder engines are fitted with an in-line injection pump, where the fuel is pressurised by individual plungers mounted on the top of the pump.

The injection pump is driven at half crankshaft speed by the timing chain. Fuel is drawn from the fuel tank, through the filter, to the injection pump, which then distributes the fuel under very high pressure to the injectors via separate delivery pipes.

The basic injection timing is set by the position of the injection pump on its mounting bracket. When the engine is running, the injection timing is advanced and retarded electronically. In addition, an injection timing device is incorporated in the pump drive sprocket.

The injectors are spring-loaded mechanical valves, which open when the pressure of the fuel supplied to them exceeds a specific limit. Fuel is then sprayed from the injector nozzle into the cylinder via a pre-chamber (indirect injection).

The engine is stopped by means of a vacuum controlled shut-off module, mounted on the upper surface of the fuel injection pump. When the facia mounted ignition key is turned to the OFF position, a vacuum switch integral with the ignition lock assembly interrupts the supply of vacuum to the shut-off module, which in turn interrupts the supply of fuel to the injection pump, stopping the engine.

Engine idle speed is controlled electronically, responding to engine load. The system increases the idle speed when the power steering, air conditioning, or automatic transmission systems are operative, in addition to increased idle speed under cold start conditions. The engine speed is monitored by an electronic control unit via a sensor mounted at the flywheel, and coolant temperature via a sensor threaded into the cylinder head. The ECU compares the actual engine speed with a mapped value stored in memory. If the two are different, the ECU drives an electromagnetic actuator which mechanically pre-loads the injection pump governor to alter the engine idle speed accordingly.

On turbocharged models, the operation of the diesel fuel injection system is identical to that of the normally-aspirated engines, however, the inlet charge pressure (turbo-boost) and exhaust gas recirculation systems are also controlled by the ECU. Air inlet temperature is monitored by a sensor inside the air duct located above the right-hand side of the radiator.

Precautions

 Warning: Many of the procedures in this Chapter require the removal of fuel lines and connections, which may result in some fuel spillage. Before carrying out any operation on the fuel system, refer to the precautions given in Safety first! at the beginning of this manual, and follow them implicitly. Always switch off the ignition before working on the fuel system.

Warning: When working on any part of the fuel system, avoid direct skin contact with diesel fuel - wear protective clothing and gloves when handling fuel system components. Ensure the work area is well ventilated. Fuel injectors operate at extremely high pressures and the jet of fuel produced at the nozzle is capable of piercing skin, with potentially fatal results. When working with pressurised injectors, take great to avoid exposing any part of the body to the fuel spray. It is recommended that any pressure testing of the fuel system components should be carried out by a diesel fuel injection specialist.

Caution: Do not allow diesel fuel to come into contact with coolant hoses - wipe off accidental spillage immediately. Hoses that have been contaminated with fuel for an extended period should be renewed. Diesel fuel systems are particularly sensitive to contamination from dirt, air and water. Pay particular attention to cleanliness when working on any part of the fuel system, to prevent the ingress of dirt. Thoroughly clean the area around fuel unions before disconnecting them. Store dismantled components in sealed containers to prevent contamination and the formation of condensation. Only use lint-free cloths and clean fuel for component cleansing.

2.1a Release the coolant expansion tank purge hose from the clip . . .

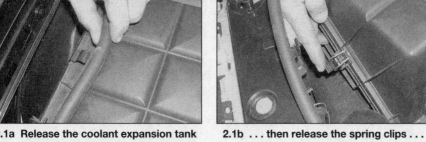

2.1b . . . then release the spring clips . . .

2.1c . . . and plastic clip securing the cover to the air cleaner body

2 Air cleaner, filter element and air ducts - removal and refitting

Air filter element

Removal

1 Release the coolant expansion tank purge hose from the clip on the air cleaner cover, then prise open each of the cover retaining clips (see illustrations).

2 Lift off the air cleaner cover and remove the air filter element (see illustration).

Refitting

3 Clean out all debris from the inside of the air cleaner assembly.

4 Fit the new filter by following the removal procedure in reverse, ensuring that the filter element is fitted the correct way up, according to the markings on its upper surface.

Air cleaner and air ducts

Removal

5 Remove the air filter element as described earlier in this Section.

Turbo-diesel engines

6 Slacken the hose clips and detach the ducting from the front of the air cleaner housing.

7 Remove the nuts that secure the air cleaner to its mounting brackets.

8 On models with an inlet air temperature sensor mounted in the air cleaner, unplug the wiring from the sensor at the connector.

9 Release the inlet elbow cup seal from the base of the air cleaner housing, then remove the air cleaner from the engine bay.

Normally aspirated engines

10 Where applicable, disconnect the vacuum line from the control flap actuator.

11 Unbolt the front and rear mounting brackets and release the air cleaner from them - recover the rubber mountings.

12 Lift the air cleaner away from the inlet manifold and recover the rubber sealing boots.

All engines

13 To remove the air ducting, loosen the clips and withdraw as necessary. Note that the air temperature sensor is located in the air duct positioned above the right-hand side of the radiator. To remove it, first disconnect the wiring, then release the plastic clips and withdraw it (see illustrations).

Refitting

14 Refitting is a reversal of removal. On completion, refit the air filter element as described earlier in this Section.

2.2 Lift the cover and remove the air filter element

3 Fuel gauge sender unit - removal and refitting

⚠️ **Warning: Observe the precautions in Section 1 before working on any component in the fuel system.**

Removal

1 This work must be carried out with the fuel tank empty. This is best achieved by waiting until the tank is almost empty through the

2.13a Disconnect the wiring . . .

2.13b . . . then release the clips and withdraw the temperature sensor

3.4a Unscrew the bolts . . .

3.4b . . . and remove the covers from the bottom front of each fuel tank half

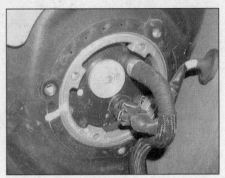

3.5 Fuel supply hose on the left-hand fuel gauge sender unit

course of normal driving. Any remaining fuel can be drained by unscrewing the drain plugs from the sender units before removing them.

2 Disconnect the battery negative (earth) lead and position it away from the terminal. The battery is located in the rear luggage compartment.

3 There are two fuel gauge sender units, each one located at the lower front of each half of the fuel tank. Chock the front roadwheels, then jack up the rear of the vehicle and support it on axle stands (see *Jacking and vehicle support*).

4 Unbolt and remove the covers from the bottom front of each tank half, for access to the sender units **(see illustrations)**.

5 Fit a hose clamp to the fuel supply hose, then loosen the clip and disconnect the hose from the left-hand fuel gauge sender unit **(see illustration)**.

6 Disconnect the fuel gauge wiring from each sender unit **(see illustration)**.

7 Unscrew the drain plugs from the sender units, and drain any remaining fuel from each half of the tank.

8 The retaining rings must now be loosened and removed. To do this, Mercedes-Benz technicians use a special tool which engages the holes in the ring. Ideally, this tool should be obtained, however it should be possible to fabricate a home-made version using metal bar and suitable sized bolts.

9 With the rings removed, carefully withdraw the sender units from the fuel tank. Recover

the special shaped gaskets. Note the location stud and groove to ensure correct refitting. When removing the left-hand sender unit, disconnect the internal pipes leading to each half of the tank.

Refitting

10 Refitting is a reversal of removal, but always renew the sender unit gaskets, and tighten the retaining rings to the specified torque.

4 Fuel tank - removal and refitting

⚠️ **Warning: Observe the precautions in Section 1 before working on any component in the fuel system.**

Removal

1 The fuel tank must be emptied before the operation can be started. This is best achieved by waiting until the tank is almost empty through the course of normal driving. If necessary, any remaining fuel can be drained after supporting the vehicle on axle stands, by removing the drain plugs from the sender units in the bottom of each half section of the fuel tank. To do this remove the covers with reference to Section 3.

2 Park the vehicle on a level surface and chock the front roadwheels. Raise the rear of

the vehicle, support it securely on axle stands (see *Jacking and vehicle support*) and remove the rear roadwheels.

3 Disconnect the battery negative (earth) lead and position it away from the terminal. The battery is located in the rear luggage compartment.

4 Remove the final drive unit as described in Chapter 8.

5 Remove the right-hand rear wheel arch liner, then loosen the clip attaching the filler neck to the fuel tank filler extension. Unscrew and remove the bolt securing the extension to the body.

6 Where necessary, remove the right-hand bracket of the anti-roll bar with reference to Chapter 10.

7 Remove the covers for access to the fuel gauge sender units at the bottom of each section of the fuel tank.

8 Fit a hose clamp to the fuel feed hose leading to the fuel pump, then loosen the union nut and disconnect the hose from the tank. Also, where applicable, disconnect the ventilation hose from the fuel tank by loosening the clip.

9 Unscrew the nut and remove the vent line support bracket.

10 Support the fuel tank with a trolley jack and a piece of wood to prevent damage.

11 Unscrew the nuts and remove the tank support straps **(see illustrations)**.

12 Where necessary, remove the sound deadening mat from the tank.

3.6 Fuel gauge wiring on the right-hand sender unit

4.11a Fuel tank inner support strap mounting nut

4.11b Fuel tank outer support strap mounting nut

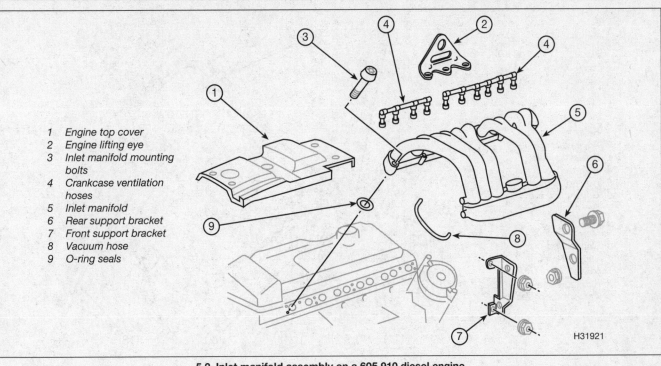

1 Engine top cover
2 Engine lifting eye
3 Inlet manifold mounting
   bolts
4 Crankcase ventilation
   hoses
5 Inlet manifold
6 Rear support bracket
7 Front support bracket
8 Vacuum hose
9 O-ring seals

H31921

5.2 Inlet manifold assembly on a 605.910 diesel engine

13 Unscrew the nuts and remove the central shield from the front of the tank.
14 Loosen the clips and disconnect the vent lines from the upper left-hand side of the tank.
15 Carefully lower the fuel tank from the underbody, and remove from under the car.
16 Unscrew the fuel strainer from the tank and recover the O-ring seal.
17 Remove the gauge sender unit as described in Section 3.
18 Swill the tank out with clean fuel. If the tank shows signs of leakage, it should either be repaired by a specialist or renewed.

 Warning: Do not attempt to repair the tank yourself by welding, soldering or brazing. The tank will contain an explosive mixture of air and fuel vapour, even when emptied of liquid fuel.

Refitting

19 Refit the fuel tank by reversing the removal procedure, but tighten all fixings to the correct torque, where specified.

5 Inlet manifold - removal and refitting

Removal

1 Loosen the clip and disconnect the air inlet duct from the inlet manifold. Where necessary, loosen the clip and disconnect the other end of the duct from the EGR valve adapter on the inlet duct, and remove the duct.
2 On normally-aspirated engines only, disconnect the crankcase ventilation hoses from the inlet manifold (see illustration).

3 Unbolt and remove the plastic cover from the top of the camshaft cover.
4 Disconnect the vacuum hose from the lower front of the inlet manifold.
5 As applicable, unscrew the bolts/nuts and remove the support bracket(s) from the inlet manifold as necessary. For improved access, remove the fuel injector pipes completely by loosening the union nuts at the injectors and injection pump.
6 Progressively unscrew the mounting bolts, then lift the inlet manifold away from the cylinder head. Note the location of the engine lifting eye on the manifold rear mounting bolts **(see illustrations)**. Recover the O-ring seals.

Refitting

7 Refitting is a reversal of removal, but fit new O-ring seals. Tighten the inlet manifold securing bolts to the specified torque.

5.6a Showing the inlet manifold on a 5-cylinder engine

5.6b Inlet manifold-to-cylinder head mounting bolts

5.6c Engine lifting eye on the inlet manifold rear mounting bolts

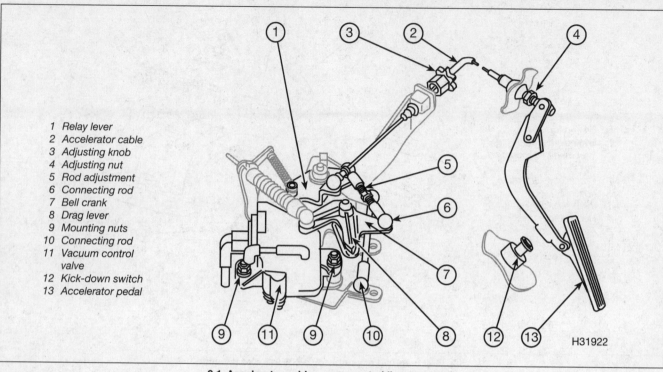

1 Relay lever
2 Accelerator cable
3 Adjusting knob
4 Adjusting nut
5 Rod adjustment
6 Connecting rod
7 Bell crank
8 Drag lever
9 Mounting nuts
10 Connecting rod
11 Vacuum control
valve
12 Kick-down switch
13 Accelerator pedal

6.1 Accelerator cable components (direct control)

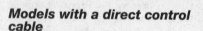

6 Accelerator cable - removal, refitting and adjustment

Models with a direct control cable

Removal

1 Working in the engine compartment, disconnect the accelerator inner cable from the relay lever on the injection pump by prising the ball socket off the ball (see illustration).
2 Release the outer cable from its support bracket by compressing the lugs on the plastic retainer and withdrawing it.
3 Working in the driver's footwell, remove the lower trim cover, then unhook the return spring.
4 Disconnect the inner cable from the pedal by pulling out the bracket together with the expansion bolt from the top of the pedal.
5 Press the accelerator cable through the rubber grommet in the bulkhead and into the engine compartment. Do not remove the rubber grommet at this stage.
6 Withdraw the cable from the engine compartment.
7 Check the condition of the rubber grommet and, if necessary, renew it by prising it from the bulkhead.

Refitting

8 Refit the cable by following the removal procedure in reverse, using a little grease to

lubricate the moving parts. On completion, adjust the operation of the cable as described in the following sub-section.

Adjustment

9 Check that the accelerator cable and linkage operate smoothly, without any stiffness or binding. Check that the cable is not kinked at any point along its length and lubricate the linkage if required.

Manual transmission models

10 With the accelerator pedal released, check that the throttle relay lever is resting against the idle stop. If not, turn the adjustment knob on the outer cable as required.
11 Have an assistant fully depress the accelerator pedal, and check that the relay lever is touching the fully open stop. If not, loosen the locknut beneath the accelerator pedal and adjust the stop as necessary. Tighten the locknut on completion.
12 Check again that the accelerator pedal opens and closes the throttle lever relay fully.

Automatic transmission models

13 Have an assistant depress the accelerator pedal to the point just before the kick-down switch (beneath the accelerator pedal) is operated. Check that the relay lever is touching the fully open stop. If not, turn the adjustment knob on the outer cable at the support bracket as required.
14 Fully release the accelerator pedal and check that the relay lever is resting against the idle stop. If not, reach up under the facia to the top of the accelerator pedal and turn the adjustment nut on the cable end fitting as required.

15 Check that the tips of the bell crank and drag lever are opposite each other. If not, turn the relay lever centre shaft as necessary.
16 The vacuum control valve must now be adjusted. First, press the inner cable end socket off the ball on the relay lever. Loosen the vacuum valve mounting nuts and turn the relay lever to the fully open position. Now turn the valve clockwise until resistance is felt, and tighten the nuts. Reconnect the inner cable end socket.

Models with remotely located cable

Removal

17 Working in the left-hand rear corner of the engine compartment, release the inner cable socket from the ball on the accelerator pedal module (see illustration).

6.17 Accelerator cable (remote) attachment to the module in the left-hand rear corner of the engine compartment

18 Release the outer cable from its support bracket by compressing the lugs on the plastic retainer.

19 Working in the driver's footwell, remove the lower trim cover, then disconnect the inner cable from the pedal by pulling out the holder with the expanding pin.

20 Press the accelerator cable through the rubber grommet in the bulkhead and into the engine compartment.

21 Withdraw the cable from the engine compartment.

22 Check the condition of the rubber grommet and if necessary renew it by prising it from the bulkhead.

Refitting

23 Refit the cable by following the removal procedure in reverse, using a little grease to lubricate the moving parts. On completion, adjust the operation of the cable as described in the following sub-section noting, however, that adjustment of the electronic module requires the use of a specialist Mercedes-Benz hand-tester. If the module has been renewed, or if its operation is suspect, the vehicle should be taken to a dealer for the adjustment.

Cable adjustment

24 Check that the accelerator cable and linkage operate smoothly, without any stiffness or binding. Check that the cable is not kinked at any point along its length and lubricate the linkage if required.

25 With the linkage in the idle position, there should be 0.5 to 1.0 mm freeplay at the end of the inner cable. If necessary, turn the adjustment nut at the end of the outer cable to achieve the correct freeplay.

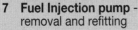
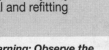

7 Fuel Injection pump -
removal and refitting

Warning: Observe the precautions in Section 1 before working on any component in the fuel system.

Note: *Following removal, the injection pump shaft must be locked in position using a specially shaped tapered locking tool. Fabrication of an accurate substitute would be very difficult and its use could risk internal damage to the injection pump. For these reasons, it is recommend that a locking tool is borrowed from a Mercedes-Benz dealer or a Bosch diesel fuel injection system specialist.*

Removal

1 Disconnect the battery negative (earth) lead and position it away from the terminal. The battery is located in the rear luggage compartment.

2 Unbolt the splash guard from under the engine compartment.

3 Refer to Section 5, Paragraph 6 of Chapter 2B and remove the auxiliary belt tensioner.

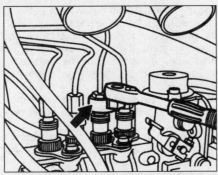

7.8 Using a crow's foot adapter to unscrew the union nuts from the injection pipes

4 With reference to Chapter 3, remove the cooling fan and shroud.

5 Remove the plastic cover from the top of the engine.

6 Remove the inlet manifold as described in Section 5.

7 Release the retaining clips from the pipes, and also unscrew the bolts securing the pipes to the side of the cylinder head.

8 Using an open ended spanner or wrench and crow's foot adapter, unscrew the union nuts at the injection pump and injectors and withdraw the injection pipes complete from the engine **(see illustration)**. Be prepared for an amount of fuel loss - pad the surrounding area with absorbent rags. Tape over or plug the apertures in the injection pump and injectors to prevent entry of dust and dirt.

9 Remove the brake vacuum pump from the timing cover with reference to Chapter 9. Note that the gasket must be renewed on refitting.

10 On models with cruise control, unbolt the cruise control actuator and position it to one side.

11 Counterhold the crankshaft, then unscrew and loosen only the injection pump sprocket centre bolt **(see illustration)**. **Do not** unscrew the bolt completely. **Note:** *The bolt has a LEFT-HAND THREAD.*

12 Using a socket and wrench on the crankshaft pulley centre bolt, turn the crankshaft in its normal direction of rotation until the engine is set to 14° + 0.5° *AFTER* top

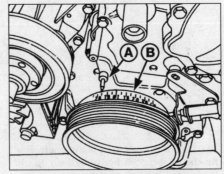

7.12 Set the engine to 14° ATDC on cylinder No 1, using the pointer (A) on the timing cover and the graduated markings (B) on the vibration damper

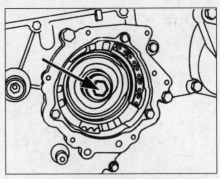

7.11 Unscrewing the injection pump sprocket centre bolt - note that the bolt has a LEFT-HAND thread

dead centre on cylinder No 1. Use the pointer on the timing cover and the graduated markings on the vibration damper to achieve the correct alignment **(see illustration)**. If necessary, an alternative method of positioning the crankshaft is to remove the oil filler cap and turn the engine until the timing mark on the inlet camshaft sprocket is visible through the filler hole. Then turn the engine to position it at 14° + 0.5° *AFTER* top dead centre on cylinder No 1.

13 Completely unscrew the injection pump sprocket centre bolt, and recover the washer.

14 Refer to Chapter 2B and remove the timing chain tensioner **(see illustration)**.

15 Depress the plastic catch and disconnect the injection pump wiring at the connector. At the same time, remove the right-hand cover and cable duct from the bulkhead.

16 Unscrew the banjo bolts, then disconnect the fuel supply, delivery and return hoses from the injection pump. Recover the copper washers and discard them - new items must be used on refitting. Clamp off the flexible section of the hoses to prevent further fuel loss.

17 Unplug all vacuum hoses from the actuators on the top and rear of the injection pump, noting their fitted positions to aid refitting later.

18 Where applicable, detach the accelerator linkage from the injection pump control lever.

19 Mark the body of the injection pump in relation to the rear surface of its mounting flange, to allow approximate alignment during refitting.

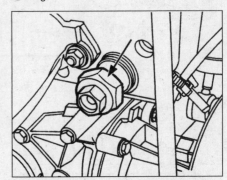

7.14 Removing the timing chain tensioner

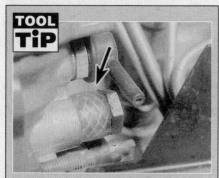

Fit a short length of hose over the banjo holt so that the drillings are covered, then thread the bolt back into its injection pump port and finger tighten it

20 Unscrew and remove the injection pump mounting bolts, while holding the square nuts stationary with a further spanner.

21 Loosen only the bolt of the start of delivery device.

22 When the injection pump is removed, it will be necessary to hold the sprocket (and timing device, where fitted) in place in the timing chain casing, so that it cannot disengage from the timing chain, but in a manner which still allows it to rotate, if the engine is turned over by hand. On later models, a special retaining cage is fitted for this purpose. Mercedes-Benz technicians use a special tool bolted to the timing cover which holds the sprocket in place. If possible, obtain this tool, however an alternative method is to use a length of metal tubing, of roughly the same outside diameter as the threaded section of the injection pump sprocket centre bolt. Slide the metal tubing through the sprocket centre hole. Pass a length of sturdy wire, or a large nylon cable-tie through the tubing, then secure it and the sprocket over the top of the timing chain casing.

23 Remove the bolt that secures the rear of the injection pump to the support bracket, then lift the injection pump away from the engine. *At the same time,* support the pump sprocket (and timing device, where fitted) to

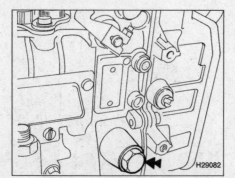

7.26 Unscrew the timing plug from the side of the injection pump

keep it in place. ***DO NOT*** *allow the sprocket to disengage from the timing chain.*

24 Unbolt the fuel thermostat from the injection pump body and position it to one side. It should not be necessary to disconnect the fuel lines from the thermostat.

25 Cover all exposed fuel unions to minimise fuel loss and prevent the ingress of dirt **(see Tool Tip)**

26 With the injection pump on a workbench, unbolt and remove the timing plug from the side of pump body **(see illustration)**.

27 Using a suitable pair of grips, turn the injection pump shaft in its normal direction of rotation, whilst observing the movement of the governor body through the timing plug hole. Continue turning the shaft until the lug on the governor body lines up with the hole. At this point, the governor body must be locked to the injection pump body using the special Mercedes-Benz locking tool, to prevent further movement of the pump shaft (refer to the note at the beginning of this Section) **(see illustration)**.
Caution: Take care to avoid damaging the surface of the injection pump shaft with the jaws of the grips.

28 Recover the O-ring seal from the front of the injection pump and discard it - a new item must be used on refitting.

Refitting

29 Refit the pump by following the

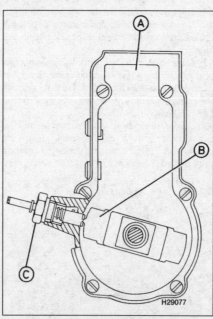

7.27 Turn the injection pump shaft until the lug on the governor body lines up with the inspection hole

A Injection pump - viewed from rear
B Governor body
C Locking tool

removal procedure in reverse, noting these points:

a) *Fit a new O-ring seal to the injection pump mating face and lubricate it lightly with clean engine oil.*
b) *Ensure that the engine is still set to 14° AFTER top dead centre on cylinder No 1 before refitting the injection pump.*
c) *Counterhold the crankshaft and tighten the injection pump sprocket to the specified torque, noting that the bolt has a LEFT-HAND THREAD.*
d) *Remove the locking tool from the injection pump timing hole (and refit the plug) before turning the engine over.*
e) *Tighten the injection pump mounting bolts to the specified torque.*
f) *Reconnect the high pressure injection pipes and tighten the union to the specified torque.*
g) *New sealing washers must be fitted to the fuel supply, delivery and return banjo bolt unions at the injection pump.*
h) *A new seal must be used when the vacuum pump is refitted - refer to Chapter 9.*
i) *On completion, have the injection pump start of delivery checked by a Mercedes-Benz dealer or garage having the necessary test equipment.*

8 Fuel lift pump - removal and refitting

 Warning: Observe the precautions in Section 1 before working on any component in the fuel system.

Note: *This Section applies to 5-cylinder engines only.*

Removal

1 Disconnect the battery negative cable and position it away from the terminal. The battery is located in the rear luggage compartment.

2 On normally-aspirated engines, refer to Section 2 and remove the air cleaner cover.

3 Clamp off the fuel supply line to the injection pump using a proprietary hose clamp. Loosen the clip and detach the fuel line from the port on the lift pump. Be prepared for an amount of fuel loss - position a container underneath the pump, and pad the surrounding area with absorbent rags.

4 Slacken the union at the top of the lift pump and detach the delivery line to the fuel filter. Again, be prepared for an amount of fuel loss.

5 When the lift pump is removed, there will be a small amount of oil loss - position a container underneath the pump in preparation for this.

6 Slacken and withdraw the retaining nuts,

then pull the lift pump away from the injection pump body **(see illustration)**. Recover the washers and the pump gasket.

Refitting

7 Refitting is a reversal of removal, noting the following points:

a) *If the pump is to be renewed, unscrew the lower half of the fuel filter delivery union from the top of the pump and transfer it to the new pump.*

b) *Use a new gasket when refitting the lift pump to the injection pump.*

c) *On completion, tighten the lift pump retaining nuts securely.*

---

9 Fuel injection pump timing device and sprocket - removal and refitting

Note: *This Section is applicable to 5-cylinder engines only.*

Removal

Note: *Following removal of the timing device and sprocket, the injection pump shaft must be locked in position using a special locking tool with a tapered end. Fabrication of an accurate substitute would be very difficult and its use could risk internal damage to the injection pump. For these reasons, it is recommend that a locking tool is borrowed from a Mercedes-Benz dealer or a Bosch diesel fuel injection system specialist.*

1 Disconnect the battery negative cable and position it away from the terminal. The battery is located in the rear luggage compartment.

2 Remove the splash guard from under the engine compartment. If necessary, apply the parking brake then jack up the front of the vehicle and support it on axle stands (see *Jacking and vehicle support*).

3 Refer to Section 5, Paragraph 6 of Chapter 2B and remove the auxiliary belt tensioner.

4 With reference to Chapter 3, remove the cooling fan and shroud.

5 On the normally aspirated 5-cylinder diesel engine (engine code 605.910) remove the inlet manifold as described in Section 5.

6 On the turbocharged 5-cylinder diesel engine (engine code 605.960) remove the air duct leading to the turbocharger.

7 Remove the camshaft cover from the cylinder head as described in Chapter 2B.

8 Refer to Chapter 9 and remove the vacuum pump from the timing cover. Note that the gasket must be renewed on refitting.

9 Using a socket and wrench on the crankshaft pulley centre bolt, turn the crankshaft in its normal direction of rotation until the engine is set to 14° AFTER top dead centre on cylinder No 1. Use the pointer on the timing cover and the graduated markings on the vibration damper to achieve the correct alignment. Refer to Section 3 Chapter 2B, if necessary.

10 Remove the timing chain tensioner as described in Chapter 2B.

8.6 View of the lift pump, from beneath the injection pump

11 Remove the injection pump as described in Section 7.

12 Using an open ended spanner or wrench and crow's foot adapter, unscrew the union nuts at the injection pump and injectors and withdraw the injection pipes complete from the engine. Be prepared for an amount of fuel loss - pad the surrounding area with absorbent rags. Tape over or plug the apertures in the injection pump and injectors to prevent entry of dust and dirt.

13 Disconnect the leak-off hoses from the injectors, noting the location of the return hose on the No 1 injector.

14 Loosen only the bolts securing the camshaft sprocket to the exhaust camshaft. Do not unscrew the bolts completely.

15 From the front of the timing cover, unbolt the injection pump centring device cage.

16 Using a dab of paint, mark the camshaft sprocket, injection pump sprocket, and timing chain in relation to each other to facilitate correct refitting.

17 Unscrew the bolts and remove the camshaft sprocket from the camshaft and timing chain. Tie the chain to one side using wire.

18 Remove the locking pin from the front of the timing cover. Mercedes-Benz technicians use a special tool to do this, incorporating a slide hammer. However, an alternative tool can be fabricated using a suitable bolt.

19 Lift the timing chain so that it is clear of the sprocket, then withdraw the sprocket together with the timing device. One method of retaining the timing chain away from the sprocket is to use a piece of thin metal plate formed into a curve so that it can be inserted under the chain **(see illustration)**.

20 Unbolt and remove the timing plug from the side of pump body.

21 Using a suitable pair of grips, turn the injection pump shaft in its normal direction of rotation, whilst observing the movement of the governor body through the timing plug hole. Continue turning the shaft until the lug on the governor body lines up with the hole. At this point, the governor body must be locked to the injection pump body using the special Mercedes-Benz locking tool, to prevent further movement of the pump shaft -

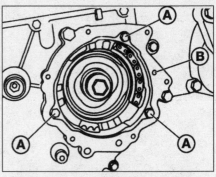

9.19 Using thin metal plate to hold the timing chain away from the injection pump sprocket

A Mounting bolts   B Locking pin

refer to the note at the beginning of this Section. This step must not be omitted, as it is the only means of ensuring correct injection pump timing during reassembly.

Caution: Do not damage the surface of the injection pump shaft with the jaws of the grips.

Refitting

22 Refitting is the reversal of removal, noting the following points:

a) *Ensure that the engine is still set to 14° AFTER top dead centre on cylinder No 1 before refitting the sprocket and timing device to the injection pump shaft.*

b) *Use the paint marks made during removal to align the injection pump sprocket and camshaft sprocket with the timing chain.*

c) *Counterhold the crankshaft and tighten the injection pump sprocket to the specified torque, noting that the bolt has a LEFT HAND THREAD.*

d) *Remove the locking tool from the injection pump timing hole (and refit the plug) before turning over the engine.*

e) *Refer to Section 8 of Chapter 2B for details of refitting the camshaft sprocket. To verify the camshaft timing, rotate the engine through two complete crankshaft revolutions and check that the camshaft and crankshaft TDC markings line up correctly.*

f) *A new seal must be used when the vacuum pump is refitted - refer to Chapter 9 for details.*

g) *On completion, have the injection pump start of delivery checked by a Mercedes-Benz dealer or garage having the necessary test equipment.*

---

10 Injectors and high pressure fuel lines - removal and refitting

 Warning: Exercise extreme caution when working on the fuel injectors. Never expose the hands or any part of the body to injector spray, as the high working pressure can cause the fuel to penetrate

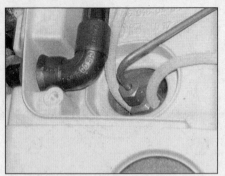

10.6 Leak-off hoses on injector No 1. Note the location of the return hose

10.7a Showing the location of the injector fuel lines on the camshaft cover

10.7b Injector pipe supports on the left-hand side of the camshaft cover

the skin, with possibly fatal results. You are strongly advised to have any work which involves testing the injectors under pressure carried out by a dealer or fuel injection specialist. Refer to the precautions given in Section 1 of this Chapter before proceeding.

General information

1 Injectors do deteriorate with prolonged use and it is reasonable to expect them to need reconditioning or renewal after 60 000 miles (100 000 km), or so. Accurate testing, overhaul and calibration of the injectors must be left to a specialist. A defective injector which is causing knocking or smoking can be located as follows.

2 Loosen the clips and temporarily remove the inlet manifold-to-air cleaner/intercooler air duct in order to remove the plastic engine top cover. With the cover removed, refit the air duct and tighten the clips. Run the engine at a fast idle. Slacken each injector union in turn, placing rag around the union to catch spilt fuel and being careful not to expose the skin to any spray. When the union on the defective injector is slackened, the knocking or smoking will stop.

Removal

Note: Take great care not to allow dirt into the injectors or fuel pipes during this procedure. Do not drop the injectors or allow the needles

at their tips to become damaged. The injectors are precision-made to fine limits and must not be handled roughly.

3 Disconnect the battery negative cable and position it away from the terminal. The battery is located in the rear luggage compartment.

4 Loosen the clips and remove the inlet manifold-to-air cleaner/intercooler air duct.

5 Undo the screws and remove the engine plastic top cover. Carefully clean around the injectors and pipe union nuts.

6 Disconnect the leak-off hoses from the injectors, noting the location of the return hose on the No 1 injector **(see illustration)**.

7 Unscrew the fuel pipe union nuts at the injectors and injection pump, then unscrew the pipe support bolts on the left-hand side of the camshaft cover and either remove the pipes as an assembly or carefully swivel them to one side of the injectors **(see illustrations)**. As each pump union nut is slackened, retain the adapter with a suitable open-ended spanner to prevent it being unscrewed from the pump. With the union nuts undone, remove the injector pipes from the engine. Cover the injector and pipe unions to prevent the entry of dirt into the system **(see Tool Tip)**.

8 Unscrew the injector, using a deep socket or box spanner, and remove it from the cylinder head **(see illustration)**.

Note: Unscrew the injector by the hexagonal section closest to the cylinder head. Do not unscrew it by the upper hexagonal section, or the injector will fall apart.

9 Recover the washer, noting which way up it is fitted.

Refitting

10 Fit a new washer to the cylinder head, then screw the injector into position and tighten it to the specified torque.

11 Refit the injector pipes and tighten the union nuts to the specified torque setting. Insert and tighten the pipe support bolts.

12 Reconnect the leak-off hoses to the injectors.

13 Refit the engine top cover and tighten the screws.

14 Refit the inlet manifold-to-air cleaner/intercooler air duct and tighten the clips.

15 Reconnect the battery negative (earth) lead and position it away from the terminal.

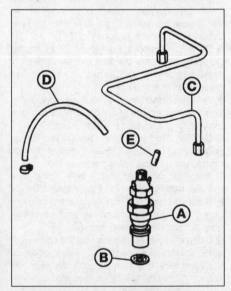

10.8 Fuel injector assembly

A	Injector body	D	Leak-off hose
B	Washer	E	End cap
C	High pressure pipe		

Cut the fingertips from an old rubber glove and secure them over the open unions with elastic bands to prevent the ingress of dirt

10.7c Injector fuel pipe union nuts on the injector pump

11 TDC sensor - removal, refitting and adjustment

Note: *A dial test indicator is required to set the TDC sensor.*

Removal

1 Disconnect the battery negative (earth) lead and position it away from the terminal. The battery is located in the rear luggage compartment.
2 Apply the parking brake, then jack up the front of the vehicle and support it on axle stands (see *Jacking and vehicle support*). Remove the engine compartment undershield.
3 Remove the viscous fan unit as described in Chapter 3.
4 With the auxiliary drivebelt still fitted, loosen the bolts securing the pulley to the coolant pump flange by half a turn each.
5 Remove the auxiliary drivebelt (and air conditioning compressor drivebelt where fitted) as described in Chapter 1B. On early models, release the auxiliary drivebelt tensioner by levering it up.
6 Unscrew the bolts and remove the pulley from the coolant pump.
7 Refer to Chapter 2B, Section 3 and set the engine to TDC.
8 Trace the wiring back from the TDC sensor to the connector and disconnect it.
9 Mark the position of the TDC sensor to aid refitting, then unscrew the mounting bolt and remove it from the timing cover.

Refitting and adjustment

10 Locate the TDC sensor on the timing cover and insert the mounting bolt loosely.
11 Reconnect the wiring.
12 The following procedure describes using a dial test indicator (DTI) to set the TDC sensor accurately.
13 Remove the injector from No 1 cylinder as described in Section 10.
14 Remove the glow plug from No 1 cylinder as described in Chapter 5C.
15 Remove the camshaft cover as described in Chapter 2B. Also remove the tubes from over the injector apertures, noting the location tags. Recover the O-ring seals. **Note:** *It may be necessary to rotate the engine in order to remove the tubes.*
16 Unscrew the pre-combustion chamber retaining ring using the special Mercedes-Benz serrated tool, if available. Alternatively, a locally-made tool may be used.
17 Remove the pre-combustion chamber. Mercedes-Benz technicians use a special slide hammer which screws into the pre-combustion chamber to do this and, if available, this should be used. It may

be possible to fabricate an alternative tool locally.
18 Screw the DTI into the pre-combustion chamber aperture, then set the engine to about 10° BTDC. Adjust the DTI so that there is approximately 5.00 mm preload.
19 Turn the engine forwards and backwards as necessary to determine the exact point of TDC. Set the DTI to TDC. From this point, turn the engine slowly clockwise until the DTI reads 3.35 mm (4-cylinder engine) or 3.23 mm (5-cylinder engines). This point indicates a crankshaft position of 20° ATDC.
20 At the 20° ATDC position, it must be possible to insert a close-fitting pin or drill through the TDC sensor bracket, into the timing hole in the crankshaft pulley or vibration damper. If it is not possible to do this, reposition the sensor until the pin drops easily into the hole, then tighten the mounting bolt.
21 Repeat the adjustment procedure and check that the pin enters the hole freely. Remove the pin on completion.
22 Before refitting the pre-combustion chamber, inspect it for cracks or scorching. If it requires renewal, the remaining pre-combustion chambers should be inspected in the same manner.
23 Unscrew the DTI, then insert the pre-combustion chamber, making sure that the lug on the collar is resting against the recess in the cylinder head.
24 Lubricate the threads of the retaining ring, then screw it in and tighten to the specified torque.
25 Refit the injector aperture tubes together with new O-rings. Make sure that the tube tags are correctly located
26 Refit the camshaft cover as described in Chapter 2B.
27 Refit the glow plug and injector to No 1 cylinder with reference to Chapter 5C and to Section 10 of this Chapter.
28 Refit the coolant pump pulley and tighten the bolts, then refit the auxiliary drivebelt (and air conditioning compressor drivebelt where fitted) with reference to Chapter 1B.
29 Refit the viscous fan unit as described in Chapter 3.
30 Refit the engine compartment undershield and lower the car to the ground.
31 Reconnect the battery negative (earth) lead and position it away from the terminal.

12 Electronic control unit - removal and refitting

Removal

1 The control unit is located on the left-hand side of the bulkhead (right-hand side on LHD models). First, disconnect the battery negative

(earth) lead and position it away from the terminal. The battery is located in the rear luggage compartment.
2 Undo the screws and remove the cover from the electronic control unit (ECU). Recover the gasket.
3 Disconnect the wiring connectors from the ECU control module by swivelling them to one side.
4 Disconnect the wiring connectors from the traction control system module by pulling out the slide locks.
5 Undo the retaining screw and withdraw the bracket, together with the two control modules, from the guides. Separate the ECU from the traction control module.
6 If necessary, remove the relay module after disconnecting the wiring.

Refitting

7 Refitting is a reversal of removal.

13 Fuel heat exchanger and thermostat - removal and refitting

⚠️ **Warning: Observe the precautions in Section 1 before working on any component in the fuel system.**

Removal

1 The fuel heat exchanger and thermostat assembly is mounted on the left-hand side of the cylinder head, behind the injection pump.
2 Remove the engine top cover.
3 Remove the inlet manifold as described in Section 5.
4 Drain approximately 2.0 litres of coolant from the cooling system.
5 Disconnect the fuel inlet and outlet hoses and recover the O-ring.
6 Unbolt the wiring support.
7 Unscrew the Nos 3 and 4 fuel pipe union nuts from the injection pump and move slightly to one side.
8 Unscrew the heat exchanger and thermostat assembly mounting bolts and withdraw the assembly from the cylinder head. Recover the gasket.

Refitting

9 Refitting is a reversal of removal.

14 Intercooler - removal and refitting

Removal

1 Remove the front bumper as described in Chapter 11.
2 Loosen the clips and disconnect the

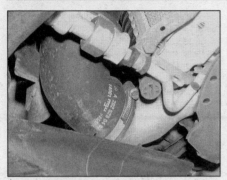

14.2a Air duct connection to the left-hand side of the intercooler

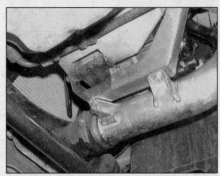

14.2b Air duct connection to the right-hand side of the intercooler

air ducts from the intercooler **(see illustrations)**.

3 Remove the radiator as described in Chapter 3.

4 On models equipped with air conditioning, unscrew the mounting bolts of the receiver/drier, then lift the condenser for access to the intercooler. Support the condenser with a block of wood.

5 Remove the air scoop from the front of the intercooler.

6 Lift the intercooler from the rubber mounting grommets.

7 Check the rubber mounting grommets in the front valance and, if necessary, renew them.

Refitting

8 Refitting is a reversal of removal. Make sure that the air duct hose clips are securely tightened, otherwise the air pressure from the turbocharger may force them off.

Chapter 4 Part C:
Emission control and exhaust systems

Contents

Degrees of difficulty

Easy, suitable for novice with little experience	Fairly easy, suitable for beginner with some experience	Fairly difficult, suitable for competent DIY mechanic	Difficult, suitable for experienced DIY mechanic	Very difficult, suitable for expert DIY or professional

Specifications

Torque wrench settings	Nm	lbf ft
Exhaust manifold to cylinder head	30	22
Exhaust mounting to transmission (diesel models)	20	15
Turbocharger hose clips	3	2
Turbocharger to exhaust manifold	20	15
Turbocharger to front exhaust pipe	20	15

1 General information

Emission control systems

All petrol engine models are designed to use unleaded petrol only, and are controlled by engine management systems that are programmed to give the best compromise between driveability, fuel consumption and exhaust gas emission. In addition, a number of systems are fitted that help to minimise other harmful emissions: a crankcase emission control system recycles crankcase blow-by gases, a catalytic converter reduces exhaust gas pollutants, and an evaporative loss emission control system reduces the release of gaseous hydrocarbons from the fuel tank. In addition, certain models are fitted with an air injection system that helps to reduce the exhaust gas pollutants produced by partially burnt fuel.

All diesel models have a crankcase emission control system and catalytic converter.

Crankcase emission control

To reduce the emission of unburned hydrocarbons from the crankcase into the atmosphere, the engine is sealed and the blow-by gases and oil vapour are drawn from inside the crankcase, through an oil separator, into the inlet tract to be burned by the engine during normal combustion. According to the speed of the engine, the gases are drawn through a restrictor into the cylinder head or into the inlet duct leading to the throttle body.

Exhaust emission control - petrol models

To minimise the amount of pollutants which escape into the atmosphere, a catalytic converter is fitted in the exhaust system. The fuelling system is of the closed-loop type, in which a lambda (oxygen) sensor in the exhaust system provides the fuel injection system ECU with constant feedback, enabling the ECU to adjust the air/fuel mixture to optimise combustion.

The lambda sensor has a heating element built-in that is controlled by the ECU through the lambda sensor relay to quickly bring the sensor's tip to its optimum operating temperature. The sensor's tip is sensitive to oxygen and relays a voltage signal to the ECU that varies according on the amount of oxygen in the exhaust gas. If the inlet air/fuel mixture is too rich, the exhaust gases are low in oxygen so the sensor sends a low voltage signal, the voltage increasing as the mixture weakens and the amount of oxygen rises in the exhaust gases. Peak conversion efficiency of all major pollutants occurs if the inlet air/fuel mixture is maintained at the chemically-correct ratio for the complete combustion of petrol of 14.7 parts (by weight) of air to 1 part of fuel (the 'stoichiometric' ratio). The sensor output voltage alters in a large step at this point, and the ECU uses the signal change as a reference point for correcting the inlet air/fuel mixture accordingly by altering the fuel injector pulse width. The system is referred to as 'closed-loop', because the exhaust gas oxygen content is constantly monitored in order to adjust the air/fuel mixture.

On certain export models, air injection is employed to help reduce the production of gaseous hydrocarbons and carbon monoxide. A mechanical air pump, driven from the

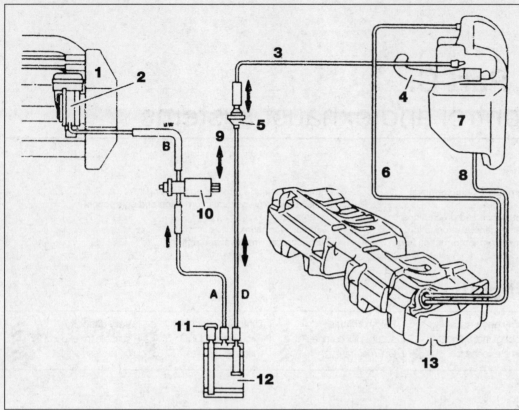

1   Inlet manifold
2   Throttle body (idle speed control actuator)
3   Air inlet and vent pipe to vent valve
4   Vent pipe to filler neck
5   Vent valve
6   Air inlet and vent pipe from fuel tank
7   Fuel expansion reservoir
8   Vent pipe for refuelling
9   HFM sequential multi-port fuel injection ignition system (HFM-SFI) control module
10 Purge switchover valve
11 Air inlet cap
12 Activated charcoal canister
13 Fuel tank
A   Activated charcoal canister/purge switchover valve pipe
B   Purge switchover valve/idle speed control actuator pipe
D   Vent valve/activated charcoal canister pipe

2.1a HFM-SFI evaporation emission control system

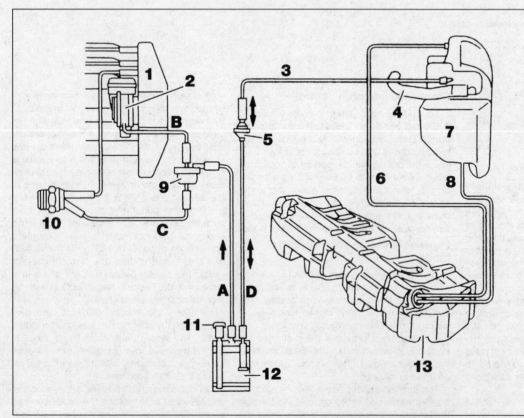

1   Inlet manifold
2   Throttle body (idle speed control actuator)
3   Air inlet and vent pipe to vent valve
4   Vent pipe to filler neck
5   Vent valve
6   Air inlet and vent pipe from fuel tank
7   Fuel expansion reservoir
8   Vent pipe for refuelling
9   Purge valve
10 Thermo valve (opens at 70°C/closes at 35°C)
11 Air inlet cap
12 Activated charcoal canister
13 Fuel tank
A   Activated charcoal canister/purge switchover valve pipe
B   Purge switchover valve/idle speed control actuator pipe
D   Vent valve/activated charcoal canister pipe

2.1b PEC evaporation emission control system

auxiliary drivebelt, forces air into the exhaust manifold where it mixes with the partially-burnt fuel particles. The oxygen-rich air combines with pollutants and allows further oxidation to take place, converting a proportion of the hydrocarbons and carbon monoxide into harmless carbon dioxide and water vapour.

Exhaust emission control - diesel models

An oxidation catalyst is fitted in the exhaust system on diesel engined models. This has the effect of removing a large proportion of the hydrocarbons and carbon monoxide present in the exhaust gas.

Evaporative loss emission control - petrol models

To minimise the escape of hydrocarbons from the fuel system into the atmosphere, an evaporative loss emission control system is fitted to all petrol models. The fuel tank filler cap is sealed and charcoal canister is mounted inside the left-hand rear wheelarch to collect the petrol vapours released from the fuel contained in the fuel tank.

The canister stores the gases until they can be drawn via the purge valve into the throttle body by inlet manifold depression, and burned by the engine during normal combustion.

The flow of fuel vapour from the charcoal canister through the purge valve to the throttle body is controlled by a thermo-valve, which prevents the purge valve from opening until the coolant temperature exceeds a preset limit. This is to ensure that the engine runs correctly when it is cold and to protect the catalytic converter from the effects of an over-rich mixture. In addition, because the purge valve is controlled by manifold vacuum, the charcoal canister is only purged when the engine is under load. This prevents an over-rich mixture from being supplied at idle, preserving idle speed stability and low speed driveability.

Exhaust systems

The exhaust system comprises the exhaust manifold (and turbocharger on turbo-diesel engines), downpipe and catalytic converter, and tailpipe and silencers. On some models the manifold and downpipe are integral. The system is suspended beneath the vehicle by rubber mountings.

The turbocharger fitted to turbo-diesel engined models is oil-cooled and has an integral charge pressure limiting valve.

2 Evaporative loss emission control system - information and component renewal

General information

1 The major components of the evaporative loss emission control system consist of a purge valve, a thermo-valve, an activated charcoal filter canister and vacuum hoses **(see illustrations)**. Fuel gases from the fuel tank and channelled to the charcoal canister, then drawn into the inlet manifold via the idle speed control actuator.

2 The purge valve is clipped to the bulkhead, at the rear of the engine bay. The charcoal canister is mounted on a bracket inside the left-hand rear wheel housing.

Charcoal canister

Removal

3 Chock the front roadwheels, then jack up the rear of the vehicle and support on axle stands (see *Jacking and vehicle support*). Remove the left-hand rear roadwheel.

4 Remove the left-hand rear wheelarch liner.

5 Disconnect the inlet and outlet pipes from the charcoal canister.

6 Unscrew the mounting bolts and remove the charcoal canister from under the wheelarch.

Refitting

7 Refitting is a reversal of removal.

Purge valve

Removal

8 Disconnect the wiring from the purge valve.

9 Disconnect the hoses from the purge valve, noting their order of connection to avoid confusion during refitting.

10 Release the valve from its clip and remove it from the engine bay.

Refitting

11 Refitting is a reversal of removal.

3 Crankcase emission control system - general information

1 The crankcase emission control system consists of a hose that connects the crankcase vent to the inlet ports of the cylinder head, a hose connecting the camshaft cover to the inlet air duct, a restrictor valve and an oil separator unit **(see illustrations)**. When the engine is operating in the idle speed to mid part-load speed, the blow-by gases in the crankcase are drawn through an oil separator and hose with a restrictor to the inlet ports of

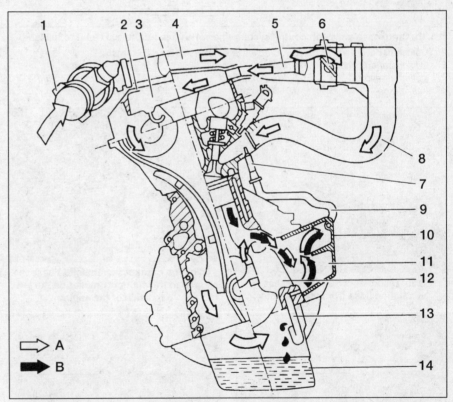

3.1a Crankcase emission control system - petrol engine (idle speed to mid-part load)

1 Hot film air mass sensor	6 Throttle body	11 Oil separation chamber (cylinder block)
2 Camshaft cover	7 Restrictor	12 Crankcase
3 Oil separation chamber (cylinder head)	8 Inlet manifold	13 Oil return pipe
4 Intake pipe	9 Crankcase ventilation hose	14 Sump
5 Crankcase ventilation pipe	10 Power steering pump mounting bracket	A Fresh air
		B Blow-by gases

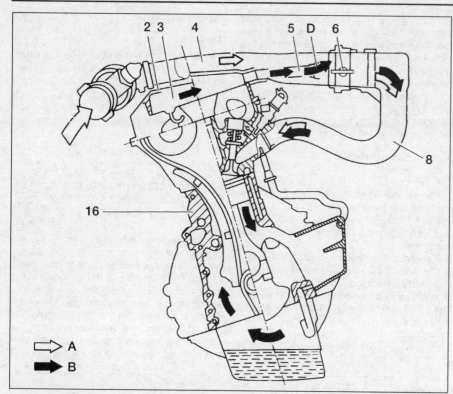

3.1b Crankcase emission control system - petrol engine (upper-part load to full load)

2	Camshaft cover	5	Crankcase ventilation pipe	A	Fresh air
3	Oil separation chamber	6	Throttle body	B	Blow-by gases
	(cylinder head)	8	Inlet manifold	D	Point of vacuum at the
4	Intake pipe	16	Crankcase		ventilation pipe

the cylinder head, where it is mixed with fresh air entering the engine through the inlet manifold. When the engine is operating at mid part-load to full load speed, the blow-by gases are drawn through the camshaft cover through a hose into the inlet air duct leading to the throttle body.

2 The components of this system require no attention other than to check at regular intervals that the hoses are free of blockages and undamaged **(see illustrations)**.

4 Exhaust manifold - removal and refitting

Removal

1 Apply the parking brake, then jack up the front of the vehicle and support it on axle stands (see *Jacking and vehicle support*). Remove the engine compartment undershield.

Petrol models

2 Disconnect the oxygen (lambda) sensor wiring at the bulkhead. Alternatively, completely remove the sensor as described in Chapter 4A, Section 10.

3 Unscrew the flange bolts securing the exhaust front pipe to the exhaust manifold, then unbolt the mounting bracket from the transmission. Recover the gasket **(see illustrations)**.

4 Unbolt the hot air shroud from the exhaust manifold **(see illustrations)**.

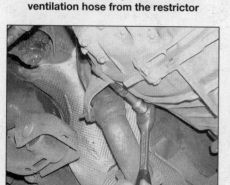

3.2a Disconnecting the crankcase ventilation hose from the restrictor

3.2b The crankcase ventilation hose is clipped to the support bracket on the left-hand side of the engine

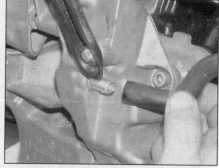

3.2c Disconnecting the crankcase ventilation hose from the oil separator

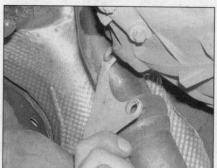

4.3a Unscrew the bolts . . .

... and remove the mounting bracket from the lower end of the manifold

4.3b

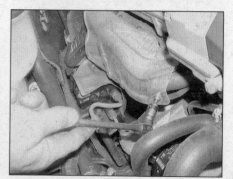

4.4a Unscrew the bolts . . .

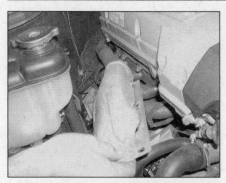

4.4b . . . and remove the hot air shroud from the exhaust manifold

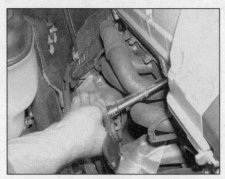

4.5 Unscrew the mounting nuts . . .

5 Progressively unscrew the nuts securing the exhaust manifold to the cylinder head **(see illustration)**.

6 Withdraw the exhaust manifold from the studs on the cylinder head, and recover the gasket **(see illustrations)**.

Diesel models

7 Loosen the clips and remove the air inlet duct leading from the air cleaner to the inlet manifold.

8 Unscrew the nuts securing the exhaust downpipe to the exhaust manifold or turbocharger, then unscrew the exhaust mounting bracket from the transmission. Support the downpipe on an axle stand or blocks of wood. Recover the gasket.

9 On turbocharged models, remove the turbocharger as described in Section 6.

10 Progressively unscrew the nuts securing the exhaust manifold to the cylinder head.

11 Withdraw the exhaust manifold from the studs on the cylinder head, and recover the gasket.

Refitting

12 Before refitting the exhaust manifold, check the studs in the cylinder head and renew them if necessary. The nuts should be renewed as a matter of course.

13 Refitting is a reversal of removal, but fit a new gasket and progressively tighten the mounting nuts to the specified torque.

---

5 Turbocharger - removal and refitting

Note: *This Section applies to the 2.5 litre turbocharged diesel engine only.*

General information

1 The turbocharger is mounted on the exhaust manifold. Lubrication is provided by a dedicated oil supply pipe that runs from a tapping on the cylinder head. Oil is returned to the sump via a return pipe that connects to the side of the cylinder block. The turbocharger unit has an integral wastegate valve and vacuum actuator diaphragm, which is used to limit the boost pressure applied to the inlet manifold.

2 The turbocharger's internal components rotate at very high speed and as such are very sensitive to contamination; a great deal of damage can be caused by small particles of dirt, particularly if they strike the delicate turbine blades. Refer to the **Caution** and **Warning** notes given below before working on or removing the turbocharger unit.

Caution: Thoroughly clean the area around all oil pipe unions before disconnecting them, to prevent the ingress of dirt. Store dismantled components in a sealed container to prevent contamination. Cover the turbocharger air inlet ducts to prevent debris entering and clean using lint-free cloths only.

Warning: Do not run the engine with the turbocharger air inlet hose disconnected, since the depression at the inlet can build up very suddenly if the engine speed is raised, and there is the risk of foreign objects being sucked in and then ejected at very high speed.

Removal

3 Disconnect the battery negative (earth) lead and position it away from the terminal. The battery is located in the rear luggage compartment.

4 Apply the parking brake, then jack up the front of the vehicle and support it on axle stands (see *Jacking and vehicle support*). Remove the engine compartment undershield.

5 Unclip and remove the air cleaner cover, then loosen the clips and remove the air duct from between the air cleaner and turbocharger.

6 Loosen the clips and remove the air duct leading from the intercooler outlet duct to the pressure regulating housing.

7 Loosen the clip and remove the pressure regulating housing from the air duct leading to the inlet manifold.

8 Unscrew the union nuts and remove the oil supply pipe from the turbocharger and cylinder head.

9 Loosen the clips and remove the intercooler charge air hose from the turbocharger.

10 Position a container beneath the oil drain pipe, then unscrew the bolts and remove the pipes and flange from the turbocharger and cylinder block. Recover the gaskets.

11 Disconnect the vacuum hoses from the wastegate actuator diaphragm housing and, where applicable, the EGR valve. Identify the hoses for position.

12 Unscrew the nuts and disconnect the exhaust downpipe from the turbocharger. Recover the gasket.

13 Unscrew the bolts and remove the turbocharger from the exhaust manifold. Recover the gasket.

Refitting

14 Refitting is a reversal of removal, but before reconnecting the oil supply pipe to the turbocharger, prime the oil inlet port with clean engine oil. Tighten all nuts and bolts securely, and to the specified torque where given. When the engine is first started, allow it to idle for at least one minute to allow the oil to circulate around the turbocharger bearings.

---

6 Exhaust system - general information and component renewal

General information

1 On all models, both petrol and diesel, the exhaust system is made up of an exhaust manifold, front pipe, a catalytic converter, and a rear tailpipe incorporating two silencers. On

4.6a . . . then withdraw the exhaust manifold from the cylinder head . . .

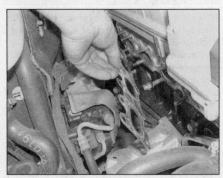

4.6b . . . and recover the gasket from the studs

6.6 Unbolting the exhaust front pipe from the lower end of the manifold (2.0 litre engine)

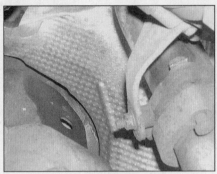

6.8 Bracket supporting the lower end of the manifold to the transmission (2.0 litre engine)

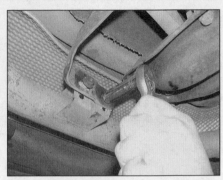

6.9 Unbolting the exhaust front pipe from the bracket on the rear of the transmission

petrol engine models, an oxygen sensor (lambda sensor) is located either on the exhaust manifold or on the front of the catalytic converter. Also on petrol engine models, note that each silencer of the factory-supplied rear section may be renewed separately by cutting the pipe between the silencers, and fitting a clamp and bolt. The pipe of the new rear silencer is of larger diameter so that it will locate over the original pipe of the front silencer, so the rearmost silencer must be renewed first.

2 The exhaust system is suspended along its entire length by rubber mountings, which are secured to the underside of the vehicle. The downpipe is secured to the transmission by means of a bracket and rubber pad.

3 The downpipe is attached to the exhaust manifold by a flange joint and gasket, secured with bolts. A clamped joint secures the front of the catalytic converter to the downpipe, and the catalytic converter is connected to the rear exhaust section by a flange joint fitted with a sealing olive.

Removal

4 Each exhaust section can be removed individually or, alternatively, the complete system can be removed as a unit.

5 Before removing any part of the system, first jack up the front or rear of the car, as applicable, and support it on axle stands (see *Jacking and vehicle support*). Alternatively (or if the complete exhaust system is being removed) position the car over an inspection pit or on car ramps.

Front pipe

6 Unscrew and remove the bolts/nuts securing the front pipe to the exhaust manifold/turbocharger **(see illustration)**.

7 Unscrew the bolts and separate the rear end of the pipe from the front of the catalytic converter. Recover the gasket where applicable.

8 Where applicable, unscrew the nut securing the lower end of the manifold to the bracket on the right-hand side of the transmission **(see illustration)**.

9 Unbolt the front pipe from the bracket on the rear of the transmission, then withdraw it from under the car **(see illustration)**.

Catalytic converter

Note: *Catalytic converters must not be disposed of as normal scrap metal as they contain precious metal which can be recycled.*

10 Support the rear section of the exhaust on an axle stand or block of wood.

11 Release the rubber mounting, then unbolt the mounting bracket from the transmission.

12 Unscrew the bolt and separate the front of the catalytic converter from the rear end of the exhaust downpipe. Where applicable recover the gasket.

13 At the rear of the catalytic converter, unscrew the bolts and separate the converter from the rear section of the exhaust system. Recover the sealing olive.

14 Withdraw the catalytic converter from under the car.

Rear pipe and silencers (as supplied in one unit by the factory)

15 Unscrew the bolts and separate the front and rear sections of the exhaust system. Recover the sealing olive.

16 Support the rear pipe and silencers, then release the rubber mountings. Lower the exhaust and remove it from under the vehicle.

17 If only one of the silencers requires renewal, use a hacksaw to cut the pipe between the silencers, 80 mm behind the intermediate silencer. Note that the new and old pipes must overlap each other by 70 to 80 mm.

Intermediate silencer (separate service part)

18 Unscrew the bolts and separate the intermediate pipe from the catalytic converter. Recover the sealing olive.

19 Unscrew the bolt from the clamp, then separate the intermediate silencer from the rear silencer. It may be necessary to tap around the joint with a hammer in order to release it. Lower the intermediate silencer and withdraw it from under the vehicle.

Rear silencer (separate service part)

20 Unscrew the bolt from the clamp, then separate the intermediate silencer from the rear silencer. It may be necessary to tap around the joint with a hammer in order to release it.

21 Support the rear silencer, then unhook the rubber mounting. Lower the silencer and withdraw it from under the vehicle.

Complete system

22 Unscrew and remove the clamp bolts securing the catalytic converter/downpipe to the exhaust manifold/turbocharger, separate and, where necessary, recover the gasket.

23 Release the rubber mounting then unbolt the mounting bracket from the transmission.

24 With the help of an assistant, support the rear of the exhaust system, then unhook the rubber mountings and lower the system to the floor. Withdraw it from under the vehicle.

Refitting

25 Each section is refitted by a reverse of the removal sequence, noting the following points.

a) *Ensure that all traces of corrosion have been removed from the flanges and renew all necessary gaskets.*

b) *Inspect the rubber mountings for signs of damage or deterioration and renew as necessary.*

c) *Renew the sealing olive between the catalytic converter and rear section.*

d) *When refitting the transmission mounting bracket to the downpipe, note that the front two holes must be used for automatic transmission models and the rear two holes must be used for manual transmission.*

e) *Prior to tightening the exhaust system joints, ensure that all rubber mountings are correctly located and that there is adequate clearance between the exhaust system and vehicle underbody.*

7   Catalytic converters - general information and precautions

The catalytic converter is a reliable and simple device, with no moving parts and as such requires no maintenance. There are, however, some facts of which an owner should be aware if the converter is to function properly for its full service life.

Petrol models

a) *DO NOT use leaded petrol (or LRP) in a car equipped with a catalytic converter - the lead will coat the precious metals, reducing their converting efficiency and will eventually destroy the converter.*

b) *Always keep the ignition and fuel systems well-maintained in accordance with the manufacturer's schedule.*

c) *If the engine develops a misfire, do not drive the car at all (or at least as little as possible) until the fault is cured.*

d) *DO NOT push- or tow-start the car - this will soak the catalytic converter in unburned fuel, causing it to overheat when the engine does start.*

e) *DO NOT switch off the ignition at high engine speeds.*

f) *DO NOT use fuel or engine oil additives - these may contain substances harmful to the catalytic converter.*

g) *DO NOT continue to use the car if the engine burns oil to the extent of leaving a visible trail of blue smoke.*

h) *Remember that the catalytic converter operates at very high temperatures. DO NOT, therefore, park the car in dry undergrowth, over long grass or piles of dead leaves after a long run.*

i) *Remember that the catalytic converter is FRAGILE - do not strike it with tools during servicing work.*

j) *The catalytic converter, used on a well-maintained and well-driven car, should last for between 50 000 and 100 000 miles - if the converter is no longer effective it must be renewed.*

Diesel models

Refer to the information given in Parts f, g, h, i and j of the petrol models information given above.

8 Air injection system - general information, pump removal and refitting

General information

1 An air injection system is fitted to some petrol engines for certain export vehicles. The system injects air into the exhaust manifold in order to promote rapid combustion of any unburnt hydrocarbons, particularly during start-up. This has the effect of quickly heating up the catalytic converter and oxygen sensor to their normal operating temperatures so that maximum engine efficiency is reached without delay. The injection pump is belt-driven from the crankshaft pulley and incorporates an electromagnetic coupling to enable the pump to be switched on and off.

Air injection pump
Removal

2 Access to the air injection pump is best achieved from under the car. Apply the parking brake, then jack up the front of the vehicle and support it on axle stands (see *Jacking and vehicle support*). Remove the engine compartment undershield.

3 Remove the auxiliary drivebelt as described in Chapter 1A.

4 Remove the plastic cover from the cooling system thermostat housing.

5 Disconnect the pump wiring, located behind the viscous fan. Also unscrew the bolt securing the earth cable to the cylinder block.

6 Release the clamp and disconnect the air hose (leading to the shut-off valve) from the pump.

7 Unscrew the mounting bolts and remove the air injection pump from the right-hand side of the cylinder block. Inspect the rubber mountings for condition and if necessary, renew them.

8 It is recommended that the air shut-off valve is renewed when renewing the air injection pump. The valve is located on the exhaust manifold.

Refitting

9 Refitting is a reversal of removal.

Chapter 5 Part A:
Starting and charging systems

Contents

Degrees of difficulty

Easy, suitable for novice with little experience		Fairly easy, suitable for beginner with some experience		Fairly difficult, suitable for competent DIY mechanic		Difficult, suitable for experienced DIY mechanic		Very difficult, suitable for expert DIY or professional	

Specifications

General
System type . . . . 12 volt, negative earth

Battery
Rating:
   Petrol engined models . . . . 46, 62 or 75 Ah
   Diesel engined models . . . . 74 or 100 Ah
Charge condition:
   Poor . . . . 12.5 volts
   Normal . . . . 12.6 volts
   Good . . . . 12.7 volts

Starter motor
Rating:
   Petrol engined models . . . . 12V, 1.4 kW
   Diesel engined models . . . . 12V, 2.2 kW

Alternator
Type:
   Models without air conditioning 40A/70A
   Models with air conditioning 45A/90A
Minimum brush length . . . . 5.0 mm

Torque wrench settings

	Nm	lbf ft
Alternator main cable nut	15	11
Alternator mounting bolt	42	31
Alternator warning wire nut	4	3
Starter motor main cable nut	14	10
Starter motor mounting bolt	42	31
Starter motor trigger wire nut	6	4

1 General information and precautions

General information

1 The engine electrical system consists mainly of the charging and starting systems. Because of their engine-related functions, these components are covered separately from the body electrical devices such as the lights, instruments, etc (which are covered in Chapter 12). On petrol engine models refer to Part B of this Chapter for information on the ignition system, and on diesel models refer to Part C for information on the pre-heating system.

2 The electrical system is of the 12 volt negative earth type.

3 The battery may be of the low maintenance or maintenance-free (sealed for life) type and is charged by the alternator, which is belt-driven from the crankshaft pulley.

4 The starter motor is of the pre-engaged type incorporating an integral solenoid. On starting, the solenoid moves the drive pinion into engagement with the flywheel ring gear before the starter motor is energised. Once the engine has started, a one-way clutch prevents the motor armature being driven by the engine until the pinion disengages from the flywheel.

Precautions

5 Further details of the various systems are given in the relevant Sections of this Chapter. While some repair procedures are given, the usual course of action is to renew the component concerned.

6 It is necessary to take extra care when working on the electrical system to avoid damage to semi-conductor devices (diodes and transistors), and to avoid the risk of personal injury. In addition to the precautions given in *Safety first!* at the beginning of this manual, observe the following when working on the system.

7 *Always remove rings, watches, etc, before working on the electrical system*. Even with the battery disconnected, capacitive discharge could occur if a component's live terminal is earthed through a metal object. This could cause a shock or nasty burn.

8 *Do not reverse the battery connections*. Components such as the alternator, electronic control units, or any other components having semi-conductor circuitry could be irreparably damaged.

9 If the engine is being started using jump leads and a slave battery, connect the batteries *positive-to-positive* and *negative-to-negative* (see *Jump Starting*). This also applies when connecting a battery charger.

10 Never disconnect the battery terminals, the alternator, any electrical wiring or any test instruments when the engine is running.

11 Do not allow the engine to turn the alternator when the alternator is not connected.

12 Never test for alternator output by 'flashing' the output lead to earth.

13 Never use an ohmmeter of the type incorporating a hand-cranked generator for circuit or continuity testing.

14 Always ensure that the battery negative lead is disconnected when working on the electrical system.

15 Before using electric-arc welding equipment on the car, disconnect the battery, alternator and components such as the fuel injection/ignition electronic control unit to protect them from the risk of damage.

16 The radio/cassette unit fitted as standard equipment by Mercedes-Benz is equipped with a built-in security code to deter thieves. If the power source to the unit is cut, the anti-theft system will activate. Even if the power source is immediately reconnected, the radio/cassette unit will not function until the correct security code has been entered. Therefore, if you do not know the correct security code for the radio/cassette unit do not disconnect the battery negative terminal of the battery or remove the radio/cassette unit from the vehicle. Refer to your Mercedes-Benz dealer for further information on whether the unit fitted to your car has a security code. Also refer to *Radio/cassette unit anti-theft system - precaution* for further information.

2 Battery - testing and charging

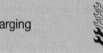

Standard and low maintenance battery - testing

1 If the vehicle covers a small annual mileage, it is worthwhile checking the specific gravity of the electrolyte every three months to determine the state of charge of the battery. Use a hydrometer to make the check and compare the results with the following table. The temperatures quoted in the table are ambient (air) temperatures. Note that the specific gravity readings assume an electrolyte temperature of 15°C (60°F); for every 10°C (18°F) below 15°C (60°F) subtract 0.007. For every 10°C (18°F) above 15°C (60°F) add 0.007.

	Above 25°C (77°F)	Below 25°C (77°F)
Fully-charged	1.210 to 1.230	1.270 to 1.290
70% charged	1.170 to 1.190	1.230 to 1.250
Discharged	1.050 to 1.070	1.110 to 1.130

2 If the battery condition is suspect, first check the specific gravity of electrolyte in each cell. A variation of 0.040 or more between any cells indicates loss of electrolyte or deterioration of the internal plates.

3 If the specific gravity variation is 0.040 or more, the battery should be renewed. If the cell variation is satisfactory but the battery is discharged, it should be charged as described later in this Section.

Maintenance-free battery - testing

4 In cases where a 'sealed for life' maintenance-free battery is fitted, topping-up and testing of the electrolyte in each cell is not possible. The condition of the battery can therefore only be tested using a battery condition indicator or a voltmeter.

5 Certain models may be fitted with a maintenance-free battery with a built-in charge condition indicator. The indicator is located in the top of the battery casing, and indicates the condition of the battery from its colour. If the indicator shows green, then the battery is in a good state of charge. If the indicator turns darker, eventually to black, then the battery requires charging, as described later in this Section. If the indicator shows clear/yellow, then the electrolyte level in the battery is too low to allow further use, and the battery should be renewed. **Do not** attempt to charge, load or jump start a battery when the indicator shows clear/yellow.

6 If testing the battery using a voltmeter, connect the voltmeter across the battery and compare the result with those given in the *Specifications* under 'charge condition'. The test is only accurate if the battery has not been subjected to any kind of charge for the previous six hours. If this is not the case, switch on the headlights for 30 seconds, then wait four to five minutes before testing the battery after switching off the headlights. All other electrical circuits must be switched off, so check that the doors and tailgate are fully shut when making the test.

7 If the voltage reading is less than 12.2 volts, then the battery is discharged, whilst a reading of 12.2 to 12.4 volts indicates a partially discharged condition.

8 If the battery is to be charged, remove it from the vehicle and charge it as described later in this Section.

Standard and low maintenance battery - charging

Note: *The following is intended as a guide only. Always refer to the manufacturer's recommendations (often printed on a label attached to the battery) before charging a battery.*

9 Charge the battery at a rate equivalent to 10% of the battery capacity (eg, for a 46 Ah battery charge at 4.6 A) and continue to charge the battery at this rate until no further rise in specific gravity is noted over a four hour period.

10 Alternatively, a trickle charger charging at the rate of 1.5 amps can safely be used overnight.

11 Specially rapid 'boost' charges which are claimed to restore the power of the battery in 1 to 2 hours are not recommended, as they can cause serious damage to the battery plates through overheating.

12 While charging the battery, note that the temperature of the electrolyte should never exceed 37.8°C (100°F).

Maintenance-free battery - charging

Note: *The following is intended as a guide only. Always refer to the maker's recommendations (often printed on a label attached to the battery) before charging a battery.*

13 This battery type takes considerably longer to fully recharge than the standard type, the time taken being dependent on the extent of discharge, but it can take anything up to three days.

14 A constant voltage type charger is required to be set, when connected, to 13.9 to 14.9 volts with a charger current below 25 amps. Using this method, the battery should be useable within three hours, giving a voltage reading of 12.5 volts, but this is for a partially discharged battery and, as mentioned, full charging can take considerably longer.

15 If the battery is to be charged from a fully discharged state (condition reading less than 12.2 volts), have it recharged by your Mercedes-Benz dealer or local automotive electrician, as the charge rate is higher and constant supervision during charging is necessary.

3 Battery - removal and refitting

Removal

1 The battery is located in the rear luggage compartment, next to the spare wheel. Open the boot lid or tailgate, then lift up the floor covering.
2 Loosen the clamp bolt and disconnect the battery negative cable from the terminal.
3 Lift the flap, then loosen the clamp bolt and disconnect the battery positive cable from the terminal.
4 Unscrew the bolts and remove the clamp plate securing the battery to the floor.
5 Detach the ventilation pipe from the battery.
6 Lift the battery from the luggage compartment.

Refitting

7 Refitting is a reversal of removal. Tighten the battery clamp plate bolt securely.

4 Alternator/charging system - testing in vehicle

Note: *Refer to the precautions given in Safety first! and in Section 1 of this Chapter before starting work.*

1 If the ignition warning light fails to illuminate when the ignition is switched on, first check the alternator wiring connections for security. If satisfactory, check that the warning light bulb has not blown, and that the bulbholder is secure in its location in the instrument panel. If the light still fails to illuminate, check the continuity of the warning light feed wire from the alternator to the bulbholder. If all is satisfactory, the alternator is at fault and should be renewed or taken to an auto-electrician for testing and repair.
2 If the ignition warning light illuminates when the engine is running, stop the engine and check that the drivebelt is intact and that the alternator connections are secure. If all is so far satisfactory, check the alternator brushes and slip rings as described in Section 6. If the fault persists, the alternator should be renewed, or taken to an auto-electrician for testing and repair.
3 If the alternator output is suspect even though the warning light functions correctly, the regulated voltage may be checked as follows.
4 Connect a voltmeter across the battery terminals and start the engine.
5 Increase the engine speed until the voltmeter reading remains steady; the reading should be approximately 12 to 13 volts, and no more than 14 volts.
6 Switch on as many electrical accessories (eg, the headlights, heated rear window and heater blower) as possible, and check that the alternator maintains the regulated voltage at around 13 to 14 volts.
7 If the regulated voltage is not as stated, the fault may be due to worn brushes, weak brush springs, a faulty voltage regulator, a faulty diode, a severed phase winding or worn or damaged slip rings. The brushes and slip rings may be checked (see Section 6), but if the fault persists, the alternator should be renewed or taken to an auto-electrician for testing and repair.

5 Alternator - removal and refitting

1 The alternator is bolted to the right hand side of the engine block and is driven by the auxiliary belt.

Removal

2 Disconnect the battery negative (earth) lead and position it away from the terminal. The battery is located in the rear luggage compartment.
3 On petrol engine models with air conditioning, and all diesel models, apply the parking brake, then jack up the front of the vehicle and support it on axle stands (see *Jacking and vehicle support*). Remove the engine compartment undershield.
4 Detach the auxiliary drivebelt from the alternator pulley with reference to Chapter 1A or 1B.
5 Prise off the protective cap and unscrew the nut securing the battery positive lead to the alternator terminal **(see illustration)**. Position the lead to one side.
6 Unscrew the nut and detach the warning light wire from the alternator terminal.
7 Unscrew and remove first the lower then the upper mounting bolt, and withdraw the alternator from its mounting bracket on the right-hand side of the engine **(see illustrations)**.
8 If necessary, remove the brush holder/voltage regulator module as described in Section 6.

Refitting

9 Refitting is a reversal of removal. Refer to Chapter 1A or 1B for details of refitting the auxiliary drivebelt.

6 Alternator - brush holder/regulator module renewal

1 Remove the alternator as described in Section 5.
2 Place the alternator on a clean work surface, with the pulley facing down.

5.5 Disconnecting the wiring from the alternator

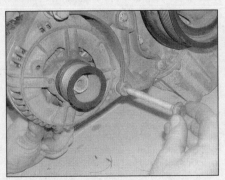
5.7a Removing the alternator lower mounting bolt . . .

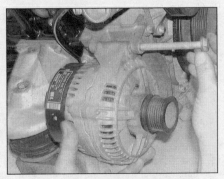
5.7b . . . and upper mounting bolt

6.4a Remove the brush holder/voltage regulator module screws (arrowed) . . .

6.4b . . . then lift the module away from the alternator

3 Undo the three screws, then prise open the clips and lift the plastic cover from the rear of the alternator.

4 Undo the two screws securing the brush holder/voltage regulator module to the alternator, then withdraw the module **(see illustrations).**

5 Measure the free length of the brush contacts - take the measurement from the manufacturers emblem etched on the side of the brush contact, to the shallowest part of the curved end face of the brush. Check the measurement with the *Specifications*; renew the module if the brushes are worn below the minimum limit.

6 Inspect the surfaces of the slip rings through the brush holder/regulator aperture. If they are dirty, carefully clean them with fine glasspaper, however, if they are excessively worn, burnt or pitted, renewal of the complete alternator may be necessary.

7 Carefully locate the new brush holder/regulator on the alternator, taking care not to break the carbon brushes, then insert and tighten the retaining screws. The new holder may incorporate pins which retain the brushes retracted while the holder is being fitted and the screws inserted, after which the pins are removed to release the brushes against the slip rings.

8 Refit the plastic cover to the alternator and retain with the three screws.

9 Refit the alternator with reference to Section 5.

7 Starting system - testing

Note: *Refer to the precautions given in Safety first! and in Section 1 of this Chapter before starting work.*

1 If the starter motor fails to operate when the ignition key is turned to the appropriate position, the following possible causes may be responsible.

a) *The battery is faulty.*
b) *The electrical connections between the switch, solenoid, battery and starter motor are somewhere failing to pass the necessary current from the battery through the starter to earth.*
c) *The solenoid is faulty.*
d) *The starter motor is mechanically or electrically defective.*

2 To check the battery, switch on the headlights. If they dim after a few seconds, this indicates that the battery is discharged - recharge (see Section 2) or renew the battery. If the headlights glow brightly, operate the ignition switch and observe the lights. If they dim, then this indicates that current is reaching the starter motor, therefore the fault must lie in the starter motor. If the lights continue to glow brightly (and no clicking sound can be heard from the starter motor solenoid), this indicates that there is a fault in the circuit or solenoid - see following paragraphs. If the starter motor turns slowly when operated, but the battery is in good condition, then this indicates that either the starter motor is faulty, or there is considerable resistance somewhere in the circuit.

3 If a fault in the circuit is suspected, disconnect the battery leads (including the earth connection to the body), the starter/solenoid wiring and the engine/transmission earth strap. Thoroughly clean the connections, and reconnect the leads and wiring, then use a voltmeter or test lamp to check that full battery voltage is available at the battery positive lead connection to the solenoid, and that the earth is sound. Smear petroleum jelly around the battery terminals to prevent corrosion - corroded connections are amongst the most frequent causes of electrical system faults.

4 If the battery and all connections are in good condition, check the circuit by disconnecting the trigger wire from the solenoid terminal. Connect a voltmeter or test lamp between the wire end and a good earth (such as the battery negative terminal), and

check that the wire is live when the ignition switch is turned to the 'start' position. If it is, then the circuit is sound - if not the circuit wiring can be checked as described in Chapter 12.

5 The solenoid contacts can be checked by connecting a voltmeter or test lamp between the battery positive feed connection on the starter side of the solenoid, and earth. When the ignition switch is turned to the 'start' position, there should be a reading or lighted bulb, as applicable. If there is no reading or lighted bulb, the solenoid is faulty and should be renewed.

6 If the circuit and solenoid are proved sound, the fault must lie in the starter motor. Begin checking the starter motor by removing it and having the brushes checked (see Section 11). If the fault does not lie in the brushes, the motor windings must be faulty. In this event, it may be possible to have the starter motor overhauled by a specialist, but check on the availability and cost of spares before proceeding, as it may prove more economical to obtain a new or exchange motor.

8 Starter motor - removal and refitting

Removal

1 The starter motor is bolted to the transmission bellhousing, at the rear of the engine on the left-hand side. Access is best achieved from under the front of the car, although on petrol engine models without air conditioning, the starter motor can be removed from above.

2 Disconnect the battery negative (earth) lead and position it away from the terminal. The battery is located in the rear luggage compartment.

3 On petrol models equipped with air conditioning, and all diesel models, apply the

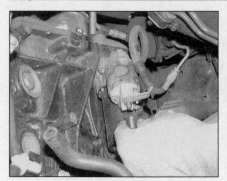

8.4a Remove the cap . . .

8.4b . . . then disconnect the main cable from the starter motor

parking brake, then jack up the front of the vehicle and support it on axle stands (see *Jacking and vehicle support*). Remove the engine compartment undershield.

4 Remove the cap then unscrew the nut and disconnect the main cable from the terminal on the starter solenoid **(see illustrations)**.

Unbolt and remove the cable support and move the cable to one side.
5 Disconnect the trigger wire from the solenoid.
6 Release the wiring from the clips on the starter motor. Where necessary, unbolt the support.

7 Using socket extensions above the transmission, unscrew the upper starter mounting bolts, then unscrew the lower mounting bolts. Remove the starter motor from the transmission bellhousing and withdraw from under the car **(see illustrations)**.

Refitting

8 Refitting is a reversal of removal.

9   Starter motor - overhaul

If the starter motor is thought to be defective, it should be removed from the vehicle and taken to an auto-electrician for assessment. In the majority of cases, new starter motor brushes can be fitted at a reasonable cost. However, check the cost of repairs first as it may prove more economical to purchase a new or exchange motor.

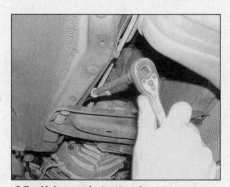

8.7a Using socket extensions to unscrew the upper starter motor mounting bolts

8.7b Unscrewing the lower starter motor mounting bolts

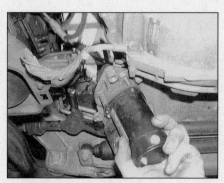

8.7c Removing the starter motor from under the car

Chapter 5 Part B:
Ignition system - petrol engines

Contents

Degrees of difficulty

Easy, suitable for novice with little experience		Fairly easy, suitable for beginner with some experience		Fairly difficult, suitable for competent DIY mechanic		Difficult, suitable for experienced DIY mechanic		Very difficult, suitable for expert DIY or professional	

Specifications

General

System type:

1.8 litre (111.920) and 2.0 litre (111.941) engines	Bosch PMS sequential, closed-loop fuel injection/ignition system
1.8 litre (111.921), 2.0 litre (111.945), 2.2 litre (111.961) and 2.3 litre (111.974) engines	Bosch HFM sequential, closed-loop fuel injection/ignition system

Ignition coil(s)

Primary winding resistance (terminals 1 and 15)	0.3 to 0.6 ohms
Secondary winding resistance (terminals 1 and 4)	5.2 to 8.5 k ohms
Dwell angle:	
At cranking speed	20 to 100 ms
At idle speed	4 to 5 ms

Spark plugs

Type and electrode gap	See Chapter 1A
Spark plug connector resistance	700 to 1300 ohms

Sensors

Crankshaft position sensor resistance	680 to 1200 ohms
Camshaft position sensor resistance	900 to 1600 ohms
Coolant temperature sensor:	
Electrical resistance:	
At 80°C	325 ohms
At 40°C	1170 ohms
At 10°C	3700 ohms
Inlet air temperature sensor:	
Electrical resistance:	
At 80°C	620 ohms
At 40°C	2600 ohms
At 10°C	9670 ohms

Torque wrench setting

	Nm	lbf ft
Camshaft position sensor	10	7
Crankshaft position sensor	10	7
Knock sensor	20	15
Spark plugs	27	20

1 General information

The PMS and HFM systems fitted to Mercedes-Benz C-Class models covered in this manual are self-contained engine management systems, which control both the fuel injection and ignition. This Chapter deals with the ignition system components only - refer to Chapter 4A for details of the fuel injection system components.

The main components of the system comprise the spark plugs, electronic ignition coils, HT leads from the coils to the spark plugs, and an electronic control unit (ECU) together with associated sensors and wiring. The basic operation is as follows: the ECU supplies a voltage to the input stage of the ignition coil which causes the primary windings to be energised. The LT (low tension) supply voltage is periodically interrupted by the ECU and this results in the collapse of the primary magnetic field, which then induces a much larger HT (high tension) voltage in the coil's secondary windings. This HT voltage is directed via the HT leads to the spark plug in the cylinder currently on its ignition stroke. The spark plug electrodes form a gap small enough for the HT voltage to arc across, and the resulting spark ignites the fuel/air mixture in the cylinder. The timing of this sequence of events is critical and is regulated solely by the ECU.

Distributorless, 'wasted spark' ignition is employed, whereby the ECU directly controls two 'double-ended' coils, each of which serves two spark plugs. The ECU triggers each coil once per ignition stroke per cylinder, so each spark plug receives a total of two sparks per cycle, and the spark generated during the exhaust stroke is therefore 'wasted'.

The ECU calculates and controls the ignition timing and dwell angle primarily according to engine speed, crankshaft position and inlet manifold depression information, received from sensors mounted on and around the engine. Other parameters that affect ignition timing are throttle position (idle and full throttle positions are sensed via a changeover switch), inlet air temperature and coolant temperature. Again, these are monitored via sensors mounted on the engine.

It should be noted that comprehensive fault diagnosis of all the engine management systems described in this Chapter is only possible with dedicated electronic test equipment. Problems with the systems operation that cannot be pinpointed by following the basic guidelines in Section 2 should therefore be referred to a Mercedes-Benz dealer for assessment. Once the fault has been identified, the removal/refitting sequences detailed in the following Sections will then allow the appropriate component(s) to be renewed as required.

2 Ignition system - testing

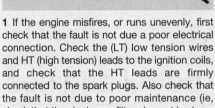

1 If the engine misfires, or runs unevenly, first check that the fault is not due a poor electrical connection. Check the (LT) low tension wires and HT (high tension) leads to the ignition coils, and check that the HT leads are firmly connected to the spark plugs. Also check that the fault is not due to poor maintenance (ie, check that the air cleaner filter element is clean, the spark plugs are in good condition and correctly gapped, and that the engine breather hoses are clear and undamaged. If the engine is running very roughly check the compression pressures as described in Chapter 2A.

2 Where misfiring occurs, check the condition of the HT leads from the ignition coils to the spark plugs. They must be clean and dry and in good condition to prevent arcing onto nearby engine parts. If the engine has covered a high mileage, it is worth considering renewing the HT leads as a set. Note that, on some engines, it is necessary to unbolt the cover from the top of the camshaft cover in order to gain access to the two ignition coils, and each coil is located directly onto the spark plugs of cylinders 1 and 3, with HT leads from the coils to the spark plugs in cylinders 2 and 4.

3 If the engine either will not turn over at all, or only turns very slowly, check the battery and starter motor as described in Chapter 5A. If the engine turns over at normal speed, connect a voltmeter across the battery terminals then note the voltage reading obtained while briefly operating the starter. If the reading obtained is less than approximately 9.5 volts, charge the battery and repeat the check.

4 If the engine turns over at normal speed but will not start, check that voltage is reaching the spark plugs as follows. Unbolt the cover from the top of the camshaft cover, then connect a timing light to one of the HT leads. Turn the engine over on the starter motor and check that the timing light flashes. **Note: *Do not check for a spark by disconnecting an HT lead and holding it a short distance from the cylinder head, as this may permanently damage the electronic ignition components in the ECU.***

5 If these checks fail to reveal the cause of the problem, the vehicle should be taken to a Mercedes-Benz dealer who will use a special test instrument in the diagnostic socket located on the left-hand side of the bulkhead in the engine compartment. The test instrument will locate the fault quickly and simply, alleviating the need to test all the system components individually which is a time consuming operation that carries a high risk of damaging the ECU.

3 HT coils - removal and refitting

Removal

1 On early models (pre 12/94) the HT ignition coils are located on the left-hand, rear side of the cylinder head, beneath the inlet manifold. On later models the HT ignition coils are located beneath a cover on top of the camshaft cover. First disconnect the battery negative (earth) lead and position it away from the terminal. The battery is located in the rear luggage compartment.

2 Loosen the clips and remove the air inlet duct from between the air cleaner and inlet manifold.

Early models

3 Unbolt the windscreen washer reservoir with reference to Chapter 12, Section 20, and position it to one side.

4 On the left-hand side of the cylinder head, next to the fuel rail, disconnect the wiring plug for the ignition coils from the socket.

5 Identify the positions of the ignition HT leads, then disconnect them from the ignition coils.

6 Unbolt the inlet manifold support bracket from the right-hand side of the engine, and disconnect the wiring at the same time.

7 Unscrew the mounting bolts securing the ignition coils to the bracket.

8 Remove the covers then unscrew the terminals and disconnect the low tension wiring. Withdraw the ignition coils from the engine.

Later models

9 Unbolt the cover from the top of the camshaft cover (see illustrations).

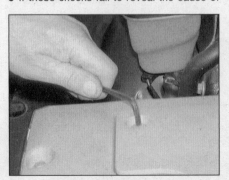

3.9a Unscrew the bolts . . .

3.9b . . . and remove the cover from the top of the camshaft cover

3.10 Removing the ignition coil wiring conduits

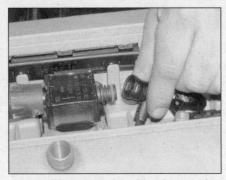

3.11a Disconnect the wiring from each ignition coil . . .

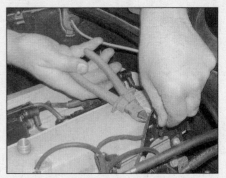

3.11b . . . release it from the cable tie . . .

3.11c . . . disconnect the wiring loom at the left-hand side of the cylinder head . . .

3.11d . . . and release the rubber grommet

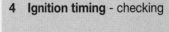

4 Ignition timing - checking

It is not possible to check the ignition timing without using special instrumentation plugged into the diagnostic socket located on the left-hand side of the bulkhead in the engine compartment. Normally, if a fault occurs in the ignition system, the ECU memory will contain a fault code, and the engine management warning light will be illuminated on the instrument panel. If this occurs, the car should be taken to a Mercedes-Benz dealer who will have the necessary equipment to diagnose the faulty component.

10 Note the location of the wiring and conduits to ensure correct refitting, then remove the conduits from their location slots **(see illustration)**.
11 Disconnect the wiring from each ignition coil, release the wiring from the cable tie, disconnect the wiring loom at the left-hand

side of the cylinder head, and release the rubber grommet **(see illustrations)**.
12 Disconnect the HT leads from the spark plugs of cylinders 2 and 4 **(see illustration)**.
13 Unbolt the ignition coils, disconnect them from spark plugs 1 and 3, and remove from the camshaft cover **(see illustrations)**.

Refitting

14 Refitting is a reversal of removal. Make sure that the HT leads are reconnected to the correct positions on the ignition coils.

5 Ignition control system components - removal and refitting

The ignition system shares components with the fuel injection system - refer to the information given in Chapter 4A, Section 10.

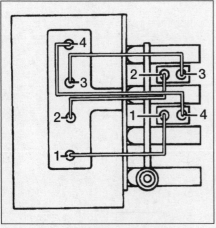

3.12 HT lead connections

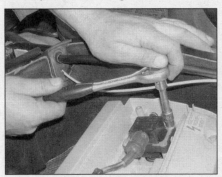

3.13a Unscrew the mounting bolts . . .

3.13b . . . and remove the ignition coils from spark plugs 1 and 3

Notes

Chapter 5 Part C:
Pre-heating system - diesel engines

Contents

Degrees of difficulty

Easy, suitable for novice with little experience	Fairly easy, suitable for beginner with some experience	Fairly difficult, suitable for competent DIY mechanic	Difficult, suitable for experienced DIY mechanic	Very difficult, suitable for expert DIY or professional

Specifications

Glow plugs
Nominal operating voltage	11.5 V
Electrical resistance	0.75 to 1.5 ohms (approx., at operating temperature)
Current consumption	14 - 16 amps (per glow plug, after approx. 8 seconds of operation)
After-heating	180 seconds up to maximum coolant temperture of 40° C

Torque wrench settings
	Nm	lbf ft
Glow plug to cylinder head	20	15
Glow plug wiring terminal	4	3

1 General information

To assist cold starting, diesel-engined models are fitted with a pre-heating system which comprises four glow plugs (one per cylinder), a glow plug control unit, a facia-mounted warning lamp, a coolant temperature sensor and the associated electrical wiring.

The glow plugs are miniature electric heating elements, encapsulated in a metal case with a probe at one end and electrical connection at the other. Each combustion chamber has one glow plug threaded into it. When the glow plug is energised, it heats up rapidly causing the temperature of the air charge drawn into each of the combustion chambers to rise. The glow plug probe is positioned directly in line with the incoming spray of fuel from the injectors. Hence the fuel passing over the glow plug probe is also heated, allowing its optimum combustion temperature to be achieved more readily. In addition, small particles of the fuel passing over the glow plugs are ignited and this helps to trigger the combustion process.

The duration of the pre-heating period is governed by the glow plug control unit. This device monitors the temperature of the engine coolant via a sensor threaded into the cylinder head and then alters the pre-heating time (the length for which the glow plugs are supplied with current) to suit the conditions.

A facia-mounted warning lamp informs the driver that pre-heating is taking place. The lamp extinguishes when sufficient pre-heating has taken place to allow the engine to be started, but power will still be supplied to the glow plugs for a further period until the engine is started. If no attempt is made to start the engine, the power supply to the glow plugs is switched off to prevent battery drain and glow plug burn-out. Note that the warning lamp will also illuminate during normal driving if a pre-heating system malfunction occurs. The system employs post-glowing (after-heating) which operates as follows. After the engine has been started, the glow plugs continue to operate for a further period of time as given in this Chapter's Specifications. This helps to improve fuel combustion whilst the engine is warming up, resulting in quieter, smoother running and reduced exhaust emissions. The duration of the after-heating period is dependant on the coolant temperature.

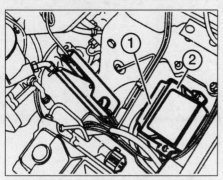

2.1 Glow plug control unit

1 Wiring connector
2 Time relay

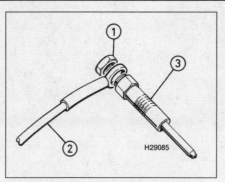

3.9 Glow plug and electrical connection

1 Terminal nut
2 Supply cable
3 Glow plug

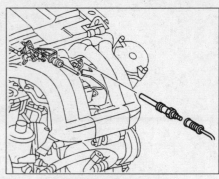

3.10 Glow plug removal

2 Glow plug control unit - removal and refitting

Removal

1 The control unit is located in the front left-hand side of the engine compartment **(see illustration)**. First, disconnect the battery negative (earth) lead and position it away from the terminal. The battery is located in the rear luggage compartment.
2 Undo the screws and remove the cover from the electronic control unit (ECU). Recover the gasket.
3 Disconnect the wiring connectors from the ECU control module by swivelling them to one side.
4 Disconnect the wiring connectors from the traction control system module by pulling out the slide locks.
5 Undo the retaining screw and withdraw the bracket, together with the two control modules, from the guides. Separate the ECU from the traction control module.
6 If necessary, remove the relay module after disconnecting the wiring.

Refitting

7 Refitting is a reversal of removal.

3 Glow plugs - testing, removal and refitting

Testing

1 If the system malfunctions, testing is ultimately by substitution of known good units,

but some preliminary checks may be made as described in the following paragraphs.
2 Connect a voltmeter or 12 volt test lamp between the glow plug supply cable and a good earth point on the engine.
Caution: Make sure that the live connection is kept well clear of the engine and bodywork.
3 Have an assistant activate the pre-heating system with the ignition key and check that battery voltage is applied to the glow plug supply cable. Note that the voltage will drop to zero when the pre-heating period ends.
4 If no supply voltage can be detected at the glow plug supply cable, then either the glow plug relay or the supply cabling must be faulty.
5 To locate a faulty glow plug, first disconnect the supply cabling from all of the glow plug terminals. Connect an ohmmeter between the first glow plug terminal and a good earthing point on the cylinder head and measure the electrical resistance of the glow plug. A reading of anything more than a few ohms indicates that the plug is defective. Repeat the test on the remaining glow plugs.
6 If a suitable ammeter is available, connect it between the glow plug and its supply cable and measure the steady state current consumption (ignore the initial current surge which will be about 50% higher). Compare the result with this Chapter's Specifications - high current consumption (or no current draw at all) indicates a faulty glow plug.
7 As a final check, remove the glow plugs and inspect them visually, as described in the following paragraphs.

Removal

8 Disconnect the battery negative (earth) lead and position it away from the terminal. The

battery is located in the rear luggage compartment.
9 Remove the nuts and washers from the glow plug terminal and disconnect the cabling **(see illustration)**.
10 Unscrew and remove the glow plug from the cylinder head **(see illustration)**.
11 Inspect the glow plug probe for signs of damage. A badly burned or charred probe indicates a faulty fuel injector (refer to Chapter 4B).

Refitting

12 Refitting is a reversal of removal, but tighten the glow plug to the specified torque.

4 Coolant temperature sensor - removal and refitting

Removal

1 The coolant temperature sensor is threaded into the left-hand side of the cylinder head.
2 Ensure that the engine has cooled completely before starting work. Disconnect the battery negative (earth) lead and position it away from the terminal. The battery is located in the rear luggage compartment.
3 With reference to Chapters 1B and 3, partially drain the cooling system.
4 Unplug the wiring from the sensor at the connector.
5 Unscrew the sensor from the cylinder head and recover the sealing washer.

Refitting

6 Refitting is a reversal of removal. On completion, refill the cooling system with reference to Chapter 1B.

Chapter 6
Clutch

Contents

Degrees of difficulty

Easy, suitable for novice with little experience	Fairly easy, suitable for beginner with some experience	Fairly difficult, suitable for competent DIY mechanic 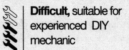	Difficult, suitable for experienced DIY mechanic	Very difficult, suitable for expert DIY or professional

Specifications

Friction disc

Lining thickness:	
New	3.6 to 4.0 mm
Wear limit	2.6 to 3.0 mm
Lining face run-out	0.5 mm maximum

Clutch pedal

Travel	157 mm

Torque wrench settings	Nm	lbf ft
Clutch pressure plate-to-flywheel bolts	25	18
Release lever ball stud	35	26

1 General information and precautions

General information

All models are fitted with a single dry plate clutch system. The main components consist of a friction disc, pressure plate (or cover), release bearing, release arm, and hydraulic master and slave cylinders.

The clutch pressure plate is bolted to the rear face of the flywheel, and the friction disc is located between the pressure plate and the flywheel friction surface. The friction disc is splined to the transmission input shaft and is free to slide along the splines. Friction lining material is riveted to each side of the disc, and the disc hub incorporates cushioning springs to absorb transmission shocks and ensure a smooth take-up of drive. The pressure plate incorporates an internal diaphragm spring mounted on a fulcrum ring. When the inner fingers of the spring are depressed, the outer perimeter draws the pressure plate away from the friction disc.

The release bearing is located on a guide sleeve at the front of the transmission, and the bearing is free to slide on the sleeve under the action of the release arm which pivots on a ball stud inside the clutch bellhousing.

The release mechanism is operated by the clutch pedal, using hydraulic pressure. The pedal acts on the hydraulic master cylinder pushrod, and hydraulic pressure operates a slave cylinder mounted on the transmission bellhousing.

When the clutch pedal is depressed, the release arm pushes the release bearing forwards, to bear against the centre of the diaphragm spring, thus pushing the centre of the diaphragm spring inwards.

When the clutch pedal is released, the diaphragm spring forces the pressure plate into contact with the friction linings on the friction disc, and simultaneously pushes the friction disc forwards on its splines, forcing it against the flywheel. The friction disc is now firmly sandwiched between the pressure plate and the flywheel, and drive is taken up.

The clutch is self-adjusting. As wear takes place on the friction disc over a period of time, the pressure plate automatically moves closer to the friction plate to compensate.

Precautions

 Warning: Dust created by clutch wear and deposited on the clutch components may contain asbestos, which is a health hazard. DO NOT blow it out with compressed air, or inhale any of it. DO NOT use petrol (or petroleum-based solvents) to clean off the dust. Brake system cleaner or methylated spirit should be used to flush the dust into a suitable receptacle. After the clutch components are wiped clean with rags, dispose of the contaminated rags and cleaner in a sealed, marked container.

 Warning: Hydraulic fluid is poisonous; wash off immediately and thoroughly in the case of skin contact, and seek immediate medical advice if any fluid is swallowed or gets into the eyes. Certain types of hydraulic fluid are inflammable, and may ignite when allowed into contact with hot components; when servicing any hydraulic system, it is safest to assume that the fluid is inflammable, and to take precautions against the risk of fire as though it is petrol that is being handled. Hydraulic fluid is also an effective paint stripper, and will attack plastics; if any is spilt, it should be washed off immediately, using copious quantities of fresh water. Finally, it is hygroscopic (it absorbs moisture from the air) - old fluid may be contaminated and unfit for further use. When topping-up or renewing the fluid, always use the recommended type, and ensure that it comes from a freshly-opened sealed container.

2 Clutch assembly - removal, inspection and refitting

Note: *Refer to the precautions given in Section 1 regarding dust.*

Removal

1 Remove the transmission, as described in Chapter 7A.
2 If the original clutch is to be refitted, make alignment marks between the clutch pressure plate assembly and the flywheel, so that the clutch can be refitted in its original position.
3 Progressively unscrew the bolts securing the clutch pressure plate assembly to the flywheel, and recover the washers (where fitted) (see illustrations).
4 Withdraw the clutch pressure plate assembly (cover) and disc from the flywheel (see illustration). Be prepared to catch the friction disc, and note which way round the friction disc is fitted - the two sides of the disc may be marked *Engine side* and *Transmission side*, or the side with the part number on faces the flywheel. The greater projecting side of the hub faces away from the flywheel.

Inspection

5 Clean the cover, disc, and flywheel. Do not inhale the dust, as it may contain asbestos which is dangerous to health.
6 Examine the fingers of the diaphragm spring for wear or scoring. If the depth of any scoring exceeds 0.3 mm, a new cover assembly must be fitted.
7 Examine the pressure plate for scoring, cracking and discoloration. Light scoring is acceptable, but if excessive, a new assembly must be fitted.
8 Examine the friction disc linings for wear cracking, and for contamination with oil or grease. Using vernier calipers, check the thickness of the linings and compare with the details given in the Specifications. Check the disc hub and splines for wear, by temporarily fitting it on the transmission input shaft. Renew the friction disc as necessary.
9 Examine the flywheel friction surface for scoring, cracking and discoloration (caused by overheating). If excessive, it may be possible to have the flywheel machined by an engineering works, otherwise it should be renewed.
10 Ensure that all parts are clean, and free of oil or grease, before reassembling. Apply just a small amount of high melting-point grease to the splines of the friction disc hub. Note

2.3a Progressively loosen the bolts securing the clutch pressure plate to the flywheel

2.3b Removing the pressure plate bolts

2.4 Removing the pressure plate and disc from the flywheel

2.13 Use the centralising tool to hold the friction disc on the flywheel

2.14 Locating the clutch pressure plate over the friction disc and onto the flywheel

3.2 Removing the clutch release bearing

that a new pressure plate may be coated with protective grease. It is only permissible to clean the grease away from the friction disc lining contact area. Removal of the grease from other areas will shorten the service life of the clutch.

11 Check the spigot bearing in the end of the crankshaft or in the centre of the flywheel. Make sure that it turns smoothly and quietly. If the transmission input shaft contact face on the bearing is worn or damaged, fit a new bearing, as described in the relevant part of Chapter 2.

Refitting

12 It is important to ensure that no oil or grease gets onto the friction disc linings, or the pressure plate and flywheel faces. It is advisable to refit the clutch assembly with clean hands, and to wipe down the pressure plate and flywheel faces with a clean rag before assembly begins.

13 Apply a smear of molybdenum disulphide grease to the splines of the friction disc hub, then offer the disc to the flywheel, with the greater projecting side of the hub facing away from the flywheel (most friction discs will have an *Engine side* marking which should face the flywheel). Hold the friction disc against the flywheel while the pressure plate assembly is offered into position, or alternatively use the centralising tool described in paragraph 15 to hold the disc on the flywheel **(see illustration)**.

14 Fit the clutch pressure plate assembly, where applicable aligning the marks with those on the flywheel **(see illustration)**.

Ensure that the pressure plate assembly locates over the dowels on the flywheel. Insert the securing bolts and washers, and tighten them finger-tight, so that the friction disc is gripped, but can still be moved.

15 The friction disc must now be centralised, to ensure correct alignment of the transmission input shaft with the spigot bearing in the crankshaft/flywheel. To do this, a proprietary tool may be used, or alternatively, use a wooden mandrel made to fit inside the friction disc hub and spigot bearing. Insert the tool through the friction disc into the spigot bearing, and make sure that it is central.

16 Tighten the clutch pressure plate bolts progressively and in diagonal sequence, until the specified torque setting is achieved, then remove the centralising tool.

17 Check the release bearing in the front of the transmission for smooth operation, and if necessary renew it with reference to Section 3.

18 Refit the transmission with reference to Chapter 7A.

3 Clutch release bearing and lever - removal, inspection and refitting

Note: *Refer to the precautions given in Section 1 regarding dust.*

Release bearing

Removal

1 Remove the transmission, as described in Chapter 7A.

2 Hold the release lever in the bellhousing, then pull the bearing from the lever, noting how the two shoulders locate in the central aperture. Slide the bearing from the guide tube **(see illustration)**.

Inspection

3 Spin the release bearing, and check it for excessive roughness. Hold the outer race, and attempt to move it laterally against the inner race. If any excessive movement or roughness is evident, renew the bearing. If a new clutch has been fitted, it is wise to renew the release bearing as a matter of course.

Refitting

4 Clean and then lightly grease the release bearing contact surfaces on the release lever. Similarly, lightly grease the guide tube **(see illustration)**.

5 Slide the bearing into position on the guide tube, then rotate the bearing until it locates in the release lever aperture.

6 Refit the transmission as described in Chapter 7A.

Release lever

Removal

7 Remove the release bearing, as described previously in this Section.

8 Pull the slave cylinder end of the release lever forwards, then slide the lever sideways to release it from the ball stud, then withdraw the lever over the guide tube **(see illustrations)**.

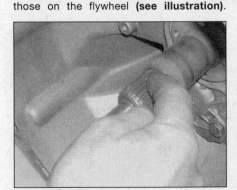

3.4 Lightly grease the guide tube before refitting the release bearing

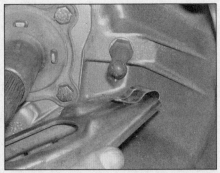

3.8a Disengaging the clutch release lever from the ball stud

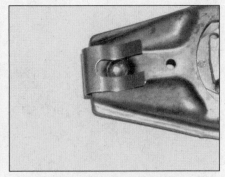

3.8b Showing the ball stud spring on the back of the release lever

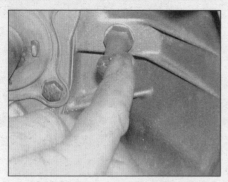

3.11 Lightly grease the ball stud

3.12 Ensure that the spring clip (arrowed) engages with the pivot pin

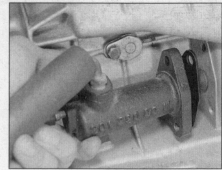

4.3a Removing the clutch slave cylinder from the transmission bellhousing

Inspection

9 Inspect the contact surfaces of the release bearing, release lever, ball stud and slave cylinder for wear. Renew the lever if excessive wear is evident.

10 Check the condition of the release lever retaining spring clip, and renew if necessary.

Refitting

11 Clean and then lightly grease the release bearing contact surfaces on the release lever, and the ball stud (see illustration). Similarly, lightly grease the guide tube.

12 Slide the release lever into position over the guide tube, then slide the end of the lever over the pivot pin, ensuring that the retaining spring clip engages around the rear of the ball stud (see illustration).

13 Refit the release bearing as described previously in this Section.

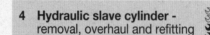

4 Hydraulic slave cylinder - removal, overhaul and refitting

Note: *Refer to the precautions given in Section 1 regarding the use of hydraulic fluid.*

Removal

1 Apply the parking brake, then jack up the front of the vehicle and support securely on axle stands (see *Jacking and vehicle support*).

2 Working beneath the right-hand side of the transmission, place a suitable container under the slave cylinder, then unscrew the fluid pipe

union, and disconnect the fluid pipe from the rear of the cylinder. Alternatively, if desired, the flexible hose can be disconnected from the rigid fluid pipe on the left-hand side of the transmission. Once the fluid has drained, plug the open ends of the pipe/hose and slave cylinder to prevent dirt ingress.

3 Unscrew the two bolts securing the slave cylinder to the transmission bellhousing, then withdraw the cylinder, complete with the pushrod. Recover the shim/spacer, noting which way round it is fitted (see illustrations).

Overhaul

4 Using a screwdriver, carefully hook out the notched retaining ring, and withdraw the pushrod assembly.

5 Tap the cylinder on a block of wood to release the piston, then remove the piston and spring (see illustrations).

6 Wash all the parts in hydraulic fluid, then lay them out for inspection (see illustration).

7 Examine the cylinder bore and piston carefully for signs of scoring or wear ridges. If these are apparent, renew the complete slave cylinder. If the condition of the components appears satisfactory, a repair kit containing new rubber seals should be obtained. Never re-use the old seals.

8 Remove the old seal from the piston, and fit the new one, using the fingers only. To ease fitting of the seal, lubricate with clean hydraulic fluid. Ensure that the sealing lip edge is towards the spring end of the piston.

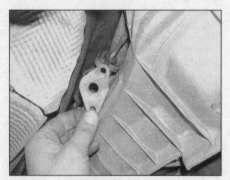

4.3b Removing the shim/spacer from the slave cylinder

4.3c Clutch slave cylinder removed from the transmission

4.5a Remove the slave cylinder piston . . .

4.5b . . . followed by the spring

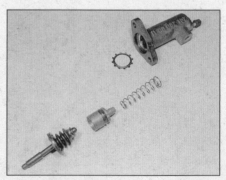

4.6 Clutch slave cylinder components

9 Lubricate the cylinder bore and insert the spring, with the larger coils towards fluid union end of the cylinder.

10 Carefully insert the piston, engaging the protruding end into the centre of the spring.

11 If necessary, fit a new dust cover to the pushrod, then insert the pushrod assembly into the cylinder. The dust cover end of the pushrod should face the piston.

12 Press a new retaining ring into position, and push it in firmly to secure the pushrod assembly.

Refitting

13 Commence refitting by placing the shim in position, with the grooved side facing towards the bellhousing.

14 Offer the slave cylinder and pushrod onto the bellhousing, ensuring that the pushrod engages with the spherical recess in the clutch release lever.

15 Refit and tighten the mounting bolts.

16 Reconnect the pipe or hose, then bleed the clutch hydraulic system as described in Section 6.

17 Lower the vehicle to the ground.

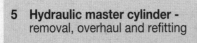

5 Hydraulic master cylinder - removal, overhaul and refitting

Note: *Refer to the precautions given in Section 1 regarding the use of hydraulic fluid.*

Removal

1 The clutch master cylinder is located inside the vehicle, attached to the clutch and brake pedal mounting bracket **(see illustration)**. Hydraulic fluid for the unit is supplied by a flexible rubber hose connected to the brake fluid reservoir in the engine compartment.

2 Disconnect the battery negative (earth) lead and position it away from the terminal. The battery is located in the rear luggage compartment.

3 Remove the lower facia trim panel from under the steering column for access to the master cylinder and pedal assembly (see Chapter 11, Section 41).

4 Pull back the floor carpet, and cover the

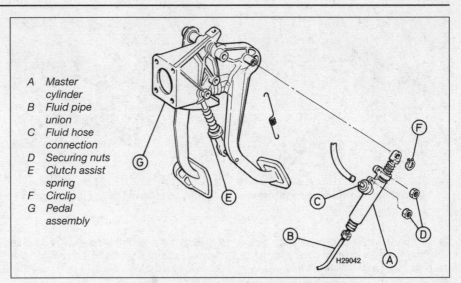

A Master cylinder
B Fluid pipe union
C Fluid hose connection
D Securing nuts
E Clutch assist spring
F Circlip
G Pedal assembly

5.1 Clutch master cylinder and pedal assembly

floor beneath the pedals to protect against fluid spillage.

5 To reduce fluid loss, draw off as much fluid as possible from the appropriate chamber of the brake fluid reservoir, using a clean syringe, until the fluid level is below the level of the clutch master cylinder supply pipe. Alternatively, fit a hose clamp to the supply pipe.

6 Place a suitable container beneath the clutch master cylinder to catch any spilt fluid.

7 Unscrew the hydraulic pipe union nut from the bottom of the clutch master cylinder, and carefully withdraw the pipe sufficiently far to release it from the cylinder. Plug the open ends of the pipe and master cylinder to prevent dirt entry and further fluid loss.

8 Unscrew the two bolts and nuts securing the master cylinder to the pedal mounting bracket.

9 Pull the clutch pedal upwards, and withdraw the clutch assist spring seat, spring and washer from the pushrod **(see illustration)**. Note, however, that some models may be fitted with a single return spring instead of the assist spring.

10 Extract the circlip and disconnect the clutch master cylinder pushrod from the pin on the pedal.

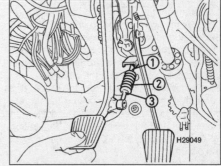

5.9 Pull the pedal upwards, and withdraw the clutch assist spring seat (1), spring (2) and washer (3) from the pushrod

11 Disconnect the fluid supply hose from the master cylinder, then withdraw the assembly from the footwell.

Overhaul

12 Ease the dust cover on the pushrod away from the cylinder body to provide access to the circlip **(see illustration)**.

13 Using circlip pliers, extract the circlip, then remove the retaining washer **(see illustrations)**.

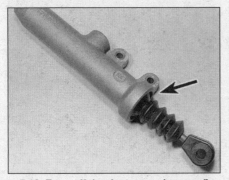

5.12 Ease off the dust cover (arrowed)

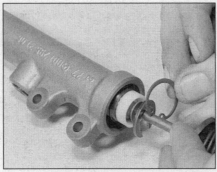

5.13a Remove the circlip ...

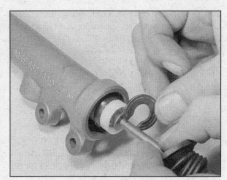

5.13b ... and the retaining washer

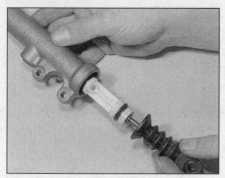

5.14a Withdraw the pushrod and piston assembly . . .

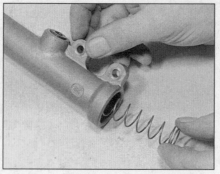

5.14b . . . followed by the piston spring

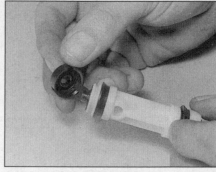

5.15 Remove the end cap and check valve from the piston

14 Withdraw the pushrod and piston assembly from the cylinder bore, followed by the piston spring (see illustrations).

15 Remove the end cap and check valve from the end of the piston (see illustration).

16 Wash all components in clean hydraulic fluid, then lay them out for inspection.

17 Examine the cylinder bore and piston carefully for signs of scoring or wear ridges. If these are evident, renew the complete master cylinder. If the condition of the components is satisfactory, a new set of rubber seals must be obtained. Never re-use the old seals.

18 Remove the old seals from the piston, and carefully fit the new ones, using the fingers only. To ease fitting of the seals, lubricate with clean hydraulic fluid. Ensure that the sealing lip of each seal is towards the spring end of the piston.

19 Lubricate the cylinder bore and the piston with hydraulic fluid, then insert the spring into the bore.

20 Place the check valve and end cap on the piston, and carefully enter the piston into the cylinder bore.

21 Fit the retaining washer over the pushrod, followed by the circlip.

22 Push the piston down the bore slightly, and engage the circlip in its groove. Ensure that the circlip is correctly seated.

23 Slide the dust cover into position, and locate its end under the edge of the cylinder.

Refitting

24 Refitting is a reversal of removal, but when reconnecting the pushrod, make sure that the shoulder is facing towards the pedal bracket. Finally bleed the hydraulic system as described in Section 6.

6 Hydraulic system - bleeding

Note: *Refer to the precautions given in Section 1 regarding the use of hydraulic fluid.*

1 The correct operation of the hydraulic system is only possible after removing all air from the circuit, and this is achieved by bleeding the system.

2 During the bleeding procedure, add only clean, unused hydraulic fluid of the recommended type. Never re-use fluid that has already been bled from the system. Ensure that sufficient fluid is available before starting work.

3 If there is any possibility of incorrect fluid being already in the system, both the clutch and brake circuits must be flushed completely with uncontaminated, correct fluid, and new seals should be fitted to the various components.

4 If hydraulic fluid has been lost from the system, or air has entered because of a leak, ensure that the fault is cured before proceeding further.

5 Apply the parking brake, then jack up the front of the vehicle and support it on axle stands (see *Jacking and vehicle support*).

6 Where applicable, remove the underbody shield for access to the right-hand side of the transmission bellhousing.

7 Remove the dust cap from the slave cylinder bleed screw, and clean away any dirt.

8 Note that the brake fluid reservoir feeds both the brake and clutch hydraulic systems.

9 Mercedes-Benz recommended that pressure-bleeding equipment is used to bleed the system. Some pressure-bleeding kits are operated by the reservoir of pressurised air contained in the spare tyre, however, note that it will probably be necessary to reduce the pressure to a lower level than normal. Refer to the instructions supplied with the kit. If a pressure-bleeding kit is not available, use the normal bleeding method described for the brake hydraulic circuit in Chapter 9.

10 By connecting a pressurised, fluid-filled container to the brake fluid reservoir, bleeding can be carried out simply by opening the bleed screw on the clutch slave cylinder, and allowing the fluid to flow out until no more air bubbles can be seen in the expelled fluid. This method has the advantage that the large reservoir of fluid provides an additional safeguard against air being drawn into the system during bleeding.

11 Collect a clean glass jar, a suitable length of plastic or rubber tubing which is a tight fit over the bleed screw, and a ring spanner to fit the screw.

12 Fit the spanner and tube to the slave cylinder bleed screw, place the other end of the tube in the jar, and pour in sufficient fluid to cover the end of the tube (see illustration).

13 Connect the pressure-bleeding equipment to the brake/clutch fluid reservoir in accordance with its manufacturer's instructions.

14 Loosen the bleed screw half a turn using the spanner, and allow fluid to drain into the jar until no more air bubbles emerge.

15 When bleeding is complete, tighten the bleed screw, and disconnect the hose and the pressure bleeding equipment.

16 Wash off any spilt fluid, check once more that the bleed screw is tightened securely, and refit the dust cap.

17 Check the hydraulic fluid level in the reservoir, and top-up if necessary (see *Weekly checks*).

18 Discard any hydraulic fluid that has been bled from the system, as it will not be fit for re-use.

19 Check the feel of the clutch pedal. If it feels at all spongy, air must still be present in the system, and further bleeding is required. Failure to bleed satisfactorily after a reasonable repetition of the bleeding procedure may be due to worn master or slave cylinder seals.

20 On completion, lower the vehicle to the ground.

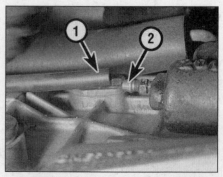

6.12 Fit a tube (1) to the slave cylinder bleed screw (2)

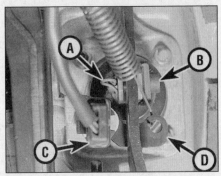
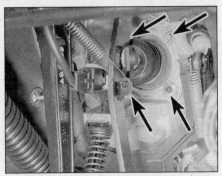

7.7 Brake pedal mounting details

A *Clevis pin locking clip*
B *Clevis pin*
C *Stop light switch wiring plug*
D *Return spring bracket*

7.10a Pedal assembly securing nuts (arrowed) . . .

7.10b . . . and securing bolt (arrowed)

7 Clutch pedal - removal and refitting

Removal

1 Disconnect the battery negative (earth) lead and position it away from the terminal.
2 Remove the driver's side lower facia trim panel to gain access to the master cylinder and pedal assembly.
3 Pull back the floor carpet, and cover the floor beneath the pedals to protect against fluid spillage.
4 To reduce fluid loss, draw off as much fluid as possible from the appropriate chamber of the brake fluid reservoir, using a clean syringe, until the fluid level is below the level of the clutch master cylinder supply pipe.
5 Place a suitable container beneath the clutch master cylinder to catch any spilt fluid.
6 Unscrew the hydraulic pipe union nut from the bottom of the clutch master cylinder, and carefully withdraw the pipe sufficiently far to release it from the cylinder. Plug the open ends of the pipe and master cylinder to prevent dirt entry and further fluid loss.
7 Carefully unhook the brake pedal return spring **(see illustration)**.
8 Disconnect the wiring plug from the stop-light switch, then unclip the switch from the bracket on the pedal assembly.
9 Remove the locking clip from the brake pedal-to-servo pushrod clevis pin, then withdraw the clevis pin.
10 Unscrew the four nuts securing the pedal assembly to the front of the bulkhead (note that these nuts also secure the brake vacuum

servo), and the single bolt securing the assembly to the top of the bulkhead **(see illustrations)**.
11 Pull the pedal assembly back from the bulkhead until the mounting bracket disengages from the studs, then lower the assembly, and disconnect the fluid hose from the clutch master cylinder (be prepared for fluid spillage).
12 Withdraw the assembly from under the facia.
13 Dismantling of the assembly is self-explanatory. Note the locations of all components to ensure correct refitting **(see illustration)**.

Refitting

14 Refitting is a reversal of removal, but check the adjustment of the stop-light switch as described in Chapter 9, and on completion bleed the clutch hydraulic system as described in Section 6.

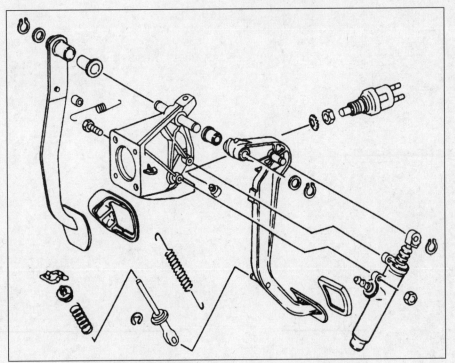

7.13 Exploded view of clutch and brake pedal assembly

Chapter 7 Part A:
Manual transmission

Contents

Degrees of difficulty

Easy, suitable for novice with little experience	**Fairly easy,** suitable for beginner with some experience	**Fairly difficult,** suitable for competent DIY mechanic	**Difficult,** suitable for experienced DIY mechanic	**Very difficult,** suitable for expert DIY or professional

Specifications

General

Type	5-speed

Transmission code:

Engine code 111.920	717.416
Engine code 111.921	717.416 or 717.460
Engine code 111.941	717.417
Engine code 111.945	717.417 or 717.422
Engine codes 111.961 and 111.974	717.417
Engine code 604.910	717.416
Engine code 605.910	717.417
Engine code 605.960	717.460

Transmission fluid

Type	See *Lubricants and fluids*
Capacity	1.5 litres

Torque wrench settings

	Nm	lbf ft
Crossmember-to-vehicle floor bolts	45	33
Fluid drain and level/filler plugs	60	44
Gearchange assembly	6	4
Engine-to-transmission bolts:		
M10 x 40	55	41
M10 x 90	45	33
M12 bolts	65	48
Transmission input shaft end cover plate securing bolts	20	15
Transmission output flange nut	160	118

1 General information

A 5-speed manual transmission is bolted to the rear of the engine. Drive is transmitted from the crankshaft via the clutch to the input shaft, which has a splined extension to accept the clutch friction disc. The transmission output shaft transmits the drive via the propeller shaft to the rear differential. The input shaft runs in line with the output shaft. The input shaft and output shaft gears are in constant mesh with the layshaft gear cluster. Selection of gears is by sliding synchromesh hubs, which lock the appropriate output shaft gears to the output shaft.

Gear selection is via a floor-mounted lever and selector mechanism incorporating three gearchange rods. The selector mechanism causes the appropriate selector fork to move its respective synchro-sleeve along the shaft, to lock the gear pinion to the synchro-hub. Since the synchro-hubs are splined to the output shaft, this locks the pinion to the shaft, so that drive can be transmitted. To ensure that gear-changing can be made quickly and quietly, a synchromesh system is fitted to all forward gears, consisting of baulk rings and spring-loaded fingers, as well as the gear pinions and synchro-hubs. The synchromesh cones are formed on the mating faces of the baulk rings and gear pinions.

2 Manual transmission fluid - draining and refilling

Note: *A hexagonal key, or a suitable alternative (see text) will be required to unscrew the transmission level/filler and drain plugs.*

1 Apply the parking brake, then jack up the front of the vehicle and support it on axle stands (see *Jacking and vehicle support*).
2 Place a suitable container beneath the transmission drain plug, at the bottom of the casing, then unscrew the plug. Unscrew the

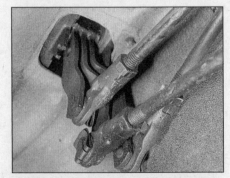

3.9 Prise off the securing clips and disconnect the gearchange rods from the gearchange lever assembly

2.2a Using a long nut and a spanner to unscrew the transmission fluid level/filler plug

level/filler plug, located on the right-hand side of the transmission, to assist draining. A hexagonal key should be used to unscrew the plugs, but a tool can be improvised using a long nut, or a length of hexagonal bar, and a spanner **(see illustrations)**.
3 Once all the fluid has drained, refit and tighten the drain plug, using a new sealing ring.
4 Fill the transmission until fluid runs from the level/filler plug hole. The level should just be up to the bottom of the level/filler plug hole. **Note:** *The vehicle must be in a level position.*
5 When the level is correct, refit the plug, and tighten to the specified torque.

3 Gearchange lever assembly - removal, refitting and adjustment

Removal

1 Apply the parking brake, then jack up the front of the vehicle and support it on axle stands (see *Jacking and vehicle support*). Select neutral.
2 Working under the vehicle, note the locations of the 1/2, 3/4 and 5/R gearchange rods on the gearchange lever extensions, then prise off the securing clips, and disconnect the rods from the gearchange lever extensions.
3 Working inside the vehicle, remove the cover from the centre console (Chapter 11) to expose the gearchange lever assembly. If required, the knob can be removed from the top of the lever by turning the retainer anti-clockwise.

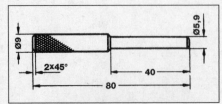

3.10 Gearchange linkage adjustment locating pin

All dimensions in mm

2.2b Transmission fluid drain plug location (arrowed)

4 Disconnect the wiring from the reversing light switch.
5 Unscrew the gearchange lever assembly securing nuts.
6 Withdraw the assembly through the floor into the vehicle interior. Recover the gasket.

Refitting

7 Refitting is a reversal of removal, but check and adjust the linkage as described in the following paragraphs. Make sure that the gearchange rod securing clips are securely refitted.

Adjustment

Note: *To check the adjustment, it will be necessary to make up a suitable locating pin - see text.*
8 Make sure that the transmission is in neutral.
9 Working under the vehicle, prise off the securing clips, and disconnect the gearchange rods from the gearchange lever extensions **(see illustration)**.
10 Make up a locating pin to the dimensions shown, ideally using steel bar **(see illustration)**.
11 Insert the locating pin through the bores provided in the gearchange lever extensions **(see illustration)**.
12 With the gearchange extensions locked in position, it should be possible to locate the gearchange rods easily onto the gearchange lever pins, with the transmission still in neutral.

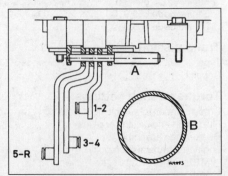

3.11 Locating pin in position in gearchange levers

A Locating pin   B Propeller shaft

4.3 Removing the cover plate and guide tube from the transmission bellhousing

If necessary, loosen the locknuts and adjust the position of the gearchange rod end fittings until the rods can be located on the lever pins.
13 When the adjustment is correct, refit the clips to secure the gearchange rods to the lever extensions, then withdraw the locating pin.
14 Lower the vehicle to the ground, then start the engine, and check the operation of the gearchange linkage. Take the vehicle on a road test, and check that all gears can be engaged easily.

4 Oil seals - renewal

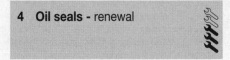

Input shaft oil seal

1 Remove the transmission as described in Section 6.
2 Remove the clutch release bearing and lever, with reference to Chapter 6.
3 Unscrew the bolts and remove the cover plate and guide tube over the input shaft **(see illustration)**.
4 Recover the spacer shim(s) **(see illustration)**.
5 Lever the oil seal from the cover plate using a screwdriver **(see illustration)**.
6 Thoroughly clean the oil seal seating in the cover plate.
7 Tap the new seal into position, using a suitable socket or tube, until the seal seats on the shoulder in the cover plate.

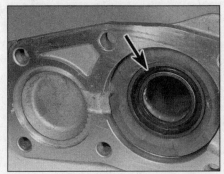

4.5 Input shaft oil seal location (arrowed) in cover plate

4.4 Recover the spacer shim(s)

8 Hold the spacer shim(s) in position using a little grease, then slide the cover plate into position over the input shaft.
9 Apply sealant to the threads of the cover plate securing bolts, then refit the bolts and tighten to the specified torque.
10 Refit the clutch release lever and bearing, with reference to Chapter 6.
11 Refit the transmission as described in Section 6.

Output flange oil seal

Note: *A new transmission output flange securing nut will be required on refitting.*
12 Disconnect the propeller shaft from the transmission output flange, with reference to Chapter 8.
13 Ensure that the transmission is in neutral.
14 Bolt a suitable holding tool to the transmission output flange. A suitable tool can be made up using two pieces of flat bar, and bolts - engage the tool with two of the bolts holes in the output flange, and use it to counterhold the flange. Note that it must be possible to gain access to the output flange nut with the tool in place.
15 Counterhold the output flange, then unscrew the flange securing nut. Discard the nut, a new one must be used on refitting **(see illustration)**.
16 Pull the output flange from the shaft, using a suitable puller if necessary.
17 Prise the oil seal from the housing using a screwdriver.
18 Thoroughly clean the oil seal seating in the rear transmission cover.

4.15 Removing the transmission output flange securing nut

19 Tap the new seal into position, using a suitable socket or tube, until the outer face of the seal is flush with the end face of the housing.
20 Refit the output flange to the output shaft, and secure using a new nut. Tighten the nut to the specified torque.
21 Reconnect the propeller shaft to the output flange, with reference to Chapter 8.

5 Reversing light switch - testing, removal and refitting

Testing

1 The reversing light circuit is controlled by a plunger-type switch located at the rear of the gear selector lever assembly under the centre console. If a fault develops in the circuit, first ensure that the circuit fuse has not blown.
2 For access to the switch, working inside the vehicle, remove the cover from the centre console (see Chapter 11) to expose the gearchange lever assembly.
3 To test the switch, disconnect the wiring connector, and use a multimeter (set to the resistance function) or a battery-and-bulb test circuit to check that there is continuity between the switch terminals only when reverse gear is selected. If this is not the case, and there are no obvious breaks or other damage to the wires, the switch is faulty, and must be renewed.

Removal

4 Proceed as described in paragraph 2.
5 Unclip the switch from the mounting bracket, and disconnect the wiring plug.

Refitting

6 Refitting is a reversal of removal.

6 Manual transmission - removal and refitting

Removal

Note: *This is a difficult operation, due to the limited access to the engine-to-transmission bolts. It is suggested that the procedure is read through thoroughly before starting the operation. Suitable ratchet extensions will be required to reach some of the engine-to-transmission bolts.*
1 Disconnect the battery negative (earth) lead and position it away from the terminal. The battery is located in the rear luggage compartment.
2 Raise the bonnet to its fully open position. To protect the bulkhead and brake pipes, place a thin sheet of wood or card (approximately 300 mm square) at the rear of the engine compartment.
3 Apply the parking brake, then jack up the front of the vehicle and support it on axle stands (see *Jacking and vehicle support*). The vehicle must be raised sufficiently high to enable the transmission to be lowered and

6.6 Unbolting the exhaust mounting bracket from the rear of the transmission

6.7a Unscrew the nuts . . .

6.7b . . . and remove the exhaust heat shield from the underbody

removed from under the vehicle. Remove the engine undershield.

4 Drain the transmission fluid with reference to Section 2.

5 Place a small, thin wooden block between the engine sump and the welded crossmember under the engine compartment.

6 Remove the complete exhaust system as described in Chapter 4C. Also unbolt the exhaust bracket from the rear of the transmission **(see illustration)**.

7 Where applicable, unbolt the exhaust heat shield from the vehicle floor for access to the propeller shaft intermediate bearing assembly **(see illustrations)**.

8 Disconnect the propeller shaft from the transmission flange with reference to Chapter 8. **Note:** *It is recommended that the self-*

locking nuts are renewed. On early models, slacken the clamp nut at the propeller shaft intermediate bearing, then slacken (do not remove) the intermediate bearing securing nuts. Push the propeller shaft rearwards as far as possible **(see illustrations)**.

9 Where a speedometer cable is fitted, unscrew the clamp bolt, pull the cable from the right-hand rear side of the transmission, and tie it to one side. Where applicable, release the cable-tie(s) securing the cable to the transmission.

10 Where a speedometer transponder is fitted, unbolt the unit from the right-hand rear side of the transmission and tie it to one side.

11 Unbolt the clutch slave cylinder from the transmission (see Chapter 6), and carefully pull it, complete with the fluid pipe, to the rear until the pushrod is clear of the transmission.

Recover the shim **(see illustrations)**. Tie the slave cylinder up, away from the transmission. **Note:** *The hydraulic fluid pipe from the clutch master cylinder loops over the transmission bellhousing, and an alternative method is to disconnect the union on the left-hand side of the transmission, and leave the pipe and slave cylinder in position while the transmission is being removed. If this course of action is taken, fit a hose clamp to the fluid supply hose leading from the brake fluid reservoir to the clutch master cylinder. Place a suitable container beneath the union to catch the fluid which will be released, and plug or cover the open ends of the pipe and hose.*

12 Prise off the securing clips, and disconnect the gear selector rods from the levers at the rear of the transmission **(see illustrations)**.

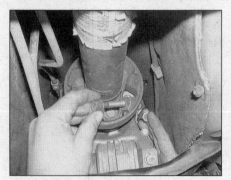

6.8a Unscrew the bolts . . .

6.8b . . . and withdraw the propeller shaft from the transmission flange

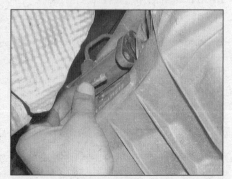

6.11a Unbolt the clutch slave cylinder . . .

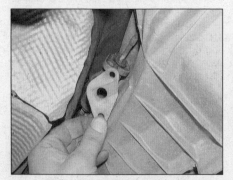

6.11b . . . and recover the shim

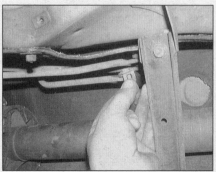

6.12a Prise off the securing clips . . .

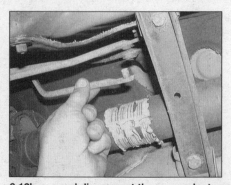

6.12b . . . and disconnect the gear selector rods

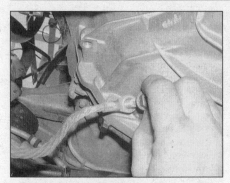

6.13 Unbolting the earth cable from the transmission

6.15a Unscrew the bolts securing the rear engine/transmission mounting bracket to the vehicle floor . . .

6.15b . . . then unscrew the mounting rubber . . .

13 Unscrew the lower transmission-to-engine bolt securing the earth cable to the transmission **(see illustration)**.

14 Support the transmission using a trolley jack and interposed block of wood.

15 Unbolt the rear engine/transmission mounting bracket from the transmission and from the vehicle floor **(see illustrations)**.

16 Remove the starter motor (see Chapter 5A).

17 Ensure that the transmission is adequately supported, then lower the assembly as far as possible, until the engine is resting on the block of wood inserted between the crossmember and the sump. Support the propeller shaft up against the underbody. Take care not to damage the brake pipes and any other components on the crossmember and at the rear of the bulkhead as the transmission is lowered.

18 Unscrew all the engine-to-transmission bolts, leaving one bolt on either side of the transmission. Access to the upper bolts is very difficult, even with the assembly tilted, and several long socket extensions will be required **(see illustration)**.

19 Unscrew the two remaining engine-to-transmission bolts, then, with the help of an assistant, pull the transmission rearwards and release the transmission input shaft from the clutch **(see illustration)**. Take care not to allow the weight of the transmission to hang on the clutch and input shaft, and where applicable take care not to damage the clutch slave cylinder and fluid pipe during this

procedure. If necessary, rotate the transmission to the left to enable the top of the bellhousing to clear the vehicle body.

20 Once the input shaft is clear of the clutch, lower the transmission to the ground and withdraw from under the vehicle **(see illustrations)**.

Refitting

21 Before refitting the transmission, check that the clutch friction disc is centralised as described in Chapter 6. Also check the clutch release components (Chapter 6) and the crankshaft spigot bearing (Chapter 2A).

22 Lubricate the transmission input shaft splines with a little molybdenum disulphide grease.

6.15c . . . and withdraw the mounting bracket

23 Support the transmission using the trolley jack and block of wood, as during removal, then raise the transmission into position beneath the vehicle. The help of an assistant is recommended.

24 Lift the transmission into position, and if the clutch slave cylinder is still in position in the vehicle, lift the fluid pipe over the transmission to ensure that it does not get trapped.

25 Move the transmission forwards, ensuring that the input shaft engages with the clutch friction disc splines (where necessary, turn the transmission to the left to enable the bellhousing to clear the vehicle floor). It may be necessary to rock the engine and transmission slightly and/or turn the

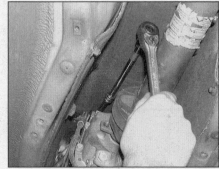

6.18 Using socket extensions to unscrew the transmission-to-engine upper mounting bolts

6.19 Separating the transmission from the rear of the engine

6.20a Withdrawing the transmission from the rear of the engine

6.20b View of the rear of the engine, with the transmission removed

crankshaft slightly, to allow the input shaft to engage. Take care not to allow the weight of the transmission to hang on the input shaft.

26 Slide the transmission forwards until the bellhousing contacts the cylinder block, making sure that the bolt holes and location dowels are correctly aligned.

27 Refit and tighten the engine-to-transmission bolts.

28 The remaining procedure is a reversal of removal, bearing in mind the following points.

a) *Where applicable, bleed the clutch hydraulic system as described in Chapter 6.*

b) *Reconnect the propeller shaft to the transmission flange with reference to Chapter 8.*

c) *Refit the exhaust system with reference to Chapter 4C.*

d) *Refill the transmission with fluid as described in Section 2.*

7 Manual transmission overhaul - general information

Overhauling a manual transmission is a difficult and involved job for the DIY home mechanic. In addition to dismantling and reassembling many small parts, clearances must be precisely measured and, if necessary, changed by selecting shims and spacers. Internal transmission components are also often difficult to obtain, and in many instances, extremely expensive. Because of this, if the transmission develops a fault or becomes noisy, the best course of action is to have the unit overhauled by a specialist repairer, or to obtain an exchange reconditioned unit. Be aware that some transmission repairs can be carried out with the transmission in the car.

Nevertheless, it is not impossible for the more experienced mechanic to overhaul the transmission, provided the special tools are available, and the job is done in a deliberate step-by-step manner, so that nothing is overlooked.

The tools necessary for an overhaul include internal and external circlip pliers, bearing pullers, a slide hammer, a set of pin punches, a dial test indicator, and possibly a hydraulic press. In addition, a large, sturdy workbench and a vice will be required.

During dismantling of the transmission, make careful notes of how each component is fitted, to make reassembly easier and more accurate.

Before dismantling the transmission, it will help if you have some idea what area is malfunctioning. Certain problems can be closely related to specific areas in the transmission, which can make component examination and replacement easier. Refer to the *Fault finding* Section at the end of this manual for more information.

Chapter 7 Part B:
Automatic transmission

Contents

Degrees of difficulty

Easy, suitable for novice with little experience		Fairly easy, suitable for beginner with some experience		Fairly difficult, suitable for competent DIY mechanic		Difficult, suitable for experienced DIY mechanic		Very difficult, suitable for expert DIY or professional	

Specifications

General
Transmission code*:

Engine code 111.920	722.421
Engine code 111.921	722.604
Engine code 111.941	722.422
Engine code 111.945	722.422
Engine code 111.961	722.428
Engine code 111.974	722.600
Engine code 604.910	722.603
Engine code 605.910	722.427
Engine code 605.960	722.604

* Refer to Chapter 2A or 2B for engine codes

Transmission fluid
Type . . . . See *Lubricants and fluids*
Capacity . . . . 5.5 litres

Torque wrench settings

	Nm	lbf ft
Crossmember-to-vehicle floor bolts	45	33
Kickdown solenoid valve	20	15
Selector lever assembly	6	4
Selector lever shift lock (722.60x transmission)	4	3
Starter inhibitor/reversing light switch	8	6
Torque converter drain plug:		
722.42x transmission	14	10
722.60x transmission	16	12
Torque converter-to-driveplate bolts	42	31
Transmission fluid main drain plug	14	10
Transmission-to-engine bolts:		
M10 bolts	55	41
M12 bolts	65	48
Vacuum box	8	6

1 General information

A Mercedes-Benz four-speed automatic transmission is available as an option on all models covered by this manual.

The transmission comprises a torque converter, an epicyclic geartrain, and hydraulically-operated brakes and clutches.

The torque converter provides a fluid coupling between the engine and transmission, and acts as a clutch, also providing a degree of torque multiplication when accelerating.

The epicyclic geartrain provides the four forward and one reverse gear ratios, according to which of its component parts are held stationary or allowed to turn. The components of the geartrain are held or released by brakes and clutches which are activated by a hydraulic control unit. A fluid pump within the transmission provides the necessary hydraulic pressure to operate the brakes and clutches.

Driver control of the transmission is by a selector lever and, on the 722.60x transmission, a two-position switch. On the 722.42x transmission, a control pressure cable, operated by movement of the accelerator pedal alters the hydraulic control pressure in the transmission, according to throttle position. The selector lever has a 'drive' position, and a 'hold' facility on 2nd and 3rd gear (722.42x transmission) or gear ratios 1, 2, 3 and 4D (722.60x transmission). The 'drive' position (D) provides automatic changing throughout the range of all forward gear ratios, and is the position selected for normal driving. An automatic kickdown facility shifts the transmission down a gear if the accelerator pedal is fully depressed. The 'hold' facility is similar to the 'drive' position, but limits the number of gear ratios available - ie, when the selector lever is in the 3 position, only the first three ratios can be used; in the 2 position, only the first two can be used, and so on. The lower ratio 'hold' is useful when travelling down steep gradients, or for preventing unwanted selection of high gears on twisty roads.

Two driving programs are provided for selection by the switch; 'economy' or 'standard'. With the switch in the 'standard' position, the vehicle will move away from a standstill in 2nd gear with a light throttle, or 1st gear with full throttle. With the switch in the 'economy' position, the vehicle will always move away from a standstill in 2nd gear, and the gearchange points will occur at lower driving speeds.

Due to the complexity of the automatic transmission, any repair or overhaul work must be left to a Mercedes-Benz dealer or automatic transmission specialist with the necessary special equipment for fault diagnosis and repair. The contents of the following Sections are therefore confined to supplying general information, and any service information and instructions that can be used by the owner.

2 Selector lever - removal, refitting and adjusting

Removal

1 Disconnect the battery negative (earth) lead and position it away from the terminal. The battery is located in the rear luggage compartment.
2 Apply the parking brake, then jack up the front of the vehicle, and support securely on axle stands (see *Jacking and vehicle support*). Move the selector lever to position P.
3 Working under the vehicle, prise off the metal retaining clip, and disconnect the selector rod from the bottom of the selector lever **(see illustration)**.

2.3 Prise off the clip securing the gear selector lever to the selector rod

4 Remove the cover from the centre console as described in Chapter 11. On some models, it may be necessary to remove the complete centre console assembly.
5 Disconnect the wiring plugs from the selector lever assembly. The plugs are for the illumination and the economy/standard switch. Additionally, on 722.60x transmissions, one plug is for the reverse gear/park lock solenoid.
6 On 722.42x transmissions, unclip and remove the park position interlock cables.
7 Unscrew the mounting bolts and lift the selector lever assembly from the floor **(see illustration)**. Recover the gasket and check it for condition. Obtain a new one if necessary.

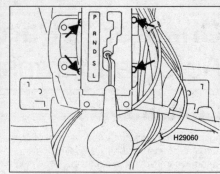

2.7 Unscrew the four gear selector lever securing screws (arrowed)

Refitting and adjusting

Models with the 722.42x transmission

8 The shift lock in the selector lever assembly incorporates cables attached to both the steering lock and parking brake pedal. After connecting all the cables, and before fitting the centre console, adjust the cables as follows. First, make sure that the selector lever is in position P and the ignition key is in position 0.
9 Refer to the accompanying illustration **(see illustration)** and pull cable 4 forwards until the locking lever 2 contacts the cam 1. Fit the cable holding clip. Now pull cable 6 forwards until the locking lever 7 contacts the cam 1. Insert and tighten the cable retaining bolt.

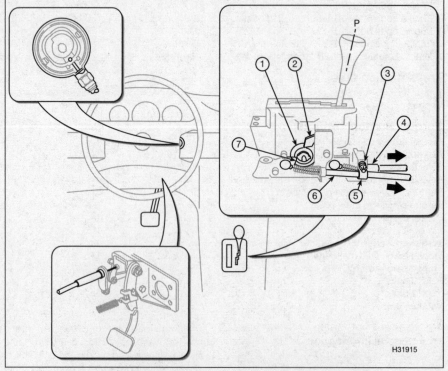

2.9 Interlock cables on the 722.42x automatic transmission

1	Cam	4	Locking lever	6	Locking lever
2	Locking lever	5	Support	7	Locking lever
3	Screw				

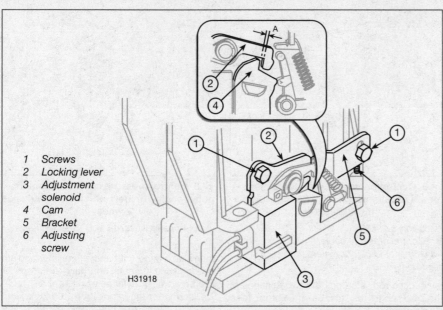

1 Screws
2 Locking lever
3 Adjustment solenoid
4 Cam
5 Bracket
6 Adjusting screw

H31918

2.11 Selector lever interlock mechanism on the 722.60x automatic transmission

10 To check the adjustment, turn the ignition key to position 1 and depress the brake pedal at least 25 mm. Check that the locking levers 2 and 7 disengage from the disc cam 1, enabling the selector lever to be moved into position N without resistance. With the brake pedal released, move the selector lever from position N to position P, and also turn the ignition key to position 0. Check that the locking levers 2 and 7 now engage the cams 1.

Models with the 722.60x transmission

Note: *Unlike the 722.42x transmission, the steering lock and parking brake interlock mechanism is separate to the selector lever on the 722.60x transmission; refer to Section 6 to carry out the adjustment.*

11 The shift lock in the selector lever assembly may be adjusted as follows before refitting the assembly. Select position N, then disconnect the wiring from the lock solenoid located on the right-hand side of the assembly. Loosen the two bolts securing the lock mechanism to the side of the assembly, then adjust the gap between the locking lever and cam to 0.2 mm by turning the adjustment screw under the front of the mechanism **(see illustration)**. Finally tighten the two bolts to the specified torque.

All models

12 Refitting of the selector lever is a reversal of removal, but tighten the mounting bolts to the specified torque, and check the adjustment of the selector rod with reference to Section 3. Make sure that there are no kinks in the cables as they are being refitted.

3 Selector rod - removal, refitting and adjustment

Removal

1 Apply the parking brake, then jack up the front of the vehicle and support it on axle stands (see *Jacking and vehicle support*).
2 Prise the securing clips from the ends of the selector rod, at the bottom of the selector lever and at the lever on the transmission, then withdraw the rod from under the vehicle.

Refitting

3 Refitting is a reversal of removal, but check and adjust the selector rod as follows.

Adjustment

Models with transmission 722.42x

4 Move the selector lever inside the vehicle to position N.
5 Working under the vehicle, release the clip and disconnect the selector rod from the bottom of the selector lever.
6 Move the selector lever on the transmission to position N.
7 Loosen the selector rod adjustment locknut **(see illustration)**, and adjust the length of the rod by turning the end fitting until, with the selector rod reconnected to the gear selector lever, there is approximately 1.0 mm clearance between the driver's gear selector lever and the N stop on the gear selector gate.
8 When the adjustment is correct, secure the selector rod to the selector lever with the metal clip, then tighten the locknut.

Models with transmission 722.60x

9 Move the selector lever inside the vehicle to position D.
10 Working under the vehicle prise off the metal retaining clip and disconnect the selector rod from the selector lever on the transmission.
11 Check that the selector lever on the transmission is in position D, and that the selector lever inside the vehicle is also in position D.
12 Check that the selector rod engages freely with the lever on the transmission. If necessary, adjust the length of the rod so that it engages correctly by loosening the Torx lockbolt. After making the adjustment, tighten the lockbolt.

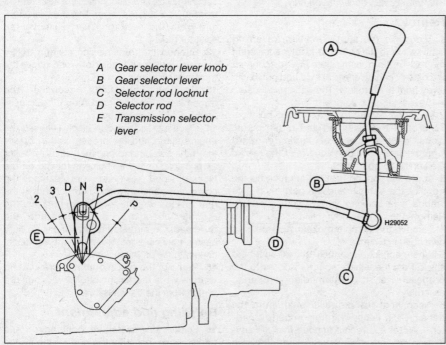

A Gear selector lever knob
B Gear selector lever
C Selector rod locknut
D Selector rod
E Transmission selector lever

H29052

3.7 Gear selector rod adjustment (transmission 722.42x)

13 When the adjustment is correct, secure the selector rod to the selector lever with the metal clip.

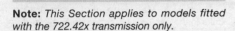

4 Control pressure cable - adjustment

Note: *This Section applies to models fitted with the 722.42x transmission only.*

Petrol engines

Note: *The accelerator cable must be correctly adjusted as described in Chapter 4A before commencing the control pressure cable adjustment.*

Models with ball head cable

1 Prise the control pressure cable ball head from the ball on the throttle linkage.
2 Push the ball head into the outer cable, then pull it out again until a slight resistance is felt. Keep the ball head at this position and check that it will locate on the linkage ball free of tension. If necessary loosen the locknut on the outer cable and reposition the cable until the ball head locates correctly.

Models with pointers on the throttle linkage

3 With the throttle in its rest position, check that the pointers on the throttle linkage are aligned with each other **(see illustration)**. If not, turn the adjustment on the outer cable to align the pointers.

Models with knurled adjuster wheel

4 Turn the adjuster wheel sufficiently to give approximately 1.0 mm of play between the cable end fitting and the spacer sleeve at the end of the adjuster.
5 Turn the adjuster wheel back until the tip of the adjuster pointer is positioned exactly above the groove in the centre of the adjuster wheel **(see illustration)**.

Diesel engines

6 Disconnect the control pressure cable end fitting from the ballstud on the throttle linkage.
7 Loosen the clamp on the throttle lever

4.7 Control pressure cable adjustment - diesel engine models

A   Control pressure cable end fitting
B   Throttle lever connecting plate

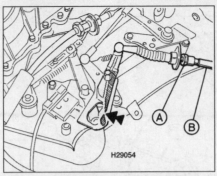

4.3 Control pressure cable adjustment - petrol engine models with pointers on the throttle linkage

A   Cable adjuster
B   Control pressure cable
Adjustment indicator pointers (arrowed) in alignment

connecting rod, then pull the two sections of the rod apart as far as the stop **(see illustration)**.
8 Pull the control pressure cable forwards until slight resistance is felt.
9 At the point where resistance is just felt, it should be possible to fit the cable end back onto the throttle linkage balljoint. If necessary, adjust the length of the connecting rod until the cable end can be easily refitted to the balljoint.

5 Starter inhibitor/reversing light switch - removal, refitting and adjustment

Note: *This Section applies to models fitted with the 722.42x transmission only.*

Removal

1 Access to the starter inhibitor/reversing light switch is difficult, and involves lowering the rear of the transmission. First disconnect the battery negative (earth) lead and position it away from the terminal. The battery is located in the rear luggage compartment.
2 Raise the bonnet to its fully open position. To protect the bulkhead and brake pipes, place a thin sheet of wood or card (approximately 300 mm square) at the rear of the engine compartment.
3 Apply the parking brake, then jack up the front of the vehicle and support it on axle stands (see *Jacking and vehicle support*). Remove the engine undershield.
4 Remove the complete exhaust system as described in Chapter 4C.
5 Where applicable, unbolt the exhaust heat shield from the vehicle floor for access to the propeller shaft intermediate bearing assembly.
6 Disconnect the propeller shaft from the transmission flange with reference to Chapter 8. **Note:** *It is recommended that the self-locking nuts are renewed.* Slacken the clamp nut at the propeller shaft intermediate bearing,

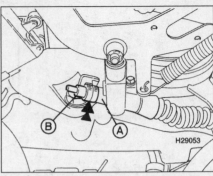

4.5 Control pressure cable adjustment - petrol engine models with knurled adjuster wheel

A   Adjuster wheel   B   Spacer sleeve

then slacken (do not remove) the intermediate bearing securing nuts, and push the propeller shaft rearwards as far as possible.
7 Disconnect the wiring from the kickdown solenoid, at the rear right-hand corner of the transmission
8 Where a speedometer cable is fitted, unscrew the clamp bolt, pull the cable from the right-hand rear side of the transmission, and tie it to one side. Where applicable, release the cable-tie(s) securing the cable to the transmission.
9 Where a speedometer transponder is fitted, unbolt the unit from the right-hand rear side of the transmission and tie it to one side.
10 Release the starter inhibitor/reversing light switch wiring connector locking clip by pushing it upwards off the connector lug. Carefully prise off the switch wiring connector, using two screwdrivers.
11 Select position N, then prise off the securing clips and disconnect the selector rod from the selector lever on the transmission, and from the selector lever. Remove the selector rod.
12 Support the transmission using a trolley jack and interposed block of wood under the transmission sump.
13 Unscrew the bolts securing the transmission/engine rear mounting cross-member to the underbody.
14 Place a small wooden block between the engine sump and the crossmember. Lower the transmission and engine assembly as far as possible, until the engine is resting on the block of wood. Take care not to damage the brake pipes and any other components at the rear of the engine compartment, as the cylinder head may be forced into the bulkhead. On models fitted with an auxiliary heater, take care not to damage the additional coolant hose on the bulkhead.
15 Remove the two mounting screws, and withdraw the starter inhibitor/reversing light switch from the transmission.

Refitting and adjustment

16 Locate the switch in position on the transmission, ensuring the peg on the switch engages with the corresponding hole in the

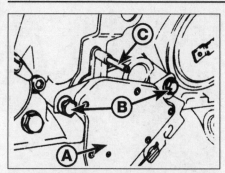

5.16 Starter inhibitor/reversing light switch adjustment - models with 722.42x transmission

A *Starter inhibitor/reversing light switch*
B *Switch securing screws*
C *4.0 mm twist drill*

selector lever **(see illustration)**. Ensure the selector lever is in position N (the positions are marked on the transmission casing).

17 Refit the mounting screws loosely, then insert a 4.0 mm diameter twist drill or rod through the switch peg and selector lever. Tighten the switch mounting screws, then remove the drill or rod.

18 Raise the jack, then refit and tighten the bolts securing the transmission/engine rear mounting crossmember to the underbody.

19 Reconnect the selector rod to the selector levers and secure with the clips.

20 Reconnect the starter inhibitor/reversing light switch wiring.

21 Refit the speedometer transponder or cable, as applicable.

22 Reconnect the wiring to the kickdown solenoid.

23 Reconnect the propeller shaft to the transmission flange with reference to Chapter 8, using new self-locking nuts.

24 Refit the exhaust heat shield where applicable.

25 Refit the exhaust system and the engine undershield.

26 Lower the vehicle to the ground and remove the bulkhead protector.

27 Reconnect the battery negative (earth) lead.

7.6 Torque converter drain plug (arrowed) aligned with transmission aperture

6 Parking lock interlock cables - removal, refitting and adjustment

Note: *This Section applies to models fitted with the 722.60x transmission only.*

Removal

1 Apply the handbrake, then jack up the front of the vehicle and support it on axle stands (see *Jacking and vehicle support*).

2 Remove the lower facia trim panel from under the steering column, and also remove the steering column shrouds.

3 With the ignition key at position 1, disconnect the interlock cable from the steering lock by compressing the tabs and moving the cable out from the side of the lock.

4 Remove the stop-lamp switch from the brake pedal bracket with reference to Chapter 9.

5 Disconnect the interlock cable from the lever link on the parking brake pedal, then compress the retainers and release the cable from the pedal bracket. Withdraw the steering lock interlock cable.

6 Disconnect the transmission interlock cable from the lever link on the parking brake pedal, then compress the retainers and release the cable from the pedal bracket.

7 Move the selector lever to position P, then, working under the vehicle, use a screwdriver to prise open the retaining clip and disconnect the interlock cable from the rear of the transmission.

8 Prise out the rubber grommet from the transmission tunnel, then release the interlock cable from its retainers and withdraw from the vehicle.

Refitting

9 Refitting is a reversal of removal, but adjust the cables as follows before refitting the lower facia trim panel.

Adjustment

Steering lock interlock cable

10 Pretension the cable at the parking brake end of the cable by depressing the button.

11 Turn the ignition key to position 1, then

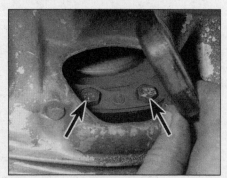

7.7 Prise out the plastic plug for access to the torque converter-to-driveplate bolts (arrowed)

have an assistant operate the parking brake pedal and move the selector lever to position D.

12 Have the assistant fully depress the parking brake pedal as far as possible, then adjust the cable by depressing the button.

Transmission interlock cable

13 Pretension the cable at the parking brake end of the cable by depressing the button.

14 Move the selector lever to position P, and turn the ignition key to position 0.

15 Adjust the cable by depressing the button.

7 Automatic transmission - removal and refitting

Removal

Note: *This is a difficult operation, due to the limited access to the engine-to-transmission bolts, and to the weight of the transmission assembly. It is suggested that the procedure is read through thoroughly before starting the operation. Suitable ratchet extensions will be required to reach some of the engine-to-transmission bolts.*

1 Disconnect the battery negative (earth) lead and position it away from the terminal. The battery is located in the rear luggage compartment.

2 Raise the bonnet to its fully open position. To protect the bulkhead and brake pipes, place a thin sheet of wood or card (approximately 300 mm square) at the rear of the engine compartment.

3 Apply the parking brake, then jack up the front of the vehicle and support it on axle stands (see *Jacking and vehicle support*). The vehicle must be raised sufficiently to enable the transmission to be lowered and removed from under the vehicle. Remove the engine undershield.

4 On 722.42x transmissions, disconnect the transmission control pressure cable from the accelerator linkage on the inlet manifold. To do this, press off the ball socket.

5 Place a suitable container beneath the transmission main fluid drain plug, then unscrew the drain plug, and drain the transmission fluid. Check the condition of the sealing ring and renew it if necessary, then refit the plug and tighten it to the specified torque.

6 Reposition the container beneath the torque converter aperture in the transmission casing. Using a socket on the crankshaft pulley/vibration damper hub, turn the crankshaft until the torque converter drain plug is aligned with the transmission aperture **(see illustration)**. Unscrew the drain plug, then drain the torque converter fluid. Check the condition of the sealing ring and renew it if necessary, then refit the plug and tighten it to the specified torque.

7 On 722.42x transmissions, prise the plastic plug from the transmission bellhousing for access to the torque converter-to-driveplate bolts **(see illustration)**. On 722.60x

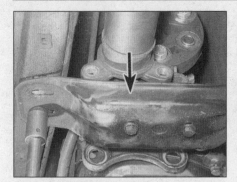

7.12 Unbolt the rear engine/transmission support bracket (arrowed)

7.15 Disconnect the wiring plug from the kickdown solenoid

7.16a Unscrew the clamp bolt . . .

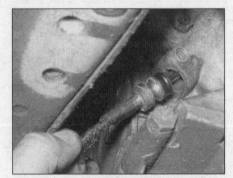

7.16b . . . and pull out the speedometer cable

transmissions, unbolt the cover from the bottom of the bellhousing.

8 Unscrew the six torque converter-to-driveplate bolts, turning the crankshaft for access to each pair of bolts in turn.

9 Remove the complete exhaust system as described in Chapter 4C. Also unbolt the exhaust support bracket from the transmission.

10 Remove the starter motor as described in Chapter 5A.

11 Support the transmission using a trolley jack and interposed block of wood under the transmission sump.

12 Unscrew the bolts securing the transmission/engine rear mounting crossmember to the underbody **(see**

illustration)**, then unscrew the nut securing the rubber mounting to the transmission, and withdraw the crossmember and mounting.

13 Where applicable, unbolt the exhaust heat shield from the vehicle floor for access to the propeller shaft intermediate bearing assembly.

14 Disconnect the propeller shaft from the transmission flange with reference to Chapter 8. **Note:** *It is recommended that the self-locking nuts are renewed*. On early models only, slacken the clamp nut at the propeller shaft intermediate bearing, then slacken (do not remove) the intermediate bearing securing nuts, and push the propeller shaft rearwards as far as possible.

15 On 722.42x transmissions, disconnect the wiring from the kickdown solenoid, at the rear right-hand corner of the transmission **(see illustration)**. On 722.60x transmissions, unbolt the cover from the right-hand side of the transmission, then disconnect the multiplug by twisting the bayonet-type plug anti-clockwise.

16 Where a speedometer cable is fitted, unscrew the clamp bolt, pull the cable from the right-hand rear side of the transmission, and tie it to one side **(see illustrations)**. Where applicable, release the cable-tie(s) securing the cable to the transmission.

17 Where a speedometer transponder is fitted, unbolt the unit from the right-hand rear side of the transmission and tie it to one side.

18 Release the starter inhibitor/reversing light

switch wiring connector locking clip by pushing it upwards off the connector lug. Carefully prise off the switch wiring connector, using two screwdrivers **(see illustration)**.

19 Prise off the securing clips, and disconnect the selector rod from the selector lever on the transmission, and from the selector lever. Remove the selector rod.

20 On 722.60x transmissions, select P then disconnect the parking lock interlock cable from the rear of the transmission using a screwdriver to prise open the retainer.

21 Disconnect the vacuum lines from the transmission **(see illustration)**. Each line is colour-coded for position to ensure correct refitting.

22 Pull up the locking clip, and remove the transmission fluid level dipstick.

23 Unscrew the bolt and remove the transmission fluid filler pipe support clamp from the cylinder head. On 722.42x transmissions, unscrew the securing bolt then pull out the pipe from the transmission **(see illustration)**. On 722.60x transmissions, unscrew the lower support bolt and the transmission-to-engine bolt securing the filler pipe bracket, then carefully tap out the pipe from the transmission and recover the O-ring seal.

24 Where applicable, unscrew the knurled locking ring, and disconnect the wiring plug from the left-hand side of the transmission.

25 Unscrew the union bolts and disconnect the transmission fluid cooler feed and return

7.18 Disconnect the starter inhibitor/reversing light switch wiring connector (arrowed)

7.21 Disconnect the vacuum lines from the vacuum unit (arrowed)

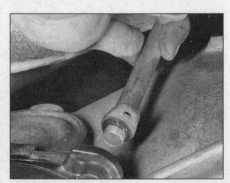

7.23 Withdraw the dipstick tube/filler pipe

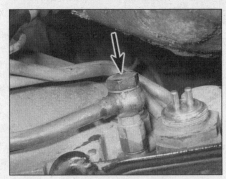

7.25 Disconnect the transmission fluid cooler pipes (arrowed)

7.27 Unscrew the transmission-to-engine bolts, noting the location of the earth strap

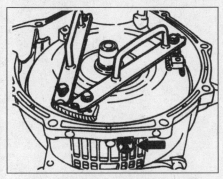

7.30 Lifting handles bolted to torque converter. Plastic holding pin arrowed

pipes from the transmission (see illustration). Recover the sealing rings, and cover or plug the open ends of the pipes and transmission to prevent dirt entry and further fluid loss. Tie the pipes to one side.

26 Place a small wooden block between the engine sump and the crossmember. Lower the transmission and engine assembly as far as possible, until the engine is resting on the block of wood. Take care not to damage the brake pipes and any other components at the rear of the engine compartment, as the cylinder head may be forced into the bulkhead. On models fitted with an auxiliary heater, take care not to damage the additional coolant hose on the bulkhead.

27 Unscrew all the transmission-to-engine bolts, leaving one bolt on either side of the transmission. Access to the upper bolts is very difficult, even with the assembly tilted, and several long ratchet extensions will be required. Note the locations of the earth strap and any support brackets (see illustration).

28 Raise the engine/transmission assembly until it is horizontal. During the removal operation, it is important that the torque converter remains fully engaged with the transmission, otherwise it may fall out and be damaged. A plastic retaining pin is fitted to the bellhousing for this purpose, however, if the pin is missing, one method of retaining the torque converter is to partially unscrew the drain plug and tie some wire or welding rod around it.

29 Unscrew the remaining two transmission-to-engine bolts, then, with the help of an assistant, withdraw the transmission rearwards as far as possible, and lower it to the ground with the jack.

 Warning: The transmission is heavy.

30 To remove the torque converter, proceed as follows (see illustration):

a) Support the transmission on wooden blocks in a vertical position, with the bellhousing and torque converter pointing vertically upwards.

b) Using an 8.0 mm Allen key, turn the torque converter plastic holding pin through a quarter-turn anti-clockwise and remove.

c) Bolt two suitable lifting handles to the torque converter, using long bolts in the torque converter-to-driveplate bolt holes, and use the handles to lift the torque converter from the transmission. Pull evenly on both handles. Alternatively, screw two long bolts into two of the torque converter-to-driveplate bolt holes, and use the bolts to lift out the torque converter. Be prepared for some fluid spillage.

d) Store the torque converter in a safe place, where it cannot be damaged.

Refitting

31 To refit the torque converter, proceed as follows:

a) Lightly grease the torque converter drive flange. Molykote grease is recommended.

b) Using the two bolts, manipulate the converter into position. Move the converter back and forth as it is fitted to ensure that it is fully engaged with the transmission input shaft and primary pump. The converter is fully engaged when the distance between the bellhousing face and torque converter driveplate face is 9.6 mm on petrol engine models or 8.7 mm on diesel engine models.

c) Refit the plastic holding pin, and turn it a quarter-turn clockwise to secure.

d) Turn the torque converter until two of the torque converter-to-driveplate bolt holes are positioned at the bottom of the transmission bellhousing.

32 Support the transmission using the trolley jack and block of wood, as during removal, then raise the transmission into position beneath the vehicle. Carefully engage the transmission with the rear of the engine, making sure that the bellhousing locates over the two dowels correctly.

33 Refit and tighten the transmission-to-engine bolts, ensuring that the earth strap and

any brackets noted during removal are in place.

34 Insert the torque converter-to-driveplate bolts, and tighten them to the specified torque. Turn the crankshaft as during removal for access to all of the bolts. Make sure that the torque converter drain plug is tightened to the specified torque.

35 Further refitting is a reversal of removal, bearing in mind the following points.

a) Use new sealing rings when connecting the transmission fluid cooler pipes.

b) Reconnect the propeller shaft as described in Chapter 8.

c) Tighten all nuts and bolts to the specified torque where given.

d) Ensure that all wires and vacuum lines are correctly reconnected and routed as noted before removal.

e) Refit the starter motor with reference to Chapter 5A.

f) Refit the exhaust system with reference to Chapter 4C.

g) Refill the transmission with fluid poured down the dipstick tube (Chapter 1A or 1B).

h) On completion, check the adjustment of the selector rod (both transmission types) and control pressure cable (722.42x transmissions only) as described in Sections 3 and 4.

8 Automatic transmission overhaul - general information

In the event of a fault occurring with the transmission, it is first necessary to determine whether it is of an electrical, mechanical or hydraulic nature, and to do this special test equipment is required. It is therefore essential to have the work carried out by a Mercedes-Benz dealer or automatic transmission specialist if a transmission fault is suspected. Do not remove the transmission from the vehicle for repair before professional fault diagnosis has been carried out, since most tests require the transmission to be in the vehicle.

Chapter 8
Final drive, driveshafts and propeller shaft

Contents

Degrees of difficulty

Easy, suitable for novice with little experience 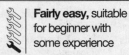	Fairly easy, suitable for beginner with some experience 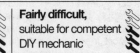	Fairly difficult, suitable for competent DIY mechanic	Difficult, suitable for experienced DIY mechanic	Very difficult, suitable for expert DIY or professional

Specifications

Final drive
Type . . . . Unsprung, casing bolted to rear suspension crossmember

Driveshaft
Type . . . . Steel shafts with ball-and-cage type constant velocity joints at each end

Propeller shaft
Type . . . . Two-piece tubular shaft with centre bearing and universal joint. Rubber coupling at front and rear joints

Torque wrench settings	Nm	lbf ft
Driveshaft		
Shaft-to-final drive flange bolts	70	52
Driveshaft retaining nut	220	162
Final drive unit		
Mounting bolts:		
Front Allen bolt	45	33
Rear collared bolt	110	81
Speed sensor bolts	8	6
Propeller shaft		
Centre bearing bracket bolts:		
Bolt with washer	25	18
Bolt with collar	30	22
Clamping nut	40	30
Flexible coupling bolt nuts:		
M10 bolts	40	30
M12 bolts	60	44
Rear cross-brace self-locking bolts	40	30
Transmission rear support bracket self-locking bolts	25	18
Roadwheels		
Wheel bolts	110	81

1 General information

Power is transmitted from the transmission to the rear axle by a two-piece propeller shaft, joined in front of the centre bearing by a 'slip joint', a sliding, splined coupling. The slip joint allows slight fore-and-aft movement of the propeller shaft. The propeller shaft is attached to the flanges of the transmission and final drive unit by flexible rubber couplings, a vibration damper being fitted between the front coupling and the shaft. The middle of the propeller shaft is supported by the centre bearing which is bolted to the vehicle body. A universal joint is located at the rear of the centre bearing, to compensate for movement of the transmission and differential on their mountings, and for any flexing of the chassis.

The final drive assembly includes the drive pinion, the ring gear, the differential and the output flanges. The drive pinion, which drives the ring gear, is also known as the differential input shaft, and is connected to the propeller shaft via an input flange. The differential is bolted to the ring gear and drives the rear wheels through a pair of output flanges bolted to driveshafts. The differential allows the wheels to turn at different speeds when cornering, although only to a limited amount on models fitted with ASD (limited-slip differential).

The driveshafts deliver power from the final drive unit output flanges to the rear wheels.

The driveshafts are equipped with constant velocity (CV) joints at each end. The inner CV joints are bolted to the differential flanges; the outer CV joints engage the splines of the wheel hubs, and are secured by a large nut.

Major repair work on the differential assembly components (drive pinion, ring-and-pinion, and differential) requires many special tools and a high degree of expertise, and therefore should not be attempted by the home mechanic. If major repairs become necessary, we recommend that they be performed by a Mercedes-Benz service department or other suitably-equipped automotive engineer.

2 Final drive unit - draining and refilling

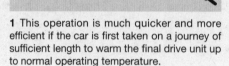

1 This operation is much quicker and more efficient if the car is first taken on a journey of sufficient length to warm the final drive unit up to normal operating temperature.
2 Park the car on level ground, switch off the ignition and apply the parking brake firmly. For improved access, jack up the rear of the car and support it securely on axle stands (see *Jacking and vehicle support*). Note that the car must be level, to ensure accuracy, when refilling and checking the oil level.
3 Wipe clean the area around the filler/level plug, which is situated on the left-hand side of the final drive unit, next to the driveshaft flange, and unscrew it **(see illustration)**.
4 Position a suitable container under the drain plug, and unscrew the plug from the right-hand side of the housing.
5 Allow the oil to drain completely into the container. If the oil is hot, take precautions against scalding. Clean both the filler/level and the drain plugs, being especially careful to wipe any metallic particles off the magnetic inserts.
6 When the oil has finished draining, clean the drain plug threads and those of the final drive casing, and refit the drain plug. If the car was raised for the draining operation, now lower it to the ground.
7 Refilling the final drive unit is an extremely awkward operation. Above all, allow plenty of

time for the oil level to settle properly before checking it. Note that the car must be parked on flat level ground when checking the oil level.
8 Refill the final drive unit with the exact amount of the specified type of oil, then check the oil level as described in Chapter 1A or 1B. If the correct amount was poured into the final drive unit and a large amount flows out on checking the level, refit the filler/level plug and take the car on a short journey so that the new oil is distributed fully around the final drive components, then check the level again on your return.

3 Final drive unit - removal and refitting

Note: *New propeller shaft rear coupling nuts, driveshaft joint bolts and final drive unit mounting bolt nuts will be required on refitting.*

Removal

1 Chock the front wheels and loosen the rear wheel bolts. Jack up the rear of the car and support it on axle stands (see *Jacking and vehicle support*). Remove both rear wheels.
2 Drain the oil from the final drive unit, as described in Section 2.
3 With reference to Chapter 4C, remove the rear section of the exhaust system, then unscrew the nuts and lower the exhaust heat shield away from the floorpan **(see illustration)**.
4 Where applicable (on models up to 1995), using a large open-ended spanner, slacken the propeller shaft clamping nut, located in front of the centre support bearing, by one turn. Use a second spanner to hold the propeller shaft stationary as the clamping nut is slackened, and take care not to damage the rubber gaiter.
5 Undo the two bolts securing the propeller shaft centre support bearing to the underbody **(see illustration)**.
6 Undo the three nuts and remove the bolts securing the propeller shaft rear flexible coupling to the differential pinion flange **(see illustration)**.

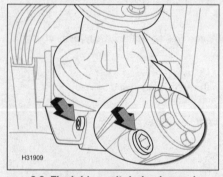

2.3 Final drive unit drain plug and filler/level plug (inset)

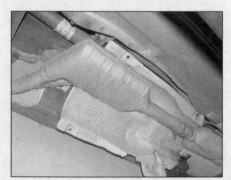

3.3 Removing the exhaust heat shield

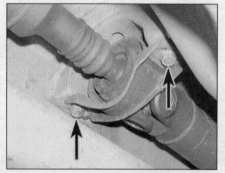

3.5 Two bolts (arrowed) securing propeller shaft centre support

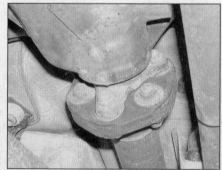

3.6 Propeller shaft flexible rear coupling

3.13 Final drive housing-to-subframe bolts

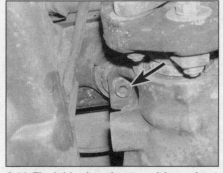

3.14 Final drive housing-to-subframe front retaining bolt (arrowed)

3.16 ABS speed sensor location (arrowed)

7 Push the propeller shaft forwards as far as it will go to disengage the pinion flange centring sleeve. Lower the disconnected propeller shaft, and rest it on the rear cross-brace.

8 On petrol models, undo the nuts/bolts securing the fuel pump shield, and remove the shield from under the car.

9 Support the fuel pump, and unhook the rubber mounting rings. Lower the fuel pump to one side, and either tie it up clear of the final drive unit, or support it so that the fuel pipes are not strained.

10 Using a suitable multi-toothed key or socket bit, unscrew the bolts securing both driveshaft inner constant velocity joints to the differential drive flanges. Make sure the tool used to loosen the bolts engages fully - clean the bolt heads first if necessary. Remove the bolts and plate washers. Mercedes-Benz recommend that new bolts and washers are obtained for reassembly - this seems wise, given their important role, and the high torque to which they are tightened.

11 Push the driveshafts outwards to clear the drive flanges and tie them up, using a length of wire, to the rear suspension camber strut.

12 Place a jack beneath the final drive housing and just take the weight of the unit.

13 Undo the collared bolts at the rear securing the final drive housing to the subframe, and remove the bolts together with the large impact washers **(see illustration)**.

14 Unscrew the Allen bolt and nut, and the nut/washer, securing the housing to the subframe at the front **(see illustration)**. When the final drive is removed, note that there are either one or two shims fitted between the Allen bolt and the housing - make sure these are recovered and refitted. Note the fitted order of all the bushes and washers as they are removed.

15 On models with the limited-slip differential (ASD), disconnect the hydraulic line from the housing, and plug the connection and pipe end fitting to prevent fluid loss or dirt entry.

16 Where applicable, the speed sensor wiring must now be disconnected. All models up to 1998 model year have one speed sensor at the front of the housing **(see illustration)**, but models up to May 1994 with traction

control (ASR) have two more, one above each driveshaft. Trace the wiring up from the final drive housing to the entry point(s) in the luggage compartment floor, and remove the rubber sealing grommet(s). Working in the luggage compartment, lift up the front section of the boot floor (this may be secured by a number of large plastic screw retainers). Disconnect the ABS wiring plug (and where applicable, the traction control/ASR wiring plug), then feed the wiring down through the holes in the floor.

17 Lower the jack slowly, and remove the final drive housing from under the car. As they become accessible, unscrew the Allen bolt securing each speed sensor, and remove the speed sensor(s) from the housing, noting the location of each.

Refitting

18 Where applicable, clean the speed sensor(s) thoroughly before refitting to the housing. Fit new O-ring seals where necessary, and tighten the sensor bolts to the specified torque.

19 To refit the unit, position it centrally within the subframe, and refit the front retaining bolt with a new nut and nut/washer finger-tight.

20 Refit the rear retaining bolt with a new impact washer, and tighten to the specified torque. Now tighten the front bolt to the specified torque as well.

21 Further refitting is a reversal of removal, noting the following points:

a) Tighten all fasteners to the specified torque, where given.
b) Delay tightening the centre bearing bolts fully until after the propeller shaft has been reconnected.
c) Lightly lubricate the threads of the new driveshaft inner constant velocity joint-to-differential drive flange bolts, refit the bolts and locking plates, and tighten to the specified torque.
d) On models with the limited-slip differential (ASD), reconnect the hydraulic line to the housing. Have the system bled by a Mercedes-Benz dealer on completion.
e) Refit the rear section of the exhaust system with reference to Chapter 4C.
f) On completion, when the car has been

lowered to the ground and is level, unscrew the housing filler/level plug and refill the final drive oil to the level of the plug orifice, using the specified lubricant (Section 2). Refit the plug and tighten securely.

4 Final drive unit oil seals - renewal

Renewal of the final drive unit oil seals is a complex task, requiring the final drive unit to be partially dismantled. This operation should therefore be entrusted to a Mercedes-Benz dealer.

5 Driveshaft - removal and refitting

Note: *A new driveshaft retaining nut and bolts will be required on refitting.*

Removal

1 Remove the wheel trim/hub cap (as applicable) and, using a hammer and pointed-nose chisel, carefully relieve the driveshaft retaining nut staking.

2 Slacken the 12-point driveshaft retaining nut with the car resting on its wheels. Note that this nut is extremely tight - ensure that the tools used to loosen it are of good quality, and a good fit. Do not remove the nut at this stage.

3 Chock the front wheels and loosen the rear wheel bolts. Jack up the rear of the car and support it on axle stands (see *Jacking and vehicle support*). Remove the relevant rear roadwheel.

4 If the left-hand driveshaft is to be removed, note that it may be necessary to remove the exhaust system tailpipe to gain the relevant clearance required to manoeuvre the shaft out of position (see Chapter 4C).

5 Slacken and remove the retaining bolts and plates securing the driveshaft to the final drive unit flange, and support the driveshaft by tying it to the vehicle underbody using a piece

5.5 Slacken and remove the retaining bolts and plates securing the driveshaft to the final drive unit flange

5.8a Lubricate the face and the threads of the new driveshaft nut with clean engine oil

5.8b Tighten the driveshaft nut to the specified torque, then stake it into the driveshaft groove

of wire **(see illustration)**. **Note:** *Do not allow the driveshaft to hang under its own weight, as the CV joint may be damaged.* Mercedes-Benz recommend that new bolts and washers are obtained for reassembly - this seems wise, given their important role, and the high torque to which they are tightened.

6 Remove the driveshaft retaining nut, and withdraw the driveshaft outer constant velocity joint from the hub assembly. If necessary, tap the joint out of the hub using a soft-faced mallet. If this fails to free it from the hub, the joint will have to be pressed out using a suitable tool which is bolted to the hub.

7 Remove the driveshaft from underneath the vehicle.

Refitting

8 Refitting is the reverse of removal, noting the following points.

  a) *Lubricate the threads and face of the new driveshaft nut and retaining bolts with clean engine oil prior to fitting* **(see illustration)**.

  b) *Fit the new retaining bolts with the retaining plates and tighten them to the specified torque.*

  c) *Once the vehicle is resting on its wheels, tighten the driveshaft retaining nut to the specified torque and stake it firmly into the driveshaft groove using a hammer and punch* **(see illustration)**.

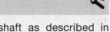

6 Driveshaft gaiters - renewal

1 Remove the driveshaft as described in Section 5.

2 Clean the driveshaft and mount it in a vice.

3 Lever off the sealing cover from the end of the inner constant velocity (CV) joint **(see illustration)**.

4 Cut/release the two inner joint gaiter retaining clips, and slide the gaiter along the driveshaft **(see illustration)**.

5 Wipe away excess grease and remove the inner joint circlip from the end of the driveshaft **(see illustration)**.

6 Securely support the joint inner member, and tap the driveshaft out of position using a hammer and suitable drift. If the joint is a tight fit, a suitable puller will be required to draw off the joint. Do not dismantle the inner joint.

7 With the joint removed, slide the gaiter off from the end of the driveshaft.

8 Release the outer joint gaiter retaining clips then slide the gaiter along the shaft and remove it.

9 Thoroughly clean the constant velocity joints using paraffin, or a suitable solvent, and dry thoroughly. Carry out a visual inspection as follows.

10 Move the inner splined driving member

from side-to-side to expose each ball in turn at the top of its track. Examine the balls for cracks, flat spots or signs of surface pitting.

11 Inspect the ball tracks on the inner and outer members. If the tracks have widened, the balls will no longer be a tight fit. At the same time check the ball cage windows for wear or cracking between the windows. If necessary, the dust covers can be removed from each joint assembly and renewed; on refitting, ensure that the joint and cover mating surfaces are clean and dry, and apply a smear of sealant to the cover surface to prevent leakage.

12 If on inspection any of the constant velocity joint components are found to be worn or damaged, it must be renewed. The inner joint is available separately but if the outer joint is worn, it will be necessary to renew the complete joint and driveshaft assembly. If the joints are in satisfactory condition, obtain new gaiter repair kits which contain gaiters, retaining clips, an inner constant velocity joint circlip and the correct type and quantity of grease required.

13 Tape over the splines on the end of the driveshaft.

14 Slide the new outer gaiter onto the end of the driveshaft.

15 Pack the outer joint with the grease supplied in the repair kit - alternatively, use a good-quality molybdenum disulphide ('moly')

6.3 Remove the sealing cover from the end of the inner CV joint

6.4 Cut the retaining clips and disengage the inner gaiter from the joint

6.5 Remove the circlip and tap/pull the inner joint off the end of the driveshaft

6.15 Pack the driveshaft outer joint with the grease supplied with the repair kit

6.16a Slide the new gaiter into position . . .

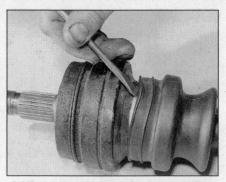

6.16b . . . then lift the gaiter outer sealing lip to equalise air pressure in the gaiter

grease **(see illustration)**. Work the grease well into the bearing tracks whilst twisting the joint, and fill the rubber gaiter with any excess.

16 Ease the gaiter over the joint and ensure that the gaiter lips are correctly located on both the driveshaft and constant velocity joint. Lift the outer sealing lip of the gaiter to equalise air pressure within the gaiter **(see illustrations)**.

17 Fit the large metal retaining clip to the gaiter. Pull the clip as tight as possible and locate its hook in one of the slots. Remove all slack from the retaining clip by compressing the raised section of the clip using special

pliers; if the special pliers are not available, **carefully** compress the clip using side-cutters, taking care not to cut the clip **(see illustrations)**. Secure the small retaining clip using the same procedure.

18 Slide the new inner joint gaiter onto the driveshaft **(see illustration)**.

19 Remove the tape from the driveshaft splines, and fit the inner constant velocity joint **(see illustration)**. Press the joint fully onto the shaft, and secure it in position with a new circlip.

20 Work the grease supplied fully into the inner joint, and fill the gaiter with any excess **(see illustration)**.

21 Ease the gaiter over the joint, and ensure that the gaiter lips are correctly located on both the driveshaft and constant velocity joint. Lift the outer sealing lip of the gaiter to equalise air pressure within the gaiter, and secure it in position with the retaining clips (see paragraph 17).

22 Ensure that the inner joint and dust cover mating surfaces are clean and dry, then apply a smear of sealant to the inner edge of the cover **(see illustration)**, and press the cover fully onto the inner joint.

23 Check that both constant velocity joints are free to move easily, then refit the driveshaft as described in Section 5.

6.17a Hook the retaining clip tightly around the gaiter . . .

6.17b . . . and remove any slack by compressing the raised section of the clip

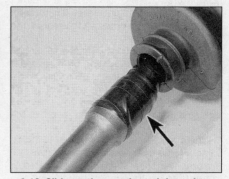

6.18 Slide on the new inner joint gaiter, then remove the protective tape (arrowed) . . .

6.19 . . . and fit the inner joint assembly

6.20 Pack the inner joint with the special grease supplied

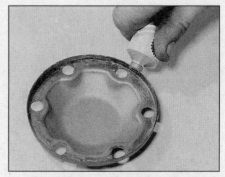

6.22 Apply a smear of sealant to the sealing cover before fitting it to the inner joint

7.3 Transmission rear support bracket

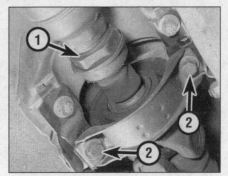

7.6 Propeller shaft threaded sleeve nut (1) and centre bearing bracket bolts (2)

7.7 Remove the flexible coupling-to-transmission flange nuts and bolts

7 Propeller shaft - removal and refitting

Note: *New propeller shaft front and rear coupling nuts will be required on refitting.*

Removal

1 Chock the front wheels. Jack up the rear of the car and support it on axle stands (see *Jacking and vehicle support*).
2 Where applicable, release the clips and fasteners, and remove the engine lower cover from under the car.
3 Unbolt and remove the transmission rear support bracket which fits across at the front of the propeller shaft tunnel **(see illustration)**, and the rear cross-brace at the rear of the propeller shaft tunnel.
4 Using the information in Chapter 4C, unbolt and remove the rear section of the exhaust system, together with the heatshield(s).
5 Place a jack with a block of wood underneath the transmission and raise the jack so that it is supporting the weight of the unit.
6 Where applicable (on models up to 1995), using a large open-ended spanner, slacken the propeller shaft clamping nut, located in front of the centre support bearing, by one turn **(see illustration)**. Use a second spanner to hold the propeller shaft stationary as the

clamping nut is slackened, and take care not to damage the rubber gaiter.
7 Make alignment marks between the shaft coupling and transmission flange, then slacken and remove the retaining nuts and bolts securing the flexible coupling to the transmission **(see illustration)**. Discard the nuts, new ones should be used on refitting.
8 Using paint or a suitable marker pen, make alignment marks between the propeller shaft coupling and final drive unit flange. Unscrew the nuts and bolts securing the coupling to the final drive unit and discard them; new ones must be used on refitting **(see illustration)**.
9 With the aid of an assistant, support the propeller shaft, then unscrew the centre support bearing bracket retaining bolts.
10 Slide the rear of the shaft forwards and disengage the shaft from the final drive unit. Free the front of the shaft from the transmission, and remove the shaft assembly from underneath the vehicle **(see illustrations)**. **Note:** *Do not separate the two halves of the shaft without first making alignment marks. If the shafts are incorrectly joined, the propeller shaft assembly may become imbalanced, leading to noise and vibration during operation. On some models, there are alignment marks already on the shaft; the raised mark on the front section must be positioned in between the two marks on the rear section universal joint.*

11 Inspect the rubber couplings, the support bearing and shaft universal joint as described in Sections 8, 9 and 10.
12 For C220 diesel models up to July 1996, the diameter of the front section of the propeller shaft has been changed, and only the larger-diameter shaft is available as a replacement part. If a new front shaft is to be fitted, note that it may therefore be necessary to also replace the transmission flange, to accept the larger shaft. Refer to your Mercedes-Benz dealer or parts supplier for advice.
13 On C180 and C200 models with automatic transmission, there appears to have been a modification relating to the vibration damper originally fitted to the shaft's front flange, which seems to be no longer fitted on later models, and may not be available as a replacement part. Details of this change were not available at the time of writing - refer to a Mercedes-Benz dealer or your parts supplier for advice.

Refitting

14 Lubricate the shaft bushes with multi-purpose grease, and the shaft splines with molybdenum disulphide grease.
15 Manoeuvre the shaft into position, aligning the marks made prior to removal, and engage the shaft with the transmission and final drive unit flanges. With the marks correctly aligned, refit the centre bearing

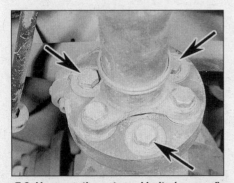

7.8 Unscrew the nuts and bolts (arrowed) securing the coupling to the final drive unit

7.10a Slide the rear of the shaft forwards and disengage the shaft from the final drive unit

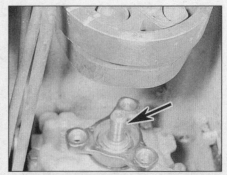

7.10b Disengage the front of the propeller shaft from the transmission flange

7.17 On refitting tighten the propeller shaft coupling bolts to the specified torque

8.8 Refit the rubber coupling, ensuring that the wording faces the damper/propeller shaft

retaining bolts, tightening them lightly only at this stage.

16 Making sure the marks are correctly aligned, insert the retaining bolts securing the rear coupling to the final drive unit and fit the new retaining nuts. Tighten the retaining nuts to the specified torque setting.

17 Make sure the front coupling is correctly aligned with the transmission flange and refit the coupling bolts. Fit the new retaining nuts and tighten them to the specified torque **(see illustration)**.

18 With both the front and rear couplings correctly tightened, tighten the centre bearing retaining bolts to the specified torque setting.

19 Where applicable, tighten the clamping nut to the specified torque, ensuring that the rubber gaiter remains correctly seated.

20 The remainder of refitting is a reversal of removal.

---

8 Propeller shaft rubber coupling - check and renewal

Check

1 Firmly apply the parking brake, then jack up the front of the car and support it on axle stands (see *Jacking and vehicle support*).

2 To improve access to the coupling,

unscrew the heatshield retaining nuts and manoeuvre the heatshield out from around the exhaust system.

3 Closely examine the rubber couplings which link the propeller shaft to the transmission and final drive, looking for signs of damage such as cracking or splitting or for signs of general deterioration. If necessary, renew the coupling as follows.

Renewal

Note: *New propeller shaft coupling nuts will be required.*

4 Remove the propeller shaft as described in Section 7.

Front coupling

5 Make alignment marks between the coupling and vibration damper (where fitted) and propeller shaft.

6 Unscrew the retaining nuts and washers, then withdraw the bolts and remove the coupling from the propeller shaft. Note carefully any additional markings or wording (which may be in German) for use when refitting. Inspect the vibration damper for signs of wear or damage, and renew if necessary.

7 Check the centring sleeve fitted to the centre of the coupling for signs of wear or damage. If necessary, the centring sleeve can be pressed out of position for renewal.

8 Fit the new rubber coupling to the shaft,

ensuring that (where applicable) any additional markings or wording are orientated as noted on removal **(see illustration)**. Insert the retaining bolts then fit the new retaining nuts and washers, and tighten them to the specified torque.

9 Refit the propeller shaft as described in Section 7.

Rear coupling

10 Unscrew the retaining nuts then withdraw the bolts and remove the coupling from the propeller shaft.

11 Fit the new coupling, then fit the retaining bolts and new nuts, tightening them to the specified torque.

12 Refit the propeller shaft as described in Section 7.

---

9 Propeller shaft support bearing - check and renewal

Check

1 Wear in the support bearing will lead to noise and vibration when the car is driven. The bearing is best checked with the propeller shaft removed (see Section 7).

2 Rotate the bearing and check that it turns smoothly with no sign of freeplay; if it's difficult to turn, or if it has a gritty feeling, renew it. Also inspect the rubber portion. If it's cracked or deteriorated, renew it.

Renewal

Note: *Bearing renewal requires the use of a puller and hydraulic press, as well as suitable spacers. If access to suitable equipment cannot be gained, entrust the task to your Mercedes-Benz dealer.*

3 Remove the propeller shaft as described in Section 7.

4 Make alignment marks between the front and rear sections of the propeller shaft, noting that on some models there are alignment marks already on the shaft; the raised mark on the front section must be positioned in between the two marks on the rear section universal joint - see Section 7 for details.

5 Where applicable (on models up to 1995), release the rubber gaiter from the clamping nut, then fully slacken the nut **(see illustration)**.

6 Separate the two halves of the propeller shaft.

7 Remove the rubber gaiter from the rear section of the shaft.

8 Using a suitable puller, draw the centre mounting assembly off the end of the shaft, noting which way around the bracket is fitted. Recover the front and rear bearing covers.

9 Support the mounting bracket assembly, and carefully press the bearing out of position using a tubular drift.

10 Inspect all components for signs of wear or damage and renew as necessary. Note that

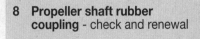

9.5 Propeller shaft centre bearing components - typical

1 *Propeller shaft*	4 *Rubber gaiter*	7 *Centre mounting*
2 *Propeller shaft*	5 *Protective cap*	8 *Bearing*
3 *Sleeve nut (up to 1995)*	6 *Protective cap*	

the bearing protective caps (models up to June 1995 only) and the rubber gaiter should be renewed regardless of their apparent condition.

11 Support the mounting bracket securely and press the new bearing fully into position using a tubular drift which bears only on the bearing outer race.

12 Remove all traces of dirt from the propeller shaft, and (on models up to June 1995) fit a new rear protective cap.

13 Ensure that the mounting bracket is positioned the correct way around and press the assembly fully onto the shaft using a tubular drift which bears only on the bearing inner race.

14 Fit the front protective cap to the shaft (models up to June 1995 only) and install the new rubber gaiter, ensuring it is correctly located in the shaft groove.

15 Lubricate the propeller shaft splines with molybdenum disulphide grease. Carefully slide the two halves of the propeller shaft together, making sure the alignment marks are correctly positioned (see paragraph 4).

16 On models up to 1995, seat the rubber gaiter in the threaded sleeve nut groove.

17 Refit the propeller shaft as described in Section 7.

10 Propeller shaft universal joint - check and renewal

Check

1 Wear in the universal joint is characterised by vibration in the transmission, noise during acceleration, and metallic squeaking and grating sounds as the bearings disintegrate. The joint can be checked with the propeller shaft still fitted.

2 Hold the front half of the propeller shaft, and try to turn the rear half of the shaft. Free play between the propeller shaft halves indicates excessive wear. If the axial movement is excessive, renew the propeller shaft.

Renewal

3 At the time of writing, no spare parts were available to enable renewal of the universal joints to be carried out. Therefore, if any joint shows signs of damage or wear the propeller shaft assembly must be renewed. Consult your Mercedes-Benz dealer or parts supplier for latest information on parts availability.

4 If renewal of the propeller shaft is necessary, it may be worthwhile seeking the advice of an automotive engineering specialist. They may be able to repair the original shaft assembly, or supply a reconditioned shaft on an exchange basis.

Chapter 9
Braking system

Contents

Degrees of difficulty

Easy, suitable for novice with little experience	Fairly easy, suitable for beginner with some experience	Fairly difficult, suitable for competent DIY mechanic 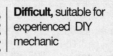	Difficult, suitable for experienced DIY mechanic	Very difficult, suitable for expert DIY or professional

Specifications

Front brakes

Disc diameter	284 mm
Disc thickness:	
1.8 litre petrol and normally-aspirated diesel models (solid discs):	
New	12.0 mm
Minimum (before repair)	10.5 mm
Minimum (limit)	10.0 mm
All other models (ventilated discs):	
New	22.0 mm
Minimum (before repair)	20.4 mm
Minimum (limit)	19.4 mm
Maximum disc runout	0.12 mm
Brake pad friction material minimum thickness	2.0 mm
Pad wear indicator actuates at	3.5 mm
Caliper bore diameter	54.0 mm

Rear brakes

Disc diameter	258 mm
Disc thickness:	
New	9.0 mm
Minimum (before repair)	7.6 mm
Minimum (limit)	7.3 mm
Maximum disc runout	0.15 mm
Brake pad friction material minimum thickness	2.0 mm
Pad wear indicator actuates at	2.5 mm
Caliper bore diameter	34.98 to 35.03 mm

Parking brake

Type .... Cable-operated brake shoes with drum machined into rear disc hub
Parking brake drum diameter .... 164 ± 0.2 mm
Brake shoe friction material thickness:
    New .... 2.65 mm
    Minimum .... 1.00 mm

Torque wrench settings

	Nm	lbf ft
ABS wheel sensor retaining bolts:		
Front sensor	22	16
Rear sensor	8	6
Brake disc retaining screw	10	7
Brake hose unions:		
Caliper unions	18	13
All other unions	14	10
Brake pad wear sensor bolt	30	22
Caliper bleed screws	7	5
Front brake caliper:		
Caliper mounting bracket-to-steering knuckle	115	85
Guide pin bolts	25	18
Master cylinder mounting nuts	20	15
Parking brake cable bolts at rear wheel	20	15
Parking brake foot pedal bolts	12	9
Rear brake caliper mounting bolts	50	37
Roadwheel bolts	110	81
Servo unit mounting nuts	15	11
Servo unit vacuum hose union nut	30	22
Vacuum pump mounting bolts	14	10

1 General information

The braking system is of the servo-assisted, dual-circuit hydraulic type. The layout is such that under normal circumstances, both circuits operate in unison. Should a hydraulic failure occur in one of the circuits, full braking force will still be available in the other circuit (operating on two diagonally-opposite roadwheels), albeit with increased pedal travel.

All models have disc brakes at the front and rear wheels as standard. An Anti-lock Braking System (ABS) is fitted as standard to all models (refer to the appropriate section for further information on the operation of the ABS). **Note:** On models equipped with electronic traction control (ASR), this function is also carried out by the ABS.

Later models are equipped with the Mercedes-Benz Brake Assist System (BAS), which ensures that, in an emergency braking situation, full braking effort is applied immediately, reducing stopping distances. Models from August 1999 onwards are also equipped with the Electronic Stability Program (ESP), which uses the braking system to help steer the car in extreme circumstances. Information on these systems was limited at time of writing and, in any case, any problems would have to be referred to a Mercedes-Benz dealer.

The front disc brakes, on all models covered by this manual, are actuated by sliding single-piston type calipers. This design

of caliper ensures that equal pressure is applied to each disc pad.

On all models, the rear disc brakes are actuated by fixed, opposed-piston calipers.

The parking brake provides an independent, mechanical means of applying the rear brakes. A drum and shoe arrangement is fitted in the centre of each rear brake disc. The parking brake is applied by a foot pedal, and is released by a hand lever on the facia panel; both controls actuate the brake shoes via cables.

Note: When servicing any part of the system, work carefully and methodically; also observe scrupulous cleanliness when overhauling any part of the hydraulic system. Always renew components (in axle sets, where applicable) if in doubt about their condition, and use only genuine Mercedes-Benz replacement parts, or at least those of known good quality. Note the warnings given in Safety first! and at relevant points in this Chapter concerning the dangers of asbestos dust and hydraulic fluid.

2 Hydraulic system - bleeding

Warning: Hydraulic fluid is poisonous; wash off immediately and thoroughly in the case of skin contact, and seek immediate medical advice if any fluid is swallowed or gets into the eyes.

Warning: Certain types of hydraulic fluid are flammable, and may ignite when brought

into contact with hot components. Hence when servicing any part of the hydraulic system, it is safest to assume that the fluid is flammable, and to take precautions against the risk of fire as though it were petrol being handled.

Warning: Hydraulic fluid is also an effective paint stripper, and will attack plastics; if any is spilt, it should be washed off immediately, using copious quantities of fresh water.

Warning: Finally, brake fluid is hygroscopic, which means that if left in an open container, it will absorb moisture from the air. This has the effect of lowering the boiling point of the fluid, rendering it unfit for use. When topping-up or renewing the fluid, always use the recommended type, and ensure that it comes from a sealed, freshly opened container.

General

1 The correct operation of any hydraulic system is only possible after removing all air from the components and circuit; this is achieved by bleeding the system.
2 During the bleeding procedure, add only clean, unused hydraulic fluid of the recommended type; never re-use fluid that has already been bled from the system. Ensure that sufficient fluid is available before starting work.
3 If there is any possibility of incorrect fluid being already in the system, the brake components and circuit must be flushed completely with uncontaminated, correct

fluid, and new seals should be fitted to the various components.

4 If hydraulic fluid has been lost from the system, or air has entered because of a leak, ensure that the fault is cured before continuing further.

5 Park the car on level ground, switch off the engine and select first or reverse gear, then chock the wheels and release the parking brake.

6 Check that all pipes and hoses are secure, unions tight and bleed screws closed. Clean any dirt from around the bleed screws.

7 Unscrew the master cylinder reservoir cap, and top the master cylinder reservoir up to the MAX level line; refit the cap loosely, and remember to maintain the fluid level at least above the MIN level line throughout the procedure, or there is a risk of further air entering the system.

8 There are a number of one-man, do-it-yourself brake bleeding kits currently available from motor accessory shops. It is recommended that one of these kits is used whenever possible, as they greatly simplify the bleeding operation, and reduce the risk of expelled air and fluid being drawn back into the system. If such a kit is not available, the basic (two-man) method must be used, which is described in detail below.

9 If a kit is to be used, prepare the car as described previously, and follow the kit manufacturer's instructions, as the procedure may vary slightly according to the type being used; generally, they are as outlined below in the relevant sub-section.

10 Whichever method is used, the same sequence must be followed (paragraphs 11 and 12) to ensure that all air is removed from the system. On completion, test the operation of the braking system exhaustively, before bringing the car back into service on the road.

Bleeding sequence

11 If the system has been only partially disconnected, and suitable precautions were taken to minimise fluid loss, it should be necessary only to bleed that part of the system.

12 If the complete system is to be bled, then it should be done working in the following sequence:

a) *Right-hand rear brake.*
b) *Left-hand rear brake.*
c) *Right-hand front brake.*
d) *Left-hand front brake.*

Note: *On early models with traction control (ASR), if the hydraulic system linking the master cylinder, hydraulic unit, pressure pump and accumulator has been disturbed, then the ASR circuit must also be bled once the main braking system has been bled (see paragraph 32).*

Bleeding - basic (two-man) method

13 Collect a clean glass jar, a suitable length of plastic or rubber tubing which is a tight fit

over the bleed screw, and a ring spanner to fit the screw. The help of an assistant will also be required.

14 Remove the dust cap from the first screw in the sequence. Fit the spanner and tube to the screw, place the other end of the tube in the jar, and pour in sufficient fluid to cover the end of the tube.

15 Ensure that the master cylinder reservoir fluid level is maintained at least above the MIN level line throughout the procedure.

16 Have the assistant fully depress the brake pedal several times to build up pressure, then maintain it on the final downstroke.

17 While pedal pressure is maintained, unscrew the bleed screw (approximately one turn) and allow the compressed fluid and air to flow into the jar. The assistant should maintain pedal pressure, following it down to the floor if necessary, and should not release it until instructed to do so. When the flow stops, tighten the bleed screw again, have the assistant release the pedal slowly, and recheck the reservoir fluid level.

18 Repeat the steps given in paragraphs 16 and 17 until the fluid emerging from the bleed screw is free from air bubbles. If the master cylinder has been drained and refilled, and air is being bled from the first screw in the sequence, allow approximately five seconds between cycles for the master cylinder passages to refill.

19 When no more air bubbles appear, tighten the bleed screw to the specified torque, remove the tube and spanner, and refit the dust cap. Do not overtighten the bleed screw.

20 Repeat the procedure on the remaining screws in the sequence, until all air is removed from the system and the brake pedal feels firm again.

Bleeding - using a one-way valve kit

21 As their name implies, these kits consist of a length of tubing with a one-way valve fitted, to prevent expelled air and fluid being drawn back into the system; some kits include a translucent container, which can be positioned so that the air bubbles can be more easily seen flowing from the end of the tube **(see illustration)**.

22 The kit is connected to the bleed screw, which is then opened. The user returns to the

2.21 Bleeding a rear brake caliper

driver's seat, depresses the brake pedal with a smooth, steady stroke, and slowly releases it; this is repeated until the expelled fluid is clear of air bubbles.

23 Note that these kits simplify work so much that it is easy to forget the master cylinder reservoir fluid level; ensure that this is maintained at least above the MIN level line at all times.

Bleeding - using a pressure-bleeding kit

24 These kits are usually operated by the reservoir of pressurised air contained in the spare tyre. However, note that it will probably be necessary to reduce the pressure to a lower level than normal; refer to the instructions supplied with the kit. **Note:** *Mercedes-Benz specify that a pressure of 2 bar (29 psi) should not be exceeded.*

25 By connecting a pressurised, fluid-filled container to the master cylinder reservoir, bleeding can be carried out simply by opening each brake caliper bleed screw in turn (in the specified sequence – see paragraph 12), and allowing the fluid to flow out until no more air bubbles can be seen in the expelled fluid.

26 This method has the advantage that the large reservoir of fluid provides an additional safeguard against air being drawn into the system during bleeding.

27 Pressure-bleeding is particularly effective when bleeding 'difficult' systems, or when bleeding the complete system at the time of routine fluid renewal.

All methods

28 When bleeding is complete, and firm pedal feel is restored, wash off any spilt fluid, tighten the bleed screws to the specified torque, and refit their dust caps.

29 Check the hydraulic fluid level in the master cylinder reservoir, and top-up if necessary (see *Weekly checks*).

30 Discard any hydraulic fluid that has been bled from the system; it will not be fit for re-use.

31 Check the feel of the brake pedal. If it feels at all spongy, air must still be present in the system, and further bleeding is required. Failure to bleed satisfactorily after a reasonable repetition of the bleeding procedure may be due to worn master cylinder seals.

Models with traction control (ASR) - up to May 1994

32 On models with traction control (ASR) up to and including May 1994, the ASR circuit must be bled after the four calipers have been bled as described above. Mercedes-Benz state that their hand-held test equipment must be plugged into the datalink socket at the left-hand rear corner of the engine compartment, in order to activate the system for it to be bled.

33 For information, the system bleed screw is mounted on the master cylinder, below the fluid reservoir.

3 Hydraulic pipes and hoses - renewal

Note: *Before starting work, refer to the warnings at the beginning of Section 2.*

1 If any pipe or hose is to be renewed, minimise fluid loss by first removing the master cylinder reservoir cap, then tightening it down onto a piece of polythene to obtain an airtight seal. Alternatively, flexible hoses can be sealed, if required, using a proprietary brake hose clamp; metal brake pipe unions can be plugged (if care is taken not to allow dirt into the system) or capped immediately they are disconnected. Place a wad of rag under any union that is to be disconnected, to catch any spilt fluid.

2 If a flexible hose is to be disconnected, unscrew the brake pipe union nut before removing the spring clip which secures the hose to its mounting bracket.

3 To unscrew the union nuts, it is preferable to obtain a brake pipe spanner of the correct size; these are available from most large motor accessory shops. Failing this, a close-fitting open-ended spanner will be required, though if the nuts are tight or corroded, their flats may be rounded-off if the spanner slips. In such a case, a self-locking wrench is often the only way to unscrew a stubborn union, but it follows that the pipe and the damaged nuts must be renewed on reassembly. Always clean a union and surrounding area before disconnecting it; this helps to prevent the entry of dirt into the hydraulic system. If disconnecting a component with more than one union, make a careful note of the connections before disturbing any of them.

4 If a brake pipe is to be renewed, it can be obtained, cut to length and with the union nuts and end flares in place, from Mercedes-Benz dealers. All that is then necessary is to bend it to shape, following the line of the original, before fitting it to the car. Alternatively, most motor accessory shops can make up brake pipes from kits, but this requires very careful measurement of the original, to ensure that the replacement is of the correct length. The safest answer is usually to take the original to the shop as a pattern.

5 On refitting, do not overtighten the union nuts. It is not necessary to exercise brute force to obtain a sound joint !

6 Ensure that the pipes and hoses are correctly routed, with no kinks, and that they are secured in the clips or brackets provided. After fitting, remove the polythene from the reservoir, and bleed the hydraulic system as described in Section 2. Wash off any spilt fluid, and check carefully for fluid leaks.

7 Finally, test the operation of the braking system exhaustively, before bringing the car back into service on the road.

4 Front brake pads - renewal

⚠️ **Warning: Renew both sets of front brake pads at the same time - never renew the pads on only one wheel, as uneven braking may result. Note that the dust created by wear of the pads may contain asbestos, which is a health hazard. Never blow it out with compressed air, and do not inhale any of it. An approved filtering mask should be worn when working on the brakes. DO NOT use petrol or petroleum-based solvents to clean brake parts; use brake cleaner or methylated spirit only.**

Note: *New caliper guide pin bolts will be required on refitting.*

1 Chock the rear wheels and firmly apply the parking brake. Loosen the front wheel bolts, then jack up the front of the car and support it on axle stands (see *Jacking and vehicle support*). Remove the appropriate front roadwheel.

2 Where applicable, release the retaining clips and unclip the pad wear sensor wiring connector cover from the caliper aperture.

3 Disconnect the wear sensor connector from the caliper housing. Unclip the wear sensor wiring from the clips under the wheelarch **(see illustrations)**.

4 On models up to September 1995, slacken and remove the lower caliper guide pin bolt, using a slim open-ended spanner to prevent the guide pin itself from rotating **(see illustration)**. Discard the guide pin bolt - a new bolt must be used on refitting. Pivot the caliper upwards away from the brake pads and mounting bracket.

5 On models from September 1995 onwards, slacken and remove both caliper guide pin bolts, and remove the caliper from the mounting bracket **(see illustrations)**. Tie the caliper to a convenient point, so that the brake hose is not strained.

6 Withdraw the two brake pads from the caliper mounting bracket, noting the correct fitted location of the wear sensor (on the inner pad). Recover the heat shield fitted around the

4.3a Disconnect the wear sensor wiring connector . . .

4.3b . . . and unclip the wiring from the clips under the wheel arch

4.4 On early models, slacken the lower guide pin bolt, holding the guide pin with an open-ended spanner

4.5a Remove the upper and lower guide pin bolts . . .

4.5b . . . and lift the caliper out of its mounting bracket

4.6a Remove the outer . . .

4.6b . . . and inner pads from the caliper mounting bracket

4.6c Remove the heat shield from the piston, where fitted

caliper piston, where applicable, noting how it is fitted (see illustrations).

7 First measure the thickness of each brake pad's friction material (excluding the metal backplate). If either pad is worn at any point to the specified minimum thickness or less, all four pads must be renewed. Also, the pads should be renewed if any of them are fouled with oil or grease. There is no satisfactory way of degreasing friction material, once contaminated. If any of the brake pads are worn unevenly, or are fouled with oil or grease, trace and rectify the cause before reassembly. Inspect the wear sensor for signs of damage, and renew if necessary. New brake pad kits are available from Mercedes-Benz dealers.

8 If the brake pads are still serviceable, carefully clean them using a clean, fine wire brush or similar, paying particular attention to the sides and back of the metal backing. Clean out the grooves in the friction material (where applicable), and pick out any large embedded particles of dirt or debris. Carefully clean the pad locations in the caliper body/mounting bracket.

9 Prior to fitting the pads, check the pins are free to slide easily in the caliper bracket, and are a reasonably tight fit. Ensure that the guide pin gaiters are undamaged. Remove all traces of locking compound from guide pin threads using a tap of the correct thread size and pitch.

> **HAYNES HiNT** *If a suitable tap is not available, clean out the holes using the old bolt with a slot cut in its threads.*

10 Brush the dust and dirt from the caliper and piston, but *do not* inhale it, as it may contain asbestos, which is a health hazard. Inspect the dust seal around the piston for damage, and the piston itself for evidence of fluid leaks, corrosion or damage. If any such deterioration is found, the caliper must be overhauled - refer to Section 8 for details.

11 If new brake pads are to be fitted, the caliper piston must be pushed back into the cylinder to make room for them. Either use a

G-clamp or similar tool, or use suitable pieces of wood as levers (see illustration). Provided that the master cylinder reservoir has not been overfilled with hydraulic fluid, there should be no spillage, but keep a careful watch on the fluid level while retracting the piston. If the fluid level rises above the MAX level line at any time, the surplus should be syphoned off or ejected through a plastic tube connected to the bleed screw (see Section 2).

> ⚠ **Warning: Do not syphon the fluid by mouth, as it is poisonous; use a syringe or an old poultry baster.**

12 Apply a smear of brake grease to the backing plate of each pad (Mercedes-Benz recommend the use of brake paste - number 001 989 10 51); do not apply excess grease or allow the grease to contact the friction material.

13 Clip the pad wear sensor (where removed) securely in position and fit the pads to the caliper mounting bracket, ensuring that their friction material is against the brake disc. Note that the pad with the wear sensor should be fitted as the outer pad. Where applicable, refit the heat shield around the caliper piston.

14 Pivot the caliper down, or refit the caliper, into position over the pads, passing the wear sensor wiring up through the caliper aperture.

15 Ensure that the pad anti-rattle springs are correctly positioned against the caliper housing, then press down on the caliper and install a new guide pin bolt (or bolts). Tighten

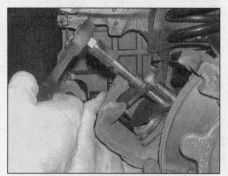

4.11 Using a proprietary tool for pushing the piston back into the caliper

the bolt(s) to the specified torque setting while retaining the guide pin with an open-ended spanner.

16 Reconnect the wear sensor wiring connector to the caliper, making sure the excess wiring is wrapped neatly around the connector. Ensure that the connector is correctly fitted, and clip the sensor cover into the caliper aperture.

17 Depress the brake pedal repeatedly, until the pads are pressed into firm contact with the brake disc, and normal (non-assisted) pedal pressure is restored.

18 Repeat the above procedure on the remaining front brake caliper.

19 Refit the roadwheels, then lower the car to the ground and tighten the roadwheel bolts to the specified torque setting.

20 Check the hydraulic fluid level as described in *Weekly checks*. Test the operation of the braking system exhaustively, before bringing the car back into service on the road.

> ⚠ **Warning: New pads will not give full braking efficiency until they have 'bedded in'. Be prepared for this - avoid hard braking, as far as possible, for the first hundred miles or so after pad renewal.**

5 Rear brake pads - renewal

> ⚠ **Warning: Renew both sets of rear brake pads at the same time - never renew the pads on only one wheel, as uneven braking may result. Note that the dust created by wear of the pads may contain asbestos, which is a health hazard. Never blow it out with compressed air, and do not inhale any of it. An approved filtering mask should be worn when working on the brakes. DO NOT use petrol or petroleum-based solvents to clean brake parts; use brake cleaner or methylated spirit only.**

1 Chock the front wheels and loosen the rear wheel bolts. Jack up the rear of the car and support it on axle stands (see *Jacking and*

5.3a Early models had two pad retaining pins . . .

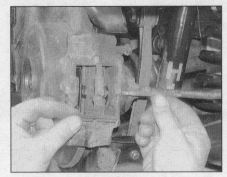

5.3b . . . later models have just one - remove the pin, and recover the anti-rattle spring

5.4 Withdrawing the rear brake pads

vehicle support). Remove the rear roadwheels.

2 Where applicable, pull the pad wear sensor wiring connectors out from the caliper body, noting the correct routing of the wiring.

3 Using a hammer and suitable punch, carefully tap out the pad retaining pin(s) towards the inside, and recover the anti-rattle spring **(see illustrations)**.

4 Slide the pads out from the caliper body, noting the correct fitted position of the wear sensors **(see illustration)**. Where applicable, recover the shims which are fitted between the pads and pistons.

5 Inspect the brake pads as described in paragraphs 7 and 8 ofSection 4. Renew the anti-rattle spring, pad retaining pin(s) and shims (as applicable) if the pads are to be renewed.

6 Prior to fitting the pads, brush the dust and dirt from the caliper and pistons, but *do not* inhale it, as it is a health hazard. Inspect the dust seals around each piston for damage, and the pistons for evidence of fluid leaks, corrosion or damage. If any such deterioration is found, the caliper must be overhauled - refer to Section 9 for details.

7 If new brake pads are to be fitted, the caliper pistons must be pushed back into the cylinder to make room for them. Carefully prise the pistons back into position using a suitable piece of wood as a lever. Provided that the master cylinder reservoir has not

been overfilled with hydraulic fluid, there should be no spillage, but keep a careful watch on the fluid level while retracting the piston. If the fluid level rises above the MAX level line at any time, the surplus should be syphoned off or ejected through a plastic tube connected to the bleed screw (see Section 2).

⚠️ *Warning: Do not syphon the fluid by mouth, as it is poisonous; use a syringe or an old poultry baster.*

8 On brake pads equipped with anti-squeal shims, **do not** apply any lubricant to the pads. Where the pad backing plates are plain and no shim is fitted, apply a smear of copper brake grease to the side edges of the pad backing plate (Mercedes-Benz recommend the use of brake paste - number 001 989 10 51); do not apply excess grease or allow the grease to contact the friction material **(see illustration)**.

9 Ensure that the wear sensors are clipped securely into the backing plate of each pad and (where applicable) fit the shims to the back of each pad.

10 Slide the brake pads and (where applicable) shims into position in the caliper, making sure the friction material of each pad is against the brake disc.

11 Fit the new anti-rattle spring to the top of the pads, making sure it is fitted the right way up.

12 Slide in the pad retaining pin(s) over the

anti-rattle spring from the inside, and tap fully into place up to the stop **(see illustration)**.

13 Ensure that the wiring is correctly routed, and connect the wear sensor connectors to the caliper body.

14 Depress the brake pedal repeatedly, until the pads are pressed into firm contact with the brake disc, and normal (non-assisted) pedal pressure is restored.

15 Repeat the above procedure on the remaining rear brake caliper.

16 Refit the roadwheels, then lower the car to the ground and tighten the roadwheel bolts to the specified torque setting.

17 Check the hydraulic fluid level as described in *Weekly checks*. Test the operation of the braking system exhaustively, before bringing the car back into service on the road.

⚠️ *Warning: New pads will not give full braking efficiency until they have 'bedded in'. Be prepared for this - and avoid hard braking, as far as possible, for the first hundred miles or so after pad renewal.*

---

6 Front brake disc - inspection, removal and refitting

Note: *Before starting work, refer to the note at the beginning of Section 4 concerning the dangers of asbestos dust.*

Inspection

Note: *If either disc requires renewal, BOTH should be renewed at the same time, to ensure even and consistent braking. New brake pads should also be fitted.*

1 Chock the rear wheels and firmly apply the parking brake. Loosen the front wheel bolts, then jack up the front of the car and support on axle stands (see *Jacking and vehicle support*). Remove the appropriate front roadwheel.

2 Slowly rotate the brake disc so that the full area of both sides can be checked; remove the brake pads if better access is required to the inboard surface. Light scoring is normal in the area swept by the brake pads, but if

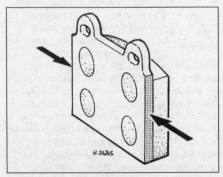

5.8 If the pads have no shims, apply lubricant to the edges of the backing plate (arrowed)

5.12 Tap the pad retaining pin(s) in from the inside

6.3 Using a micrometer to measure the brake disc thickness

6.5 Checking disc run-out with a dial gauge (rear disc shown - procedure for front disc similar)

Removal

Note: *New brake caliper mounting bolts and disc retaining screws will be required on refitting.*

7 Unscrew the two bolts securing the brake caliper mounting bracket to the steering knuckle, then slide the caliper assembly off the disc **(see illustrations)**. Discard the bolts; new ones must be used on refitting.

8 Unclip the pad wear sensor wiring from the clips under the wheelarch. Using a piece of wire or a nylon cable-tie, attach the caliper to the front suspension coil spring, to avoid placing any strain on the hydraulic brake hose or the caliper wiring.

9 Slacken and remove the screw securing the brake disc to the hub **(see illustration)**. Discard the screw, as a new one should be used on refitting.

10 Remove the disc from the hub, noting the correct fitted location of its locating pins **(see illustration)**. If it is tight, lightly tap its rear face with a hide or plastic mallet.

heavy scoring or cracks are found, the disc must be renewed.

3 It is normal to find a lip of loose rust and brake dust around the disc's perimeter; this can be scraped off if required. However, if a lip of solid material has formed due to excessive wear of the brake pad swept area, then the disc thickness must be measured using a micrometer **(see illustration)**. Take measurements at several places around the disc, and at the inside and outside edges of the pad swept area; if the disc has worn at *any* point to the specified minimum thickness or less, the disc must be renewed.

4 If the disc is thought to be warped, it can be checked for run-out, but first eliminate wheel bearing play as the cause of the problem, with reference to Chapter 10, Section 2.

5 To check the disc run-out, fit large, plain washers under the heads of two of the wheel bolts, then bolt them to the hub through the disc. Position the wheel bolts diagonally opposite each other, to ensure that the disc seats evenly, then tighten the bolts securely. Either use a dial gauge mounted on any convenient fixed point, while the disc is slowly rotated, or use feeler blades to measure (at several points all around the disc) the clearance between the disc and a fixed point, such as the caliper mounting bracket **(see illustration)**. If the measurements obtained are at the specified maximum or beyond, the disc is excessively warped, and must be renewed.

6 Check the disc for cracks, especially around the wheel bolt holes, and any other wear or damage, and renew if necessary.

Refitting

11 Prior to refitting, remove all traces of old locking compound from the caliper bolt hole threads in the hub by running a tap of the correct thread size and pitch down them. Clean the disc retaining screw threads in the hub in the same way.

> **HAYNES HiNT** *If a suitable tap is not available, clean out the holes using an old bolt/screw with a slot cut in its threads*

12 Ensure that the mating surfaces of the disc and hub are clean and flat, and that the disc locating pins are in position. If a new disc has been fitted, use a suitable solvent to wipe any preservative coating from the disc. Apply a thin coat of high-temperature grease to the mating surface of the hub, but ensure that the surface of the disc is not contaminated.

13 Fit the disc to the hub, making sure it is correctly located with the pins. Fit the new disc retaining screw and tighten it to the specified torque setting.

14 Slide the caliper into position over the

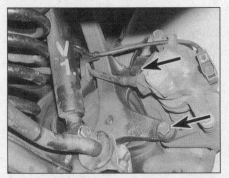

6.7a Unscrew the caliper mounting bracket bolts (arrowed) . . .

6.7b . . . then remove the bolts and discard them

6.7c Slide the caliper and bracket off the disc

6.9 Loosening the brake disc retaining screw

6.10 Removing the brake disc

7.3 Removing the rear brake disc

disc, making sure the pads pass either side of the disc.

15 Fit the new caliper mounting bracket bolts and tighten them to the specified torque setting. Clip the pad wear sensor wiring back into position.

16 Refit the roadwheel, then lower the car to the ground and tighten the roadwheel bolts to the specified torque. On completion, repeatedly depress the brake pedal until normal (non-assisted) pedal pressure returns. Test the operation of the braking system exhaustively, before bringing the car back into service on the road.

7 Rear brake disc - inspection, removal and refitting

Note: Before starting work, refer to the note at the beginning of Section 4 concerning the dangers of asbestos dust.

Inspection

Note: If either disc requires renewal, BOTH should be renewed at the same time, to ensure even and consistent braking. New brake pads should also be fitted.

1 Firmly chock the front wheels, then loosen the rear wheel bolts. Jack up the rear of the car and support it on axle stands (see *Jacking and vehicle support*). Remove the appropriate rear roadwheel.

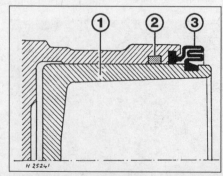

8.8 Sectional view of piston, caliper body and seals

1 Piston   2 Piston (fluid) seal   3 Dust seal

8.2 Use a brake hose clamp, a G-clamp or a similar tool to clamp the flexible hose

2 Inspect the disc as described in Section 6 (see paragraph 2).

Removal

3 Refer to Section 6, noting that there is only one disc locating pin. Ensure that the parking brake is fully released before trying to remove the disc **(see illustration)**. If the disc is still tight on the shoes with the brake fully released, slacken the parking brake adjustment as described in Section 13.

Refitting

4 Refer to Section 6. On completion, adjust the parking brake as described in Section 13. Test the operation of the braking system exhaustively, before bringing the car back into service on the road.

8 Front brake caliper - removal, overhaul and refitting

Note: Before starting work, refer to the note at the beginning of Section 2 concerning the dangers of hydraulic fluid, and to the warning at the beginning of Section 4 concerning the dangers of asbestos dust.

Removal

Note: New brake caliper guide pin bolts will be required on refitting.

1 Chock the rear wheels and firmly apply the parking brake. Loosen the front wheel bolts, then jack up the front of the car and support it on axle stands (see *Jacking and vehicle support*). Remove the appropriate front roadwheel.

2 Minimise fluid loss by first removing the master cylinder reservoir cap, and then tightening it down onto a piece of polythene, to obtain an airtight seal. Alternatively, use a brake hose clamp or a similar tool to clamp the flexible hose **(see illustration)**. Do not use a G-clamp or any other device with flat jaws as this may pinch the hose, leading to premature failure.

3 Clean the area around the union, then loosen the brake hose union nut at the caliper.

4 Remove the brake pads as described in Section 4.

5 If not already removed, slacken and remove the upper guide pin bolt, then unscrew the caliper and remove it from the end of the brake hose.

Overhaul

6 With the caliper on the bench, wipe away all traces of dust and dirt, but *avoid inhaling the dust, as it is a health hazard.*

 HAYNES HiNT *If the piston cannot be withdrawn by hand, it can be pushed out by applying compressed air to the brake hose union hole. Only low pressure should be required, such as that generated by a foot pump. Place a block of wood between the end of the piston and the caliper body to prevent damage to the piston as it pops out of its bore - also take great care not to trap your fingers when this happens.*

7 Withdraw the partially-ejected piston from the caliper body, and remove the dust seal.

8 Using a soft blunt instrument, such as the end of a pen cap, extract the piston hydraulic seal, taking great care not to damage the caliper bore **(see illustration)**.

9 Thoroughly clean all components, using only methylated spirit, isopropyl alcohol or clean hydraulic fluid. Never use mineral-based solvents such as petrol or paraffin, as they will attack the hydraulic system's rubber components. Dry the components immediately, using compressed air or a clean, lint-free cloth. Use compressed air to blow clear the fluid passages.

10 Check all components, and renew any that are worn or damaged. Check particularly the cylinder bore and piston; these should be renewed (note that this means the renewal of the complete body assembly) if they are scratched, worn or corroded in any way. Similarly check the condition of the guide pins and their bushes; both pins should be undamaged and (when cleaned) a reasonably tight sliding fit in the bushes. If there is any doubt about the condition of any component, renew it.

11 If the assembly is fit for further use, obtain the appropriate repair kit; the components are available from Mercedes-Benz dealers in various combinations. All rubber seals should be renewed as a matter of course; these should never be re-used.

12 On reassembly, ensure that all components are clean and dry.

13 Soak the piston and the new piston (fluid) seal in clean hydraulic fluid. Smear clean fluid on the cylinder bore surface.

14 Fit the new piston (fluid) seal, using only your fingers (no tools) to manipulate it into the cylinder bore groove.

15 Fit the new dust seal to the rear of the piston, and seat the outer lip of the seal in the caliper body groove. Carefully ease the piston

squarely into the cylinder bore using a twisting motion. Press the piston fully into position and seat the inner lip of the dust seal in the piston groove.

16 If the guide pins are being renewed, lubricate the pin shafts with the special grease supplied in the repair kit and fit the gaiters to the pin grooves. Insert the pins into the caliper bracket and seat the gaiters correctly in the bracket grooves.

Refitting

17 Remove all traces of old locking compound from the caliper guide pin/bolt hole threads (as applicable) by running a tap of the correct thread size and pitch down them.

 If a suitable tap is not available, clean out the holes using an old bolt with a slot cut in its threads

18 Screw the caliper fully onto the flexible hose union.
19 Offer the caliper up to the mounting bracket and fit the new upper guide pin bolt, tightening it to the specified torque setting.
20 Tighten the brake hose union nut to the specified torque and remove the brake hose clamp or polythene (as applicable).
21 Refit the brake pads as described in Section 4 and bleed the hydraulic system as described in Section 2. Note that, providing the precautions described were taken to minimise brake fluid loss, it should only be necessary to bleed the relevant front brake.
22 Refit the roadwheel, then lower the car to the ground and tighten the roadwheel bolts to the specified torque. On completion, check the hydraulic fluid level as described in *Weekly checks*. Test the operation of the braking system exhaustively, before bringing the car back into service on the road.

9 Rear brake caliper - removal, overhaul and refitting

Note: *Before starting work, refer to the note at the beginning of Section 2 concerning the dangers of hydraulic fluid, and to the warning at the beginning of Section 4 concerning the dangers of asbestos dust.*

Removal

Note: *New caliper mounting bolts will be required on refitting.*
1 Firmly chock the front wheels, then loosen the rear wheel bolts. Jack up the rear of the car and support it on axle stands (see *Jacking and vehicle support*). Remove the appropriate rear roadwheel.
2 Minimise fluid loss by first removing the master cylinder reservoir cap, and then tightening it down onto a piece of polythene, to obtain an airtight seal. Alternatively, use a

proprietary brake hose clamp to seal off the flexible hose leading to the caliper. Do not use a G-clamp, or any other device with flat jaws, as this may pinch the hose, leading to premature failure.
3 Clean the area around the union, then loosen the brake hose union nut.
4 Remove the brake pads as described in Section 5.
5 Slacken and remove the caliper mounting bolts **(see illustration)**, then unscrew the caliper from the end of the flexible hose and remove it from the car. Discard the mounting bolts - they should be renewed whenever they are disturbed.
Caution: Never slacken the bolts securing the two halves of the caliper together. If the bolts are slackened and the caliper is body is dismantled, the assembly may leak after reassembly.
6 With the caliper on the bench, wipe away all traces of dust and dirt, but *avoid inhaling the dust, as it is a health hazard.*
7 Make identification markings between each piston and its relative bore in the caliper to avoid interchanging the pistons on reassembly.

 *Check that all the pistons move easily before withdrawing them completely. If any piston cannot be withdrawn by hand, insert a piece of wood (approximately 28 mm thick) into the caliper body and push out the pistons by applying compressed air to the brake hose union hole. Only low pressure should be required, such as that generated by a foot pump. Ensure that all pistons are pushed out simultaneously until they are in contact with the wood, then remove the wood from the caliper. This avoids the possibility of having one piston left in the caliper, which will be very difficult to remove.*

8 Withdraw the partially-ejected piston from the caliper body, and remove the dust seals.
9 Using a small screwdriver, extract the

9.5 Slacken and remove the caliper mounting bolts (arrowed)

piston hydraulic seal, taking great care not to damage the caliper bore.

Overhaul

10 Thoroughly clean all components, using only methylated spirit, isopropyl alcohol or clean hydraulic fluid. Never use mineral-based solvents such as petrol or paraffin, as they will attack the hydraulic system's rubber components. Dry the components immediately, using compressed air or a clean, lint-free cloth. Use compressed air to blow the fluid passages clear.
11 Check all components, and renew any that are worn or damaged. Check particularly the cylinder bore and piston; these should be renewed (note that this means the renewal of the complete body assembly) if they are scratched, worn or corroded in any way. If you have any doubts about the condition of a component, it is safest to renew it.
12 If the assembly is fit for further use, obtain the appropriate repair kit; the components are available from Mercedes-Benz dealers in various combinations. All rubber seals should be renewed as a matter of course; these should never be re-used.
13 On reassembly, ensure that all components are clean and dry and that each piston is refitted in its original bore.
14 Working on the first piston, soak it and the new piston (fluid) seal in clean hydraulic fluid. Smear clean fluid on the cylinder bore surface.
15 Fit the new piston (fluid) seal, using only your fingers (no tools) to manipulate it into the cylinder bore groove **(see illustration)**.
16 Fit the new dust seal to the piston groove and carefully ease the piston squarely into its respective cylinder bore using a twisting motion. Press the piston fully into position and seat the outer lip of the dust seal in the caliper body.
17 Repeat the previous operations on the remaining piston(s).
18 Prior to pushing the pistons fully into the caliper, position each one so that its raised section will be positioned uppermost when the caliper is refitted. Mercedes-Benz dealers

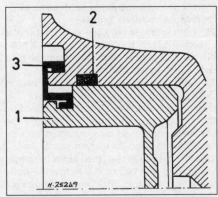

9.15 Rear brake caliper piston and dust seal arrangement

1 Piston   2 Piston seal   3 Dust cap

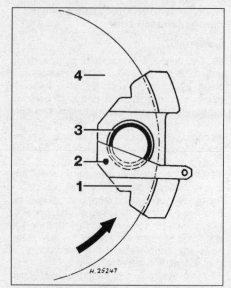

9.18 Correct positioning of piston in the rear brake caliper

1 Caliper
2 Special positioning tool
3 Piston
4 Disc

use a special gauge to ensure that the piston is correctly positioned **(see illustration)**. The raised section of the piston ensures the pad contacts the disc at a slight angle and reduces the possibility of the break squeal.

Refitting

19 Remove all traces of old locking compound from the caliper bolt hole threads by running a tap of the correct thread size and pitch down them.

HAYNES HiNT *If a suitable tap is not available, clean out the holes using an old bolt with a slot cut in its threads*

20 Screw the caliper fully onto the flexible hose union, using a new sealing washer where applicable.
21 Slide the caliper assembly into position, then fit the new mounting bolts and tighten them to the specified torque.
22 Tighten the brake hose union nut to the specified torque and remove the brake hose clamp (or the polythene sheet from the fluid reservoir as applicable).
23 Refit the brake pads as described in Section 5 and bleed the hydraulic system as described in Section 2. Note that, providing the precautions described were taken to minimise brake fluid loss, it should only be necessary to bleed the relevant rear brake.
24 Refit the roadwheel, then lower the car to the ground and tighten the roadwheel bolts to the specified torque. On completion, check the hydraulic fluid level as described in *Weekly checks*. Test the operation of the braking system exhaustively, before bringing the car back into service on the road.

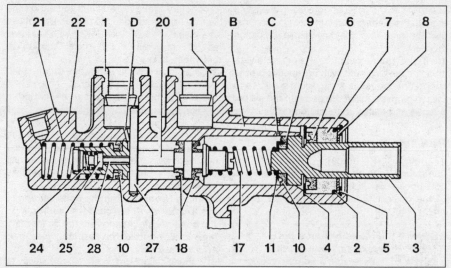

10.9 Cross-sectional view of typical master cylinder assembly - Teves model shown, others similar

1 Mounting seals	9 Seal	25 Valve seal
2 Sealing ring	10 Seal	27 Secondary piston pin
3 Primary piston	11 Spring seat	28 Valve pin
4 Stop washer	17 Spring	B Fluid supply bore
5 Circlip	20 Secondary piston	C Compensating bore
6 Seal	21 Spring	D Filling and compensating
7 Bush	22 Cylinder body	bore
8 Washer	24 Valve spring	

10 Master cylinder - removal, overhaul and refitting

Removal

Note: *Before starting work, refer to the warning at the beginning of Section 2 concerning the dangers of hydraulic fluid.*
1 Disconnect the battery negative terminal.
2 Disconnect the wiring connector from the brake fluid level sender unit.
3 Remove the master cylinder reservoir cap, and syphon the hydraulic fluid from the reservoir. Alternatively, open any convenient bleed screw in the system, and gently pump the brake pedal to expel the fluid through a plastic tube connected to the screw.

 Warning: Do not syphon the fluid by mouth, as it is poisonous; use a syringe or an old poultry baster

4 Disconnect the fluid hose(s) from the side of the reservoir and plug the hose end(s) to minimise fluid loss.
5 Carefully ease the fluid reservoir out from the top of the master cylinder. Recover the reservoir seals and plug the cylinder ports to prevent dirt entry.
6 Wipe clean the area around the brake pipe unions on the side and front of the master cylinder, and place absorbent rags beneath the pipe unions to catch any surplus fluid. Make a note of the correct fitted positions of the unions, then unscrew the union nuts and

carefully withdraw the pipes. Plug or tape over the pipe ends and master cylinder orifices, to minimise the loss of brake fluid, and to prevent the entry of dirt into the system. Wash off any spilt fluid immediately with cold water.
7 Slacken and remove the two nuts and washers securing the master cylinder to the vacuum servo unit, then withdraw the unit forwards and away from servo unit. **Note:** *Do not tilt the master cylinder until it is disengaged from the servo unit pushrod, otherwise the servo unit will be damaged.* Remove the sealing ring from the rear of the master cylinder.

Overhaul

8 Mercedes-Benz state that the 'switchover' type of master cylinder, fitted to all models, must not be repaired. It is therefore unlikely that any spare parts or repair kits are available. Consult your Mercedes-Benz dealer or parts supplier for up-to-date information.

Refitting

9 Remove all traces of dirt from the master cylinder and servo unit mating surfaces, and fit a new sealing ring to the rear of the master cylinder body **(see illustration)**.
10 Fit the master cylinder to the servo unit, ensuring that the servo unit pushrod enters the master cylinder bore centrally, and keeping the master cylinder horizontal until it is fully engaged. Refit the master cylinder retaining nuts and tighten them to the specified torque.
11 Wipe clean the brake pipe unions, then

refit them to the master cylinder ports and tighten them to the specified torque.

12 Ease the fluid reservoir into position in the master cylinder and reconnect the fluid hose(s).

13 Refill the master cylinder reservoir with new fluid, and bleed the complete hydraulic system as described in Section 2. Test the operation of the braking system exhaustively, before bringing the car back into service on the road.

11 Vacuum servo unit - testing, removal and refitting

Testing

1 To test the operation of the servo unit, depress the footbrake several times with the engine off, to exhaust the vacuum from the servo. Now start the engine whilst keeping the pedal firmly depressed. There should be a noticeable 'give' in the brake pedal as the engine starts and the vacuum builds up.

2 Allow the engine to run for at least two minutes, then switch it off. If the brake pedal is now depressed it should feel normal, but further applications should result in the pedal feeling progressively firmer, with the pedal stroke decreasing on each application.

3 If the servo does not operate as described, first inspect the servo unit check valve as described in Section 12.

4 If the servo unit still fails to operate satisfactorily, the fault lies within the unit itself. Repairs to the unit are not possible - if faulty, the servo unit must be renewed.

Removal

Note: *New retaining nuts will be required on refitting.*

5 Remove the master cylinder as described in Section 10.

6 Unscrew the end fitting and disconnect the vacuum hose from the servo unit; see Section 12. On some models, the end fitting is simply prised out.

7 On models with the brake assist system (BAS), disconnect the wiring plugs from the BAS diaphragm travel sensor and release switch solenoid valve.

8 Remove the driver's side lower facia panel as described in Chapter 11, Section 41.

9 Unhook the brake pedal return spring, then remove the spring retaining clip and slide out the clevis pin securing the brake pedal to the servo unit pushrod.

10 Slacken and remove the servo unit retaining nuts, then return to the engine compartment and remove the servo unit from the car.

Refitting

11 Prior to refitting, check the condition of the gasket which is glued to the rear of the servo unit. If the gasket shows signs of wear or damage, cut it off and stick on a new one.

12 Manoeuvre the servo unit into position in the engine compartment.

13 From inside the car, ensure that the servo unit pushrod is correctly engaged with the brake pedal, then fit the servo retaining nuts and tighten them to the specified torque.

14 Apply a smear of grease to the servo pushrod clevis pin, and secure it in position with the spring clip. Hook the pedal return spring back into position.

15 Refer to Section 18 and remove the stop-light switch, then refit it as described. This resets the switch, and will ensure that it works correctly on completion.

16 Refit the driver's side lower facia panel (see Chapter 11, Section 41).

17 Where applicable, reconnect the wiring to the BAS components.

18 Reconnect the vacuum hose to the servo, either by screwing in the end fitting or by pressing it in firmly until it is fully seated.

19 Refit the master cylinder as described in Section 10. On completion, start the engine and check for air leaks at the vacuum hose-to-servo unit connection; check the operation of the braking system before using the car on the road.

12 Vacuum servo unit check valve - removal, testing and refitting

Removal

1 Slacken the union nut and disconnect the vacuum hose from the servo unit.

2 Trace the hose back, then disconnect it from the inlet manifold/pump connection (as applicable) and remove the hose and valve assembly from the engine compartment.

Testing

3 Examine the vacuum hose, check the valve for signs of damage, and renew if necessary.

4 The valve may be tested by blowing through the hose in both directions; air should flow through the valve in one direction only - when blown through from the servo unit end of the hose. Renew the hose assembly if this is not the case.

Refitting

5 Ensuring that the hose is correctly routed, securely reconnect it to the manifold/pump (as applicable). Connect the hose to the servo unit and tighten the union nut to the specified torque.

6 On completion, start the engine and check the valve to servo unit connection for signs of air leaks. Test the operation of the braking system exhaustively before bringing the car back into service on the road.

13 Parking brake - adjustment

1 The parking brake cable is self-adjusting on all models. The following procedure is intended merely to compensate for wear of the shoe friction material, which should occur at a very slow and even rate and make routine adjustment unnecessary.

2 The parking brake should be fully applied before ten clicks are heard from the ratchet mechanism. Before deciding that shoe adjustment is required, confirm that the cables are operating correctly, and are not broken or seized. After several years' service, it is possible that the parking brake cables may have stretched too far for compensation by the automatic adjuster.

3 On models with steel wheels, remove one wheel bolt from each rear wheel.

4 On models with alloy wheels, both rear wheels must be removed for this adjustment. Loosen the rear wheel bolts before jacking up the car.

5 Firmly chock the front wheels, then jack up the rear of the car and support it on axle stands (see *Jacking and vehicle support*). Release the parking brake completely. On models with alloy wheels, remove both rear wheels.

6 Turn the wheel or hub so that access can be gained to the parking brake shoe adjuster, situated between the parking brake shoes, at the top.

7 Using a long slim screwdriver engaged in the teeth of the adjuster, turn the adjuster until the parking brake shoes make contact and the wheel can no longer be turned **(see illustrations)**. Repeat the procedure on the other rear wheel. To apply the brake shoes,

13.7a Position the wheel bolt hole as described in text and adjust the parking brake shoes . . .

13.7b . . . by rotating the adjuster ring (arrowed) with a flat-bladed screwdriver (shown with disc removed)

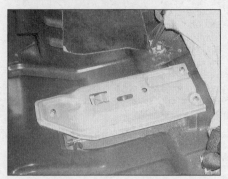

14.2 Cover plate fitted over handbrake automatic adjuster assembly

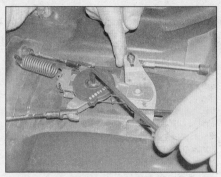

14.3 Preloading the automatic adjuster using an Allen key

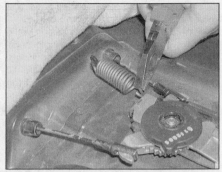

14.4 Unhooking the cable return spring

the adjuster on the left-hand wheel is turned from the bottom upwards, with that on the right-hand wheel being turned from the top downwards.

8 Noting the exact number of strokes required to do so, back off the brake shoe adjuster so that the rear wheel is completely free to turn. Repeat the procedure on the other rear wheel, turning the adjuster by exactly the same amount.

9 Check the operation of the parking brake by gradually applying it, and confirm that the rear wheels both start to 'drag' at the same point. Also check that the parking brake is fully applied before ten clicks are heard from the ratchet.

10 On completion, refit the rear wheels (where removed) and lower the car to the ground. Tighten the wheel bolt(s) to the specified torque.

14 Parking brake pedal - removal and refitting

Removal

1 Remove the rear seat cushion as described in Chapter 11.

2 Remove the three securing nuts from the access cover under the cushion, and lift out the cover (see illustration).

3 Preload the rear cable automatic adjuster by inserting an Allen key into the top of the locking eccentric pin. Turn the pin clockwise using the Allen key through approximately half a turn, at the same time pushing the adjuster rearwards until the spring clip at the rear clicks into the eccentric (see illustration).

4 Unhook the rear cable return spring from the cable adjuster (see illustration).

5 Remove the driver's side lower facia panel as described in Chapter 11, Section 41, and detach the carpet as required for access to the parking brake pedal.

6 Pull on the cable inner to gain some slack, then unhook the cable end fitting from the pedal (see illustration). Removing the cable outer completely requires that the clamping ring be destroyed (obtain a new ring for refitting) - also recover the rubber grommet.

7 The pedal bracket can now be withdrawn from its location. The bracket is secured by two or three bolts, depending on model - it is recommended that the lowest bolt is only loosened, not removed (see illustration). Note that the Torx bolts on the pedal bracket should not be loosened. Unhook the pedal bracket from the facia support bar for access to the wiring and hand control cable.

8 Disconnect the parking brake warning light switch wiring connector from the top of the pedal bracket, with reference to Section 17.

9 Unhook the hand control cable outer and end fitting with reference to Section 15, then

remove the cable outer from the location next to the warning light switch.

10 Remove the pedal bracket completely from the car, unhooking it from the lower mounting bolt if it was not removed.

Refitting

11 Refitting is a reversal of removal, noting the following points:

a) Use a new clamping ring to secure the cable outer to the pedal bracket, locating the ring into the groove in the cable.

b) To reset the rear cable automatic adjuster, use a screwdriver to lift up the spring clip at the rear of the assembly, and allow the eccentric to turn to its required position (see illustration).

c) Operate the parking brake several times to reset the automatic adjustment, and to confirm correct operation.

15 Parking brake cables - removal and refitting

Hand control cable
Removal

1 Remove the driver's lower facia panel as described in Chapter 11, Section 41.

2 Pull out the parking brake handle to its fullest extent.

3 Release the handle from behind, and

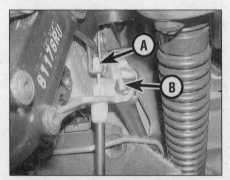

14.6 Parking brake pedal cable end fitting (A) and one of the pedal bracket mounting bolts (B)

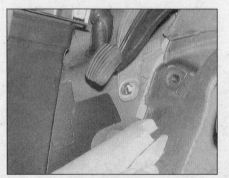

14.7 Parking brake pedal bracket lower mounting bolt

14.11 Using a screwdriver to lift the spring clip and reset the automatic adjuster

15.3a Release the handle from the facia . . .

15.3b . . . then unhook the cable inner, and release the cable outer

15.5a Using a small screwdriver, prise the cable outer locking clip to the left . . .

unhook it from its location in the facia. Press the cable inner to the right and upwards to release the end fitting from the handle, then disconnect the cable inner and outer from the handle **(see illustrations)**.

4 The cable runs over the main foot pedals - trace the line of the cable, releasing it from any clips or cable-ties.

5 The cable outer is secured to the parking brake foot pedal bracket by a clip, which must be prised to the left before the cable can be lifted upwards and removed. Unhook the end fitting from the pedal **(see illustrations)**.

Refitting

6 Refitting is a reversal of removal. Check for correct operation on completion.

Foot pedal cable

Removal

7 Remove the rear seat cushion as described in Chapter 11.

8 Remove the three securing nuts from the access cover under the cushion, and lift out the cover **(see illustration)**.

9 Preload the rear cable automatic adjuster by inserting an Allen key into the top of the locking eccentric pin. Turn the pin clockwise using the Allen key through approximately half a turn, at the same time pushing the adjuster rearwards until the spring clip at the rear clicks into the eccentric **(see illustration)**.

10 Unhook the rear cable return spring from the cable adjuster **(refer to illustration 14.4)**.

11 Remove the locking clip and pin securing

the cable end fitting from the intermediate lever under the rear seat **(see illustrations)**.

12 Remove the cable outer from the floorpan

15.5b . . . then release the cable outer from the pedal bracket

15.8 Removing the access cover from the handbrake automatic adjuster

15.11a Prise off the locking clip . . .

by releasing the clamping ring (which may have to be destroyed - obtain a new ring for refitting) **(see illustration)**.

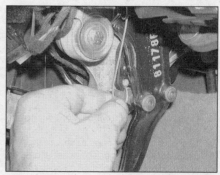

15.5c Unhook the cable end fitting from the pedal

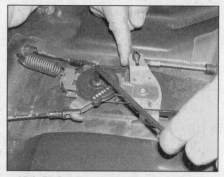

15.9 Preloading the automatic adjuster using an Allen key

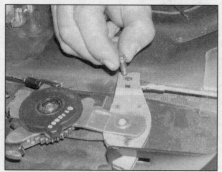

15.11b . . . then remove the cable securing pin

15.12 Prise out the cable clamping ring from the floorpan

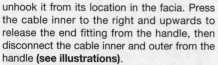

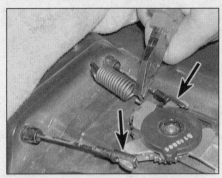

15.20 Unhooking the cable return spring - note cable end fittings (arrowed)

13 Remove the driver's side lower facia panel as described in Chapter 11, Section 41, and detach the carpet as required for access to the parking brake pedal.

14 Unhook the cable end fitting from the parking brake pedal **(refer to illustration 14.6)**. Remove the cable outer from the pedal bracket by releasing the clamping ring (which may have to be destroyed - obtain a new ring for refitting) - also recover the rubber grommet.

Refitting

15 Refitting is a reversal of removal, noting the following points:

a) *Use new clamping rings to secure the cable outer to the pedal bracket and intermediate lever bracket, locating the ring into the groove in the cable.*

b) *To reset the rear cable automatic adjuster, use a screwdriver to lift up the spring clip at the rear of the assembly,*

15.22 Prise out the cable clamping rings from the floorpan

and allow the eccentric to turn to its required position (refer to illustration 14.11).

c) *Operate the parking brake several times to reset the automatic adjustment, and to confirm correct operation.*

Rear cables

Removal

16 Remove the relevant set of parking brake shoes as described in Section 16 and detach the expander mechanism from the end of the cable.

17 Remove the cable outer from the rear hub by unscrewing the mounting bolt securing the cable endplate.

18 Remove the rear seat cushion as described in Chapter 11.

19 Remove the three securing nuts from the access cover under the cushion, and lift out the cover.

20 Unhook the rear cable return spring from the cable adjuster **(see illustration)**.

21 Unhook the front cable end fitting from the intermediate lever under the rear seat, then unhook both rear cables from the cable equaliser bracket.

22 Remove the rear cable outers from the fittings on the floorpan by releasing the clamping rings (which may have to be destroyed - obtain new rings for refitting) **(see illustration)**.

Refitting

23 Refitting is a reversal of the removal procedure, securing the cable to the hub with a new bolt. On completion, check the operation of the parking brake as described in paragraph 9 of Section 13.

---

16 Parking brake shoes - removal and refitting

Removal

1 Remove the rear brake disc as described in Section 7, making a note of the correct fitted position of all components **(see illustration)**.

2 Remove the rear seat cushion as described in Chapter 11.

3 Remove the three securing nuts from the access cover under the cushion, and lift out the cover.

4 Preload the rear cable automatic adjuster by inserting an Allen key into the top of the locking eccentric pin. Turn the pin clockwise using the Allen key through approximately half a turn, at the same time pushing the adjuster rearwards until the spring clip at the rear clicks into the eccentric **(refer to illustration 15.9)**.

5 Using a pair of thin-nosed pliers, compress the shoe retaining springs then rotate them through 90° and remove them from the backplate. Access to the springs can be gained through the hub flange holes **(see illustration)**.

6 Carefully unhook and remove the parking brake shoe lower return spring, noting which

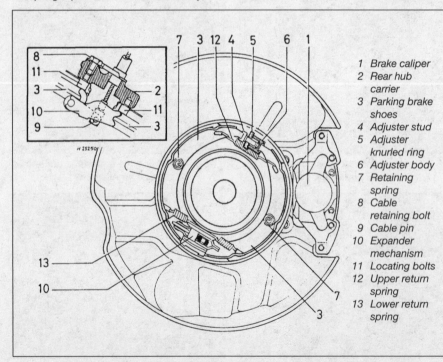

16.1 Layout of parking brake shoe components (left-hand side shown)

1 Brake caliper
2 Rear hub carrier
3 Parking brake shoes
4 Adjuster stud
5 Adjuster knurled ring
6 Adjuster body
7 Retaining spring
8 Cable retaining bolt
9 Cable pin
10 Expander mechanism
11 Locating bolts
12 Upper return spring
13 Lower return spring

16.5 Remove the retaining springs . . .

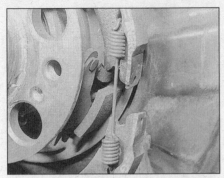

16.6 . . . then unhook the lower return spring, noting which way around it is fitted . . .

16.7 . . . and remove the parking brake shoe assembly from the vehicle

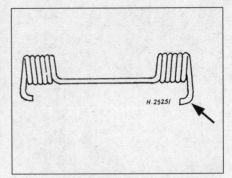

16.14 Ensure the lower return spring is fitted with its longer hook (arrowed) engaged with the upper parking brake shoe

way round the spring is fitted - it is not symmetrical **(see illustration)**.

7 Free the lower ends of the shoes from the lower expander plate, and remove the assembly from the car **(see illustration)**.

8 With the assembly on a bench, note each component's correct fitted location, then unhook the upper return spring and separate the shoes and adjuster assembly.

9 Inspect the parking brake shoes for signs of wear or contamination, and renew if necessary. It is recommended that the return springs are renewed as a matter of course. Check the shoe friction material thickness; shoes with anything less than the minimum friction material given in this Chapter's Specifications should be renewed.

10 With the shoes removed, clean and inspect the condition of the shoe adjuster and expander mechanisms, and renew them if they show signs of wear or damage. If all is well, apply a fresh coat of brake grease (Mercedes-Benz recommend Molykote Paste U or G-Rapid) to the threads of the adjuster and sliding surfaces of the lower expander mechanism. Do not allow the grease to contact the shoe friction material.

Refitting

11 Prior to installation, clean the backplate, and apply a thin smear of high-temperature brake grease (see paragraph 10) or anti-seize compound to all those surfaces of the backplate which bear on the shoes. Do not allow the lubricant to foul the friction material.

12 Assemble the shoes and the adjuster mechanism, noting that the adjuster must be fitted with its knurled ring at the front of the adjuster (facing in the direction of travel). Fully retract the adjuster and fit the upper return spring.

13 Manoeuvre the assembly into position and engage the lower end of each shoe with the expander mechanism.

14 Fit the shoe lower return spring, making sure it locates with its larger hooked end in the upper shoe **(see illustration)**.

15 Ensure that the shoes are correctly positioned, and secure them with the retaining springs.

16 Check all components are correctly fitted, and centralise the parking brake shoes.

17 To reset the rear cable automatic adjuster, use a screwdriver to lift up the spring clip at the rear of the assembly, and allow the eccentric to turn to its required position.

18 Operate the parking brake several times to reset the automatic adjustment, and to confirm correct operation.

19 Refit the brake disc as described in Section 7. Prior to refitting the roadwheel, check the parking brake adjustment as described in Section 13.

17 Parking brake warning light switch - removal and refitting

Removal

1 Remove the driver's side lower facia panel as described in Chapter 11, Section 41.

2 The warning light switch is mounted on top of the parking brake pedal bracket.

3 Lift the plastic cover fitted over the switch, then squeeze together the retaining lugs and lift the switch away **(see illustration)**.

4 Disconnect the wiring plug from the switch, and remove the switch from the car **(see illustration)**.

Refitting

5 Refitting is a reversal of removal. Check for correct operation on completion.

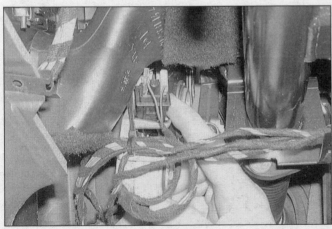

17.3 Squeeze the switch retaining lugs to remove it from above the foot pedal

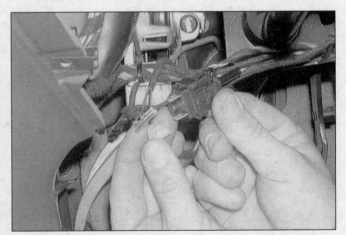

17.4 With the switch removed, disconnect its wiring plug

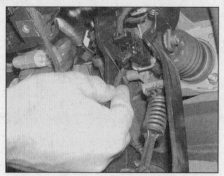

18.2a Remove the lower wiring plug . . .

18.2b . . . and the upper wiring plug, noting which fits where

18 Stop-light switch - removal and refitting

Note: *Correct operation of the stop-light switch is essential. Without the signal from the stop-light switch that the brakes have been applied, the ABS will not function. Similarly, if the signal from the switch is delayed (due to the switch plunger sticking, for example), there will be a corresponding delay in operation of the ABS.*

Removal

1 Remove the driver's side lower facia panel as described in Chapter 11, Section 41.
2 Ensure that the ignition is switched off, then disconnect the wiring plug(s) from the stop-light switch **(see illustrations)**.
3 Depress the lug on the side of the switch body, then rotate the switch and withdraw it from the pedal mounting bracket **(see illustration)**.

Refitting

4 Fully extend the stop-light switch plunger from the switch body to reset the switch **(see illustration)**.
5 Fully depress the brake pedal and hold it in position, then manoeuvre the switch into position. Rotate the switch until the locking lug clips into position. Slowly release the brake pedal and allow it to return to its stop. This will automatically adjust the stop-light switch.

6 Reconnect the wiring connector, and check the operation of the stop-lights. The stop-lights should illuminate after the brake pedal has travelled approximately 5 mm. If the switch is not functioning correctly, it is faulty and must be renewed; no other adjustment is possible.
7 On completion, refit the driver's side lower facia panel (see Chapter 11, Section 41).

19 Anti-lock braking system (ABS) - general information

Note: *On models equipped with traction control, the ABS unit is a dual-function unit, and performs both the anti-lock braking system (ABS) and traction control (ASR) system functions. On later models with the Electronic Stability Program (ESP), the ABS unit is also used to modulate the brakes as required.*

Models without traction control (ASR) or ESP

1 ABS is fitted to all models as standard. The system comprises the following components:
  a) *A hydraulic unit, which contains either three or four hydraulic solenoid valves (one for each front brake, and one for both rear brakes, or one for each brake from 1998 model year) and the electrically-driven return pump.*
  b) *Three or four roadwheel sensors (one for each front wheel, and one for both rear*

wheels, or one for each wheel from 1998 model year). The sensors for each front wheel are fitted to the hubs, as are the sensors for each rear wheel, on models from 1998 model year onwards. Models prior to 1998 have one sensor for both rear wheels, and this sensor is mounted on the final drive unit.
  c) *The electronic control unit (ECU), located in the module box at the left-hand rear of the engine compartment (left as seen from the driver's seat).*

2 The purpose of the system is to prevent the wheel(s) locking during heavy braking and/or slippery road conditions. This is achieved by automatic release of the brake on the relevant wheel, followed by re-application of the brake. On models prior to 1998 model year, in the case of the rear wheels, both brakes are applied at the same time.
3 The solenoids are controlled by the ECU, which itself receives signals from the wheel sensors, which monitor the speed of rotation of each wheel. By comparing these signals with that from the speedometer sensor on the transmission, the ECU can determine the speed at which the vehicle is travelling. It can then use this speed to determine when a wheel is decelerating at an abnormal rate compared to the speed of the vehicle, and therefore predicts when a wheel is about to lock.
4 During normal operation, the system functions in the same way as a non-ABS braking system.
5 If the ECU senses that a wheel is about to lock, it operates the relevant solenoid valve in the hydraulic unit, which then isolates from the master cylinder the relevant brake caliper(s) on the wheel(s) which is/are about to lock - effectively sealing-in the hydraulic pressure.
6 If the speed of rotation of the wheel continues to decrease at an abnormal rate, the ECU switches on the electrically-driven return pump which pumps the hydraulic fluid back into the master cylinder, releasing pressure on the brake caliper(s) so that the brake is released. Once the speed of rotation of the wheel returns to an acceptable rate, the pump stops; the solenoid valve opens, allowing the hydraulic master cylinder pressure to return to the caliper, which then re-applies the brake. This cycle can be carried out at up to 10 times a second.
7 The action of the solenoid valves and return pump creates pulses in the hydraulic circuit. When the ABS system is functioning, these pulses can be felt through the brake pedal.
8 The operation of the ABS system is entirely dependent on electrical signals. To prevent the system responding to any inaccurate signals, a built-in safety circuit monitors all signals received by the ECU. If an inaccurate signal or low battery voltage is detected, the ABS system is automatically shut down, and the warning light on the instrument panel is illuminated to inform the driver that the ABS

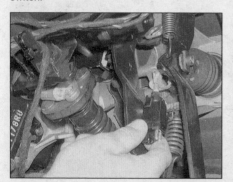

18.3 Rotate the switch body, and remove it from the pedal bracket

18.4 Pull the switch plunger out fully to reset it

system is not operational. Normal braking should still be available, however.

9 If a fault does develop in the ABS system, the vehicle must be taken to a Mercedes-Benz dealer for fault diagnosis and repair.

Models with traction control (ASR) and/or ESP

10 On models with traction control (ASR) and/or the stability program (ESP), the hydraulic unit performs the traction control and stability program functions as well as the anti-lock braking.

11 On models with ASR and/or ESP, a modified hydraulic unit and electronic control unit is fitted. The ABS electronic control unit (ECU) is linked to the engine management ECU, to operate the throttle valve position actuator.

12 The braking side of the system works as described above. On models with ASR up to May 1994, a speed sensor is fitted above each rear driveshaft on the final drive housing - these two sensors are unique to the ASR system. On later models, the two additional sensors are deleted, and rear axle speed is monitored solely by the rear wheel ABS sensor(s).

13 The traction control system prevents the rear wheels from losing traction by either gently applying the brake or by closing the throttle valve, depending on the speed of the vehicle. In extreme cases, a combination of both may be used.

14 On the braking side of the system, if a wheel is about to lose traction, the hydraulic unit uses the hydraulic pressure stored in the accumulator to gently apply the brake on the relevant wheel. Once the risk of wheel spin has passed, the hydraulic unit allows the fluid to return to the accumulator and releases the brake, allowing the wheel to rotate freely again.

15 On the throttle side of the system, if traction is about to be lost, the engine management ECU operates the throttle valve actuator and closes the throttle valve, decreasing the engine power output. Once the risk of wheel spin has passed, the actuator returns the throttle valve to its normal

position and returns control of the throttle to the driver.

16 On models with the stability program (ESP), the traction control system is further refined to help retain control of the car during cornering. An accelerometer fitted above the rear axle monitors the lateral (cornering) forces on the car. If the car starts to slide sideways, the system reacts by gently applying one of the brakes to help steer the car - if appropriate, the throttle valve is also closed.

17 In the same way as for the ABS, the vehicle must be taken to a Mercedes-Benz dealer for testing if a fault develops in the traction control (ASR) or ESP systems.

> ⚠ **Warning: Diagnosis of the faults within ABS/ASR/ESP systems requires access to dedicated test equipment. For safety reasons, owners are strongly advised against attempting to investigate complex problems with these systems using standard workshop equipment.**

20 Anti-lock braking system (ABS) components - removal and refitting

> ⚠ **Warning: If any of the ABS system components have been disturbed or renewed, the operation of the system must be** *verified before the vehicle is brought back into service. This procedure must be carried out using dedicated test equipment, and as such should be entrusted to a Mercedes-Benz dealer.*
> **Note:** *Before starting work, refer to the note at the beginning of Section 2 concerning the dangers of hydraulic fluid.*

Hydraulic unit
Removal

1 Disconnect the battery negative cable and position it away from the terminal.

2 Unscrew the master cylinder reservoir filler cap and top-up the reservoir to the MAX mark (see Chapter 1A or 1B). Place a piece of polythene over the filler neck, and securely refit the cap. This will minimise brake fluid loss during subsequent operations. As a precaution, place absorbent rags beneath the hydraulic unit.

3 Disconnect the unit wiring connector(s). The main connector is secured using a sliding locking clip - slide the clip upwards to release the connector pins, and free it from the hydraulic unit. Undo the retaining nut/bolt and disconnect the earth strap **(see illustrations)**.

4 Wipe clean the area around the hydraulic unit brake pipe unions, then make a note of how the pipes are arranged to use as a reference on refitting. Unscrew the union nuts and carefully withdraw the pipes **(see illustration)**. Plug or tape over the pipe ends and unit orifices, to minimise the loss of brake

20.3a Slide the locking clip upwards . . .

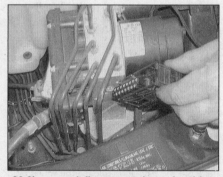

20.3b . . . and disconnect the main wiring plug from the front . . .

20.3c . . . then squeeze together the locking tabs and disconnect the smaller plug at the rear

20.3d Unscrew the nut and disconnect the earth strap

20.4 Unscrew the union nuts and disconnect the fluid pipes

fluid and to prevent the entry of dirt into the system. Wash off any spilt fluid immediately with cold water.

5 On early models, turn the plastic mounting sleeves, and release the hydraulic unit from its mounting bracket. If necessary, slide off the mounting bushes and remove them.

6 On later models, the hydraulic unit is rubber mounted. Carefully prise the unit upwards to free it from the mountings.

Note: *Do not attempt to dismantle the modulator block hydraulic assembly; overhaul of the unit is not possible.*

Refitting

7 Refitting is the reverse of the removal procedure, noting the following points.

a) *Examine the mountings for signs of wear or damage, and renew if necessary.*

b) *When refitting the plastic mounting sleeves, note that the lugs must face downwards.*

c) *Refit the brake pipes to their respective unions, and tighten the union nuts to the specified torque.*

d) *Ensure that the wiring is correctly routed and securely connected. Where applicable, slide the locking clip fully into place.*

e) *On completion prior to refitting the battery, bleed the complete braking system as described in Section 2.*

Electronic control unit (ECU)

Models up to July 1996

Removal

8 The control unit is located inside the car, in the passenger's front footwell.

9 Referring to Chapter 11 if necessary, remove the facia lower trim panel. The control unit is mounted on a hinged panel - release the fasteners securing the panel, and lower it for access to the control unit.

10 Make sure that the ignition is switched off (take out the key), then release the wiring plug locking levers and disconnect the two wiring plugs from the ECU.

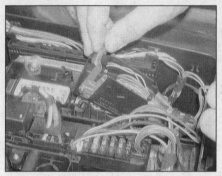

20.16a On this model, lift the levers to release the engine management ECU plugs

11 Unscrew the retaining nuts/bolts and remove the ECU from the car.

Models from August 1996 onwards

Removal

12 The control unit is located in the control module box in the left-hand rear corner of the engine compartment.

13 Remove the screws securing the module box lid, then take off the lid for access to the control units.

14 Typically, the module box only contains one other ECU apart from the ABS unit - the one for the engine management system. The engine management ECU can be identified by tracing the wiring harness from the connector plugs back towards the throttle housing.

15 On most models, the ABS control unit must be removed with the engine management ECU, and then separated.

16 Make sure that the ignition is switched off (take out the key), then release the wiring plug locking levers and disconnect the two wiring plugs from each ECU, as applicable. The locking levers either lift up and hinge out of the way, or slide sideways to release the connector pins **(see illustrations)**.

17 Remove the small cross-head screw inside the module box which secures the ECUs in position **(see illustration)**.

18 Lift the ECUs from the module box, taking care not to catch any other wiring, and remove them from the car.

19 Where applicable, unscrew the retaining

20.16b The ABS ECU wiring plugs are released by sliding sideways

screws, and separate the ABS control unit from the engine management ECU **(see illustration)**.

Refitting - all models

20 Refitting is the reverse of removal, ensuring that the wiring plugs are securely reconnected.

Front wheel sensor

Note: *New sensor retaining bolt(s) and where applicable, a new plastic centring sleeve, will be required on refitting*

Removal

21 Chock the rear wheels and firmly apply the parking brake. Loosen the front wheel bolts, then jack up the front of the car and support on axle stands (see *Jacking and vehicle support*). Remove the appropriate front roadwheel.

22 Ensure that the ignition switch is turned off (take out the key), then trace the wiring back from the sensor to the connector. Free the sensor wiring from any relevant retaining clips or ties, noting its correct routing, so that it is free to be removed.

23 Unclip the wiring connector from its retaining clip and disconnect it from the main harness. On later models, the pad wear sensor wiring connector appears at first to be attached to the connector for the ABS sensor, but the two connectors can be prised apart using a small screwdriver **(see illustrations)**.

20.17 Removing the small screw which secures the ECUs

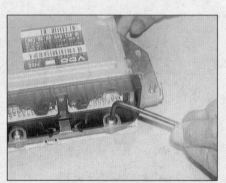

20.19 Removing the screws which secure the two ECUs together

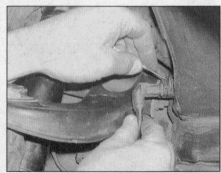

20.23a Prise the pad wear and ABS sensor wiring plugs from the rear of the wheel arch . . .

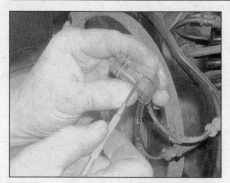

20.23b . . . then prise up the retaining clip with a screwdriver . . .

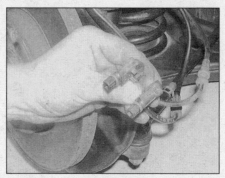

20.23c . . . and separate the two plugs for removal

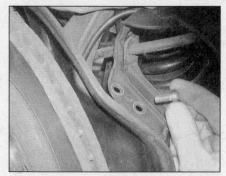

20.24 Removing one of the bolts securing the sensor plate to the steering knuckle

24 Slacken and remove the bolt(s) securing the sensor mounting plate to the top of the steering knuckle **(see illustration)**.
25 The sensor itself must now be prised out of its mounting in the brake disc splash shield. Access is not easy, and care must be taken not to damage the rubber seal or plastic sleeve (where fitted). Remove the sensor and lead assembly from the car **(see illustrations)**.
26 On models up to September 1995, examine the sensor sealing ring for signs of wear or damage, and renew as necessary.
27 On models from September 1995 onwards, recover the plastic centring sleeve and discard it; a new sleeve must be used on reassembly. Note, however, that our 1998 model year car did not appear to have such a sleeve, and it may have been discontinued in production.
28 Discard the sensor retaining bolt(s); new bolts must be fitted whenever they are disturbed.

Refitting

29 Prior to refitting, ensure that the mating surfaces of the sensor and steering knuckle are clean and dry, and apply a thin coat of multi-purpose grease to them (Mercedes-Benz recommend the use of MB long-life grease).
30 Ensure that the sensor tip and reluctor rings are clean and free from debris, and fit

the sealing ring or centring sleeve to the sensor, as applicable.
31 Insert the sensor fully into the location in the disc splash shield.
32 Align the sensor mounting plate with the hole(s) in the top of the steering knuckle, and insert the new mounting bolt(s). Tighten the bolt(s) to the specified torque **(see illustration)**.
33 Secure the wiring in position with all the necessary clips and ties, making sure it is correctly routed. Ensure that the connector sealing ring is in good condition, then connect the wiring and clip the connector into its retaining clip.
34 Refit the roadwheel, then lower the car to the ground and tighten the roadwheel bolts to the specified torque.

Rear wheel sensor

Removal - up to 1998 model year

Note: *A new sensor retaining bolt will be required on refitting.*
35 Chock the front wheels, then jack up the rear of the car and support it on axle stands (see *Jacking and vehicle support*).
36 The sensor is located at the front of the final drive housing, on the left-hand side **(see illustration)**. Unscrew the sensor retaining bolt, and remove the sensor and sealing ring from the final drive unit. Renew the sealing

ring if it shows signs of damage or deterioration. Discard the retaining bolt; the bolt must be renewed whenever it is disturbed.
37 Trace the wiring up from the sensor to the rubber grommet in the floorpan, noting how it is routed and freeing it from any retaining clips. Prise out the grommet, taking care not to damage the wires.
38 Lift up the boot carpet, then remove the three fasteners and lift out the cover panel for access to the sensor wiring. From the floorpan aperture, trace the wiring to its connector plug, and disconnect it **(see**

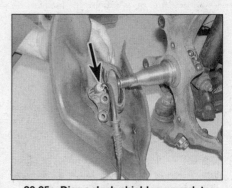

20.25a Disc splash shield removed, to show front wheel ABS sensor location (arrowed)

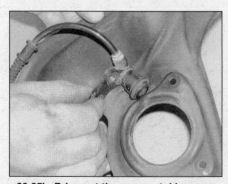

20.25b Prise out the sensor, taking care not to damage the rubber seal

20.32 Tightening the ABS sensor plate bolts

20.36 Rear wheel ABS sensor location (arrowed) on final drive unit

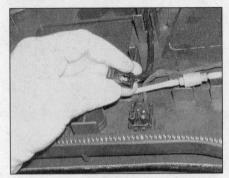

20.38 Disconnect the wiring plug for the ABS sensor

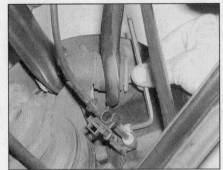

20.41 Using an Allen key to unscrew the sensor retaining bolt

20.42 Withdrawing the sensor from its location

illustration). Feed the plug, wiring and grommet down through the floorpan, and recover it from under the car.

Removal - 1998 model year onwards

39 Loosen the relevant rear wheel bolts, chock the front wheels, then jack up the rear of the car and support it on axle stands (see *Jacking and vehicle support*). Remove the rear wheel.

40 Unclip the sensor wiring from the clip on the suspension arm.

41 Using an Allen key, loosen and remove the sensor retaining bolt **(see illustration)**.

42 Prise the sensor out from its location, noting that it is quite a tight fit. Recover the sealing ring, where applicable **(see illustration)**.

43 Trace the wiring up from the sensor to the rubber grommet in the floorpan, noting how it is routed and freeing it from any retaining clips. Prise out the grommet, taking care not to damage the wires.

44 Lift up the boot carpet, then remove the three fasteners and lift out the cover panel for access to the sensor wiring. From the floorpan aperture, trace the wiring to its connector plug, and disconnect it **(see illustrations)**. Feed the plug, wiring and grommet down through the floorpan, and recover it from under the car.

Refitting - all models

45 Ensure that the sensor and its location are clean and dry, and fit the sealing ring to the sensor.

46 Ease the sensor into position, then fit the new retaining bolt and tighten it to the specified torque setting.

47 Feed the wiring back up through the floorpan then, from inside the car, connect it to the main harness. Ensure that the wiring is correctly routed, and secure it in position with all the relevant clips. Refit the rubber grommet to the floorpan aperture.

48 On completion, lower the car to the ground.

Additional rear wheel sensors - early models with ASR

Note: *A new sensor retaining bolt and final drive unit mounting bolt nuts will be required on refitting. A sensor sealing ring will also be required.*

Removal

49 Models with traction control (ASR) up to May 1994 have two additional rear wheel sensors fitted to the top of the final drive housing, one above each driveshaft. Access to these sensors is very limited unless the final drive unit is lowered, as described below, but may be possible with patience. Refer to Chapter 8, Section 3 for more information on final drive unit removal and refitting.

50 Chock the front wheels, then jack up the rear of the car and support it on axle stands (see *Jacking and vehicle support*).

51 Position a jack with a block of wood on its head underneath the final drive unit, and raise the jack until it is supporting the weight of the final drive.

52 Undo the collared bolts at the rear securing the final drive housing to the subframe, and remove the bolts together with the large impact washers.

53 Unscrew the Allen bolt and nut, and the nut/washer, securing the housing to the subframe at the front. When the final drive is removed, note that there are either one or two shims fitted between the Allen bolt and the housing - make sure these are recovered and refitted. Note the fitted order of all the bushes and washers as they are removed.

54 Carefully lower the final drive unit until the propeller shaft contacts the rear cross-brace at the rear of the propeller shaft tunnel.

55 Slacken and remove each sensor's retaining bolt, and withdraw the sensors from the top of the final drive unit, along with the sealing rings, which should be renewed.

56 Trace the wiring up from the sensors to the rubber grommet in the floorpan, noting how it is routed and freeing it from any retaining clips. Prise out the grommet, taking care not to damage the wires.

57 Lift up the boot carpet, then remove the three fasteners and lift out the cover panel for access to the sensor wiring. From the floorpan aperture, trace the wiring to its connector plugs, and disconnect it. Feed the plugs, wiring and grommet down through the floorpan, and recover it from under the car.

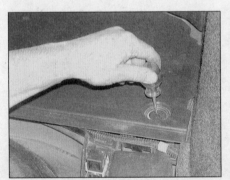

20.44a Unscrew the plastic fasteners . . .

20.44b . . . then lift up the front section of the boot floor . . .

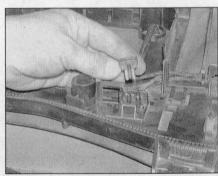

20.44c . . . and disconnect the wiring plug for the ABS sensor

Refitting

58 Ensure that the sensor and final drive surfaces are clean and dry, and fit a new sealing ring to each sensor.

59 Insert the sensors into the final drive unit, making sure they are correctly seated, then fit the new retaining bolts and tighten to the specified torque setting.

60 Ensure that the upper and lower front mounting rubber and washers are correctly positioned, then carefully raise the final drive unit back into position.

61 Insert the final drive unit mounting bolts and fit the new nuts. Tighten the mounting bolts to the specified torque setting (see Chapter 8 Specifications).

62 Feed the wiring back up through the floorpan then, from inside the car, connect it to the main harness. Ensure that the wiring is correctly routed, and secure it in position with all the relevant clips. Refit the rubber grommet to the floorpan aperture.

63 On completion, lower the car to the ground.

Front reluctor rings

64 The front reluctor rings are fixed onto the rear of wheel hubs. Examine the rings for damage such as chipped or missing teeth. If renewal is necessary, the complete hub assembly must be renewed as described in Chapter 10.

Rear reluctor ring(s)

Up to 1998 model year

65 The rear reluctor ring (fitted to all models, at the front of the final drive housing) is an integral part of the final drive unit. With the sensor removed, examine the ring for signs of damage such as chipped or missing teeth, and renew as necessary. If renewal is necessary, the final drive unit will have to be overhauled by a Mercedes-Benz dealer or other suitable specialist.

66 The reluctor rings for the additional rear sensors (fitted to early models with ASR) are pressed onto the rear driveshafts. Given their location, it will be necessary to remove the driveshaft(s) to inspect the reluctor rings. It may then be necessary to fit a new driveshaft if the ring is found to be damaged.

1998 model year onwards

67 The rear reluctor rings are fixed onto the rear of wheel hubs. Examine the rings for damage such as chipped or missing teeth. If renewal is necessary, the hub carrier must be renewed, as described in Chapter 10.

Over-voltage protection relay

Removal

68 On models up to July 1996, the over-voltage protection relay is on the right-hand side of the engine compartment. On models after August 1996, the relay is in the fuse/relay box on the left-hand side of the engine compartment.

69 Prior to removal, ensure that the ignition is switched off (take out the key). On later models, remove the fusebox cover.

70 Undo the retaining screw (where fitted), then unplug the relay and remove it from the engine compartment.

Refitting

71 On refitting, ensure that the relay and wiring connector terminals are clean and dry.

ABS relays

Removal

72 On models up to July 1996, the ABS relays are located under the facia panel, on the driver's side. On models after August 1996, the ABS relays are in the fuse/relay box on the left-hand side of the engine compartment. A further ABS relay is located in the luggage compartment, and on most models, is black or white - do not confuse it

with the fuel pump relay, where applicable, which is green and has a fuse attached.

73 To gain access to the relays, remove the driver's side lower facia panel (Chapter 11, Section 41), or take off the fusebox lid, or remove the three plastic fasteners and lift up the front section of the boot floor, as applicable.

74 Ensure that the ignition is switched off (take out the key), then pull the relevant relay out from its location.

Refitting

75 Refitting is a reversal of removal, ensuring that the relays are pushed securely into position.

21 Vacuum pump (diesel models) - testing, removal and refitting

Testing

1 The operation of the braking system vacuum pump can be checked using a vacuum gauge.

2 Disconnect the vacuum pipe from the pump, and connect the gauge to the pump union using a suitable length of hose.

3 Start the engine and allow it to idle, then measure the vacuum created by the pump. As a guide, a minimum of approximately 500 mm Hg should be recorded. If the vacuum registered is significantly less than this, it is likely that the pump is faulty. However, seek the advice of a Mercedes-Benz dealer before condemning the pump.

Removal

4 Remove the cooling fan as described in Chapter 3.

5 Remove the auxiliary drivebelt as described in Chapter 1A or 1B.

6 Slacken the union nut and disconnect the vacuum hose from the top of the pump, which is mounted on the front of the cylinder block (see illustration).

7 Slacken and remove the pump retaining bolts and remove it from the cylinder block. Recover the pump gasket and discard it.

Refitting

8 Refitting is the reverse of removal, using a new gasket and making sure the pump drive flange is correctly engaged.

9 Tighten the vacuum pump mounting bolts to the specified torque.

22 Brake assist system (BAS) components - removal and refitting

Electronic control unit

Note: On models with the stability program (ESP) system, the brake assist ECU is incorporated into the ESP control unit. Details

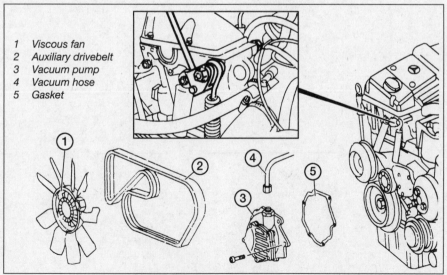

1 Viscous fan
2 Auxiliary drivebelt
3 Vacuum pump
4 Vacuum hose
5 Gasket

21.6 Vacuum pump details

of the ESP system were not available at time of writing.

Removal

1 The brake assist ECU is located adjacent to the vacuum servo unit. Before removing the ECU, make sure the ignition is switched off (take out the key).

2 Press and release the brake pedal several times, to dissipate the vacuum in the servo unit.

3 Noting their locations, disconnect the three wiring plugs from the control unit.

4 Carefully unclip the unit from its mounting, and slide it out of position.

Refitting

5 Refitting is a reversal of removal, ensuring the wiring connections are correctly and securely remade, and that the control unit is securely clipped back into position.

Diaphragm travel sensor

Removal

6 Press and release the brake pedal several times, to dissipate the vacuum in the servo unit. This is essential to avoid the possibility of the sensor's sealing ring from being sucked into the servo unit.

7 Using a pair of suitable circlip pliers, release the circlip securing the sensor to the servo unit.

8 Ease the sensor out of its location in the front of the servo unit, and recover the sealing O-ring.

9 Trace the wiring back to the connector on the control unit, and disconnect it. Noting how the wiring is routed, release it from any retaining clips and remove the sensor from the car.

Refitting

10 Fit a new O-ring to the sensor, and 'lubricate' it with a little methylated spirit to ease fitting (it is important that the O-ring makes a good seal, and that it does not fall into the servo unit).

11 Ease the sensor back into position, and secure using a new circlip.

12 Route the sensor wiring as noted on removal, and reconnect it at the control unit.

13 Start the engine, and operate the brake pedal a few times. Switch off the engine, and listen for any sounds of air leaking in the vicinity of the servo unit.

Chapter 10
Suspension and steering

Contents

Degrees of difficulty

| Easy, suitable for novice with little experience | | Fairly easy, suitable for beginner with some experience | | Fairly difficult, suitable for competent DIY mechanic | | Difficult, suitable for experienced DIY mechanic | | Very difficult, suitable for expert DIY or professional | |

Specifications

Front suspension

Type . . . . Independent, double wishbone with coil springs and telescopic shock absorbers. Anti-roll bar fitted to most models

Rear suspension

Type . . . . Independent, multi-link with coil springs and telescopic shock absorbers. Anti-roll bar fitted to most models

Steering

Type . . . . Power-assisted steering box with drag link, idler arm and track rod arrangement. Steering damper fitted to track rod

Front hub bearing
Endfloat . . . .   0.01 to 0.02 mm

Wheel alignment and steering angles
Front wheel:
  Camber angle:
    Classic/Elegance . . . .   -0° 35' ± 20'
    Esprit/Sport . . . .   -0° 55' ± 20'
  Castor angle (wheels turned):
    Classic/Elegance . . . .   4° 40' ± 30'
    Esprit/Sport . . . .   5° 10' ± 30'
  Toe setting (total) . . . .   0° 25' ± 10' toe-in
Rear wheel:
  Camber angle . . . .   -1° 30' ± 30'
  Toe setting (total) . . . .   0° 33' ± 7' toe-in

Roadwheels
Type . . . .   Pressed-steel or aluminium alloy (depending on model)
Size . . . .   6.5J x 15, 7J x 15, or 7J x 16

Tyres
Roadwheels size:
  6.5J x 15 wheels . . . .   195/65 R 15
  7J x 15 wheels . . . .   205/60 R 15
  7J x 16 wheels . . . .   205/55 R 16
Tyre pressures . . . .   Refer to end of *Weekly checks*

Torque wrench settings

	Nm	lbf ft
Front suspension		
Anti-roll bar body bracket bolts	60	44
Anti-roll bar mounting clamp nuts:		
M8 nuts	20	15
M10 nuts	40	30
Brake dust shield bolts to steering knuckle	22	16
Hub nut clamp bolt	8	6
Lower arm:		
Pivot bolt nut	120	89
Supporting joint (balljoint) nuts	105	77
Shock absorber:		
Lower mounting nut/bolt	55	41
Upper mounting locknut	30	22
Upper mounting nut	18	13
Upper arm:		
Balljoint nut to steering knuckle	45	33
Pivot bolt nut	65	48
Rear suspension		
Anti-roll bar:		
Mounting clamp bolts	28	21
Connecting link:		
Upper nut	30	22
Lower bolt nut	20	15
Control arms:		
Pivot bolt nuts:		
M10 nuts	40	30
M12 nuts	70	52
Lower rear (track) arm balljoint nut	35	26
Lower arm:		
Inner pivot bolt	70	52
Outer pivot bolt	120	89
Rear subframe mounting bolts	90	66
Shock absorber:		
Upper mounting nut	15	11
Upper mounting locknut	30	22
Lower mounting bolt nut	55	41

Torque wrench settings

	Nm	lbf ft
Steering		
Drag link balljoint nut	50	37
Drop arm clamp bolt	55	41
Engine mounting to subframe	25	18
Idler arm:		
Balljoint nut	50	37
Pivot bolt nut	30	22
Power steering hose unions:		
Return hose	40	30
Supply hose:		
M14 fitting	30	22
M16 fitting	40 to 50	30 to 37
Power steering pump:		
Mounting bolts	25	18
Pulley bolts	30	22
Steering box mounting bolts	70	52
Steering column:		
Lower mounting nuts	8	6
Shaft clamp bolt	25	18
Upper mounting bolts	20	15
Steering damper bolt nuts	40	30
Steering wheel bolt	80	59
Track rod:		
Balljoint nut	50	37
Inner balljoint clamp bolt	20	15
Roadwheels		
Roadwheel bolts	110	81

1 General information

The independent front suspension incorporates coil springs and telescopic shock absorbers. The shock absorbers are located by transverse lower suspension arms, which use rubber inner mounting bushes, and incorporate a supporting joint (double balljoint) at the outer ends. The front steering knuckles, which carry the brake calipers and the hub/disc assemblies, are connected to the upper and lower suspension arms through balljoints (see illustration). The upper suspension arms are attached to the vehicle body at their inner ends via pivot bolts. A front anti-roll bar is fitted to most models. The anti-roll bar is rubber-mounted and is connected to both lower arms by mounting clamps.

The independent rear suspension also incorporates coil springs and telescopic shock absorbers. The shock absorbers are located by transverse lower suspension arms, which use rubber mounting bushes. The hub assemblies are fastened to the lower arms, and are joined to the rear subframe by the three control arms; two upper arms and a lower one. Coil springs are fitted between the lower arms and vehicle body (see illustration). A rear anti-roll bar is fitted to most models. The anti-roll bar is rubber-

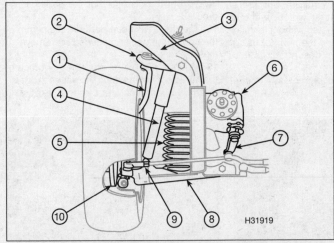

1.1 Cross-sectional view of the front suspension

1 Steering knuckle
2 Upper arm
3 Suspension mounting
4 Shock absorber
5 Coil spring
6 Steering box
7 Drop arm
8 Lower arm
9 Track rod end
10 Brake disc

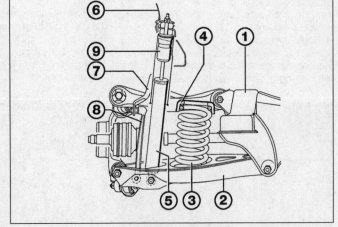

1.2 Cross-sectional view of the rear suspension

1 Subframe
2 Lower arm
3 Coil spring
4 Spring seat
5 Shock absorber
6 Body
7 Anti-roll bar
8 Connecting link
9 Bump stop

mounted and is connected to both lower arms by connecting links.

The steering column shaft is in two sections, with a clamp bolt securing the upper and lower shafts.

The steering box is mounted onto the bulkhead. The steering box is connected to one of the steering knuckles directly by a track rod, and is connected to the other steering knuckle by a drag link, idler arm and track rod linkage. The track rod and drag link have a balljoint at each of their ends. The track rod balljoint ends are threaded to facilitate adjustment.

Power-assisted steering is standard on all models. The hydraulic steering system is powered by a belt-driven pump which is driven off the crankshaft pulley.

Note: *Many of the suspension and steering components are secured in position with self-locking nuts and bolts. Whenever a self-locking nut or bolt is disturbed, it must be discarded and a new nut/bolt fitted.*

2 Front hub bearing - checking and adjustment

1 Mercedes-Benz recommend the use of a dial gauge to check the hub endfloat, as a means of checking the bearing adjustment. While this is certainly the method for assuring the maximum accuracy, a competent mechanic will be able to check and adjust the bearing by feel.
2 If the bearing is worn to the extent that the droning noise can be heard inside the car, there is no point trying to 'adjust' the bearing to reduce the noise. Fit a new bearing as described in Section 3.

Without a dial gauge

3 Chock the rear wheels and firmly apply the parking brake. Jack up the front of the car and support it on axle stands (see *Jacking and vehicle support*).
4 Grasp the wheel at the top and bottom, and shake it to assess freeplay **(see illustration)**. Repeat the check with the wheel held on the left and right sides. A very small amount of

2.4 Shake the wheel to assess play in the bearing

play may be noticed, but if the play is excessive, the bearings should be adjusted as described below.
5 If adjustment is required, the wheel must be removed. This will probably entail lowering the car temporarily to loosen the wheel bolts, then raising the car once more.
6 Taking care not to damage the pad friction material or the disc surface, use a large flat-bladed screwdriver to push the brake pads and pistons back into the caliper, away from the disc so that the pads do not drag.
7 Tap or prise the grease cap out from the centre of the hub **(see illustration)**. If the cap is damaged on removal, it must be renewed.
8 Using an Allen key or socket, slacken the hub nut clamp bolt so that the nut is free to turn **(see illustration)**.
9 Rotate the brake disc and at the same time lightly tighten the hub nut until the disc starts to become difficult to turn **(see illustration)**. From this point, slacken the hub nut by approximately one-third of a turn, then tap the end of the hub spindle with a soft-faced mallet to relieve the tension on the bearing.
10 Slacken the hub nut fully, then very lightly tighten it by hand only until resistance is felt. A few attempts may be required, but there should be a clear point at which, without effort, all freeplay is eliminated without loading the bearing. Do not tighten the hub nut using tools, or any tighter than described, as this will quickly destroy it.
11 Tighten the hub nut clamp bolt to the specified torque.

2.7 Tap the grease cap out from the centre of the hub (brake disc removed)

12 Pack the grease cap with fresh grease, and tap it fully back into place **(see illustration)**.
13 Refit the wheel, then lower the car to the ground and tighten the wheel bolts to the specified torque. Depress the brake pedal repeatedly until normal pedal pressure returns.
14 If a new bearing has been fitted, re-check the adjustment within approximately 500 miles.

With a dial gauge

15 Chock the rear wheels and firmly apply the parking brake. Loosen the front wheel bolts, then jack up the front of the car and support it on axle stands (see *Jacking and vehicle support*). Remove the relevant front roadwheel.
16 Using spacers if necessary, refit two of the wheel bolts (to locate the brake disc), positioning them on opposite sides, and tightening them securely.
17 Taking care not to damage the pad friction material or the disc surface, use a large flat-bladed screwdriver to push the brake pads and pistons back into the caliper, away from the disc so that the pads do not drag.
18 Tap the grease cap out from the centre of the hub. If the cap is damaged on removal, it must be renewed.
19 Mount a dial gauge onto the front face of the hub/disc, and position the gauge probe so that it is in contact with the end of the axle

2.8 Unscrew the hub nut clamp bolt using an Allen key

2.9 Turn the hub/disc slowly while lightly tightening the hub nut

2.12 Tap the grease cap back into place, working around the edge

2.19 Using a dial gauge to check the hub bearing endfloat adjustment

3.3 Slacken and remove the hub nut

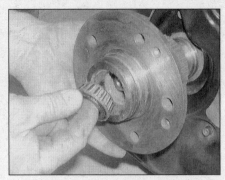

3.4 Remove the hub outer bearing

shaft (see illustration). Zero the gauge scale, then grasp the disc at two opposite points and pull it in and out. Note the reading obtained on the gauge, and check that the hub bearing endfloat is within the limits given in the *Specifications* at the start of this Chapter.

20 If all is well, remove the dial gauge. Pack the grease cap with grease, and tap the cap into position. Remove the wheel bolts and refit the roadwheel, then lower the car to the ground and tighten the wheel bolts to the specified torque. Depress the brake pedal several times until normal, non-assisted pedal pressure returns prior to taking the car on the road.

21 If adjustment is required, use an Allen key to slacken the hub retaining nut clamp bolt until the retaining nut is free to turn.

22 Rotate the brake disc while lightly tightening the hub nut, until the disc starts to become difficult to turn. From this point, slacken the hub nut by approximately one-third of a turn, then tap the end of the hub spindle with a soft-faced mallet to relieve the tension on the bearing.

23 Check the hub bearing endfloat as described in paragraph 19. If necessary adjust the endfloat by rotating the hub nut as required.

24 Recheck the bearing endfloat, then refit all disturbed components as described in paragraph 20.

25 If a new bearing has been fitted, re-check the adjustment within approximately 500 miles.

3 Front hub and bearing - removal, overhaul and refitting

Note: *The hub assembly should not be removed unless the bearings are to be renewed; the hub bearing inner race is a press-fit on the steering knuckle, and removal of the hub will almost certainly damage the bearings. A press will be required to dismantle and rebuild the assembly; if such a tool is not available, a large bench vice and spacers (such as large sockets) will serve as an adequate substitute. The bearing's inner races are an interference fit on the hub; if the inner race remains on the hub when it is pressed out of the hub carrier, a knife-edged bearing puller will be required to remove it.*

Removal

1 Remove the front brake disc, disc shield and ABS sensor as described in Chapter 9.

2 Tap the grease cap out from the centre of the hub. If the cap is damaged on removal, it must be renewed.

3 Slacken the hub nut clamp bolt, then slacken and remove the hub nut from the axle **(see illustration)**. Remove the thrustwasher (where fitted).

4 Take off the hub outer bearing, and place it to one side where it can be kept clean **(see illustration)**.

5 The front hub assembly can now be

withdrawn from the steering knuckle. If the hub assembly is a tight fit on the axle, a puller will be required to draw it off.

6 If the inner bearing race remains on the steering knuckle, a knife-edge type puller will be required to remove it. With the race removed, slide off the hub oil seal.

7 Inspect the steering knuckle axle shaft for signs of damage, and renew if necessary (see Section 4).

Overhaul

8 Remove the inner race from the outer bearing.

9 Where necessary, carefully lever out the oil seal from the rear of the hub assembly and drift out the inner bearing.

10 Support the front of the hub assembly and tap the outer bearing inner race out of position using a hammer and punch passed through the hub.

11 Turn the hub over and remove the inner bearing outer race in the same way **(see illustration)**.

12 Thoroughly clean the hub, removing all traces of dirt and grease, and polish away any burrs or raised edges which might hinder reassembly. Check for cracks or any other signs of wear or damage, and renew if necessary. Ensure that the ABS sensor ring is in good condition.

13 On reassembly, apply a light coating of grease to the bearing outer race and hub contact surfaces. Also work the grease well into the inner bearing tracks.

14 Securely support the hub, and locate the inner bearing outer race in the hub. Press the race fully into position, ensuring that it enters the hub squarely, using a tubular spacer (such as a large socket) which bears only on the outer edge of the race.

15 Turn the hub over and fit the outer bearing inner race in the same way.

16 Fit the inner bearing to the inner race. Fit the oil seal to the rear of the hub, making sure its sealing lip is facing inwards, and press it squarely into position **(see illustration)**.

17 Pack the hub assembly about two-thirds full of grease. The outer bearing is best fitted once the hub assembly has been fitted to the steering knuckle.

3.11 Tap out the inner bearing outer race using a suitable punch

3.16 Tap the rear oil seal squarely into the hub, using a suitable socket

4.4a Unscrew the track rod balljoint nut . . .

4.4b . . . release the balljoint taper using a separator tool . . .

4.4c . . . and remove the track rod end from the steering knuckle

Refitting

18 Apply a smear of grease to the hub rear oil seal lip, and locate the hub assembly onto the steering knuckle shaft.

19 Pack the outer bearing with grease, working it well into the bearing tracks. Fit the outer bearing into position over the steering knuckle pin, and slide it fully into the hub location.

20 Screw on the hub nut. Rotate the hub assembly whilst using the hub nut to press the hub assembly onto the steering knuckle axle. Once the hub assembly is correctly seated, adjust the hub bearing endfloat as described in Section 2 and tighten the hub nut clamp bolt to the specified torque.

21 Pack the grease cap with grease, then tap it squarely into position.

4.5a Unscrew the upper arm balljoint nut . . .

22 Refit the brake disc and shield, and the ABS front wheel sensor, as described in Chapter 9.

| 4 | Front steering knuckle assembly - removal and refitting |

Note: *Refer to the note at the end of Section 1 before proceeding.*

⚠️ *Warning: The shock absorbers must remain in position during removal of the steering knuckle. If the shock absorber is removed once the steering knuckle has been removed, the coil spring pressure will be released uncontrollably, with great risk of personal injury.*

Removal

1 Chock the rear wheels and firmly apply the parking brake. Loosen the front wheel bolts, then jack up the front of the car and support it on axle stands (see *Jacking and vehicle support*). Remove the relevant front roadwheel.

2 If the steering knuckle is to be renewed, remove the hub assembly as described in Section 3. With the hub and brake disc removed, the brake dust shield can also be removed, which greatly improves access for removing the steering knuckle.

3 If the steering knuckle assembly is to be refitted, slacken and remove the two bolts

securing the brake caliper mounting bracket to the knuckle, then slide the caliper assembly off the disc. **Note:** *Discard the caliper bolts, new ones must be used on refitting.* Using a piece of wire or string, tie the caliper to the front suspension coil spring, to avoid placing any strain on the hydraulic brake hose. Also remove the ABS wheel sensor as described in Chapter 9.

4 Slacken and remove the nut securing the track rod balljoint to the steering knuckle, and release the balljoint tapered shank using a universal balljoint separator **(see illustrations)**.

5 Similarly, release the balljoint securing the steering knuckle to the suspension upper arm **(see illustrations)**.

6 Loosen and remove the nut which secures the lower suspension arm supporting joint (right-angled balljoint) to the steering knuckle **(see illustration)**.

7 In theory, it should now be possible to separate the supporting joint from the steering knuckle, so that the steering knuckle can be removed. However, in practice, we found in the workshop that the taper on the supporting joint-to-knuckle connection was so tight that it was simpler to split the supporting joint balljoint from the lower arm, and remove the steering knuckle complete with supporting joint, as described below. If required, the supporting joint can then be driven from the knuckle with the knuckle supported in a sturdy vice.

4.5b . . . release the balljoint taper using a separator tool . . .

4.5c . . . and remove the balljoint from the steering knuckle

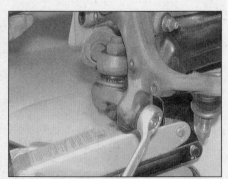

4.6 Unscrew the supporting joint nut

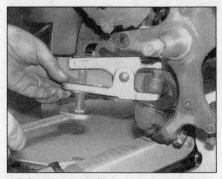

4.8 Loosen the balljoint nut, then separate the balljoint

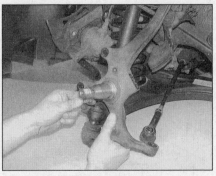

4.9 Take off the balljoint nut, and remove the steering knuckle from the car

4.13a Refit the balljoint to the lower arm . . .

8 Remove the nut which secures the suspension arm supporting joint (right-angled balljoint) to the lower arm. Release the balljoint tapered shank using a universal balljoint separator **(see illustration)**.

9 Remove the steering knuckle from the car **(see illustration)**. Inspect the knuckle for signs of wear or damage, and renew as necessary.

Refitting

10 Prior to refitting, clean the threads of the steering knuckle bolt holes by running a tap of the correct thread size and pitch down them.

 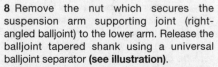

HAYNES HiNT *If a suitable tap is not available, clean out the holes using one of the old bolts with slots cut in its threads.*

11 Thoroughly clean the balljoint tapers and their locating holes, making sure that no lubricant is present, which would prevent the tapers from locking firmly into position. Clean the balljoint threads if necessary, using a wire brush.

12 Check all the balljoint rubbers for signs of damage or perishing. If the rubber has split, this will lead to loss of lubricant and dirt entry, which will destroy the joint. If any balljoints are suspect, take the opportunity to fit new components.

13 If the lower supporting joint was removed with the steering knuckle (and then separated), refit the balljoint to the lower arm, and secure with a new nut, tightening it by hand only at this stage **(see illustrations)**.

14 Engage the knuckle with the lower arm

supporting joint. Fit a new nut and tighten it by hand only at this stage **(see illustration)**.

15 Reconnect the track rod balljoint to the steering knuckle. Fit a new nut and tighten it to the specified torque; press downwards on the track rod end as this is done, to lock the balljoint taper and prevent the threaded section from turning **(see illustrations)**.

16 Locate the upper arm balljoint into the knuckle. Fit a new nut, and tighten it to the specified torque. We found it necessary to lever down the upper arm as this is done, to prevent the threads from turning **(see illustrations)**.

17 Once the upper arm balljoint nut has been tightened, go back and tighten the lower arm supporting joint nuts to the specified torque.

18 On models where the hub was not

4.13b . . . and secure with a new nut - hold the balljoint shank with an Allen key

4.14 Fit the steering knuckle to the lower arm, and fit a new supporting joint nut

4.15a Refit the track rod to the steering knuckle, using a new nut . . .

4.15b . . . and tighten the nut to the specified torque

4.16a Lever down on the upper arm . . .

4.16b . . . while tightening the balljoint nut to the specified torque

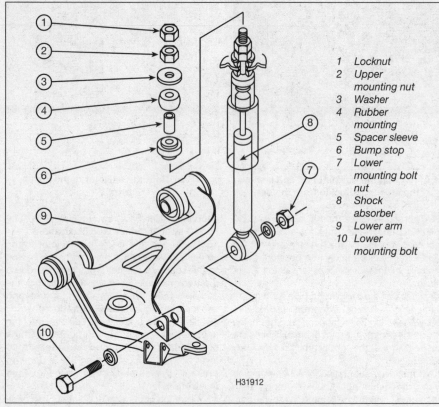

1 Locknut
2 Upper mounting nut
3 Washer
4 Rubber mounting
5 Spacer sleeve
6 Bump stop
7 Lower mounting bolt nut
8 Shock absorber
9 Lower arm
10 Lower mounting bolt

H31912

5.3 Front shock absorber mounting details

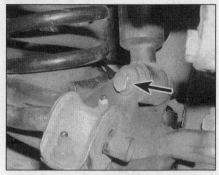

5.4 Front shock absorber lower mounting bolt (arrowed)

disturbed, remove all traces of locking compound and slide the caliper into position over the disc, making sure the pads pass either side of the disc. Fit the new mounting bolts and tighten them to the specified torque setting (see Chapter 9). Also refer to Chapter 9 when refitting the ABS wheel sensor.

19 Where removed, refit the hub assembly as described in Section 3.

20 Refit the roadwheel, then lower the car to the ground and tighten the wheel bolts to the specified torque.

21 Where new parts have been fitted, it is advisable to have the front wheel toe setting ('tracking') checked on completion.

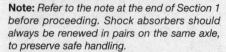

5 Front suspension shock absorber - removal and refitting

Note: *Refer to the note at the end of Section 1 before proceeding. Shock absorbers should always be renewed in pairs on the same axle, to preserve safe handling.*

Removal

1 Chock the rear wheels, and firmly apply the parking brake. Loosen the front wheel bolts, then jack up the front of the car and support it on axle stands (see *Jacking and vehicle support*). Remove the relevant front roadwheel.

2 Slacken and remove the nut from the shock absorber lower mounting bolt on the suspension lower arm. Recover the washer.

3 Retain the shock absorber upper mounting nut with an open-ended spanner, and slacken and remove the locknut. Unscrew the upper mounting nut, taking care to ensure that the shock absorber body/piston rod does not rotate, and lift off the large washer and rubber bush **(see illustration)**.

4 Remove the lower mounting bolt **(see illustration)**, tapping it out with a pin punch if necessary, noting which way round it fits. Recover the washer which fits under the bolt head.

5 Compress the shock absorber a little if necessary, and release it from the lower mounting. When free of the lower mounting, tilt the shock absorber at an angle to release the upper mounting, and remove it from under the car. Take off the dust cover, and recover the spacer sleeve and bump stop from the top of the threaded section, noting how they fit.

6 Examine the shock absorber for signs of fluid leakage. Check the piston for signs of pitting along its entire length, and check the shock body for signs of damage.

7 While holding it in an upright position, test the operation of the shock absorber by moving the piston through a full stroke, and then through short strokes of 50 to 100 mm. In both cases, the resistance felt should be smooth and continuous. If the resistance is

jerky, or uneven, or if there is any visible sign of wear or damage to the shock absorber, renewal is necessary.

8 Inspect all other components for signs of damage or deterioration, and renew any that are suspect.

Refitting

9 If a new shock absorber is being fitted, gently compress and release the unit a few times, to prime it before fitting.

10 Slide the bump stop onto the shock absorber piston, then refit the dust cover and spacer.

11 Manoeuvre the unit into position so that the threaded top section passes through the hole in the inner wing. Engage the lower mounting loosely with the mounting point on the lower arm, and fully insert the lower mounting bolt with its washer.

12 Working from above, fit the rubber bush and large washer, then screw on the first of the two upper mounting nuts, and tighten it by hand only.

13 Fit the new nut and washer to the lower mounting bolt, and tighten it by hand only.

14 Refit the wheel, lower the car to the ground, and tighten the wheel bolts to the specified torque.

15 With the car resting on its wheels, push down on the front wing, then release it. Repeat this a few times, to settle the components.

16 Tighten the shock absorber upper mounting nut to the specified torque, making sure the piston rod does not turn. Fit the new locknut over the first nut, and tighten it to its specified torque, while counter-holding the first nut.

17 Tighten the lower mounting nut to the specified torque, holding the bolt against rotation if necessary.

6 Front suspension coil spring - removal and refitting

Note: *Refer to the note at the end of Section 1 before proceeding. Springs should always be renewed in pairs on the same axle, to preserve safe handling.*

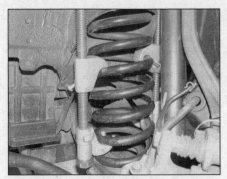

6.2 Spring compressor fitted to front coil spring

7.7a Lower arm front . . .

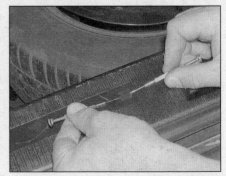

7.7b . . . and rear pivot bolt and nut

Removal

 Warning: A suitable tool to hold the coil spring in compression must be obtained. Adjustable coil spring compressors are readily available, and are recommended for this operation. Any attempt to remove the spring without such a tool is likely to result in damage or personal injury.

1 Chock the rear wheels, and firmly apply the parking brake. Loosen the front wheel bolts, then jack up the front of the car and support it on axle stands (see *Jacking and vehicle support*). Remove the relevant front roadwheel.

2 Fit the spring compressor, and compress the coil spring until all tension is relieved from the spring seats **(see illustration)**.

3 Position a jack and block of wood beneath the lower arm, and raise the jack head until the arm is securely supported.

4 Retain the shock absorber upper mounting nut with an open-ended spanner, and slacken and remove the locknut. Unscrew the upper mounting nut, taking care to ensure that the shock absorber body/piston rod does not rotate, and lift off the large washer and rubber bush.

5 Carefully lower the lower suspension arm until it is possible to the remove the coil spring and upper spring seat. Recover the metal shim from the spring seat, noting how it fits.

6 Inspect the coil spring for signs of wear or damage, and renew if necessary. The upper spring seat should also be renewed if it is damaged or shows signs of deterioration.

Refitting

7 If new springs are required, note that later models were fitted with modified springs - consult your Mercedes-Benz dealer or parts supplier for advice. The springs should always be renewed in pairs in any case.

8 Ensure that the lower arm spring seat is clean, then fit the upper spring seat to the coil spring and manoeuvre the spring into position. Make sure that the metal shim is fitted as noted on removal.

9 Locate the lower end of the spring correctly against the stop on the lower arm seat. Align the upper spring seat with the body mounting

and carefully raise the lower arm whilst also aligning the shock absorber upper mounting with the body.

10 Check that the spring is correctly located, then fit the rubber bush and large washer to the shock absorber upper mounting. Screw on the first of the two upper mounting nuts, and tighten it by hand only.

11 Remove the jack from beneath the lower arm then carefully release the spring compressor, whilst making sure both its upper and lower ends are correctly located.

12 Refit the roadwheel, then lower the car to the ground and tighten the wheel bolts to the specified torque.

13 With the car resting on its wheels, first tighten the shock absorber upper mounting nut to the specified torque. Fit the new locknut over the first nut, and tighten it to its specified torque, while counter-holding the first nut.

7 Front suspension lower arm - removal, overhaul and refitting

Note: *Refer to the note at the end of Section 1 before proceeding.*

Removal

1 Chock the rear wheels, and firmly apply the parking brake. Loosen the front wheel bolts, then jack up the front of the car and support it on axle stands (see *Jacking and vehicle support*). Remove the relevant front roadwheel.

2 Slacken and remove the retaining nuts securing the anti-roll bar mounting clamp to the front of the lower arm, and remove the mounting rubber.

3 Remove the spring as described in Section 6.

4 Unscrew the nut (and recover the washer) from the shock absorber lower mounting bolt. Remove the lower mounting bolt, tapping it out with a pin punch if necessary, and noting which way round it fits. Recover the washer which fits under the bolt head.

5 Compress the shock absorber a little if necessary, and release it from the lower mounting. When free of the lower mounting,

tilt the shock absorber at an angle to release the upper mounting, and remove it from under the car. Recover the spacer sleeve and upper mounting bush from the top of the threaded section, noting how they fit.

6 Remove the nut which secures the supporting joint (right-angled balljoint) to the lower arm. Release the balljoint tapered shank using a universal balljoint separator.

7 Slacken and remove the lower arm pivot bolt nuts, and remove the bolts and washers, noting which way around the bolts are inserted **(see illustrations)**. The lower arm can then be removed from underneath the car.

Overhaul

8 Thoroughly clean the lower arm and the area around the arm mountings, removing all traces of dirt and underseal if necessary. Check carefully for cracks, distortion or any other signs of wear or damage, paying particular attention to the mounting bushes.

9 In theory, the lower arm can be mounted in a large vice (with protected jaws), and the bushes pressed or driven out using a suitable drift. The new bushes, lubricated with a little liquid soap (or washing-up liquid) can then be pressed or drawn in using a long bolt and several large washers and spacers.

10 In practice, if either bush requires renewal, it may be best to take the lower arm to a Mercedes-Benz dealer or suitably-equipped garage. Mercedes-Benz do not actually state that a press is required, but on a car which has covered many miles, removing the old bushes may be extremely difficult without appropriate tools.

11 Inspect the supporting joint (double balljoint) for signs of wear, and for damage to the balljoint gaiters. If necessary, unscrew the remaining balljoint nut and separate the joint from the arm using a balljoint separator.

12 Thoroughly clean the balljoint tapers and their locating holes, making sure that no lubricant is present, which would prevent the tapers from locking firmly into position. Clean the balljoint threads if necessary, using a wire brush.

13 Check the threads on the pivot bolts, and clean using a wire brush if necessary.

8.2a Using a balljoint separator tool . . .

8.2b . . . release the upper arm balljoint

Refitting

14 Offer up the lower arm, and insert the front and rear pivot bolts and washers. Fit the new nuts, tightening them lightly only at this stage.

15 Reconnect the lower arm balljoint (supporting joint), and secure with a new balljoint nut, tightened to the specified torque.

16 Make sure that the spacer sleeve and upper bush are fitted to the top of the shock absorber, then manoeuvre the unit into position so that the threaded top section passes through the hole in the inner wing. Engage the lower mounting loosely with the mounting point on the lower arm, and fully insert the lower mounting bolt with its washer.

17 Working from above, fit the shock absorber rubber bush and large washer, then screw on the first of the two upper mounting nuts, and tighten it by hand only.

18 Fit the new nut and washer to the shock absorber lower mounting bolt, and tighten it by hand only.

19 Refit the spring as described in Section 6.

20 Slide the rubber mounting onto the end of the anti-roll bar and locate it in the lower arm clamp. Fit the mounting clamp, then screw on the new nuts and tighten them to the specified torque.

21 Refit the roadwheel, then lower the car to the ground and tighten the wheel bolts to the specified torque.

22 With the car resting on its wheels, rock it to settle the lower arm in position.

23 Tighten the shock absorber upper mounting nut to the specified torque. Fit the new locknut over the first nut, and tighten it to its specified torque, while counter-holding the first nut. Tighten the lower mounting nut to the specified torque, holding the bolt against rotation if necessary.

24 Tighten the lower arm pivot nuts to the specified torque, holding the bolts against rotation if necessary.

Note: *It is recommended that the front steering angles (camber and castor) and wheel alignment (toe-in, or 'tracking') are checked at the earliest possible opportunity by a Mercedes-Benz dealer or other suitably-equipped garage.*

8 Front suspension upper arm - removal and refitting

Note: *Refer to the note at the end of Section 1 before proceeding. The shock absorbers must remain in position during removal of the upper arm.*

Removal

1 Chock the rear wheels, and firmly apply the parking brake. Loosen the front wheel bolts, then jack up the front of the car and support it on axle stands (see *Jacking and vehicle support*). Remove the relevant front roadwheel.

2 Unscrew and remove the nut from the upper arm balljoint at the top of the steering

knuckle, then release the balljoint tapered shank using a universal balljoint separator **(see illustrations)**.

3 Using wire or a cable-tie, secure the steering knuckle to the shock absorber, to prevent it from tilting outwards. Make sure that the wiring and brake hose are not strained.

4 Working in the engine compartment, unscrew and remove the nut from the upper arm pivot bolt, holding the bolt against rotation if necessary. The nut and bolt are not easy to get to, and depending on which side is being worked on, it may be necessary to unbolt the washer bottle or expansion tank (where fitted) for improved access **(see illustration)**.

5 Withdraw the pivot bolt, and remove the upper arm from the car.

6 Check the arm for signs of damage, distortion or cracking. If any damage is noted, a new arm should be fitted - no parts are available separately.

7 Check the threads on the pivot bolt, and clean using a wire brush if necessary.

8 Inspect the balljoint for signs of wear, and for damage to the balljoint gaiter. If the balljoint is worn, or the gaiter damaged, a new arm will be needed, but check with your Mercedes-Benz dealer or parts supplier first.

9 Thoroughly clean the balljoint taper and its locating hole in the top of the steering knuckle, making sure that no lubricant is present, which would prevent the taper from locking firmly into position. Clean the balljoint threads if necessary, using a wire brush.

Refitting

10 Offer the arm into position, and insert the pivot bolt. Fit a new nut, and tighten by hand only at this stage.

11 Remove the wire or cable-tie securing the steering knuckle to the shock absorber, then engage the upper arm balljoint with the top of the steering knuckle. Fit a new balljoint nut, and tighten it to the specified torque. We found it necessary to lever down the upper arm as this is done, to prevent the threads from turning **(see illustration)**.

12 Refit the roadwheel, and lower the car to the ground. Tighten the wheel bolts to the specified torque.

13 With the car now resting on its wheels, rock it to settle the upper arm into position.

14 Tighten the pivot bolt nut to the specified torque, holding the bolt against rotation if necessary.

9 Front suspension anti-roll bar - removal and refitting

Note: *Refer to the note at the end of Section 1 before proceeding.*

Removal

1 Chock the rear wheels, and firmly apply the parking brake. Loosen the front wheel bolts,

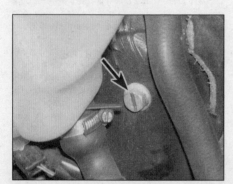

8.4 Front suspension upper arm pivot bolt (arrowed)

8.11 If necessary, lever down on the upper arm as the balljoint nut is tightened

9.3 Release the anti-roll bar clamp on the suspension lower arm . . .

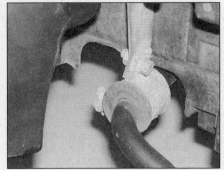

9.4 . . . and on the body brackets

9.8 Renewing an anti-roll bar mounting rubber

then jack up the front of the car and support it on axle stands (see *Jacking and vehicle support*). Remove both the front roadwheels.

2 Make alignment marks between the mounting bushes and anti-roll bar.

3 Unscrew the retaining nuts and remove the mounting clamps securing the anti-roll bar to the suspension lower arms **(see illustration)**.

4 Slacken and remove the nuts and bolts securing the mounting clamps to the body brackets, and remove the clamps **(see illustration)**.

5 Free the anti-roll bar and manoeuvre it out from underneath the car. If necessary, the mounting brackets can then be unbolted and removed from the vehicle body.

6 Inspect the mounting rubbers for signs of damage or deterioration, and renew as necessary.

Refitting

7 Where necessary, refit the anti-roll bar mounting brackets to the vehicle body and tighten the retaining bolts to the specified torque.

8 Lubricate the mounting bushes with soapy water (or washing-up liquid) and slide them into position **(see illustration)**.

9 Align the mounting rubbers with the marks made prior to removal, and manoeuvre the anti-roll bar into position.

10 Engage the mounting rubbers with the body brackets, and refit the mounting clamps. Insert the clamp bolts and fit the new nuts, tightening them lightly only.

11 Locate the outer mounting rubbers in the lower arm brackets, then fit the mounting clamps and screw on the new clamp nuts.

12 Ensure that the marks made prior to removal are correctly aligned, then tighten all the clamp nuts to the specified torque setting.

13 Fit the roadwheels, then lower the car to the ground and tighten the wheel bolts to the specified torque.

10 Rear hub carrier - removal and refitting

Note: *Refer to the note at the end of Section 1 before proceeding.*

Removal

1 Remove the wheel trim or hub cap, then using a hammer and pointed-nose chisel, carefully relieve the driveshaft retaining nut staking (where applicable).

2 Slacken the driveshaft retaining nut with the car resting on its wheels. Note that this nut is extremely tight - ensure that the tools used to loosen it are of good quality, and a good fit. Do not remove the nut at this stage.

3 Chock the front wheels, and loosen the rear wheel bolts. Jack up the rear of the car and support it on axle stands (see *Jacking and vehicle support*). Remove the relevant rear roadwheel.

4 With reference to Chapter 9 , carry out the following:
  a) *Unbolt the brake caliper and suspend it out of the way.*
  b) *Remove the brake disc.*
  c) *Unhook the relevant rear parking brake cable from the equaliser bracket.*

5 Undo the retaining screws and unclip the protective cover from the base of the suspension lower arm.

6 Position a jack and block of wood underneath the lower arm, and raise the jack until it is supporting the weight of the arm.

7 Slacken and remove the nut and pivot bolt securing the lower arm to the hub carrier.

8 Support the hub carrier assembly, then slacken and remove the nuts and pivot bolts securing the upper and lower control arms to the hub carrier, with reference to Section 14 **(see illustration)**. **Note:** *To preserve the rear wheel alignment settings, mark the position of the eccentric screw and cam, before removing the upper and lower control arms.*

9 Remove the driveshaft retaining nut completely, and withdraw the hub assembly from the end of the driveshaft joint. If necessary, tap the joint out of the hub using a soft-faced mallet. If this fails to free it from the hub, the joint will have to be pressed out using a suitable tool which is bolted to the hub.

10 Remove the hub assembly and support the driveshaft by hanging it from the vehicle underbody using a piece of wire. **Note:** *Do not allow the driveshaft to hang under its own weight, as the CV joint may be damaged.*

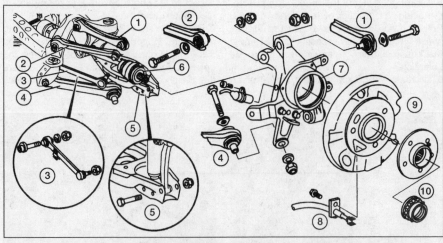

10.8 Rear suspension and hub carrier details

1	Camber control arm	5	Lower arm	8	Parking brake cable
2	Torque control arm	6	Driveshaft	9	Disc splash shield
3	Track control arm	7	Hub carrier	10	Driveshaft nut
4	Thrust control arm				

10.14 Lubricate the new driveshaft nut before fitting it

Refitting

11 Manoeuvre the hub assembly into position, and engage it with the driveshaft joint.

12 Align the hub assembly with the control arms and (where necessary) insert the pivot bolts. Fit a new nut to each of the pivot bolts and the balljoint, tightening them lightly only at this stage.

13 Insert the lower arm pivot bolt and fit the new retaining nut, tightening it lightly only. **Note:** *To preserve the rear wheel alignment, observe the alignment markings made on the control arm eccentric screw and cam. If no marks were made during removal, position the screw at the centre of its range of adjustment.*

14 Lubricate the threads of the new driveshaft nut with clean engine oil, and screw the nut onto the driveshaft end **(see illustration)**. Lightly tighten the nut at this stage - it is safer to tighten and stake the nut once the car is resting on its wheels.

15 Refit the brake disc and caliper, and reconnect the parking brake cable, as described in Chapter 9.

16 Refit the protective cover to the lower arm, and securely tighten its retaining screws.

17 Refit the roadwheel, then lower the car to the ground and tighten the wheel bolts to the specified torque.

18 With the car resting on its wheels, rock it to settle the hub carrier in position, then tighten the control arm and lower arm outer pivot bolt/balljoint nuts to their specified torque settings.

19 Tighten the driveshaft retaining nut to the specified torque (see Chapter 8 Specifications) and stake it firmly into the driveshaft groove using a hammer and punch.

Note: *It is recommended that the rear wheel alignment is checked at the earliest possible opportunity by a Mercedes-Benz dealer or other suitably-equipped garage.*

11 Rear hub bearing - renewal

Note: *A press and suitable tubular spacers will be required to dismantle and rebuild the assembly; if such a tool is not available, a large bench vice and spacers (such as large sockets) will serve as an adequate substitute. The bearing's inner races are an interference fit on the hub flange; if the inner race remains on the hub flange when it is pressed out of position, a knife-edged bearing puller will be required to remove it.*

1 Remove the rear hub carrier as described in Section 10.

2 Securely support the hub carrier and carefully press the hub flange out from the centre of the bearing. If the bearing inner race remains on the flange, remove it with a knife-edge bearing puller.

3 Remove the hub bearing retaining circlip from the hub carrier.

4 Support the hub carrier, and press the hub bearing out of position using a suitable tubular spacer.

5 Thoroughly clean the hub carrier bore, removing all traces of dirt and grease. Polish away any burrs or raised edges which might hinder reassembly. Renew the circlip if there is any doubt about its condition.

6 On reassembly, apply a light film of clean

engine oil to the bearing outer race, to aid installation.

7 Locate the bearing in the hub carrier and press it fully into position, ensuring that it enters the carrier squarely, using a suitable tubular spacer which bears only on the bearing outer race.

8 Secure the bearing in position with the circlip, making sure it is correctly located in the hub carrier groove.

9 Securely support the bearing inner race, and press the hub flange fully into the bearing.

10 Check the bearing rotates freely, then refit the rear hub carrier as described in Section 10.

12 Rear suspension shock absorber - removal, testing and refitting

Note: *Refer to the note at the end of Section 1 before proceeding. Shock absorbers should always be renewed in pairs on the same axle, to preserve safe handling.*

Removal

1 Chock the front wheels, and loosen the rear wheel bolts. Jack up the rear of the car and support it on axle stands (see *Jacking and vehicle support*). To improve access, remove the rear roadwheel.

2 Undo the retaining screws and unclip the protective cover from the base of the suspension lower arm **(see illustrations)**.

3 Position a jack and block of wood underneath the lower arm, and raise the jack until it is supporting the weight of the arm.

4 Remove the luggage compartment side trim panel (see Chapter 11, Section 41) to gain access to the shock absorber upper mounting **(see illustration)**.

5 Retain the shock absorber upper mounting nut with an open-ended spanner, then slacken and remove the locknut. Unscrew the upper mounting nut, taking care to ensure that the shock absorber body/piston rod does

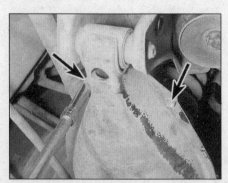

12.2a Undo the retaining screws (arrowed) . . .

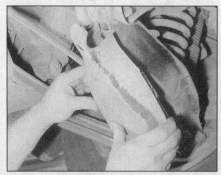

12.2b . . . and remove the protective cover from the base of the lower arm

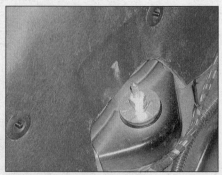

12.4 Rear shock absorber upper mounting (Estate model shown)

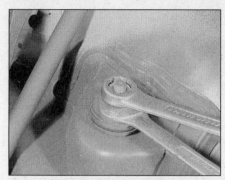

12.5a Remove the two nuts . . .

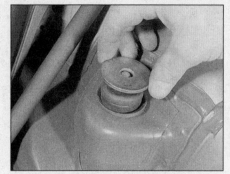

12.5b . . . the washer . . .

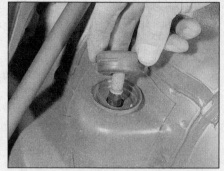

12.5c . . . and then the rubber mounting

not rotate, and lift off the large washer and rubber bush **(see illustrations)**.

 Warning: Do not attempt to remove the shock absorber upper mounting nuts unless the lower arm is securely supported by the jack.

6 From underneath the car, slacken and remove the shock absorber lower mounting bolt nut **(see illustration)**, and withdraw the bolt and washers.

7 Carefully lower the suspension arm slightly, then manoeuvre the shock absorber out from underneath the wheelarch. Take off the dust cover, and recover the spacer sleeve and bump stop from the top of the shock absorber **(see illustration)**.

Testing

8 Examine the shock absorber for signs of fluid leakage. Check the piston for signs of pitting along its entire length, and check the body for signs of damage.

9 While holding it in an upright position, test the operation of the shock absorber by moving the piston through a full stroke, and then through short strokes of 50 to 100 mm. In both cases, the resistance felt should be smooth and continuous. If the resistance is jerky, or uneven, or if there is any visible sign of wear or damage, renewal is necessary.

10 Inspect all other components for signs of damage or deterioration, and renew any that are suspect.

Refitting

11 If a new shock absorber is being fitted, gently compress and release the unit a few times, to prime it before fitting.

12 Slide the bump stop onto the shock absorber piston, then refit the dust cover and spacer.

13 Manoeuvre the unit into position so that the threaded top section passes through the hole at the top of the wheelarch. Raise the lower arm slightly if necessary, and engage the lower mounting loosely with the mounting point on the lower arm; fully insert the lower mounting bolt with its washer.

14 Working from above, fit the rubber bush and large washer, then screw on the first of

the two upper mounting nuts, and tighten it by hand only.

15 Fit the new nut and washer to the lower mounting bolt, and tighten it by hand only.

16 Refit the roadwheel, then lower the car to the ground and tighten the wheel bolts to the specified torque.

17 With the car resting on its wheels, push down on the front wing, then release it. Repeat this a few times, to settle the components.

18 Tighten the shock absorber upper mounting nut to the specified torque, making sure the piston rod does not turn. Fit the new locknut over the first nut, and tighten it to its specified torque, while counter-holding the first nut.

19 Refit the luggage compartment trim panel.

20 Tighten the lower mounting nut to the specified torque, holding the bolt against rotation if necessary.

21 Refit the protective cover to the lower arm, and securely tighten its retaining screws.

13 Rear suspension coil spring - removal and refitting

 Warning: A suitable tool to hold the coil spring in compression must be obtained. Adjustable coil spring compressors are readily-available, and are recommended for this operation. Any attempt to remove the spring without such a tool is likely to result in damage or personal injury.

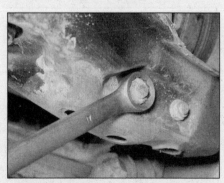

12.6 Unscrew the nut and withdraw the shock absorber lower mounting bolt

Note: *Refer to the note at the end of Section 1 before proceeding.*

Removal

1 Chock the front wheels, and loosen the rear wheel bolts. Jack up the rear of the car and support it on axle stands (see *Jacking and vehicle support*). Remove the relevant rear roadwheel.

2 Fit the spring compressor, and compress the coil spring until all tension is relieved from the spring seats.

3 Undo the retaining screws and remove the protective cover from the base of the lower suspension arm.

4 Position a jack and block of wood beneath the arm, and raise the jack head until the arm is securely supported.

5 Slacken and remove the nut, and withdraw the pivot bolt securing the lower suspension arm to the rear subframe. Also slacken and remove the nut and bolt securing the anti-roll bar connecting link to the lower arm.

6 Carefully lower the lower suspension arm until it is possible to remove the coil spring and upper spring seat.

7 Inspect the coil spring for signs of wear or damage, and renew if necessary. The upper spring seat should also be renewed if it is damaged or shows signs of deterioration.

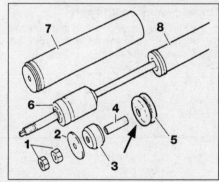

12.7 Rear shock absorber upper mounting components

1	Locknut and mounting nut	4	Spacer
2	Washer	5	Mounting rubber
3	Mounting rubber	6	Bump stop
		7	Dust cover
		8	Shock absorber

Refitting

8 Ensure that the lower arm spring seat is clean, then fit the upper spring seat to the coil spring and manoeuvre the spring into position.
9 Locate the lower end of the spring correctly against the stop on the lower arm seat. Align the upper spring seat with the body mounting, and carefully raise the lower arm whilst also aligning it with the subframe.
10 Check that the spring is correctly located, then insert the lower arm pivot bolt. Fit a new nut to the pivot bolt, tightening it lightly only at this stage. Refit the anti-roll bar connecting link bolt, and tighten the new retaining nut to the specified torque.
11 Remove the jack from beneath the lower arm, then carefully release the spring compressor whilst making sure both its upper and lower ends are correctly located.
12 Refit the roadwheel, then lower the car to the ground and tighten the wheel bolts to the specified torque.
13 With the car resting on its wheels, rock it to settle the spring and lower arm in position.
14 Tighten the lower arm pivot bolt nut to the specified torque setting.
15 Refit the protective cover to the lower arm, and securely tighten its retaining screws.

14 Rear suspension control arms - removal and refitting

Note: *Refer to the note at the end of Section 1 before proceeding.*

Removal

Note: *If more than one control arm is to be removed at the same time, support the lower arm with a jack and block of wood.*
1 Chock the front wheels, and loosen the rear wheel bolts. Jack up the rear of the car and support it on axle stands (see *Jacking and vehicle support*). Remove the relevant rear roadwheel.

Upper camber control arm

2 Slacken and remove the nut, and withdraw the pivot bolt securing the arm to the hub carrier **(see illustration)**.

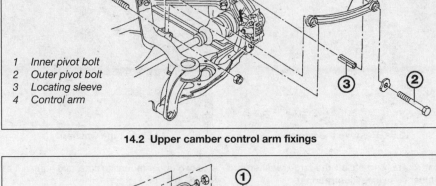

1 Inner pivot bolt
2 Outer pivot bolt
3 Locating sleeve
4 Control arm

14.2 Upper camber control arm fixings

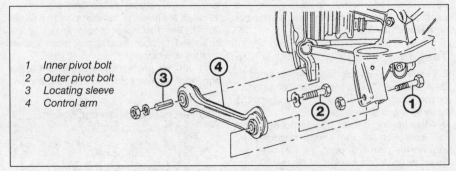

1 Inner pivot bolt
2 Outer pivot bolt
3 Control arm

14.5 Upper torque control arm fixings

1 Inner pivot bolt
2 Outer pivot bolt
3 Locating sleeve
4 Control arm

14.6 Lower thrust control arm fixings

3 Slacken and remove the nut and pivot bolt securing the control arm to the subframe, and remove the arm from the car. If necessary, tap out the locating sleeve from the control arm hub carrier bush.
4 Inspect the control arm for signs of damage, paying particular attention to the rubber bushes, and renew if necessary. Also renew the pivot bolts if they show signs of wear.

Upper torque control arm

5 Remove the arm as described in paragraphs 2 to 4, ignoring the remark about the locating sleeve **(see illustration)**.

Lower thrust control arm

6 Remove the arm as described in paragraphs 2 to 4 **(see illustration)**.

Lower track control arm

7 Prior to removal, make alignment marks between the arm inner pivot bolt, the eccentric washers and the subframe. This will be necessary to ensure that the rear wheel toe setting remains correct on refitting.
8 Slacken and remove the nut and eccentric washer, and withdraw the pivot bolt securing the arm to the subframe **(see illustration)**.
9 Unscrew the nut from the balljoint shank,

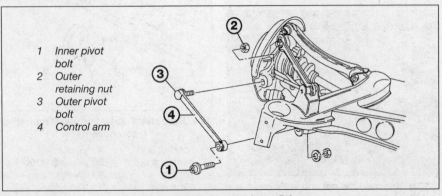

1 Inner pivot bolt
2 Outer retaining nut
3 Outer pivot bolt
4 Control arm

14.8 Lower track control arm fixings

then free the balljoint from the hub carrier and remove the arm from the car. If necessary, use a balljoint separator to free the balljoint shank from the carrier.

10 Inspect the control mounting bush for signs of damage or deterioration. Also check that the balljoint is free to move easily, and that its gaiter is undamaged. Renew the control arm if necessary.

Refitting

Upper camber control arm

11 Where necessary, tap the locating sleeve back into position in the arm hub carrier bush.
12 Locate the arm in position and insert the pivot bolts. Fit the new nuts to the pivot bolts, tightening them lightly only at this stage.
13 Refit the rear roadwheel, then lower the car to ground and tighten the wheel bolts to the specified torque.
14 With the car resting on its wheels, rock it to settle the control arm in position, then tighten both pivot bolt nuts to the specified torque setting.

Upper torque control arm

15 Refit the arm as described in paragraphs 11 to 14.

Lower thrust control arm

16 Refit the arm as described in paragraphs 11 to 14.

Lower track control arm

17 Manoeuvre the arm into position, then insert the inner pivot bolt, eccentric washer and fit the new retaining nut. Align the marks made prior to removal and lightly tighten the nut.
18 Fit the new retaining nut to the balljoint shank, and tighten it to the specified torque setting.
19 Refit the rear roadwheel then lower the car to ground and tighten the wheel bolts to the specified torque.
20 With the car resting on its wheels, rock it to settle the control arm in position.
21 Check that the marks on the subframe, pivot bolt and eccentric washer are still correctly aligned, then tighten the pivot bolt nut to the specified torque setting.
Note: *It is recommended that the rear wheel alignment is checked at the earliest possible opportunity.*

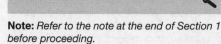

15 Rear suspension lower arm - removal, overhaul and refitting

Note: *Refer to the note at the end of Section 1 before proceeding.*

Removal

1 Chock the front wheels, and loosen the rear wheel bolts. Jack up the rear of the car and support it on axle stands (see *Jacking and vehicle support*). Remove the relevant rear roadwheel.

15.4 Unscrew the retaining nut and bolt and detach the anti-roll bar connecting link from the lower arm

2 Undo the retaining screws/clips and remove the protective cover from the base of the lower arm.
3 Fit a spring compressor to the coil spring, and compress the spring to relieve the tension from its upper and lower seats (see Section 13).
4 Slacken and remove the nut and bolt securing the anti-roll bar connecting link to the lower arm **(see illustration)**.
5 Position a jack (with a block if required) beneath the lower arm, and raise the jack until it is supporting the weight of the arm.
6 Slacken and remove the shock absorber lower mounting bolt nut, and withdraw the bolt and washers.
7 Unscrew the nut from the lower arm outer pivot bolt and withdraw the bolt. Carefully lower the arm slightly until it is possible to withdraw the coil spring and spring seat **(see illustrations)**.
8 Unscrew the nut, then withdraw the inner pivot bolt and washers and remove the lower arm from underneath the car **(see illustration)**.

Overhaul

9 Thoroughly clean the lower arm and the area around the arm mountings, removing all traces of dirt and underseal.
10 Check carefully for cracks, distortion or any other signs of wear or damage, paying particular attention to the mounting bushes. If either bush requires renewal, the lower arm

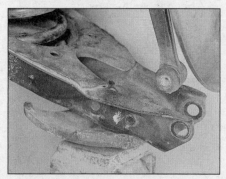

15.7b Carefully lower the arm using the jack, until it is possible to withdraw the coil spring and spring seat

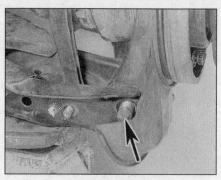

15.7a Remove the lower arm outer pivot bolt (arrowed)

should be taken to a Mercedes-Benz dealer or suitably-equipped garage. A hydraulic press and suitable spacers are required to press the bushes out of position and install the new ones.

Refitting

11 Offer up the lower arm, and insert the inner pivot bolt and washers. Fit the new nut to the bolt, tightening it lightly only at this stage.
12 Ensure that the lower arm spring seat is clean, then fit the upper spring seat to the coil spring and manoeuvre the spring into position.
13 Locate the lower end of the spring correctly against the stop on the lower arm seat. Align the upper spring seat with the body mounting, and carefully raise the lower arm whilst also aligning it with the hub carrier, anti-roll bar link and the shock absorber.
14 Check that the coil spring is correctly located, then insert the lower arm outer pivot bolt. Fit the new retaining nut to the bolt, tightening it lightly only at this stage.
15 Align the lower end of the shock absorber with the arm, and insert the mounting bolt. Fit a new nut to the bolt, tightening it lightly only at this stage.
16 Insert the anti-roll bar connecting link bolt, then fit the new retaining nut and tighten lightly.
17 Refit the rear roadwheel, then lower the car to ground and tighten the wheel bolts to the specified torque.

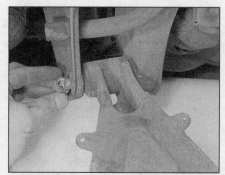

15.8 Unscrew the nut, withdraw the inner pivot bolt and washers and remove the lower arm from underneath the vehicle

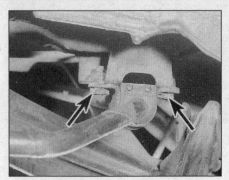

16.3 Rear anti-roll-to-body mounting clamp bolts (arrowed)

18.4 Disconnect the wiring around the steering wheel

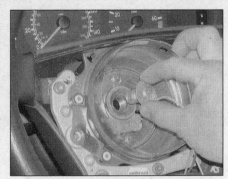

18.5 Removing the steering wheel retaining bolt

18 With the car resting on its wheels, rock it to settle all disturbed components in position.
19 Tighten the lower arm pivot bolts, shock absorber lower mounting nut and the anti-roll bar connecting link bolt to their specified torque settings.
20 Refit the protective cover to the lower arm, and securely tighten its retaining screws.

16 Rear suspension anti-roll bar - removal and refitting

Note: *Refer to the note at the end of Section 1 before proceeding.*

Removal

1 Chock the front wheels, and loosen the rear wheel bolts. Jack up the rear of the car and support it on axle stands (see *Jacking and vehicle support*). To improve access, remove the rear roadwheels.
2 Slacken and remove the nut securing each connecting link to the anti-roll bar.
3 Make alignment marks between the mounting bushes and anti-roll bar, then slacken the two anti-roll bar mounting clamp retaining bolts and remove the clamps **(see illustration)**. Remove the rubber mountings from the anti-roll bar, noting which way around they are fitted. Try and manoeuvre the anti-roll bar out of position from underneath the car, noting that it is likely that the following work will be required to gain the necessary clearance to remove the bar.
4 Referring to Chapter 8, disconnect the propeller shaft from the final drive unit, and slacken the propeller shaft centre bearing bolts so the shaft assembly is free to move.
5 Securely support the weight of the rear subframe assembly on a jack, with a block of wood positioned on its head, positioned underneath the final drive unit.
6 Ensure that the subframe assembly is securely supported, then slacken and remove the mounting bolts and washers securing the subframe to the vehicle body. Carefully lower the subframe assembly slightly until it is possible to withdraw the anti-roll bar from underneath the car. **Note:** *Take great care not*

to place any strain on the rear sensor wiring as the assembly is lowered. If necessary, unbolt the sensor(s) from the final drive unit or disconnect the sensor wiring inside the luggage area (see Chapter 9).

Refitting

7 Manoeuvre the anti-roll bar into position, and engage it with the connecting links.
8 Where necessary, raise the subframe assembly back into position, then fit the new mounting bolts and washers and tighten them to the specified torque. Reconnect the propeller shaft to the final drive unit, and tighten the centre mounting bolts as described in Chapter 8.
9 Fit the mounting rubbers to the anti-roll bar, positioning them so their splits are facing forwards, and align them with the marks made prior to removal. Locate the flat of each rubber against the vehicle body, then refit the mounting clamps and screw in the new clamp bolts.
10 Fit the new nuts to the connecting links, tighten them to the specified torque setting, then tighten the mounting clamp bolts to the specified torque setting.
11 Refit the rear roadwheels, then lower the car to the ground and tighten the wheel bolts to the specified torque settings.

17 Rear suspension anti-roll bar connecting link - removal and refitting

Note: *Refer to the note at the end of Section 1 before proceeding.*

Removal

1 Chock the front wheels, and loosen the rear wheel bolts. Jack up the rear of the car and support it on axle stands (see *Jacking and vehicle support*). Remove the relevant rear roadwheel.
2 Undo the retaining screws and remove the protective cover from the base of the lower arm.
3 Slacken and remove the nut securing the connecting link to the anti-roll bar.

4 Unscrew the nut and bolt securing the connecting link to the lower arm and remove it from the car. Inspect the connecting link for signs of wear or damage, and renew if necessary.

Refitting

5 Manoeuvre the connecting link into position, and fit the connecting link lower retaining bolt.
6 Fit a new nut to the connecting link stud, tighten it to the specified torque, then fit the new nut to the lower retaining bolt and tighten it to the specified torque.
7 Refit the protective cover to the lower arm, and securely tighten its retaining screws.
8 Refit the roadwheel, then lower the car to the ground and tighten the wheel bolts to the specified torque.

18 Steering wheel - removal and refitting

Note: *Refer to the note at the end of Section 1 before proceeding.*

Removal

1 Set the front wheels in the straight-ahead position, and remove the ignition key. Push the steering column fully inwards.
2 Disconnect the battery earth lead, and position the lead away from the terminal.
3 Remove the airbag unit from the centre of the steering wheel as described in Chapter 12.
4 Disconnect the wiring for the horn contacts, airbag contact unit, and steering angle sensor (models with Electronic Stability Program - ESP). Note the position of all the wiring plugs, or label them to aid refitting **(see illustration)**.
5 Slacken and remove the steering wheel retaining bolt **(see illustration)**.
6 If marks do not already exist, mark the steering wheel and steering column shaft in relation to each other, then lift the steering wheel off the column splines. If it is tight, tap it up near the centre, using the palm of your hand, or twist it from side-to-side, whilst

18.6 Release the steering wheel from its splines, and remove it

19.5 Removing the column upper trim

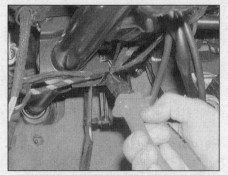

19.8 Cut through the cable-ties as necessary to release the wiring harness from the column

pulling upwards to release it from the shaft splines **(see illustration)**.

 Do not fully unscrew the steering wheel retaining bolt so the wheel will not fly off when it comes free.

Refitting

7 Refitting is the reverse of removal, noting the following points:

a) *If the contact unit has been rotated with the wheel removed, centralise it by pressing down on the contact unit and gently rotating its centre fully anti-clockwise. From this position, rotate the centre back through three complete rotations in a clockwise direction.*

b) *Coat the steering wheel horn contact ring with a smear of petroleum jelly and refit the wheel, making sure the contact unit wiring is correctly routed.*

c) *Ensure that the locating peg at the top of the steering column engages correctly with the recess in the contact unit, as the steering wheel is refitted.*

d) *Engage the wheel with the column splines, aligning the marks made on removal, and tighten the steering wheel retaining bolt to the specified torque setting.*

e) *Reconnect the wiring using the notes made on dismantling.*

f) *Refit the airbag unit as described in Chapter 12.*

g) *If the ESP warning light flashes when the ignition is switched on, turn the steering wheel fully from lock-to-lock. This should reset the steering wheel sensor, and extinguish the warning light.*

19 Steering column - removal, inspection and refitting

Removal

Note: *Refer to the note at the end of Section 1 before proceeding.*

1 Disconnect the battery earth lead, and position the lead away from the terminal.

2 Remove the steering wheel as described in Section 18.

3 Take off the airbag wiring contact unit with reference to Chapter 12.

4 Remove the steering lock as described in Section 20.

5 Remove the steering column combination switches as described in Chapter 12, and lift off the steering column upper trim **(see illustration)**.

6 Remove the instrument panel with reference to Chapter 12.

7 Working in the engine compartment, using paint or a suitable marker pen, make alignment marks between the lower end of the

steering column and the coupling. Note that on some models it will be necessary to unbolt the steering box heatshield(s) to gain access to the coupling.

8 Release the wiring harness from the steering column, noting that it may be necessary to cut through some of the cable-ties used **(see illustration)**.

9 Slacken and remove the socket-headed clamp bolt securing the coupling to the steering column shaft **(see illustration)**.

10 Slacken and remove the steering column upper mounting bolts (which are accessed through the instrument panel aperture) and the lower mounting nuts (at the base of the column, above the foot pedals) **(see illustration)**.

11 Free the steering column gaiter bush from the bulkhead, and carefully pull the column and shaft into the car, separating the shaft and the lower coupling **(see illustration)**. Do not use excessive force, or the lower section of the shaft may be damaged.

12 As the column separates, take care that the lower mounting bush and thrustwasher do not fall out. Note their fitted positions in case they fall out at a later stage.

Inspection

13 The steering column incorporates a telescopic safety feature. In the event of a front-end crash, the lower section of the shaft collapses and prevents the steering wheel injuring the driver. Before refitting the steering

19.9 Unscrewing the column shaft clamp bolt

19.10 Remove the column upper mounting bolts (arrowed)

19.11 Removing the steering column (seen with facia panel removed)

column, examine the column and mountings for signs of damage and deformation, and renew as necessary.

14 Check the steering shaft for signs of free play in the column bushes. If any damage or wear is found on the steering column bushes, the column should be overhauled. Overhaul of the column is a complex task requiring several special tools, and should be entrusted to a Mercedes-Benz dealer.

Refitting

15 Prior to refitting, lubricate the column lower bush with multi-purpose grease.

16 Aligning the marks made on removal, manoeuvre the steering column into position, feeding the lower end through the bulkhead and engaging the lower shaft with the coupling. Make sure that the wiring harness is routed correctly as the column is fitted.

17 Ensure that the column gaiter bush is correctly located in the bulkhead, then refit and tighten the steering column lower mounting nuts, then the upper mounting bolts.

18 Fit a new clamp bolt to the coupling, and tighten it to the specified torque.

19 Where necessary, secure the wiring harness to the column, using new cable-ties.

20 Refit the column trim, then refit the combination switches and instrument panel as described in Chapter 12.

21 Refit the steering lock as described in Section 20.

22 Refit the airbag contact unit as described in Chapter 12.

23 Refit the steering wheel as described in Section 18.

20 Steering lock/ignition switch - removal and refitting

1 Models from 1998 model year onwards are equipped with the Mercedes-Benz Driver Authorisation System (DAS), one feature of which is an 'electronic' key. The procedures relating to models with DAS differ from earlier models, as described below.

Models without DAS

Lock cylinder

2 Using a small screwdriver, carefully prise

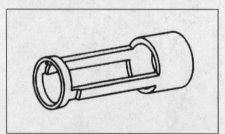

20.4 Mercedes tool used to depress the lock cylinder locking plate

off the trim panel from around the lock cylinder.

3 On later models, prise out the immobiliser transponder coil, taking care not to damage it or its wiring.

4 Mercedes-Benz dealers use a special tool (No 202589001400) to depress the circular locking plate around the lock cylinder **(see illustration)**. It is possible to make up a substitute tool using a piece of welding wire bent at the end into a small circle - the tool must be shaped so that it can depress and turn the locking plate, with the ignition key inserted in the lock cylinder.

5 Insert the ignition key, then fit the tool and depress the locking plate. Turn the key to position I.

6 Keeping the key in position I, turn the tool 90° anti-clockwise to rotate the locking plate **(see illustration)**.

7 Withdraw the lock cylinder using the ignition key. **Note:** *The switch must not be turned from position I while the lock cylinder is removed, or the steering lock will be permanently engaged.*

8 Remove the ignition key, then withdraw the lock cylinder from the locking plate.

9 Prior to refitting, lubricate the outside of the lock cylinder with a little long-life grease. Mercedes-Benz dealers use a special lock cylinder grease for this, which is sprayed on.

10 Insert the lock cylinder through the circular locking plate, then insert the key up to its stop in the lock cylinder. The lock cylinder tumblers must be completely retracted before fitting.

11 Offer the cylinder into the lock housing, aligning the indentations in the lock cylinder with the recesses in the housing.

12 When the lock cylinder is in position, use the removal tool to turn the locking plate 90° clockwise, until the plate is heard or felt to lock into place.

13 Turn the ignition key back to the 0 position.

14 On later models, refit the immobiliser transponder coil, again taking care not to damage it or its wiring.

15 Finally, clip the trim panel back into place.

16 Check the lock and lock cylinder for correct operation.

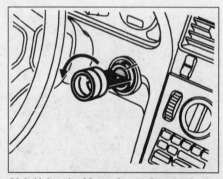

20.6 Using the Mercedes tool to rotate the locking plate (left-hand-drive model shown)

Complete switch assembly

17 Disconnect the battery negative terminal.

18 Remove the instrument panel as described in Chapter 12.

19 Remove the driver's side lower facia panel as described in Chapter 11, Section 41.

20 Remove the lock cylinder as described previously in this Section. **Note:** *The switch must not be turned from position I while the lock cylinder is removed, or the steering lock will be permanently engaged.*

21 Disconnect the wiring plug for the 'lights-on' warning buzzer, at the base of the switch.

22 Disconnect the main wiring plug from the rear of the switch - it may be helpful to make an alignment mark between the switch and plug, for use on reassembly.

23 On diesel models, make alignment marks between the vacuum hoses and switch, and disconnect the hoses from the side of the switch body.

24 On models with automatic transmission, it will be necessary to unscrew the selector mechanism interlock cable from the lock assembly.

25 Slacken the switch clamp bolt, then depress the detent pin and remove the switch assembly from the column.

26 The various peripheral components attached to the switch can now be removed if necessary, noting how they are fitted.

27 Refitting is the reverse of removal, noting the following:

a) *Ensure that the switch remains in position I until the lock cylinder has been refitted.*

b) *When refitting the switch to the column, ensure that the detent pin locks into position in the column hole; securely tighten the clamp bolt.*

c) *Ensure that the wiring is correctly routed and securely reconnected.*

d) *On diesel models, ensure that the vacuum hoses are connected the right way around.*

Ignition/starter wiring block

28 Remove the switch assembly as described previously in this Section.

29 Undo the retaining screws and remove the wiring block from the rear of the switch.

30 Fit the wiring block, ensuring its locating lug is correctly engaged with the cut-out in the switch body. Refit the retaining screws and tighten them securely.

31 Refit the switch assembly as described in paragraph 27.

Models with DAS

Ignition switch

32 Disconnect the battery negative terminal, and position the lead away from the terminal.

33 Remove the driver's lower facia panel as described in Chapter 11, Section 41.

34 Unscrew the chrome trim ring from the front of the switch, tapping it round with a

20.34a Use a small screwdriver to unscrew . . .

20.34b . . . and remove the switch trim ring

20.35 Disconnect the wiring plugs from the switch (one of three shown)

small screwdriver if necessary (take care not to damage the finish) **(see illustrations)**.

35 Release the switch from the facia panel, then disconnect the wiring plugs from the rear of the switch, noting their locations **(see illustration)**.

36 Refitting is a reversal of removal, noting the following points:

a) *Make sure that the switch wiring is correctly and securely reconnected.*

b) *Engage the lug on the right-hand rear of the switch aperture with the cut-out on the front face of the switch, then screw on the trim ring to secure.*

Steering lock

37 Disconnect the battery negative terminal, and position the lead away from the terminal.

38 Remove the driver's lower facia panel as described in Chapter 11, Section 41.

39 Unscrew the nut and tap out the lock retaining bolt, noting how it is fitted **(see illustrations)**.

40 Disengage the lock from the column, and disconnect the wiring plug **(see illustration)**. Note that the lock is electrically activated, via a signal from the keyfob.

41 Refitting is a reversal of removal.

20.39a Unscrew and remove the lock mounting bolt nut . . .

20.39b . . . and remove the specially-shaped bolt

21 Steering box - removal, overhaul and refitting

Note: *Refer to the note at the end of Section 1 before proceeding.*

Removal

1 Chock the rear wheels, firmly apply the parking brake, then jack up the front of the car

and support on axle stands (see *Jacking and vehicle support*).

2 Set the front wheel in the straight-ahead position, and lock the column in position using the steering lock (take out the ignition key). **Note:** *Do not rotate the column whilst the steering box is removed, or the airbag contact unit will be damaged.*

3 Using brake hose clamps, clamp the power steering fluid supply and return hoses near the steering box to minimise fluid loss **(see illustration)**.

20.40 Disconnect the wiring plug from the lock

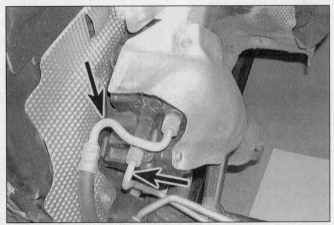

21.3 View of the steering box with the engine removed - fluid pipes arrowed

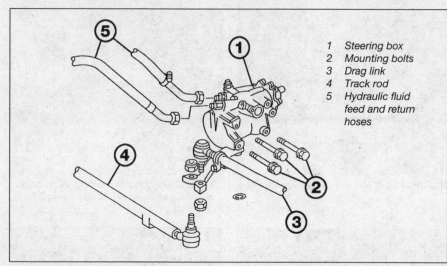

1 Steering box
2 Mounting bolts
3 Drag link
4 Track rod
5 Hydraulic fluid feed and return hoses

21.4 Steering box and associated components

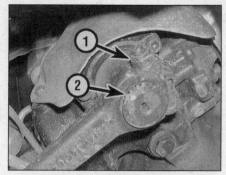

22.3 Steering box drop arm clamp bolt nut (1) and circlip (2)

4 Mark the fluid hose unions to ensure that they are correctly positioned on reassembly, then slacken and remove the hose union nuts **(see illustration)**. Be prepared for fluid spillage, and position a suitable container beneath the hoses whilst unscrewing the nuts. Plug the hose ends and steering box orifices, to prevent fluid leakage and to keep dirt out of the hydraulic system.

5 Using paint or a suitable marker pen, make alignment marks between the lower end of the steering column shaft, coupling/clamp, and the steering box pinion. Note that on some models it will be necessary to unbolt the steering box heatshield(s) to gain access to the coupling.

6 Slacken and remove the socket-headed clamp bolt, then separate the steering column shaft from the coupling.

7 Unscrew the nuts securing the track rod and drag link balljoints to the steering box drop arm. Free the balljoints from the drop arm, if necessary, using a universal balljoint separator.

8 From underneath the wheelarch, slacken and remove the three steering box mounting bolts and manoeuvre the steering box out from underneath the car.

Overhaul

9 Examine the steering box assembly for signs of wear or damage. If overhaul of the steering box assembly is necessary, the task must be entrusted to a Mercedes-Benz dealer. The only service item which is easily replaced is the steering box seal which can be renewed as described in Section 23.

Refitting

10 If a new steering box is being fitted, it will be necessary position the steering pinion correctly prior to fitting the box. To do this, align the index mark on the steering gear pinion with the mark on the steering box housing.

11 Manoeuvre the steering box assembly

into position. Align the marks made on removal (original box) or ensure that the pinion remains correctly centred (new box) and engage the pinion with the rubber coupling.

12 Engage the lower end of the steering column shaft with the coupling, taking care not to use force, otherwise the shaft lower section may be damaged.

13 Fit the new steering box mounting bolts, and tighten them to the specified torque.

14 Fit a new coupling clamp bolt, and tighten it to the specified torque.

15 Insert the drag link and track rod balljoints into the steering box drop arm. Fit new balljoint retaining nuts and tighten them to the specified torque.

16 Reconnect the power steering fluid hoses to the steering box and tighten the union nuts securely. Remove the fluid hose clamps. On completion, refill and bleed the hydraulic system as described in Section 25.

22 Steering box drop arm - removal and refitting

Note: *Refer to the note at the end of Section 1 before proceeding.*

Removal

1 Chock the rear wheels, firmly apply the parking brake, then jack up the front of the car and support on axle stands (see *Jacking and vehicle support*).

2 Unscrew the nuts securing the track rod and drag link balljoints to the steering box drop arm. Free the balljoints from the drop arm, using a universal balljoint separator if necessary.

3 Slacken and remove the drop arm clamp bolt and nut, and remove the retaining circlip **(see illustration)**.

4 Prior to removal, measure the distance between the top edge of the drop arm and the steering box housing, and note this down.

Also check that the pinion mark which aligns with the drop arm clamp split is clearly visible; if not, make an alignment mark.

5 Using a universal puller, draw the drop arm off from the steering box pinion, and remove it from underneath the car. Whilst the arm is removed, inspect the steering box lower seal for signs of leakage, and renew if necessary.

Refitting

6 Remove all traces of old locking compound from the steering box pinion and drop arm, and ensure that the splines are clean and dry.

7 Apply a smear of locking compound (Mercedes-Benz recommend the use of Loctite 270) to the splines of the drop arm.

8 Engage the drop arm with the steering box pinion splines, ensuring that the index mark on the pinion is correctly aligned with the arm clamp split.

9 Press the drop arm onto the steering box, until the distance between its upper edge and the housing is as was noted prior to removal.

10 Insert the drop arm clamp bolt, then fit the new nut and tighten it to the specified torque setting. Secure the arm in position by fitting the circlip, making sure it is correctly located in the pinion groove.

11 Reconnect the balljoints to the drop arm, then fit the new retaining nuts and tighten them to the specified torque. Lower the car to the ground.

23 Steering box lower seal - renewal

1 Remove the drop arm as described in Section 22.

2 Remove the upper circlip from the steering box pinion, then carefully lever the seal out of position, taking great care to mark the pinion or housing.

3 Remove all trace of dirt from the housing and pinion and tape over the pinion splines.

4 Ease the new seal over the end of the steering box pinion, and press it squarely into the steering box housing.

5 Remove the tape from the pinion splines then fit the upper circlip, making sure it is correctly located in the pinion groove.

6 Refit the drop arm as described in Section 22.

7 On completion, bleed the power steering system as described in Section 25.

24 Power steering pump - removal and refitting

Removal

1 To reduce the amount of fluid spillage, syphon off as much of the power steering fluid from the reservoir as possible, taking care not to introduce dirt into the system. Alternatively, attach fluid hose clamps to the supply and return hoses before disconnecting the unions.

2 Chock the rear wheels, firmly apply the parking brake, then jack up the front of the car and support on axle stands (see *Jacking and vehicle support*).

3 Working as described in Chapter 1A or 1B, release the drivebelt tension and unhook the drivebelt from the pump pulley, noting that the pulley retaining bolts should be slackened prior to releasing the tension.

4 Where necessary, remove the air inlet hose to improve access to the pump (see relevant part of Chapter 4).

5 On models with the ZF pump, unscrew the retaining bolts and remove the pulley from the power steering pump, noting which way round it is fitted **(see illustration)**.

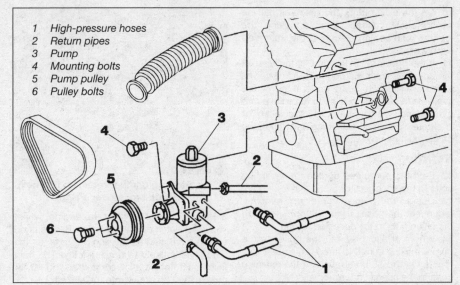

1 High-pressure hoses
2 Return pipes
3 Pump
4 Mounting bolts
5 Pump pulley
6 Pulley bolts

24.5 ZF power steering pump details

6 On models with the LUK pump, the pulley does not have to be removed - for reference, it is a press-fit, after unscrewing the centre nut; if a new pump is to be fitted, the pulley may have to be removed using a suitable puller **(see illustration)**.

7 Wipe clean the area around the pump unions, and make identification marks between the hydraulic pipes and hoses and the pump.

8 Slacken the union nuts and disconnect the hoses from the pump (or fluid reservoir). Be prepared for fluid spillage, and position a suitable container beneath the hoses whilst unscrewing the nuts. Plug the hose ends and steering pump orifices, to prevent fluid leakage and to keep dirt out of the hydraulic system.

9 Slacken and remove the power steering pump mounting bolts, and remove the pump assembly from the engine compartment **(see illustrations)**.

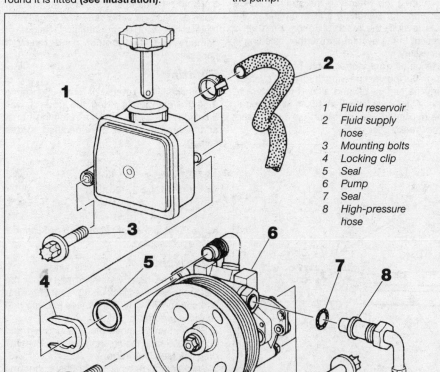

1 Fluid reservoir
2 Fluid supply hose
3 Mounting bolts
4 Locking clip
5 Seal
6 Pump
7 Seal
8 High-pressure hose

24.6 LUK power steering pump details

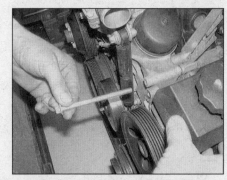

24.9a Remove the mounting bolts . . .

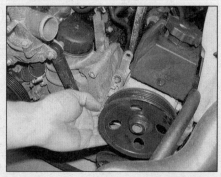

24.9b . . . and remove the power steering pump

10 On the LUK pump, the reservoir can be separated if wished, after removing the locking clip which secures the reservoir supply pipe.

11 If the power steering pump is faulty, seek the advice of your Mercedes-Benz dealer as to the availability of spare parts. If spares are available, it may be possible to have the pump overhauled by a suitable specialist or alternately obtain an exchange unit. If not, the pump must be renewed.

Refitting

12 Refit the pump and tighten the mounting bolts to the specified torque.

13 Using the marks made on removal, reconnect the hoses to the pump, tightening the union nuts to the specified torque.

14 Where applicable, refit the pulley to the pump, making sure it is fitted the correct way round. On the ZF pump, tighten the retaining bolts to the specified torque.

15 Fit the drivebelt and tension as described in Chapter 1A or 1B.

16 On completion, refill the reservoir and bleed the hydraulic system as described in Section 25.

25 Power steering system - bleeding

1 With the engine stopped, fill the fluid reservoir to within 10 mm of the top of the reservoir. Use only the specified type of fluid (see end of *Weekly checks*).

2 With the engine stopped, slowly move the steering from lock-to-lock several times to purge out the trapped air, then top-up the level in the fluid reservoir. Repeat this procedure until the fluid level in the reservoir does not drop any further.

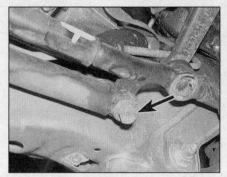

26.2a Steering damper retaining bolt next to the drop arm (driver's side) . . .

3 Have an assistant start the engine, whilst you keep watch on the fluid level. Be prepared to add more fluid as the engine starts, as the fluid level is likely to drop quickly. The fluid level must not be allowed to drop too far, or more air will be drawn into the system.

4 With the engine running at idle speed, turn the steering wheel slowly two or three times approximately 45° to the left and right of the centre, then turn the wheel twice from lock-to-lock. Do not hold the wheel on either lock, as this imposes strain on the hydraulic system. Repeat this procedure until bubbles cease to appear in fluid reservoir.

5 If, when turning the steering, an abnormal noise is heard from the fluid lines, it indicates that there is still air in the system. Check this by turning the wheels to the straight-ahead position and switching off the engine. If the fluid level in the reservoir rises, then air is present in the system and further bleeding is necessary.

6 Once all traces of air have been removed from the power steering hydraulic system, turn the engine off and allow the system to cool. Once cool, check that fluid level is up to the maximum mark, topping-up if necessary (see *Weekly checks*).

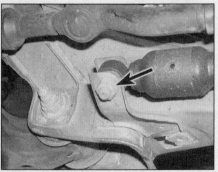

26.2b . . . and retaining nut at the opposite end (arrowed)

26 Steering damper - removal and refitting

Note: *Refer to the note at the end of Section 1 before proceeding.*

Removal

1 Chock the rear wheels, firmly apply the parking brake, then jack up the front of the car and support on axle stands (see *Jacking and vehicle support*).

2 Slacken and remove the damper retaining nuts and bolts and remove the damper, noting which way around it is fitted **(see illustrations)**.

3 Inspect the damper assembly for signs of wear or damage, and renew if necessary. Inspect the rubber mountings for signs of damage and deterioration, and renew if necessary.

Refitting

4 Refitting is the reverse of removal ensuring that the damper is fitted the correct way around. Fit new nuts to the retaining bolts, and tighten them to the specified torque setting.

27 Steering drag link - removal and refitting

Note: *Refer to the note at the end of Section 1 before proceeding.*

Removal

1 Chock the rear wheels, firmly apply the parking brake, then jack up the front of the car and support on axle stands (see *Jacking and vehicle support*).

2 Slacken and remove the retaining nut and bolt, and detach the steering damper from the drag link **(see illustration)**.

3 Slacken and remove the nuts securing the drag link balljoints to the steering box and idler arm. Free the balljoints, using a balljoint separator if necessary, and remove the drag link from underneath the car.

4 Check that the link balljoints move freely

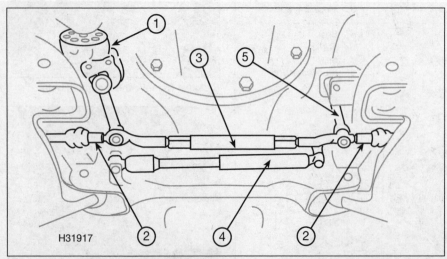

27.2 Steering linkage details (left-hand-drive model shown)

1	Steering box	3	Drag link
2	Track rod	4	Steering damper

5 Idler arm

H31917

28.4 View of the idler arm with the engine removed

without any sign of roughness. Also check that the balljoint gaiters show no sign of deterioration, and are free from cracks and splits. If the balljoints are worn or damaged, the drag link assembly must be renewed. If only the gaiter appears to be damaged, renew it and pack the balljoint with fresh grease.

Refitting

5 Ensure that the balljoint shanks are clean and dry, then refit the drag link. Fit new balljoint nuts, and tighten them to the specified torque.
6 Reconnect the steering damper to the drag link, and insert the retaining bolt. Fit a new nut to the bolt and tighten it to the specified torque setting. Lower the car to the ground.

28 Steering idler arm - removal and refitting

Note: Refer to the note at the end of Section 1 before proceeding.

Removal

1 Chock the rear wheels, firmly apply the parking brake, then jack up the front of the car and support on axle stands (see Jacking and vehicle support).
2 Slacken and remove the securing nuts, and detach the drag link and track rod balljoints from the idler arm. If necessary, free the balljoints using a balljoint separator.
3 Where fitted, unscrew the retaining nuts and bolt(s), and remove the heatshield from the arm pivot.
4 Unscrew the idler arm pivot bolt nut and remove the washer (see illustration). Withdraw the pivot bolt then remove the idler arm, along with the bush which is fitted between the arm and pivot.
5 Inspect the idler arm for signs of damage, and renew as necessary. Check the arm pivot bushes for signs of wear or deterioration, and renew if necessary.
6 The main bush can be removed from the pivot end of the idler arm by loosening the clamp bolt and sliding out the bush. The new bush is fitted with the idler arm offset pointing

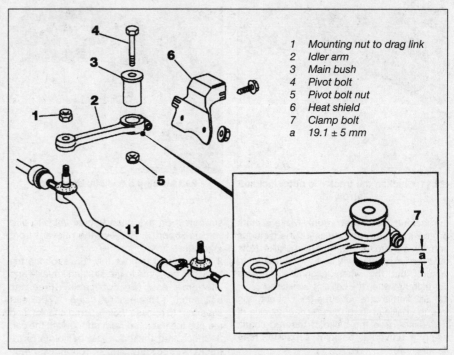

1 Mounting nut to drag link
2 Idler arm
3 Main bush
4 Pivot bolt
5 Pivot bolt nut
6 Heat shield
7 Clamp bolt
a 19.1 ± 5 mm

28.6 Idler arm details (left-hand drive model shown)

towards the bush collar, and at the position shown (see illustration). Tighten the clamp bolt securely.

Refitting

7 Offer up the idler arm, and insert the pivot bolt. Fit the washer and new nut to the pivot bolt, tightening it to the specified torque, then refit the heatshield.
8 Ensure that the balljoint shanks are clean and dry, and locate them in the idler arm. Fit the new balljoint nut, tighten it to the specified torque setting, then lower the car to the ground.

29 Track rod balljoint - removal and refitting

Note: Refer to the note at the end of Section 1 before proceeding.

Inner balljoint

Removal

1 Chock the rear wheels, firmly apply the parking brake, then jack up the front of the car and support on axle stands (see Jacking and vehicle support).
2 Clean the inner end of the track rod, and slacken the balljoint clamp bolt. Make a mark on the track rod, and measure the distance from the mark to the centre of the balljoint. Note this measurement down, as it will be needed to ensure that the wheel alignment remains correctly set when the balljoint is installed.
3 Slacken and remove the balljoint nut, and

free the balljoint from the idler/drop arm (as applicable). If necessary, free the balljoint tapered shank using a universal balljoint separator.
4 Counting the exact number of turns necessary to do so, unscrew the balljoint from the track rod end.
5 Carefully clean the balljoint and the threads - the balljoint taper must not have any lubricant on it, otherwise it will not lock into position. Renew the balljoint if its movement is sloppy or too stiff, is excessively worn, or is damaged in any way; carefully check the stud taper and threads.

Refitting

6 Screw the balljoint into the track rod by the number of turns noted on removal. This should position the balljoint at the relevant distance from the track rod mark that was noted prior to removal.
7 Refit the balljoint shank to the idler/drop arm (as applicable), then fit a new retaining nut and tighten it to the specified torque.
8 Tighten the balljoint clamp bolt to the specified torque then lower the car to the ground.
9 Check and, if necessary, adjust the front wheel toe setting as described in Section 31.

Outer balljoint

Removal

10 Chock the rear wheels, and loosen the front wheel bolts. Jack up the front of the car and support it on axle stands (see Jacking and vehicle support). Remove the relevant front roadwheel.
11 Clean the end of the track rod and slacken

29.11 Slacken the track rod outer locknut (arrowed)

29.12 Using a balljoint separator

29.17 Tighten the balljoint nut to the specified torque

the locknut (see illustration). Make a mark on the track rod, and measure the distance from the mark to the centre of the balljoint. Note this measurement down, as it will be needed to ensure that the wheel alignment remains correctly set when the balljoint is installed.

12 Slacken and remove the balljoint nut, and free the balljoint from the steering knuckle. If necessary, free the balljoint tapered shank using a universal balljoint separator (see illustration).

13 Counting the **exact** number of turns necessary to do so, unscrew the balljoint from the track rod end.

14 Carefully clean the balljoint and the threads - the balljoint taper must not have any lubricant on it, otherwise it will not lock into position. Renew the balljoint if its movement is sloppy or too stiff, is excessively worn, or is damaged in any way; carefully check the stud taper and threads.

Refitting

15 If necessary, transfer the locknut onto the new track rod balljoint.

16 Screw the balljoint into the track rod by the number of turns noted on removal. This should position the balljoint at the relevant distance from the track rod mark that was noted prior to removal.

17 Refit the balljoint shank to the steering knuckle, then fit a new retaining nut and tighten it to the specified torque (see illustration).

18 Refit the roadwheel, then lower the car to the ground and tighten the roadwheel bolts to the specified torque.

19 Check and, if necessary, adjust the front wheel toe setting as described in Section 31, then securely tighten the locknut.

30 Track rod - removal and refitting

Note: *Refer to the note at the end of Section 1 before proceeding.*

Removal

1 Chock the rear wheels, and loosen the front wheel bolts. Jack up the front of the car and support it on axle stands (see *Jacking and vehicle support*). Remove the relevant front roadwheel.

2 Slacken and remove the nuts securing the track rod balljoints to the steering knuckle and idler/drop arm (as applicable). Free the balljoints, if necessary using a balljoint separator to release their tapered shanks, and remove the track rod from underneath the car.

3 Check that the track rod balljoints move freely, without any sign of roughness. Also check that the balljoint gaiters show no sign of deterioration, and are free from cracks and splits. If the balljoints are worn or damaged, they must be renewed as described in Section 29. If just the gaiters appear to be damaged, renew the gaiters and pack the balljoint(s) with fresh grease.

Refitting

4 Ensure that the balljoint shanks are clean and dry - remove all traces of lubricant. If a new track rod assembly is being fitted, check that the length of the rod is correctly set prior to installation, using the old track rod as a guide.

5 Manoeuvre the track rod into position, ensuring it is the correct way around (the inner balljoint is the one secured in position with the clamp, and the outer balljoint by a locknut and clamping ring), and engage the balljoint shanks in the steering knuckle and arm.

6 Fit the new retaining nuts to the balljoints, and tighten them to the specified torque.

7 Lower the car to the ground. On completion, check the front wheel toe setting as described in Section 31.

31 Wheel alignment and steering angles - general information

Definitions

A car's steering and suspension geometry is defined in four basic settings - all angles are expressed in degrees (toe settings are also expressed as a measurement); the steering axis is defined as an imaginary line drawn through the axis of the suspension strut, extended where necessary to contact the ground.

Camber is the angle between each roadwheel and a vertical line drawn through its centre and tyre contact patch, when viewed from the front or rear of the car. Positive camber is when the roadwheels are tilted outwards from the vertical at the top; negative camber is when they are tilted inwards.

The front camber angle is adjusted by slackening and rotating the lower arm front pivot bolt, and can be adjusted using a camber angle gauge. The rear wheel camber is not adjustable and is given for reference only; while it can be checked using a checking gauge, if the figure obtained is significantly different from that specified, the vehicle must be taken for careful checking by a professional, as the fault can only be caused by wear or damage to the body or suspension components.

Castor is the angle between the steering axis and a vertical line drawn through each roadwheel's centre and tyre contact patch, when viewed from the side of the car. Positive castor is when the steering axis is tilted so that it contacts the ground ahead of the vertical; negative castor is when it contacts the ground behind the vertical.

The front castor angle is adjusted by slackening and rotating the lower arm rear pivot bolt, and can be adjusted using a castor angle gauge. The rear wheel castor is not adjustable.

Toe is the difference, viewed from above, between lines drawn through the roadwheel centres and the car's centre-line. 'Toe-in' is when the roadwheels point inwards, towards each other at the front, while 'toe-out' is when they splay outwards from each other at the front.

The front wheel toe setting is adjusted by screwing the track rod in or out of its balljoints, to alter the effective length of the track rod assembly.

Rear wheel toe setting is also adjustable. The toe setting is adjusted by slackening and rotating the lower rear (track) control arm inner pivot bolt.

Checking and adjustment

Due to the special measuring equipment necessary to check the wheel alignment and steering angles, and the skill required to use it properly, the checking and adjustment of these settings is best left to a Mercedes-Benz dealer or similar expert. Note that most tyre-fitting shops now possess sophisticated checking equipment.

Front wheel toe setting

To check the toe setting, a tracking gauge must first be obtained. Two types of gauge are available, and can be obtained from motor accessory shops. The first type measures the distance between the front and rear inside edges of the roadwheels, with the vehicle stationary. The second type, known as a 'scuff plate', measures the actual position of the contact surface of the tyre, in relation to the road surface, with the vehicle in motion. This is achieved by pushing or driving the front tyre over a plate, which then moves slightly according to the scuff of the tyre, and shows this movement on a scale. Both types have their advantages and disadvantages, but either can give satisfactory results if used correctly and carefully.

Make sure that the steering is in the straight-ahead position when making measurements.

If adjustment is necessary, apply the parking brake then jack up the front of the vehicle and support it securely on axle stands (see *Jacking and vehicle support*).

First clean the track rod threads; if they are corroded, apply penetrating fluid before starting adjustment. Slacken the inner balljoint clamp bolt and outer balljoint locknut.

Alter the length of the track rod, by screwing it into or out of the balljoints by rotating the track rod using a pair of grips; shortening the track rod length will reduce toe-in/increase toe-out.

When the setting is correct, hold the track rod and tighten the inner balljoint clamp bolt to the specified torque setting; securely tighten the locknut.

If after adjustment, the steering wheel spokes are no longer horizontal when the wheels are in the straight-ahead position, remove the steering wheel and reposition it (see Section 18).

Check that the toe setting has been correctly adjusted by lowering the vehicle to the ground and re-checking the toe setting; re-adjust if necessary.

Front wheel camber and castor setting

If access to camber and castor angle measuring equipment can be gained, the camber and castor angles can be checked as follows. Both camber and castor angles should be adjusted simultaneously, since any alteration to the camber also affects the castor and *vice versa*.

Attach the gauges to the vehicle and check the camber and castor angles are within the specified limits.

If adjustment is necessary, slacken the mounting clamps securing the anti-roll bar to both front suspension lower arms. Also slacken the lower arm pivot bolt nuts.

Rotate the pivot bolts until both camber and castor angles are correctly set, then hold the bolt stationary and tighten the pivot bolt nuts to the specified torque.

Check that both the camber and castor angles are correctly set, then tighten the anti-roll bar mounting clamp nuts to the specified torque and remove the gauges.

Rear wheel toe setting

The procedure for checking the rear toe setting is same as described for the front wheel toe setting.

To adjust the setting, slacken the lower track control arm inner pivot bolt nut. Rotate the pivot bolt until the toe setting is correctly set, then hold the pivot bolt stationary and tighten the pivot bolt nut to the specified torque.

Check that the toe setting has been correctly adjusted by lowering the vehicle to the ground and re-checking the toe setting; re-adjust if necessary.

Chapter 11
Bodywork and fittings

Contents

Degrees of difficulty

Easy, suitable for novice with little experience	**Fairly easy,** suitable for beginner with some experience	**Fairly difficult,** suitable for competent DIY mechanic 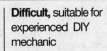	**Difficult,** suitable for experienced DIY mechanic	**Very difficult,** suitable for expert DIY or professional

Specifications

Torque wrench settings	Nm	lbf ft
Bonnet hinge bolts	12	9
Boot lid/tailgate hinge bolts	10	7
Bumper mounting nuts	20	15
Door check strap bolt	25	18
Door hinge bolts	37	27
Front seat belt mounting bolts	35	26
Front seat mounting bolts	50	37
Rear seat belt mounting bolts	30	22

1 General description

The body is of unitary all-steel construction, and incorporates computer-calculated impact crumple zones at the front and rear, with a central safety cell passenger compartment. During manufacture the body is dip-primed, fully sealed and undercoated, then painted with multi-layered base and top-coats.

The bodyshell on all models covered by this manual is of four-door Saloon or five-door Estate configuration.

A number of structural components and body panels are made of galvanised steel to provide a high level of protection against corrosion. Extensive use is also made of plastic materials, mainly in the interior, but also in exterior components. The front and rear bumpers are moulded from a synthetic material that is very strong and yet light. Plastic components such as wheelarch liners are fitted to the underside of the vehicle to further improve corrosion resistance.

2 Maintenance - bodywork and underframe

The general condition of a vehicle's bodywork is the one thing that significantly affects its value. Maintenance is easy but needs to be regular. Neglect, particularly after minor damage, can lead quickly to further deterioration and costly repair bills. It is important also to keep watch on those parts of the vehicle not immediately visible, for instance the underside, inside all the wheelarches and the lower pan of the engine compartment.

The basic maintenance routine for the bodywork is washing - preferably with a lot of water, from a hose. This will remove all the loose solids which may have stuck to the vehicle. It is important to flush these off in such a way as to prevent grit from scratching the finish. The wheelarches and underframe need washing in the same way to remove any accumulated mud which will retain moisture and tend to encourage rust. Paradoxically, the best time to clean the underframe and wheelarches is in wet weather when the mud is thoroughly wet and soft. In very wet weather the underframe is usually cleaned of large accumulations automatically and this is a good time for inspection.

Periodically, except on vehicles with a wax-based underbody protective coating, it is a good idea to have the whole of the underframe of the vehicle steam cleaned, engine compartment included, so that a thorough inspection can be carried out to see what minor repairs and renovations are necessary. Steam cleaning is available at many garages and is necessary for removal of the accumulation of oily grime which sometimes is allowed to become thick in certain areas. If steam cleaning facilities are not available, there are one or two excellent grease solvents available which can be brush applied. The dirt can then be simply hosed off. Note that these methods should not be used on vehicles with wax-based underbody protective coating or the coating will be removed. Such vehicles should be inspected annually, preferably just prior to winter, when the underbody should be washed down and any damage to the wax coating repaired. Ideally, a completely fresh coat should be applied. It would also be worth considering the use of such wax-based protection for injection into door panels, sills, box sections, etc, as an additional safeguard against rust damage where such protection is not provided by the vehicle manufacturer.

After washing paintwork, wipe off with a chamois leather to give an unspotted clear finish. A coat of clear protective wax polish will give added protection against chemical pollutants in the air. If the paintwork sheen has dulled or oxidised, use a cleaner/polisher combination to restore the brilliance of the shine. This requires a little effort, but such dulling is usually caused because regular washing has been neglected. Care needs to be taken with metallic paintwork, as special non-abrasive cleaner/polisher is required to avoid damage to the finish. Always check that the door and ventilator opening drain holes and pipes are completely clear so that water can be drained out. Bright work should be treated in the same way as paint work. Windscreens and windows can be kept clear of the smeary film which often appears by the use of a proprietary glass cleaner. Never use any form of wax or other body or chromium polish on glass.

3 Maintenance - upholstery and carpets

Mats and carpets should be brushed or vacuum cleaned regularly to keep them free of grit. If they are badly stained remove them from the vehicle for scrubbing or sponging and make quite sure they are dry before refitting. Seats and interior trim panels can be kept clean by wiping with a damp cloth. If they do become stained (which can be more apparent on light coloured upholstery) use a little liquid detergent and a soft nail brush to scour the grime out of the grain of the material. Do not forget to keep the headlining clean in the same way as the upholstery. When using liquid cleaners inside the vehicle do not over-wet the surfaces being cleaned. Excessive damp could get into the seams and padded interior causing stains, offensive odours or even rot. If the inside of the vehicle gets wet accidentally it is worthwhile taking some trouble to dry it out properly, particularly where carpets are involved. *Do not leave oil or electric heaters inside the vehicle for this purpose.*

4 Minor body damage - repair

Repair of minor scratches in bodywork

If the scratch is very superficial, and does not penetrate to the metal of the bodywork, repair is very simple. Lightly rub the area of the scratch with a paintwork renovator, or a very fine cutting paste, to remove loose paint from the scratch and to clear the surrounding bodywork of wax polish. Rinse the area with clean water.

In the case of metallic paint, the most commonly-found scratches are not in the paint, but in the lacquer top coat, and appear white. If care is taken , these can sometimes be rendered less obvious by very careful use of paintwork renovator (which would otherwise not be used on metallic paintwork); otherwise, repair of these scratches can be achieved by applying lacquer with a fine brush.

Apply touch-up paint to the scratch using a fine paint brush; continue to apply fine layers of paint until the surface of the paint in the scratch is level with the surrounding paintwork. Allow the new paint at least two weeks to harden, then blend it into the surrounding paintwork by rubbing the scratch area with a paintwork renovator or a very fine cutting paste. Finally, apply wax polish.

Where the scratch has penetrated right through to the metal of the bodywork, causing the metal to rust, a different repair technique is required. Remove any loose rust from the bottom of the scratch with a penknife, then apply rust-inhibiting paint to prevent the formation of rust in the future. Using a rubber or nylon applicator, fill the scratch with bodystopper paste. If required, this paste can be mixed with cellulose thinners to provide a very thin paste which is ideal for filling narrow scratches. Before the stopper-paste in the scratch hardens, wrap a piece of smooth cotton rag around the top of a finger. Dip the finger in cellulose thinners, and then quickly sweep it across the surface of the stopper-paste in the scratch; this will ensure that the surface of the stopper-paste is slightly hollowed. The scratch can now be painted over as described earlier in this Section.

Repair of dents in bodywork

When deep denting of the vehicle's bodywork has taken place, the first task is to pull the dent out, until the affected bodywork almost attains its original shape. There is little point in trying to restore the original shape completely, as the metal in the damaged area will have stretched on impact and cannot be reshaped fully to its original contour. It is better to bring the level of the dent up to a point which is about 3 mm below the level of the surrounding bodywork. In cases where the dent is very shallow anyway, it is not worth trying to pull it out at all. If the underside of the dent is accessible, it can be hammered out gently from behind, using a mallet with a wooden or plastic head. Whilst doing this, hold a suitable block of wood firmly against the outside of the panel to absorb the impact from the hammer blows and thus prevent a large area of the bodywork from being 'belled-out'.

Should the dent be in a section of the bodywork which has a double skin or some other factor making it inaccessible from behind, a different technique is called for. Drill several small holes through the metal inside the area - particularly in the deeper section. Then screw long self-tapping screws into the holes just sufficiently for them to gain a good purchase in the metal. Now the dent can be pulled out by pulling on the protruding heads of the screws with a pair of pliers.

The next stage of the repair is the removal of the paint from the damaged area, and from an inch or so of the surrounding 'sound' bodywork. This is accomplished most easily by using a wire brush or abrasive pad on a power drill. although it can be done just as effectively by hand using sheets of abrasive paper. To complete the preparation for filling, score the surface of the bare metal with a screwdriver or the tang of a file, or alternatively, drill small holes in the affected area. This will provide a really good 'key' for the filler paste.

To complete the repair see the Section on filling and re-spraying.

Repair of rust holes or gashes in bodywork

Remove all paint from the affected area and from an inch or so of the surrounding 'sound' bodywork, using an abrasive pad or a wire brush on a power drill. If these are not available a few sheets of abrasive paper will do the job just as effectively. With the paint removed you will be able to gauge the severity of the corrosion and therefore decide whether to renew the whole panel (if this is possible) or to repair the affected area. New body panels are not as expensive as most people think and it is often quicker and more satisfactory to fit a new panel than to attempt to repair large areas of corrosion.

Remove all fittings from the affected area except those which will act as a guide to the original shape of the damaged bodywork. Then, using tin snips or a hacksaw blade, remove all loose metal and any other metal badly affected by corrosion. Hammer the edges of the hole inwards in order to create a slight depression for the filler paste.

Wire-brush the affected area to remove the powdery rust from the surface of the remaining metal. Paint the affected area with rust -inhibiting paint - if the back of the rusted area is accessible, treat this also.

Before filling can take place it will be necessary to block the hole in some way. This can be achieved by the use of aluminium or plastic mesh, or aluminium tape.

Aluminium or plastic mesh is probably the best material to use for a large hole. Cut a piece to the approximate size and shape of the hole to be filled, then position it in the hole so that its edges are below the level of the surrounding bodywork. It can be retained in position by several blobs of filler paste around its periphery.

Aluminium tape should be used for small or very narrow holes. Pull a piece off the roll and trim it to the approximate size and shape required, then pull off the backing paper (if used) and stick the tape over the hole; it can be overlapped if the thickness of one piece is insufficient. Burnish down the edges of the tape with the handle of a screwdriver or similar, to ensure that the tape is securely attached to the metal underneath.

Bodywork repairs - filling and re-spraying

Before using this Section, see the Sections on dent, deep scratch, rust holes and gash repairs.

Many types of bodyfiller are available, but generally speaking those proprietary kits which contain a tin of filler paste and a tube of resin hardener are best for this type of repair. A wide, flexible plastic or nylon applicator will be found invaluable for imparting a smooth and well-contoured finish to the surface of the filler.

Mix up a little filler on a clean piece of card or board - measure the hardener carefully (follow the maker's instructions on the pack) otherwise the filler will set too rapidly or too slowly. Using the applicator, apply the filler paste to the prepared area; draw the applicator across the surface of the filler to achieve the correct contour and to level the filler surface. As soon as a contour that approximates to the correct one is achieved, stop working the paste - if you carry on too long, the paste will become sticky and begin to 'pick up' on the applicator. Continue to add thin layers of filler paste at twenty-minute intervals until the level of the filler is just proud of the surrounding bodywork.

Once the filler has hardened, excess can be removed using a metal plane or file. From then on, progressively finer grades of abrasive paper should be used, starting with a 40-grade production paper and finishing with a 400-grade (or higher) wet-and-dry paper. Always wrap the abrasive paper around a flat rubber, cork, or wooden block - otherwise the surface of the filler will not be completely flat. During the smoothing of the filler surface, the wet-and-dry paper should be periodically rinsed in water. This will ensure that a very smooth finish is imparted to the filler at the final stage.

At this stage the 'dent' should be surrounded by a ring of bare metal, which in turn should be encircled by the finely 'feathered' edge of the good paintwork. Rinse the repair area with clean water, until all of the dust produced by the rubbing-down operation has gone.

Spray the whole repair area with a light coat of primer - this will show up any imperfections in the surface of the filler. Repair these imperfections with fresh filler paste or bodystopper, and once more smooth the surface with abrasive paper. If bodystopper is used, it can be mixed with cellulose thinners to form a really thin paste which is ideal for filling small holes. Repeat this spray-and-repair procedure until you are satisfied that the surface of the filler, and the feathered edge of the paintwork are perfect. Clean the repair area with clean water, and allow to dry fully.

The repair area is now ready for final spraying. Paint spraying must be carried out in a warm, dry, windless and dust-free atmosphere. This condition can be created artificially if you have access to a large indoor working area, but if you are forced to work in the open, you will have to pick your day very carefully. If you are working indoors, dousing the floor in the work area with water will help to settle the dust which would otherwise be in the atmosphere. If the repair area is confined to one body panel, mask off the surrounding panels; this will help to minimise the effects of a slight mis-match in paint colours. Bodywork fittings (eg: rubbing strips, door handles, etc) will also need to be masked off. Use genuine masking tape and several thicknesses of newspaper for the masking operations.

Before commencing to spray, agitate the aerosol can thoroughly, then spray a test area (an old tin, or similar) until the technique is mastered. Cover the repair area with a thick coat of primer; the thickness should be built up using several thin layers of paint rather than one thick one. Using 400-grade (or higher) wet-and-dry paper, rub down the surface of the primer until it is really smooth. While doing this, the work area should be thoroughly doused with water, and the wet-and-dry paper periodically rinsed in water. Allow to dry before spraying on more paint.

Spray on the top coat, again building up the thickness by using several thin layers of paint. Start spraying at the top of the repair area and then, using a side-to-side motion, work downwards until the whole repair area and about 2 inches of the surrounding original paintwork is covered. Remove all masking material 10 to 15 minutes after spraying on the final coat of paint.

Allow the new paint at least two weeks to harden, then, using a paintwork renovator or a very fine cutting paste, blend the edges of the paint into the existing paintwork. Finally, apply wax polish.

Plastic components

With the use of more and more plastic body components by the vehicle manufacturers (eg: bumpers, spoilers, and in some cases major body panels), rectification of more serious damage to such items has become a matter of either entrusting repair work to a specialist in this field, or renewing complete components. Repair of such damage by the DIY owner is not really feasible, owing to the cost of the equipment and materials required for effecting such repairs. The basic technique involves making a groove along the line of the crack in the plastic using a rotary burr in a power drill. The damaged part is then welded back together by using a hot-air gun to heat up and fuse a plastic filler rod into the groove. Any excess plastic is then removed and the area rubbed down to a smooth finish. It is important that a filler rod of the correct plastic is used, as body components can be made of a variety of different types (eg: polycarbonate, ABS, polypropylene).

Damage of a less serious nature (abrasions, minor cracks etc) can be repaired by the DIY owner using a two-part epoxy filler repair material. Once mixed in equal proportions, this is used in similar fashion to the bodywork filler used on metal panels. The filler is usually cured in twenty to thirty minutes, ready for sanding and painting.

If the owner is renewing a complete component himself, or if he has repaired it with epoxy filler, he will be left with the problem of finding a suitable paint for finishing which is compatible with the type of plastic used. At one time the use of a universal paint was not possible, owing to the complex range of plastics encountered in body component applications. Standard paints, generally speaking, will not bond to plastic or rubber satisfactorily. However, it is now possible to

obtain a plastic body parts finishing kit which consists of a preprimer treatment, a primer and coloured top coat. Full instructions are normally supplied with a kit, but basically the method of use is to first apply the pre-primer to the component concerned and allow it to dry for up to 30 minutes. Then the primer is applied and left to dry for about an hour before finally applying the special coloured top coat. The result is a correctly-coloured component where the paint will flex with the plastic or rubber, a property that standard paint does not normally possess.

5 Major body damage - repair

Where serious damage has occurred, or large areas need renewal due to neglect, it means that complete new panels will need welding in, and this is best left to professionals. If the damage is due to impact, it will also be necessary to completely check the alignment of the bodyshell, and this can only be carried out accurately by a Mercedes-Benz dealer using special jigs. If the body is left misaligned, it is primarily dangerous as the car will not handle properly, and secondly, uneven stresses will be imposed on the steering, suspension and possibly transmission, causing abnormal wear, or complete failure, particularly to such items as the tyres.

6 Bonnet - removal and refitting

Removal

1 Raise the bonnet to the vertical position by pulling the catch on each hinge inwards **(see illustration)**, and lifting the bonnet until the lugs engage in the second slot on the hinge.
2 Press the retaining catches and remove the plastic cover panels at the base of the bonnet - these fit over the washer hose connections, and the wiring plugs for the heated washer jets **(see illustration)**.
3 Disconnect the windscreen washer hose(s) at the check valve on the right-hand side, and release the hose clips on the bonnet hinge **(see illustration)**.
4 Pull the wiring for the heated washer jets out of the bonnet cavity adjacent to the jet(s) and disconnect the wiring plug connections **(see illustration)**.
5 Tie a length of string to the main feed cable and pull the wiring out of the bonnet cavity from the hinge end. As soon as the end of the string appears, untie it and remove the wire, leaving the string in place. When refitting, tie the cable to the string to draw it back into position. Use a similar method to remove the washer supply hose.
6 Mark the position of the hinge bolts on both sides **(see illustration)**, so that the bonnet can be refitted in its original position.
7 With the help of an assistant to support the bonnet, loosen and withdraw the hinge bolts, and carefully lift off the bonnet.

Refitting

8 Refitting is a reversal of removal, noting the following points:
a) Tie the washer jet supply hose and wiring to the drawstring, and pull the wires/hoses through the bonnet into place. Reconnect the wiring plug(s) and hose(s) securely.
b) Lower the bonnet and check its fit and alignment. If necessary, adjust the bonnet position as described in Section 7.
c) Tighten the bonnet hinge bolts to the specified torque.

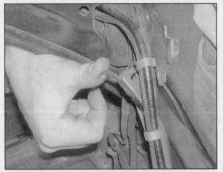

6.1 Pull the bonnet hinge catches inwards and raise the bonnet to the vertical position

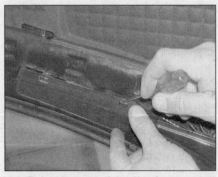

6.2 Releasing one of the plastic covers at the base of the bonnet

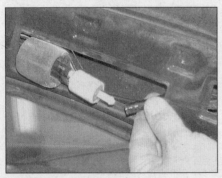

6.3 Disconnect the washer hose at the check valve

6.4 Pull out the heated washer jet wiring plug, and disconnect it

6.6 Bonnet hinge bolts (arrowed)

7.2 Bonnet lock striker plate

7.11 Bonnet rubber buffer (arrowed) behind bonnet hinge

7.13 Bonnet rubber buffer above headlight

7 Bonnet - adjustment

1 With the bonnet closed, check the gap between the bonnet and front wings on both sides (transverse adjustment), the alignment of the front edge of the bonnet with the front edge of the wing when looking down (longitudinal adjustment), and the height of the bonnet front edge and top edge in relation to the wing (height adjustment). The help of an assistant would be useful when adjusting the bonnet.

Transverse adjustment

2 Open the bonnet and slacken the two bolts securing the lock striker plate to the bonnet **(see illustration)**.
3 By trial and error, move the striker plate until an equal gap exists between the bonnet and the front wings on each side.

Longitudinal adjustment

4 Remove the bonnet support strut as described in Section 9, then lower and close the bonnet.
5 Remove the plastic covering from under the wheelarch, on the side being adjusted, for access to the bonnet hinge retaining nuts.
6 From within the engine compartment, slacken the locknut and screw down the bonnet rubber buffer behind the hinge.
7 Slacken the bonnet hinge retaining bolts from under the wheelarch.
8 With the bonnet closed, position it in such a way that when viewed from the front looking down, the edge of the bonnet and the edge of the front wing are in alignment.
9 Tighten the hinge nuts and bolts with the bonnet closed and correctly aligned.
10 Refit the wheelarch covering and bonnet support strut, then check the height adjustment.

Height adjustment

11 From within the engine compartment, slacken the locknut and screw down the bonnet rubber buffer behind the hinge **(see illustration)**.
12 Slacken the hinge retaining bolts.
13 By trial and error, move the bonnet as necessary, tightening the hinge bolts each time until the bonnet upper edge and front wing edge are aligned. Rubber buffers are also fitted above each headlight **(see illustration)**.
14 Now raise the rubber buffer a few turns at a time until the front edge of the bonnet and the edge of the wing, when viewed from the front, are aligned. Tighten the buffer locknut when adjustment is correct.

8 Bonnet hinge - removal and refitting

Removal

1 Remove the bonnet as described in Section 6.
2 Remove the plastic wheelarch covering from under the wheelarch for access to the hinge retaining nuts.
3 Undo the four hinge retaining nuts and remove the hinge.

Refitting

4 Refitting is the reverse sequence to

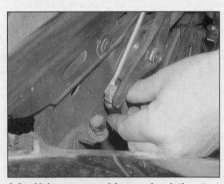

9.2a Using a screwdriver, unhook the strut retaining clip . . .

removal. Adjust the bonnet as described in Section 7 after fitting.

9 Bonnet support strut - removal and refitting

Removal

1 Raise the bonnet to the vertical position by pulling the catch on each hinge inwards, and lifting the bonnet until the lugs engage in the second slot on the hinge.
2 Extract the strut retaining clip, then unhook and remove the strut **(see illustrations)**.

Refitting

3 Refitting is the reverse sequence to removal.

10 Bonnet release cable - removal and refitting

Removal

1 Open the bonnet. If the bonnet release cable has broken, it is probably best to seek the advice of a Mercedes-Benz dealer as to the best course of action.

9.2b . . . and remove the strut from its location

10.2a Remove the handle retaining screw . . .

10.2b . . . then use pliers if necessary to gain slack on the cable, and disconnect the end fitting

10.8 Disconnecting the release cable at the bonnet lock

2 Undo the screw and remove the release handle, then disconnect the cable end fitting **(see illustrations)**.
3 Push out the rubber grommet at the cable entry point on the bulkhead.
4 Tie string to the release cable so that, as the cable is pulled through the bulkhead, it will pull the string with it.
5 Moving to the engine compartment, trace the route of the cable for use when refitting. Unclip and remove the trim panels for access to the cable where it enters the bulkhead and the bonnet lock itself.
6 On most models, it will be necessary to unbolt and remove the upper crossmember for access to the lock end of the cable. Refer to the bonnet lock removal procedure in Section 11.

7 If not already done, remove the cover from the bonnet lock.
8 Disconnect the release cable at the lock lever and support bracket **(see illustration)**.
9 Where applicable, release the cable from the plastic guide channel which runs along the inside of the crossmember **(see illustration)**.
10 Pull out the cable in a forward direction. When the drawstring appears through the bulkhead, untie it and remove the cable from the car, leaving the string in place.

Refitting

11 Refitting is the reverse sequence to removal - use the string to draw the new cable through the bulkhead into the car. With the help of an assistant, make sure that the lock is working satisfactorily before closing the bonnet.

11 Bonnet lock - removal and refitting

Removal

1 Release the two spring catches which secure the top of the radiator to the crossmember, and remove the rubber pads fitted below **(see illustrations)**.
2 Where applicable, prise out the round plastic clip which secures the plastic trim piece to the top of the crossmember **(see illustration)**.
3 Prise off the cover panel fitted over the radiator crossmember front support, and remove the top bolt to free the support from the crossmember **(see illustrations)**.

10.9 Remove the release cable from the plastic guide channel

11.1a Release and remove the two spring catches . . .

11.1b . . . and pull off the rubber pads beneath

11.2 Remove the clip securing the crossmember trim

11.3a Unclip the cover panel from the crossmember front support . . .

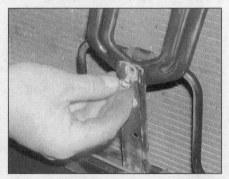

11.3b . . . and remove the top bolt beneath

11.4 Remove the two crossmember securing bolts at each end

11.5 Prise off the plastic clips from the top of the crossmember

11.6 Remove the crossmember, and unclip the plastic conduit from underneath

11.7 Disconnecting the alarm microswitch wiring plug

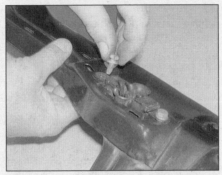

11.8a Unscrew and remove the lock mounting bolts . . .

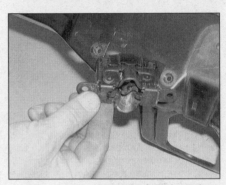

11.8b . . . and remove the lock from the crossmember

4 Unscrew the two retaining bolts at either end of the crossmember which fits over the top of the radiator (see illustration).

5 Prise off the several small oblong plastic clips which are used to secure the bonnet release cable and alarm microswitch wiring plastic conduit to the underside of the crossmember (see illustration).

6 Carefully lift away the crossmember, and turn it over. Unclip the plastic conduit from the underside of the crossmember (see illustration).

7 Where applicable, disconnect the alarm microswitch wiring plug (see illustration).

8 Unhook the release cable inner end fitting and cable outer from the lock, then unscrew the two lock mounting bolts and remove the lock from the crossmember (see illustrations).

Refitting

9 Refitting is the reverse sequence to removal. Minor adjustment of the closing action can be carried out by adjusting the position of the lock striker on the underside of the bonnet.

12 Radiator grille - removal and refitting

Removal

1 Open the bonnet and, from the inside at the front, undo the eight grille retaining screws.

Take off the two rubber seals at the top of the grille (see illustrations).

2 Remove the grille surround and grille from the bonnet, taking care not to damage the paintwork (see illustration).

3 Move the grille assembly to a bench, and rest it on a soft surface.

4 Work around the edge of the assembly and remove the combination clips/screw mountings. Also remove the screw at the base of the assembly.

5 Separate the grille from the chrome frame. If required, the horizontal strips can also be unclipped and removed from the grille.

Refitting

6 Refitting is the reverse sequence to removal.

12.1a Remove the grille retaining screws . . .

12.1b . . . and take off the rubber seals

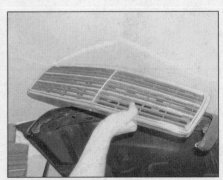

12.2 Removing the radiator grille assembly

13.1 Inside the bonnet, turn the emblem retaining clip to the right . . .

13.2 . . . and remove the emblem from the bonnet

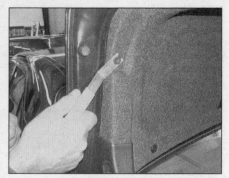

14.2a Remove the trim clips using a forked tool

13 Bonnet emblem -
removal and refitting

Removal

1 From the underside of the bonnet, turn the emblem retaining clip 90° clockwise - the clip has raised sides to make it easier to grip with pliers **(see illustration)**.
2 Pull the emblem upwards out of the bonnet to remove **(see illustration)**.

Refitting

3 Refitting is the reverse sequence to removal, ensuring that the retaining clip is securely engaged.

14 Boot lid (Saloon) -
removal and refitting

Removal

1 Disconnect the battery negative terminal.
2 Unclip and remove the trim panel from inside the boot lid, for access to the hinges and wiring, etc. Prise out the plastic retaining clips using a wide-bladed screwdriver or forked tool. The mountings for the warning triangle are removed by depressing the catch with a small screwdriver **(see illustrations)**.
3 Remove the push-in clips securing the wiring harness duct to the right-hand hinge, and remove the duct **(see illustrations)**. Partially remove the right-hand trim panel as required.
4 Remove the screws securing the boot lid lock, and withdraw the lock sufficiently to disconnect the wiring plug and vacuum line from it - refer to Section 15 if necessary.
5 Trace the wiring for the number plate lights, and disconnect the wiring plugs from the lights.
6 Unclip the boot light switch from its location, and disconnect its wiring plug **(see illustrations)**.
7 Release the cable-ties securing the wiring harness to the inside of the boot lid, and remove the harness and vacuum hose from the boot lid, noting its routing for use when refitting.
8 Mark the outline of the hinges on the boot lid using a pencil.
9 Place some rags beneath the lower corners of the boot lid and, with the help of an assistant, undo the hinge retaining bolts **(see illustration)**. Remove the boot lid upwards out of the restraining hooks, and out from the car.

Refitting

10 Refitting is the reverse sequence to

14.2b Remove the warning triangle mounting clips using a screwdriver

14.3a Remove the plastic clip . . .

14.3b . . . and unclip the wiring harness duct from the hinge

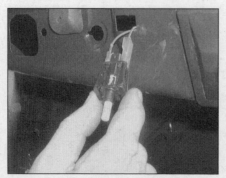

14.6a Unclip the boot light switch . . .

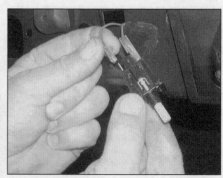

14.6b . . . and disconnect the wiring plugs

14.9 Boot lid hinge retaining bolts (arrowed)

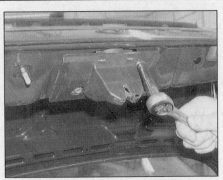

15.2a Unscrew the lock mounting bolts . . .

15.2b . . . and withdraw the lock from the boot lid

15.2c Recover the rubber seal from around the lock barrel

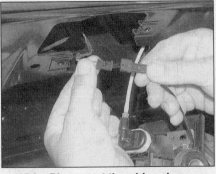

15.3a Disconnect the wiring plug . . .

15.3b . . . and vacuum line from the lock

removal, but align the hinges with the outline marks made prior to removal before tightening the bolts. Adjust the lock striker plate as necessary to achieve satisfactory opening and closing of the boot lid.

15 Boot lid lock (Saloon) - removal and refitting

Removal

1 Unclip and remove the trim panel from inside the boot lid. Prise out the plastic retaining clips using a wide-bladed screwdriver or forked tool. The mountings for

the warning triangle are removed by depressing the catch with a small screwdriver.
2 Undo the lock mounting bolts and withdraw the lock. Recover the rubber seal which fits around the lock barrel (see illustrations).
3 Disconnect the wiring plug (where applicable) and the central locking vacuum line from the lock assembly, and remove the lock from the boot lid (see illustrations).
4 If required, the lock housing can be separated from the latch by prising up the locating lugs with a small screwdriver (see illustration).
5 To remove the lock microswitch or actuator, refer to Section 29.

Refitting

6 Refitting is the reverse sequence to

removal. Adjust the lock striker plate as necessary to achieve satisfactory opening and closing of the boot lid.

16 Tailgate and support struts (Estate) - removal and refitting

Removal

1 Disconnect the battery negative terminal.
2 Prise out the trim clips securing the tailgate inner trim panel in position; unclip and remove the panel from the inside of the tailgate. Also unclip and remove the trim from around the tailgate window (see illustrations).
3 Disconnect the wiring plug, washer hose

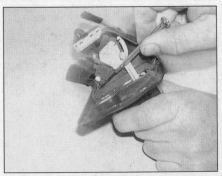

15.4 Prise up the lock housing locating lugs with a small screwdriver

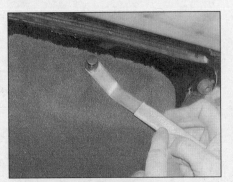

16.2a Prise out the trim securing clips using a forked tool . . .

16.2b . . . and lower the tailgate trim panel

16.2c Unclip and remove the top . . .

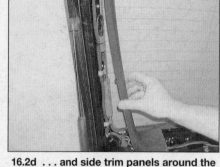

16.2d . . . and side trim panels around the rear window

16.5 Tailgate strut upper retaining clip

and central locking vacuum hose from their connections at the top of the tailgate. Where necessary, tie string to the hoses/wiring, so that as the hoses/wiring are pulled out of the tailgate, it will pull the string with it, leaving the string in position.

4 Mark the fitted positions of the hinges on the tailgate, so that the tailgate can be accurately aligned when refitting.

5 Have an assistant support the tailgate, then prise off the tailgate strut upper retaining clips, and remove the tailgate support struts, pulling them off their lower ball fittings on the body if required (see illustration).

6 Still supporting the tailgate, loosen and remove the tailgate hinge bolts, and with the help of an assistant, remove the tailgate from the car.

Refitting

7 Refitting is a reversal of removal. If necessary, adjust the tailgate to achieve a good fit. The hinge and lock striker plate can be loosened and the components moved as required; there are also two adjustable rubber buffers fitted to the lower edge of the tailgate.

17 Tailgate lock (Estate) - removal and refitting

1 Disconnect the battery negative terminal.

2 Prise out the trim clips securing the tailgate inner trim panel in position; unclip and remove the panel from the inside of the tailgate.

3 Unscrew the nuts on the inside of the tailgate which secure the tailgate lock handle trim strip. The nuts are supposed to remain in place on the inside of the tailgate, but we found that they came off quite easily in practice (see illustrations).

4 Disconnect the two wiring connectors from behind each number plate light (note how they are fitted), and remove the trim from outside (see illustrations).

5 Unhook the lock operating rod from the lock assembly, noting how it fits (see illustration).

6 Unscrew and remove the lock assembly mounting screws, and withdraw the assembly from the tailgate (see illustrations).

7 If required, unscrew the retaining bolts and remove the lock handle from the tailgate.

17.3a Unscrew the nuts securing the handle trim strip . . .

17.3b . . . the nuts should remain in position, but this one did not

17.4a Disconnecting the number plate light wiring

17.4b Removing the handle trim strip from the outside of the tailgate

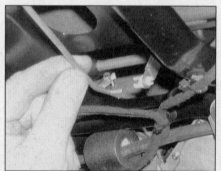

17.5 Unhook the lock operating rod

17.6a Unscrew the lock mounting screws . . .

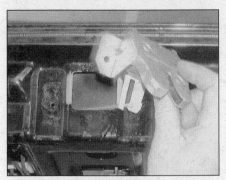

17.6b . . . and remove the lock from the
tailgate

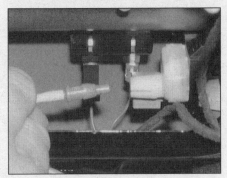

17.7a Disconnect the vacuum line . . .

17.7b . . . then unscrew and remove the
handle retaining screws . . .

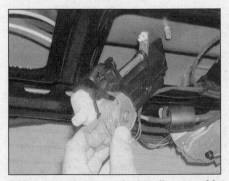

17.7c . . . and remove the handle assembly
from the tailgate

17.8 Handle assembly removed, showing
lock cylinder retaining circlip (arrowed)

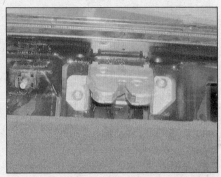

17.9 Tailgate latch retaining bolts

Disconnect the central locking vacuum line
from the handle assembly, and remove it (see
illustrations).

8 The lock cylinder can be unclipped from the
handle, once the retaining circlip has been
prised off (see illustration).

9 Also if required, the tailgate latch can be
unbolted and removed from the base of the
tailgate, after removing the two retaining bolts
(see illustration).

Refitting

10 Refitting is a reversal of removal. Take
care when refitting the tailgate lock handle
trim strip that the studs do not knock off the
nuts on the inside of the tailgate, as they pass
through the holes (see paragraph 3). If

necessary, adjust the tailgate lock striker
on completion to achieve satisfactory
operation.

18 Bumpers -
removal and refitting

Front bumper

1 Chock the rear wheels and firmly apply the
parking brake, then jack up the front of the car
and support it on axle stands (see *Jacking and
vehicle support*).

2 On models equipped with front foglights,

disconnect the foglight wiring from the light
units, and tie it up out of the way.

3 Where the Parktronic parking aid system is
fitted, trace the wiring harness from the
sensors fitted to the inside of the bumper, and
disconnect it at the plug(s).

4 Working from below, unclip and remove the
lower trim panels from the front of the bumper
at either side (see illustration).

5 On models with an outside temperature
gauge, the temperature sensor fits on the rear
of the bumper left-hand lower trim panel.
Disconnect the wiring plug from the sensor,
and remove the sensor itself from its holder
(see illustrations).

6 Remove the front section of the wheelarch

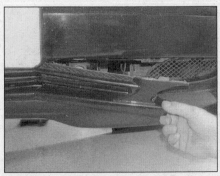

18.4 Prise out and remove the bumper
lower trim panels

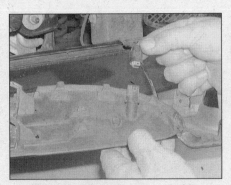

18.5a Disconnect the sensor wiring
plug . . .

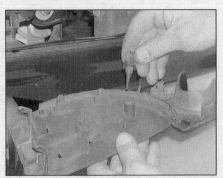

18.5b . . . and remove the sensor from the
panel

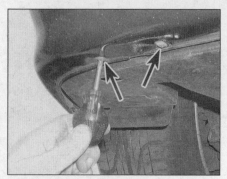

18.6a Front section of wheelarch liner is secured by two screws to the bumper . . .

18.6b . . . two bolts at the rear . . .

18.6c . . . one bolt from below . . .

liner, for access to the bumper side mounting nuts. The wheelarch liner is secured to the lower edge of the bumper by two screws, and by four bolts - two at the rear of the liner, one from below, and one from the side **(see illustrations)**.

7 Unscrew and remove the two nuts each side which secure the bumper to the mounting brackets **(see illustration)**. On some models, note that a bumper retaining catch is fitted to the mounting bracket.

8 Open the bonnet, and remove the two bumper securing nuts and washers visible in the radiator grille aperture. Immediately below these two nuts are two further nuts and washers, accessed through the bumper trim panel apertures **(see illustrations)**.

9 With all mounting nuts removed, release the retaining catches (see paragraph 7) and with the help of an assistant, pull the bumper forwards off its guides **(see illustration)**.

10 Refitting is a reversal of removal. Tighten the mounting nuts to the specified torque.

Rear bumper

11 Where the Parktronic parking aid system is fitted, working under the rear bumper, trace the wiring harness from the sensors fitted to the inside of the bumper, and disconnect it at the plug.

12 From inside the luggage compartment, unclip and pull back the left- and right-hand trim panels.

13 On Saloon models, unscrew the two bumper retaining nuts on each side of the rear crossmember; if necessary, remove the foam inserts either side. Recover the washers **(see illustration)**.

14 On Estate models, remove the two bolts at the rear of the luggage area (these are also used to secure the load lashing

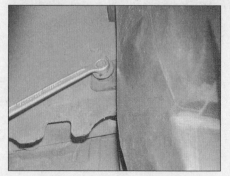

18.6d . . . and one from the side

18.6e Withdraw the liner front section from under the wheelarch

18.7 Bumper side mounting nuts (arrowed)

18.8a Remove the nuts at the base of the radiator grille aperture . . .

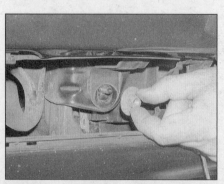

18.8b . . . and those visible inside the bumper lower trim panel apertures

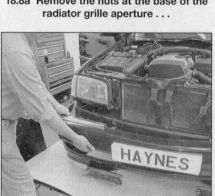

18.9 Removing the front bumper

18.13 Remove the two bumper retaining nuts (arrowed)

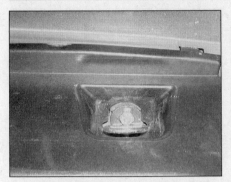

18.14a Load lashing eye retaining bolt

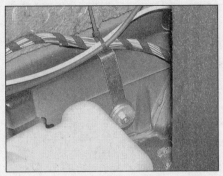

18.14b Bumper side mounting nut - note earth plate beneath

18.15a Prise off the trim cover . . .

eyes). Also remove the nuts in the well on each side which secure the bumper sides to the body. Depending on model and equipment, note that the nuts also secure an earthing plate - make sure this is refitted correctly on completion **(see illustrations)**.

15 Remove the small plastic cover in the centre trim panel which allows access to the bumper centre mounting nut. Unscrew the nut, and recover the washer **(see illustrations)**.

16 Where applicable, prise out the clip which secures the left-hand side of the bumper to the base of the wheelarch liner **(see illustration)**.

17 Carefully unhook each bumper end from the wheelarch on either side **(see illustration)**

18 With the help of an assistant, carefully pull the bumper rearwards to release it from the side mounting guides, and remove it from the car **(see illustration)**.

19 Refitting is a reversal of removal. Tighten the mounting nuts to the specified torque.

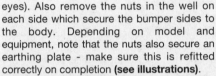

19 Door trim panel -
removal and refitting

⚠ **Warning: On models equipped with side airbags, one airbag unit is housed in each front door trim panel. Although removing the door trim panel should not involve disturbing the airbag unit in any way, it is still wise to be aware of the precautions to**

18.15b . . . for access to the centre mounting nut

be observed when working with the airbag system.

Before carrying out any operations on the airbag system, disconnect the battery negative terminal and wait at least 15 minutes to allow the system capacitors to discharge. When operations are complete, make sure no one is inside the vehicle when the battery is reconnected.

Airbags must not be subjected to temperatures in excess of 90°C (194°F). When an airbag is removed, ensure that it is stored the correct way up to prevent possible inflation.

Do not allow any solvents or cleaning agents to contact the airbag assemblies. They must be cleaned using only a damp cloth.

Airbags are sensitive to impact. If they

18.16 Prise out the clip from the base of the left-hand wheelarch

are dropped or damaged, they should be enewed.

Removal

1 On models equipped with side airbags, ensure that the ignition switch is off (take out the key). Disconnect the battery negative lead, and position the lead away from the battery terminal (Mercedes-Benz recommend covering up the terminal, to prevent accidental reconnection). Wait for at least 15 minutes before proceeding.

2 On cars with manually-operated window regulators, slide the regulator handle trim off the handle, after releasing the detent by pressing down with a small screwdriver. Withdraw the regulator handle and the trim disc **(see illustrations)**.

3 Remove the screw at the rear of the door securing the door lock trim panel, and slide

18.17 Unclip the bumper end from the bodywork

18.18 Removing the rear bumper

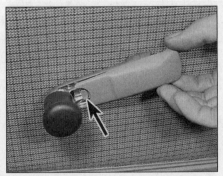

19.2a Remove the window handle trim by pressing down the detent (arrowed)

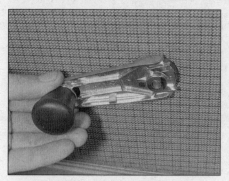

19.2b Withdraw the handle from the splines . . .

19.2c . . . and recover the trim disc

19.3a Remove the securing screw . . .

the panel downwards to remove it **(see illustrations)**.

4 Prise out the door lock handle recess panel

using a suitable screwdriver, taking care not to mark the panel. Remove the panel over the door lock handle **(see illustration)**.

Early models

5 Remove the cross-head screw behind the door lock handle recess panel just removed **(see illustration)**.

6 On front door trim panels, prise off the small round trim panel below the front of the armrest, and unscrew the cross-head screw behind it **(see illustrations)**.

7 On rear door trim panels, remove the cross-head screw from below the door armrest **(see illustration)**.

Later models

8 Carefully prise off the outer cover from the door pull, and remove the two screws behind it **(see illustrations)**.

9 On front door trim panels with side

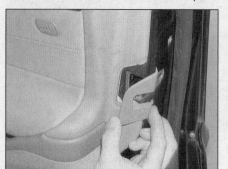

19.3b . . . and slide out the lock trim panel

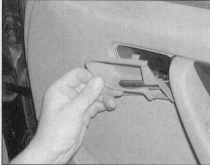
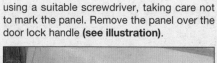

19.4 Prise out and remove the handle recess panel

19.5 Remove the screw behind the handle recess panel

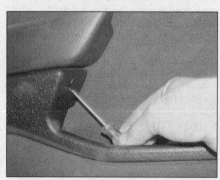

19.6a Prise out the round cover panel . . .

19.6b . . . and remove the screw from the armrest

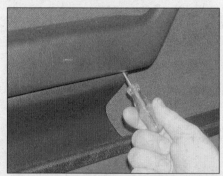

19.7 Removing the rear door trim panel screw below the armrest

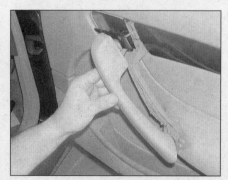

19.8a Remove the door pull cover . . .

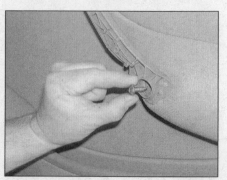

19.8b . . . and remove the screws behind it

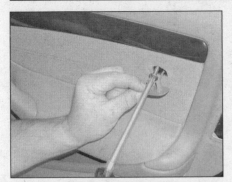

19.9 Prise off the SRS panel, and remove the screw behind it

19.10 Prise off the trim panel using a wide-bladed tool

19.11 Lift the panel, to clear the lock operating knob

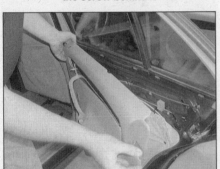

19.12a Removing a rear door trim panel

19.12b On rear doors, and front doors without side airbags, unhook the lock operating rod

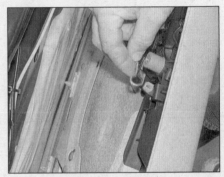

19.12c On front doors with side airbags, unhook the lock operating cable

airbags, prise off the small SRS trim piece and remove the screw behind it **(see illustration)**.

All models

10 Using a wide-bladed or wedge tool, carefully prise off the door trim panel, working progressively around the edge of the panel until all the clips have been released **(see illustration)**. Do not use excessive force, otherwise the clips will be broken.

11 Lift the trim panel slightly, and free it from the window channel at the top. Further lift the panel, to clear the lock operating knob at the top **(see illustration)**.

12 Carefully withdraw the panel from the door, sufficiently to gain access to the lock handle operating mechanism. On models without side airbags, open the retaining clip

which secures the end of the lock operating rod, and detach the rod from the handle. On models with side airbags, unhook the lock operating cable **(see illustrations)**.

13 Where applicable, disconnect the wiring plug(s) from the window switch(es). Check that there is nothing else attached to the door trim panel, then remove it from the car.

14 If desired (if the door internal components are to be worked on), the waterproofing sheet must now be removed from the door. To remove the sheet completely, first remove the door speaker as described in Chapter 12. If great care is taken, the sheet can simply be peeled off, and re-used **(see illustration)**.

Refitting

15 Refitting is the reverse sequence to

removal. On models with side airbags, close the front doors, making sure that no-one is inside the car, and check that the ignition switch is still off, before reconnecting the battery negative lead.

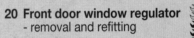

20 Front door window regulator
- removal and refitting

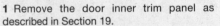

Removal

1 Remove the door inner trim panel as described in Section 19.

2 Prise up and remove the inner and outer window channel sealing strips at the top of the door, taking care not to damage the door paintwork **(see illustrations)**.

19.14 Peeling off the waterproofing sheet

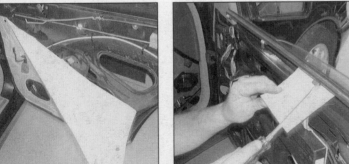

20.2a Prise up the inner sealing strip, taking care to protect the paintwork . . .

20.2b . . . and remove the strip from the door

20.2c Removing the outer sealing strip

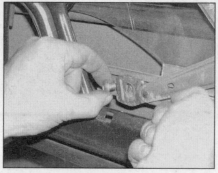

20.4 Unscrew and remove the regulator arm bolt

20.6a Drill off the pop-rivet heads . . .

3 Lower the window until the bolt securing the regulator arm to the window regulator channel is accessible through the aperture at the front of the door.
4 With the window supported, undo the regulator arm-to-channel retaining bolt **(see illustration)**.
5 Manoeuvre the window out of the sliding channels, disengaging first the front then the rear regulator arm, and lift it up out of the regulator, sliding it up to the top of the door. Support the window in this position either by using a wooden wedge between the window and door, or by using masking tape over the top of the door frame.
6 Drill out the regulator pop-rivets, then

manoeuvre the regulator arms downwards and out through the door aperture **(see illustrations)**.
7 On models with electric windows, disconnect the wiring plug from the window motor as it becomes accessible, then remove the regulator completely **(see illustrations)**.
8 If required, also remove the rivets securing the rear guide channel, and remove it through the door aperture **(see illustration)**.

Refitting

9 Refitting is the reverse sequence to removal. Lubricate the regulator sliding channels when reassembling.

21 Front door window glass - removal and refitting

Removal

1 Remove the door inner trim panel as described in Section 19.
2 Lower the window until the bolt securing the regulator arm to the window regulator channel is accessible through the aperture at the front of the door.
3 With the window supported, undo the regulator arm-to-channel retaining bolt **(refer to illustration 20.4)**.
4 Prise up and remove the inner and outer window channel sealing strips at the top of the door, taking care not to damage the door paintwork **(refer to illustrations 20.2a, 20.2b and 20.2c)**.
5 Slide the window forwards out of the regulator channel at the front, then down out of the front guide channel.
6 Disengage the window from the rear regulator arm and rear guide channel, then tilt it forwards before lifting it up and removing it to the outside of the door **(see illustration)**.

Refitting

7 Refitting is the reverse sequence to

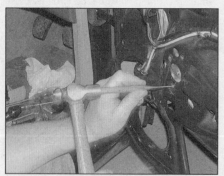

20.6b . . . then tap out the rivets using a suitable punch

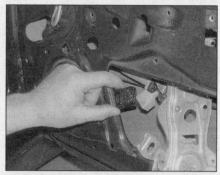

20.7a Disconnect the motor wiring plug (where applicable) . . .

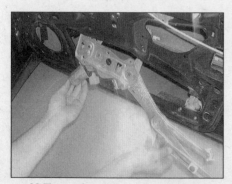

20.7b . . . then remove the regulator through the door aperture

20.8 Removing the rear guide channel

21.6 Removing the front window glass

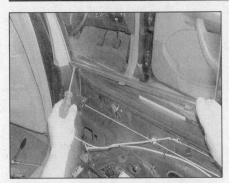

22.2a Prising up the inner sealing strip . . .

22.2b . . . and removing the outer strip

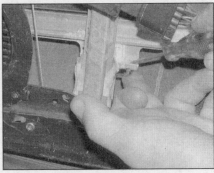

22.4a Using a small screwdriver . . .

removal. Lubricate the regulator sliding channels when reassembling, and ensure that the window glass is correctly engaged in the front and rear guide channels.

22 Rear door window regulator - removal and refitting

Removal

1 Remove the door inner trim panel as described in Section 19.
2 Carefully prise up the inner and outer sealing strips at the top of the door panel, taking care not to damage the paintwork (see illustrations).
3 Lower the window until the guide member of the regulator guide rail is accessible through the aperture in the top centre of the door panel.
4 With the window supported, remove the locking clip securing the window glass to the guide member of the regulator guide rail (see illustrations).
5 Slide the window to the rear to disengage it from the regulator, then slide it up to the top of the door. Support the window in this position either by using a wooden wedge between the window and the door, or by using masking tape over the top of the door

frame and onto the glass on the inside and outside.
6 On models with electric windows, disconnect the wiring plug from the window motor (see illustration).
7 Drill out the regulator pop-rivets (see illustration), then manoeuvre the regulator out through the door aperture.

Refitting

8 Refitting is the reverse sequence to removal. Lubricate the regulator sliding channels when reassembling.

23 Rear door window glass - removal and refitting

Removal

1 Remove the door inner trim panel as described in Section 19.
2 Open the window until the guide member of the regulator guide rail is accessible through the aperture in the top centre of the door panel.
3 With the window supported, remove the locking clip securing the window glass to the guide member of the regulator guide rail (refer to illustrations 22.4a and 22.4b).
4 Carefully prise up the inner and outer

sealing strips at the top of the door panel, taking care not to damage the paintwork (refer to illustrations 22.2a and 22.2b).
5 Move the window glass to the rear to release the channel at the bottom of the glass from the guide member, and temporarily lower it into the base of the door, taking care not to scratch the glass.
6 Working progressively around the window aperture in the door, prise off the window guide strip, and slide it down and out of the door frame (see illustration).
7 Remove the upper and lower screw securing the rear section of the window guide channel (which also secures the fixed glass in place), then pull the guide channel off the

22.4b . . . prise off the glass-to-regulator locking clip

22.6 Disconnect the window motor wiring plug (where applicable)

22.7 Regulator pop-rivets (arrowed)

23.6 Removing the window guide strip

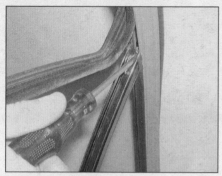

23.7a Remove the rear guide channel upper screw . . .

23.7b . . . and lower guide screw . . .

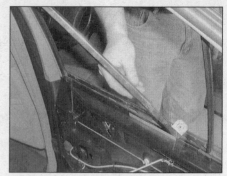

23.7c . . . and remove the guide channel from the door

fixed glass and out of the door frame **(see illustrations)**.

23.8 Removing the rear door window glass

8 Lift the window glass upwards and remove it from the door frame **(see illustration)**.

Refitting

9 Refitting is the reverse sequence to removal. Lubricate the window guide channels with liquid soap (eg, washing-up liquid) to make refitting to the door aperture easier.

24 Rear door fixed quarter-light - removal and refitting

Removal

1 Refer to Section 23 and carry out the

operations listed in paragraphs 1 to 7 inclusive.
2 Ease the quarter-light forwards to release the rubber seal, and remove it from the door **(see illustration)**.

Refitting

3 Refitting is the reverse sequence to removal, but lubricate the quarter-light sealing channels with a soapy solution to ease insertion.

25 Front door exterior handle - removal and refitting

Removal

1 Pull off the door seal in the area around the door lock.
2 Using a 4 mm Allen key inserted through the plug hole, undo the lock cylinder retaining grub screw **(see illustration)**.
3 Push the lock cylinder rearwards to disengage the internal tang, and withdraw it outwards from the door handle. Where applicable, unclip the wiring plug from the lock cylinder, and disconnect the plug from the infra-red remote sensor **(see illustrations)**.
4 Push the door exterior handle to the rear, while at the same time pulling outwards, then disengage the tangs at the front from the mounting bracket; recover the rubber gaskets

24.2 Removing the rear quarter-light glass

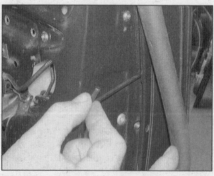

25.2 Using an Allen key to loosen the lock cylinder screw

25.3a Withdraw the lock cylinder . . .

25.3b . . . unclip the wiring plug . . .

25.3c . . . and disconnect it

25.4a Withdraw the handle from the door, and recover the gasket at the rear . . .

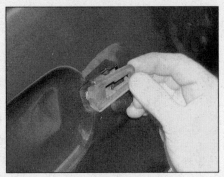

25.4b . . . and at the front of the handle

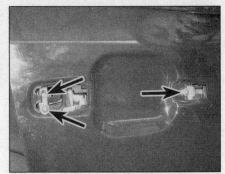

25.5a Loosen (or remove) the three screws (arrowed) . . .

from the front and rear of the handle **(see illustrations)**.

5 If required, the handle inner mounting bracket can only be removed once the door inner trim panel has been removed as described in Section 19. The bracket is removed by loosening three screws (two at the rear, one at the front, under the rubber gasket) and sliding the bracket forwards to disengage the screws **(see illustrations)**.

Refitting

6 To make fitting the handle easier, the lock eccentric adjuster screw should be turned fully outwards (anti-clockwise). The eccentric adjuster is accessed through another hole in the rear edge of the door, below the hole for the Allen screw **(see illustration)**. Note that it may be found that the handle can be refitted without adjusting the eccentric.

7 Fit the rubber gaskets between the handle and the door. When inserting the handle, ensure that the rear operating leg slides behind the wire spring of the mounting bracket as well as the lock lever, then slide the handle forwards to secure.

8 Where applicable, reconnect the wiring to the infra-red sensor, and clip it to the lock cylinder.

9 Insert the lock cylinder, ensuring that the operating rod locates correctly into the lock, and press it home.

10 Tighten the lock cylinder grub screw using

the Allen key inserted into the hole at the rear of the door.

11 If the lock eccentric adjuster has been disturbed, adjust it as follows via the hole in the rear edge of the door. Pull on the exterior handle until resistance is felt, indicating that the lock is about to release. The handle 'free travel' should be approximately 2 mm. Adjust this travel using the eccentric until the handle operation is correct.

12 On completion, refit the door seal and check the operation of the lock and handle.

26 Front door lock - removal and refitting

Removal

1 Remove the door inner trim panel as described in Section 19, and the front door exterior handle as described in Section 25.

2 Disengage the door window from the regulator, as described in Section 20, paragraphs 2 to 4. Move the regulator as necessary to remove the lock assembly, or alternatively remove the regulator completely, as described in Section 20.

3 Release the inner door handle connecting rod (or cable, on models with side airbags)

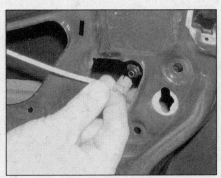

25.5b . . . and withdraw the inner bracket through the door aperture

from the door guide, then disengage it from the lock lever **(see illustration)**.

4 Release the clip securing the rod for the door lock button, and remove the rod from the rear of the lock.

5 Trace the vacuum line along the door panel, and disconnect it at the central locking solenoid **(see illustration)**.

6 Where applicable, trace the door lock wiring harness along the door panel to the lock switch. Press the lock switch securing lug outwards, and remove the switch from the housing.

7 Drill out the two pop-rivets at the top and bottom of the window rear guide rail, and

25.6 Door lock eccentric adjuster screw (arrowed)

26.3 Unhooking the lock operating cable from the lock lever

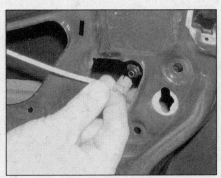

26.5 Disconnect the vacuum line from the lock

26.7 Drill out the pop-rivets at the top and bottom of the rear guide rail

26.8 Removing the door lock inner cover screw

26.9a Remove the lock securing screws . . .

26.9b . . . and withdraw the lock and cover from the door aperture

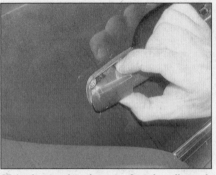

27.1a Loosening the rear door handle grub screw

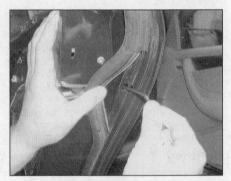

27.1b Removing the plastic trim from behind the rear door handle

remove the guide rail from the door **(see illustration)**.

8 Unscrew and remove the lock inner cover retaining screw from the door inner panel **(see illustration)**.

9 Remove the three lock securing screws from the rear edge of the door, and withdraw the lock assembly and cover down the rear edge of the door until it can be withdrawn through the door aperture **(see illustrations)**. Where applicable, disconnect the anti-theft alarm wiring plug as the lock is removed, and separate the cover from the lock assembly.

Refitting

10 Refitting is the reverse sequence to

removal. Check the lock operation before refitting the door inner trim panel.

27 Rear door exterior handle - removal and refitting
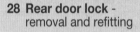

1 The procedure is the same as for the front door handle as described in Section 25, except that on some models, a 3 mm Allen key will be required to unscrew the handle grub screw at the rear edge of the door. In addition, there is no lock cylinder to remove. Instead, remove the plastic trim covering by pushing it to the rear **(see illustrations)**.

28 Rear door lock - removal and refitting

Removal

1 Remove the door inner trim panel as described in Section 19, and the door exterior handle and inner bracket as described in Section 27.

2 Release the inner door handle connecting rod from the door guide, then disengage it from the lock lever **(see illustration)**.

3 Release the clip securing the rod for the door lock button, and remove the rod from the

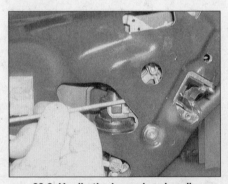

28.2 Unclip the inner door handle connecting rod from the lock

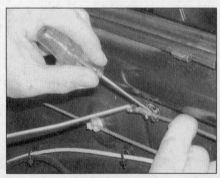

28.3a Unclip the door lock button rod from the door . . .

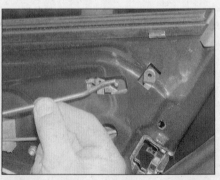

28.3b . . . and unhook it from the door lock

28.3c Unscrew the lock button rod pivot screw . . .

28.3d . . . and remove the rod and button

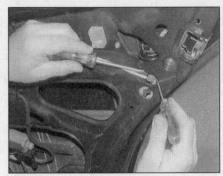

28.4a Using a pair of small screwdrivers . . .

rear of the lock. Unscrew and remove the plastic screw securing the door lock button pivot, and remove the rod and button from the door **(see illustrations)**.

4 Trace the vacuum line along the door panel, and prise off the connection at the central locking solenoid. We had to use two screwdrivers for this, one inserted through the door aperture from the side, as the connection is very tight - care must be taken not to damage the plastic fitting **(see illustrations)**.

5 Unscrew and remove the lock cover retaining screw from the door inner panel **(see illustration)**.

6 Remove the three lock securing screws from the rear edge of the door, and withdraw the lock and cover assembly downwards, tilting it slightly and following the rear edge of the door until the assembly can be withdrawn through the door aperture **(see illustrations)**. Where applicable, disconnect the anti-theft alarm wiring plug as the lock is removed.

7 Once the assembly is removed, the plastic cover can be unclipped for access to the lock components **(see illustration)**.

Refitting

8 Refitting is the reverse sequence to removal. Check the lock operation before refitting the door inner trim panel.

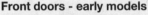

29 Central locking system components - removal and refitting

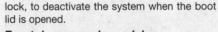

Lock switches

1 On most models, only the front door locks have switches, which activate the complete system when either front door is locked/unlocked. All four doors, the boot lid/tailgate and fuel filler flap all have vacuum-operated actuators, to carry out the physical locking/unlocking operation.

2 On Saloon models up to December 1994, an additional switch is fitted to the boot lid

28.4b . . . release the vacuum line from the door lock

lock, to deactivate the system when the boot lid is opened.

Front doors - early models

3 Remove the door inner trim panel as described in Section 19.

4 Trace the door lock wiring harness along the door panel to the lock switch. Press the lock switch securing lug outwards, and remove the switch from the housing.

5 There is no connector plug in the switch wiring harness, so renewal of the switch requires that the harness is cut. Mercedes-Benz recommend that the cut is made approximately 150 mm from the switch.

6 Taking care to correctly identify the wiring, solder the relevant wires on the new switch

28.5 Remove the lock inner cover screw

28.6a Remove the lock securing screws . . .

28.6b . . . and withdraw the lock assembly down the rear edge of the door

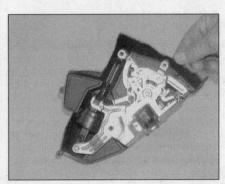

28.7 Removing the lock assembly plastic cover

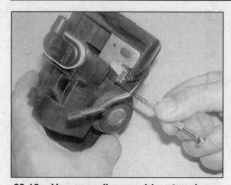

29.10a Use a small screwdriver to release the securing lug . . .

29.10b . . . and remove the boot lid lock switch

29.14 Remove the screw at the base of the actuator

29.15 Unclip the interior lock button control rod

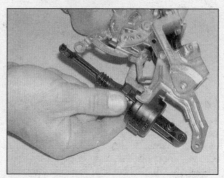

29.16 Unhook and remove the actuator

and the old harness together, and insulate the joints.

7 Attach the switch to the lock housing, then refit the door trim panel as described in Section 19.

Front doors - later models

8 On models with the Mercedes-Benz Driver Authorisation System (DAS), the lock switches are incorporated in the lock barrels. Refer to the exterior handle removal procedure in Section 25.

Boot lid

9 Remove the boot lid lock as described in Section 15.

10 With the switch wiring disconnected, the switch itself can be unclipped from the lock assembly by pressing the securing lug upwards (see illustrations).

11 Refitting is a reversal of removal.

Actuators

Front doors

12 On early models, the actuators can be removed as described for the rear doors, below. On later models, although it appears to be possible to separate the front door lock actuator from the lock, after several attempts in the workshop, we concluded that this is not a DIY operation, and may not in fact be possible without damaging the components. If a front door lock actuator fails, seek the advice of a Mercedes-Benz dealer or parts supplier.

Rear doors

13 Remove the door lock, complete with actuator, from the front or rear doors as

applicable, as described in Section 26 or 28.

14 Remove the screw at the base of the actuator - depending on model, this is either a cross-head or Torx type (see illustration).

15 At the top of the actuator, unclip the control rod from the interior lock button rod (see illustration).

16 Unhook the actuator from the lock assembly to remove (see illustration).

17 Refitting is the reverse sequence to removal.

Boot lid

18 Remove the boot lid lock as described in Section 15.

19 To remove the actuator, it must be

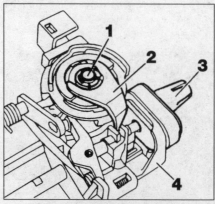

29.23 Tailgate actuator details

1	Circlip	3	Actuator
2	Operating arm	4	Frame

unclipped from the carrier bracket. Two of the clips are at the base of the bracket, which can be released with a small screwdriver; the remaining two clips wrap around at the top, and are released by pressing sideways.

20 The main body of the actuator can now be pulled off the bracket, and the lock operating lever separated by lifting up the locking clip on the actuator shaft.

21 Refitting is a reversal of removal. Make sure that the actuator lock operating lever is correctly engaged with the lock, and that the actuator is clipped securely in place, before refitting the lock.

Tailgate

22 Remove the tailgate lock as described in Section 17.

23 Release the circlip which secures the actuator operating arm to the lock, then unhook the lower end of the arm from the actuator body, noting how it is engaged (see illustration).

24 Unclip the actuator from its location on the lock assembly, and withdraw it.

25 Refitting is a reversal of removal.

Fuel filler flap

26 Open the boot lid or tailgate, and remove the inner trim panel from the right-hand side of the luggage area for access to the fuel filler flap actuator.

27 Prise off the vacuum hose from the actuator - Mercedes-Benz recommend the use of a 7 mm open-end spanner for this, but access is very limited (see illustration).

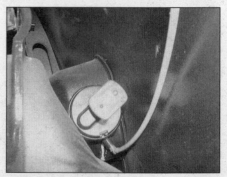

29.27 View of the fuel filler flap actuator from inside the luggage compartment

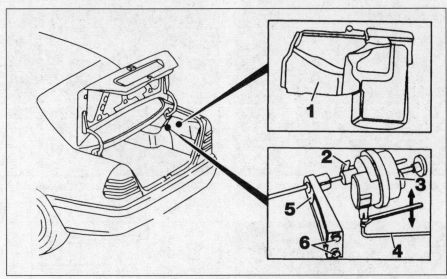

29.28 Fuel filler flap actuator details

| 1 | Liner | 3 | Actuator | 5 | Bracket |
| 2 | Mounting tab | 4 | Vacuum line | 6 | Bolts |

28 Loosen but do not remove the two bolts on the actuator bracket (see illustration).

29 Detach the actuator and its bracket from the support strut, then press down the raised tab between the actuator body and bracket to release the actuator.

30 Refitting is a reversal of removal. Check the operation of the flap before refitting the trim panel.

Vacuum pump

31 Disconnect the battery negative lead.

32 Open the boot lid or tailgate, and remove the inner trim panel from the right-hand side of the luggage area.

33 The pump is housed inside a foam soundproofing box. Carefully withdraw the box from its recess, and open it to access the pump (see illustrations).

34 Disconnect the wiring plugs, noting their locations (see illustration).

35 To disconnect the multiple vacuum hose connection, pull the tab on the side of the pump outwards (see illustration).

36 When completely disconnected, remove the unit from the car.

37 Refitting is the reverse sequence to removal.

Infra-red receivers

38 The receivers are only fitted to those locks which are equipped with lock switches, ie, the front doors and, on early models, the boot lid.

39 The receivers for the front doors are incorporated into the lock cylinders, and may be removed as described in Section 25, paragraphs 1 to 3.

40 To remove the boot lid lock receiver, first remove the boot lid lock as described in Section 15. The receiver simply unclips from the side of the lock assembly.

Control module

Models up to July 1996

41 On early models without the Driver Authorisation System (DAS), the module is located either in the luggage compartment, behind the spare wheel, or at the front of the front passenger's footwell (see illustration).

42 Disconnect the battery negative lead.

43 Gain access to the module either by lifting the boot floor covering, or by removing the facia lower trim panel and releasing the passenger side front carpet.

44 Release the locking catches on the 12-pin and 2-pin connectors respectively, and disconnect the wiring.

45 Release the module from its location, and remove it from the car.

46 Refitting is a reversal of removal.

Models from August 1996 onwards

47 The module is located behind the instrument panel, or behind the driver's front

29.33a Withdraw the foam box . . .

29.33b . . . and open it for access to the pump

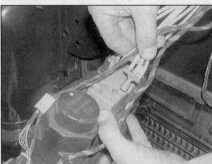

29.34 Disconnect the wiring plugs from the pump

29.35 Disconnect the multiple vacuum hose connection

29.41 Central locking control module location on the right-hand side of the luggage compartment

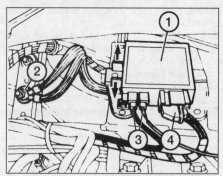

29.47a Infra-red control module behind the instrument panel

1 Module
2 Earth connection
3 2-pin connectors
4 18-pin connector

29.47b Infra-red control module at front of driver's door

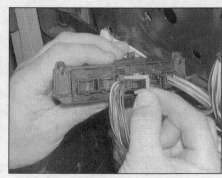

29.50 The 18-pin connector is released by lifting the locking lever

door trim panel **(see illustrations)**. Note that, where applicable, the other 'module' in the driver's door is the side airbag, which is riveted in position.

48 Disconnect the battery negative lead.

49 Remove the instrument panel as described in Chapter 12, or remove the driver's door trim panel as described in Section 19.

50 Disconnect the wiring plugs from the module - the 18-pin connector is secured by a locking lever **(see illustration)**. Where necessary, unscrew the nut securing the earth leads.

51 Release the retaining lugs (they either squeeze together, or are pressed apart), and remove the module from the car **(see illustration)**.

52 Refitting is a reversal of removal.

Main facia switch

53 Refer to Chapter 12.

29.51 The module on the driver's door is released by squeezing the lugs together

here - rest the door carefully on a trolley jack or axle stand temporarily, making sure the door paintwork is suitably protected.

6 Unclip the rubber gaiter fitted around the door wiring connector, then separate the connector halves **(see illustration)**.

7 Move the door away from the A-pillar, and rest it carefully against the car, making sure that the paintwork is protected.

8 Refitting is the reverse sequence to removal, noting the following points:

a) Locate the door onto the centring bolts on each hinge when fitting initially, prior to inserting and tightening the hinge bolts.

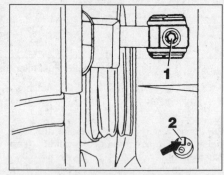

30.2 Door check strap bolt (1) and access hole (2) for square socket (arrowed)

b) Tighten the hinge bolts and door check strap bolt to the specified torque.

c) Make sure that the door wiring connector is locked into position by turning the square socket anti-clockwise.

d) Adjustments can be made at the hinges and at the door striker to provide an equal gap all round the door, and to align the contour of the door panel with that of the front wing.

Front door - later models

9 Pull off the door seal at the front of the door aperture, in the vicinity of the kick panel in the footwell.

10 Prise out the screw cover from the centre of the kick panel, and remove the screw beneath it **(see illustration)**.

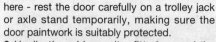

30 Doors - removal and refitting

Front door - early models

1 Fully open the window.

2 Open the door fully and remove the cover from the hole just below the door check strap, to expose the square socket which is used to unlock the wiring connector plug **(see illustration)**.

3 Mercedes-Benz dealers use a special square-ended tool which locates in the square socket - when the tool is turned clockwise, the wiring connector is unlocked. It may be possible to improvise this tool by using a close-fitting flat-bladed screwdriver in the square hole.

4 Prise out the rubber seal from the door check strap location, and remove the bolt securing the door check strap.

5 Unscrew the upper and lower bolts on each hinge, and move the door slightly away from the A-pillar. The help of an assistant is useful

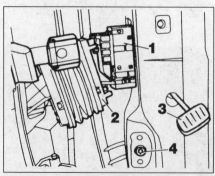

30.6 Front door removal details - early models

1 Wiring connector
2 Rubber gaiter
3 Mercedes square-ended tool
4 Centering bolt

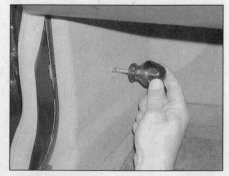

30.10 Remove the screw from the centre of the kick panel

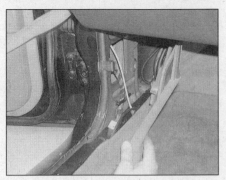

30.11 Removing the kick panel

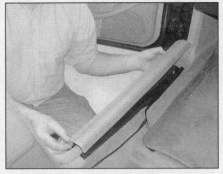

30.12 Remove the sill trim panel for access to the door wiring

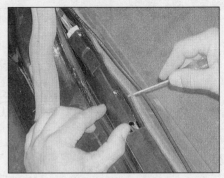

30.13a Prise open the wiring harness cover . . .

11 Unclip the kick panel and remove it **(see illustration)**. On the driver's side, the kick panel has a locating lug at the front - slide the panel rearwards to disengage it.
12 Unclip the door sill trim panel **(see illustration)**. This panel is secured by clips which are an extremely tight fit, and care should be taken that the panel itself, or those surrounding it, are not damaged.
13 With the sill trim panel removed, open the cover on the wiring harness inside the sill, and disconnect the wiring and vacuum hoses to the door **(see illustrations)**.
14 Prise out the rubber seal from the door check strap location, and remove the bolt securing the door check strap **(see illustrations)**.

15 Detach the large rubber gaiter either from the door or the body.
16 Unscrew the upper and lower bolts on each hinge **(see illustration)**, and move the door slightly away from the A-pillar. Feed the wiring and vacuum hoses out through the rubber gaiter. The help of an assistant is useful here - rest the door carefully on a trolley jack or axle stand temporarily, making sure the door paintwork is suitably protected.
17 Refitting is the reverse sequence to removal, noting the following points:
a) Locate the door onto the centring bolts on each hinge when fitting initially, prior to inserting and tightening the hinge bolts.
b) Tighten the hinge bolts and door check strap bolt to the specified torque.

c) Make sure that the wiring and vacuum hoses are securely and correctly reconnected.
d) Adjustments can be made at the hinges and at the door striker to provide an equal gap all round the door, and to align the contour of the door panel with that of the front wing.

Rear door - early models

18 Open the door window to its fullest extent.
19 Detach the large rubber gaiter either from the door or the body.
20 Using a hooked tool or stout piece of bent wire, pull apart the wiring connector retainer visible inside the rubber gaiter **(see illustration)**.

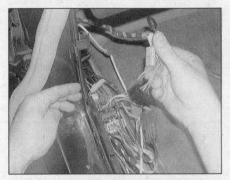

30.13b . . . then disconnect the wiring . . .

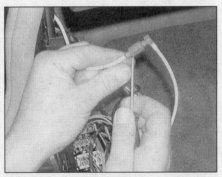

30.13c . . . and vacuum hoses to the door

30.14a Remove the rubber seal . . .

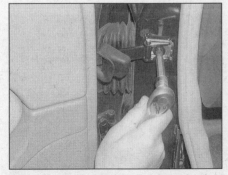

30.14b . . . then unbolt the door check strap

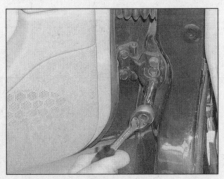

30.16 Removing the door hinge bolts

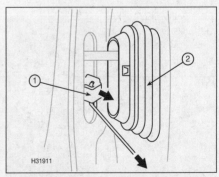

30.20 Insert a piece of bent wire into the connector retainer (1) inside rubber gaiter (2) and pull to separate

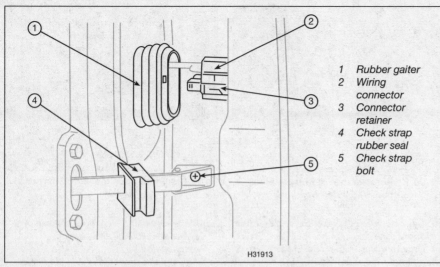

1   Rubber gaiter
2   Wiring connector
3   Connector retainer
4   Check strap rubber seal
5   Check strap bolt

30.21 Rear door removal details - early models

21 Prise out the rubber seal from the door check strap location, and remove the bolt securing the door check strap **(see illustration)**.

22 Support the door, then unscrew and remove the hinge pin bolts.

23 Unscrew the upper and lower bolts on each hinge, and move the door slightly away from the B-pillar. Feed the wiring and vacuum hoses out through the rubber gaiter. The help of an assistant is useful here - rest the door carefully on a trolley jack or axle stand temporarily, making sure the door paintwork is suitably protected.

24 Refitting is the reverse sequence to removal, noting the following points:

a) *Locate the door onto the centring bolts on each hinge when fitting initially, prior to inserting and tightening the hinge bolts.*

b) *Tighten the hinge bolts and door check strap bolt to the specified torque.*

c) *Make sure that the wiring and vacuum hoses are securely and correctly reconnected.*

d) *Adjustments can be made at the hinges and at the door striker to provide an equal gap all round the door, and to align the door panel.*

Rear door - later models

25 Open the door window to its fullest extent.

26 Unclip and remove the B-pillar trim panel as described in Section 41.

27 Noting their fitted positions carefully for refitting, disconnect the wiring plug(s) and vacuum hose at the base of the B-pillar which lead into the door panel **(see illustrations)**.

28 Detach the large rubber gaiter either from the door or the body.

29 Prise out the rubber seal from the door check strap location, and remove the bolt securing the door check strap **(see illustrations)**.

30 Unscrew and remove the nuts from the base of the hinge pins, and recover the washers **(see illustration)**.

31 Pull out the hinge pins, and move the door slightly away from the B-pillar. Feed the wiring and vacuum hoses out through the rubber gaiter. The help of an assistant is useful here - rest the door carefully on a trolley jack or axle stand temporarily, making sure the door paintwork is suitably protected.

32 Refitting is the reverse sequence to removal, noting the following points:

a) *Locate the door onto the centring bolts on each hinge when fitting initially, prior to inserting the hinge pins.*

b) *Securely tighten the hinge pin nuts and door check strap bolt.*

c) *Make sure that the wiring and vacuum hoses are securely and correctly reconnected.*

d) *Adjustments can be made at the hinges and at the door striker to provide an equal gap all round the door, and to align the door panel.*

31 Windscreen and fixed glass - removal and refitting

Due to the methods of attachment, and the special equipment required to complete the

30.27a Disconnect the wiring plug(s) . . .

30.27b . . . and vacuum hose leading to the door

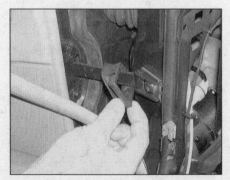

30.29a Prise out the rubber seal . . .

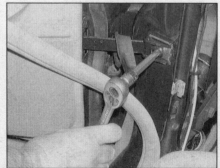

30.29b . . . and unbolt the rear door check strap

30.30 Unscrewing the hinge pin nuts

32.2 Using a cranked screwdriver to hook back the C-shaped mirror cover retainer plate

32.3 Slide off the mirror cover

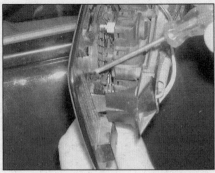

32.4a Use a screwdriver to prise down the spring 'leg' . . .

task successfully, removal and refitting of the windscreen, rear/tailgate window (and rear side windows on Estate models) should be entrusted to a dealer or an automotive glass replacement specialist.

Removal of the fixed glass in the rear doors is covered in Section 24.

32 Door mirror glass - renewal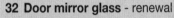

Removal

1 Fully open the window. Carefully push the mirror forwards against the tension of the spring, to gain access to the mirror internal components.

2 Working through the gap thus created on the inside of the mirror, use a small screwdriver to slide back the C-shaped spring plate which retains the mirror outer cover **(see illustration)**.

3 With the retainer released, let the mirror return to its rest position, and slide off the mirror cover, noting how it fits **(see illustration)**.

4 Unhook the mirror glass retaining spring, situated at the top of the mirror glass on the inside **(see illustrations)**.

5 Carefully prise the mirror glass off the drive, and disconnect the wiring plug for the heating element **(see illustration)**.

Refitting

6 Refitting is a reversal of removal. Before refitting the mirror cover, return the cover retaining spring plate to its original position. The cover also has a retaining lug inside, which must engage correctly with the mirror body when it is fitted.

33 Door mirror assembly - removal and refitting

Removal

1 Fully open the window. Carefully push the mirror forwards against the tension of the spring, to gain access to the mirror internal components.

2 Working through the gap thus created on the inside of the mirror, use a small screwdriver to slide back the C-shaped spring plate which retains the mirror outer cover.

3 With the retainer released, let the mirror return to its rest position, and slide off the mirror cover for access to the mounting screws.

4 Support the mirror, then unscrew and remove the three screws on the inside edge of the mirror **(see illustration)**.

5 Move the mirror out of its location, and disconnect the wiring plug **(see illustration)**.

Refitting

6 Refitting is a reversal of removal. Before refitting the mirror cover, return the cover retaining spring plate to its original position. The cover also has a retaining lug inside, which must engage correctly with the mirror body when it is fitted.

34 Front seats - removal and refitting

Removal

1 Move the seat fully to the front. Although not essential, removing the seat is made

32.4b . . . then lift it out and up, to release the glass

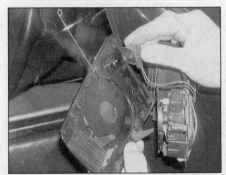

32.5 Disconnecting the mirror heating wiring plug

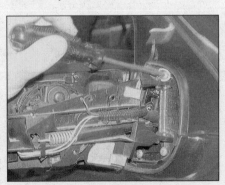

33.4 Remove the mirror mounting screws . . .

33.5 . . . then pull the mirror out, and disconnect the motor wiring plug

34.1 Press the catch inwards, and pull the head restraint out of the seat

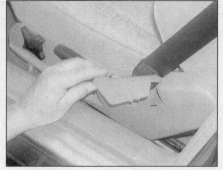

34.2 Unclip the trim from the seat belt end fitting

34.3 Unbolt the seat belt end fitting from the seat

easier by pulling the head restraint out from the top of the seat **(see illustration)**.

2 Carefully unclip the trim surrounding the end of the seat belt attachment to the seat **(see illustration)**.

3 Unscrew the seat belt mounting bolt from the seat, and recover any washers and spacers, noting their order of fitting **(see illustration)**.

4 Using a Torx socket, unscrew the bolts at the rear of each seat slide rail **(see illustration)**. Note the fitted positions of the rearward travel limiter stops in the seat slide rail - these may fall out when the seat is removed, and they must be installed in the correct positions.

5 Move the seat fully to the rear.

6 Release the covers on the front of each seat slide rail by pressing the retaining tabs upwards. Unscrew the Torx bolts at the front of each seat slide rail **(see illustrations)**.

7 Disconnect the seat wiring connector at the front of the seat, noting its location for refitting **(see illustration)**. Depending on the level of equipment fitted, there may be more than one plug - make sure that all wiring is disconnected before lifting the seat out.

8 Lift the seat and remove it from the car **(see illustration)**.

Refitting

9 Refitting is the reverse sequence to removal. Make sure that the travel limiter stops are correctly fitted to the rear section of

the slide rails, as noted in paragraph 4. Tighten the seat belt end fittings and seat mounting bolts to the specified torque.

35 Rear seat - removal and refitting

Saloon

Models with fixed rear seat

1 Push in the detent clip on the left- and right-hand sides of the seat bench at the bottom, while at the same time lifting up the seat bench **(see illustrations)**.

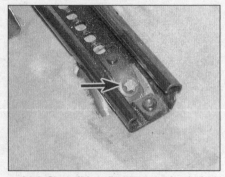

34.4 Seat slide rail rear mounting bolt (arrowed)

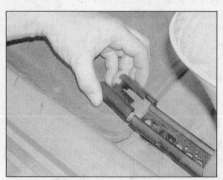

34.6a Slide off the covers . . .

34.6b . . . and remove the front mounting bolts

34.7 Disconnect the wiring plug from the front of the seat

34.8 Removing the front seat

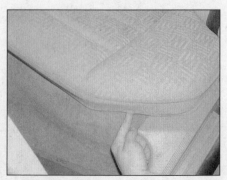

35.1a Press in the seat retaining clip . . .

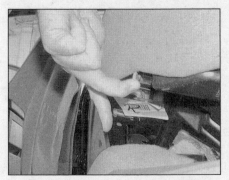

35.1b . . . and lift up the seat bench

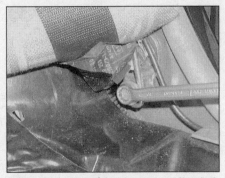

35.3a Unscrew the backrest mounting bolt at each side . . .

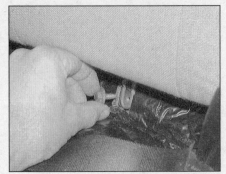

35.3b . . . and the one in the centre

2 Withdraw the seat bench, unhooking it from the metal tabs on the car body, and remove it from the car.
3 To remove the backrest, undo the three retaining bolts at the bottom of the back seat **(see illustrations)**.
4 Push the backrest upwards to disengage the three metal tabs at the top, then remove the backrest from the car **(see illustration)**. If required, remove the insulating mat fitted behind and below the rear seat.
5 Refitting is the reverse sequence to removal, noting the following points:
   a) When refitting the backrest, make sure that the insulating mat is fitted first.
   b) Ensure that the seat belts are not trapped as the seat is installed, and that the belts and buckles are fed through properly.
   c) Ensure in all cases that the metal tabs engage with the locations in the backrest and seat bench.

Models with folding rear seat

6 Push in the detent clip on the left- and right-hand sides of the seat bench at the bottom, while at the same time lifting up the seat bench.
7 Withdraw the seat bench, unhooking it from the metal tabs on the car body, and remove it from the car.
8 Remove the screw securing each backrest side cushion in place, then lift the side cushions upwards to release them from their upper retaining tabs.

9 Unlock the seat backrests, and fold them forward.
10 Remove the screws securing the boot carpet retaining plate, just behind the rear seat, and lift the front of the carpet for access to the backrest hinges.
11 Loosen and remove the hinge nuts and bolts, and remove the two sections of backrest from the car.
12 Refitting is the reverse sequence to removal, noting the following points:
   a) Tighten the hinge nuts and bolts securely.
   b) Ensure that the seat belts are not trapped as the seat is installed, and that the belts and buckles are fed through properly.
   c) Ensure that the metal tabs securing the seat side cushions engage correctly.

Estate

13 Push in the detent clip on the left- and right-hand sides of the seat bench at the bottom, while at the same time lifting up the seat bench.
14 Withdraw the seat bench, unhooking it from the metal tabs on the car body, and remove it from the car.
15 Remove the bolt securing each backrest side cushion in place, then lift the side cushions upwards to release them from their upper retaining tabs **(see illustrations)**.
16 Unlock the seat backrests, and fold them forward.
17 Lift the front of the boot carpet for access to the backrest hinges **(see illustration)**.
18 Unscrew and remove the bolts securing the backrest outer hinges **(see illustration)**.

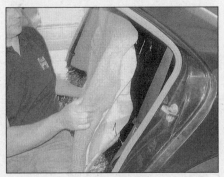

35.4 Lift the backrest upwards, and remove it

35.15a Remove the bolt at the base of the side cushion . . .

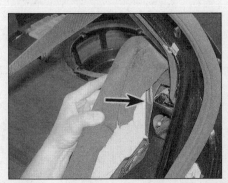

35.15b . . . then lift the cushion to release the metal hook at the top

35.17 Lift up the front section of the boot carpet

35.18 Backrest outer hinge bolts

35.19 Backrest upper pivot bolt and nut (arrowed)

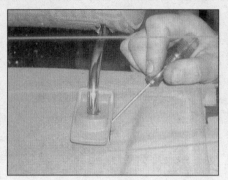

36.2a Using a screwdriver, prise out the plastic covers . . .

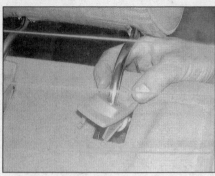

36.2b . . . and slide them up the head restraint stalks

19 Unscrew the upper pivot bolt between the sections of backrest **(see illustration)**, then unfold the backrests back to vertical.

20 Unscrew the centre seat belt end fitting bolt from the floor, noting the locations of any washers and spacers.

21 Loosen, but do not remove, the lower pivot bolt between the sections of backrest.

22 The two sections of backrest can now be lifted from their locations, and removed from the car.

23 Refitting is the reverse sequence to removal, noting the following points:

a) *Tighten the hinge nuts and bolts securely.*

b) *Ensure that the seat belts are not trapped as the seat is installed, and that the belts and buckles are fed through properly.*

c) *Tighten the seat belt end fitting bolt to the specified torque.*

d) *Ensure that the metal tabs securing the seat side cushions engage correctly.*

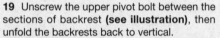

36 Rear head restraints - removal and refitting

Removal

1 Make sure that the head restraint is in the vertical position.

2 Push the plastic covers at the base of each head restraint stalk forwards, then use a screwdriver either side to press in and release the cover securing tabs. Slide the covers out

of position and up the stalks **(see illustrations)**.

3 Use a small screwdriver to lift the small black locking levers now exposed **(see illustration)**. The levers need only be lifted very slightly, as the 'removal' position is between the two locked positions.

4 Pulling gently on the head restraint, slide it to the rear and out of the guides.

Refitting

5 Refitting is a reversal of removal, ensuring that the head restraint locks fully into place. Check the operation of the head restraint folding function on completion.

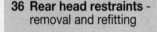

37 Seat belts - removal and refitting

⚠ **Warning: All models are equipped with spring-loaded automatic tensioning devices fitted to the front seat belt inertia reel assemblies. The belt tensioners are triggered by the airbag system, in the event of an accident. For safety reasons, no attempt should be made to dismantle the front seat belt inertia reels, and no electrical testing should be performed on any of the wiring associated with the airbag or belt tensioner system - work of this nature must be entrusted to a Mercedes-Benz dealer.**

Although no specific precautions are given by the manufacturer, it seems prudent to treat the seat belt tensioner with as much care as an airbag unit (see Chapter 12). Therefore, do not drop or strike the tensioner, nor subject it to extremes of heat. If there is any doubt about the condition of the seat belt or tensioner, refer to a Mercedes-Benz dealer - DO NOT attempt to dismantle the belt reel or tensioner, as this could be highly dangerous. If any noise has been noted from the seat belt mechanism, do not attempt to cure this by applying lubricants of any kind. A noise from the tensioner may indicate an internal fault, or it may be that the unit has 'fired', and is therefore no longer operative.

Front belts

1 Disconnect the battery negative lead, and position the lead away from the battery terminal.

2 Pull off the door rubber sealing weatherstrip around the centre pillar.

3 Where applicable, unclip the cover from the alarm system interior sensor **(see illustration)**.

4 Using a screwdriver, release the four upper clips securing the B-pillar trim panel to the car body **(see illustration)**.

5 Pull the upper section of the trim panel upwards, to release it from the lower section.

6 Loosen and remove the alarm sensor

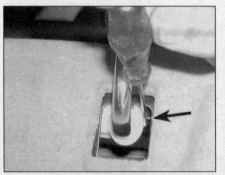

36.3 Lift the locking lever (arrowed) to release the head restraint

37.3 Unclip the alarm interior sensor cover

37.4 Release the clips securing the upper trim panel

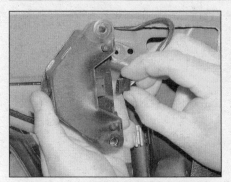

37.6 Remove the alarm sensor screws, then disconnect the wiring plug and remove it

37.7 Unclip the trim panel lower section, and remove it

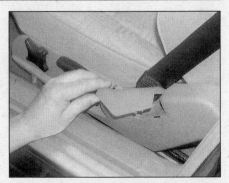

37.8 Unclip the seat belt trim panel from the front seat

retaining screws, then disconnect the sensor unit and remove it from the car **(see illustration)**.

7 Unclip the lower section of the B-pillar trim panel, and slide it upwards out of the sill trim panels **(see illustration)**.

8 Carefully unclip the trim surrounding the end of the seat belt attachment to the seat **(see illustration)**.

9 Unscrew the seat belt mounting bolt from the seat, and recover any washers and spacers, noting their order of fitting **(see illustration)**.

10 Feed the end of the seat belt through the upper section of the trim panel, and remove the panel completely **(see illustration)**.

11 Unscrew and remove the seat belt upper

mounting bolt, and recover the washers and spacers fitted around it, noting their fitted sequence **(see illustration)**.

12 Disconnect the wiring plug from the seat belt inertia reel/belt tensioner assembly **(see illustration)**.

13 Unscrew and remove the inertia reel mounting bolt, and recover any washers or spacers used, noting their fitted sequence.

14 Remove the seat belt from the car, noting the precautions listed at the start of this Section.

15 Refitting is the reverse sequence to removal, noting the following points:

a) Tighten the seat belt mounting bolts to the specified torque.

b) When refitting the B-pillar trim panel,

engage the seat belt height adjuster lug with the inside of the adjuster lever **(see illustration)**. Where applicable, refit the screws and wiring plug to the alarm sensor before fitting the panel over it.

Front belt stalks

16 Remove the relevant front seat as described in Section 34.

17 Unscrew the bolt at the rear securing the stalk side trim panel, and remove the panel.

18 Release the wiring from the cable-ties as necessary, then unclip the inner cover from the belt stalk.

19 Disconnect the wiring plug from the seat belt stalk.

20 Unscrew the seat belt stalk mounting bolt **(see illustration)**, noting the fitted sequence

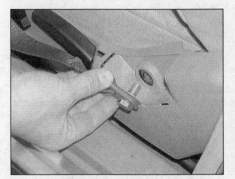

37.9 Unbolt the seat belt end fitting

37.10 Feed the seat belt end fitting through the upper trim panel

37.11 Seat belt upper mounting bolt

37.12 Prise off the wiring plug from the inertia reel - mounting bolt arrowed

37.15 Engage the seat belt height adjuster correctly when refitting the trim panel

37.20 Front seat belt stalk mounting bolt (arrowed)

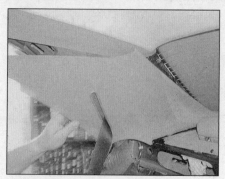

37.26 Removing the C-pillar trim panel

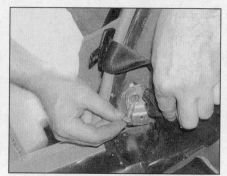

37.27 Unbolt and remove the seat belt lower mounting

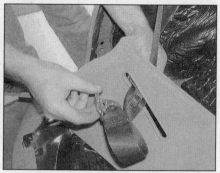

37.28 Feed the seat belt through the C-pillar trim panel

of any washers, and remove the stalk from the car.

21 Refitting is a reversal of removal. Tighten the stalk mounting bolt to the specified torque, and secure the wiring using new cable-ties.

Rear belts

Note: *Where fitted, the centre seat belt is incorporated into the seat itself, and can only be removed by dismantling the seat, which includes removing the seat covering. This job is considered beyond the scope of this manual, and is best entrusted to a Mercedes-Benz dealer.*

Saloon models

22 Remove the rear seat bench and backrest as described in Section 35.

23 Pull off the door rubber sealing weatherstrip around the front edge of the C-pillar trim panel.

24 Using a screwdriver, and taking care not to damage the panel or surrounding trim, release the three securing clips at the front edge of the panel.

25 Release the panel retaining clip at the top rear corner of the panel by moving the panel sideways, towards the centre of the car.

26 Finally, release the panel lower securing clips by lifting the panel upwards **(see illustration)**.

27 Unscrew the seat belt end fitting bolt from the floor, recovering any washers or spacers used. Unhook the end plate from the recess in the car body **(see illustration)**.

28 Feed the end of the seat belt through the trim panel, and remove the panel completely **(see illustration)**.

29 Unbolt and remove the seat belt upper mounting bolt, recovering any washers or spacers used **(see illustration)**.

30 Unscrew and remove the bolts securing the seat belt guide to the rear pillar, and remove the guide **(see illustrations)**.

31 Unscrew and remove the inertia reel mounting bolt, and remove the seat belt from the car, feeding the belt through the sound insulation panel **(see illustration)**.

32 If required, the rear seat belt stalks can be unbolted from the floor and removed **(see illustration)**.

33 Refitting is a reversal of removal. Tighten the seat belt mounting bolts to the specified torque.

Estate models

34 Remove the rear seat bench and backrest as described in Section 35.

35 Unclip and remove the luggage compartment side trim panels as described in Section 41.

36 Unclip the cover fitted over the seat belt upper mounting bolt. Unscrew and remove the seat belt upper mounting bolt, inertia reel mounting bolt, and lower mounting bolt **(see illustrations)**. In all cases, note the fitted sequence of any washers or spacers used. Remove the seat belt from the car.

37 If required, the rear seat belt stalks can be

37.29 Unscrew and remove the seat belt upper mounting bolt

37.30a Unscrew the bolts . . .

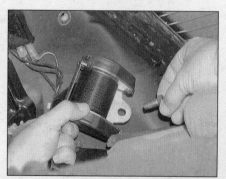

37.30b . . . and remove the belt guide

37.31 Unscrew the inertia reel mounting bolt, and remove the seat belt

37.32 Rear seat belt stalk mounting bolt (arrowed)

37.36a Unclip the cover from the upper mounting . . .

37.36b . . . then unscrew the mounting bolt

37.36c Seat belt inertia reel mounting bolt (arrowed)

unbolted from the floor and removed, once the insulating mat is lifted out.
38 Refitting is a reversal of removal. Tighten the seat belt mounting bolts to the specified torque.

38 Sunroof - general information

A sliding sunroof, either mechanically- or electrically-operated, is available as a factory-fitted option. Adjustment or repair of the sunroof or its component parts should be left to a dealer, as the complexity of the unit and the need for special tools and equipment renders these operations beyond the scope of the average owner.

39 Centre console - removal and refitting

Removal

1 On manual transmission models, prise out and release the gear lever boot from the console cover, and slide the boot up the lever **(see illustration)**.
2 On automatic transmission models, prise up the plastic frame surrounding the selector level panel, which is secured by two clips on either side.
3 Carefully prise up the console centre panel from around the gear/selector lever - there are two clips either side **(see illustration)**.

Mercedes-Benz recommend only levering through the gear/selector lever aperture to release the clips; whatever method is used, take care to avoid damaging or marking the trim panels by protecting them with rag or card.
4 Lift the panel off over the gear/selector lever, and disconnect the wiring connector(s). Models from September 1995 onwards have just one connector, but it may be advisable to mark the positions of the connectors found on earlier models **(see illustrations)**.
5 Prise out and remove the oddments tray in front of the gear/selector lever **(see illustration)**. On early models, this is secured by two screws in the base of the tray.
6 Remove the screw in each corner at the base of the facia centre panel **(see illustration)**.

39.1 Prise up the gear lever boot

39.3 Remove the console centre panel

39.4a Later models have just one wiring connector . . .

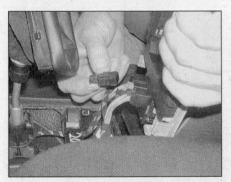

39.4b . . . but early models have more, and may need to be marked for position

39.5 Unclip and remove the oddments tray

39.6 Remove the two screws inside the oddments tray aperture

39.7 Removing the screws (arrowed) securing the storage tray below the radio

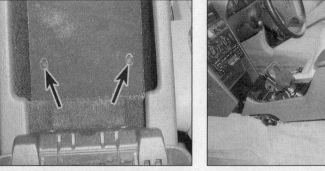

39.8 Remove the two screws (arrowed) in the storage bin between the front seats

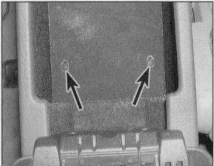

39.10 Removing the centre console

7 Unscrew and remove the two screws securing the storage compartment below the radio, then carefully prise down the top edge of the compartment to release it from the facia centre panel, and pull it out of the facia. Withdraw the ashtray, disconnecting the lighting wiring plug as this is done **(see illustration)**.
8 Depending on model, either lift up the centre armrest, or remove the carpet in the base of the storage compartment between the front seats. Unscrew and remove the two screws in the base of the compartment **(see illustration)**.
9 Where applicable, remove the two remaining screws behind the gear/selector lever aperture.
10 Lift and tilt the console to separate the sliding joint connections at the front, where it joins the centre of the facia panel. Lift the

console over the gear/selector lever, and remove it from the car **(see illustration)**.

Refitting
11 Refitting is the reverse sequence to removal.

40 Glovebox - removal and refitting

Removal
1 Disconnect the battery negative terminal.
2 Unscrew and remove the glovebox catch retaining screws, and remove the catch **(see illustrations)**.
3 On models without a passenger airbag,

prise out the glovebox light from the top of the glovebox, disconnect the wiring and remove the light.
4 Remove the expanding rivets from the glovebox aperture by prising out the rivet expander with a screwdriver, then remove the expander and rivet body **(see illustration)**.
5 Release the clips at the top and bottom of the glovebox, using a thin wedge tool or slim screwdriver, taking care not to damage the glovebox or facia.
6 Withdraw the glovebox. On models with a passenger airbag, disconnect the wiring plug from the glovebox light **(see illustration)**. Pull the light wiring through the aperture and remove the glovebox from the facia.

Refitting
7 Refitting is the reverse sequence to removal.

41 Trim panels - removal and refitting

A-pillar trim panel
1 Pull away the door seal weatherstrip on the front body pillar on both sides.
2 Remove both front pillar trim panels by pushing the panel in the area of the retaining clips away from the pillar using a plastic wedge or small screwdriver - three clips are used altogether **(see illustration)**. Take care not to damage or mark the panel.

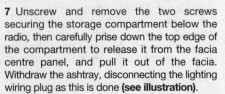

40.2a Loosen and remove the screws . . .

40.2b . . . and remove the glovebox catch

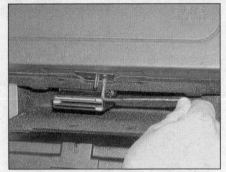

40.4 Using a forked tool to prise up the glovebox retaining rivets

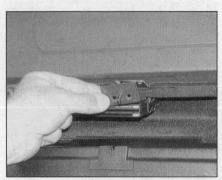

40.6 Withdraw the glovebox, and disconnect the light wiring plug

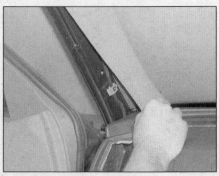

41.2 Prise the trim panel away from its retaining clips

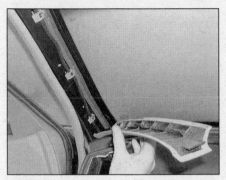

41.3 Release the upper clip, and remove the A-pillar trim

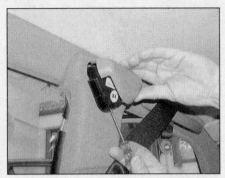

41.6 Unclip the alarm interior sensor cover

41.7 Release the clips securing the upper trim panel

3 When the three main clips have been released, slide the panel downwards to release the upper locating lug, and remove it from the car (see illustration).
4 Refitting is a reversal of removal.

B-pillar trim panel

5 Pull off the door rubber sealing weatherstrip around the centre pillar.
6 Where applicable, unclip the cover from the alarm system interior sensor (see illustration).
7 Using a screwdriver, release the four upper clips securing the B-pillar trim panel to the car body (see illustration). Pull the upper section of the trim panel upwards, to release it from the lower section.
8 Loosen and remove the alarm sensor retaining screws, then disconnect the sensor unit and remove it from the car (see illustration).
9 Carefully unclip the trim surrounding the end of the seat belt attachment to the seat (see illustration).
10 Unscrew the seat belt mounting bolt from the seat, and recover any washers and spacers, noting their order of fitting (see illustration).
11 Feed the end of the seat belt through the upper section of the trim panel, and remove the panel completely (see illustration).
12 If required, unclip the lower section of the

B-pillar trim panel, and slide it upwards out of the sill trim panels (see illustration).
13 Refitting is the reverse sequence to removal, noting the following points:
a) Tighten the seat belt mounting bolts to the specified torque.
b) When refitting the B-pillar trim panel, engage the seat belt height adjuster lug with the inside of the adjuster lever. Where applicable, refit the screws and wiring plug to the alarm sensor before fitting the panel.

C-pillar trim panel

Saloon

14 Removing the panel is made easier if the

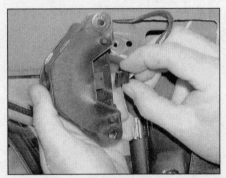

41.8 Remove the alarm sensor screws, then disconnect the wiring plug and remove it

rear seat side cushion is removed first, as described in Section 35.
15 Pull off the door rubber sealing weatherstrip around the front edge of the panel.
16 Using a screwdriver, and taking care not to damage the panel or surrounding trim, release the three securing clips at the front edge of the panel.
17 Release the panel retaining clip at the top rear corner of the panel by moving the panel sideways, towards the centre of the car.
18 Finally, release the panel lower securing clips by lifting the panel upwards (see

41.9 Unclip the seat belt trim panel from the front seat

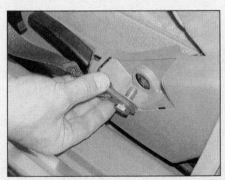

41.10 Unbolt the seat belt end fitting

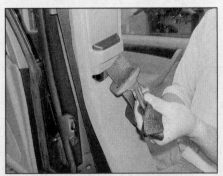

41.11 Feed the seat belt end fitting through the upper trim panel

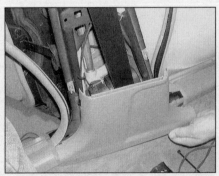

41.12 If required, unclip the trim panel lower section, and remove it

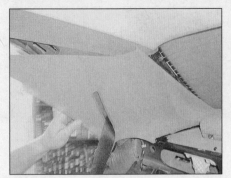

41.18 Removing the C-pillar trim panel

41.19 Unbolt and remove the seat belt lower mounting

41.20 Feed the seat belt through the C-pillar trim panel

illustration). Recover the insulation panel fitted inside the trim panel.

19 Unscrew the seat belt lower mounting bolt, recovering any washers or spacers used **(see illustration)**.

20 Feed the end of the seat belt through the trim panel, and remove the panel completely **(see illustration)**.

21 Refitting is a reversal of removal. Tighten the seat belt mountings to the specified torque.

Estate

22 Unclip the cover from the seat belt upper mounting bolt, then unscrew and remove the bolt, noting the fitted sequence of the washers and spacers **(see illustrations)**.

23 Pull off the tailgate rubber seal from the door aperture, around the side of the trim panel to be removed.

24 Using a thin wedge or slim screwdriver, and taking care not to mark the panel, unclip the panel retaining clips and remove the panel, releasing its lower edge from the side trim panel **(see illustration)**.

25 Refitting is a reversal of removal. Tighten the seat belt mountings to the specified torque.

D-pillar trim panel (Estate)

26 Unscrew and remove the Allen bolt which secures the hook for the luggage net, and remove the hook from the trim panel **(see illustration)**.

27 Pull off the tailgate rubber seal from the tailgate aperture, around the side of the trim panel to be removed.

28 Using a thin wedge or slim screwdriver,

and taking care not to mark the panel, unclip the panel retaining clips and remove the panel **(see illustration)**. If difficulty is experienced, it will be necessary to locally remove the C-pillar trim panel and luggage area side trim panel, using the appropriate removal procedures in this Section.

29 Refitting is a reversal of removal.

Lower facia panels

Driver's side

30 Lift up the door sill weatherstrip and pull off the door seal in the vicinity of the trim panel.

31 Turn the plastic fastener which retains the air vent 90° anti-clockwise, pull out the fastener, and remove the vent panel **(see illustration)**.

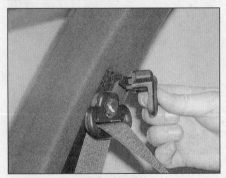

41.22a Unclip the cover from the upper mounting . . .

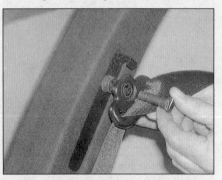

41.22b . . . then unscrew the mounting bolt

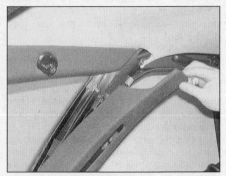

41.24 Unclip and remove the C-pillar trim panel

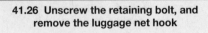

41.26 Unscrew the retaining bolt, and remove the luggage net hook

41.28 Unclip and remove the D-pillar trim panel

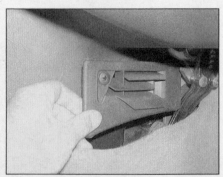

41.31 Removing the vent panel below the facia

41.33a Remove the bonnet release handle screw . . .

41.33b . . . then remove the handle and unhook the release cable

41.34 Removing one of the panel retaining screws

32 At the base of the lower facia panel, unscrew the plastic fastener and remove it.

33 Remove the screw securing the bonnet release handle, then remove the handle and unhook the bonnet release cable **(see illustrations)**.

34 Remove the six screws on the underside of the panel **(see illustrations)**.

35 On models with an adjustable steering column, pull the cover off the adjuster lever, and remove the housing screw beneath.

36 Unhook the trim panel locating lug from the front of the instrument panel, and remove the panel from the car **(see illustration)**.

37 Refitting is a reversal of removal.

Passenger side

38 Turn the plastic fastener which retains the air vent 90° anti-clockwise, pull out the

fastener, and remove the vent panel **(see illustration)**.

39 Remove the three screws from the underside of the panel **(see illustration)**.

40 Withdraw the panel rearwards, unhooking the two locating lugs at the front edge of the panel, and remove it from the car **(see illustration)**.

41 Refitting is a reversal of removal.

Door trim panels

42 See Section 19.

Luggage area side trim panels

Saloon

43 Release the clips at the corners of the trim panel by turning them through 90°, then prise them out.

44 Peel the panel away from the side of the boot, and remove it from the car **(see illustration)**.

45 Refitting is a reversal of removal.

Estate

46 Remove the rear seat side cushion on the side concerned, referring to Section 35.

47 Fold the rear seat backrest forwards.

48 Lift out the rear section of the boot floor panel.

49 Remove the tailgate sill trim panel; prise up and removing the upper clips, then remove the bolts securing the luggage tie-down hooks on the inside edge. Also unclip the trim panel which surrounds the tailgate lock striker **(see illustrations)**.

50 Remove the Torx bolts which secure the luggage tie-down hooks at the front of the

41.36 Removing the driver's lower facia panel (steering wheel removed for clarity)

41.38 Removing the passenger side vent panel

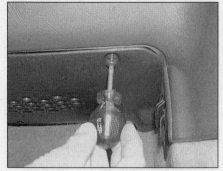

41.39 Remove the three panel securing screws . . .

41.40 . . . then lower the panel and remove it

41.44 Removing the luggage area side trim panel - Saloon

41.49a Using a screwdriver, prise up . . .

41.49b . . . and remove the clips securing the tailgate sill trim panel

41.49c Unscrew the bolts securing the luggage tie-down hooks, and remove the hooks

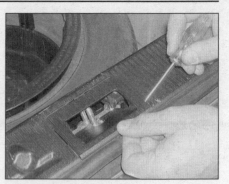

41.49d Unclip the trim panel surrounding the tailgate lock striker

41.49e Removing the tailgate sill trim panel

41.50a Remove the bolt securing the front tie-down hooks, and remove the hook and plate

boot floor. Remove the hooks and mounting plates, and lift out the front section of the boot floor panel **(see illustrations)**.

51 Pull off the tailgate rubber seal from the tailgate aperture, around the end of the trim panel to be removed.

52 Unscrew and remove the hooks at the rear of the panel for the luggage cover, taking care not to mix them up, as they are handed **(see illustration)**.

53 Release the clips at the corners of the trim panel by turning them through 90°, then prise them out.

54 The panel must be lifted upwards to release the three clips at the top of the panel. Lift the panel out, and remove it from the car **(see illustration)**.

55 Refitting is a reversal of removal.

Rear shelf (Saloon)

56 Remove the rear seat as described in Section 35 and the rear seat head restraints as described in Section 36.

57 Remove the C-pillar trim panels as described previously in this Section.

58 Unscrew and remove the screws from the front edge of the shelf. On later models, the shelf is retained by plastic rivets, which can be released by tapping out the centre sections with a punch - recover the centre sections for use when refitting **(see illustrations)**.

59 Lift the shelf at the front, and pull to

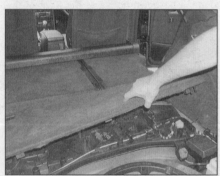

41.50b Lift out the front section of the boot floor panel

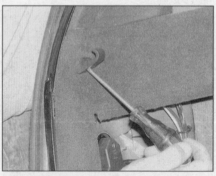

41.52 Remove the luggage cover hooks at the rear of the side trim panel

41.54 Removing the luggage area side trim panel - Estate

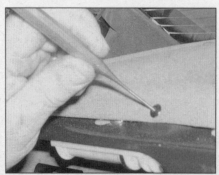

41.58a Tap the centre of the rivets through with a punch

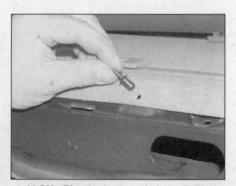

41.58b Plastic rivet ready for refitting

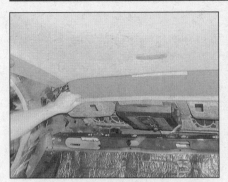

41.59 Lift the shelf at the front, and remove it

41.61a Using a forked tool to prise out the securing clip

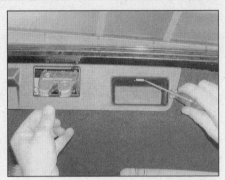

41.61b Release the plastic tab inside the handle recess, and remove the panel

remove it, disengaging the rear locating lugs **(see illustration)**. Disconnect the rear speaker wiring as necessary, noting its location.

60 Refitting is a reversal of removal.

Tailgate trim panel - Estate

61 Prise out the clip securing the tailgate lock/handle cover, then use a screwdriver to release the plastic tab in the handle recess **(see illustrations)**. Unhook and remove the tailgate lock/handle cover.

62 Prise out the plastic clips at the edges of the main trim panel, then lift the panel slightly, and unhook the clips securing the top edge of the panel **(see illustrations)**.

63 If required, the three sections of trim surrounding the rear window can be prised free of their retaining clips using a plastic wedge or wide-bladed tool **(see illustrations)**.

64 Refitting is a reversal of removal.

Other trim panels - general

65 The interior trim panels are secured using either screws or various types of trim fasteners, usually studs or clips.

66 Check that there are no other panels overlapping the one to be removed, or other components hindering removal; usually there is a sequence that has to be followed, and this will only become obvious on close inspection.

67 Some of the interior panels will additionally be retained by the screws which are used to secure other items, such as the grab handles.

68 Remove all visible retainers such as screws, noting that these may be hidden under small plastic caps. If the panel will not come free, it is held by internal clips or fasteners. These are usually situated around the edges of the panel, and can be prised up to release them; note, however, that they can break quite easily, so replacements should be available. The best way of releasing such clips is to use a large flat-bladed screwdriver or other wide-bladed tool. Note that in many cases, the adjacent sealing strip must be prised back to release a panel.

69 When removing a panel, **never** use excessive force or the panel may be damaged; always check carefully that all fasteners or other relevant components have

been removed or released before attempting to withdraw a panel.

70 Refitting is a reversal of removal; secure the fasteners by pressing them firmly into place and ensure that all disturbed components are correctly secured to prevent rattles.

Carpets

71 Carpet removal and refitting is reasonably straightforward, but is very time-consuming because all adjoining trim panels must be removed first, as must components such as the seats, centre console and seat belt lower anchorages.

Headlining

72 The headlining is clipped to the roof, and can be withdrawn only once all fittings such

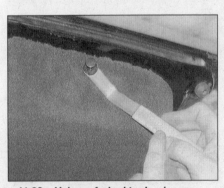

41.62a Using a forked tool, prise up . . .

41.62b . . . and remove the clips around the panel edges

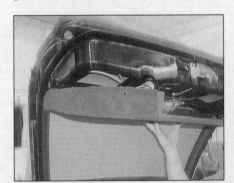

41.62c Unhook the top edge of the panel, and remove it

41.63a Removing the tailgate window trim panel top section . . .

41.63b . . . and one of the side sections

42.4 Release the A-pillar trim panel lower clip

42.6 Remove the screws (arrowed) above and below the radio aperture

42.7a Unclip the panel from the facia . . .

as grab handles, sun visors, sunroof (if fitted), fixed window glass, and related trim panels have been removed and the relevant sealing strips have been prised clear.

73 Note that headlining removal and refitting requires considerable skill and experience if it is to be carried out without damage, and is therefore best entrusted to a dealer or automotive upholstery specialist.

42 Facia -
removal and refitting

Removal

1 Remove the steering column as described in Chapter 10.

2 Remove the instrument panel and the radio/cassette player as described in Chapter 12.
3 Remove the glovebox as described in Section 40.
4 Remove the A-pillar trim panels as described in Section 41. Release the lower clip from the A-pillar on each side, to provide clearance for the facia to be removed **(see illustration)**.
5 Remove the centre console as described in Section 39.
6 Remove the two screws above and below the radio aperture in the facia **(see illustration)**.
7 Pull the lower edge of the facia centre panel outwards, then unhook the side and top edges from the facia. Unclip the cover which

fits over the switch panel wiring plugs. Noting their locations, disconnect the wiring from the switches, and remove the panel complete with switches **(see illustrations)**.
8 Remove the facia lower trim panels on the driver's and passenger's sides, as described in Section 41.
9 Using a small screwdriver inserted through the vent grilles, release the tabs securing the speakers at either end of the facia. Lift up each speaker and disconnect the wiring plug **(see illustrations)**.
10 Unscrew and remove the two screws in each speaker aperture which secure the facia vents. Lift up the two retaining tabs at the base of each vent, and remove them from the ends of the facia **(see illustrations)**.
11 The centre vents are secured by two

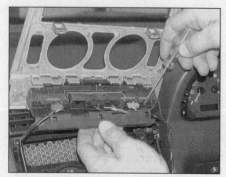

42.7b . . . then open the cover to access the wiring plugs . . .

42.7c . . . and disconnect the wiring plugs from the switches

42.9a Release the speaker securing tabs . . .

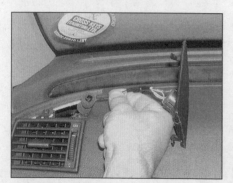

42.9b . . . then lift out the speaker and disconnect the wiring plug

42.10a Remove the vent securing screws . . .

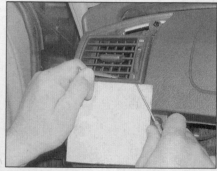

42.10b . . . lift the lower retaining tabs . . .

42.10c . . . then remove the vents from the facia

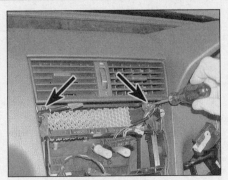

42.11a Remove the lower screws (arrowed) . . .

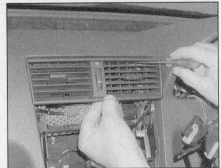

42.11b . . . then release the upper tabs and remove the centre vents

screws at the bottom, and two clips at the top. Remove the screws and prise the clips downwards, then pull the centre vents from the facia **(see illustrations)**.

12 Remove the heater control panel as described in Chapter 3.

13 Remove the main light switch as described in Chapter 12. Carefully unclip the light switch panel and withdraw it from the facia, then unclip the headlight adjuster connector plug and remove the panel completely **(see illustration)**.

14 Using the information in the relevant Section of Chapter 9, unhook the parking brake cable from the facia operating handle. Pull the parking brake handle out of the facia, and remove it **(see illustration)**.

15 Remove the facia mounting bolt on the driver's side end of the facia **(see illustration)**.

16 Unclip the small trim panel from the passenger's end of the facia, and remove the facia mounting bolt beneath **(see illustration)**.

17 Prise out the two trim covers at either end of the facia windscreen vent, and remove the facia mounting bolts (and washers) beneath each one **(see illustrations)**.

18 Remove the two facia mounting bolts from the base of the facia, on the passenger's side **(see illustration)**.

19 Unclip the wiring harness from the central

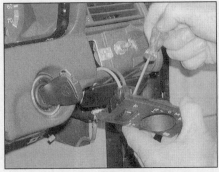

42.13 Remove the light switch panel and disconnect the headlight adjuster connector

42.14 Remove the parking brake handle, and detach the cable

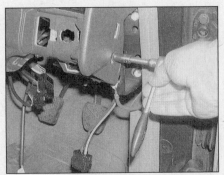

42.15 Remove the facia mounting bolt from the driver's side

42.16 Prise out the panel at the passenger side to access the facia mounting bolt

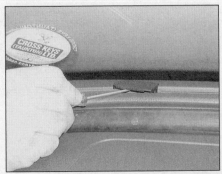

42.17a Prise up the covers at either end of the windscreen vent . . .

42.17b . . . and remove the mounting bolt beneath each

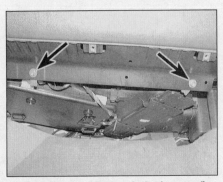

42.18 Remove the two bolts (arrowed) under the passenger side of the facia

42.19 Unclip the wiring harness from the centre of the facia

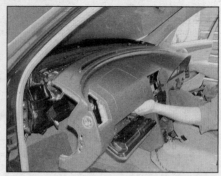

42.20 Withdraw the facia panel to the rear, and remove it from the car

section of the facia panel, and make sure that it is moved clear **(see illustration)**.

20 With the aid of an assistant, lift the facia panel slightly and withdraw it rearwards **(see illustration)**.

21 On models with a passenger airbag, take care not to damage the airbag as the facia panel is withdrawn.

22 As the facia panel is removed, take care to ensure that nothing is still attached, and feed the wiring carefully through the various apertures, noting how it is routed for refitting.

Refitting

23 Refitting is the reverse of removal, noting the following points:

a) *Ensure that all wiring is correctly routed, and is not trapped as the facia is refitted. The aid of an assistant will be useful.*

b) *When reconnecting the battery, make sure that no-one is inside the car because of the potential risk of air bag deployment.*

c) *On completion, check that all the electrical components and switches function correctly.*

Chapter 12
Body electrical system

Contents

Degrees of difficulty

Easy, suitable for novice with little experience	Fairly easy, suitable for beginner with some experience	Fairly difficult, suitable for competent DIY mechanic	Difficult, suitable for experienced DIY mechanic	Very difficult, suitable for expert DIY or professional

Specifications

System type .... 12-volt, negative earth

Battery
Type .... 12-volt lead-acid, 46 to 100 Ah depending on model

Bulbs — **Wattage**
Exterior lights
Headlight:
  Dipped beam .... 55 (H7 type) or 35 (Xenon bulb)
  Main beam .... 55 (H1 type)
Front foglight .... 55 (H1 type)
Front sidelight 5
Direction indicator .... 21 (amber)
Direction indicator side repeater .... 5 (amber)
Stoplight 21
Rear foglight/taillight 21/4
Reversing light 21
Number plate light 5
Interior light
Front courtesy lights 10
Rear courtesy lights 10
Luggage compartment light 10
Instrument panel:
  Illumination bulbs 3
  Warning light bulbs 1.5

Torque wrench settings	Nm	lbf ft
Driver's airbag screws	6	4
Windscreen wiper motor:		
Mounting bolts	5	4
Spindle nut	19	14

1 General information and precautions

⚠️ **Warning: Before carrying out any work on the electrical system, read through the precautions given in Safety first! at the beginning of this manual and in Chapter 5A.**

The electrical system is of the 12-volt negative-earth type. Power for the lights and all electrical accessories is supplied by a lead-acid type battery, which is located below the luggage area floor, and is charged by the alternator.

This Chapter covers repair and service procedures for the various electrical components not associated with the engine. Information on the battery, alternator and starter motor can be found in Chapter 5A.

It should be noted that prior to working on any component in the electrical system, the battery negative terminal should first be disconnected, to prevent the possibility of electrical short-circuits and/or fires.

2 Electrical fault finding - general information

Note: *Refer to the precautions given in Safety first! and in Chapter 5A before starting work. The following tests relate to testing of the main electrical circuits, and should not be used to test delicate electronic circuits (such as anti-lock braking systems), particularly where an electronic control module (ECU) is used.*

General

1 A typical electrical circuit consists of an electrical component, any switches, relays, motors, fuses, fusible links or circuit breakers related to that component, and the wiring and connectors which link the component to both the battery and the chassis. To help to pinpoint a problem in an electrical circuit, wiring diagrams are included at the end of this Chapter.

2 Before attempting to diagnose an electrical fault, first study the appropriate wiring diagram to obtain a complete understanding of the components included in the particular circuit concerned. The possible sources of a fault can be narrowed down by noting if other components related to the circuit are operating properly. If several components or circuits fail at one time, the problem is likely to be related to a shared fuse or earth connection.

3 Electrical problems usually stem from simple causes, such as loose or corroded connections, a faulty earth connection, a blown fuse, a melted fusible link, or a faulty relay (refer to Section 3 for details of testing relays). Visually inspect the condition of all fuses, wires and connections in a problem circuit before testing the components. Use the wiring diagrams to determine which terminal connections will need to be checked in order to pinpoint the trouble spot.

4 The basic tools required for electrical fault finding include a circuit tester or voltmeter (a 12-volt bulb with a set of test leads can also be used for certain tests); a self-powered test light (sometimes known as a continuity tester); an ohmmeter (to measure resistance); a battery and set of test leads; and a jumper wire, preferably with a circuit breaker or fuse incorporated, which can be used to bypass suspect wires or electrical components. Before attempting to locate a problem with test instruments, use the wiring diagram to determine where to make the connections.

5 To find the source of an intermittent wiring fault (usually due to a poor or dirty connection, or damaged wiring insulation), a 'wiggle' test can be performed on the wiring. This involves wiggling the wiring by hand to see if the fault occurs as the wiring is moved. It should be possible to narrow down the source of the fault to a particular section of wiring. This method of testing can be used in conjunction with any of the tests described in the following sub-Sections.

6 Apart from problems due to poor connections, two basic types of fault can occur in an electrical circuit - open-circuit, or short-circuit.

7 Open-circuit faults are caused by a break somewhere in the circuit, which prevents current from flowing. An open-circuit fault will prevent a component from working, but will not cause the relevant circuit fuse to blow.

8 Short-circuit faults are caused by a 'short' somewhere in the circuit, which allows the current flowing in the circuit to 'escape' along an alternative route, usually to earth. Short-circuit faults are normally caused by a breakdown in wiring insulation, which allows a feed wire to touch either another wire, or an earthed component such as the bodyshell. A short-circuit fault will normally cause the relevant circuit fuse to blow.

Finding an open-circuit

9 To check for an open-circuit, connect one lead of a circuit tester or voltmeter to either the negative battery terminal or a known good earth.

10 Connect the other lead to a connector in the circuit being tested, preferably nearest to the battery or fuse.

11 Switch on the circuit, bearing in mind that some circuits are live only when the ignition switch is moved to a particular position.

12 If voltage is present (indicated either by the tester bulb lighting or a voltmeter reading, as applicable), this means that the section of the circuit between the relevant connector and the battery is problem-free.

13 Continue to check the remainder of the circuit in the same fashion.

14 When a point is reached at which no voltage is present, the problem must lie between that point and the previous test point with voltage. Most problems can be traced to a broken, corroded or loose connection.

Finding a short-circuit

15 To check for a short-circuit, first disconnect the load(s) from the circuit (loads are the components which draw current from a circuit, such as bulbs, motors, heating elements, etc).

16 Remove the relevant fuse from the circuit, and connect a circuit tester or voltmeter to the fuse connections.

17 Switch on the circuit, bearing in mind that some circuits are live only when the ignition switch is moved to a particular position.

18 If voltage is present (indicated either by the tester bulb lighting or a voltmeter reading, as applicable), this means that there is a short-circuit.

19 If no voltage is present, but the fuse still blows with the load(s) connected, this indicates an internal fault in the load(s).

Finding an earth fault

20 The battery negative terminal is connected to 'earth' - the metal of the engine/transmission and the car body - and most systems are wired so that they only receive a positive feed, the current returning through the metal of the car body. This means that the component mounting and the body form part of that circuit. Loose or corroded mountings can therefore cause a range of electrical faults, ranging from total failure of a circuit, to a puzzling partial fault. In particular, lights may shine dimly (especially when another circuit sharing the same earth point is in operation), motors (eg, wiper motors or the heater fan motor) may run slowly, and the operation of one circuit may have an apparently-unrelated effect on another.

21 Note that on many vehicles, earth straps are used between certain components, such as the engine/transmission and the body, usually where there is no metal-to-metal contact between components due to flexible rubber mountings, etc.

22 To check whether a component is properly earthed, disconnect the battery and connect one lead of an ohmmeter to a known good earth point. Connect the other lead to the wire or earth connection being tested. The resistance reading should be zero; if not, check the connection as follows.

23 If an earth connection is thought to be faulty, dismantle the connection and clean back to bare metal both the bodyshell and the wire terminal or the component earth connection mating surface. Be careful to remove all traces of dirt and corrosion, then use a knife to trim away any paint, so that a clean metal-to-metal joint is made.

24 On reassembly, tighten the joint fasteners securely; if a wire terminal is being refitted, use serrated washers between the terminal

3.2a Unclip and remove the fusebox cover . . .

3.2b . . . for access to the main fuses

3.2c Additional fuses are found in the module box . . .

and the bodyshell to ensure a clean and secure connection. When the connection is remade, prevent the onset of corrosion in the future by applying a coat of petroleum jelly or silicone-based grease or by spraying on (at regular intervals) a proprietary ignition sealer or a water-dispersant lubricant.

3 Fuses and relays - general information

Main fuses

1 Most of the fuses are situated in the main fusebox, located at the rear of the engine compartment on the left-hand side. Additional fuses may be located in the module box, situated at the right-hand rear of the engine compartment, and/or in the luggage compartment, in front of the battery.
2 To gain access to the fuses, unclip and remove the fusebox cover; on some models, the lid is secured by a locking bar. To gain access to the luggage compartment fusebox, lift up the floor covering **(see illustrations)**.
3 A list of the circuits each fuse protects is

given on the label attached to the inside of the fusebox cover.
4 To remove a fuse, first switch off the circuit concerned (or the ignition), then pull the fuse out of its terminals **(see illustration)**. The wire within the fuse should be visible; if the fuse is blown it will be broken or melted.
5 Always renew a fuse with one of an identical rating; never use a fuse with a different rating from the original or substitute anything else. Never renew a fuse more than once without tracing the source of the trouble. The fuse rating is stamped on top of the fuse; note that the fuses are also colour-coded for easy recognition.
6 If a new fuse blows immediately, find the cause before renewing it again; a short to earth as a result of faulty insulation is most likely. Where a fuse protects more than one circuit, try to isolate the defect by switching on each circuit in turn (if possible) until the fuse blows again. Always carry a supply of spare fuses of each relevant rating on the vehicle; a spare of each rating should be clipped into the base of the fusebox.

Relays

7 Most of the relays are situated in the main

3.2d . . . and in the luggage compartment auxiliary fusebox, near the battery

fusebox, located at the rear of the engine compartment on the left-hand side. Additional relays may be located in the module box, situated at the right-hand rear of the engine compartment, and/or in the luggage compartment, near the battery **(see illustration)**.
8 To gain access to the relays in the engine compartment, the fusebox cover must first be unclipped. Remove the screws securing the

3.4 Removing a fuse - note the application list inside the fusebox cover

3.7 On early models, the fuel pump relay is located next to the battery

3.8a After removing the fusebox cover, unscrew the surround . . .

3.8b . . . and lift it clear of the fusebox . . .

3.8c . . . for access to the relays

fusebox cover surround, and lift off the larger cover (see illustrations).

9 If a circuit or system controlled by a relay develops a fault and the relay is suspect, operate the system; if the relay is functioning it should be possible to hear it click as it is energised. If this is the case the fault lies with the components or wiring of the system. If the relay is not being energised then either the relay is not receiving a main supply or a switching voltage or the relay itself is faulty. Testing is by the substitution of a known good unit but be careful; while some relays are identical in appearance and in operation, others look similar but perform different functions.

4.3a Disconnect the wiper motor wiring plug from inside the fusebox . . .

10 To renew a relay, first ensure that the ignition switch is off. The relay can then simply be pulled out from the socket and the new relay pressed in.

4 Fuse and module boxes - removal and refitting

Fuseboxes

Removal

1 Disconnect the battery negative terminal.
2 Unclip and remove the fusebox cover, then (where applicable) remove the screws securing the relay cover beneath it, and remove the relay cover.
3 Disconnect the wiring plug for the wiper motor, then lift up the wiring harness to release it from the side of the fusebox (see illustrations).
4 Remove the fusebox mounting screws or nuts, and withdraw the fusebox as far as the wiring will allow, without straining it (see illustration).
5 Label the positions of all the wiring connectors as necessary before disconnecting any of them. Most will, however, only reconnect one way.
6 Working methodically, disconnect the

wiring connections from the fusebox (or sections of fusebox, on later models), and remove the fusebox from the car. If required, the engine compartment main fusebox case can be removed after unscrewing the retaining nuts.

Refitting

7 Refitting is the reverse sequence to removal, ensuring that all the wiring is correctly and securely reconnected.

Module box

Removal

Note: *It is essential that there is no power applied to the modules when their connector plugs are disconnected, or they could suffer permanent damage. It is even possible for the modules to be damaged if their terminals are subjected to static electricity - take care to avoid direct contact with the module pins once they have been disconnected.*

8 Disconnect the battery negative terminal.
9 Unscrew and remove the screws securing the module box cover in the left-hand rear corner of the engine compartment (left as seen from the driver's seat), and remove the cover.
10 Release the locking levers securing the module wiring connectors (note that some of the levers slide sideways), and disconnect the wiring from above the module box, noting

4.3b . . . then detach the wiring harness from the fusebox, to permit removal

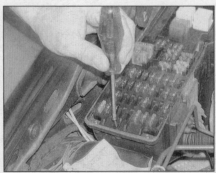

4.4a Remove the securing screws . . .

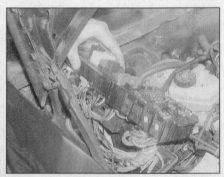

4.4b . . . then lift out the top section of the fusebox

4.10a Release the locking levers, and disconnect the module wiring plugs . . .

4.10b . . . where levers are not used, the plugs slide sideways to remove

4.11 Removing the module securing screw

how it is fitted **(see illustrations)**. Label the connectors if necessary, to avoid confusion when refitting.

11 The modules themselves can be lifted out with their mounting bracket, which is secured by one screw at the side **(see illustration)**.

12 Locate the datalink connector at the front of the module box. On early models, loosen the horizontal screw adjacent to the connector, then remove the four screws which locate it from above. Later models have just two screws, removed from above **(see illustrations)**.

13 Remove the screws securing the upper section of the module box, then lift it out, turning it to the right to detach the wiring connectors **(see illustration)**.

14 Remove the passenger side lower facia panel as described in Chapter 11, Section 41.

15 Carefully pull the wiring harness for the modules through into the passenger footwell, noting how it is routed.

16 The lower section of the module box can now be removed, after unscrewing the retaining nuts.

Refitting

17 Refitting is a reversal of removal. Make sure that all wiring connections are correctly and securely remade.

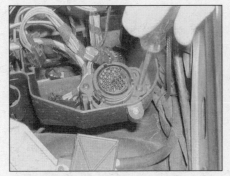

4.12a Remove the two screws . . .

4.12b . . . and remove the datalink connector

4.13a Remove the upper section of the module box . . .

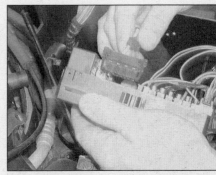

4.13b . . . and disconnect the wiring connectors from it as necessary

5 Steering column combination switch - removal and refitting

Removal

1 Disconnect the battery negative terminal.
2 Remove the driver's side lower facia panel as described in Chapter 11, Section 41.
3 Remove the steering wheel as described in Chapter 10.
4 Remove the airbag contact unit as described in Section 30.
5 Undo the three screws securing the combination switch to the steering column **(see illustration)**.
6 Partially remove the combination switch (and cruise control switch, where applicable) for access to the wiring multi-plug **(see illustration)**.

5.5 Remove the three switch securing screws (arrowed)

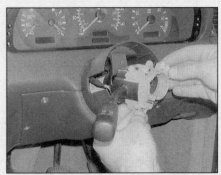

5.6 Withdraw the switch assembly

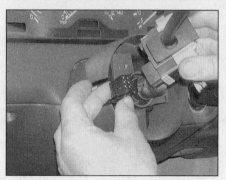

5.7 Disconnect the switch multi-plug

5.8 Unclip the airbag contact unit wiring plug

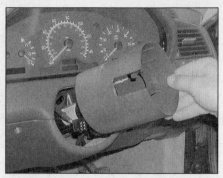

5.9 Removing the column upper surround

7 Release the switch multi-plug from its location, and separate the connector halves (see illustration). On models with cruise control, similarly release and disconnect the multi-plug connector for the cruise control switch.

8 Unclip the wiring plug for the airbag contact unit, and move it to one side (see illustration).

9 If required, lift off the column surround, and remove it (see illustration).

Refitting

10 Refitting is the reverse sequence to removal.

6 Facia and centre console switches - removal and refitting

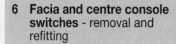

1 Before removing any switches, disconnect the battery negative terminal, and reconnect on completion.

Facia switches

2 Remove the radio/cassette player as described in Section 24.

3 Remove the two screws above and below the radio aperture in the facia (see illustration).

4 Pull the lower edge of the facia centre panel outwards, and unhook the top edge (see illustration).

5 Open the cover fitted over the wiring connectors, then disconnect the wiring from the relevant switch. If preferred, disconnect the wiring from all the switches, and remove the panel from the facia (see illustrations).

6 Unclip the wiring plug surround from the rear of the switches, and remove it (see illustration).

7 Unclip the relevant switch from the panel, and remove it (see illustration).

8 Refitting is a reversal of removal.

Headlight main switch

9 Remove the driver's side lower facia panel as described in Chapter 11, Section 41.

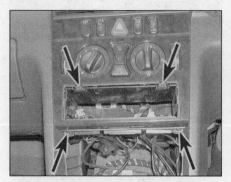

6.3 Remove the screws (arrowed) above and below the radio aperture

6.4 Unclip the panel from the facia, then lift up the bottom edge

6.5a Open the cover for access to the wiring plugs . . .

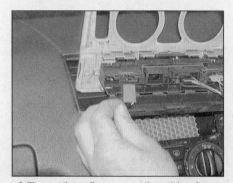

6.5b . . . then disconnect the wiring from one or all of the switches, as required

6.6 Unclip and remove the wiring plug surround

6.7 Removing the hazard warning light switch assembly

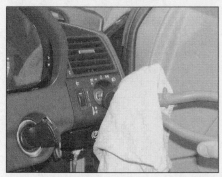

6.10a Using pliers and a cloth to protect the finish . . .

6.10b . . . pull off the headlight switch knob

6.11 Using pliers to unscrew the switch retaining nut

10 Using pliers and a protective cloth, carefully pull off the switch knob **(see illustrations)**.
11 Unscrew and remove the nut below the switch knob **(see illustration)**.
12 Carefully unclip the light switch panel and withdraw it from the facia. Unclip the headlight beam adjuster from the panel **(see illustrations)**.
13 Twist the switch to release the securing lugs, and remove the switch from the panel **(see illustration)**.
14 Disconnect the wiring plug from the rear of the main switch. If required, the switch light bulb can be removed from the centre of the switch by pulling it out **(see illustrations)**.
15 Refitting is a reversal of removal.

Headlight beam adjuster

16 Carry out the operations described in paragraphs 9 to 12.
17 Disconnect the vacuum connections from the rear of the switch. If this does not prove possible, note that the vacuum hoses run along the rear of the facia panel, and can be disconnected at a join in the vacuum pipes behind the passenger side kick panel.
18 Refitting is the reverse sequence to removal.

Centre console switches

19 On manual transmission models, prise out and release the gear lever boot from the console cover, and slide the boot up the lever **(see illustration)**.

6.12a Unclip the switch panel from the facia . . .

6.12b . . . and release the headlight adjuster control from the panel

6.13 Reach in behind the switch, and twist it to release it from the facia

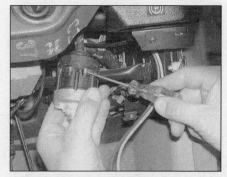

6.14a Using a screwdriver, prise the switch wiring connector . . .

6.14b . . . and separate it from the switch

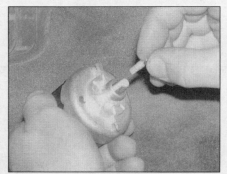

6.14c If necessary, the light switch bulb can be pulled out of its holder

6.19 Release the gear lever boot frame from the console

6.21 Removing the console centre panel

6.23 On models from 1995 to 1997, disconnect three wiring plugs to remove the switch assembly

6.24 Models from June 1997 onwards have just one small plug to disconnect

20 On automatic transmission models, prise up the plastic frame surrounding the selector level panel, which is secured by two clips on either side.

21 Carefully prise up the console centre panel from around the gear/selector lever - there are two clips either side. Mercedes-Benz recommend only levering through the gear/selector lever aperture to release the clips; whatever method is used, take care to avoid damaging or marking the trim panels by protecting them with rag or card (see illustration).

22 On early models, disconnect the wiring multi-plug from the base of the switch, then press it out of the panel from below.

23 On models from September 1995 to July 1997, disconnect the three wiring plugs from the one-piece switch assembly (see illustration).

24 On models from July 1997 onwards, disconnect the single wiring plug from the one-piece switch assembly (see illustration).

25 The one-piece switch assembly is released from the console panel by sliding back the two elongated catches at either side, and removing the retaining clip from the rear (see illustrations). The switches are not available individually, and if one is faulty, a new switch assembly will be required.

26 Refitting is the reverse sequence to removal.

Roof console switches

27 Prise out the light lenses from the roof console (see illustration).

28 Release the console retaining catches using a screwdriver in the prise points provided (at the front of the assembly on models with a sunroof, or at the rear on models without a sunroof) (see illustrations). The catches should release quite easily - note that the other two holes on the roof console only provide access to the console panel plastic hinges.

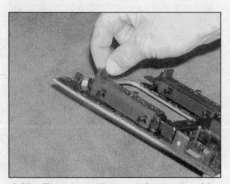

6.25a To remove the one-piece assembly, slide back the clips either side . . .

6.25b . . . then remove the clip at the rear . . .

6.25c . . . and separate the switch assembly from the console panel

6.27 Prise out and remove the light lenses from the roof console

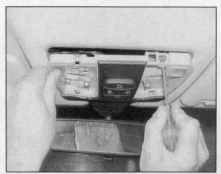

6.28a Release the catches at the rear of the console - models without sunroof . . .

6.28b . . . or at the front of the console, on sunroof-equipped models

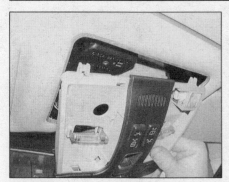

6.29 Remove the console from the roof aperture, and unhook the hinges

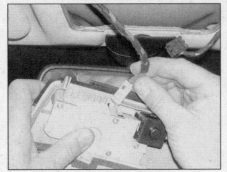

6.30a Disconnect the lighting wiring plugs . . .

6.30b . . . and the sunroof switch wiring plug, where applicable

29 Prise down the console from its location, and unhook the hinges **(see illustration)**.
30 Disconnect the wiring plugs from the roof console, noting their locations for refitting **(see illustrations)**.
31 Some of the switches can be unclipped and removed from the console, while others are integral with it **(see illustration)**.
32 Refitting is a reversal of removal.

---

7 Door courtesy light switches - removal and refitting

Removal

1 Disconnect the battery negative terminal.
2 It is possible to prise out the switches from their locations without any preliminary dismantling, but this carries a high risk of damaging the surrounding paintwork, and damaging the switch locating lugs, which would mean the switch would not fit back into position. It is recommended that the removal procedures are followed, to avoid these problems.

Front door switch

3 Remove the B-pillar trim panels as described in Chapter 11, Section 41.

4 Disconnect the wiring plug from the rear of the switch **(see illustration)**.
5 Depress the upper securing lug, and release the switch from the body **(see illustrations)**.

Rear door switch

6 Either prise back the seat cushion for access to the switch, or remove the rear seat side cushion (models with folding rear seat only).
7 Peel away the cloth tape from the rear of the switch **(see illustration)**.
8 Disconnect the wiring plug from the rear of the switch **(see illustration)**.
9 Depress the upper securing lug, and

6.31 Removing the sunroof switch

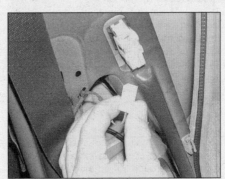

7.4 Disconnect the switch wiring

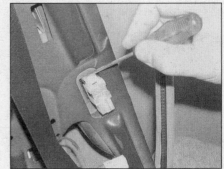

7.5a Release the securing lug at the top . . .

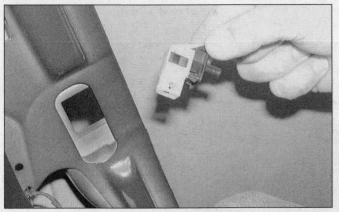

7.5b . . . then remove the switch from the B-pillar

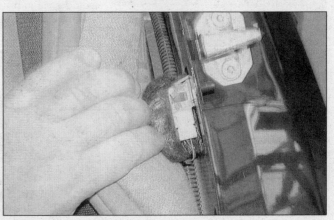

7.7 Peel back the cloth tape at the rear of the switch

7.8 Disconnect the switch wiring

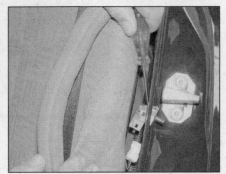

7.9a Depress the lug at the top to release the switch . . .

7.9b . . . then remove the switch from the car

release the switch from the body **(see illustrations)**.

Refitting

10 Refitting is the reverse sequence to removal. Check for correct operation on reassembly.

8 Instrument panel - removal and refitting

Removal

1 Disconnect the battery negative terminal.
2 Remove the steering wheel as described in Chapter 10.

8.4a Reach up behind the panel . . .

Method 1

3 Remove the driver's lower facia panel as described in Chapter 11, Section 41.
4 If care is taken, it should now be possible to reach up behind the instrument panel, and push it out of the facia **(see illustrations)**
5 When they are accessible, release the locking levers securing the two wiring connectors, and disconnect the wiring from the rear of the panel **(see illustration)**.

Method 2

6 If the above method (used successfully on our project vehicle) does not work, it may be necessary to use this method, which involves special tools.
7 The instrument panel is removed by inserting two wire hooks, one either side, at the base of the panel. The Mercedes-Benz tools for this are available under part no 140589023300, but it is possible to make substitutes from thin, stiff wire.
8 The tools should be approximately 15 cm long, with 1 cm at the ends bent over at 45°.
9 Insert the tools at the sides of the instrument panel, roughly in line with the centres of the instruments **(see illustration)**. Insert the tools by approximately 8 cm, then twist them through 90° so that the bent ends wrap around the rear of the panel.
10 Pull the tools carefully rearwards until the ends engage in the locking ribs behind the instrument panel.

11 Pulling on each tool alternately (do not pull both together), extract the panel a little at a time on each side until it is clear of the facia panel. Splay the tools apart slightly, so that the ends do not slip out of the ribs behind the panel.
12 When they are accessible, release the locking clips securing the two wiring connectors, and disconnect the wiring from the rear of the panel.

Refitting

13 Offer the panel into position, and reconnect the wiring plugs, securing each with its locking clip.
14 Make sure the panel is lined up squarely with the facia aperture, and press it gently into place until the securing clips are felt to engage.
15 Where applicable, refit the driver's lower facia panel as described in Chapter 11.
16 Refit the steering wheel as described in Chapter 10.
17 On completion, check for correct operation of all instruments and warning lights.

9 Instrument panel components - removal and refitting

1 Remove the instrument panel as described in the previous Section.

8.4b . . . and push the instrument panel out gently from behind

8.5 Release the locking lever on each connector, and remove

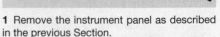

8.9 Insert the hooked tools into the holes on either side of the instrument panel

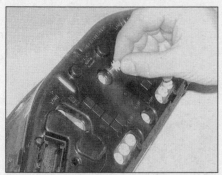

9.2 Twist and remove the bulbholders from behind the panel

9.5 Releasing the panel surround clips with a screwdriver

9.6 Removing the panel from the surround

Panel illumination and warning light bulbs

2 Turn the bulbholders anti-clockwise and remove them from the rear of the instrument panel **(see illustration)**.

3 Remove the illumination bulbs by pulling them out of their holders. The warning light bulbs (except for the alternator warning light) are renewed complete with their holders.

4 Refit the bulbholders by pushing down and turning clockwise.

Instrument panel surround

5 The surround is secured by several plastic clips around its edge, which can be released using a small screwdriver **(see illustration)**.

6 When the clips have been released, pull the panel free of the surround **(see illustration)**.

7 Refitting is a reversal of removal. Where applicable, make sure that the trip reset and clock adjustment knobs are refitted correctly. We found that the warning light colour panels at either end of the instrument panel tend to fall out as the surround is refitted.

Instruments

8 At the time of writing, no details were available concerning renewal of individual instruments, and indeed, this appears not to be possible. If one instrument is suspected of being defective, remove the instrument panel, and take it to a Mercedes-Benz dealer or automotive electrician for testing. Consult your dealer or parts supplier for advice regarding the availability of replacement parts.

Speedometer operation

9 All models are fitted with an electronic speedometer, and a conventional speedometer cable is not used. The signal for the speedometer is derived from the ABS wheel sensors, of which there are three on early models, and four on later models. The ABS control unit takes the average speed from the wheel sensors, and this is fed to the speedometer. Therefore, in the event of a query on the operation of the speedometer, check the connections to all wheel sensors, and to the ABS control unit, as well as all the ABS wiring; refer to Chapter 9 as necessary.

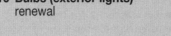

10 Bulbs (exterior lights) - renewal

General

1 Whenever a bulb is renewed, note the following points:

a) *Disconnect the battery negative lead before starting work (see Section 1).*

b) *Remember that if the light has just been in use, the bulb may be extremely hot.*

c) *Always check the bulb contacts and holder, ensuring that there is clean metal-to-metal contact between the bulb and its live(s) and earth. Clean off any corrosion or dirt before fitting a new bulb.*

d) *Wherever bayonet-type bulbs are fitted, ensure that the live contact(s) bear firmly against the bulb contact.*

e) *Always ensure that the new bulb is of the correct rating and that it is completely*

clean before fitting it; this applies particularly to headlight/foglight bulbs (see below).

f) *With quartz halogen bulbs (headlights and similar applications), use a tissue or clean cloth when handling the bulb; do not touch the bulb glass with the fingers. Even small quantities of grease from the fingers will cause blackening and premature failure. If a bulb is accidentally touched, clean it with methylated spirit and a clean rag.*

Headlight

2 From within the engine compartment, release the clip(s) securing the light unit cover in place, then tip the cover to the rear and remove it. Early models have a one-piece cover which fits over the main and dipped beam bulb access points; later models have two separate covers - the main beam bulb is behind the inner cover **(see illustrations)**.

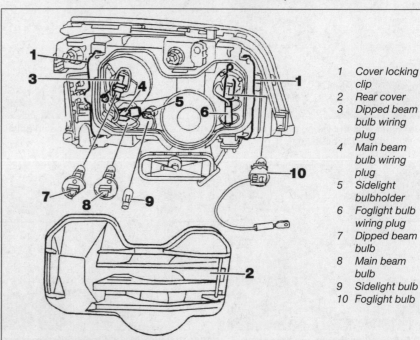

1 Cover locking clip
2 Rear cover
3 Dipped beam bulb wiring plug
4 Main beam bulb wiring plug
5 Sidelight bulbholder
6 Foglight bulb wiring plug
7 Dipped beam bulb
8 Main beam bulb
9 Sidelight bulb
10 Foglight bulb

10.2a Headlight bulb details on early models with one-piece rear cover

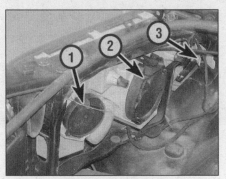

10.2b View of the right-hand headlight rear covers, with air cleaner removed

1   Inner cover (main beam bulb)
2   Outer cover (dipped beam, foglight, sidelight bulbs)
3   Indicator light unit retaining clamp

3 Carefully pull off the wiring connector from the relevant bulb **(see illustrations)**.
4 Release the bulb retaining clip by squeezing the clip arms together and swinging downward **(see illustration)**.
5 Withdraw the bulb from the light unit **(see illustration)**. Take care not to touch the glass with your fingers.

 Use a tissue or clean cloth when handling the bulb. If the glass is touched, wipe the bulb with a rag moistened with methylated spirit.

10.2c To renew the dipped beam bulb, remove the outer cover . . .

6 Refitting is the reverse sequence to removal, but ensure that the tags on the bulb plate engage with the recesses in the light unit.

Sidelight

7 Remove the headlight unit cover as described in paragraph 2. On models with two covers, the sidelight bulb is located behind the outer cover.

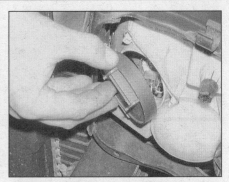

10.2d . . . the main beam bulb is behind the inner cover

8 Pull out the sidelight bulbholder **(see illustration)**.
9 Pull out the wedge-base bulb from its holder **(see illustration)**.
10 Refitting is the reverse sequence to removal.

Foglight

Headlight-mounted

11 Remove the headlight unit cover as described in paragraph 2. On models with two covers, the foglight bulb is located behind the outer cover.
12 Disconnect the bulb electrical lead at the

10.3a Removing the wiring plug from the dipped beam bulb . . .

10.3b . . . and from the main beam bulb

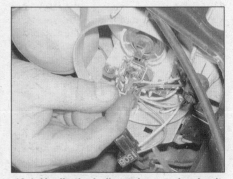

10.4 Unclip the bulb retainer, and swing it clear of the bulb

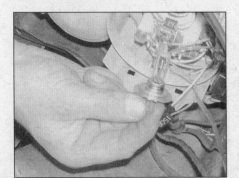

10.5 Removing the dipped beam bulb (main beam bulb similar)

10.8 Pull the sidelight bulbholder from the headlight

10.9 Pull out the wedge-base bulb

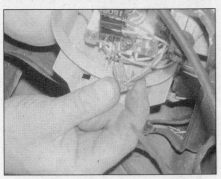

10.12 Disconnect the foglight bulb wiring connector

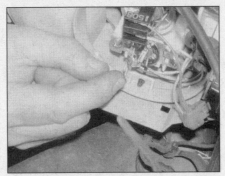

10.13 Release the bulb retaining clip, and swing it aside

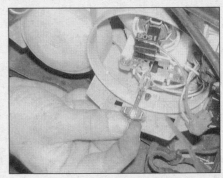

10.14 Removing the foglight bulb

connector **(see illustration)**. On models with one cover, the foglight bulb is the innermost bulb.

13 Compress the retaining clip arms and swing the clip to the side **(see illustration)**.

14 Withdraw the bulb from the light unit **(see illustration)**. Take care not to touch the glass with your fingers (see **Haynes Hint**).

15 Refitting is the reverse sequence to removal.

Bumper-mounted

16 To improve access, make sure that the parking brake is firmly applied, then jack up the front of the car and support on axle stands (see *Jacking and vehicle support*).

17 Unclip and remove the cover from the rear of the light unit, for access to the bulb.

18 Disconnect the wiring from the bulb, then release the spring clip and remove the bulb from the light unit.

19 Refitting is a reversal of removal.

Front direction indicator

20 Open the bonnet.

21 At the rear of the light unit, compress the light unit retaining clamp and push the indicator light unit forwards to gain access to the wiring plug **(see illustrations)**.

22 Twist the bulbholder anti-clockwise to release it from the light unit **(see illustration)**.

23 Depress and turn the bulb anti-clockwise

to remove it from the bulbholder **(see illustration)**.

24 Refitting is a reversal of removal. Ensure that the two light unit lugs engage in the slots next to the headlight when refitting.

Front direction indicator side repeater

25 Carefully slide the side repeater light forwards, then release its rear edge from the body side panel and withdraw it **(see illustration)**.

26 Withdraw the bulbholder from the light unit, and pull the bulb from the holder **(see illustrations)**.

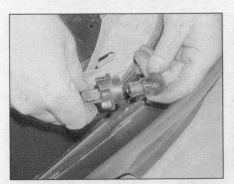

10.21a Compress the legs of the indicator retaining clamp to release it . . .

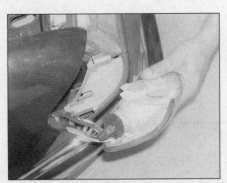

10.21b . . . then remove the light unit forwards

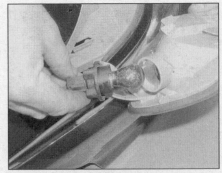

10.22 Twist the bulbholder to release it from the light unit

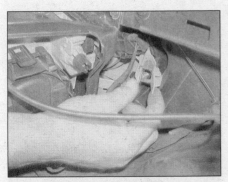

10.23 Twist and remove the indicator light bulb

10.25 Slide the light unit forwards, and unhook its rear edge

10.26a Pull the bulbholder from the light unit . . .

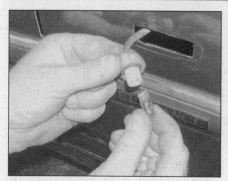

10.26b ... then pull out the wedge-base bulb from the holder

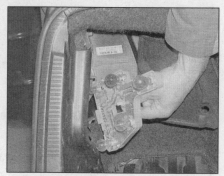

10.29 Removing the bulbholder from the rear light cluster - Saloon

10.30 Removing the rear foglight/tail light bulb

27 Refitting is the reverse sequence to removal.

Rear light cluster bulbs

Saloon

28 From inside the luggage compartment, release the trim clips where necessary, and remove the carpeted trim panel from the area around the rear light.

29 Turn the bulbholder catch until it is horizontal, then withdraw the bulbholder from the light unit (see illustration).

30 Remove the relevant bulb by turning anti-clockwise slightly (see illustration). The bulb numbers and their wattages are shown adjacent to each bulb location.

31 Refitting is the reverse sequence to removal.

Estate

32 From inside the luggage compartment, release the trim clips where necessary, and remove the carpeted trim panel from the area around the rear light.

33 Press the bulbholder catch downwards to release, then withdraw the bulbholder from the rear of the light unit (see illustration).

34 Remove the relevant bulb by turning anti-clockwise slightly (see illustration). The bulb numbers and their wattages are shown adjacent to each bulb location.

35 Refitting is the reverse sequence to removal.

Number plate light

Saloon models

36 Unclip and remove the trim panel from inside the boot lid. Prise out the plastic retaining clips using a wide-bladed screwdriver or forked tool. The mountings for the warning triangle are removed by depressing the catch with a small screwdriver (see illustrations).

37 Reach inside the boot lid apertures and unclip the relevant bulb from the number plate light concerned (see illustration).

Estate models

38 Undo the two retaining screws and withdraw the lens unit (see illustrations).

10.33 Removing the rear light cluster bulbholder - Estate

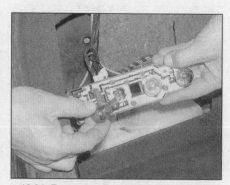

10.34 Removing the rear indicator bulb

10.36a Remove the trim clips using a forked tool

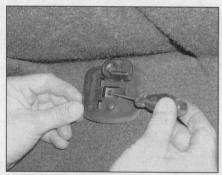

10.36b Remove the warning triangle mounting clips using a screwdriver

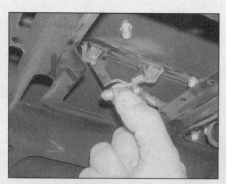

10.37 Remove the number plate light bulbs from inside the boot lid

10.38a Unscrew and remove the retaining screws ...

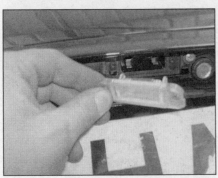

10.38b . . . and remove the light unit and bulb

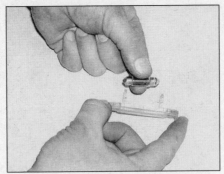

10.39 Removing the number plate light bulb - Estate model

11.2 Prise out the light unit lens

39 Spread the contacts and remove the festoon-type bulb **(see illustration)**.
40 Refitting is the reverse sequence to removal.

High-level stop-light

41 The 'bulbs' in the high-level stop-light are LEDs, and are not available separately. If the light unit stops working, check the wiring and fuse first. If the light unit is defective, remove it as described in Section 12 for renewal.

11 Bulbs (interior lights) - renewal

11.3 Take out the festoon-type bulb

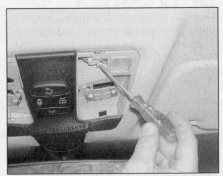

11.4a Prise out the bulbholder sideways . . .

General

1 Whenever a bulb is renewed, note the following points:
 a) *Disconnect the battery negative lead before starting work (see Section 1).*
 b) *Remember that if the light has just been in use, the bulb may be extremely hot.*
 c) *Always check the bulb contacts and holder, ensuring that there is clean metal-to-metal contact between the bulb and its live(s) and earth. Clean off any corrosion or dirt before fitting a new bulb.*
 d) *Wherever bayonet-type bulbs are fitted, ensure that the live contact(s) bear firmly against the bulb contact.*
 e) *Always ensure that the new bulb is of the*

correct rating and that it is completely clean before fitting it; this applies particularly to headlight/foglight bulbs (see below).
 f) *With quartz halogen bulbs (headlights and similar applications), use a tissue or clean cloth when handling the bulb; do not touch the bulb glass with the fingers. Even small quantities of grease from the fingers will cause blackening and premature failure. If a bulb is accidentally touched, clean it with methylated spirit and a clean rag.*

Interior courtesy lights

Front

2 Carefully prise out the relevant lens unit,

taking care only to prise at the points on the inner edges of the lens **(see illustration)**.
3 To remove the courtesy light bulb, spread the contacts and remove the festoon-type bulb **(see illustration)**.
4 To remove the map reading light bulb, prise the bulbholder out sideways, and pull out the wedge-base bulb **(see illustrations)**.
5 Refitting is the reverse sequence to removal.

Rear

6 Carefully prise out the light unit from the headlining **(see illustration)**.
7 Where applicable, open the hinged cover inside the light unit, for access to the bulb. Spread the bulb contacts and remove the bulb **(see illustrations)**.
8 Refitting is a reversal of removal.

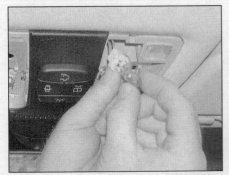

11.4b . . . and pull out the map reading light bulb

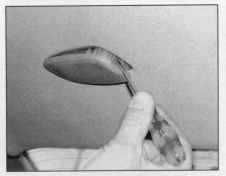

11.6 Prise the light unit out of the headlining

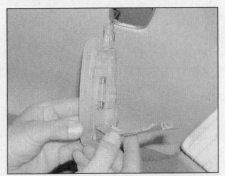

11.7a Open the hinged cover inside the light . . .

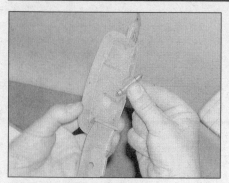

11.7b . . . then pull the festoon-type bulb from its contacts

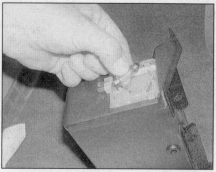

11.14 Removing the glovebox light bulb (model with passenger airbag shown)

11.16 Prise the luggage compartment light down from its location

Sun visor illumination

9 Fold down the sun visor and carefully prise off the cover on the left-hand and right-hand recesses.
10 Spread the contacts and remove the festoon-type bulb.
11 Refitting is the reverse sequence to removal.

Glovebox light

12 On models with a passenger airbag, remove the glovebox as described in Chapter 11.
13 On models without a passenger airbag, prise the light lens unit down out of its location.
14 Spread the contacts and remove the festoon-type bulb (see illustration).
15 Refitting is the reverse sequence to removal.

Luggage compartment light

16 Carefully prise off the lens, for access to the festoon-type bulb (see illustration).
17 Spread the bulb contacts and remove the bulb (see illustration).
18 Refitting is a reversal of removal.

Selector lever illumination light

19 Prise up the plastic frame surrounding the selector level panel, which is secured by two clips on either side.
20 Carefully prise up the console centre panel from around the selector lever - there are two clips either side. Mercedes-Benz

recommend only levering through the selector lever aperture to release the clips; whatever method is used, take care to avoid damaging or marking the trim panels by protecting them with rag or card.
21 Lift the panel off over the selector lever, disconnecting any wiring connectors as necessary. Note the positions of all wiring connectors, attaching labels if necessary for identification.
22 Remove the illumination bulb from its holder.
23 Refitting is a reversal of removal.

Door entry lights

24 Prise out the light unit from the rear edge of the door, and disconnect the wiring plug.
25 Remove the bulb from its holder by depressing and twisting it anti-clockwise.
26 Refitting is a reversal of removal.

12 Exterior lights - removal and refitting

Note: Disconnect the battery negative lead before removing any light unit.

Front direction indicator light

1 Open the bonnet.
2 At the rear of the light unit, compress the light unit retaining clamp and push the indicator light unit forwards to gain access to the wiring plug (see illustrations).

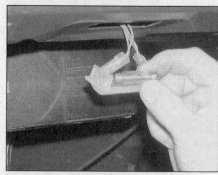

11.17 Remove the festoon-type bulb from its contacts

3 Disconnect the wiring plug at the rear of the unit, and withdraw the light completely (see illustration).
4 Refitting is a reversal of removal. Ensure that the two light unit lugs engage in the slots next to the headlight when refitting.

Headlight unit

5 Remove the front direction indicator light as described previously.
6 On models with headlight wipers, first operate the system, and allow the headlight wipers to return to their 'parked' position. Lift up the cover on the wiper arm, unscrew the nut, and pull the headlight wiper arm from its spindle.
7 Remove the two screws securing the trim strip below the headlight, then carefully withdraw the trim from the front of the car

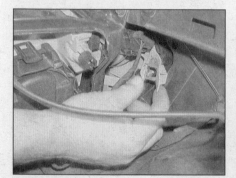

12.2a Compress the legs of the indicator retaining clamp to release it . . .

12.2b . . . then remove the light unit forwards to access the wiring plug

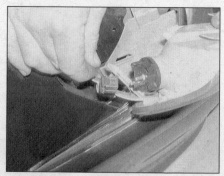

12.3 Disconnect the wiring plug and remove the indicator

12.7a Remove the inner screw . . .

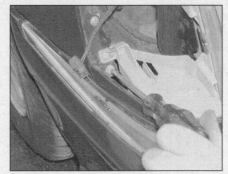

12.7b . . . and the outer screw . . .

12.7c . . . and move the headlight trim strip to one side

(see illustrations). On some models, the trim strip cannot be removed completely, and must be left hanging by the rubber strip.
8 On models up to 1998 model year, unscrew and remove the three headlight mounting bolts. There is a bolt fitted either side at the rear, and a further bolt on top of the light unit.
9 From 1998 model year onwards, four screws are used to secure the headlight. Two are accessed from the indicator light aperture (one from the front, and one from the side of the headlight), with a further screw removed from above, on the crossmember. The fourth screw is on the radiator side of the headlight, and is removed after prising out a small plastic cover panel (see illustrations).
10 Pull the headlight forwards and remove it from the car, taking care not to scratch the bumper (see illustrations).

11 Disconnect the wiring multi-plug at the rear of the light unit; also disconnect the vacuum hose - this may need to be prised off,

using a suitable screwdriver (see illustrations).
12 Refitting is the reverse sequence to removal.

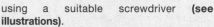

12.9a Headlight screws in the indicator aperture - one from the front . . .

12.9b . . . and one from the side

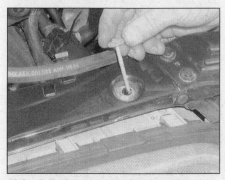

12.9c A further screw is fitted at the top . . .

12.9d . . . while to access the fourth screw, prise out . . .

12.9e . . . and remove this trim panel

12.10a Pull the headlight forwards . . .

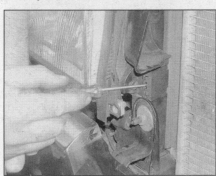

12.10b . . . noting as it is removed how it is located

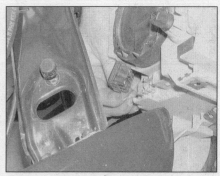

12.11a Disconnect the wiring plug from the base of the headlight . . .

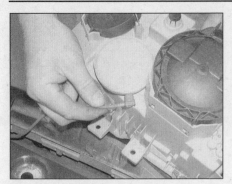

12.11b . . . and the vacuum hose from the headlight adjuster

12.16 Disconnecting the wiring plug from the rear light cluster

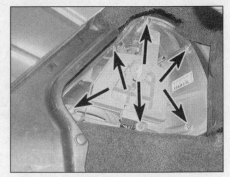

12.17a Rear light cluster securing nuts (arrowed)

On models with headlight wipers, make sure the system is still in the parked position, and engage the wiper arm in the appropriate (horizontal) position. Have the headlight beam alignment checked on completion.

Front foglight (bumper-mounted)

13 To improve access, make sure that the parking brake is firmly applied, then jack up the front of the car and support on axle stands (see *Jacking and vehicle support*).
14 Disconnect the wiring from the rear of the light unit, then remove the retaining screws and withdraw the light unit from the bumper.

15 Refitting is a reversal of removal. On completion, have the beam alignment checked and adjusted if necessary.

Rear light cluster

Saloon

16 Remove the bulbholder from the rear of the light unit as described in Section 10. Alternatively, disconnect the wiring plug from the bulbholder (see illustration).
17 Unscrew and remove the six nuts at the rear of the light unit (see illustrations).
18 To release the lens from the reflector, squeeze together the two lugs on the back of

the light unit, and recover the lens from outside. Check that the rubber seal is removed with the lens (see illustrations).
19 If required, the reflector part of the light unit can be manoeuvred out to the outside, noting that some trial-and-error is needed before it will come out (see illustration).
20 Refitting is the reverse sequence to removal. Ensure that the seal is correctly located in the lens groove - fit a new one, if necessary, to prevent leaks into the boot.

Estate

21 Remove the bulbholder from the rear of the light unit as described in Section 10.

12.17b Using a suitable spanner, unscrew . . .

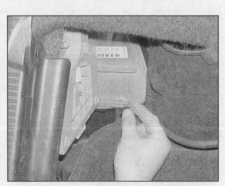

12.17c . . . and remove the light cluster nuts

12.18a Squeeze the two lugs to release the lens . . .

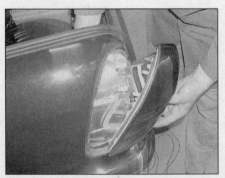

12.18b . . . then withdraw the lens from the outside . . .

12.18c . . . and recover the rubber seal

12.19 Removing the light cluster reflector

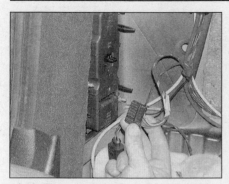

12.21 Disconnecting the bulbholder wiring plug

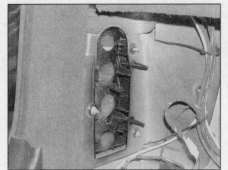

12.22a Unscrew the three nuts . . .

12.22b . . . and remove the light unit from the outside

Alternatively, disconnect the wiring plug from the bulbholder (see illustration).

22 Unscrew the three nuts at the rear of the light unit, and withdraw it from the car (see illustrations). Where applicable, recover the seal fitted between the light unit and the body.

23 Refitting is the reverse sequence to removal.

High-level stop-light

Saloon

24 Carefully unclip the light unit rear cover - there is a retaining clip on either side (see illustration).

25 With the cover removed, disconnect the wiring plug, then press together the clips at either end of the unit, and lift it off its mounting base on the rear shelf (see illustrations).

26 If the mounting base is to be removed, remove the rear shelf as described in Chapter 11, Section 41.

27 Refitting is a reversal of removal.

Estate

28 The high-level stop-light is incorporated in the rear spoiler, which must first be removed.

29 Using the information in Chapter 11, Section 41, unclip the tailgate upper trim panel.

30 Disconnect the wiring plug for the light unit, then remove the nuts securing the spoiler to the tailgate (see illustrations), and lift the spoiler off the rear of the car.

31 The light unit is secured by three screws - remove the screws and separate the light from the spoiler.

32 Refitting is a reversal of removal.

Number plate light

Saloon

33 Gain access to the inside of the light unit, as described for bulb removal in Section 10. The bulb does not have to be removed, but there is less chance of damaging the bulb if it is.

12.24 Unclip the cover from the rear of the high-level stop-light

12.25a Disconnect the wiring plug . . .

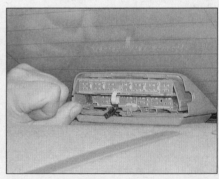

12.25b . . . then release the catch at either end . . .

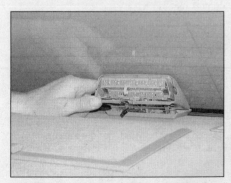

12.25c . . . and remove the unit from the rear shelf

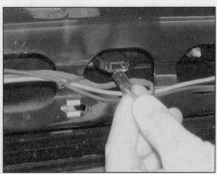

12.30a Disconnect the wiring plug for the high-level stop-light . . .

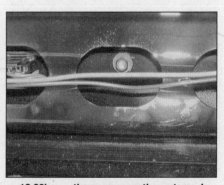

12.30b . . . then unscrew the nuts and remove the tailgate spoiler

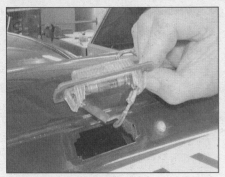

12.34 Release the retaining clips at either end, and remove the number plate light

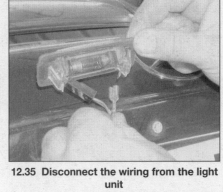

12.35 Disconnect the wiring from the light unit

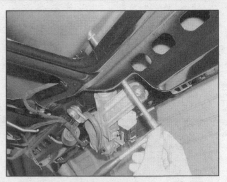

12.40a Unscrew the nuts securing the handle trim strip . . .

34 The light unit is secured by two clips, which must be released from inside the boot lid - withdraw the light from its location **(see illustration)**.

35 Disconnect the wiring connectors when they become accessible, and remove the light unit from the car **(see illustration)**.

36 Refitting is a reversal of removal.

Estate

37 Remove the bulb as described in Section 10.

38 The rear halves of the two light units are incorporated in the tailgate lock handle trim strip, and may be removed as follows.

39 Remove the tailgate inner trim panel as described in Chapter 11, Section 41.

40 Unscrew the nuts on the inside of the tailgate which secure the tailgate lock handle

trim strip. The nuts are supposed to remain in place on the inside of the tailgate, but we found that they came off quite easily in practice **(see illustrations)**.

41 Disconnect the two wiring connectors from behind each number plate light (note how they are fitted), and remove the trim from outside **(see illustrations)**.

42 Refitting is a reversal of removal.

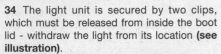

13 Headlight glass - removal and refitting

Removal

1 Remove the headlight as described in the previous Section.

2 Carefully pull off the outer seal from the headlight glass.

3 Prise off the metal clips or lift up the plastic tabs securing the glass to the headlight shell, and remove the glass **(see illustration)**. Recover the seal fitted between the glass and the headlight shell.

Refitting

4 Refitting is the reverse sequence to removal. Use new seals if necessary (this is recommended, to prevent the ingress of water) and ensure that the glass is securely retained by the clips/tabs.

14 Headlights - alignment

See Chapter 1A or 1B.

15 Headlight height adjustment system - description and component renewal

Description

1 The headlights are provided with a beam height adjustment system to enable the driver to regulate the beam height from inside the car to cater for different vehicle loading. Later models with xenon headlight bulbs have an automatic adjuster facility, and the manual control is not fitted.

2 The system is operated by vacuum supplied from the central locking system vacuum pump.

3 Control of the system is by a three-position switch adjacent to the lighting switch on the facia. The vacuum supplied to the headlight adjusting unit is regulated according to switch position. The adjusting unit consists of a diaphragm which is connected to the movable headlight lens by means of a pullrod having a stroke of approximately 3.0 mm. Vacuum applied to the diaphragm causes it to deflect, which in turn moves the pullrod to raise or lower the headlight beams.

4 Apart from periodically checking the

12.40b . . . the nuts should remain in position, but this one did not

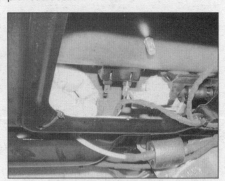

12.41a Disconnecting the number plate light wiring

12.41b Removing the handle trim strip from the outside of the tailgate

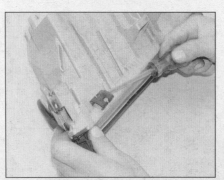

13.3 Prising off one of the headlight glass securing clips

15.7a Twist the adjusting unit clockwise . . .

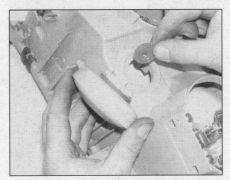

15.7b . . . and remove it from the headlight, recovering the spacer

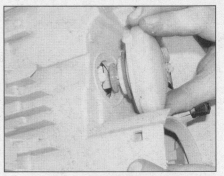

15.8a Refitting the adjusting unit

condition of the vacuum hoses, the system does not require any maintenance or adjustment in service.

Component renewal

Adjuster switch

5 Refer to Section 6.

Headlight adjusting unit

6 Remove the headlight unit as described in Section 12.

7 To remove the adjusting unit, twist it to release the bayonet fitting on the rear of the headlight, then pull firmly outwards to disengage the ball fitting. Recover the orange aligning spacer, which will probably fall off as the unit is removed **(see illustrations)**.

8 Refitting is a reversal of removal, noting the following points:

a) *Reconnecting the ball fitting is a tricky operation, and will probably require several attempts **(see illustration)**. Grease the fittings to aid assembly.*

b) *When refitting the adjusting unit, note that it should be turned anti-clockwise so that the arrow marks on the rear of the headlight comes into alignment with the vacuum connection **(see illustration)**.*

c) *Refit the headlight as described in Section 12.*

---

16 Headlight wiper motor - removal and refitting

Removal

1 Remove the headlight unit as described in Section 12.

2 Disconnect the motor wiring plug, then pull off the washer hose from the base of the motor.

3 Unscrew the two mounting bolts, and remove the motor from the car.

Refitting

4 Refitting is a reversal of removal. When refitting the wiper arm, make sure the system is still in the parked position, and engage the arm in the appropriate (horizontal) position.

---

17 Wiper arms - removal and refitting

1 Before removing the wiper arms, ensure that the motor is in the 'parked' position by switching on the wiper, then switching it off halfway through its sweep - the arm should continue its sweep and return to the parked position.

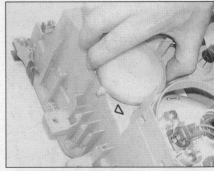

15.8b Turn the adjusting unit until the arrow mark is aligned with the vacuum hose connection

Windscreen wiper

2 Prise up the cover from the end of the wiper arm, for access to the arm retaining bolt **(see illustration)**.

3 Using a suitable Allen key, unscrew the wiper arm bolt, and slide the arm out **(see illustrations)**. Hold the spring-loaded lower section of the arm as this is done, otherwise it may strike the glass with some force.

4 Refitting is a reversal of removal. Tighten the wiper arm retaining bolt securely, then check for correct operation.

Tailgate wiper

5 Prise up the cover from the end of the wiper

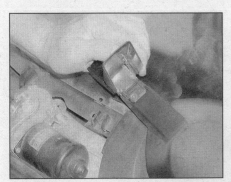

17.2 Lift up the cover for access to the wiper arm bolt

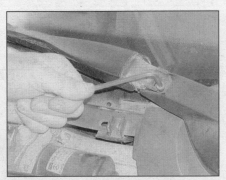

17.3a Using an Allen key, unscrew the wiper arm bolt . . .

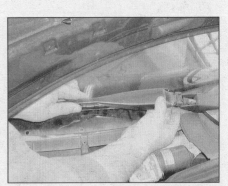

17.3b . . . then slide out the wiper arm

17.5 Lift up the cover for access to the wiper arm nut

17.6a Unscrew and remove the wiper arm nut . . .

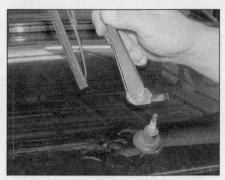

17.6b . . . and slide the wiper arm off its splines

arm, for access to the arm retaining nut **(see illustration)**.

6 Remove the nut, then pull the wiper arm away from the tailgate, and remove it **(see illustrations)**. Take care not to damage the washer jet.

7 Refitting is a reversal of removal. Tighten the wiper arm retaining nut securely, then check for correct operation.

Headlight wiper

8 Lift up the cover on the wiper arm, unscrew the nut, and pull the headlight wiper arm from its spindle.

9 Refitting is a reversal of removal.

18.3a Using a screwdriver, prise up the panel to release the clips . . .

18.3b . . . and remove the two sections of trim from below the windscreen

---

18 Windscreen wiper motor and linkage - removal and refitting

Removal

1 Remove the wiper arm as described in the previous Section.

2 Open the bonnet, and raise it to the vertical position by releasing the catch on the side of each bonnet hinge - an assistant is useful here.

3 Release the clips securing the two halves of the windscreen cowl panel trim **(see illustrations)**.

4 Undo the ten screws (four each side, two below the wiper arm) and two plastic nuts securing the upper section of the windscreen cowl panel, then release the clips and withdraw the cowl panel from the base of the windscreen **(see illustrations)**.

5 Remove the semi-circular cover below the wiper arm **(see illustration)**.

6 Remove the covers from the right-hand

18.4a Remove the screws . . .

18.4b . . . and the plastic nuts . . .

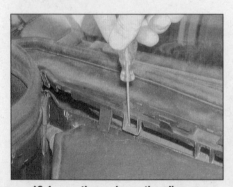

18.4c . . . then release the clips . . .

18.4d . . . and remove the upper section of the windscreen cowl panel

18.5 Remove the semi-circular panel below the wiper arm

18.6a Unclip and remove the front section of the fusebox cover . . .

18.6b . . . the rear section is secured by a number of screws

18.7a Disconnect the wiper motor wiring plug . . .

fusebox - the front cover unclips, while the rear cover is secured by a number of small screws **(see illustrations)**.

7 Trace the wiring harness back from the wiper motor, and disconnect its wiring plug from inside the fusebox. Lift out the harness, and release the grommet from the side of the fusebox, so that it can be removed with the motor **(see illustrations)**.

8 Remove the two wiper assembly mounting nuts, then release the plastic clamp around the rubber mounting underneath the wiper motor **(see illustrations)**.

9 Carefully withdraw the wiper assembly from its mountings, taking care not to damage

either the bonnet or the windscreen **(see illustration)**.

Refitting

10 Refitting is the reverse sequence to removal.

11 On completion, check the distance between the lower section of the wiper arm (the wiper arm gear head) and the windscreen, when the wiper arm is in the vertical position. The distance should be approximately 5 mm - if necessary, this dimension can be adjusted using the bolt on the base of the wiper assembly which secures the rubber mounting.

19 Windscreen wiper motor - removal and refitting

Removal

1 Remove the wiper motor and linkage assembly from the car as described in the previous Section.

2 Before proceeding, confirm that the linkage is in the parked position. This can be done by checking that the mark on the wiper arm gear head appears in the cut-out in the housing **(see illustration)**.

18.7b . . . and unclip the wiring harness from the fusebox

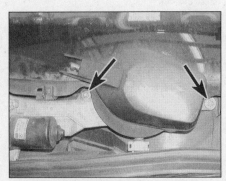

18.8a Windscreen wiper assembly mounting nuts (arrowed) . . .

18.8b . . . unscrew and remove the mounting nuts . . .

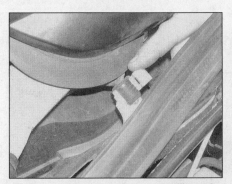

18.8c . . . and release the plastic clip at the base of the wiper motor

18.9 Remove the wiper assembly from its mountings

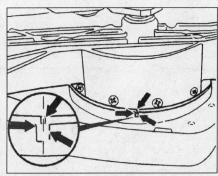

19.2 Wiper motor linkage in parked position

20.3a Disconnect the washer pump wiring plug . . .

20.3b . . . then release the hose clip . . .

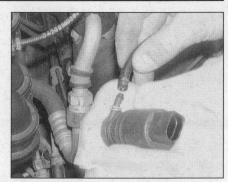

20.3c . . . and pull off the washer pump hose

3 Unscrew the retaining nut and remove the bellcrank arm from the motor spindle.
4 Undo the three bolts and remove the motor from the linkage bracket.

Refitting

5 Refitting is the reverse sequence to removal, but with the linkage and motor in the parked position, the bellcrank and linkage must be parallel with each other as the bellcrank is fitted to the motor spindle.

20 Washer system components - removal, refitting and adjustment

1 The windscreen washer system consists of a water reservoir located at the left-hand side of the engine compartment, an electric pump attached to the reservoir and two double nozzle jets located on each side of the bonnet. A water level indicator is also fitted to the reservoir to inform the driver of low water supply in the reservoir.
2 Estate models have a separate reservoir and pump located on the left-hand side of the luggage area.

Removal

Windscreen washer

3 To remove the reservoir, disconnect the wiring and water hoses at the pump, and also the wiring plug at the water level sensor (see illustrations).

4 Unscrew the plastic cap nut, then lift the reservoir up and out of its locating stub (see illustrations).
5 The pump is a push fit in the reservoir, and can be removed by carefully prising it out (drain the reservoir first) (see illustration). The pump is a sealed unit, and cannot be repaired.
6 To remove the water level sensor, prise it out of its location. Recover the rubber seal (see illustrations).
7 A check valve is located in the water hose alongside the right-hand front suspension strut turret. The valve can be removed after detaching the hoses.
8 To remove the jets, disconnect the water hose and electrical connection from within the

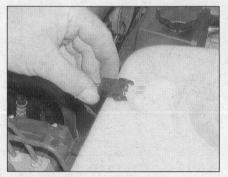

20.3d Disconnect the wiring plug from the water level sensor

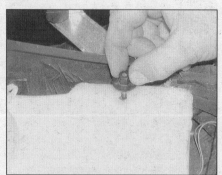

20.4a Unscrew the plastic cap nut . . .

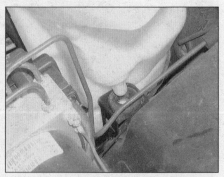

20.4b . . . then lift the reservoir up out of its locating stub

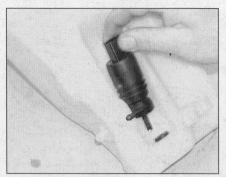

20.5 Prise out the washer pump, and remove it

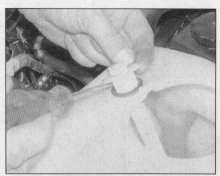

20.6a Prise the water level sensor out of the reservoir . . .

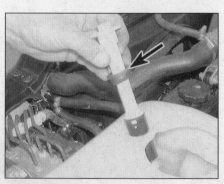

20.6b . . . and remove it - note the rubber seal (arrowed)

20.8a Disconnect the wiring connections . . .

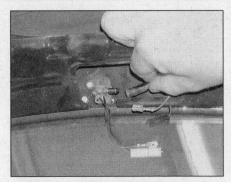

20.8b . . . and the washer hose from the washer jet

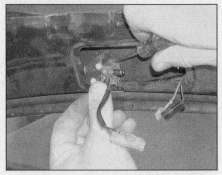

20.9a Using a screwdriver, release the retaining lugs . . .

aperture on the inside of the bonnet **(see illustrations)**.

9 Release the retaining lugs, then push the jet upwards and withdraw it from the bonnet **(see illustrations)**.

Tailgate washer

10 To remove the reservoir, open the access flap in the luggage area side trim panel.

11 Lift the reservoir up and out of its location. Disconnect the wiring and water hoses at the pump, and where applicable, the wiring plug at the water level indicator **(see illustrations)**.

12 The pump is a push fit in the reservoir, and can be removed by carefully prising it out. The pump is a sealed unit, and cannot be repaired.

13 To remove the tailgate washer jet, remove the tailgate trim panel as described in Chapter 11, Section 41.

14 Open the cover adjacent to the jet location. Hold the fluid hose, then twist and pull the jet out of position.

15 When refitting the jet, twist it until it catches, then press it into place. Check that the jet is facing the tailgate glass.

Refitting and adjustment

16 Refitting all the components is the reverse sequence to removal.

17 Adjust the nozzles using a pin, so that the

20.9b . . . then push the jet out of the bonnet

water contacts the windscreen/tailgate centrally. When adjusting the windscreen jets, allow for the downforce created by the airflow over the bonnet and windscreen, when the car is in forward motion.

21 Rain sensor - removal and refitting

1 Some later models are equipped with a rain sensor - an infra-red device mounted on the inside of the windscreen (above the interior

20.11a Disconnect the washer pump wiring plug . . .

mirror) which detects the presence of rain droplets on the windscreen, and activates the windscreen wipers automatically.

Removal

2 Carefully unclip the cover from the rear of the sensor.

3 Unhook the retaining clips at either side by prising them outwards, and remove the sensor from its lens.

4 The lens is glued to the inside of the windscreen, and no attempt should be made to remove it. If it is damaged, seek the advice of a Mercedes-Benz dealer.

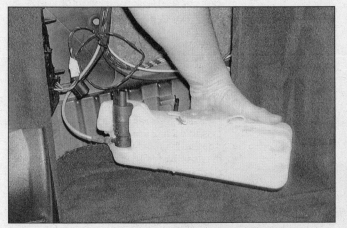

20.11b . . . and lift out the washer reservoir

20.11c To remove the washer pump, disconnect the hose and prise it out of the reservoir

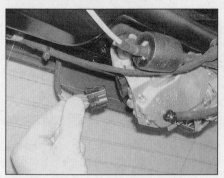

22.3a Disconnect the wiring plug . . .

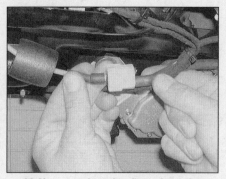

22.3b . . . and washer hose from the tailgate wiper motor

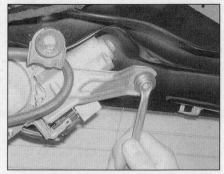

22.4 Removing the wiper motor mounting bolts

Refitting

5 Refitting is a reversal of removal. On completion, check the operation of the sensor by turning the ignition on and spraying some water onto the windscreen.

22 Tailgate wiper motor - removal and refitting

Removal

1 Remove the wiper arm as described in Section 17.
2 Remove the tailgate trim panel as described in Chapter 11, Section 41.
3 Disconnect the wiper motor wiring plug, and pull off the washer hose **(see illustrations)**.
4 Remove the three motor mounting bolts, and withdraw the motor from the tailgate **(see illustration)**. Recover the rubber sealing grommet from the tailgate glass.

Refitting

5 Refitting is a reversal of removal. Fit a new sealing grommet if necessary when refitting the motor.

23 Horns - removal and refitting

1 Early Classic models are fitted with just one horn unit, on the left-hand side. All high-specification models, and those made after September 1996, have twin horns, one on each side.

Removal

2 Disconnect the battery negative terminal.
3 Chock the rear wheels, then apply the parking brake. Jack up the front of the car, and support it on axle stands (see *Jacking and vehicle support*).
4 Release the screws and clips, and remove the wheelarch liner on the side concerned.
5 Where applicable, remove the cooling air duct for the front brakes.
6 Disconnect the horn wiring connector(s), then unscrew the mounting bolt and remove the horn unit from the front of the car **(see illustration)**.

Refitting

7 Refitting is the reverse sequence to removal. Check for correct operation on completion.

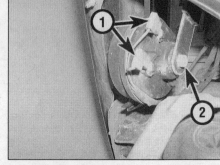

23.6 Horn unit viewed from below
1 Wiring connectors
2 Mounting bolt

24 Radio/cassette player - removal and refitting

Note: *This Section relates principally to radio equipment fitted as standard by Mercedes-Benz, or supplied and fitted by Mercedes-Benz dealers.*

Removal

1 Disconnect the battery negative terminal.

Mercedes-Benz audio equipment

2 To release the retaining catches on either side of the radio, two special removal tools are required. These tools resemble keys, and would have been provided (typically, in the glovebox) with the car when new. If the tools are no longer with the car, a Mercedes-Benz dealer (or car audio dealer) should be able to help. It is not advisable to try fabricating substitute tools, as damage may be caused to the radio if these are used.
3 Insert the removal tools into the slots until they can be felt to engage with the catches. Now pull the unit out of its aperture **(see illustration)**.
4 Disconnect the electrical connections and aerial lead at the rear of the radio and push the retaining clips inward to release the removal tools. Remove the unit from the car.

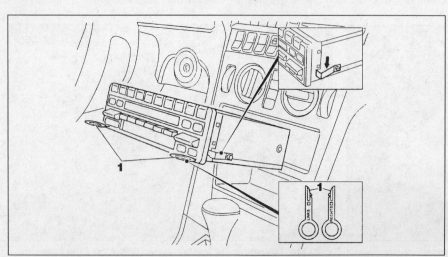

24.3 Removing a Mercedes radio/cassette unit with the special tools (1)

24.8 Using the removal tools to pull out the radio/cassette

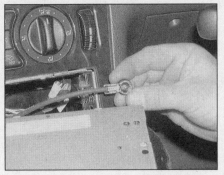

24.9a Disconnect the aerial lead . . .

24.9b . . . and the power supply/speaker wiring plugs

Other audio equipment (typical)

5 Typically, an aftermarket radio/cassette player will require the more standard removal tools to be used. The round holes to accept these tools will either be visible at either end of the unit front panel, or there will be two end plates to prise off for access to the tool holes.

6 The standard removal tools are widely available from car accessory outlets, and are two pieces of thick wire, bent into an elongated C-shape, with shaped ends to engage the retaining catches at either side of the radio unit.

7 Fit the tools into the holes provided, and push them firmly into place until the retaining catches are felt to release.

8 Using the tools as 'handles', pull the unit slowly out of the facia until the wiring is accessible (see illustration).

9 Disconnect the electrical connections and aerial lead from the rear of the unit, noting their locations, and remove it from the car (see illustrations). If required, the removal tools can be unhooked and removed - they are not required for refitting.

Radio mounting cage

10 Usually, there will be a metal cage still fitted to the radio aperture (on some models, the main wiring for the radio is attached to the cage, not to the radio itself). If the radio has been removed as part of another procedure (such as facia panel removal), the cage should also be removed.

11 The cage is secured in the aperture by a number of metal tabs, which are bent over the inside edge of the facia aperture, to prevent removal. Careful use of a small screwdriver will release the tabs and allow the cage to be removed (see illustration).

Refitting

12 If the mounting cage was removed, offer it back into position, and bend over the metal tabs used to retain the cage originally, until it is securely held in place.

13 Reconnect the wiring to the radio, then push the radio/cassette player back into its aperture until the catches engage.

14 On models with a coded unit, it will be necessary to re-activate the code once the battery has been reconnected. The code will have been provided (like the removal tools) with the car when new. Again, a Mercedes-Benz dealer or car audio specialist may be able to help if the code has been lost.

25 Speakers - removal and refitting

Facia-mounted speakers

1 The front speakers are located at each side of the facia at the top.

2 Using a small screwdriver inserted through the vent grilles, release the tabs securing the speakers at either end of the facia (see

illustration). Alternatively, prise the edge of the speaker cover with a plastic wedge, taking care not to damage the top of the facia.

3 Lift up the speaker and disconnect the wiring plug (see illustration).

4 Refitting is the reverse sequence to removal.

Front door speakers

5 Remove the front door trim panel as described in Chapter 11 - this is necessary to gain access to the speaker wiring plug, which is located at the top of the panel, and is not accessible through the (removable) speaker cover.

6 Unscrew and remove the speaker retaining screws, then withdraw the speaker from its location (see illustration).

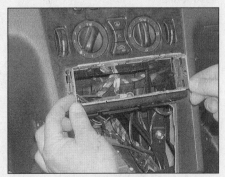

24.11 Removing the radio mounting cage

25.2 Using a screwdriver to release the speaker retaining tabs

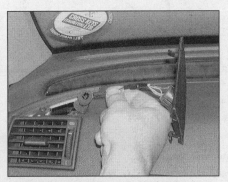

25.3 Disconnect the speaker wiring plug, and remove the speaker

25.6 Unscrew the three speaker retaining screws, and withdraw the speaker

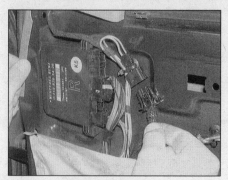

25.7 The speaker wiring plug is located at the top of the door

25.9 Remove the four speaker screws

25.10 Disconnect the speaker wiring plug, and remove the speaker

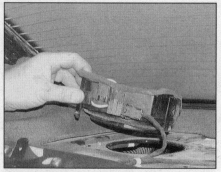

25.12 Remove the speaker and housing from the shelf

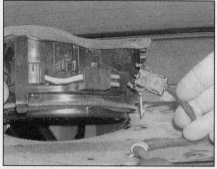

25.13 Disconnecting the speaker wiring

7 Disconnect the speaker wiring plug, and remove the speaker from the car **(see illustration)**.

Rear door speakers

8 Remove the rear door trim panel as described in Chapter 11.

9 Unscrew and remove the speaker retaining screws, then withdraw the speaker from its location **(see illustration)**.
10 Trace the speaker wiring to the speaker wiring plug, and disconnect it **(see illustration)**. Remove the speaker from the car.

Rear shelf speakers

11 On Saloon models, remove the rear shelf as described in Chapter 11, Section 41.
12 Unclip the speaker housing from the rear shelf, and remove complete with the speaker **(see illustration)**.
13 Disconnect the speaker wiring, labelling it if necessary to ensure correct refitting **(see illustration)**. Note that there is a risk of severe damage to the speakers if the wiring is wrongly connected.
14 Refitting is the reverse sequence to removal.

Bass module (Estate)

15 Where fitted, the bass module is located on the left-hand side of the luggage area.
16 Unscrew and remove the two nuts and one bolt securing the module, and withdraw it from its location.
17 Disconnect the wiring connector from the module, and remove it from the car.
18 Refitting is a reversal of removal.

26 Radio aerial and associated components - removal and refitting

Aerial

1 Early Saloon models have the aerial located in the left-hand rear wing, but on later models, the aerial is incorporated into the rear window glass.

Early Saloon

Aerial motor unit
2 Disconnect the battery negative terminal.
3 Remove the inner trim covering on the left-hand side of the luggage compartment.
4 Unscrew and remove the bolt securing the aerial earth lead, and the aerial motor unit mounting bolt **(see illustration)**.
5 Carefully draw the aerial unit down into the luggage area, feeding the aerial mast down through the rubber grommet in the rear wing.
6 Disconnect the aerial lead and power supply connection from the aerial motor, and remove the unit from the car.
7 Refitting is the reverse sequence to

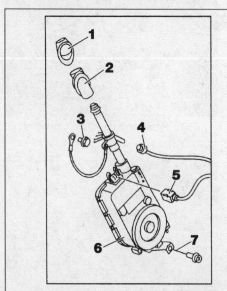

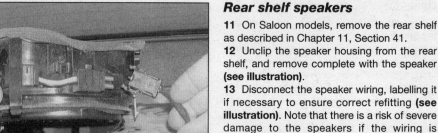

26.4 Aerial motor unit details

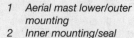

1 Aerial mast lower/outer mounting	3 Earth lead mounting bolt	6 Aerial motor unit
	4 Aerial RF lead	7 Mounting bolt
2 Inner mounting/seal	5 Wiring connector	

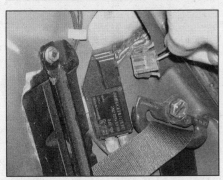

26.18a Disconnect the main wiring plug from the side . . .

26.18b . . . and the two smaller connectors from below

26.18c If necessary, unbolt and remove the seat belt guide plate . . .

removal. Check the condition of the aerial rubber grommet, and renew it, if necessary, to prevent water leaking into the car.

Aerial mast

8 Completely unscrew the nut at the base of the aerial mast, and if possible, remove it over the top of the mast.

9 Have an assistant switch on the radio. As the mast extends, pull it upwards to remove it and the toothed plastic drive cable completely from the rear wing. Note which way round the teeth on the drive cable are facing. Also recover the rubber seal from the base of the mast.

10 Feed in the drive cable on the new mast as far as possible, with the teeth facing the same way as noted on removal.

11 Have the assistant switch off the radio, and the aerial motor should draw in the new cable completely. Some trial-and-error may be required until this is achieved.

12 With the mast fully inserted, fit the rubber seal to the rear wing, and screw on the lower mounting and nut, tightening it securely. Re-check the operation of the aerial on completion.

Later Saloon, and Estate

13 On later Saloons, the aerial is in the form of two vertical 'bars' in the rear window demister - the aerial cannot be changed without changing the rear window glass.

14 On Estate models, the FM aerial is effectively the grid for the rear window

demister, and the AM aerial is incorporated into the left-hand rear window glass. As a result, the aerial cannot be renewed without changing the relevant pieces of glass.

15 On models where the aerial is incorporated into the rear glass, an amplifier is fitted to boost the signal; Estate models also have a noise suppression capacitor fitted.

Aerial amplifier

Saloon

16 The aerial amplifier is located at the top of the right-hand C-pillar.

17 Remove the rear C-pillar trim panel as described in Chapter 11, Section 41, for access to the amplifier unit.

18 Unscrew the retaining bolt, then disconnect the wiring from the unit and remove it from the car. To gain access to the mounting bolt, it may prove necessary to unbolt and remove the seat belt guide plate (see illustrations).

19 Refitting is a reversal of removal.

Estate

20 The aerial amplifier is located in the roof, on the left-hand side of the car, behind the D-pillar trim panel.

21 Unclip the D-pillar trim panel using the information in Chapter 11, Section 41.

22 Disconnect the three wiring plugs from the amplifier, labelling them if necessary so that they are correctly reconnected (see illustration).

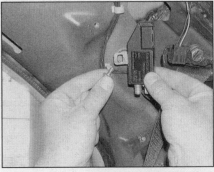

26.18d . . . then unscrew the mounting bolt and remove the amplifier

23 Unscrew the amplifier retaining bolt and remove it from the car.

24 Refitting is a reversal of removal.

Rear window noise suppressor - Estate

25 Referring to Chapter 11, Section 41, if necessary, unclip and remove the trim panels at the top and left-hand sides of the tailgate window.

26 Unscrew the nut securing the rear window demister earth lead (see illustration).

27 At the top of the tailgate, pull back the foam covering the suppressor wiring connector, and disconnect it (see illustration).

28 Unclip the suppressor from the side of the tailgate, and remove it from the car.

29 Refitting is a reversal of removal.

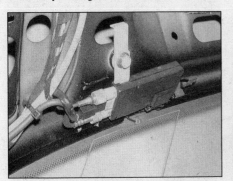

26.22 Aerial amplifier unit on Estate models

26.26 Rear window demister earth connection (arrowed)

26.27 Suppressor wiring plug (arrowed)

27 Amplifier (audio system) - removal and refitting

Removal

1 Disconnect the battery negative terminal.
2 On Estate models with the bass module fitted, the module fits over the amplifier, and so must be removed first, as described in Section 25.
3 Remove the inner trim covering on the left-hand side of the luggage compartment.
4 Disconnect the wiring connectors from the amplifier, noting their locations.
5 Unscrew and remove the amplifier fasteners, and remove the amplifier from the car.

Refitting

6 Refitting is a reversal of removal.

28 Anti-theft alarm system - general information

Note: *This information is applicable only to the anti-theft alarm system fitted by Mercedes-Benz as standard equipment.*

All models are fitted with an anti-theft alarm system as standard equipment. The alarm has switches on all the doors (including the boot lid), the bonnet, the audio unit and the ignition switch, and also a tilt switch which is sensitive to shocks. If the boot lid, bonnet or either of the doors are opened or the ignition switch or audio unit are switched on whilst the alarm is set, or if the tilt switch senses the vehicle is being tampered with, the alarm horn will sound and the hazard warning lights will flash. The alarm also has an immobiliser function which makes the ignition/starter (as applicable) system inoperable whilst the alarm is triggered.

On later models, the scope of alarm functions is increased, with switchable interior motion sensors and anti-jacking/tilt sensor

The alarm is set using the key in the front door lock or boot/tailgate lock; on later models, the alarm is also set when the doors are locked using the remote central locking device. The LED on the centre console will flash to indicate that the alarm system is operational.

Models from June 1997 onwards are equipped with the Mercedes-Benz Driver Authorisation System (DAS). This advanced security system does away with a conventional key for locking and unlocking the doors and, instead, a sophisticated electronic remote-control handset/electronic key is provided. Without this handset, the engine cannot be started.

Should the alarm system become faulty, the vehicle should be taken to a Mercedes-Benz

dealer for examination. They will have access to a special diagnostic tester which will quickly trace any fault present in the system.

29 Airbag system - general information and precautions

A driver's airbag is fitted as standard to all models, and a passenger airbag was made standard equipment on all models from August 1995. From June 1997, the airbag system was expanded further, with the fitment as standard of front side airbags to all models - these being fitted in the front door trim panels.

Airbag units have the word AIRBAG or SRS-AIRBAG stamped on them. The airbag system comprises of the airbag unit(s) (each with a gas generator), the control unit (with an integral impact sensor) and a warning light in the instrument panel. The airbag control unit features 'intelligent' software, and also operates the front seat belt tensioner mechanisms at the same time as the airbag (see Chapter 11, Section 37).

The driver's and passenger's front airbags will only be triggered in the event of a heavy frontal impact above a predetermined force; depending on the point of impact (rear impacts will not usually trigger the airbag system). The side airbags will only be triggered if the car is hit from the side, and only on the side from which the car has been hit. The passenger airbags and seat belt tensioner will only be triggered if the passenger seat is occupied - a sensor built into the seat cushion informs the control unit of this. Light impacts, such as those which might be sustained when parking, will not trigger the system.

The airbag is inflated within milliseconds, and forms a safety cushion between the driver, steering wheel and door, or between the passenger, facia and door, depending on the severity of the accident. This prevents contact between the upper body and wheel/facia/door, and therefore greatly reduces the risk of injury. The airbag then deflates almost immediately.

Every time the ignition is switched on, the airbag control unit performs a self-test. The self-test takes approximately 4 seconds and during this time the airbag warning light in the instrument panel is illuminated. After the self-test has been completed the warning light should go out. If the warning light fails to come on, remains illuminated after the initial period or comes on at any time when the vehicle is being driven, there is a fault in the airbag system. The vehicle should be taken to a Mercedes-Benz dealer for examination at the earliest possible opportunity.

 Warning: Before carrying out any operations on the airbag system, first switch off the ignition (ideally, take out the

key). Disconnect the battery negative terminal, and position the lead away from the battery terminal (Mercedes-Benz recommend covering up the terminal, to prevent accidental reconnection). Wait 15 minutes after disconnecting the battery for the capacitive charge in the system to dissipate. When operations are complete, make sure no one is inside the vehicle when the battery is reconnected.

Note that the airbag(s) must not be subjected to temperatures in excess of 100°C. When an airbag is removed, ensure that it is stored the correct way up to prevent possible inflation.

Do not allow any solvents or cleaning agents to contact the airbag assemblies. They must be cleaned using only a damp cloth.

The airbags and control unit are both sensitive to impact. If dropped or damaged, they should be renewed.

Disconnect the airbag control unit wiring plug prior to using arc-welding equipment on the vehicle.

30 Airbag system components - removal and refitting

Note: *Refer to the warnings given in Section 29 before carrying out the following operations.*

1 Turn the ignition key to position 0, then disconnect the battery negative cable, and position it away from the terminal.

Driver's airbag

Removal

2 Slacken and remove the two airbag Torx retaining screws from the rear of the steering wheel, rotating the wheel as necessary to gain access to the screws **(see illustration)**.
3 Return the steering wheel to the straight-ahead position, then carefully lift the airbag assembly away from the steering wheel and disconnect the wiring connector from the rear

30.2 Remove the two Torx screws from behind the steering wheel

30.3a Carefully lift the airbag unit from the wheel . . .

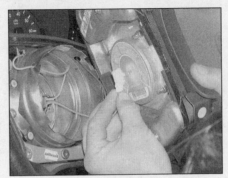

30.3b . . . and disconnect the wiring connector at the rear

30.9a Disconnect the wiring plug, then unscrew the mounting nuts (two arrowed) . . .

of the unit **(see illustrations)**. Note that the airbag must not be knocked or dropped, and should be stored the correct way up (padded surface uppermost).

Refitting

4 Ensure that the wiring connector is securely reconnected (it should engage audibly), and seat the airbag unit centrally in the steering wheel, making sure the wire does not become trapped.
5 Fit the retaining screws and tighten them to the specified torque setting, noting the left-hand retaining screw should be tightened first.
6 Ensure no one is inside the vehicle, and reconnect the battery. Turn on the ignition switch and check the operation of the airbag warning light, whilst turning the steering wheel from full left lock to full right lock.
7 Mercedes-Benz state that, if the airbag has been deployed, a new steering wheel should be fitted.

Passenger airbag

Removal

8 Remove the facia panel as described in Chapter 11.
9 Disconnect the airbag wiring plug at the side of the unit, then unscrew the four securing nuts and remove the airbag unit from the facia **(see illustrations)**.

Refitting

10 Refitting is a reversal of removal. Tighten the airbag retaining nuts securely, and ensure

that the wiring plug is fully reconnected. Refit the facia as described in Chapter 11.
11 Mercedes-Benz state that, if the airbag has been deployed, a new facia panel should be fitted.

Side airbag

Removal

12 Remove the door trim panel as described in Chapter 11.
13 Disconnect the airbag wiring plug, then drill out the retaining rivets and remove the airbag unit **(see illustration)**.

Refitting

14 Refitting is a reversal of removal. Secure the airbag using new pop-rivets, and ensure that the wiring plug is fully reconnected. Refit the door trim panel as described in Chapter 11.

Airbag control unit

15 Removal and refitting of the control unit should be entrusted to a Mercedes-Benz dealer. On refitting, the control unit must be tested using special Mercedes-Benz diagnostic equipment to ensure that the system is operating correctly. For reference, the control unit is mounted underneath the front of the centre console **(see illustration)**.

Airbag wiring contact unit

Removal

16 Remove the steering wheel as described in Chapter 10.

17 Remove the driver's side lower facia panel as described in Chapter 11, Section 41.
18 Trace the wiring back from the contact unit, freeing it from all the relevant retaining clips, and disconnect it from the main wiring harness.
19 Loosen the contact unit screws just sufficiently so that the unit is freed from the top of the steering column and can be removed; this will lock the contact unit in position and prevent it from being rotated whilst it is removed. Hold the rear of the unit tight against the front as it is removed, or the two halves will separate - once removed, tape the front and rear halves together **(see illustrations)**. **Note:** *Do not fully remove the retaining screws and dismantle the contact unit.*

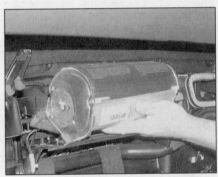

30.9b . . . and remove the passenger airbag from the car

30.13 Side airbag unit on door inner frame

30.15 Airbag control unit location

30.19a Loosen the contact unit screws . . .

30.19b . . . and remove the unit, holding it together

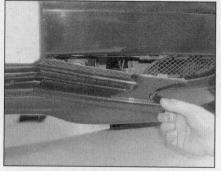

32.2a Unclip the left-hand lower trim panel from the front bumper . . .

32.2b . . . and disconnect the wiring plug from the sensor

Refitting

20 Prior to refitting, ensure that the contact unit is correctly centralised. This shouldn't be a problem if the retaining screws have not been disturbed. If there is any doubt about the unit position, screw the retaining screws fully into position in the contact unit, and rotate the contact unit insert in a clockwise direction until resistance is felt. From this point, rotate the insert back through two to two-and-a-half rotations until the fixing screws are aligned with the holes, then unscrew the screws slightly to lock the unit in position.

21 Slide the contact ring into position, making sure its wiring is correctly routed, and engage the recess at the centre of the contact ring with the corresponding lug on the steering column. Check that the wiring plug on the wheel boss aligns with that on the contact unit. Ensure that the contact ring is correctly engaged with the column and securely tighten its retaining screws.

22 Reconnect the wiring connectors and refit the remaining components by reversing the removal sequence.

31 Parktronic system - general information

Available as an option, the Parktronic system is an ultrasonic parking aid. The system uses ultrasonic sensors in the front and rear bumpers to transmit a signal which then bounces off any objects in range in front of or behind the car. The sensors receive the reflected signal, and the control unit can then calculate the distance of the object from the car. The system works at speeds up to 9 mph (15 km/h). The resulting distance information is conveyed to the driver by visual display and audio signal.

There are six sensors in the front bumper, and four at the rear. The control unit is located under the luggage area floor. The audio/visual warning units are located in the instrument panel incorporated in the rear interior light.

When the ignition is switched on, the system performs a self-test. If the system develops a fault, this will be indicated by just the red sections of the visual warning units staying on. In the event of a fault, first check the connections at the bumper-mounted sensors, as these may be subject to dirt and water entry. After checking this, and the wiring as far as possible, it is advisable to take the car to a Mercedes-Benz dealer for testing using diagnostic equipment.

32 Outside temperature sensor - removal and refitting

Removal

1 The outside temperature sensor is clipped to the left-hand side of the grille below the front bumper, and the sensor display is incorporated into the instrument panel.

2 To remove the sensor, unclip the trim panel from the bumper and disconnect the sensor wiring plug (see illustrations). On early models, it appears that the sensor cannot be disconnected, and that the wiring harness for it remains in the vehicle. If the sensor cannot easily be disconnected, it may be more convenient to cut the wiring to the sensor at a suitable point, and to solder on a new sensor.

3 Unclip the sensor from its location on the trim panel, and remove it (see illustration).

Refitting

4 Refitting is a reversal of removal.

5 Note that, if the sensor display is faulty, renewal is a job for a Mercedes-Benz dealer

or automotive electrician. The sensor is part of the instrument panel, which can be removed as described in Section 8, but removing the display completely requires that its wiring is separated from the instrument panel wiring multi-plug, which is a delicate operation.

33 Wiring diagrams - general information

1 The wiring diagrams which follow only offer limited coverage of the electrical systems fitted to the C-class.

2 At the time of writing, no more wiring diagrams were available from Mercedes-Benz, so the inclusion of more information has not been possible.

3 Bear in mind that, while wiring diagrams offer a useful quick-reference guide to the vehicle electrical systems, it is still possible to trace faults, and to check for supplies and earths, using a simple multi-meter. Refer to the general fault finding methods described in Section 2 of this Chapter (ignoring the references to wiring diagrams, if one is not provided for the system concerned).

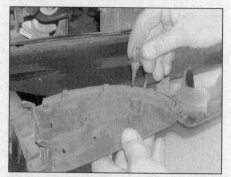

32.3 Unclip the sensor from the trim panel, and remove it

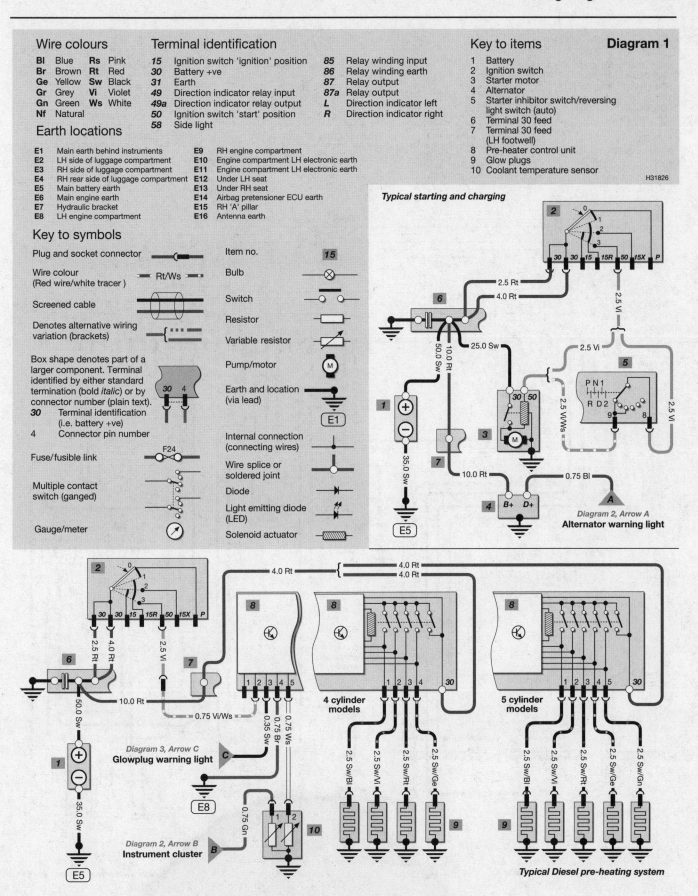

Wire colours

Bl	Blue	**Rs**	Pink
Br	Brown	**Rt**	Red
Ge	Yellow	**Sw**	Black
Gr	Grey	**Vi**	Violet
Gn	Green	**Ws**	White
Nf	Natural		

Earth locations

E1	Main earth behind instruments	E9	RH engine compartment
E2	LH side of luggage compartment	E10	Engine compartment LH electronic earth
E3	RH side of luggage compartment	E11	Engine compartment LH electronic earth
E4	RH rear side of luggage compartment	E12	Under LH seat
E5	Main battery earth	E13	Under RH seat
E6	Main engine earth	E14	Airbag pretensioner ECU earth
E7	Hydraulic bracket	E15	RH 'A' pillar
E8	LH engine compartment	E16	Antenna earth

Key to symbols

Plug and socket connector

Wire colour
(Red wire/white tracer)   Rt/Ws

Screened cable

Denotes alternative wiring
variation (brackets)

Box shape denotes part of a
larger component. Terminal
identified by either standard
termination (bold *italic*) or by
connector number (plain text).
30   Terminal identification
(i.e. battery +ve)
4   Connector pin number

Fuse/fusible link   F24

Multiple contact
switch (ganged)

Gauge/meter

Item no.   15

Bulb

Switch

Resistor

Variable resistor

Pump/motor   M

Earth and location
(via lead)   E1

Internal connection
(connecting wires)

Wire splice or
soldered joint

Diode

Light emitting diode
(LED)

Solenoid actuator

Terminal identification

15	Ignition switch 'ignition' position	85	Relay winding input
30	Battery +ve	86	Relay winding earth
31	Earth	87	Relay output
49	Direction indicator relay input	87a	Relay output
49a	Direction indicator relay output	L	Direction indicator left
50	Ignition switch 'start' position	R	Direction indicator right
58	Side light		

Key to items

Diagram 1

1 Battery
2 Ignition switch
3 Starter motor
4 Alternator
5 Starter inhibitor switch/reversing
   light switch (auto)
6 Terminal 30 feed
7 Terminal 30 feed
   (LH footwell)
8 Pre-heater control unit
9 Glow plugs
10 Coolant temperature sensor

H31826

Typical starting and charging

2.5 Rt
4.0 Rt
25.0 Sw
10.0 Rt
50.0 Sw
35.0 Sw
2.5 Vi
2.5 Vi
2.5 Vi/Ws
2.5 Vi
10.0 Rt
0.75 Bl
B+ D+
E5

Diagram 2, Arrow A
Alternator warning light

4.0 Rt
4.0 Rt
2.5 Rt
4.0 Rt
2.5 Vi
50.0 Sw
10.0 Rt
35.0 Sw
0.75 Vi/Ws
0.75 Sw
0.35 Sw
0.75 Br
0.75 Ws

4 cylinder models

2.5 Sw/Bl   2.5 Sw/Vi   2.5 Sw/Rt   2.5 Sw/Ge

5 cylinder models

2.5 Sw/Bl   2.5 Sw/Vi   2.5 Sw/Rt   2.5 Sw/Ge   2.5 Sw/Gn

Diagram 3, Arrow C
Glowplug warning light   C

E8

0.75 Gn

Diagram 2, Arrow B
Instrument cluster   B

E5

Typical Diesel pre-heating system

Wire colours

Bl	Blue	Rs	Pink
Br	Brown	Rt	Red
Ge	Yellow	Sw	Black
Gr	Grey	Vi	Violet
Gn	Green	Ws	White
Nf	Natural		

Key to items

1 Battery
2 Ignition switch
6 Terminal 30 feed
15 Fuse/relay box
16 Instrument cluster
  a = bulb failure warning light
  b = brake system warning light
  c = alternator warning light
  d = high beam warning light
  e = LH indicator warning light
  f = RH indicator warning light
  g = instrument illumination
  h = multi-function display unit

16 Instrument cluster (continued)
  i = ABS warning light
  j = ADS warning light
  k = pad wear warning light
  l = low coolant warning light
  m = low washer fluid warning light
  n = traction control warning light
  o = road condition warning light
  p = pre-heater warning light
  q = diesel engine management warning light
  r = airbag warning light
17 Handbrake switch
18 Bulb failure control unit

19 Oil level switch
20 Outside air temperature sensor
21 Low brake fluid sender
22 LH pad wear sensor
23 RH pad wear sensor
24 Low washer fluid sensor
25 Low coolant sensor
26 Fuel gauge sender (LH side)
27 Fuel gauge sender (RH side)

Diagram 2

H31827

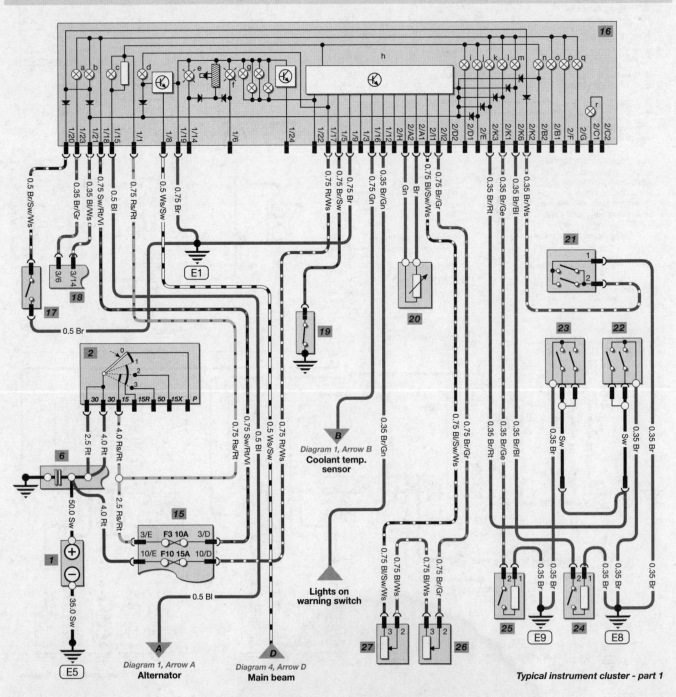

Typical instrument cluster - part 1

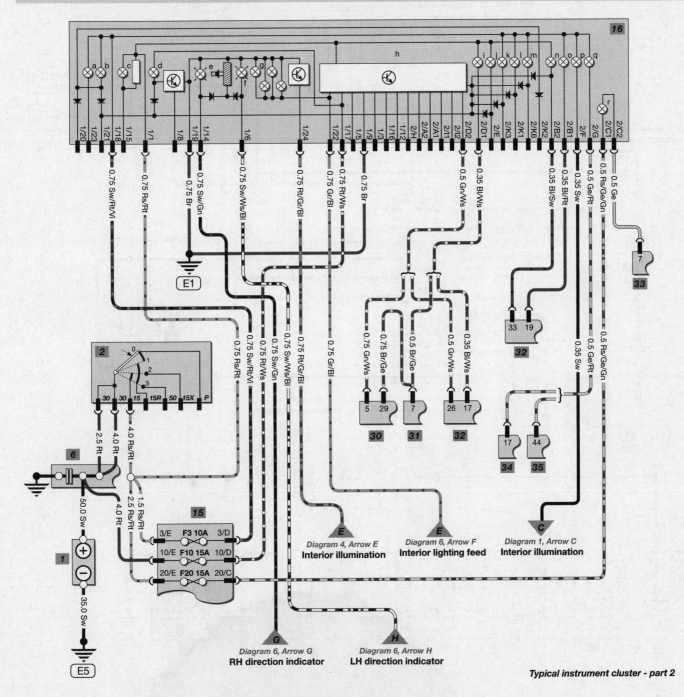

Wire colours

Bl	Blue	Rs	Pink
Br	Brown	Rt	Red
Ge	Yellow	Sw	Black
Gr	Grey	Vi	Violet
Gn	Green	Ws	White
Nf	Natural		

Key to items

1   Battery
2   Ignition switch
6   Terminal 30 feed
15 Fuse/relay box
16 Instrument cluster
   a = bulb failure warning light
   b = brake system warning light
   c = alternator warning light
   d = high beam warning light
   e = LH indicator warning light
   f = RH indicator warning light
   g = instrument illumination
   h = multi-function display unit

16 Instrument cluster (continued)
   i = ABS warning light
   j = ADS warning light
   k = pad wear warning light
   l = low coolant warning light
   m = low washer fluid warning light
   n = traction control warning light
   o = road condition warning light
   p = pre-heater warning light
   q = diesel engine management warning light
   r = airbag warning light
30 Anti-lock brake ECU
31 Anti-lock brake hydraulic unit

32 Traction control ECU
33 Airbag control unit
34 Diesel engine management ECU
   (M605 models)
35 Diesel engine management ECU
   (M604 models)

Diagram 3

H31828

Typical instrument cluster - part 2

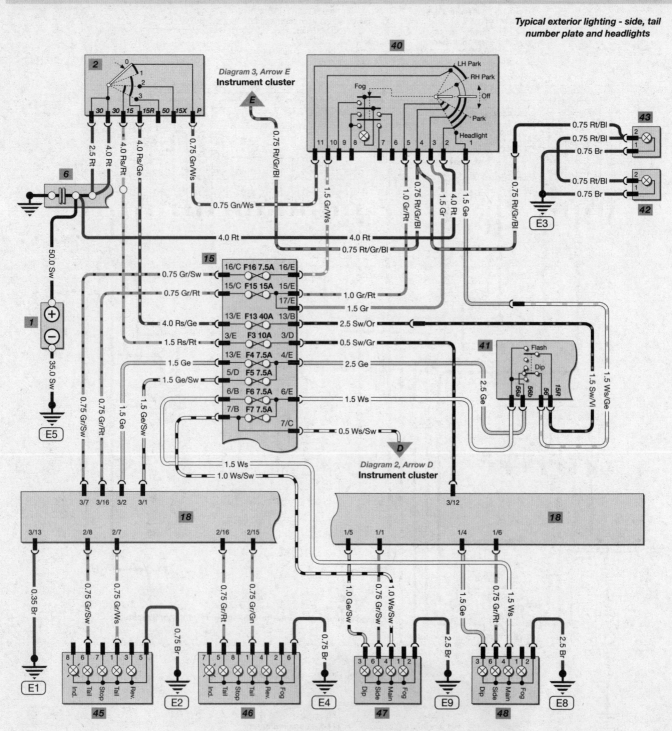

Wire colours

Bl	Blue	Rs	Pink
Br	Brown	Rt	Red
Ge	Yellow	Sw	Black
Gr	Grey	Vi	Violet
Gn	Green	Ws	White
Nf	Natural		

Key to items

1 Battery
2 Ignition switch
6 Terminal 30 feed
15 Fuse/relay box
18 Bulb failure control unit
40 Light switch
41 Combined switch
42 LH number plate light
43 RH number plate light
45 LH tail light unit
46 RH tail light unit
47 LH headlight unit
48 RH headlight unit

Diagram 4

H31829

Typical exterior lighting - side, tail number plate and headlights

Wire colours

Bl	Blue	Rs	Pink
Br	Brown	Rt	Red
Ge	Yellow	Sw	Black
Gr	Grey	Vi	Violet
Gn	Green	Ws	White
Nf	Natural		

Key to items

1 Battery
2 Ignition switch
5 Starter inhibitor/reversing light switch (auto)
6 Terminal 30 feed
15 Fuse/relay box
18 Bulb failure control unit
45 LH tail light unit
46 RH tail light unit
50 Stop light switch
51 Reversing light switch (manual)
52 High level brake light

Diagram 5

H31830

*Typical exterior lighting
- stop and reversing lights*

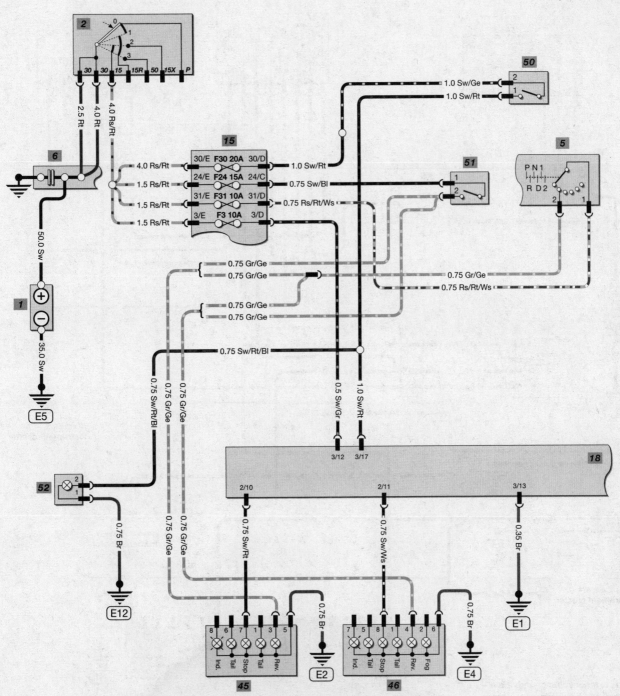

Wire colours

Bl	Blue	Rs	Pink
Br	Brown	Rt	Red
Ge	Yellow	Sw	Black
Gr	Grey	Vi	Violet
Gn	Green	Ws	White
Nf	Natural		

Key to items

1 Battery
2 Ignition switch
6 Terminal 30 feed
15 Fuse/relay box
41 Combined switch

45 LH tail light unit
46 RH tail light unit
55 Hazard warning light switch
56 Combined relay (flasher relay)
57 LH front direction indicator

58 RH front direction indicator

Diagram 6

H31831

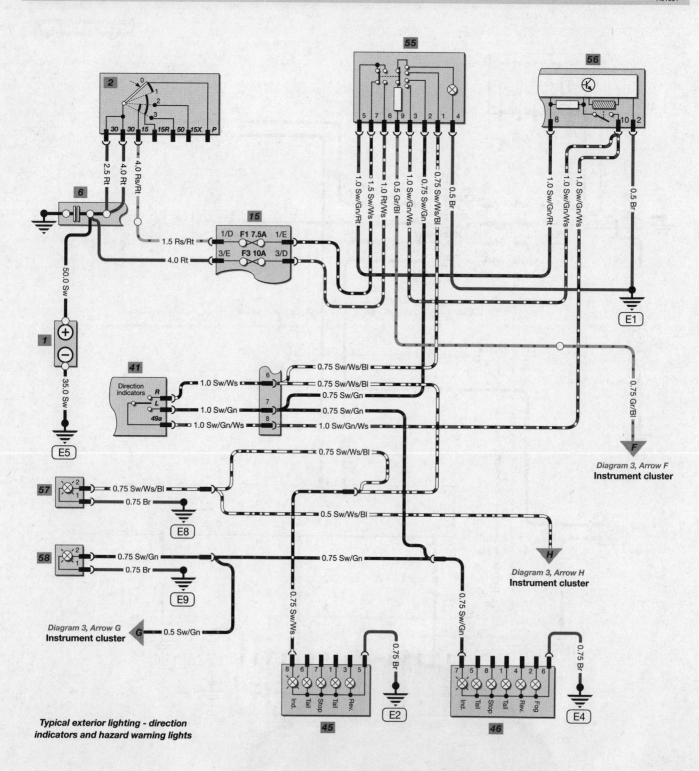

*Typical exterior lighting - direction
indicators and hazard warning lights*

Wire colours

Bl	Blue	Rs	Pink
Br	Brown	Rt	Red
Ge	Yellow	Sw	Black
Gr	Grey	Vi	Violet
Gn	Green	Ws	White
Nf	Natural		

Key to items

1 Battery
2 Ignition switch
6 Terminal 30 feed
15 Fuse/relay box
40 Light switch
45 LH tail light unit
46 RH tail light unit
47 LH headlight unit
48 RH headlight unit
49 Trailer control unit
50 Additional trailer fusebox
51 Trailer socket

Diagram 7

H31832

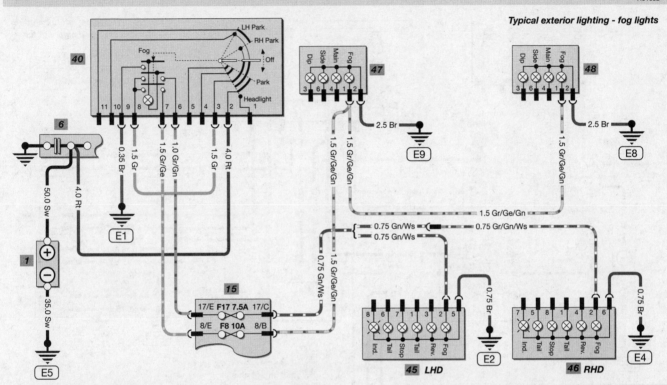

Typical exterior lighting - fog lights

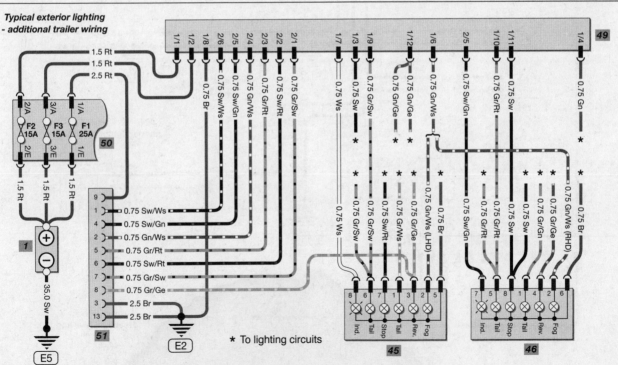

Typical exterior lighting - additional trailer wiring

* To lighting circuits

Wire colours

Bl	Blue	Rs	Pink
Br	Brown	Rt	Red
Ge	Yellow	Sw	Black
Gr	Grey	Vi	Violet
Gn	Green	Ws	White
Nf	Natural		

Key to items

1 Battery
2 Ignition switch
6 Terminal 30 feed
15 Fuse/relay box
40 Light switch
70 Roof light with delay and map reading light
71 Central locking pneumatic multifunction unit
72 Anti-dazzle interior mirror control unit
73 LH rear door switch
74 RH rear door switch
75 Rear roof light
76 Luggage compartment light
77 Luggage compartment lights switch
78 LH front door switch
79 RH front door switch
80 Glove box light
81 Transmission switch stage illumination
82 Cigar lighter

Diagram 8

H31833

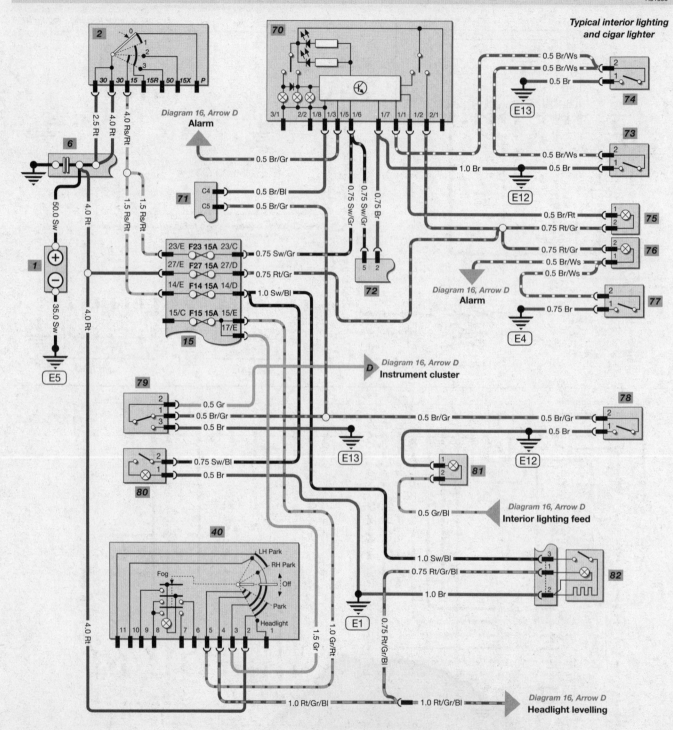

Typical interior lighting and cigar lighter

Wire colours

Bl	Blue	Rs	Pink
Br	Brown	Rt	Red
Ge	Yellow	Sw	Black
Gr	Grey	Vi	Violet
Gn	Green	Ws	White
Nf	Natural		

Key to items

1	Battery	90	Knock sensor
2	Ignition switch	91	Idle speed control motor
6	Terminal 30 feed	92	Ignition coil (cylinders 1 & 4)
85	Passenger fusebox	93	Ignition coil (cylinders 2 & 3)
86	Luggage compartment fusebox	94	Spark plug
87	Main relay	95	Mass air flow sensor
88	Fuel injection control unit	96	Camshaft position sensor
89	Camshaft control valve	97	Coolant temperature sensor

98	Oil level control switch
99	Crank angle sensor
100	Canister purge valve
101	Fuel injectors
102	Fuel pump relay
103	Fuel pump
104	Diagnostic connector
105	Lambda sensor

Diagram 9

H31834

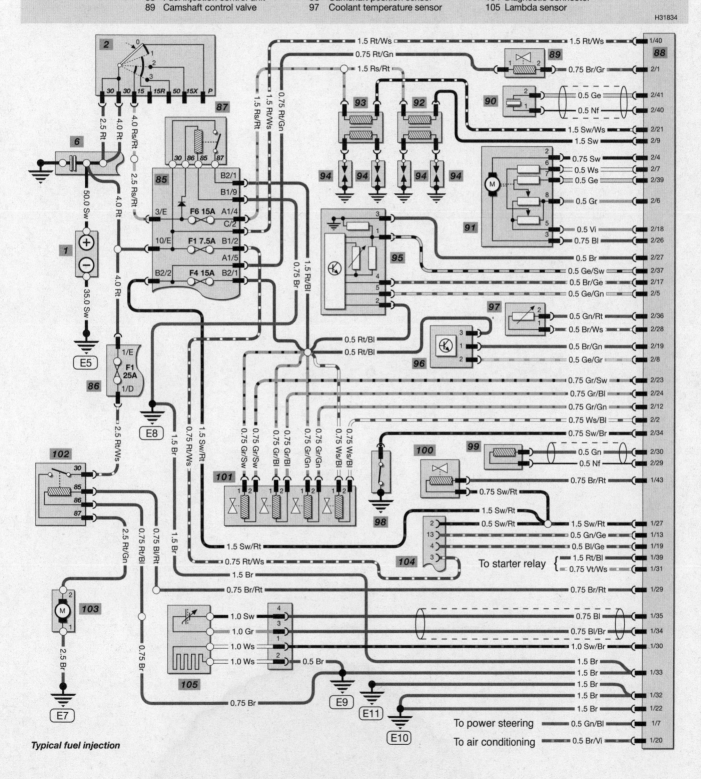

Typical fuel injection

Notes

Dimensions and weights

Note: *All figures are approximate, and may vary according to model. Refer to manufacturer's data for exact figures.*

Dimensions

Overall length . . . . 4487 mm
Overall width . . . . 1720 mm
Overall height (unladen):
   Classic and Elegance . . . . 1424 mm
   Esprit and Sport . . . . 1395 mm
Wheelbase . . . . 2690 mm

Weights

Kerb weight:
   Petrol engine models . . . . 1350 to 1380 kg
   Diesel engine models . . . . 1390 to 1480 kg
Maximum gross vehicle weight:
   Petrol engine models . . . . 1830 to 1860 kg
   Diesel engine models . . . . 1870 to 1960 kg

Conversion factors

Length (distance)

Inches (in)	x 25.4	= Millimetres (mm)	x 0.0394	= Inches (in)
Feet (ft)	x 0.305	= Metres (m)	x 3.281	= Feet (ft)
Miles	x 1.609	= Kilometres (km)	x 0.621	= Miles

Volume (capacity)

Cubic inches (cu in; in³)	x 16.387	= Cubic centimetres (cc; cm³)	x 0.061	= Cubic inches (cu in; in³)
Imperial pints (Imp pt)	x 0.568	= Litres (l)	x 1.76	= Imperial pints (Imp pt)
Imperial quarts (Imp qt)	x 1.137	= Litres (l)	x 0.88	= Imperial quarts (Imp qt)
Imperial quarts (Imp qt)	x 1.201	= US quarts (US qt)	x 0.833	= Imperial quarts (Imp qt)
US quarts (US qt)	x 0.946	= Litres (l)	x 1.057	= US quarts (US qt)
Imperial gallons (Imp gal)	x 4.546	= Litres (l)	x 0.22	= Imperial gallons (Imp gal)
Imperial gallons (Imp gal)	x 1.201	= US gallons (US gal)	x 0.833	= Imperial gallons (Imp gal)
US gallons (US gal)	x 3.785	= Litres (l)	x 0.264	= US gallons (US gal)

Mass (weight)

Ounces (oz)	x 28.35	= Grams (g)	x 0.035	= Ounces (oz)
Pounds (lb)	x 0.454	= Kilograms (kg)	x 2.205	= Pounds (lb)

Force

Ounces-force (ozf; oz)	x 0.278	= Newtons (N)	x 3.6	= Ounces-force (ozf; oz)
Pounds-force (lbf; lb)	x 4.448	= Newtons (N)	x 0.225	= Pounds-force (lbf; lb)
Newtons (N)	x 0.1	= Kilograms-force (kgf; kg)	x 9.81	= Newtons (N)

Pressure

Pounds-force per square inch (psi; lbf/in²; lb/in²)	x 0.070	= Kilograms-force per square centimetre (kgf/cm²; kg/cm²)	x 14.223	= Pounds-force per square inch (psi; lbf/in²; lb/in²)
Pounds-force per square inch (psi; lbf/in²; lb/in²)	x 0.068	= Atmospheres (atm)	x 14.696	= Pounds-force per square inch (psi; lbf/in²; lb/in²)
Pounds-force per square inch (psi; lbf/in²; lb/in²)	x 0.069	= Bars	x 14.5	= Pounds-force per square inch (psi; lbf/in²; lb/in²)
Pounds-force per square inch (psi; lbf/in²; lb/in²)	x 6.895	= Kilopascals (kPa)	x 0.145	= Pounds-force per square inch (psi; lbf/in²; lb/in²)
Kilopascals (kPa)	x 0.01	= Kilograms-force per square centimetre (kgf/cm²; kg/cm²)	x 98.1	= Kilopascals (kPa)
Millibar (mbar)	x 100	= Pascals (Pa)	x 0.01	= Millibar (mbar)
Millibar (mbar)	x 0.0145	= Pounds-force per square inch (psi; lbf/in²; lb/in²)	x 68.947	= Millibar (mbar)
Millibar (mbar)	x 0.75	= Millimetres of mercury (mmHg)	x 1.333	= Millibar (mbar)
Millibar (mbar)	x 0.401	= Inches of water (inH₂O)	x 2.491	= Millibar (mbar)
Millimetres of mercury (mmHg)	x 0.535	= Inches of water (inH₂O)	x 1.868	= Millimetres of mercury (mmHg)
Inches of water (inH₂O)	x 0.036	= Pounds-force per square inch (psi; lbf/in²; lb/in²)	x 27.68	= Inches of water (inH₂O)

Torque (moment of force)

Pounds-force inches (lbf in; lb in)	x 1.152	= Kilograms-force centimetre (kgf cm; kg cm)	x 0.868	= Pounds-force inches (lbf in; lb in)
Pounds-force inches (lbf in; lb in)	x 0.113	= Newton metres (Nm)	x 8.85	= Pounds-force inches (lbf in; lb in)
Pounds-force inches (lbf in; lb in)	x 0.083	= Pounds-force feet (lbf ft; lb ft)	x 12	= Pounds-force inches (lbf in; lb in)
Pounds-force feet (lbf ft; lb ft)	x 0.138	= Kilograms-force metres (kgf m; kg m)	x 7.233	= Pounds-force feet (lbf ft; lb ft)
Pounds-force feet (lbf ft; lb ft)	x 1.356	= Newton metres (Nm)	x 0.738	= Pounds-force feet (lbf ft; lb ft)
Newton metres (Nm)	x 0.102	= Kilograms-force metres (kgf m; kg m)	x 9.804	= Newton metres (Nm)

Power

Horsepower (hp)	x 745.7	= Watts (W)	x 0.0013	= Horsepower (hp)

Velocity (speed)

Miles per hour (miles/hr; mph)	x 1.609	= Kilometres per hour (km/hr; kph)	x 0.621	= Miles per hour (miles/hr; mph)

Fuel consumption*

Miles per gallon, Imperial (mpg)	x 0.354	= Kilometres per litre (km/l)	x 2.825	= Miles per gallon, Imperial (mpg)
Miles per gallon, US (mpg)	x 0.425	= Kilometres per litre (km/l)	x 2.352	= Miles per gallon, US (mpg)

Temperature

Degrees Fahrenheit = (°C x 1.8) + 32   Degrees Celsius (Degrees Centigrade; °C) = (°F - 32) x 0.56

It is common practice to convert from miles per gallon (mpg) to litres/100 kilometres (l/100km), where mpg x l/100 km = 282

Spare parts are available from many sources, including maker's appointed garages, accessory shops, and motor factors. To be sure of obtaining the correct parts, it will sometimes be necessary to quote the vehicle identification number. If possible, it can also be useful to take the old parts along for positive identification. Items such as starter motors and alternators may be available under a service exchange scheme - any parts returned should be clean.

Our advice regarding spare parts is as follows.

Officially-appointed garages

This is the best source of parts which are peculiar to your car, and which are not otherwise generally available (eg, badges, interior trim, certain body panels, etc). It is also the only place at which you should buy parts if the vehicle is still under warranty.

Accessory shops

These are very good places to buy materials and components needed for the maintenance of your car (oil, air and fuel filters, light bulbs, drivebelts, greases, brake pads, touch-up paint, etc). Components of this nature sold by a reputable shop are usually of the same standard as those fitted by the car manufacturer.

Besides components, these shops also sell tools and general accessories, usually have convenient opening hours, charge lower prices, and can often be found close to home. Some accessory shops have parts counters where components needed for almost any repair job can be purchased or ordered.

Motor factors

Good factors will stock all the more important components which wear out comparatively quickly, and can sometimes supply individual components needed for the overhaul of a larger assembly (eg, brake seals and hydraulic parts, bearing shells, pistons, valves). They may also handle work such as cylinder block reboring, crankshaft regrinding, etc.

Tyre and exhaust specialists

These outlets may be independent, or members of a local or national chain. They frequently offer competitive prices when compared with a main dealer or local garage, but it will pay to obtain several quotes before making a decision. When researching prices, also ask what 'extras' may be added - for instance, fitting a new valve and balancing the wheel are both commonly charged on top of the price of a new tyre.

Other sources

Beware of parts or materials obtained from market stalls, car boot sales or similar outlets. Such items are not invariably sub-standard, but there is little chance of compensation if they do prove unsatisfactory. In the case of safety-critical components such as brake pads, there is the risk not only of financial loss, but also of an accident causing injury or death.

Second-hand components or assemblies obtained from a car breaker can be a good buy in some circumstances, but this sort of purchase is best made by the experienced DIY mechanic.

Vehicle identification numbers

Modifications are a continuing and unpublicised process in vehicle manufacture, quite apart from major model changes. Spare parts manuals and lists are compiled upon a numerical basis, the individual vehicle identification numbers being essential to correct identification of the component concerned.

When ordering spare parts, always give as much information as possible. Quote the model number, chassis number, engine number and, where applicable, the spare parts number, as appropriate.

The *Vehicle Identification Number (VIN)* plate appears at the base of the B-pillar, and is visible with the driver's door open **(see illustration)**. The VIN also appears on the crossmember in front of the driver's seat, and is visible through the access panel in the carpet. Some models will also have the VIN etched into the glass, and some models also have the VIN on a small plate visible from outside through the passenger side of the windscreen **(see illustration)**.

The *body number and paint code* are marked on a coloured plate attached to the bonnet crossmember **(see illustration)**.

The *engine number* is either stamped onto the rear of the cylinder block, near the transmission mounting face, or onto the front of the left-hand face of the cylinder block, depending on engine type **(see illustration)**.

VIN plate on driver's door pillar

VIN visible through windscreen

The body number and paint code appear on the bonnet crossmember

The engine number (arrowed) appears above the transmission mounting face

Whenever servicing, repair or overhaul work is carried out on the car or its components, observe the following procedures and instructions. This will assist in carrying out the operation efficiently and to a professional standard of workmanship.

Joint mating faces and gaskets

When separating components at their mating faces, never insert screwdrivers or similar implements into the joint between the faces in order to prise them apart. This can cause severe damage which results in oil leaks, coolant leaks, etc upon reassembly. Separation is usually achieved by tapping along the joint with a soft-faced hammer in order to break the seal. However, note that this method may not be suitable where dowels are used for component location.

Where a gasket is used between the mating faces of two components, a new one must be fitted on reassembly; fit it dry unless otherwise stated in the repair procedure. Make sure that the mating faces are clean and dry, with all traces of old gasket removed. When cleaning a joint face, use a tool which is unlikely to score or damage the face, and remove any burrs or nicks with an oilstone or fine file.

Make sure that tapped holes are cleaned with a pipe cleaner, and keep them free of jointing compound, if this is being used, unless specifically instructed otherwise.

Ensure that all orifices, channels or pipes are clear, and blow through them, preferably using compressed air.

Oil seals

Oil seals can be removed by levering them out with a wide flat-bladed screwdriver or similar implement. Alternatively, a number of self-tapping screws may be screwed into the seal, and these used as a purchase for pliers or some similar device in order to pull the seal free.

Whenever an oil seal is removed from its working location, either individually or as part of an assembly, it should be renewed.

The very fine sealing lip of the seal is easily damaged, and will not seal if the surface it contacts is not completely clean and free from scratches, nicks or grooves. If the original sealing surface of the component cannot be restored, and the manufacturer has not made provision for slight relocation of the seal relative to the sealing surface, the component should be renewed.

Protect the lips of the seal from any surface which may damage them in the course of fitting. Use tape or a conical sleeve where possible. Lubricate the seal lips with oil before fitting and, on dual-lipped seals, fill the space between the lips with grease.

Unless otherwise stated, oil seals must be fitted with their sealing lips toward the lubricant to be sealed.

Use a tubular drift or block of wood of the appropriate size to install the seal and, if the seal housing is shouldered, drive the seal down to the shoulder. If the seal housing is unshouldered, the seal should be fitted with its face flush with the housing top face (unless otherwise instructed).

Screw threads and fastenings

Seized nuts, bolts and screws are quite a common occurrence where corrosion has set in, and the use of penetrating oil or releasing fluid will often overcome this problem if the offending item is soaked for a while before attempting to release it. The use of an impact driver may also provide a means of releasing such stubborn fastening devices, when used in conjunction with the appropriate screwdriver bit or socket. If none of these methods works, it may be necessary to resort to the careful application of heat, or the use of a hacksaw or nut splitter device.

Studs are usually removed by locking two nuts together on the threaded part, and then using a spanner on the lower nut to unscrew the stud. Studs or bolts which have broken off below the surface of the component in which they are mounted can sometimes be removed using a stud extractor. Always ensure that a blind tapped hole is completely free from oil, grease, water or other fluid before installing the bolt or stud. Failure to do this could cause the housing to crack due to the hydraulic action of the bolt or stud as it is screwed in.

When tightening a castellated nut to accept a split pin, tighten the nut to the specified torque, where applicable, and then tighten further to the next split pin hole. Never slacken the nut to align the split pin hole, unless stated in the repair procedure.

When checking or retightening a nut or bolt to a specified torque setting, slacken the nut or bolt by a quarter of a turn, and then retighten to the specified setting. However, this should not be attempted where angular tightening has been used.

For some screw fastenings, notably cylinder head bolts or nuts, torque wrench settings are no longer specified for the latter stages of tightening, "angle-tightening" being called up instead. Typically, a fairly low torque wrench setting will be applied to the bolts/nuts in the correct sequence, followed by one or more stages of tightening through specified angles.

Locknuts, locktabs and washers

Any fastening which will rotate against a component or housing during tightening should always have a washer between it and the relevant component or housing.

Spring or split washers should always be renewed when they are used to lock a critical component such as a big-end bearing retaining bolt or nut. Locktabs which are folded over to retain a nut or bolt should always be renewed.

Self-locking nuts can be re-used in non-critical areas, providing resistance can be felt when the locking portion passes over the bolt or stud thread. However, it should be noted that self-locking stiffnuts tend to lose their effectiveness after long periods of use, and should then be renewed as a matter of course.

Split pins must always be replaced with new ones of the correct size for the hole.

When thread-locking compound is found on the threads of a fastener which is to be re-used, it should be cleaned off with a wire brush and solvent, and fresh compound applied on reassembly.

Special tools

Some repair procedures in this manual entail the use of special tools such as a press, two or three-legged pullers, spring compressors, etc. Wherever possible, suitable readily-available alternatives to the manufacturer's special tools are described, and are shown in use. In some instances, where no alternative is possible, it has been necessary to resort to the use of a manufacturer's tool, and this has been done for reasons of safety as well as the efficient completion of the repair operation. Unless you are highly-skilled and have a thorough understanding of the procedures described, never attempt to bypass the use of any special tool when the procedure described specifies its use. Not only is there a very great risk of personal injury, but expensive damage could be caused to the components involved.

Environmental considerations

When disposing of used engine oil, brake fluid, antifreeze, etc, give due consideration to any detrimental environmental effects. Do not, for instance, pour any of the above liquids down drains into the general sewage system, or onto the ground to soak away. Many local council refuse tips provide a facility for waste oil disposal, as do some garages. If none of these facilities are available, consult your local Environmental Health Department, or the National Rivers Authority, for further advice.

With the universal tightening-up of legislation regarding the emission of environmentally-harmful substances from motor vehicles, most vehicles have tamperproof devices fitted to the main adjustment points of the fuel system. These devices are primarily designed to prevent unqualified persons from adjusting the fuel/air mixture, with the chance of a consequent increase in toxic emissions. If such devices are found during servicing or overhaul, they should, wherever possible, be renewed or refitted in accordance with the manufacturer's requirements or current legislation.

OIL CARE
FOLLOW THE CODE

OIL BANK LINE
0800 66 33 66
www.oilbankline.org.uk

Note: It is antisocial and illegal to dump oil down the drain. To find the location of your local oil recycling bank, call this number free.

The jack supplied with the vehicle tool kit should **only** be used for changing the roadwheels in an emergency - see *Wheel changing* at the front of this book. When carrying out any other kind of work, raise the vehicle using a heavy-duty hydraulic (or 'trolley') jack, and always supplement the jack with axle stands positioned under the vehicle jacking points. If the roadwheels do not have to be removed, consider using wheel ramps - these can be placed under the wheels once the vehicle has been raised using a hydraulic jack, and the vehicle lowered onto the ramps so that it is resting on its wheels.

Only ever jack the vehicle up on a solid, level surface. If there is even a slight slope, take great care that the vehicle cannot move as the wheels are lifted off the ground. Jacking up on an uneven or gravelled surface is not recommended, as the weight of the vehicle will not be evenly distributed, and the jack may slip as the vehicle is raised.

As far as possible, do not leave the vehicle unattended once it has been raised, particularly if children are playing nearby.

Before jacking up the front of the car, ensure that the parking brake is firmly applied, and engage first gear (or P). When jacking up the rear of the car, place wooden chocks in front of the front wheels.

The jack supplied with the vehicle locates in the holes provided in the sill. Unscrew the access plug and insert the jack fully into the hole in the sill. Ensure that the jack head is correctly engaged before attempting to raise the vehicle.

When using a hydraulic jack or axle stands, the jack head or axle stand head may be placed directly under one of the jacking points - a large rubber support block is provided on the base of the sill, at the front and rear, for this purpose **(see illustrations)**. It is still advisable to use a block of wood between the jack head or axle stand, and the rubber block, to avoid damage to the sill. **Do not** jack the vehicle under any other part of the sill, engine sump, floor pan, or directly under any of the steering or suspension components.

To raise the front of the vehicle, position a block of wood on the jack head and position the jack underneath the centre of the front suspension subframe crossmember (where applicable, remove the plastic undertray first). If one side of the vehicle is to be raised, the jack can be positioned to one side of the crossmember, but **not** under the front suspension arms **(see illustration)**. Lift the vehicle to the required height and support it on axle stands positioned underneath the front rubber support blocks, which are located directly underneath the vehicle jack location holes in the sill. The vehicle can also be lifted under the front rubber support blocks, and supported under the front crossmember.

To raise the rear of the vehicle, position a block of wood on the jack head, and position the jack underneath one of the rear rubber support blocks directly underneath the vehicle jack location holes in the sill. Lift the vehicle to the required height and support it on axle stands positioned underneath the triangular-shaped flanges just behind and inboard of the rubber support blocks **(see illustration)** - do not confuse the metal flanges with the plastic fuel tank! Although not necessarily recommended by Mercedes, it is generally accepted that a jack or axle stand (with a block of wood) may be placed directly under the final drive unit - ie that, with care, the final drive may be used as a jacking or support point.

Providing care is taken (and a block of wood is used to spread the load), reinforced areas of the floorpan, particularly those in the region of suspension mountings, may be used as support points. Consult a Mercedes dealer for advice before using anything other than the approved jacking points, however.

Never work under, around, or near a raised vehicle, unless it is adequately supported on stands. Do not rely on a jack alone, as even a hydraulic jack could fail under load. Makeshift methods should not be used to lift and support the car during servicing work.

Jack head positioned under rubber support block

Axle stand under rubber support block

Axle stand under one side of the front suspension crossmember

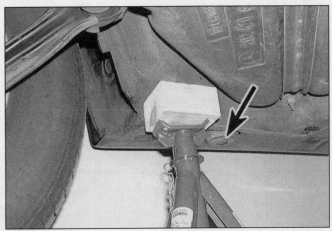

Axle stand under rear flange, inboard of rubber support block (arrowed)

Disconnecting the battery

Several of the systems require battery power to be available at all times (permanent live). This is either to ensure their continued operation (such as the clock), or to maintain electronic memory settings which would otherwise be erased. Whenever the battery is to be disconnected therefore, first note the following points, to ensure there are no unforeseen consequences:

a) *Firstly, on any vehicle with central door locking, it is a wise precaution to remove the key from the ignition, and to keep it with you. This avoids the possibility of the key being locked inside the car, should the central locking engage when the battery is reconnected.*

b) *The radio/cassette unit fitted as standard equipment by Mercedes is equipped with a built-in security code, to deter thieves. If the power source to the unit is cut, the anti-theft system will activate. Even if the power source is immediately reconnected, the radio/cassette unit will not function until the correct security code has been entered. Therefore, if you do not know the correct security code for the radio/cassette unit, **do not** disconnect either of the battery terminals, or remove the radio/cassette unit from the vehicle.*

The code appears on a code card supplied with the car when new. Details for entering the code appear in the vehicle handbook. Should the code have been misplaced or forgotten, on production of proof of ownership, a Mercedes dealer or in-car entertainment specialist may be able to help.

c) *The engine management system ECU is of the 'self-learning' type, meaning that, as it operates, it adapts to changes in operating conditions, and stores the optimum settings found (this is especially true for idle settings). When the battery is disconnected, these 'learned' settings are lost, and the ECU reverts to the base factory settings. When the engine is restarted, it may idle and run roughly until the ECU has 're-learned' the best settings. To further this 'learning' process, take the car for a road test of at least 15 minutes' duration, covering as many engine speeds and loads as possible, and concentrating on the 2000 to 4000 rpm range. On completion, let the engine idle for at least 10 minutes, turning the steering wheel occasionally and switching on high-current-draw equipment such as*

the heater fan or heated rear window.

d) *After the battery has been reconnected, the electric windows and sunroof closed positions must be re-programmed by closing the windows and sunroof, and holding the operating switch in the closed position for a few seconds.*

Devices known as 'memory-savers' or 'code-savers' can be used to avoid some of the above problems. Precise details of use vary according to the device used. Typically, it is plugged into the cigar lighter socket, and is connected by its own wiring to a spare battery; the vehicle battery is then disconnected from the electrical system, leaving the memory-saver to pass sufficient current to maintain audio unit security codes and other memory values, and also to run permanently-live circuits such as the clock.

 Warning: Some of these devices allow a considerable amount of current to pass, which can mean that many of the vehicle's systems are still operational when the main battery is disconnected. If a memory-saver is used, ensure that the circuit concerned is actually 'dead' before carrying out any work on it!

Introduction

A selection of good tools is a fundamental requirement for anyone contemplating the maintenance and repair of a motor vehicle. For the owner who does not possess any, their purchase will prove a considerable expense, offsetting some of the savings made by doing-it-yourself. However, provided that the tools purchased meet the relevant national safety standards and are of good quality, they will last for many years and prove an extremely worthwhile investment.

To help the average owner to decide which tools are needed to carry out the various tasks detailed in this manual, we have compiled three lists of tools under the following headings: *Maintenance and minor repair*, *Repair and overhaul*, and *Special*. Newcomers to practical mechanics should start off with the *Maintenance and minor repair* tool kit, and confine themselves to the simpler jobs around the vehicle. Then, as confidence and experience grow, more difficult tasks can be undertaken, with extra tools being purchased as, and when, they are needed. In this way, a *Maintenance and minor repair* tool kit can be built up into a *Repair and overhaul* tool kit over a considerable period of time, without any major cash outlays. The experienced do-it-yourselfer will have a tool kit good enough for most repair and overhaul procedures, and will add tools from the *Special* category when it is felt that the expense is justified by the amount of use to which these tools will be put.

Maintenance and minor repair tool kit

The tools given in this list should be considered as a minimum requirement if routine maintenance, servicing and minor repair operations are to be undertaken. We recommend the purchase of combination spanners (ring one end, open-ended the other); although more expensive than open-ended ones, they do give the advantages of both types of spanner.

- ☐ *Combination spanners:*
  Metric - 8 to 19 mm inclusive
- ☐ *Adjustable spanner - 35 mm jaw (approx.)*
- ☐ *Spark plug spanner (with rubber insert) - petrol models*
- ☐ *Spark plug gap adjustment tool - petrol models*
- ☐ *Set of feeler gauges*
- ☐ *Brake bleed nipple spanner*
- ☐ *Screwdrivers:*
  Flat blade - 100 mm long x 6 mm dia
  Cross blade - 100 mm long x 6 mm dia
  Torx - various sizes (not all vehicles)
- ☐ *Combination pliers*
- ☐ *Hacksaw (junior)*
- ☐ *Tyre pump*
- ☐ *Tyre pressure gauge*
- ☐ *Oil can*
- ☐ *Oil filter removal tool*
- ☐ *Fine emery cloth*
- ☐ *Wire brush (small)*
- ☐ *Funnel (medium size)*
- ☐ *Sump drain plug key (not all vehicles)*

Repair and overhaul tool kit

These tools are virtually essential for anyone undertaking any major repairs to a motor vehicle, and are additional to those given in the *Maintenance and minor repair* list. Included in this list is a comprehensive set of sockets. Although these are expensive, they will be found invaluable as they are so versatile - particularly if various drives are included in the set. We recommend the half-inch square-drive type, as this can be used with most proprietary torque wrenches.

The tools in this list will sometimes need to be supplemented by tools from the *Special* list:

- ☐ *Sockets (or box spanners) to cover range in previous list (including Torx sockets)*
- ☐ *Reversible ratchet drive (for use with sockets)*
- ☐ *Extension piece, 250 mm (for use with sockets)*
- ☐ *Universal joint (for use with sockets)*
- ☐ *Flexible handle or sliding T "breaker bar" (for use with sockets)*
- ☐ *Torque wrench (for use with sockets)*
- ☐ *Self-locking grips*
- ☐ *Ball pein hammer*
- ☐ *Soft-faced mallet (plastic or rubber)*
- ☐ *Screwdrivers:*
  Flat blade - long & sturdy, short (chubby), and narrow (electrician's) types
  Cross blade – long & sturdy, and short (chubby) types
- ☐ *Pliers:*
  Long-nosed
  Side cutters (electrician's)
  Circlip (internal and external)
- ☐ *Cold chisel - 25 mm*
- ☐ *Scriber*
- ☐ *Scraper*
- ☐ *Centre-punch*
- ☐ *Pin punch*
- ☐ *Hacksaw*
- ☐ *Brake hose clamp*
- ☐ *Brake/clutch bleeding kit*
- ☐ *Selection of twist drills*
- ☐ *Steel rule/straight-edge*
- ☐ *Allen keys (inc. splined/Torx type)*
- ☐ *Selection of files*
- ☐ *Wire brush*
- ☐ *Axle stands*
- ☐ *Jack (strong trolley or hydraulic type)*
- ☐ *Light with extension lead*
- ☐ *Universal electrical multi-meter*

Sockets and reversible ratchet drive

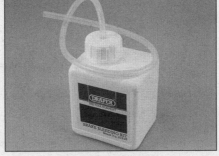

Brake bleeding kit

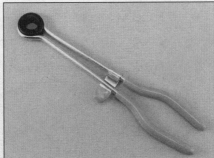

Torx key, socket and bit

Hose clamp

Angular-tightening gauge

Special tools

The tools in this list are those which are not used regularly, are expensive to buy, or which need to be used in accordance with their manufacturers' instructions. Unless relatively difficult mechanical jobs are undertaken frequently, it will not be economic to buy many of these tools. Where this is the case, you could consider clubbing together with friends (or joining a motorists' club) to make a joint purchase, or borrowing the tools against a deposit from a local garage or tool hire specialist. It is worth noting that many of the larger DIY superstores now carry a large range of special tools for hire at modest rates.

The following list contains only those tools and instruments freely available to the public, and not those special tools produced by the vehicle manufacturer specifically for its dealer network. You will find occasional references to these manufacturers' special tools in the text of this manual. Generally, an alternative method of doing the job without the vehicle manufacturers' special tool is given. However, sometimes there is no alternative to using them. Where this is the case and the relevant tool cannot be bought or borrowed, you will have to entrust the work to a dealer.

- ☐ Angular-tightening gauge
- ☐ Valve spring compressor
- ☐ Valve grinding tool
- ☐ Piston ring compressor
- ☐ Piston ring removal/installation tool
- ☐ Cylinder bore hone
- ☐ Balljoint separator
- ☐ Coil spring compressors (where applicable)
- ☐ Two/three-legged hub and bearing puller
- ☐ Impact screwdriver
- ☐ Micrometer and/or vernier calipers
- ☐ Dial gauge
- ☐ Stroboscopic timing light
- ☐ Dwell angle meter/tachometer
- ☐ Fault code reader
- ☐ Cylinder compression gauge
- ☐ Hand-operated vacuum pump and gauge
- ☐ Clutch plate alignment set
- ☐ Brake shoe steady spring cup removal tool
- ☐ Bush and bearing removal/installation set
- ☐ Stud extractors
- ☐ Tap and die set
- ☐ Lifting tackle
- ☐ Trolley jack

Buying tools

Reputable motor accessory shops and superstores often offer excellent quality tools at discount prices, so it pays to shop around.

Remember, you don't have to buy the most expensive items on the shelf, but it is always advisable to steer clear of the very cheap tools. Beware of 'bargains' offered on market stalls or at car boot sales. There are plenty of good tools around at reasonable prices, but always aim to purchase items which meet the relevant national safety standards. If in doubt, ask the proprietor or manager of the shop for advice before making a purchase.

Care and maintenance of tools

Having purchased a reasonable tool kit, it is necessary to keep the tools in a clean and serviceable condition. After use, always wipe off any dirt, grease and metal particles using a clean, dry cloth, before putting the tools away. Never leave them lying around after they have been used. A simple tool rack on the garage or workshop wall for items such as screwdrivers and pliers is a good idea. Store all normal spanners and sockets in a metal box. Any measuring instruments, gauges, meters, etc, must be carefully stored where they cannot be damaged or become rusty.

Take a little care when tools are used. Hammer heads inevitably become marked, and screwdrivers lose the keen edge on their blades from time to time. A little timely attention with emery cloth or a file will soon restore items like this to a good finish.

Working facilities

Not to be forgotten when discussing tools is the workshop itself. If anything more than routine maintenance is to be carried out, a suitable working area becomes essential.

It is appreciated that many an owner-mechanic is forced by circumstances to remove an engine or similar item without the benefit of a garage or workshop. Having done this, any repairs should always be done under the cover of a roof.

Wherever possible, any dismantling should be done on a clean, flat workbench or table at a suitable working height.

Any workbench needs a vice; one with a jaw opening of 100 mm is suitable for most jobs. As mentioned previously, some clean dry storage space is also required for tools, as well as for any lubricants, cleaning fluids, touch-up paints etc, which become necessary.

Another item which may be required, and which has a much more general usage, is an electric drill with a chuck capacity of at least 8 mm. This, together with a good range of twist drills, is virtually essential for fitting accessories.

Last, but not least, always keep a supply of old newspapers and clean, lint-free rags available, and try to keep any working area as clean as possible.

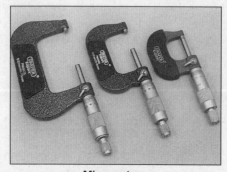
Micrometers

Dial test indicator ("dial gauge")

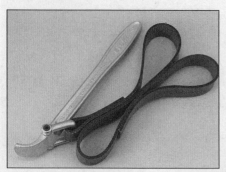
Strap wrench

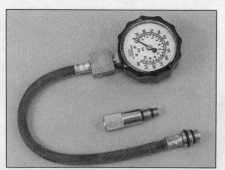
Compression tester

Fault code reader

This is a guide to getting your vehicle through the MOT test. Obviously it will not be possible to examine the vehicle to the same standard as the professional MOT tester. However, working through the following checks will enable you to identify any problem areas before submitting the vehicle for the test.

Where a testable component is in borderline condition, the tester has discretion in deciding whether to pass or fail it. The basis of such discretion is whether the tester would be happy for a close relative or friend to use the vehicle with the component in that condition. If the vehicle presented is clean and evidently well cared for, the tester may be more inclined to pass a borderline component than if the vehicle is scruffy and apparently neglected.

It has only been possible to summarise the test requirements here, based on the regulations in force at the time of printing. Test standards are becoming increasingly stringent, although there are some exemptions for older vehicles.

An assistant will be needed to help carry out some of these checks.

The checks have been sub-divided into four categories, as follows:

1 Checks carried out **FROM THE DRIVER'S SEAT**

2 Checks carried out **WITH THE VEHICLE ON THE GROUND**

3 Checks carried out **WITH THE VEHICLE RAISED AND THE WHEELS FREE TO TURN**

4 Checks carried out on **YOUR VEHICLE'S EXHAUST EMISSION SYSTEM**

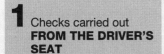

1 Checks carried out **FROM THE DRIVER'S SEAT**

Handbrake

☐ Test the operation of the handbrake. Excessive travel (too many clicks) indicates incorrect brake or cable adjustment.
☐ Check that the handbrake cannot be released by tapping the lever sideways. Check the security of the lever mountings.

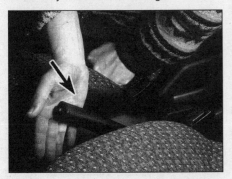

Footbrake

☐ Depress the brake pedal and check that it does not creep down to the floor, indicating a master cylinder fault. Release the pedal, wait a few seconds, then depress it again. If the pedal travels nearly to the floor before firm resistance is felt, brake adjustment or repair is necessary. If the pedal feels spongy, there is air in the hydraulic system which must be removed by bleeding.

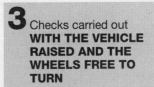

☐ Check that the brake pedal is secure and in good condition. Check also for signs of fluid leaks on the pedal, floor or carpets, which would indicate failed seals in the brake master cylinder.
☐ Check the servo unit (when applicable) by operating the brake pedal several times, then keeping the pedal depressed and starting the engine. As the engine starts, the pedal will move down slightly. If not, the vacuum hose or the servo itself may be faulty.

Steering wheel and column

☐ Examine the steering wheel for fractures or looseness of the hub, spokes or rim.
☐ Move the steering wheel from side to side and then up and down. Check that the steering wheel is not loose on the column, indicating wear or a loose retaining nut. Continue moving the steering wheel as before, but also turn it slightly from left to right.
☐ Check that the steering wheel is not loose on the column, and that there is no abnormal

movement of the steering wheel, indicating wear in the column support bearings or couplings.

Windscreen, mirrors and sunvisor

☐ The windscreen must be free of cracks or other significant damage within the driver's field of view. (Small stone chips are acceptable.) Rear view mirrors must be secure, intact, and capable of being adjusted.

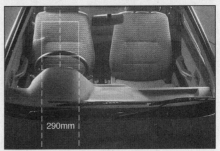

☐ The driver's sunvisor must be capable of being stored in the "up" position.

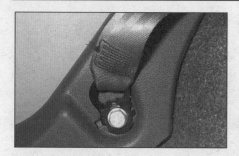

Seat belts and seats

Note: *The following checks are applicable to all seat belts, front and rear.*

☐ Examine the webbing of all the belts (including rear belts if fitted) for cuts, serious fraying or deterioration. Fasten and unfasten each belt to check the buckles. If applicable, check the retracting mechanism. Check the security of all seat belt mountings accessible from inside the vehicle.

☐ Seat belts with pre-tensioners, once activated, have a "flag" or similar showing on the seat belt stalk. This, in itself, is not a reason for test failure.

☐ The front seats themselves must be securely attached and the backrests must lock in the upright position.

Doors

☐ Both front doors must be able to be opened and closed from outside and inside, and must latch securely when closed.

2 Checks carried out WITH THE VEHICLE ON THE GROUND

Vehicle identification

☐ Number plates must be in good condition, secure and legible, with letters and numbers correctly spaced – spacing at (A) should be at least twice that at (B).

☐ The VIN plate and/or homologation plate must be legible.

Electrical equipment

☐ Switch on the ignition and check the operation of the horn.

☐ Check the windscreen washers and wipers, examining the wiper blades; renew damaged or perished blades. Also check the operation of the stop-lights.

☐ Check the operation of the sidelights and number plate lights. The lenses and reflectors must be secure, clean and undamaged.

☐ Check the operation and alignment of the headlights. The headlight reflectors must not be tarnished and the lenses must be undamaged.

☐ Switch on the ignition and check the operation of the direction indicators (including the instrument panel tell-tale) and the hazard warning lights. Operation of the sidelights and stop-lights must not affect the indicators - if it does, the cause is usually a bad earth at the rear light cluster.

☐ Check the operation of the rear foglight(s), including the warning light on the instrument panel or in the switch.

☐ The ABS warning light must illuminate in accordance with the manufacturers' design. For most vehicles, the ABS warning light should illuminate when the ignition is switched on, and (if the system is operating properly) extinguish after a few seconds. Refer to the owner's handbook.

Footbrake

☐ Examine the master cylinder, brake pipes and servo unit for leaks, loose mountings, corrosion or other damage.

☐ The fluid reservoir must be secure and the fluid level must be between the upper (**A**) and lower (**B**) markings.

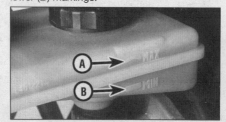

☐ Inspect both front brake flexible hoses for cracks or deterioration of the rubber. Turn the steering from lock to lock, and ensure that the hoses do not contact the wheel, tyre, or any part of the steering or suspension mechanism. With the brake pedal firmly depressed, check the hoses for bulges or leaks under pressure.

Steering and suspension

☐ Have your assistant turn the steering wheel from side to side slightly, up to the point where the steering gear just begins to transmit this movement to the roadwheels. Check for excessive free play between the steering wheel and the steering gear, indicating wear or insecurity of the steering column joints, the column-to-steering gear coupling, or the steering gear itself.

☐ Have your assistant turn the steering wheel more vigorously in each direction, so that the roadwheels just begin to turn. As this is done, examine all the steering joints, linkages, fittings and attachments. Renew any component that shows signs of wear or damage. On vehicles with power steering, check the security and condition of the steering pump, drivebelt and hoses.

☐ Check that the vehicle is standing level, and at approximately the correct ride height.

Shock absorbers

☐ Depress each corner of the vehicle in turn, then release it. The vehicle should rise and then settle in its normal position. If the vehicle continues to rise and fall, the shock absorber is defective. A shock absorber which has seized will also cause the vehicle to fail.

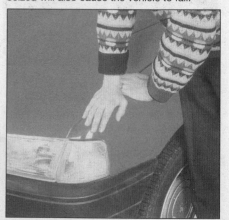

Exhaust system

☐ Start the engine. With your assistant holding a rag over the tailpipe, check the entire system for leaks. Repair or renew leaking sections.

3 Checks carried out **WITH THE VEHICLE RAISED AND THE WHEELS FREE TO TURN**

Jack up the front and rear of the vehicle, and securely support it on axle stands. Position the stands clear of the suspension assemblies. Ensure that the wheels are clear of the ground and that the steering can be turned from lock to lock.

Steering mechanism

☐ Have your assistant turn the steering from lock to lock. Check that the steering turns smoothly, and that no part of the steering mechanism, including a wheel or tyre, fouls any brake hose or pipe or any part of the body structure.
☐ Examine the steering rack rubber gaiters for damage or insecurity of the retaining clips. If power steering is fitted, check for signs of damage or leakage of the fluid hoses, pipes or connections. Also check for excessive stiffness or binding of the steering, a missing split pin or locking device, or severe corrosion of the body structure within 30 cm of any steering component attachment point.

Front and rear suspension and wheel bearings

☐ Starting at the front right-hand side, grasp the roadwheel at the 3 o'clock and 9 o'clock positions and rock gently but firmly. Check for free play or insecurity at the wheel bearings, suspension balljoints, or suspension mountings, pivots and attachments.
☐ Now grasp the wheel at the 12 o'clock and 6 o'clock positions and repeat the previous inspection. Spin the wheel, and check for roughness or tightness of the front wheel bearing.

☐ If excess free play is suspected at a component pivot point, this can be confirmed by using a large screwdriver or similar tool and levering between the mounting and the component attachment. This will confirm whether the wear is in the pivot bush, its retaining bolt, or in the mounting itself (the bolt holes can often become elongated).

☐ Carry out all the above checks at the other front wheel, and then at both rear wheels.

Springs and shock absorbers

☐ Examine the suspension struts (when applicable) for serious fluid leakage, corrosion, or damage to the casing. Also check the security of the mounting points.
☐ If coil springs are fitted, check that the spring ends locate in their seats, and that the spring is not corroded, cracked or broken.
☐ If leaf springs are fitted, check that all leaves are intact, that the axle is securely attached to each spring, and that there is no deterioration of the spring eye mountings, bushes, and shackles.

☐ The same general checks apply to vehicles fitted with other suspension types, such as torsion bars, hydraulic displacer units, etc. Ensure that all mountings and attachments are secure, that there are no signs of excessive wear, corrosion or damage, and (on hydraulic types) that there are no fluid leaks or damaged pipes.
☐ Inspect the shock absorbers for signs of serious fluid leakage. Check for wear of the mounting bushes or attachments, or damage to the body of the unit.

Driveshafts (fwd vehicles only)

☐ Rotate each front wheel in turn and inspect the constant velocity joint gaiters for splits or damage. Also check that each driveshaft is straight and undamaged.

Braking system

☐ If possible without dismantling, check brake pad wear and disc condition. Ensure that the friction lining material has not worn excessively, (A) and that the discs are not fractured, pitted, scored or badly worn (B).

☐ Examine all the rigid brake pipes underneath the vehicle, and the flexible hose(s) at the rear. Look for corrosion, chafing or insecurity of the pipes, and for signs of bulging under pressure, chafing, splits or deterioration of the flexible hoses.
☐ Look for signs of fluid leaks at the brake calipers or on the brake backplates. Repair or renew leaking components.
☐ Slowly spin each wheel, while your assistant depresses and releases the footbrake. Ensure that each brake is operating and does not bind when the pedal is released.

☐ Examine the handbrake mechanism, checking for frayed or broken cables, excessive corrosion, or wear or insecurity of the linkage. Check that the mechanism works on each relevant wheel, and releases fully, without binding.

☐ It is not possible to test brake efficiency without special equipment, but a road test can be carried out later to check that the vehicle pulls up in a straight line.

Fuel and exhaust systems

☐ Inspect the fuel tank (including the filler cap), fuel pipes, hoses and unions. All components must be secure and free from leaks.

☐ Examine the exhaust system over its entire length, checking for any damaged, broken or missing mountings, security of the retaining clamps and rust or corrosion.

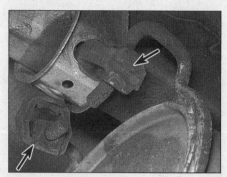

Wheels and tyres

☐ Examine the sidewalls and tread area of each tyre in turn. Check for cuts, tears, lumps, bulges, separation of the tread, and exposure of the ply or cord due to wear or damage. Check that the tyre bead is correctly seated on the wheel rim, that the valve is sound and properly seated, and that the wheel is not distorted or damaged.

☐ Check that the tyres are of the correct size for the vehicle, that they are of the same size and type on each axle, and that the pressures are correct.

☐ Check the tyre tread depth. The legal minimum at the time of writing is 1.6 mm over at least three-quarters of the tread width. Abnormal tread wear may indicate incorrect front wheel alignment.

Body corrosion

☐ Check the condition of the entire vehicle structure for signs of corrosion in load-bearing areas. (These include chassis box sections, side sills, cross-members, pillars, and all suspension, steering, braking system and seat belt mountings and anchorages.) Any corrosion which has seriously reduced the thickness of a load-bearing area is likely to cause the vehicle to fail. In this case professional repairs are likely to be needed.

☐ Damage or corrosion which causes sharp or otherwise dangerous edges to be exposed will also cause the vehicle to fail.

4 Checks carried out on YOUR VEHICLE'S EXHAUST EMISSION SYSTEM

Petrol models

☐ Have the engine at normal operating temperature, and make sure that it is in good tune (ignition system in good order, air filter element clean, etc).

☐ Before any measurements are carried out, raise the engine speed to around 2500 rpm, and hold it at this speed for 20 seconds. Allow the engine speed to return to idle, and watch for smoke emissions from the exhaust tailpipe. If the idle speed is obviously much too high, or if dense blue or clearly-visible black smoke comes from the tailpipe for more than 5 seconds, the vehicle will fail. As a rule of thumb, blue smoke signifies oil being burnt (engine wear) while black smoke signifies unburnt fuel (dirty air cleaner element, or other carburettor or fuel system fault).

☐ An exhaust gas analyser capable of measuring carbon monoxide (CO) and hydrocarbons (HC) is now needed. If such an instrument cannot be hired or borrowed, a local garage may agree to perform the check for a small fee.

CO emissions (mixture)

☐ At the time of writing, for vehicles first used between 1st August 1975 and 31st July 1986 (P to C registration), the CO level must not exceed 4.5% by volume. For vehicles first used between 1st August 1986 and 31st July 1992 (D to J registration), the CO level must not exceed 3.5% by volume. Vehicles first

used after 1st August 1992 (K registration) must conform to the manufacturer's specification. The MOT tester has access to a DOT database or emissions handbook, which lists the CO and HC limits for each make and model of vehicle. The CO level is measured with the engine at idle speed, and at "fast idle". The following limits are given as a general guide:

> At idle speed -
> CO level no more than 0.5%
> At "fast idle" (2500 to 3000 rpm) -
> CO level no more than 0.3%
> (Minimum oil temperature 60°C)

☐ If the CO level cannot be reduced far enough to pass the test (and the fuel and ignition systems are otherwise in good condition) then the carburettor is badly worn, or there is some problem in the fuel injection system or catalytic converter (as applicable).

HC emissions

☐ With the CO within limits, HC emissions for vehicles first used between 1st August 1975 and 31st July 1992 (P to J registration) must not exceed 1200 ppm. Vehicles first used after 1st August 1992 (K registration) must conform to the manufacturer's specification. The MOT tester has access to a DOT database or emissions handbook, which lists the CO and HC limits for each make and model of vehicle. The HC level is measured with the engine at "fast idle". The following is given as a general guide:

> At "fast idle" (2500 to 3000 rpm) -
> HC level no more than 200 ppm
> (Minimum oil temperature 60°C)

☐ Excessive HC emissions are caused by incomplete combustion, the causes of which can include oil being burnt, mechanical wear and ignition/fuel system malfunction.

Diesel models

☐ The only emission test applicable to Diesel engines is the measuring of exhaust smoke density. The test involves accelerating the engine several times to its maximum unloaded speed.

Note: *It is of the utmost importance that the engine timing belt is in good condition before the test is carried out.*

☐ The limits for Diesel engine exhaust smoke, introduced in September 1995 are:

Vehicles first used before 1st August 1979:
> Exempt from metered smoke testing, but must not emit "dense blue or clearly visible black smoke for a period of more than 5 seconds at idle" or "dense blue or clearly visible black smoke during acceleration which would obscure the view of other road users".

Non-turbocharged vehicles first used after 1st August 1979: 2.5m⁻¹

Turbocharged vehicles first used after 1st August 1979: 3.0m⁻¹

☐ Excessive smoke can be caused by a dirty air cleaner element. Otherwise, professional advice may be needed to find the cause.

Engine

- [ ] Engine fails to rotate when attempting to start
- [ ] Engine rotates, but will not start
- [ ] Engine difficult to start when cold
- [ ] Engine difficult to start when hot
- [ ] Starter motor noisy or excessively-rough in engagement
- [ ] Engine starts, but stops immediately
- [ ] Engine idles erratically
- [ ] Engine misfires at idle speed
- [ ] Engine misfires throughout the driving speed range
- [ ] Engine hesitates on acceleration
- [ ] Engine stalls
- [ ] Engine lacks power
- [ ] Engine backfires
- [ ] Oil pressure warning light illuminated with engine running
- [ ] Engine runs-on after switching off
- [ ] Engine noises

Cooling system

- [ ] Overheating
- [ ] Overcooling
- [ ] External coolant leakage
- [ ] Internal coolant leakage
- [ ] Corrosion

Fuel and exhaust systems

- [ ] Excessive fuel consumption
- [ ] Fuel leakage and/or fuel odour
- [ ] Excessive noise or fumes from exhaust system

Clutch

- [ ] Pedal travels to floor - no pressure or very little resistance
- [ ] Clutch fails to disengage (unable to select gears)
- [ ] Clutch slips (engine speed increases, with no increase in vehicle speed)
- [ ] Judder as clutch is engaged
- [ ] Noise when depressing or releasing clutch pedal

Manual transmission

- [ ] Noisy in neutral with engine running
- [ ] Noisy in one particular gear
- [ ] Difficulty engaging gears
- [ ] Jumps out of gear
- [ ] Vibration
- [ ] Lubricant leaks

Automatic transmission

- [ ] Fluid leakage
- [ ] Transmission fluid brown, or has burned smell
- [ ] General gear selection problems
- [ ] Transmission will not downshift (kickdown) with accelerator pedal fully depressed
- [ ] Engine will not start in any gear, or starts in gears other than Park or Neutral
- [ ] Transmission slips, shifts roughly, is noisy, or has no drive in forward or reverse gears

Differential and propeller shaft

- [ ] Vibration when accelerating or decelerating
- [ ] Low-pitched whining, increasing with road speed

Braking system

- [ ] Vehicle pulls to one side under braking
- [ ] Noise (grinding or high-pitched squeal) when brakes applied
- [ ] Excessive brake pedal travel
- [ ] Brake pedal feels spongy when depressed
- [ ] Excessive brake pedal effort required to stop vehicle
- [ ] Judder felt through brake pedal or steering wheel when braking
- [ ] Brakes binding
- [ ] Rear wheels locking under normal braking

Suspension and steering

- [ ] Vehicle pulls to one side
- [ ] Wheel wobble and vibration
- [ ] Excessive pitching and/or rolling around corners, or during braking
- [ ] Wandering or general instability
- [ ] Excessively-stiff steering
- [ ] Excessive play in steering
- [ ] Lack of power assistance
- [ ] Tyre wear excessive

Electrical system

- [ ] Battery will not hold a charge for more than a few days
- [ ] Ignition/no-charge warning light remains illuminated with engine running
- [ ] Ignition/no-charge warning light fails to come on
- [ ] Lights inoperative
- [ ] Instrument readings inaccurate or erratic
- [ ] Horn inoperative, or unsatisfactory in operation
- [ ] Windscreen wipers inoperative, or unsatisfactory in operation
- [ ] Windscreen washers inoperative, or unsatisfactory in operation
- [ ] Electric windows inoperative, or unsatisfactory in operation
- [ ] Central locking system inoperative, or unsatisfactory in operation

Introduction

The vehicle owner who does his or her own maintenance according to the recommended service schedules should not have to use this section of the manual very often. Modern component reliability is such that, provided those items subject to wear or deterioration are inspected or renewed at the specified intervals, sudden failure is comparatively rare. Faults do not usually just happen as a result of sudden failure, but develop over a period of time. Major mechanical failures in particular are usually preceded by characteristic symptoms over hundreds or even thousands of miles. Those components which do occasionally fail without warning are often small and easily carried in the vehicle.

With any fault-finding, the first step is to decide where to begin investigations. Sometimes this is obvious, but on other occasions, a little detective work will be necessary. The owner who makes half a dozen haphazard adjustments or replacements may be successful in curing a fault (or its symptoms), but will be none the wiser if the fault recurs, and ultimately may have spent more time and money than was necessary. A calm and logical approach will be found to be more satisfactory in the long run. Always take into account any warning signs or abnormalities that may have been noticed in the period preceding the fault - power loss, high or low gauge readings, unusual smells, etc - and remember that failure of components such as fuses or spark plugs may only be pointers to some underlying fault.

The pages which follow provide an easy-reference guide to the more common problems which may occur during the operation of the vehicle. These problems and their possible causes are grouped under headings denoting various components or systems, such as Engine, Cooling system, etc. The general Chapter which deals with the problem is also shown in brackets; refer to the relevant Part of that Chapter for system-specific information. Whatever the fault, certain basic principles apply. These are as follows:

Verify the fault. This is simply a matter of being sure that you know what the symptoms are before starting work. This is particularly important if you are investigating a fault for someone else, who may not have described it very accurately.

Don't overlook the obvious. For example, if the vehicle won't start, is there fuel in the tank? (Don't take anyone else's word on this particular point, and don't trust the fuel gauge either!) If an electrical fault is indicated, look for loose or broken wires before digging out the test gear.

Cure the disease, not the symptom. Substituting a flat battery with a fully-charged one will get you off the hard shoulder, but if the underlying cause is not attended to, the new battery will go the same way. Similarly, changing oil-fouled spark plugs for a new set will get you moving again, but remember that the reason for the fouling (if it wasn't simply an incorrect grade of plug) will have to be established and corrected.

Don't take anything for granted. Particularly, don't forget that a 'new' component may itself be defective (especially if it's been rattling around in the boot for months), and don't leave components out of a fault diagnosis sequence just because they are new or recently-fitted. When you do finally diagnose a difficult fault, you'll probably realise that all the evidence was there from the start.

Consider what work, if any, has recently been carried out. Many faults arise through careless or hurried work. For instance, if any work has been performed under the bonnet, could some of the wiring have been dislodged or incorrectly routed, or a hose trapped? Have all the fasteners been properly tightened? Were new, genuine parts and new gaskets used? There is often a certain amount of detective work to be done in this case, as an apparently-unrelated task can have far-reaching consequences.

Engine

Engine fails to rotate when attempting to start

- [ ] Battery terminal connections loose or corroded (*Weekly checks*)
- [ ] Battery discharged or faulty (Chapter 5A)
- [ ] Broken, loose or disconnected wiring in the starting circuit (Chapter 5A)
- [ ] Defective starter solenoid or switch (Chapter 5A)
- [ ] Defective starter motor (Chapter 5A)
- [ ] Starter pinion or flywheel ring gear teeth loose or broken (Chapters 2A, 2B or 2C and 5A)
- [ ] Engine earth strap broken or disconnected (Chapter 2C)

Engine rotates, but will not start

- [ ] Fuel tank empty
- [ ] Battery discharged (engine rotates slowly) (Chapter 5A)
- [ ] Battery terminal connections loose or corroded (*Weekly checks*)
- [ ] Immobiliser fault (Chapter 12)
- [ ] Ignition components damp or damaged - petrol models (Chapters 1A and 5B)
- [ ] Broken, loose or disconnected wiring in the ignition circuit - petrol models (Chapters 1A and 5B)
- [ ] Worn, faulty or incorrectly-gapped spark plugs - petrol models (Chapter 1A)
- [ ] Preheating system faulty - diesel models (Chapter 5C)
- [ ] Fuel injection system faulty - petrol models (Chapter 4A)
- [ ] Stop solenoid faulty - diesel models (Chapter 4B)
- [ ] Air in fuel system - diesel models (Chapter 4B)
- [ ] Major mechanical failure (eg camshaft drive) (Chapter 2A, 2B or 2C)

Engine difficult to start when cold

- [ ] Battery discharged (Chapter 5A)
- [ ] Battery terminal connections loose or corroded (*Weekly checks*)
- [ ] Worn, faulty or incorrectly-gapped spark plugs - petrol models (Chapter 1A)
- [ ] Preheating system faulty - diesel models (Chapter 5C)
- [ ] Fuel injection system faulty - petrol models (Chapter 4A)
- [ ] Other ignition system fault - petrol models (Chapters 1A and 5B)
- [ ] Low cylinder compressions (Chapter 2A, 2B or 2C)

Engine difficult to start when hot

- [ ] Air filter element dirty or clogged (Chapter 1A or 1B)
- [ ] Fuel injection system faulty - petrol models (Chapter 4A)
- [ ] Low cylinder compressions (Chapter 2A, 2B or 2C)

Starter motor noisy or excessively-rough in engagement

- [ ] Starter pinion or flywheel ring gear teeth loose or broken (Chapters 2A, 2B or 2C and 5A)
- [ ] Starter motor mounting bolts loose or missing (Chapter 5A)
- [ ] Starter motor internal components worn or damaged (Chapter 5A)

Engine starts, but stops immediately

- [ ] Loose or faulty electrical connections in the ignition circuit - petrol models (Chapters 1A and 5B)
- [ ] Vacuum leak at the throttle body or inlet manifold - petrol models (Chapter 4A)
- [ ] Blocked injector/fuel injection system faulty - petrol models (Chapter 4A)
- [ ] Stop solenoid faulty - diesel models (Chapter 4B)
- [ ] Air in fuel system - diesel models (Chapter 4B)

Engine idles erratically

- [ ] Air filter element clogged (Chapter 1A or 1B)
- [ ] Vacuum leak at the throttle body, inlet manifold or associated hoses - petrol models (Chapter 4A)
- [ ] Worn, faulty or incorrectly-gapped spark plugs - petrol models (Chapter 1A)
- [ ] Uneven or low cylinder compressions (Chapter 2A, 2B or 2C)
- [ ] Camshaft lobes worn (Chapter 2A, 2B or 2C)
- [ ] Timing chain incorrectly fitted (Chapter 2A or 2B)
- [ ] Blocked injector/fuel injection system faulty - petrol models (Chapter 4A)
- [ ] Faulty injector(s) - diesel models (Chapter 4B)

Engine (continued)

Engine misfires at idle speed

- ☐ Worn, faulty or incorrectly-gapped spark plugs - petrol models (Chapter 1A)
- ☐ Faulty spark plug HT leads - petrol models (Chapter 1A)
- ☐ Vacuum leak at the throttle body, inlet manifold or associated hoses - petrol models (Chapter 4A)
- ☐ Blocked injector/fuel injection system faulty - petrol models (Chapter 4A)
- ☐ Faulty injector(s) - diesel models (Chapter 4B)
- ☐ Uneven or low cylinder compressions (Chapter 2A, 2B or 2C)
- ☐ Disconnected, leaking, or perished crankcase ventilation hoses (Chapter 4C)

Engine misfires throughout the driving speed range

- ☐ Fuel filter choked (Chapter 1A or 1B)
- ☐ Fuel pump faulty, or delivery pressure low - petrol models (Chapter 4A)
- ☐ Fuel tank vent blocked, or fuel pipes restricted (Chapter 4A, 4B or 4C)
- ☐ Vacuum leak at the throttle body, inlet manifold or associated hoses - petrol models (Chapter 4A)
- ☐ Worn, faulty or incorrectly-gapped spark plugs - petrol models (Chapter 1A)
- ☐ Faulty spark plug HT leads - petrol models (Chapter 1A)
- ☐ Faulty ignition coils - petrol models (Chapter 5B)
- ☐ Faulty injector(s) - diesel models (Chapter 4B)
- ☐ Uneven or low cylinder compressions (Chapter 2A, 2B or 2C)
- ☐ Blocked injector/fuel injection system fault - petrol models (Chapter 4A)

Engine hesitates on acceleration

- ☐ Worn, faulty or incorrectly-gapped spark plugs - petrol models (Chapter 1A)
- ☐ Vacuum leak at the throttle body, inlet manifold or associated hoses (Chapter 4A)
- ☐ Blocked injector/fuel injection system fault - petrol models (Chapter 4A)
- ☐ Faulty injector(s) - diesel models (Chapter 4B)

Engine stalls

- ☐ Vacuum leak at the throttle body, inlet manifold or associated hoses - petrol models (Chapter 4A)
- ☐ Fuel filter choked (Chapter 1A or 1B)
- ☐ Fuel pump faulty, or delivery pressure low - petrol models (Chapter 4A)
- ☐ Fuel tank vent blocked, or fuel pipes restricted (Chapter 4A, 4B or 4C)
- ☐ Blocked injector/fuel injection system fault - petrol models (Chapter 4A)
- ☐ Faulty injector(s) - diesel models (Chapter 4B)

Engine lacks power

- ☐ Timing chain incorrectly fitted (Chapter 2A, 2B or 2C)
- ☐ Fuel filter choked (Chapter 1A or 1B)
- ☐ Fuel pump faulty, or delivery pressure low - petrol models (Chapter 4A)
- ☐ Uneven or low cylinder compressions (Chapter 2A, 2B or 2C)
- ☐ Worn, faulty or incorrectly-gapped spark plugs - petrol models (Chapter 1A)

- ☐ Vacuum leak at the throttle body, inlet manifold or associated hoses - petrol models (Chapter 4A)
- ☐ Blocked injector/fuel injection system fault - petrol models (Chapter 4A)
- ☐ Faulty injector(s) - diesel models (Chapter 4B)
- ☐ Injection pump timing incorrect - diesel models (Chapter 4B)
- ☐ Brakes binding (Chapters 1A or 1B and 9)
- ☐ Clutch slipping (Chapter 6)

Engine backfires

- ☐ Timing chain incorrectly fitted (Chapter 2A, 2B or 2C)
- ☐ Vacuum leak at the throttle body, inlet manifold or associated hoses - petrol models (Chapter 4A)
- ☐ Blocked injector/fuel injection system fault - petrol models (Chapter 4A)

Oil pressure warning light illuminated with engine running

- ☐ Low oil level, or incorrect oil grade (*Weekly checks*)
- ☐ Faulty oil pressure sensor
- ☐ Worn engine bearings and/or oil pump (Chapter 2C)
- ☐ High engine operating temperature (Chapter 3)
- ☐ Oil pressure relief valve defective (Chapter 2A, 2B or 2C)
- ☐ Oil pick-up strainer clogged (Chapter 2A, 2B or 2C)

Engine runs-on after switching off

- ☐ Excessive carbon build-up in engine (Chapter 2C)
- ☐ High engine operating temperature (Chapter 3)
- ☐ Fuel injection system fault - petrol models (Chapter 4A)
- ☐ Faulty stop solenoid - diesel models (Chapter 4B)

Engine noises

Pre-ignition (pinking) or knocking during acceleration or under load

- ☐ Ignition timing incorrect/ignition system fault - petrol models (Chapters 1A and 5B)
- ☐ Incorrect grade of spark plug - petrol models (Chapter 1A)
- ☐ Incorrect grade of fuel (Chapter 4A)
- ☐ Vacuum leak at the throttle body, inlet manifold or associated hoses - petrol models (Chapter 4A)
- ☐ Excessive carbon build-up in engine (Chapter 2C)
- ☐ Blocked injector/fuel injection system fault - petrol models (Chapter 4A)

Whistling or wheezing noises

- ☐ Leaking inlet manifold or throttle body gasket - petrol models (Chapter 4A)
- ☐ Leaking exhaust manifold gasket or pipe-to-manifold joint (Chapter 1A or 1B and 4C)
- ☐ Leaking vacuum hose (relevant parts of Chapters 4, 5 and 9)
- ☐ Blowing cylinder head gasket (Chapter 2A, 2B or 2C)

Tapping or rattling noises

- ☐ Worn valve gear or camshafts (Chapter 2A, 2B, or 2C)
- ☐ Ancillary component fault (water pump, alternator, etc) (Chapters 3, 5A, etc)

Knocking or thumping noises

- ☐ Worn big-end bearings (regular heavy knocking, perhaps less under load) (Chapter 2C)
- ☐ Worn main bearings (rumbling and knocking, perhaps worsening under load) (Chapter 2C)
- ☐ Piston slap (most noticeable when cold - engine worn) (Chapter 2C)
- ☐ Ancillary component fault (water pump, alternator, etc) (Chapters 3, 5A, etc)

Cooling system

Overheating

- ☐ Insufficient coolant in system (*Weekly checks*)
- ☐ Thermostat faulty - not opening (Chapter 3)
- ☐ Radiator core blocked, or grille restricted (Chapter 3)
- ☐ Cooling fan or viscous coupling faulty (Chapter 3)
- ☐ Inaccurate temperature gauge sender unit (Chapter 3)
- ☐ Airlock in cooling system (Chapter 3)
- ☐ Pressure cap faulty (Chapter 3)

Overcooling

- ☐ Thermostat faulty - not closing, or thermostat missing (!) (Chapter 3)
- ☐ Inaccurate temperature gauge sender unit (Chapter 3)
- ☐ Viscous coupling faulty (Chapter 3)

External coolant leakage

- ☐ Deteriorated or damaged hoses or hose clips (Chapter 1A or 1B and 3)
- ☐ Radiator core or heater matrix leaking (Chapter 3)
- ☐ Pressure cap faulty (Chapter 3)
- ☐ Coolant pump internal seal leaking (Chapter 3)
- ☐ Coolant pump gasket leaking (Chapter 3)
- ☐ Boiling due to overheating (Chapter 3)
- ☐ Core plug leaking (Chapter 2C)

Internal coolant leakage

- ☐ Leaking cylinder head gasket (Chapter 2A or 2B)
- ☐ Cracked cylinder head or cylinder block (Chapter 2C)

Corrosion

- ☐ Infrequent draining and flushing (Chapter 1A or 1B)
- ☐ Incorrect coolant mixture or inappropriate coolant type (*Weekly checks*)

Fuel and exhaust systems

Excessive fuel consumption

- ☐ Air filter element dirty or clogged (Chapter 1A or 1B)
- ☐ Fuel injection system fault - petrol models (Chapter 4A)
- ☐ Faulty injector(s) - diesel models (Chapter 4B)
- ☐ Ignition timing incorrect/ignition system fault - petrol models (Chapters 1A and 5B)
- ☐ Tyres under-inflated (*Weekly checks*)

Fuel leakage and/or fuel odour

- ☐ Damaged or corroded fuel tank, pipes or connections (Chapter 4A, 4B or 4C)

Excessive noise or fumes from exhaust system

- ☐ Leaking exhaust system or manifold joints (Chapters 1A or 1B and 4C)
- ☐ Leaking, corroded or damaged silencers or pipe (Chapters 1A or 1B and 4C)
- ☐ Broken mountings causing body or suspension contact (Chapter 1A or 1B)

Clutch

Pedal travels to floor - no pressure or very little resistance

- ☐ Hydraulic fluid level low/air in the hydraulic system (Chapter 6)
- ☐ Broken clutch release bearing or fork (Chapter 6)
- ☐ Broken diaphragm spring in clutch pressure plate (Chapter 6)

Clutch fails to disengage (unable to select gears)

- ☐ Clutch disc sticking on gearbox input shaft splines (Chapter 6)
- ☐ Clutch disc sticking to flywheel or pressure plate (Chapter 6)
- ☐ Faulty pressure plate assembly (Chapter 6)
- ☐ Clutch release mechanism worn or incorrectly assembled (Chapter 6)

Clutch slips (engine speed increases, with no increase in vehicle speed)

- ☐ Clutch disc linings excessively worn (Chapter 6)
- ☐ Clutch disc linings contaminated with oil or grease (Chapter 6)
- ☐ Faulty pressure plate or weak diaphragm spring (Chapter 6)

Judder as clutch is engaged

- ☐ Clutch disc linings contaminated with oil or grease (Chapter 6)
- ☐ Clutch disc linings excessively worn (Chapter 6)
- ☐ Faulty or distorted pressure plate or diaphragm spring (Chapter 6)
- ☐ Worn or loose engine or gearbox mountings (Chapter 2A, 2B or 2C)
- ☐ Clutch disc hub or gearbox input shaft splines worn (Chapter 6)

Noise when depressing or releasing clutch pedal

- ☐ Worn clutch release bearing (Chapter 6)
- ☐ Worn or dry clutch pedal bushes (Chapter 6)
- ☐ Faulty pressure plate assembly (Chapter 6)
- ☐ Pressure plate diaphragm spring broken (Chapter 6)
- ☐ Broken clutch disc cushioning springs (Chapter 6)

Manual transmission

Noisy in neutral with engine running

☐ Input shaft bearings worn (noise apparent with clutch pedal released, but not when depressed) (Chapter 7A)*
☐ Clutch release bearing worn (noise apparent with clutch pedal depressed, possibly less when released) (Chapter 6)

Noisy in one particular gear

☐ Worn, damaged or chipped gear teeth (Chapter 7A)*

Difficulty engaging gears

☐ Clutch fault (Chapter 6)
☐ Worn or damaged gearchange linkage (Chapter 7A)
☐ Incorrectly-adjusted gearchange linkage (Chapter 7A)
☐ Worn synchroniser units (Chapter 7A)*

Vibration

☐ Lack of oil (Chapter 1A or 1B)
☐ Worn bearings (Chapter 7A)*

Jumps out of gear

☐ Worn or damaged gearchange linkage (Chapter 7A)
☐ Incorrectly-adjusted gearchange linkage (Chapter 7A)
☐ Worn synchroniser units (Chapter 7A)*
☐ Worn selector forks (Chapter 7A)*

Lubricant leaks

☐ Leaking differential output oil seal (Chapter 7A)
☐ Leaking housing joint (Chapter 7A)*
☐ Leaking input shaft oil seal (Chapter 7A)*

Although the corrective action necessary to remedy the symptoms described is beyond the scope of the home mechanic, the above information should be helpful in isolating the cause of the condition, so that the owner can communicate clearly with a professional mechanic.

Automatic transmission

Note: *Due to the complexity of the automatic transmission, it is difficult for the home mechanic to properly diagnose and service this unit. For problems other than the following, the vehicle should be taken to a dealer service department or automatic transmission specialist. Do not be too hasty in removing the transmission if a fault is suspected, as most of the testing is carried out with the unit still fitted.*

Fluid leakage

☐ Automatic transmission fluid is usually dark red in colour. Fluid leaks should not be confused with engine oil, which can easily be blown onto the transmission by airflow.
☐ To determine the source of a leak, first remove all built-up dirt and grime from the transmission housing and surrounding areas using a degreasing agent, or by steam-cleaning. Drive the vehicle at low speed, so airflow will not blow the leak far from its source. Raise and support the vehicle, and determine where the leak is coming from. The following are common areas of leakage:
a) Transmission fluid pan (Chapter 1A or 1B and 7B)
b) Dipstick tube (Chapter 1A or 1B and 7B)
c) Transmission-to-fluid cooler pipes/unions (Chapter 7B)

Transmission fluid brown, or has burned smell

☐ Transmission fluid level low, or fluid in need of renewal (Chapter 1A or 1B)

Transmission will not downshift (kickdown) with accelerator pedal fully depressed

☐ Low transmission fluid level (Chapter 1A or 1B)
☐ Incorrect selector rod adjustment (Chapter 7B)

General gear selection problems

☐ Chapter 7B deals with checking and adjusting the selector rod on automatic transmissions. The following are common problems which may be caused by a poorly-adjusted selector rod:
a) Engine starting in gears other than Park or Neutral.
b) Indicator panel indicating a gear other than the one actually being used.
c) Vehicle moves when in Park or Neutral.
d) Poor gear shift quality or erratic gear changes.
☐ Refer to Chapter 7B for the selector rod adjustment procedure.

Engine will not start in any gear, or starts in gears other than Park or Neutral

☐ Incorrect starter/inhibitor switch adjustment (Chapter 7B)
☐ Incorrect selector rod adjustment (Chapter 7B)

Transmission slips, shifts roughly, is noisy, or has no drive in forward or reverse gears

☐ There are many probable causes for the above problems, but the home mechanic should be concerned with only one possibility - fluid level. Before taking the vehicle to a dealer or transmission specialist, check the fluid level and condition of the fluid as described in Chapter 1. Correct the fluid level as necessary, or change the fluid and filter if needed. If the problem persists, professional help will be necessary.

Differential and propeller shaft

Vibration when accelerating or decelerating

☐ Worn universal joint (Chapter 8)
☐ Bent, distorted or unbalanced propeller shaft (Chapter 8)

Low-pitched whining, increasing with road speed

☐ Worn differential (Chapter 8)

Braking system

Note: *Before assuming that a brake problem exists, make sure that the tyres are in good condition and correctly inflated, that the front wheel alignment is correct, and that the vehicle's load is distributed evenly. Apart from checking the condition of all pipe and hose connections, any faults occurring on the anti-lock braking system should be referred to a Mercedes-Benz dealer for diagnosis.*

Vehicle pulls to one side under braking

- ☐ Worn, defective, damaged or contaminated brake pads on one side (Chapters 1A or 1B and 9)
- ☐ Seized or partially-seized brake caliper piston (Chapters 1A or 1B and 9)
- ☐ A mixture of brake pad lining materials fitted between sides (Chapters 1A or 1B and 9)
- ☐ Brake caliper mounting bolts loose (Chapter 9)
- ☐ Worn or damaged steering or suspension components (Chapters 1A or 1B and 10)

Noise (grinding or high-pitched squeal) when brakes applied

- ☐ Brake pad friction lining material worn down to metal backing (Chapters 1A or 1B and 9)
- ☐ Excessive corrosion of brake disc (may be apparent after the vehicle has been standing for some time (Chapters 1A or 1B and 9)
- ☐ Foreign object (stone chipping, etc) trapped between brake disc and shield (Chapters 1A or 1B and 9)

Brake pedal feels spongy when depressed

- ☐ Air in hydraulic system (Chapters 1A or 1B and 9)
- ☐ Deteriorated flexible rubber brake hoses (Chapters 1A or 1B and 9)
- ☐ Master cylinder mounting nuts loose (Chapter 9)
- ☐ Faulty master cylinder (Chapter 9)

Excessive brake pedal travel

- ☐ Faulty master cylinder (Chapter 9)
- ☐ Air in hydraulic system (Chapters 1A or 1B and 9)
- ☐ Faulty vacuum servo unit (Chapter 9)

Excessive brake pedal effort required to stop vehicle

- ☐ Faulty vacuum servo unit (Chapter 9)
- ☐ Disconnected, damaged or insecure brake servo vacuum hose (Chapter 9)
- ☐ Primary or secondary hydraulic circuit failure (Chapter 9)
- ☐ Seized brake caliper piston (Chapter 9)
- ☐ Brake pads incorrectly fitted (Chapters 1A or 1B and 9)
- ☐ Incorrect grade of brake pads fitted (Chapters 1A or 1B and 9)
- ☐ Brake pad linings contaminated (Chapters 1A or 1B and 9)
- ☐ Faulty vacuum pump - diesel models (Chapter 9)

Judder felt through brake pedal or steering wheel when braking

- ☐ Excessive run-out or distortion of discs (Chapters 1A or 1B and 9)
- ☐ Brake pad linings worn (Chapters 1A or 1B and 9)
- ☐ Brake caliper mounting bolts loose (Chapter 9)
- ☐ Wear in suspension or steering components or mountings (Chapters 1A or 1B and 10)

Brakes binding

- ☐ Seized brake caliper piston (Chapter 9)
- ☐ Incorrectly-adjusted parking brake mechanism (Chapter 9)
- ☐ Faulty master cylinder (Chapter 9)

Rear wheels locking under normal braking

- ☐ Rear brake pad linings contaminated (Chapters 1A or 1B and 9)
- ☐ Rear brake discs warped (Chapters 1A or 1B and 9)

Suspension and steering

Note: *Before diagnosing suspension or steering faults, be sure that the trouble is not due to incorrect tyre pressures, mixtures of tyre types, or binding brakes.*

Vehicle pulls to one side

- ☐ Defective tyre (*Weekly checks*)
- ☐ Excessive wear in suspension or steering components (Chapters 1A or 1B and 10)
- ☐ Incorrect front wheel alignment (Chapter 10)
- ☐ Accident damage to steering or suspension components (Chapter 1A or 1B)

Wheel wobble and vibration

- ☐ Front roadwheels out of balance (vibration felt mainly through the steering wheel) (Chapters 1A or 1B and 10)
- ☐ Rear roadwheels out of balance (vibration felt throughout the vehicle) (Chapters 1A or 1B and 10)
- ☐ Roadwheels damaged or distorted (Chapters 1A or 1B and 10)
- ☐ Faulty or damaged tyre (*Weekly checks*)
- ☐ Worn steering or suspension joints, bushes or components (Chapters 1A or 1B and 10)
- ☐ Wheel bolts loose (Chapters 1A or 1B and 10)

Excessive pitching and/or rolling around corners, or during braking

- ☐ Defective shock absorbers (Chapters 1A or 1B and 10)
- ☐ Broken or weak spring and/or suspension component (Chapters 1A or 1B and 10)
- ☐ Worn or damaged anti-roll bar or mountings (Chapter 10)

Wandering or general instability

- ☐ Incorrect front wheel alignment (Chapter 10)
- ☐ Worn steering or suspension joints, bushes or components (Chapters 1A or 1B and 10)
- ☐ Roadwheels out of balance (Chapters 1A or 1B and 10)
- ☐ Faulty or damaged tyre (*Weekly checks*)
- ☐ Wheel bolts loose (Chapters 1A or 1B and 10)
- ☐ Defective shock absorbers (Chapters 1A or 1B and 10)

Excessively-stiff steering

- ☐ Seized steering linkage balljoint or suspension balljoint (Chapters 1A or 1B and 10)
- ☐ Broken or incorrectly-adjusted auxiliary drivebelt - power steering (Chapter 1A or 1B)
- ☐ Incorrect front wheel alignment (Chapter 10)
- ☐ Steering box or linkage damaged (Chapter 10)

Excessive play in steering

- ☐ Worn steering column intermediate shaft coupling joint (Chapter 10)
- ☐ Worn steering linkage balljoints (Chapters 1A or 1B and 10)
- ☐ Worn steering box (Chapter 10)
- ☐ Worn steering or suspension joints, bushes or components (Chapters 1A or 1B and 10)

Lack of power assistance

- ☐ Broken or incorrectly-adjusted auxiliary drivebelt (Chapter 1A or 1B)
- ☐ Incorrect power steering fluid level (*Weekly checks*)
- ☐ Restriction in power steering fluid hoses (Chapter 1A or 1B)
- ☐ Faulty power steering pump (Chapter 10)
- ☐ Faulty steering box (Chapter 10)

Tyre wear excessive

Tyres worn on inside or outside edges

☐ Tyres under-inflated (wear on both edges) (*Weekly checks*)
☐ Incorrect camber or castor angles (wear on one edge only) (Chapter 10)
☐ Worn steering or suspension joints, bushes or components (Chapters 1A or 1B and 10)
☐ Excessively-hard cornering
☐ Accident damage

Tyre treads exhibit feathered edges

☐ Incorrect toe setting (Chapter 10)

Tyres worn in centre of tread

☐ Tyres over-inflated (*Weekly checks*)

Tyres worn on inside and outside edges

☐ Tyres under-inflated (*Weekly checks*)

Tyres worn unevenly

☐ Tyres/wheels out of balance (Chapter 1A or 1B)
☐ Excessive wheel or tyre run-out (Chapter 1A or 1B)
☐ Worn shock absorbers (Chapters 1A or 1B and 10)
☐ Faulty tyre (*Weekly checks*)

Electrical system

Note: *For problems associated with the starting system, refer to the faults listed under 'Engine' earlier in this Section.*

Battery will not hold a charge more than a few days

☐ Battery defective internally (Chapter 5A)
☐ Battery terminal connections loose or corroded (*Weekly checks*)
☐ Auxiliary drivebelt worn or incorrectly adjusted (Chapter 1A or 1B)
☐ Alternator not charging at correct output (Chapter 5A)
☐ Alternator or voltage regulator faulty (Chapter 5A)
☐ Short-circuit causing continual battery drain (Chapters 5A and 12)

Ignition/no-charge warning light remains illuminated with engine running

☐ Auxiliary drivebelt broken, worn, or incorrectly adjusted (Chapter 1A or 1B)
☐ Alternator brushes worn, sticking, or dirty (Chapter 5A)
☐ Alternator brush springs weak or broken (Chapter 5A)
☐ Internal fault in alternator or voltage regulator (Chapter 5A)
☐ Broken, disconnected, or loose wiring in charging circuit (Chapter 5A)

Ignition/no-charge warning light fails to come on

☐ Warning light bulb blown (Chapter 12)
☐ Broken, disconnected, or loose wiring in warning light circuit (Chapter 12)
☐ Alternator faulty (Chapter 5A)

Lights inoperative

☐ Bulb blown (Chapter 12)
☐ Corrosion of bulb or bulbholder contacts (Chapter 12)
☐ Blown fuse (Chapter 12)
☐ Faulty relay (Chapter 12)
☐ Broken, loose, or disconnected wiring (Chapter 12)
☐ Faulty switch (Chapter 12)

Instrument readings inaccurate or erratic

Instrument readings increase with engine speed

☐ Faulty voltage regulator (Chapter 12)

Fuel or temperature gauges give no reading

☐ Faulty gauge sender unit (Chapters 3 and 4A, 4B or 4C)
☐ Wiring open-circuit (Chapter 12)
☐ Faulty gauge (Chapter 12)

Fuel or temperature gauges give continuous maximum reading

☐ Faulty gauge sender unit (Chapters 3 and 4A, 4B or 4C)
☐ Wiring short-circuit (Chapter 12)
☐ Faulty gauge (Chapter 12)

Horn inoperative, or unsatisfactory in operation

Horn operates all the time

☐ Horn push either earthed or stuck down (Chapter 12)
☐ Horn cable-to-horn push earthed (Chapter 12)

Horn fails to operate

☐ Blown fuse (Chapter 12)
☐ Cable or cable connections loose, broken or disconnected (Chapter 12)
☐ Faulty horn (Chapter 12)

Horn emits intermittent or unsatisfactory sound

☐ Cable connections loose (Chapter 12)
☐ Horn mountings loose (Chapter 12)
☐ Faulty horn (Chapter 12)

Windscreen wiper inoperative, or unsatisfactory in operation

Wiper fails to operate, or operates very slowly

☐ Wiper blade stuck to screen, or linkage seized or binding (*Weekly checks* and Chapter 12)
☐ Blown fuse (Chapter 12)
☐ Cable or cable connections loose, broken or disconnected (Chapter 12)
☐ Faulty relay (Chapter 12)
☐ Faulty wiper motor (Chapter 12)

Wiper blade sweeps over too large or too small an area of the glass

☐ Wiper arm incorrectly positioned on spindles (Chapter 1)
☐ Excessive wear of wiper linkage (Chapter 12)
☐ Wiper motor or linkage mountings loose or insecure (Chapter 12)

Wiper blade fails to clean the glass effectively

☐ Wiper blade rubber worn or perished (*Weekly checks*)
☐ Wiper arm tension spring broken, or arm pivot seized (Chapter 12)
☐ Insufficient windscreen washer additive (*Weekly checks*)

Windscreen washers inoperative, or unsatisfactory in operation

One or more washer jets inoperative

☐ Blocked washer jet (Chapter 1A or 1B and 12)
☐ Disconnected, kinked or restricted fluid hose (Chapter 12)
☐ Insufficient fluid in washer reservoir (*Weekly checks*)

Washer pump fails to operate

☐ Broken or disconnected wiring or connections (Chapter 12)
☐ Blown fuse (Chapter 12)
☐ Faulty washer switch (Chapter 12)
☐ Faulty washer pump (Chapter 12)

Washer pump runs for some time before fluid is emitted from jets

☐ Faulty one-way valve in fluid supply hose (Chapter 12)

Electric windows inoperative, or unsatisfactory in operation

Window glass will only move in one direction

☐ Faulty switch (Chapter 12)

Window glass slow to move

☐ Regulator seized or damaged (Chapter 11, Sections 19 and 21)
☐ Door internal components or trim fouling regulator (Chapter 11)
☐ Faulty motor (Chapter 11)

Window glass fails to move

☐ Blown fuse (Chapter 12)
☐ Faulty relay (Chapter 12)
☐ Broken or disconnected wiring or connections (Chapter 12)
☐ Faulty motor (Chapter 11, Sections 19 and 21)

A

ABS (Anti-lock brake system) A system, usually electronically controlled, that senses incipient wheel lockup during braking and relieves hydraulic pressure at wheels that are about to skid.

Air bag An inflatable bag hidden in the steering wheel (driver's side) or the dash or glovebox (passenger side). In a head-on collision, the bags inflate, preventing the driver and front passenger from being thrown forward into the steering wheel or windscreen.

Air cleaner A metal or plastic housing, containing a filter element, which removes dust and dirt from the air being drawn into the engine.

Air filter element The actual filter in an air cleaner system, usually manufactured from pleated paper and requiring renewal at regular intervals.

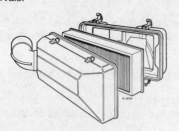

Air filter

Allen key A hexagonal wrench which fits into a recessed hexagonal hole.

Alligator clip A long-nosed spring-loaded metal clip with meshing teeth. Used to make temporary electrical connections.

Alternator A component in the electrical system which converts mechanical energy from a drivebelt into electrical energy to charge the battery and to operate the starting system, ignition system and electrical accessories.

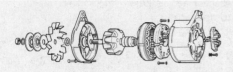

Alternator (exploded view)

Ampere (amp) A unit of measurement for the flow of electric current. One amp is the amount of current produced by one volt acting through a resistance of one ohm.

Anaerobic sealer A substance used to prevent bolts and screws from loosening. Anaerobic means that it does not require oxygen for activation. The Loctite brand is widely used.

Antifreeze A substance (usually ethylene glycol) mixed with water, and added to a vehicle's cooling system, to prevent freezing of the coolant in winter. Antifreeze also contains chemicals to inhibit corrosion and the formation of rust and other deposits that

would tend to clog the radiator and coolant passages and reduce cooling efficiency.

Anti-seize compound A coating that reduces the risk of seizing on fasteners that are subjected to high temperatures, such as exhaust manifold bolts and nuts.

Anti-seize compound

Asbestos A natural fibrous mineral with great heat resistance, commonly used in the composition of brake friction materials. Asbestos is a health hazard and the dust created by brake systems should never be inhaled or ingested.

Axle A shaft on which a wheel revolves, or which revolves with a wheel. Also, a solid beam that connects the two wheels at one end of the vehicle. An axle which also transmits power to the wheels is known as a live axle.

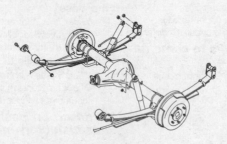

Axle assembly

Axleshaft A single rotating shaft, on either side of the differential, which delivers power from the final drive assembly to the drive wheels. Also called a driveshaft or a halfshaft.

B

Ball bearing An anti-friction bearing consisting of a hardened inner and outer race with hardened steel balls between two races.

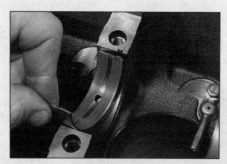

Bearing

Bearing The curved surface on a shaft or in a bore, or the part assembled into either, that permits relative motion between them with minimum wear and friction.

Big-end bearing The bearing in the end of the connecting rod that's attached to the crankshaft.

Bleed nipple A valve on a brake wheel cylinder, caliper or other hydraulic component that is opened to purge the hydraulic system of air. Also called a bleed screw.

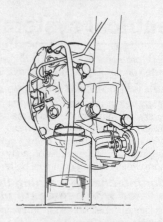

Brake bleeding

Brake bleeding Procedure for removing air from lines of a hydraulic brake system.

Brake disc The component of a disc brake that rotates with the wheels.

Brake drum The component of a drum brake that rotates with the wheels.

Brake linings The friction material which contacts the brake disc or drum to retard the vehicle's speed. The linings are bonded or riveted to the brake pads or shoes.

Brake pads The replaceable friction pads that pinch the brake disc when the brakes are applied. Brake pads consist of a friction material bonded or riveted to a rigid backing plate.

Brake shoe The crescent-shaped carrier to which the brake linings are mounted and which forces the lining against the rotating drum during braking.

Braking systems For more information on braking systems, consult the *Haynes Automotive Brake Manual*.

Breaker bar A long socket wrench handle providing greater leverage.

Bulkhead The insulated partition between the engine and the passenger compartment.

C

Caliper The non-rotating part of a disc-brake assembly that straddles the disc and carries the brake pads. The caliper also contains the hydraulic components that cause the pads to pinch the disc when the brakes are applied. A caliper is also a measuring tool that can be set to measure inside or outside dimensions of an object.

Camshaft A rotating shaft on which a series of cam lobes operate the valve mechanisms. The camshaft may be driven by gears, by sprockets and chain or by sprockets and a belt.

Canister A container in an evaporative emission control system; contains activated charcoal granules to trap vapours from the fuel system.

Canister

Carburettor A device which mixes fuel with air in the proper proportions to provide a desired power output from a spark ignition internal combustion engine.

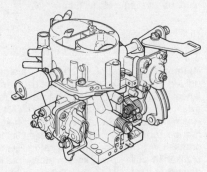

Carburettor

Castellated Resembling the parapets along the top of a castle wall. For example, a castellated balljoint stud nut.

Castellated nut

Castor In wheel alignment, the backward or forward tilt of the steering axis. Castor is positive when the steering axis is inclined rearward at the top.

Catalytic converter A silencer-like device in the exhaust system which converts certain pollutants in the exhaust gases into less harmful substances.

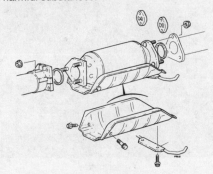

Catalytic converter

Circlip A ring-shaped clip used to prevent endwise movement of cylindrical parts and shafts. An internal circlip is installed in a groove in a housing; an external circlip fits into a groove on the outside of a cylindrical piece such as a shaft.

Clearance The amount of space between two parts. For example, between a piston and a cylinder, between a bearing and a journal, etc.

Coil spring A spiral of elastic steel found in various sizes throughout a vehicle, for example as a springing medium in the suspension and in the valve train.

Compression Reduction in volume, and increase in pressure and temperature, of a gas, caused by squeezing it into a smaller space.

Compression ratio The relationship between cylinder volume when the piston is at top dead centre and cylinder volume when the piston is at bottom dead centre.

Constant velocity (CV) joint A type of universal joint that cancels out vibrations caused by driving power being transmitted through an angle.

Core plug A disc or cup-shaped metal device inserted in a hole in a casting through which core was removed when the casting was formed. Also known as a freeze plug or expansion plug.

Crankcase The lower part of the engine block in which the crankshaft rotates.

Crankshaft The main rotating member, or shaft, running the length of the crankcase, with offset "throws" to which the connecting rods are attached.

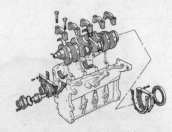

Crankshaft assembly

Crocodile clip See Alligator clip

D

Diagnostic code Code numbers obtained by accessing the diagnostic mode of an engine management computer. This code can be used to determine the area in the system where a malfunction may be located.

Disc brake A brake design incorporating a rotating disc onto which brake pads are squeezed. The resulting friction converts the energy of a moving vehicle into heat.

Double-overhead cam (DOHC) An engine that uses two overhead camshafts, usually one for the intake valves and one for the exhaust valves.

Drivebelt(s) The belt(s) used to drive accessories such as the alternator, water pump, power steering pump, air conditioning compressor, etc. off the crankshaft pulley.

Accessory drivebelts

Driveshaft Any shaft used to transmit motion. Commonly used when referring to the axleshafts on a front wheel drive vehicle.

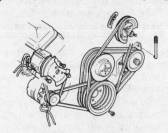

Driveshaft

Drum brake A type of brake using a drum-shaped metal cylinder attached to the inner surface of the wheel. When the brake pedal is pressed, curved brake shoes with friction linings press against the inside of the drum to slow or stop the vehicle.

Drum brake assembly

E

EGR valve A valve used to introduce exhaust gases into the intake air stream.

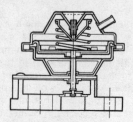

EGR valve

Electronic control unit (ECU) A computer which controls (for instance) ignition and fuel injection systems, or an anti-lock braking system. For more information refer to the *Haynes Automotive Electrical and Electronic Systems Manual.*

Electronic Fuel Injection (EFI) A computer controlled fuel system that distributes fuel through an injector located in each intake port of the engine.

Emergency brake A braking system, independent of the main hydraulic system, that can be used to slow or stop the vehicle if the primary brakes fail, or to hold the vehicle stationary even though the brake pedal isn't depressed. It usually consists of a hand lever that actuates either front or rear brakes mechanically through a series of cables and linkages. Also known as a handbrake or parking brake.

Endfloat The amount of lengthwise movement between two parts. As applied to a crankshaft, the distance that the crankshaft can move forward and back in the cylinder block.

Engine management system (EMS) A computer controlled system which manages the fuel injection and the ignition systems in an integrated fashion.

Exhaust manifold A part with several passages through which exhaust gases leave the engine combustion chambers and enter the exhaust pipe.

Exhaust manifold

F

Fan clutch A viscous (fluid) drive coupling device which permits variable engine fan speeds in relation to engine speeds.

Feeler blade A thin strip or blade of hardened steel, ground to an exact thickness, used to check or measure clearances between parts.

Feeler blade

Firing order The order in which the engine cylinders fire, or deliver their power strokes, beginning with the number one cylinder.

Flywheel A heavy spinning wheel in which energy is absorbed and stored by means of momentum. On cars, the flywheel is attached to the crankshaft to smooth out firing impulses.

Free play The amount of travel before any action takes place. The "looseness" in a linkage, or an assembly of parts, between the initial application of force and actual movement. For example, the distance the brake pedal moves before the pistons in the master cylinder are actuated.

Fuse An electrical device which protects a circuit against accidental overload. The typical fuse contains a soft piece of metal which is calibrated to melt at a predetermined current flow (expressed as amps) and break the circuit.

Fusible link A circuit protection device consisting of a conductor surrounded by heat-resistant insulation. The conductor is smaller than the wire it protects, so it acts as the weakest link in the circuit. Unlike a blown fuse, a failed fusible link must frequently be cut from the wire for replacement.

G

Gap The distance the spark must travel in jumping from the centre electrode to the side

Adjusting spark plug gap

electrode in a spark plug. Also refers to the spacing between the points in a contact breaker assembly in a conventional points-type ignition, or to the distance between the reluctor or rotor and the pickup coil in an electronic ignition.

Gasket Any thin, soft material - usually cork, cardboard, asbestos or soft metal - installed between two metal surfaces to ensure a good seal. For instance, the cylinder head gasket seals the joint between the block and the cylinder head.

Gasket

Gauge An instrument panel display used to monitor engine conditions. A gauge with a movable pointer on a dial or a fixed scale is an analogue gauge. A gauge with a numerical readout is called a digital gauge.

H

Halfshaft A rotating shaft that transmits power from the final drive unit to a drive wheel, usually when referring to a live rear axle.

Harmonic balancer A device designed to reduce torsion or twisting vibration in the crankshaft. May be incorporated in the crankshaft pulley. Also known as a vibration damper.

Hone An abrasive tool for correcting small irregularities or differences in diameter in an engine cylinder, brake cylinder, etc.

Hydraulic tappet A tappet that utilises hydraulic pressure from the engine's lubrication system to maintain zero clearance (constant contact with both camshaft and valve stem). Automatically adjusts to variation in valve stem length. Hydraulic tappets also reduce valve noise.

I

Ignition timing The moment at which the spark plug fires, usually expressed in the number of crankshaft degrees before the piston reaches the top of its stroke.

Inlet manifold A tube or housing with passages through which flows the air-fuel mixture (carburettor vehicles and vehicles with throttle body injection) or air only (port fuel-injected vehicles) to the port openings in the cylinder head.

J

Jump start Starting the engine of a vehicle with a discharged or weak battery by attaching jump leads from the weak battery to a charged or helper battery.

L

Load Sensing Proportioning Valve (LSPV) A brake hydraulic system control valve that works like a proportioning valve, but also takes into consideration the amount of weight carried by the rear axle.

Locknut A nut used to lock an adjustment nut, or other threaded component, in place. For example, a locknut is employed to keep the adjusting nut on the rocker arm in position.

Lockwasher A form of washer designed to prevent an attaching nut from working loose.

M

MacPherson strut A type of front suspension system devised by Earle MacPherson at Ford of England. In its original form, a simple lateral link with the anti-roll bar creates the lower control arm. A long strut - an integral coil spring and shock absorber - is mounted between the body and the steering knuckle. Many modern so-called MacPherson strut systems use a conventional lower A-arm and don't rely on the anti-roll bar for location.

Multimeter An electrical test instrument with the capability to measure voltage, current and resistance.

N

NOx Oxides of Nitrogen. A common toxic pollutant emitted by petrol and diesel engines at higher temperatures.

O

Ohm The unit of electrical resistance. One volt applied to a resistance of one ohm will produce a current of one amp.

Ohmmeter An instrument for measuring electrical resistance.

O-ring A type of sealing ring made of a special rubber-like material; in use, the O-ring is compressed into a groove to provide the sealing action.

O-ring

Overhead cam (ohc) engine

Overhead cam (ohc) engine An engine with the camshaft(s) located on top of the cylinder head(s).

Overhead valve (ohv) engine An engine with the valves located in the cylinder head, but with the camshaft located in the engine block.

Oxygen sensor A device installed in the engine exhaust manifold, which senses the oxygen content in the exhaust and converts this information into an electric current. Also called a Lambda sensor.

P

Phillips screw A type of screw head having a cross instead of a slot for a corresponding type of screwdriver.

Plastigage A thin strip of plastic thread, available in different sizes, used for measuring clearances. For example, a strip of Plastigage is laid across a bearing journal. The parts are assembled and dismantled; the width of the crushed strip indicates the clearance between journal and bearing.

Plastigage

Propeller shaft The long hollow tube with universal joints at both ends that carries power from the transmission to the differential on front-engined rear wheel drive vehicles.

Proportioning valve A hydraulic control valve which limits the amount of pressure to the rear brakes during panic stops to prevent wheel lock-up.

R

Rack-and-pinion steering A steering system with a pinion gear on the end of the steering shaft that mates with a rack (think of a geared wheel opened up and laid flat). When the steering wheel is turned, the pinion turns, moving the rack to the left or right. This movement is transmitted through the track rods to the steering arms at the wheels.

Radiator A liquid-to-air heat transfer device designed to reduce the temperature of the coolant in an internal combustion engine cooling system.

Refrigerant Any substance used as a heat transfer agent in an air-conditioning system. R-12 has been the principle refrigerant for many years; recently, however, manufacturers have begun using R-134a, a non-CFC substance that is considered less harmful to the ozone in the upper atmosphere.

Rocker arm

Rocker arm A lever arm that rocks on a shaft or pivots on a stud. In an overhead valve engine, the rocker arm converts the upward movement of the pushrod into a downward movement to open a valve.

Rotor In a distributor, the rotating device inside the cap that connects the centre electrode and the outer terminals as it turns, distributing the high voltage from the coil secondary winding to the proper spark plug. Also, that part of an alternator which rotates inside the stator. Also, the rotating assembly of a turbocharger, including the compressor wheel, shaft and turbine wheel.

Runout The amount of wobble (in-and-out movement) of a gear or wheel as it's rotated. The amount a shaft rotates "out-of-true." The out-of-round condition of a rotating part.

S

Sealant A liquid or paste used to prevent leakage at a joint. Sometimes used in conjunction with a gasket.

Sealed beam lamp An older headlight design which integrates the reflector, lens and filaments into a hermetically-sealed one-piece unit. When a filament burns out or the lens cracks, the entire unit is simply replaced.

Serpentine drivebelt A single, long, wide accessory drivebelt that's used on some newer vehicles to drive all the accessories, instead of a series of smaller, shorter belts. Serpentine drivebelts are usually tensioned by an automatic tensioner.

Serpentine drivebelt

Shim Thin spacer, commonly used to adjust the clearance or relative positions between two parts. For example, shims inserted into or under bucket tappets control valve clearances. Clearance is adjusted by changing the thickness of the shim.

Slide hammer A special puller that screws into or hooks onto a component such as a shaft or bearing; a heavy sliding handle on the shaft bottoms against the end of the shaft to knock the component free.

Sprocket A tooth or projection on the periphery of a wheel, shaped to engage with a chain or drivebelt. Commonly used to refer to the sprocket wheel itself.

Starter inhibitor switch On vehicles with an automatic transmission, a switch that prevents starting if the vehicle is not in Neutral or Park.

Strut See MacPherson strut.

T

Tappet A cylindrical component which transmits motion from the cam to the valve stem, either directly or via a pushrod and rocker arm. Also called a cam follower.

Thermostat A heat-controlled valve that regulates the flow of coolant between the cylinder block and the radiator, so maintaining optimum engine operating temperature. A thermostat is also used in some air cleaners in which the temperature is regulated.

Thrust bearing The bearing in the clutch assembly that is moved in to the release levers by clutch pedal action to disengage the clutch. Also referred to as a release bearing.

Timing belt A toothed belt which drives the camshaft. Serious engine damage may result if it breaks in service.

Timing chain A chain which drives the camshaft.

Toe-in The amount the front wheels are closer together at the front than at the rear. On rear wheel drive vehicles, a slight amount of toe-in is usually specified to keep the front wheels running parallel on the road by offsetting other forces that tend to spread the wheels apart.

Toe-out The amount the front wheels are closer together at the rear than at the front. On front wheel drive vehicles, a slight amount of toe-out is usually specified.

Tools For full information on choosing and using tools, refer to the *Haynes Automotive Tools Manual.*

Tracer A stripe of a second colour applied to a wire insulator to distinguish that wire from another one with the same colour insulator.

Tune-up A process of accurate and careful adjustments and parts replacement to obtain the best possible engine performance.

Turbocharger A centrifugal device, driven by exhaust gases, that pressurises the intake air. Normally used to increase the power output from a given engine displacement, but can also be used primarily to reduce exhaust emissions (as on VW's "Umwelt" Diesel engine).

U

Universal joint or U-joint A double-pivoted connection for transmitting power from a driving to a driven shaft through an angle. A U-joint consists of two Y-shaped yokes and a cross-shaped member called the spider.

V

Valve A device through which the flow of liquid, gas, vacuum, or loose material in bulk may be started, stopped, or regulated by a movable part that opens, shuts, or partially obstructs one or more ports or passageways. A valve is also the movable part of such a device.

Valve clearance The clearance between the valve tip (the end of the valve stem) and the rocker arm or tappet. The valve clearance is measured when the valve is closed.

Vernier caliper A precision measuring instrument that measures inside and outside dimensions. Not quite as accurate as a micrometer, but more convenient.

Viscosity The thickness of a liquid or its resistance to flow.

Volt A unit for expressing electrical "pressure" in a circuit. One volt that will produce a current of one ampere through a resistance of one ohm.

W

Welding Various processes used to join metal items by heating the areas to be joined to a molten state and fusing them together. For more information refer to the *Haynes Automotive Welding Manual.*

Wiring diagram A drawing portraying the components and wires in a vehicle's electrical system, using standardised symbols. For more information refer to the *Haynes Automotive Electrical and Electronic Systems Manual.*

Preserving Our Motoring Heritage

<
The Model J Duesenberg Derham Tourster. Only eight of these magnificent cars were ever built – this is the only example to be found outside the United States of America

Almost every car you've ever loved, loathed or desired is gathered under one roof at the Haynes Motor Museum. Over 300 immaculately presented cars and motorbikes represent every aspect of our motoring heritage, from elegant reminders of bygone days, such as the superb Model J Duesenberg to curiosities like the bug-eyed BMW Isetta. There are also many old friends and flames. Perhaps you remember the 1959 Ford Popular that you did your courting in? The magnificent 'Red Collection' is a spectacle of classic sports cars including AC, Alfa Romeo, Austin Healey, Ferrari, Lamborghini, Maserati, MG, Riley, Porsche and Triumph.

A Perfect Day Out

Each and every vehicle at the Haynes Motor Museum has played its part in the history and culture of Motoring. Today, they make a wonderful spectacle and a great day out for all the family. Bring the kids, bring Mum and Dad, but above all bring your camera to capture those golden memories for ever. You will also find an impressive array of motoring memorabilia, a comfortable 70 seat video cinema and one of the most extensive transport book shops in Britain. The Pit Stop Cafe serves everything from a cup of tea to wholesome, home-made meals or, if you prefer, you can enjoy the large picnic area nestled in the beautiful rural surroundings of Somerset.

>
John Haynes O.B.E., Founder and Chairman of the museum at the wheel of a Haynes Light 12.

<
Graham Hill's Lola Cosworth Formula 1 car next to a 1934 Riley Sports.

The Museum is situated on the A359 Yeovil to Frome road at Sparkford, just off the A303 in Somerset. It is about 40 miles south of Bristol, and 25 minutes drive from the M5 intersection at Taunton.
Open 9.30am - 5.30pm (10.00am - 4.00pm Winter) 7 days a week, *except Christmas Day, Boxing Day and New Years Day*
Special rates available for schools, coach parties and outings Charitable Trust No. 292048